Formation *and* Development *for* Catholic School Leaders

Volume III

The Principal as *Managerial* Leader

Formation *and* Development *for* Catholic School Leaders

Expectations in the Areas of Personnel Management, Institutional Management, and Finance and Development

Volume III
The Principal as *Managerial* Leader

Maria J. Ciriello, OP, Ph.D., Author/Editor
Dean of the School of Education
University of Portland, Oregon

Department of Education
United States Catholic Conference
Washington, D.C.

2nd Edition

In its planning document, as approved by the general membership of the United States Catholic Conference in November 1992, the Department of Education was authorized to prepare materials for the preparation of educational leaders. This second edition of *The Principal as Managerial Leader*, containing references to the *Catechism of the Catholic Church*, is the third of a three-volume series, *Formation and Development for Catholic School Leaders*. It is a collaborative project with the National Catholic Educational Association in consultation with NCEA/CACE members from Catholic colleges and universities, approved by the Most Reverend Francis B. Schulte, Chairman of the Committee on Education, and authorized for publication by the undersigned.

Monsignor Dennis M. Schnurr
General Secretary
NCCB/USCC

First Printing, July 1994
Revised Printing, June 1998

ISBN 1-57455-079-9

Acknowledgments

American Association of School Administrators

Lewis, A. 1991. Turning theories into research and practice. In *Learning styles: Putting research and common sense into practice*, Chapter 3, 19-32. Reprinted with permission of the American Association of School Administrators, Arlington, Va. Copyright © 1991 by AASA. All rights reserved.

American Federation of Teachers

Bruer, J. T. 1993. The mind's journey from novice to expert. *American Educator* 38(Summer):6–15. Reprinted with permission of the American Federation of Teachers. Copyright © 1993 by AFT. All rights reserved.

Association for Supervision and Curriculum Development

Smith, W. F., and R. L. Andrews. 1989. *Instructional leadership: How principals make a difference*, 46–48. Reprinted with permission of the Association for Supervision and Curriculum Development, Alexandria, Va. Copyright © 1989 by ASCD. All rights reserved.

Ellsworth, P. C., and V. G. Sindt. 1994. Helping 'aha' to happen: The contributions of Irving Sigel. *Educational Leadership* 51(May):40–44. (Excerpt p. 43.) Reprinted with permission of the Association for Supervision and Curriculum Development, Alexandria, Va. Copyright © 1994 by ASCD. All rights reserved.

Diocese of Galveston-Houston

Hennessy, C., C. A. Solomon, K. Mitchell, S. Plasek, D. A. Clifford, and T. Bogar. 1997. *Administrator's handbook of regulations* [Federal Programs Section 1–4, Special Education Section, 1–3]. Reprinted with permission of the Catholic School Office, Diocese of Galveston-Houston. Copyright © 1997 by the Diocese of Galveston-Houston. All rights reserved.

ERIC Clearinghouse on Educational Management

Fielding, G., and H. D. Schalock. 1985. *Promoting the professional development of teachers and administrators*. School Management Digest Series. ERIC/CEM No. 31, 7–9, 13–15, 66–67. Public Domain. Order from EDRS, 7420 Fullerton #110, Springfield, VA 22153.

Jossey-Bass

Knox, A. B. 1986. *Helping adults learn*, Chapter 2: Understanding Adult Learners, 15–31. Reprinted with permission of Jossey-Bass. Copyright © 1986 by Jossey-Bass Inc., Publishers. All rights reserved.

National Association of Elementary School Principals

Gettys, D. J. 1994. Technology trends: Integrating technology in education: The principal's role. *Principal* 73(4):52–53. Reprinted with permission of NAESP. Copyright © 1994 by the National Association of Elementary School Principals. All rights reserved.

National Catholic Educational Association

Bailey, R., U. Butler, and M. Kearney. 1991. Development of the Catholic school board. In *Capital wisdom: Papers from the Principals Academy 1991*, 39–44. Reprinted with permission of the National Catholic Educational Association. Copyright © 1991 by NCEA. All rights reserved.

Balfe, M., M. Lanning, A. Meese, and A. M. Walsh. 1991. Enrollment: Securing our future. In *Capital wisdom: Papers from the Principals Academy 1991*, 11–20. Reprinted with permission of the National Catholic Educational Association. Copyright © 1991 by NCEA. All rights reserved.

Brigham, F. H. 1993. *Technology and Chapter 1: Solutions for Catholic school participation*, 7, 10, 18, 19. Reprinted with permission of the National Catholic Educational Association. Copyright © 1993 by NCEA. All rights reserved.

Burke, R. 1984. The annual budget. In *Elementary school finance manual*, 22–27, 28, 31, 43, 45, 49, 54–59. Reprinted with permission of the National Catholic Educational Association. Copyright © 1984 by NCEA. All rights reserved.

———. 1984. Long range planning. In *Elementary school finance manual*, 84–89. Reprinted with permission of the National Catholic Educational Association. Copyright © 1984 by NCEA. All rights reserved.

CACE/NABE Governance Task Force. 1987. *A primer on educational governance in the Catholic Church*, ed. J. S. O'Brien, 7–16. Reprinted with permission of the National Catholic Educational Association. Copyright © 1987 by NCEA. All rights reserved.

Cappel, C. 1989. A reflection on the spirituality of the principal. In *Reflections on the role of the Catholic school principal*, ed. R. J. Kealey, 26–27. Reprinted with permission of the National Catholic Educational Association. Copyright © 1989 by NCEA. All rights reserved.

Doyle, R., N. Kinate, A. Langan, and M. Swanson. 1991. Evaluation of the school's Catholicity. In *Capital wisdom: Papers from the Principals Academy 1991*, 1–6. Reprinted with permission of the National Catholic Educational Association. Copyright © 1991 by NCEA. All rights reserved.

Drahmann, T. 1985. *Governance and administration in the Catholic school*, 15–16, 16–18, 27–30. Reprinted with permission of the National Catholic Educational Association. Copyright © 1985 by NCEA. All rights reserved.

Drahmann, T., and A. Stenger. 1989. *The Catholic school principal: An outline for action*, 17, 25–26. Reprinted with permission of the National Catholic Educational Association. Copyright © 1989 by NCEA. All rights reserved.

Glatthorn, A. A., and C. R. Shields. 1983. *Differentiated supervision for Catholic schools*, 2, 8–12. Reprinted with permission of the National Catholic Educational Association. Copyright © 1983 by NCEA. All rights reserved.

James, R., J. Perkowski, and M. Sesko. 1991. In the beginning: Orientation of the new teacher. In *Capital wisdom: Papers from the Principals Academy 1991*, 22–25. Reprinted with permission of the National Catholic Educational Association. Copyright © 1991 by NCEA. All rights reserved.

John, R., and M. J. Wagner. 1991. Looking for saints: Hiring Catholic school teachers. In *Capital wisdom: Papers from the Principals Academy 1991*, 55–59. Reprinted with permission of the National Catholic Educational Association. Copyright © 1991 by NCEA. All rights reserved.

Kabat, M., M. C. Valenteen, and W. Langley. 1991. Computers in the school: Working hard or hardly working? In *Capital wisdom: Papers from the Principals Academy 1991*, 45–47. Reprinted with permission of the National Catholic Educational Association. Copyright © 1991 by NCEA. All rights reserved.

McLaughlin, T. 1985. *Catholic school finance and Church-State relations*, 19, 28, 34–37, 44–52, 53–54. Reprinted with permission of the National Catholic Educational Association. Copyright © 1985 by NCEA. All rights reserved.

Ristau, K. 1989. The role of the principal in the ongoing education of teachers. In *Reflections on the role of the Catholic school principal*, ed. R. J. Kealey, 60–65. Reprinted with permission of the National Catholic Educational Association. Copyright © 1989 by NCEA. All rights reserved.

Shaughnessy, M. A. 1989. *School handbooks: Some legal considerations*, 1–3, 11–15, 19–20, 24–27, 28–30, 62–68, 76. Reprinted with permission of the National Catholic Educational Association. Copyright © 1991 by NCEA. All rights reserved.

———. 1991. *A primer on school law: A guide for board members in Catholic schools*, 5–13, 16–22, 29–34. Reprinted with permission of the National Catholic Educational Association. Copyright © 1991 by NCEA. All rights reserved.

Shea, M. 1986. Personnel selection. In *Personnel issues and the Catholic school administrator*, ed. J. S. O'Brien and M. McBrien, 25–27. Reprinted with permission of the National Catholic Educational Association. Copyright © 1986 by NCEA. All rights reserved.

Sheehan, L. 1990. *Building better boards: A handbook for board members in Catholic education*, 1–5, 7–9, 26–31, 40–44, 70–74. Reprinted with permission of the National Catholic Educational Association. Copyright © 1990 by NCEA. All rights reserved.

———. 1986. Policies and practices of governance and accountability. In *Personnel issues and the Catholic school administrator*, ed. J. S. O'Brien and M. McBrien, 1–11. Reprinted with permission of the National Catholic Educational Association. Copyright © 1986 by NCEA. All rights reserved.

Thomas, J. A., and B. Davis. 1989. The principal as part of the pastoral team. In *Reflections on the role of the Catholic school principal*, ed. R. J. Kealey, 45–54. Reprinted with permission of the National Catholic Educational Association. Copyright © 1989 by NCEA. All rights reserved.

Yeager, R. J. 1985. Steps toward development. In *Elementary school finance manual*, 120–26. Reprinted with permission of the National Catholic Educational Association. Copyright © 1985 by NCEA. All rights reserved.

National Press Publications

Adapted from *How to manage conflict: Leadership success series*, by W. Hendricks, 1–3, 6–14, 15–22. Reprinted with permission of National Press Publications, 6901 W. 63rd Street, Overland Park, KS 66202, 800-255-4436. Copyright © 1989. All rights reserved.

Adapted from *The supervisor's handbook*, by M. R. Truitt, 16–20, 46–49, 55–57, 61–63. Reprinted with permission of National Press Publications, 6901 W. 63rd Street, Overland Park, KS 66202, 800-255-4436. Copyright © 1991. All rights reserved.

Contents

Foreword

A Brief History

For many years, the identification and preparation of talented and qualified leadership for Catholic schools had been primarily the responsibility and priority of religious congregations whose members together with some priests served as principals.

Since the Second Vatican Council, staffing patterns of Catholic schools have changed dramatically. Today the majority of both teachers and principals are lay women and men. The tasks of identifying and preparing Catholic school principals have developed largely through the efforts of the education leaders in Catholic colleges and universities.

In 1982, with a grant from the Knights of Columbus Michael J. McGivney Fund for New Initiatives in Catholic Education, the National Catholic Educational Association (NCEA) began a project to study new approaches, to recommend new directions, and to identify needs for training materials. In 1985, the results of this work were published by NCEA in *Those Who Would Be Catholic School Principals: Their Recruitment, Preparation, and Evaluation* (Manno 1985).

Recognizing that many potential Catholic school administrators are not able to participate in the on-site programs of Catholic colleges and universities, a joint committee from the United States Catholic Conference (USCC) Department of Education, the National Catholic Educational Association Department of Chief Administrators of Catholic Education (CACE), and the National Catholic Graduate Educational Leadership Programs (NCGELP) of Colleges and Universities met for several years to develop alternative means to prepare school leaders. In particular, the goal was to help dioceses prepare those who aspire to be Catholic school principals and who are without the means and/or resources to earn traditional degrees at Catholic colleges.

Out of the efforts of the joint committee a set of forty-five competencies for Catholic school principals was developed. The competencies address three roles: Spiritual leader, Educational leader, and Managerial leader. NCEA/CACE received a final report from the joint committee in October 1991 and endorsed the project.

At that point, Regina Haney, OSF, of NCEA assumed responsibility for developing an assessment process for future administrators. Lourdes Sheehan, RSM, of USCC agreed to coordinate the preparation of training modules based on the agreed-upon competencies.

Maria Ciriello, OP, Ph.D., of the Department of Education at The Catholic University of America, was hired as the project-director in November 1991. Her first step was to form an advisory committee composed of persons with both practical and theoretical experience in Catholic school administration. The members of the committee who lent guidance to the project and who critiqued drafts of the writing are: Nancy Gilroy, assistant superintendent of the Catholic Schools Division of the Archdiocese of Baltimore; Joel Konzen, SM, principal of Saint Michael Academy in Austin, Texas; Dr. Elizabeth Meegan, OP, superintendent of schools in the Diocese of Pittsburgh; Dr. Jerome Porath, superintendent of schools in the Archdiocese of Los Angeles; Bernadine Robinson, OP, experienced principal from the Diocese of Cleveland; Dr. Mary Frances Taymens, SND, assistant superintendent of schools in the Archdiocese of Washington and the vice-president of the Executive Committee of the NCEA Department of Secondary Schools; Gary Wilmer, principal of Saint Charles Borromeo Elementary School in the Archdiocese of St. Paul and Minneapolis and north central states regional representative of the NCEA Department of Elementary Schools.

Because Sr. Maria and the Advisory Committee were concerned that the knowledge and experience of persons dedicated to and successful in Catholic school administration have input into the project, a two-step process was developed. First, the [arch]dioceses were surveyed to determine the present practice concerning the preparation of Catholic school administrators. Of the sixty dioceses replying, few had systematic programs in place. Virtually all respondents indicated a need for support in developing such programs. Second, over three hundred persons well versed in Catholic school administration were invited to submit proposals addressing competencies to prepare Catholic school administrators.

Obviously, as this brief history illustrates, this publication, *Formation and Development for Catholic School Leaders: A Three-Volume Preparation Program for Future and Neophyte Principals*, owes its existence to the interest and the hard work of a great many people. Among all the persons already noted, Lourdes Sheehan, RSM, former Secretary for Education, USCC, deserves special recognition for her support and facilitation at every stage of the work. Other people who provided invaluable support services were Patricia Bain, administrative assistant at the USCC and Phyllis Kokus, manager of publications/sales at the NCEA. In addition this project is indebted to Bernadette Sykes of the USCC who spent many hours organizing the copyrighted material and ensuring that it was properly managed.

Added Feature to this Second Edition

The original edition of this first volume, concerning managerial leadership, was developed largely through the collaborative efforts of Kay Alewine and Maria Ciriello, OP, Ph.D. (Ann) Nancy Gilroy, Lawrence E. Leak, Lourdes Sheehan, RSM, and Joel Konzen, SM, contributed the concept papers.

The added feature in this edition is listing the sections of the *National Catechetical Directory* and the *Catechism of the Catholic Church* that relate to the specific competencies. I am indebted to Catherine Dooley, OP, who selected the appropriate sections from the *Directory* and the *Catechism* which are included.

Two additional volumes complete this program of study. The volume on educational leadership addresses competencies related to the leadership and the curriculum and instruction issues in Catholic schools. The volume on spiritual leadership addresses competencies related to faith development, building Christian community, moral and ethical development, and history and philosophy in Catholic schools.

Supplementary Resources

Self-assessment Survey: This instrument is keyed to correspond to the nine areas of responsibility involved in Catholic school leadership addressed in this three-volume series. Designed to be self-administered and self-scored, this guide will assist individuals to estimate their current knowledge and skills, and guide subsequent study.

Handbook: A companion publication designed to be a compact reference for pastors and parish school committees to enhance their understanding of the responsibilities of the parish school principal is also available. Called *Expectations for the Catholic School Principal: A Handbook for Pastors and Parish School Committees* it contains a brief description of the position of the principal. Major components include the concept papers reprinted from the three volumes and new, additional chapters addressing the relationship of the pastor and superintendent to the parish school. All chapters include reflection questions and bibliography.

Finally, this work is dedicated to the countless committed, successful Catholic school principals, past and present. This program hopes to extend your work by nurturing future principals of Catholic schools.

Thank you.

Maria J. Ciriello, OP, Ph.D.
Dean of the School of Education
University of Portland, Oregon

Introduction

How does a diocese prepare those who aspire to be Catholic school principals? How does a religious community provide a guided internship experience for its future administrators? How does a person interested in administration in a Catholic school system prepare? How does a practicing Catholic school administrator "update," renew, improve, or gain other insights?

In an effort to address the task of developing Catholic school leaders, a committee was formed of persons associated with the USCC Department of Education, NCEA/CACE, and the National Catholic Graduate Educational Leadership Programs (NCGELP) of Catholic Colleges and Universities. The fruits of this committee were a set of competencies encompassing the basic knowledge and skills expected of well-prepared Catholic school administrators.

The content of the individual competencies is the focus of the learning experiences presented in *Formation and Development for Catholic School Leaders* in this and two other companion volumes. These three volumes in the series constitute a program of study which may be pursued either by an individual or by a group to prepare to become a Catholic school administrator.

Each volume addresses that portion of the competencies that applies most directly to one of the three Catholic school leadership roles: educational, spiritual, and managerial. Briefly, the contents of each publication are as follows:

> **Volume I**—Educational leadership role, which includes two areas of responsibility: 1. promoting vision using principles of good leadership and 2. directing the curricular and instructional aspects of the school.

> **Volume II**—Spiritual leadership role, which encompasses four areas of responsibility: 1. faith development, 2. Christian community building, 3. moral and ethical formation, and 4. familiarity with the history and philosophy of Catholic schools.

> **Volume III**—Managerial leadership role, which comprises three areas of responsibility: 1. personnel, 2. the institution, and 3. finance and development skills.

The purpose of this preparation program of study is to provide the learner with some theoretical insight into the context of Catholic school administration and some practical direction toward gaining systematic experience which will prepare and enhance one's ability to be a competent Catholic school leader.

In this managerial leadership volume, the theoretical perspective is developed in a chapter preceding each practical experience chapter. Nancy Gilroy and Lawrence Leak provide pertinent insights into the recruitment, selection, and development of Catholic school personnel. They remind administrators of the importance to working to establish a learning culture in the school so that each staff member finds sustained personal satisfaction, challenge, support, and continued professional renewal. Lourdes Sheehan, RSM, addresses the importance of fostering constructive relationships with agencies that affect the working of the school. She clearly differentiates between the different governance structure of the parish, interparish, diocesan, and private school. Joel Konzen, SM, presents a systematic account of the issues involved in assuring the financial viability of the school. His premise is that careful financial management and fostering development opportunities are critical to the continuation of the school's religious and academic mission.

An Overview of Catholic School Leadership Expectations

The following outline is presented to help the reader understand the scope of the complete program of study envisioned for the preparation for the Catholic school principal. This overview contains the expectations of the Catholic school principal related to three roles: educational, spiritual, and managerial leadership. Each role has several areas of responsibility. Each area of responsibility is further delineated by specific competencies.

Expectations for the Catholic School Principal

ROLE: THE PRINCIPAL AS *EDUCATIONAL LEADER*

Area of responsibility: *Leadership*

L1. Demonstrates symbolic and cultural leadership skills in developing a school climate reflecting Catholic identity
L2. Applies a Catholic educational vision to the daily activities of the school
L3. Promotes healthy staff morale
L4. Recognizes and fosters leadership ability among staff
L5. Interprets and uses research to guide action plans
L6. Identifies and effects needed change
L7. Attends to personal growth and professional development

Area of responsibility: *Curriculum and Instruction*

C1. Demonstrates a knowledge of the content and the methods of religious education
C2. Knows of the developmental stages of children and youth
C3. Recognizes and provides for cultural and religious differences
C4. Provides leadership in curriculum development, especially for the integration of Christian values
C5. Demonstrates an understanding of a variety of educational and pedagogical skills
C6. Recognizes and accommodates the special learning needs of children within the inclusive classroom
C7. Supervises instruction effectively
C8. Demonstrates an understanding of effective procedures for evaluating the learning of students
C9. Demonstrates the ability to evaluate the general effectiveness of the learning program of the school

ROLE: THE PRINCIPAL AS *SPIRITUAL LEADER*

Area of responsibility: *Faith Development*

F1. Nurtures the faith development of faculty and staff through opportunities for spiritual growth
F2. Ensures quality Catholic religious instruction of students
F3. Provides opportunities for the school community to celebrate faith
F4. Supports and fosters consistent practices of Christian service

Area of responsibility: *Building Christian Community*

B1. Fosters collaboration between the parish(es) and the school
B2. Recognizes, respects, and facilitates the role of parents as primary educators
B3. Promotes Catholic community

Area of responsibility: *Moral and Ethical Development*

M1. Facilitates the moral development and maturity of children, youth, and adults
M2. Integrates gospel values and Christian ethics into the curriculum, policies, and life of the school

Area of responsibility: *History and Philosophy*

H1. Knows the history and purpose of Catholic schools in the United States
H2. Utilizes church documents and Catholic guidelines and directives
H3. Develops and implements statements of school philosophy and mission that reflect the unique Catholic character of the school

ROLE: PRINCIPAL AS *MANAGERIAL LEADER*

Area of responsibility: *Personnel Management*

P1. Recruits, interviews, selects, and provides an orientation for school staff

P2. Knows and applies principles of adult learning and motivation

P3. Knows and applies the skills of organizational management, delegation of responsibilities, and communication skills

P4. Uses group process skills effectively with various school committees

P5. Manages conflicts effectively

P6. Evaluates staff

Area of responsibility: *Institutional Management*

I1. Provides for an orderly school environment and promotes student self-discipline

I2. Understands Catholic school governance structures and works effectively with school boards

I3. Recognizes the importance of the relationship between the school and the diocesan office

I4. Recognizes the importance of the relationship between the school and religious congregation(s)

I5. Knows civil and canon law as it applies to Catholic schools

I6. Understands state requirements and government-funded programs

I7. Understands the usefulness of current technologies

Area of responsibility: *Finance and Development*

D1. Demonstrates skills in planning and managing the school's financial resources toward developing and monitoring an annual budget

D2. Understands the basic strategies of long-range planning and applies them in developing plans for the school

D3. Provides for development in the broadest sense, including effective public relations programs (parish[es], church, and broader community) and a school marketing program

D4. Seeks resources and support beyond the school (and parish[es])

Who Will Profit from These Experiences?

Anyone interested in pursuing a self-study program to gain current knowledge and professional insights into Catholic education administration will benefit from the series of readings and activities presented here. However, the impetus for this program of training and formation grew out of the recognition that most persons do not have the opportunity to attend a Catholic college or university which offers programs to prepare Catholic school leaders. Most current and aspiring Catholic school administrators have, by necessity, received their formal education in public or non-Catholic private institutions of higher learning. Yet the expectations and responsibilities of Catholic and public school administrators are radically different. Because, by nature, these degree and certification programs do not address the unique circumstances and integral mission orientation of Catholic schools, public school administration sequences (though often excellent in their own right) are simply not adequate for Catholic school administrators.

The following set of experiences is presented to address primarily the unique mission of the Catholic school and the special demands placed upon Catholic school administrators. These activities presume that the learner has or is obtaining a graduate degree in education administration.

The appropriate use of this material is to supplement the standard education degree. These training and formation activities are in no way intended to replace or supplant standard professional preparation in education administration.

Since the following set of experiences presumes that the participant will possess prior or concurrent experience studying education administration topics, it does not pretend to be comprehensive in its treatment of any particular area of responsibility or competency. Rather, these activities are intended to build on previous knowledge and to lend a specifically "Catholic" perspective to all aspects of administration.

How to Use These Experiences

In the pages that follow each area of responsibility that is part of a leadership role is treated as a separate, freestanding learning unit. The design of each unit/area of responsibility is the same:

1. An **overview** is presented that lists the competencies included.
2. A separate **rationale** is provided to clarify the importance of each specific competency for a Catholic school administrator.
3. **Learning activities**, including integral readings, and interactions with experienced professionals are prescribed.
4. **Outcome activities** are listed to provide the learner opportunities to demonstrate mastery of the specific competency.
5. A **bibliography** organized by competency and citing additional sources of information relevant to the particular area of responsibility is included to help the learner extend personal knowledge and insights.
6. **Reprints**[*] of many of the selections listed in the integral readings sections are included. Special permission was obtained for these reprints which should be used solely by the learner. No permission is granted for duplication of these materials. Any attempt to do so is against the law.
7. Each volume concludes with a **general bibliography** of all the sources cited in the volume.

Because people's background, life experiences, and past professional opportunities will differ widely, it is assumed that the appropriate configuration of preparation experiences will be shaped to the particular needs of the individual. Since not every aspirant will need additional education in every competency/expectation in all three roles of leadership, the experiences are deliberately designed to contain some redundancy in presentation. Such overlap is intended to provide consistency and to present each competency as a discrete part of the larger area of responsibility. The intention of this format is to make it easier to "pick and choose" those competencies that are the "best fit" for an individual's needs, while maintaining the integrity of focus of each set of learning activities.

This study program is designed to encourage the development of an active *portfolio* record containing examples of learning and outcome activities indicating both the depth and breadth of preparation experience. Such a portfolio should be a valuable resource:

1. for the applicant seeking a specific position or to give evidence of updating, and
2. for the employing agency to evaluate the candidate's readiness to assume a position.

The learning activities and proof of mastery for each of the competencies also will depend upon the structure and circumstances of the study program. Accordingly, two models are suggested:

Model I—*The experiences are being completed under the direction of a diocese or a religious community.* The diocese or religious community may choose to provide a structured program with a person or persons appointed to direct and monitor the learning activities and to review and evaluate the outcome activities of those learners participating in the program. The learners, in turn, will be expected to participate in the activities assigned and to present evidence of mastery by completing the designated outcome activities.

Model II—*The learner is an individual pursuing this study program on his/her own.* In this case, the learner is urged to seek out individual(s) who have knowledge and experience with elementary and/or secondary Catholic school administration to act as mentor(s).

Regardless of the mode used to pursue this study program, the learner is encouraged to keep an ongoing *journal* of all reading and learning experiences. Such a record will serve as an invaluable resource when one assumes administrative responsibilities.

Integral to education administration is the protracted expectation for the leader to be constantly interacting with various constituencies. One of the best ways to prepare for this demand is in a social, rather than individual or isolated, context. For that reason, the learner is encouraged to seek out a *mentor*. The stimulation of working with one or more persons willing and able to share ideas and expertise while providing guidance and support will add immeasurably to the learner's confidence and experience.

---

[*]   Editor's note: Chapter notations in any of these reprints refer only to that individual excerpt.

Personnel Management

The Principal's Role in Personnel Management

(Ann) Nancy Gilroy and Lawrence E. Leak, Ph.D.

We demand that innovation, experimentation, risk taking, collaboration, and collegiality be the hallmark of Catholic school leadership.

—*National Congress: Catholic Schools for the 21st Century: Exectuive Summary, 1992, p. 30.*

Introduction

The Catholic school is an important and significant institution in our society. It is a functional community (Coleman and Hoffer 1987) where youthful, inexperienced minds are exposed to the intellectual discipline and moral values, rooted in the Christian heritage, which will serve the individual throughout life. Not only society as a whole, but also the life of each individual is influenced by the quality of schools embodied in the quality of teaching and the quality of instruction. While the learner, as the primary beneficiary, seriously affects schooling outcomes, the critical component in determining the quality of the school lies with the leadership of the principal (Sergiovanni 1987).

Schein (1992) contends that an important role for leaders is developing "a learning organization" that is capable of perpetual diagnosis leading to higher levels of excellence. Prudent personnel management practices enable Catholic school principals to exercise considerable responsibility for establishing a collegial learning culture among the school's instructional team.

In learning organizations, a value-based mission guides action and governs the behavior of its members. Values serve to shape and reinforce a constancy of purpose and shared learning culture (Schein 1992). Because Catholic schools are faith-filled, value-based communities, they provide ideal environments for the formulation of learning organizations.

By working together principals and teachers establish a learning culture in which each staff member finds sustained personal satisfaction, challenge, support, and continued professional renewal. Thus the importance of the principal's role with respect to personnel management is based upon three basic assumptions:

- Education takes place in individual Catholic schools through dedicated school personnel who offer educational experiences that are consistent with the unique mission of the Catholic schools.
- Personal enrichment, professional development, and Christian formation are lifelong quests requiring sustained personal and organizational commitment.
- There is no substitute for the teacher who models the Christian message.

In carrying out the mission of the Catholic school, the principal leads the community—students, teachers, and parents—toward the formation of values consistent with the Catholic tradition and improved educational outcomes. The requirements of personnel management are often unrelenting, demanding enormous amounts of energy and time. Prudent attention to these issues is an important part of the principal's leadership efforts. Principals will accomplish little without the cooperation and dedication of others. The success of the school relies on the competent and committed performance of many people. When principals selectively recruit teachers and carefully facilitate their growth, they empower the effective functioning of the school (Sergiovanni 1987) as both an educational institution and a Christian community.

Personnel search and selection

Within any learning organization culture, one of the most important responsibilities of the leader is securing new personnel who are capable and willing to support the mission of the institution. Convey (1992) notes that finding the "right fit" in choosing Catholic school personnel will affect the teacher's satisfaction, success, and longevity as well as student achievement. Therefore, the selection of instructional personnel is a crucial function of the Catholic school leader.

The selection process begins with the recruitment of candidates. Deliberate attention should be given to extending this invitation to a cross-section of individuals reflective of the multicultural perspective of the Catholic Church (*National Congress* 1992). This is particularly critical in schools that boast of a culturally and ethnically diverse population. In some dioceses, recruitment is managed through central services with a list of possible candidates forwarded to the local administrator. When no such service is available, the principal will often advertise the position. Although word of mouth and local church bulletins are cost-effective means of circulating news of the opening, more formal searching through the local colleges and universities might be more fruitful.

No attempt to provide guidance in evaluating the candidate's academic preparedness or intellectual competency is made here. Those dimensions can be ascertained through careful scrutiny of transcripts and letters of recommendation. The more difficult qualities to ascertain in the interview process are those somewhat illusive traits that identify an individual's capacity to perform appropriately for teaching in the unique environment of the Catholic school.

There are many people who are committed to teaching; however, only a small percentage of them are equipped and dedicated to teaching in a Catholic school. Convey (1992, p. 111) summarizes three special qualifications for Catholic school teachers. Catholic school teachers must be

- witnesses to the faith (*Lay Catholics in Schools: Witness to Faith* 1982, no. 29), by being committed to helping students develop Christian beliefs and values;
- willing to model for their students "how these beliefs and values shape and inform spiritual, moral, and lifestyle choices" (Benson and Guerra 1985, p. 2);
- alert for opportunities to initiate the appropriate dialogue between faith and culture (*Lay Catholics in Schools: Witness to Faith* 1982, no. 29).

Regardless of religious affiliation, this mission orientation makes an important difference in the work-satisfaction of the teacher in a Catholic school where work conditions and expectations are different from those encountered in other school systems (Ciriello 1988). During the recruitment phase principals who include "mission-orientated incentives" (Tarr, Ciriello, and Convey 1993) widen their chances of attracting candidates who will value the unique opportunities offered in the Catholic school environment. The opportunities to build community with peers and students and to experience faith experiences such as shared prayer are two mission-orientated incentives that will appeal to some applicants. The degree to which an applicant is motivated by a desire to be in an environment that is compatible with personal values (Ciriello 1988) and committed to teaching in a Catholic school is significant to future performance and should be assessed during the interview (SRI Gallup 1991).

Research conducted through SRI Gallup (1991) identified ten themes that characterize the effective Catholic school teacher:

- **Dedication:** committed to teaching and to Catholic education
- **Achiever:** driven to make things happen, to make students feel "smart"
- **Relator:** causes students to want to learn and to be receptive to Catholic values
- **Developer:** motivates students to go beyond themselves
- **Empathy:** aware of the students' feelings; helping students feel their ideas matter
- **Student Rapport:** enjoys youngsters, has an interest in students' lives
- **Stimulator:** has an intensely active style which results in a "positive hum" among students
- **Faith:** integrates one's career choice with strong religious beliefs
- **Concept:** knows what is important for students and plans how to achieve it in the classroom
- **Responsibility:** views teaching as total commitment which may entail going beyond "the call of duty"

These themes call for a number of qualities to be discerned in the interview:

Listening and **observation** are critical qualities of the Catholic school teacher in order to perceive the student as an individual with a unique learning style and pace (SRI Gallup 1991). What strategies has the applicant for learning about the students individually? How will the applicant seek to learn the uniqueness of each child?

Positive morale in the classroom is critical to the learning environment (SRI Gallup 1991). How will the teacher promote an atmosphere of camaraderie and compassion in the classroom? How will each child be encouraged to see him/herself as a special child of God and valuable member of the class?

Motivating students toward self-actualization and having high expectations of all students is critical to students' success (SRI Gallup 1991). Does the applicant indicate the importance of ensuring each child's progress? What measures will the teacher take to encourage the individual gifts of each child?

A sense of **humor** is an important way to activate children. Does the applicant display a sense of humor or a playful spirit? Does the applicant understand the place of humor as a way to encourage learning?

The **time** commitment required of any teacher is significantly more than the average eight-hour day. The Catholic school teacher must attend to the whole child in its spiritual as well intellectual development. This responsibility may require the teacher to spend additional time on collateral activities in addition to regular teaching responsibilities. What indications does the applicant give of a willingness to participate in all aspects of the school program?

Efficient **planning** and **organization** are critical for Catholic school teachers in order to bring out the best in the students (SRI Gallup 1991). How does the teacher go about instructional planning? What evidence does the teacher give that the focus of planning and organization should emphasize the welfare of the students rather than the smooth running of the classroom?

It is important to underscore the significance of determining the individual's strong **faith orientation** during the selection process. This quality identifies a great deal about the internal motivation of the applicant for the position. The teacher with a strong faith theme will promote the spiritual growth of the student, the primary function of the Catholic school (SRI Gallup 1991). Ideally, the teacher who demonstrates an understanding of the catechetical documents and dogma of the Catholic Church will be well fortified to integrate gospel values into daily lessons. However, some promising candidates may lack this formal knowledge. It will be the responsibility of the principal to supply experiences and resources to compensate for this lack.

Finally, although it is sometimes awkward to discuss something as personal as one's prayer life, it is important that the principal during the search process ensure that the prospective teacher has an ongoing sense of the sacred in his/her life. The candidate should understand the additional responsibility associated with being a Catholic school teacher. "It is important to explore with applicants their personal values and orientation toward the mission . . ." (Tarr, Ciriello, and Convey 1993). As the person in most direct contact with the student, the teacher must model an exemplary **Christian life style** and be prepared to share his/her values with young people.

Staff development

Hiring is just the first step toward developing an effective faculty. Ongoing formation is critical if the teacher is to catch "glimpses of God" in his/her work (Droel 1989). Since teachers are constantly called upon to "give" in the course of their day, it is important that they be able to "receive" to sustain their sense of ministry. Programs for personal growth, professional growth, and religious growth create opportunities for replenishment of spirit and result in higher levels of teacher commitment (Tarr, Ciriello, and Convey 1993). The effective principal provides, throughout the year, various opportunities for the teachers to be stimulated, motivated, and enriched. McBride (1981) provides an excellent resource for designing Christian formation programs. In all cases, such programs ought to be empowering, developed through consensus, and respectful of adult learning principles.

As the principal values the teachers and fosters an environment of mutual trust, the teachers will reciprocate with loyalty (Covey 1991). The effective principal creates a culture in which teachers feel a sense of empowerment in carrying out the mission of the Catholic school. This is important because organizations that empower enable the individual to feel competent (Bennis 1985). Teachers begin to feel a part of something larger than themselves and begin to identify with the institution.

The effective leader employs a consensus form of decision making in the process of developing a personnel development program (Covey 1991). The staff, those who are most impacted by these programs, work with the administrator in planning such programs and in formulating goals and objectives to achieve the overarching vision and mission.

The principal's efforts will be fruitful when appeals to the teacher tap the intrinsic reward system out of which the teacher operates (Sergiovanni 1992). Adult learners bring their best effort to a task when their interest is piqued and they feel that they are able to make a significant contribution to an endeavor. Sergiovanni claims that the common mentality of "what gets rewarded, gets done" discourages people from becoming self-managed and self-motivated. Such a reward system is not primary to Catholic school teachers who are challenged by the call of the ministry to serve and who find satisfaction in their labors.

Personnel appraisal for ongoing professional renewal

Personnel appraisal and professional renewal are central to improving schools. Since we are dynamic creatures, ever in the process of renewal, rarely arriving at fixed points, periodic appraisal enables us to assess where we are in order to move toward perfecting our professional and personal practice. Catholic school principals use appraisal to support teachers professionally. Principals can significantly influence teachers' performance and career path with systematic appraisal combined with systematic professional staff development activities (Joyce and Showers 1995).

While considering the variety of existing models of personnel appraisal and professional renewal systems, it is important to respect the tenant that teachers' commitment to personnel appraisal is directly related to their involvement in all aspects of the system or process. Castetter (1986) suggests six general stages in a systematic assessment and renewal program that includes teacher involvement:

First, Catholic school principals must capture the essence of a teacher's responsibilities. These responsibilities form the basis for developing the appraisal process. Many of these responsibilities formed the basis of the hiring interview and should be quite familiar to the teacher. The responsibilities appropriately reflect the unique faith environment of the school and will include objective as well as subjective information concerning the teacher's involvement in the community and spiritual life of the school. The task-related responsibilities are qualities that can be observed and measured by those assigned to conduct performance appraisals.

Second, school principals and teachers create the performance goals together. Teachers must be given a great deal of input toward the formulation of performance goals because they hold the key to goal attainment. Obviously, these goals should be clear, realistic, within the teacher's power to control, linked to the mission of the school, and project a desired end result. By working with teachers to establish goals, principals can: 1) clarify work-related behavior, 2) communicate performance expectations, 3) emphasize delegating and empowerment strategies, 4) establish a foundation for personnel appraisal and professional renewal, and 5) articulate the teacher's role in carrying out the mission.

Third, information is gathered with appropriate care respecting the moral and legal implications for personnel appraisal processes. Gathering information requires thoughtful attention to teacher behavior. Catholic school principals should be mindful of the multiple sources of objective data readily available for assessing teacher performance.

Fourth, the performance of teachers is assessed. The principal and teacher dialogue about task-related activities that lead to goal attainment. A number of issues can cause the assessment of teacher performance to become quite complex. Issues such as task difficulty, task interdependence, and uncontrollable circumstances are multiple contributors to performance goals. For principals, attempting to balance individual fairness with organizational consistency can prove to be a constant personnel management challenge. As we have noted, there are many non-task dimensions to the Catholic teacher's role which must also be assessed. This requires both sensitivity and candor from the principal. If such feedback is not provided, the role of the Catholic school teacher is functionary and not, therefore, supportive of the Catholic school culture.

Fifth, there is communication of assessment findings. This step is probably the most intensive step of the process and one that requires the greatest amount of sensitivity from Catholic school principals. Moreover, it is most important to remember that this step is also an information-gathering point of the appraisal and renewal process where clarifying data from both parties are shared and considered. Teachers need to feel invited to respond to the principal's analysis and dialogue about any discrepancies which may emerge. Care must be given to bring closure to those matters.

Sixth, professional renewal, the final step of the process, is a continuous activity involving personal planning, action, and energy. Individualized professional renewal plans build upon the job-related strengths of the individual teachers and seek to enhance their knowledge, skills, and abilities. Renewal plans consider the religious dimension of the school as integral to the formulation of personal goals and objectives. Catholic school principals who model their commitment to professional renewal by participating in developmental activities can significantly influence the professional renewal route teachers travel.

Process skills for personnel management

Catholic school principals make a difference in their schools through facilitating change and improvement by providing leadership in a faith context to teachers, students, and parents. Catholic school principals are also managers as they maintain the stability and security of a school organization. Both dimensions of leadership (change) and management (stability) result in the role of the principalship being a dynamic opportunity and responsibility calling for a continuous interplay between change and stability.

Since the personnel are the heart and soul of any institution, the principal relies on "people skills" to nudge the school organization to increasing levels of effectiveness. Among the many skills deserving the attention of Catholic school principals, group process and team building skills, along with delegation and empowerment skills, are often cited as the most essential for effective personnel management. In addition conflict management skills are essential to any effective administrator.

Group process and team-building skills. Work-related activity done in school environments organized around groups or teams which foster social and professional interaction is essential for institutionalizing change in schools (Sergiovanni 1987). Educationally, just as students are grouped for instruction, so too, organizing teachers by grade-level groups or teams is an effective way to accomplish educational objectives. Research indicates that one of the impediments to school improvement is teacher isolation (Sergiovanni 1987). Enhancing the group process and team-building skills of Catholic school principals and teachers for purposes of improving personnel relations and creating superior standards of academic excellence enhances morale and encourages creativity (Cunningham and Gresso 1994) and supports school improvement (Sergiovanni 1987).

Team building is an effective strategy for bringing school personnel together around a common mission. Productive utilization of group process and team building allows teachers and administrators to interact in ways that are innovative and creative. Scholtes (1988) states that successful teams have several common characteristics: 1) clarity in team goals, 2) an improvement plan linked to an organizational mission, 3) clearly defined team member roles, 4) clear communication processes, 5) beneficial team member behavior, 6) ground rules and decision-making procedures, and 7) significant contributions by all team members.

Among the beneficial aspects of team building is creating an environment where teachers are empowered to build lasting solutions to complex problems (Maeroff 1993). Catholic school teachers, who view themselves as knowledgeable sources of imaginative solutions, generate an amazing pool of creative energy. In addition, Catholic school principals who develop, nurture, and sustain a culture that taps the knowledge, expertise, and spiritual energy of teachers are practicing collegiality which is a fundamental principle of collaboration espoused by the Catholic Church (Reid 1990).

Delegation and empowerment skills. "Give a man a fish and you feed him for a day. Teach a man to fish and you feed him for a lifetime." This Chinese proverb captures the essence of delegation and empowerment. As Catholic school principals work to build productive teams of teachers, they set the stage for teachers to assume more responsibility.

Secretan (1993) believes "the highest-quality decisions are made in organizations where power is diffused and responsibility is moved to the lowest appropriate levels" (p. 229). This concept is the definition of the principle of subsidiarity first espoused in Catholic circles by Pope Pius XI (Reid 1990) and since reaffirmed in the documents of the Second Vatican Council. Catholic school leaders who employ collegiality and subsidiarity not only employ reliable management skills but also model two important principles that are basic to Catholic culture.

In a nurturing environment, Catholic school teachers, as competent professionals, are capable and willing to make high-quality decisions about ways to maintain excellence. Through delegation and empowerment, principals convey the values of trust and professional respect to personnel who have chosen to be members of a faith community. Secretan (1993) contends that delegation "is a statement of respect and love for others." But he cautions that "delegation can be successful only when the delegator has a caring eye and a teaching heart" (p. 248). Delegation and empowerment drive the motivational desires of professionals (Secretan 1993). Catholic school principals motivate their teaching personnel by enabling individuals to exercise their unique gifts and through the power of total staff involvement.

To delegate effectively, Catholic school principals should be mindful of the following points:

- match assignments with the knowledge, skills, and abilities of the individuals or teams;
- delegate gradually as confidence and competence of individuals build;
- delegate the whole assignment and avoid attempts to micro-manage individuals or teams;
- communicate and negotiate for specific assignment outcome;
- delegate task-related, decision-making, and problem-solving authority to individuals/team members;
- express positive expectations for success.

Conflict management. It is a fact of life that, even in the most satisfying environment, conflicts will emerge between and among people. To foster a constructive environment the principal seeks not only to create conditions that minimize conflicts, but also to facilitate the resolution of conflicts as they emerge (SRI Gallup 1990).

Always mindful of the fact that the Catholic school is a faith community which values the individual and which respects the diversity among people, the principal has a variety of tactics to use in conflict management. The effective principal manages the inevitable conflicts that arise by taking into consideration the needs of the individuals involved. The administrator listens carefully and gives priority to the concerns of the individual teacher (SRI Gallup 1990). Seeking the common ground upon which the different members of the school community meet is a way of managing conflict.

In some cases administrators believe that the greatest attention ought to be given to those tasks that enable the job to be accomplished. But when task accomplishment is stressed at the expense of consideration of the persons involved, hurt feelings and low morale may result (Hersey and Blanchard 1984). Catholic school teachers respond more positively when they perceive that they are working *with* the principal rather than *for* the principal (Ciriello 1988). Conflict is minimized and tasks effectively completed when individuals are treated as professionals (Sergiovanni 1992).

The words of Abraham in Genesis: "Let there be no strife between you and me . . . for we are kinsmen," (Gn 13:8) serves well as a model of harmony to motivate the Catholic school principal and teacher to find peaceful resolutions to conflict so that ultimately the student will experience true community.

Conclusion and reflection

The selection of Catholic school teachers must consider the unique culture of the Catholic school, a culture which will be shaped by the very process of selection. Training is available to assist principals in this critical task (cf: SRI Gallup 1990).

Recent studies indicate that Catholic school teachers have high levels of satisfaction in their ministry (Tarr, Ciriello, and Convey 1993). Many factors contribute to this: collegial processes, involvement in shaping the future of the school, high degree of autonomy in the classroom, good relationship with administration. This experience of job satisfaction results in commitment and dedication which are the hallmark of Catholic schools. The principal creates the climate in which this is made possible.

Contemporary school leaders shape a culture in which moral commitment between principal and teacher becomes a norm. Catholic schools, a significant part of the Church's educative ministry, are institutions built on a strong foundation of faith. Within these schools are educators who desire to make contributions that enhance the intellectual and spiritual development of students. Catholic school principals transform their schools into innovative learning organizations by valuing and developing their staffs.

Reflection Questions

1. Considering your personal leadership style, to what extent will you encourage the instructional staff to be involved in shaping the vision and carrying out the mission of the school? What are the advantages and disadvantages of your perspective?

2. Give specific examples of ways to motivate teachers extrinsically and intrinsically?

3. What aspects of group dynamics enhance consensus decision making?

4. What is the responsibility of the administrator when conflicts arise between the administrator and teacher?

5. How would you describe the "learning culture" of a specific school with which you are familiar?

6. What are specific ways a principal can demonstrate sensitivity to the uniqueness of the individual teacher?

7. How can the principal provide for the ongoing Christian formation of the teacher?

8. What significant questions in an interview will elicit information about the prospective teacher's behavior in various situations?

9. What are activities that provide continuous professional development for school personnel?

10. What kind of information might be included on an appraisal form for a new teacher and a continuing teacher?

11. What efforts can be made to select and sustain a culturally diverse staff?

12. What specific interview questions would provide information about a teacher's prayer life, value-orientation, and mission-orientation?

Resources

Bennis, W. 1985. *Leaders*. New York: Harper and Row.

Benson, P. L., and M. J. Guerra. 1985. *Sharing the faith: The beliefs and values of Catholic high school teachers*. Washington, D.C.: National Catholic Educational Association.

Castetter, W. B. 1986. *The personnel function in educational administration*. 4th ed. New York: MacMillan.

Ciriello, M. J. 1988. Teachers in Catholic school: A study of commitment. Ph.D. diss., The Catholic University of America, 1987. Abstract in *Dissertations Abstracts International* 48:8514A.

Ciriello, M. J., and J. J. Convey. 1993. Catholic higher education and diocesan school departments collaborating to strengthen leadership. *Current Issues in Catholic Higher Education* 14(1):34–39.

Clifton, D., and P. Nelson. 1992. *Soar with your strengths*. New York: Delacourte Press.

Coleman, J. S., and T. Hoffer. 1987. *Public and private high schools: The impact of communities*. New York: Basic Books.

Congregation for Catholic Education. 1977. *The Catholic school*. Washington, D.C.: United States Catholic Conference.

———. 1982. *Lay Catholics in schools: Witnesses to faith*. Boston: Daughters of St. Paul.

Convey, J. J. 1992. *Catholic schools make a difference*. Washington, D.C.: National Catholic Educational Association.

Covey, S. R. 1991. *Principle-centered leadership*. New York: Simon and Schuster.

Cunningham, W. G., and D. W. Gresso. 1994. *Cultural leadership: The culture of excellence in education*. Needham, Mass.: Allyn and Bacon.

Droel, W. 1989. *The spirituality of work: Teachers*. Chicago: National Center for the Laity.

Hersey, P., and K. H. Blanchard. 1984. *The management of organizational behavior*, 4th ed. Englewood Cliffs, N.J.: Prentice-Hall.

Joyce, B., and B. Showers. 1995. Student achievement through staff development: Fundamentals of school renewal. White Plains, N.Y.: Longman.

Larson, C. E., and F. M. LaFasto. 1991. *Teamwork*. Newbury Park, Calif.: Sage Publications.

Leak, L., B. McKay, P. Splain, P. Walker, and C. Held. 1990. *Professional development resource book for school principals*. College Park, Md.: University of Maryland Printing Service.

Maeroff, G. I. 1993. Team building. *Phi Delta Kappan* 74 (7):512–19.

McBride, A. A. 1981. *The Christian formation of Catholic educators, A CACE monograph*. Washington, D.C.: National Catholic Educational Association.

National Catholic Educational Association. 1982. *Code of ethics for the Catholic school teacher*. Washington, D.C.

National Conference of Catholic Bishops. 1990. *In support of Catholic elementary and secondary schools*. Washington, D.C.: United States Catholic Conference.

National Congress: Catholic Schools for the 21st Century. 1992. *Leadership of and on behalf of Catholic schools*. In *National congress: Catholic schools for the 21st century: Executive summary*, eds. M. Guerra, R. Haney, and R. Kealey. Washington, D.C.: National Catholic Educational Association.

Reid, D. G., ed. 1990. *Dictionary of Christianity in America*. Downers Grove, Ill.: Intervarsity Press.

Schein, E. 1992. *Organizational culture and leadership*. 2d ed. San Francisco: Jossey-Bass Publishers.

Scholtes, P. 1989. *The team handbook*. Madison, Wis.: Joiner Associates.

Secretan, L. H. K. 1993. *Managerial moxie*. Rocklin, Calif.: Prima Publishing.

Sergiovanni, T. J. 1987. *The principalship: A reflective practice perspective*. Boston: Allyn and Bacon.

———. 1992. *Moral leadership: Getting to the heart of school improvement*. San Francisco: Jossey-Bass Publishers.

SRI Gallup. 1990. Themes of the Catholic school principal. In *The Catholic school principal perceiver: Concurrent validity report*. Lincoln, Neb.: Human Resources for Ministry Institute.

———. 1991. Themes of the Catholic school teacher. In *The Catholic school principal perceiver: Concurrent validity report*. Lincoln, Neb.: Human Resources for Ministry Institute.

Tarr, H. C. 1990a. *Teacher values and commitment orientations*. A Report to the Archdiocese of Boston Strategic Planning Study for Schools, October 29, 1990. Washington, D.C.: The Catholic University of America.

———. 1990b. *Teacher satisfaction, attitudes and attributions*. A Report for the Archdiocese of Boston Strategic Planning Study for Schools, December 21, 1990. Washington, D.C.: The Catholic University of America.

Tarr H. C., M. J. Ciriello, and J. J. Convey. 1993. Commitment and satisfaction among parochial school teachers: Findings from Catholic education. *Journal of Research on Christian Education* 2(1):41–63.

Area of Responsibility: Personnel Management

Kay Alewine and Maria Ciriello, OP, Ph.D.

In *The Heart and Soul of Effective Management*, Hind states,

> Christ was the most effective executive in the history of the human race. The results He achieved are second to none. In three years, He defined a mission and formed the strategies and plans to carry it out. With a staff of twelve unlikely men, He organized Christianity. . . . He recruited, trained, and motivated twelve ordinary men to become extraordinary. He is the greatest manager and developer of people ever (Hind 1989, pp. 13–14).

One of the most challenging aspects of being the principal of a Catholic school lies in the development of people. A measure of true success lies in the principal's ability to see and enhance the gifts in others and to provide the opportunities for others' gifts to be used for the benefit of the school program. Recruiting, assessing, developing, and evaluating a wide variety of personnel who fill increasingly more technical positions in the modern Catholic school calls for specific skills on the part of the administrator. Other aspects of management required of Catholic school leaders include group dynamics skills, budgeting processes, canon and civil law, public relations, governance, current technology, and long-range and strategic planning.

As the ability of parishes to subsidize the financial needs of schools declines, the principal is expected to assume more responsibility for the budget and often for securing additional sources of funding to keep the school open. Thus Catholic school leaders are faced with the challenge of mastering managerial skills that have become increasing complex and sophisticated in the past twenty-five years.

Four beliefs espoused by the participants of the National Congress for the 21st Century (*Executive Summary*, Guerra, Haney, and Kealey 1992) indicate the high standard expected of Catholic school leaders in their work with personnel:

- "The Catholic school creates a supportive and challenging climate which affirms the dignity of all persons within the school community" (p. 17).

- "Formation in the basic mission, principles, and traditions of Catholic education is essential for all involved in Catholic school leadership (and for teachers)" (p. 25).

- "Leadership in and on behalf of the Catholic school involves a shift from vertical models to collegial models" (p. 29).

- "The recruitment, selection, and formation of leaders (and teachers) is essential to the future of the Catholic school" (p. 29).

The principal as managerial leader of personnel in a Catholic school is called to the following expectations:

P1. To *recruit, interview, select,* and *orient* the school *staff*

P2. To know and apply the *principles of adult learning and motivation*

P3. To know and apply the skills of *organizational management, delegation* of responsibilities, and *communication*

P4. To use *group process skills* effectively with various school committees

P5. To *manage conflicts* effectively

P6. To *evaluate* the *staff*

The following pages address each expectation in personnel management separately. In an introduction a rationale is presented to clarify the importance of the expectation as a basic competency for the Catholic school administrator. Learning activities, including readings and interactions with experienced professionals, are prescribed. To foster optimum growth and insight the learner is encouraged to seek a mentor and to make every effort to interact with personnel actively involved in the day-to-day functioning of Catholic educational institutions. A written record (journal) of all related readings and activities is integrated to enhance personal development and to provide a systematic chronicle of professional experiences. Finally, outcome activities are listed to give the learner opportunities to demonstrate mastery of the specific competency.

Role: Principal as Managerial Leader

Area: Personnel Management

Competency: P1
School Staff Selection and Orientation

One of the critical responsibilities of the principal as manager is the adequate and appropriate staffing of the school.

> For it is . . . the lay persons, believers or not, who will substantially determine whether or not a school realizes its aims and accomplishes its objectives (*Lay Catholics in Schools: Witnesses to Faith* 1982, no. 1).

Yearly, principals must recruit, interview, and hire staff members for both teaching and non-teaching positions. Frequent changes in laws regarding hiring practices require principals to become and remain well informed. Because salaries in Catholic schools are often less than those in public schools, recruiting quality teachers entails a marketing approach similar to that for recruiting students.

Once hired, staff members require a period of orientation and induction. When feasible, a mentoring program will facilitate integration into the new position and environment. Designing an effective staff orientation program is a challenge for any principal. The newcomer must become familiar with the physical environment of the school, particularly the specific work space, be it classroom or office. Introduction to co-workers, exposure to policies and practices, and a thorough presentation on employee responsibilities, expectations, and rights are components of the induction process.

Besides these rather mundane but important issues, staff members need a firm grounding in the mission and goals of the Catholic school. It is important that all those employed by the school appreciate the ministerial dimension of their work. Assigning a mentor and having meetings for new personnel periodically throughout the first semester or year are excellent ways to provide ongoing support to the newcomer.

Fuller (1969) notes that the concerns of beginning teachers center on their own adequacy and survival. Meeting the initial personal needs of the newcomer will facilitate a smooth transition to the work place and enable the new staff person to adjust more readily. As initial adjustment issues are dealt with, the teacher will have more energy to devote to the central concern of the school—the welfare of the students.

To support and give evidence of professional growth in recruiting, interviewing, selecting, and orienting the school staff, the learner will engage in the listed activities under the direction of the diocese (Model I) or through a self-directed program and/or with the guidance of a mentor (Model II).

The primary means of keeping a consistent record of activities is to keep an ongoing JOURNAL which would contain

1) a *Dated Log* section recording when activities were undertaken and completed,

2) a *Reading/Response* section in which notes from suggested readings and the response reactions are systematically organized, and

3) an *Experience(Activity)/Reflection* section in which one records ideas and insights gained through interacting with people or seeking out additional information in the course of completing the activities.

Learning Activities: P1
School Staff Selection and Orientation

1. Read the following and respond with reactions in a journal.* Ideally, you should discuss these readings and your reactions with a mentor. These integral readings are reprinted for your convenience on pages 32–36.

James, R., J. Perkowski, and M. Sesko. 1991. In the beginning: Orientation of the new teacher. In *Capital wisdom: Papers from the Principals Academy 1991*, 22–25. Washington, D.C.: National Catholic Educational Association.

John, R., and M. J. Wagner. 1991. Looking for saints: Hiring Catholic school teachers. In *Capital wisdom: Papers from the Principals Academy 1991*, 55–59. Washington, D.C.: National Catholic Educational Association.

Shea, M. 1986. Personnel selection. In *Personnel issues and the Catholic school administrator*, ed.

J. S. O'Brien and M. McBrien, 25–27. Washington, D.C.: National Catholic School Educational Association.

* In your journal, note insights you gained into the recruiting, interviewing, selection, and orientation of school staff. What strategies for recruiting teachers have you noted? What marketing techniques are used now to attract quality teachers to a Catholic school? What features of Catholic schools attract good teachers? What are some of the challenges or obstacles Catholic school principals face in staffing a school? What challenges do you foresee in the next few years in regard to hiring new staff members for Catholic schools in your area? What questions do you have regarding these tasks?

2. Visit the principals of one or two area Catholic schools. Inquire about the strategies used to attract good teachers to their schools.
   a. How is the interview structured? What are the advantages and disadvantages of involving teachers and, in the case of high schools, department chairs in this process? How might they be involved?
   b. What strategies or tools do they use during the interview process to determine the potential each candidate has for working in their schools?
   c. What qualities do principals look for first in the applicants?
   d. How have interview techniques—especially the extent and kinds of questions asked—changed over the past few years? Why?
   e. What legal issues need to be considered when formulating the interview questions?
   f. What are some of the "red flags" principals watch for in interviewing applicants?
   g. Do interview techniques vary when selecting clerical and other personnel, as compared with teaching personnel? If so, how?
   h. What roles do returning teachers, personnel, school board members, and parents play in recruiting staff members for the school?

   i. What kind of support program, if any, is available in the school for new personnel? What are the goals of the support program, and how long does it function for each staff member?
   j. What differences or additional requirements exist in planning staff orientation for new personnel, as compared with returning personnel?
   k. What annual turnover in staff do the schools experience? What are the reasons for the turnover?
   l. Besides the interview, what other means of appraisal does the principal use (a demonstration lesson, reactions to touring the building, etc.)?
   m. What tools or materials does the principal use in designing and implementing an orientation for new personnel?
   n. What assistance for staffing the school is provided to local principals by the diocesan office? What tools are provided by the diocese (application forms, suggested questions or strategies for interviews, policies regarding hiring procedures)?

3. Visit with a teacher new to the school and a teacher who is in his or her second year with the school.
   a. What are their perceptions of the hiring and selection process?
   b. Is there some type of support program for newcomers? To what degree has it been helpful? What features of the support program would they keep? What features would they delete or add to make the program more effective?
   c. If no support program is provided, how do they get the information they need? What kind of support would they like to have in place?
   d. How do they rate the induction and orientation experience for their first year at the school?
   e. What are some of the major concerns they have, as beginning teachers or as experienced professionals new to this Catholic school?

4. Obtain copies of the following from the diocesan office:

- application form,
- recommended interview questions,
- policies regarding hiring procedures,
- sample teacher contract, and
- related staff handbook policies.

Critique these documents regarding

a. effectiveness and practicality for use in staff selection,

b. legal implications, and

c. input from the principals and teachers you interviewed.

All opinions must be accompanied by a rationale.

As a result of study, reflection, and interaction with knowledgeable individuals, the learner will be able to complete the following activities. The quality of response to these activities should give some indication of the level of expertise the learner is able to bring to the situation.

Outcome Activities: P1
School Staff Selection and Orientation

1. As a first-year principal, you have been asked to serve on a committee with veteran principals, teachers, clergy, and the superintendent to revise the existing diocesan policies and procedures for hiring teachers and professional staff. The superintendent mentioned that your insights as a newcomer to the diocesan system will lend objectivity and a fresh perspective. Based on your recent study, what recommendations would you make to the group?

2. You are a principal who has not had a formal orientation program for teachers new to the school. However, the school is growing, and the replacement of required personnel is becoming problematic. You feel that the time has come to establish a formal orientation program for all new staff members.

a. Design a staff orientation program, being careful to meet the needs of beginning teachers and professionals new to a Catholic school (both Catholics and personnel of other faiths).

b. Include

i) goals and objectives of the program,

ii) major strategies for development and implementation,

iii) a timeline for implementation,

iv) copies of materials and tools that relate to the project (if obtaining copies is not feasible, provide complete bibliographic information), and

v) a list of necessary resources.

Role: Principal as Managerial Leader

Area: Personnel Management

Competency: P2
Principles of Adult Learning and Motivation

Every aspect of school management that deals with people or assimilating and communicating information will be enhanced by a knowledge of adult learning principles. In particular, at least four areas of personnel management require that the principal have a sophisticated understanding of human personality and behavior:

- making appropriate staff selections,

- designing and implementing staff development programs,

- developing an orderly school environment, and

- assessing staff needs and competencies.

Malcolm Knowles (1970), a leader in research into adult development, identified four critical characteristics of adult patterns of learning. First, with maturity, the adult self-concept becomes more self-directive. Second, adults have amassed experiences that are resources to be called on in new learning situations. Third, adults learn more readily as the tasks relate to role expectations. Fourth, adult learners are more interested in the immediate application of new information than in accumulating abstract knowledge.

To support and give evidence of professional growth in the principles of adult learning and motivation, the learner will engage in the listed activities under the direction of the diocese (Model I) or through a self-directed program and/or with the guidance of a mentor (Model II).

The primary means of keeping a consistent record of activities is to keep an ongoing JOURNAL which would contain

1) a *Dated Log* section recording when activities were undertaken and completed,

2) a *Reading/Response* section in which notes from suggested readings and the response reactions are systematically organized, and

3) an *Experience(Activity)/Reflection* section in which one records ideas and insights gained through interacting with people or seeking out additional information in the course of completing the activities.

Learning Activities: P2
Principles of Adult Learning and Motivation

1. Read the following and respond with reactions in a journal.* Ideally, you should discuss these readings and your reactions with a mentor. These integral readings are reprinted for your convenience on pages 37–84.

Fielding, G., and H. D. Schalock. 1985. *Promoting the professional development of teachers and administrators*. School Management Digest Series. Eugene, Ore.: ERIC Clearinghouse on Educational Management, College of Education, University of Oregon, 7–9, 13–15.

Knox, A. B. 1990. Understanding adult learners. In *Helping adults learn*, 15–31. San Francisco: Jossey-Bass.

Lewis, A. 1991. Turning theories into research and practice. In *Learning styles: Putting research and common sense into practice*, 19–32. Arlington, Va.: American Association of School Administrators.

National Conference of Catholic Bishops. 1979. *Sharing the light of faith: National catechetical directory for Catholics of the United States*. Washington, D.C.: United States Catholic Conference, nos. 182–89.

Ristau, K. 1989. The role of the principal in the ongoing education of teachers. In *Reflections on the role of the Catholic school principal*, ed. R. J. Kealey, 60–65. Washington, D.C.: National Catholic Educational Association.

Silver, H. F., and J. R. Hanson. 1980. Understanding myself as a learner. In *Teacher self-assessment*, 63–81. Moorestown, N.J.: Hanson Silver and Associates, Inc.

Silver, H. F., and J. R. Hanson. 1980. Understanding myself as a teacher. In *Teacher self-assessment*, 95–110. Moorestown, N.J.: Hanson Silver and Associates, Inc.

* In your journal, note insights concerning (a) the basic kinds of adult learners and (b) the relationships between personality style, learning

style, and working style of adults. What have you been able to determine about your own learning style? What transitions or changes do our learning styles undergo from childhood to adulthood? In what ways do learning styles change as adults mature chronologically and professionally? What questions do you have?

2. Visit one or two Catholic schools to learn about the importance of understanding the principles of adult learning, as perceived by area principals.
   a. At what point did the principal become aware of the importance of understanding the various kinds of adult learners?
   b. How has this understanding changed or modified the strategies the principal uses in staffing a school? in putting together inter-disciplinary teams? in assigning task force committees to work on school projects?
   c. What implications do the principles of adult learning have for staff development?
   d. What efforts has the principal made to offer inservice training for the staff regarding their own and student learning styles?
   e. What tools or inventories does the principal use to determine personality and learning styles? How is this information used?
   f. What changes have principals noticed since applying their understanding of adult learners to the daily operations of the school?
   g. How have understanding and applying the principles of adult learning helped the principal in working with other school groups, such as the school board and the parent-teacher organization?
   h. In what other areas does the principal see this knowledge to be useful?
   i. How do the staff members motivate themselves? How do they instigate their own self-development?
   If the principal is unaware of or skeptical about learning styles research, how does he or she get to know and adjust to the individuals on the staff? How does the principal maximize the gifts and talents of all personnel?

As a result of study, reflection, and interaction with knowledgeable individuals, the learner will be able to complete the following activities. The quality of response to these activities should give some indication of the level of expertise the learner is able to bring to the situation.

Outcome Activities: P2
Principles of Adult Learning and Motivation

1. You have just been assigned to be principal of a small Catholic school. This is your first experience as an educational administrator, and you are new to this community. Although you have met a few of the staff, the school board, and the parent club officers in an informal social setting, you do not know them well. You are concerned about establishing positive and productive working relationships.

   Describe the strategies and tools you would use in getting to know the staff, the school board, and the officers of the parent-teacher organization.
   a. What are your goals in embarking on such a course of action?
   b. How would you use this information to develop informal or formal learning style profiles of key individuals?
   c. What messages might your efforts convey to the recipients?
   d. How do you think this knowledge would affect your working style for the year, as regards staff development? school board formation? developing leadership in the parent-teacher organization?
   e. Include in your response
      i) your rationale for your strategies and plans and
      ii) specific steps and tools you would use in determining the personality, learning, and working styles of the individuals involved.

2. The diocese has solicited the ideas of current principals regarding topics to be included when orienting newly hired administrators to the diocese.
   a. Devise a proposal that outlines content and activities to introduce neophyte principals to adult learning theory, and techniques for motivating teachers toward excellence.
   b. Include a list of relevant sources.

Role: Principal as Managerial Leader

Area: Personnel Management

Competency: P3
Organizational Management, Delegation, and Communication Skills

Until after Vatican II, many Catholic schools were managed single-handedly by the principal. When the school was affiliated with a parish, the attitude of the pastor was often "Let Sister take care of the school. My job is to take care of the parish." If there was a parent organization, it was concerned with providing room mothers for the classrooms or helping with the candy sale rather than substantive issues. Catholic school boards and parish council education committees were rarities. This model of top-down decision making and management was similar to that practiced in business and industry at the time. The one "in charge" was expected to have all the answers and to make all the decisions, for the good of the organization.

This notion of autonomous, authoritarian leadership is out-of-date and counterproductive to the welfare of the school and the individuals associated with it. It militates against the community to which we all aspire. Today, the effective Catholic school leader realizes that the best interests of the school are served by implementing a collaborative style of leadership that includes productive communication and meaningful delegation of responsibilities to enhance the talents of many people and groups.

Michelon (1972), in describing the essentials of manager-worker relations, notes that effective communication builds interpersonal commitment, strengthens individual motivation, improves understanding of goals and objectives, and makes a random group of people into a team headed in a common direction. Productive communication is needed to set the stage for delegation. It requires the manager to reverse roles. Rather than taking initiative, the manager needs to listen on the wavelength of the worker and be empathetic about the worker's concerns. True teamwork is only possible with communication.

McKinney (1987) speaks eloquently about the benefits of collaboration. She believes each person has a "piece of the wisdom" and that together much more can be accomplished for Catholic schools and parishes than any one person can do alone.

To support and give evidence of professional growth in the skills of organizational management, delegating responsibilities, and communicating with various groups, the learner will engage in the listed activities under the direction of the diocese (Model I) or through a self-directed program and/or with the guidance of a mentor (Model II).

The primary means of keeping a consistent record of activities is to keep an ongoing JOURNAL which would contain

1) a *Dated Log* section recording when activities were undertaken and completed,

2) a *Reading/Response* section in which notes from suggested readings and the response reactions are systematically organized, and

3) an *Experience(Activity)/Reflection* section in which one records ideas and insights gained through interacting with people or seeking out additional information in the course of completing the activities.

Learning Activities: P3
Organizational Management, Delegation, and Communication Skills

1. Read the following and respond with reactions in a journal.* Ideally, you should discuss these readings and your reactions with a mentor. These integral readings are reprinted for your convenience on pages 85–92.

Cappel, C. 1989. A reflection on the spirituality of the principal. In *Reflections on the role of the Catholic school principal*, ed. R. J. Kealey, 26–27. Washington, D.C.: National Catholic Educational Association.

Fielding, G., and H. D. Schalock. 1985. *Promoting the professional development of teachers and administrators*. School Management Digest Series. Eugene, Ore.: ERIC Clearinghouse on Educational Management, College of Education, University of Oregon, 66–67.

Smith, W. F., and R. L. Andrews. 1989. *Instructional leadership: How principals make a difference*.

Alexandria, Va.: Association for Supervision and Curriculum Development, 46–48.

Sparks, G. J. 1986. The Catholic school administrator. In *The Catholic school administrator—A book of readings*, ed. E. M. Bushman and G. J. Sparks, 283–91. Portland, Ore.: Catholic Leadership Company.

Truitt, M. R. 1991. Time management. In *The supervisor's handbook*, 55–57, 61–63. Shawnee Mission, Kans.: National Press.

Also, read the following sections from the *Catechism*.

Libreria Editrice Vaticana. 1994. *Catechism of the Catholic Church*. Washington, D.C.: United States Catholic Conference.

Nos. 1897–1917: Understanding the rightful place of authority in human life and how it contributes to the common good encourages responsibility and participation in working toward the good of others and society.

* In your journal, note insights you have gleaned. What questions do you have about delegation—especially in regard to dividing large duties into smaller tasks and matching the skills required with related gifts of individuals? What skills are necessary or important when putting together instructional teams, committees, staff, and school groups to accomplish certain tasks? What options do principals have when designing task forces? What is the role of the principal in directing teams? How does this role change according to the task involved? How do leaders cope with and compensate for the ineffectiveness of a team or individual team members? What motivates people, especially those who are school-oriented? What techniques appear to be the most effective and practical? What have you learned about effective communication? What are some of the major attributes of effective communicators, delegators, and motivators?

2. Reflect on a specific instance in your past when you were part (not the leader) of a group that was given a task to accomplish. How did the style and manner of communication with the group enhance or deter the accomplishment of the task? What managerial support was the group afforded? How could it have been improved or refined? With your new insights and having some distance from the situation, what would you do differently as a group member?

If you could repeat the situation as the leader or facilitator of the group, what would you do differently?

3. Interview one or two principals, or persons in parish administration, about their management practices. Here are some questions to ask:
   a. What specific processes do you employ to get things accomplished?
   b. In the past ten years, what has changed in the scope of the organization? Have these changes influenced your management style? in what ways?
   c. Did you feel prepared to assume this role? If not, how did you prepare for it? What programs were available to help?
   d. How have you learned the art of effective delegation?
   e. What techniques or strategies do you use to motivate others and develop human potential? How do you deal with ineffective people?
   f. What are your most effective communication strategies?
   g. How do you integrate the scope of organizational management and effective time management?
   h. What percentage of your time do you spend daily, weekly, and monthly in organizational management, as compared with your duties as an educational or spiritual leader? How do you reconcile the contrast in the roles of leader and maintainer?
   i. How does one determine when a decision or task should be made or performed by the leader, and when it should be made with others?
   j. For an administrative team at the elementary or secondary level, what measures do you take to develop team spirit? How often does the team meet? How is the agenda developed? How do they support one another?

4. Obtain written communications from a Catholic school (newsletters, teacher bulletins, public relations brochures). What types of information are conveyed? What is the tone? What comments and suggestions would you make about the pieces?

5. If the diocese has a principal's handbook, examine the sections that deal with organizational management. To what extent have the steps for organizational management been standardized for the diocesan schools? What and how much flexibility are individual principals allowed in management? What training does the diocese provide to assist principals in developing organizational management skills?

As a result of study, reflection, and interaction with knowledgeable individuals, the learner will be able to complete the following activities. The quality of response to these activities should give some indication of the level of expertise the learner is able to bring to the situation.

Outcome Activities: P3
Organizational Management, Delegation, and Communication Skills

1. List and prioritize the qualities of sound organizational management. Focus on the context of servant leadership and the level of accountability expected of those who serve in the ministry of the Catholic school administration, as Christ's representatives to the public. Include a rationale for the qualities you have listed.

2. *Scenario*

   The following scenario could describe an elementary school, a middle school, or a secondary school. Determine for yourself the level of school, and then describe how you would prepare for the opening of school.

   You have just been hired as the principal of a school of approximately 300 students. For various reasons, past principals have been very autocratic in their management styles, which has resulted in an almost total dependency on the principal to make all decisions. Some decisions have made parents and staff unhappy or angry.

The former principal takes you on a tour of the building and discusses the preparations she has made for the following year. She shows you the teacher, parent, and student handbooks and comments that all three need to be updated for next year. In particular, the responsibilities of the staff need to be assigned. She says, "The teachers are fairly structured and will expect to know exactly what you want them to do."

She relates that the parents have been asking for a change in the grading policy. Some are complaining that including grades in non-academic subjects, such as religion, art, and physical education, in the general average is unfair. The parents base this argument on the fact that grades in art and physical education are based on skills, and religion is more a way of life. As they say, "How do you grade life?" Finally, she notes that the students have been complaining about the boring dress code and want it changed.

You leave the visit with your head spinning—so much to organize, decide, and get ready before school begins.

a. What are your goals and objectives as the new principal of the school?
b. What particular managerial skills are called for in this scenario? How will you prioritize the tasks to be accomplished?
c. Specify a plan for updating the handbooks. Who would you consult? Include a timeline for accomplishing your plan.
d. Specify how you will be responsive to the needs and concerns of the teachers, the parents, and the students that were mentioned by the outgoing principal.
e. What would you change? Why?
f. Justify your decisions on the basis of what you have learned from your readings, experiences, and interviews with knowledgeable individuals.

Role: Principal as Managerial Leader

Area: Personnel Management

Competency: P4
Group Process Skills

One of the most important and time-consuming tasks of the Catholic school principal is working effectively with committees. A sound knowledge and understanding of group decision making is critical. In today's world, there are any number of secular models for group decision making. While many of these models are interesting and some have been successful, they rarely take into account the faith dimension necessary for solving problems in a Catholic setting.

An effective leader actively seeks to develop experience and skills, to build collegiality, and to arrive at consensus when making decisions and functioning as a group. Whether as a member of the staff, the school board, the home and school association, or the parish council, the principal must always wear two hats: He or she is the principal but is also a member of that particular group with the incumbent rights and responsibilities. At these times, the principal must be as active in dialogue and reflection as any other member, while keeping the delicate balance between leader and committee member. Such times may call for uncommon courage, honesty, and integrity in sharing dreams, fears, and personal strengths or weaknesses with other group members.

To work effectively with groups, the principal must be able to understand group dynamics. Sheehan (1990) lists the benefits of group decision making and wisely notes the potential costs of working with groups for the principal. For example, the time and energy required to work as a team can be costly, especially with an already overcrowded schedule. Striving for consensus is a worthy goal that requires much more time for discussion and reflection than a unilateral decision. While the process may be greatly slowed, the results of consensus—further unification and stability of the group—are frequently worth the sacrifices required.

To support and give evidence of professional growth in using group process skills with all school groups, the learner will engage in the listed activities under the direction of the diocese (Model I) or through a self-directed program and/or with the guidance of a mentor (Model II).

The primary means of keeping a consistent record of activities is to keep an ongoing JOURNAL which would contain

1) a *Dated Log* section recording when activities were undertaken and completed,
2) a *Reading/Response* section in which notes from suggested readings and the response reactions are systematically organized, and
3) an *Experience(Activity)/Reflection* section in which one records ideas and insights gained through interacting with people or seeking out additional information in the course of completing the activities.

Learning Activities: P4
Group Process Skills

1. Read the following and respond with reactions in a journal.* Ideally, you should discuss these readings and your reactions with a mentor. These integral readings are reprinted for your convenience on pages 93–100.

   Sheehan, L. 1990. Decision-making. In *Building better boards: A handbook for board members in Catholic education*, 70–74. Washington, D.C.: National Catholic Educational Association.

   Thomas, J. A., and B. Davis. 1989. The principal as part of the pastoral team. In *Reflections on the role of the Catholic school principal*, ed. R. J. Kealey, 45–54. Washington, D.C.: National Catholic Educational Association.

   Truitt, M. R. 1991. *The supervisor's handbook*. Shawnee Mission, Kans.: National Press, 16–20.

   Also, read the following sections from the *Catechism*.
   Libreria Editrice Vaticana. 1994. *Catechism of the Catholic Church*. Washington, D.C.: United States Catholic Conference.

   No. 1724: Freedom and grace are complementary. As we respond to grace, we grow in freedom and confidence. The grace of the Holy Spirit enables us to be free to be collaborators in God's work.

   No. 1738: The freedom we exercise in our relationships with others is a right that is essential to our dignity.

Nos. 1886–88: Through society we fulfill our human vocation. We call on our spiritual and moral capacities to effect social change.

* In your journal, note insights gained concerning (a) group leadership, (b) steps in reaching consensus, and (c) strategies for conflict resolution. What questions do you have about working effectively with groups? What ideas do you have for putting together effective groups? What strategies would you use to resolve conflicts among group members?

2. Talk with one or two Catholic school leaders to learn about the group process skills they use.

   a. What types of groups are they typically involved with in the course of their work? What is their role in each of these groups?

   b. What skills or strategies are needed to work with groups in general? Are particular strategies needed with specific groups? What determines the strategy used?

   c. What changes have they noted in the frequency with which they work with groups? Have their styles of leadership in groups changed over the past several years?

   d. What strategies do the principals use to track the progress and effectiveness of committees and groups?

   e. What are the advantages and disadvantages in working with particular groups, and groups in general?

3. Visit one or two group officers or committee chairs (e.g., a staff, board, or parent organization). What responsibilities and accountability do they have? What strategies do they use to make decisions? What strategies are used to communicate internally as a group, with the principal, and with the school, parish, and public communities? How are conflicts among members resolved?

4. Get permission to attend a school board meeting or committee meeting, and observe the dynamics of the group. What roles do people take at the meeting? How do they come to a decision? How are conflicts resolved?

As a result of study, reflection, and interaction with knowledgeable individuals, the learner will be able to complete the following activities. The quality of response to these activities should give some indication of the level of expertise the learner is able to bring to the situation.

Outcome Activities: P4
Group Process Skills

1. List and discuss the various roles persons take when part of a group. How might the leader's behavior affect the group? What should the leader keep in mind when working with a group?

2. Discuss the qualities and costs of striving for consensus, especially in regard to other forms of group decision making. List and discuss the steps for reaching consensus. What strategies are available to resolve an issue or make a decision if consensus is not possible?

3. *Elementary School Scenario*

   It is mid-July. A friend of yours has been hired as the principal of a school of 150 students. One of the last decisions made by the outgoing principal was to summarily and unilaterally change the style and colors of the uniforms for all students. Students were measured in May. The clothing is to be ordered and paid for during the summer. The new uniforms are to be worn the first full week of school in September. This decision has polarized families and even the staff of the school.

   Your friend said that the former principal left her a note concerning the situation. In summary, the facts were these:

   ■ The principal had a disagreement with the former uniform company and signed a contract with the new one.
   ■ The new company would give the students more clothing selections at about the same cost.
   ■ The company could not match the style or colors of the old uniforms, so the principal decided on the new ones.

- The new company needed to be guaranteed a certain number of orders to give the school the a reasonable price. Consequently, the principal said all students must be in the new uniforms in September.

Your friend confides that she had hoped to start the school year off on a positive note. She is upset that the parents and staff seem to be more concerned about the uniforms than what the children will be learning. Her incoming calls indicate that the issue is generating considerable heat and energy and that people want her to reverse the decision. She is convinced that the real issue is how the decision was made rather than the decision itself. Your friend comes to you for advice.

a. How would you help her sort out the problem and develop a strategy to address it?
b. What groups would you encourage her to involve?
c. What process would you suggest for the groups?
d. Justify your response on the basis of what you have learned from your readings, experiences, and interviews with knowledgeable individuals.

4. *Secondary School Scenario*

It is November. You are the new principal of a secondary school with 500 students. There are 30 full-time and 6 part-time teachers on the faculty.

You hired 3 teachers this fall who had just completed their student teaching the previous year. The most experienced teacher on the staff has been at the school for 20 years. The average years of teaching experience is 10.

You have visited each teacher and formally conducted one cycle of clinical supervision. Except for the newcomers, who attempted some limited cooperative learning strategies, you are dismayed at the overwhelming number of classes that were essentially lectures. Although the students were reasonably attentive and taking notes, you sensed real boredom and lack of involvement. How will you encourage the teachers to vary their teaching strategies? What group process skills will you call into play? Describe in detail the plan and process you will employ. Justify your response.

Role: Principal as Managerial Leader

Area: Personnel Management

Competency: P5
Managing Conflicts

Even in the best of situations, conflicts will arise among personnel. The principal's expertise in helping those involved to confront and resolve concerns in a healthy, positive manner is crucial to maintaining a strong, viable staff. The key to managing conflicts lies in the administrator's ability to put aside personal feelings and self-interests (Hind 1989).

One key to effective management of conflicts is to realize that within any organization, conflicts will occasionally occur. However, some problems will not naturally resolve when left to themselves but will grow out of proportion unless they are confronted. When serious problems remain unsettled, staff members can become polarized, ineffective, and even demoralized. Therefore, it is important for the leader to be able to draw upon coping strategies to deal with the conflict before it gets out of hand.

Good communication skills and the ability to confront difficult people and problems in a constructive manner are essential to any effective management program (Hendricks 1989). As Catholic school principals, we have a responsibility to foster healthy interactions that support the community and "build up the Body of Christ."

To support and give evidence of professional growth in managing conflicts effectively, the learner will engage in the listed activities under the direction of the diocese (Model I) or through a self-directed program and/or with the guidance of a mentor (Model II).

The primary means of keeping a consistent record of activities is to keep an ongoing JOURNAL which would contain

1) a *Dated Log* section recording when activities were undertaken and completed,
2) a *Reading/Response* section in which notes from suggested readings and the response reactions are systematically organized,

3) an *Experience(Activity)/Reflection* section in which one records ideas and insights gained through interacting with people or seeking out additional information in the course of completing the activities.

Learning Activities: P5
Managing Conflicts

1. Read the following and respond with reactions in a journal.* Ideally, you should discuss these readings and your reactions with a mentor. These integral readings are reprinted for your convenience on pages 101–110.

   Drahmann, T. 1985. Kill the umpire. In *Governance and administration in the Catholic school*, 27–30. Washington, D.C.: National Catholic Educational Association.
   Hendricks, W. 1989. *How to manage conflict.* Leadership Success Series. Shawnee Mission, Kans.: National Press, 1–3, 6–14, 15–22.
   Shaughnessy, M. A. 1989. *School handbooks: Some legal considerations.* Washington, D.C.: National Catholic Educational Association, 76.

   Also, read the following sections from the *Catechism.*
   Libreria Editrice Vaticana. 1994. *Catechism of the Catholic Church.* Washington, D.C.: United States Catholic Conference.

   Nos. 1822–29: Practicing charity means loving God above all things and our neighbors as ourselves.
   Nos. 2302–06: Safeguarding peace entails denouncing anger and hatred.

   * In your journal, note insights concerning effective management of conflicts. What is your natural style in handling conflicts? Do you need further study to learn to manage your own self-control and response to difficult situations? What questions do you have? What are the relationships between a person's personality, working style, and ability to handle conflicts? Do you have strategies in mind to help diffuse another's anger? Are you aware of strategies that could be used to resolve conflict constructively?

2. Interview one or two persons involved in Catholic school leadership or parish leadership. Here are some questions to ask:

a. How do you characterize your approach to solving problems and managing conflicts?

b. What strategies do you have to avoid conflicts and to deal with confrontations when they occur?

c. How has your ability to handle difficult situations changed since being in leadership?

d. What kinds of preventive strategies do you use to solve problems before they become crucial issues?

e. How does the diocesan office train and support principals in managing conflict situations? Is there a grievance policy in place for administrators, staff, students or parents? What role does the diocese play in the grievance process? What training or services does the diocese provide to leadership personnel if conflicts escalate beyond grievance to legal action?

f. Do you have an intervention team in place that can assist with less complicated or serious conflicts?

3. Seek out three or four employees or volunteers at Catholic schools or parish DRE programs. Talk with them separately; ask them about the things in their work and ministry that bring about conflict. Then ask them how they would like to have the conflict resolved. Were there similarities in the responses? How did the strategies they proposed for settling conflict compare with the suggestions given in the readings, or interviews with the principals? What do you conclude from this experience?

4. As conflict escalates, crises may erupt. What are the components of an effective crisis management plan?

As a result of study, reflection, and interaction with knowledgeable individuals, the learner will be able to complete the following activities. The quality of response to these activities should give some indication of the level of expertise the learner is able to bring to the situation.

Outcome Activities: P5
Managing Conflicts

Prepare a basic plan of intervention for each of the following scenarios.

a. What are the issues involved in the situation?

b. What are possible causes for the difficulty?

c. What is your goal in resolving this conflict? What is the desirable end? Might this situation be resolved in such a way that all parties feel they were treated fairly and benefited from the resolution of the conflict?

d. Include all the steps you would take in the intervention.

i) Who would you involve?

ii) Specify the types of information you would gather before, during, and after the implementation of your plan of action.

e. How would you determine that the situation was satisfactorily resolved for all concerned?

1. You have just hired a young teacher, Teacher 3A, who is professionally prepared with a master's degree and has demonstrated competence in her past three years of teaching. Teacher 3A is teaching one section of a grade. You have encouraged your staff to work together whenever possible by providing common planning time for teachers of similar grade levels. Teacher 3B, her partner, is a tenured teacher who has been on your staff for several years. Teacher 3B is very competent, but she has a bachelor's degree and has not updated her credentials in the last few years. Teacher 3B is low-keyed and lacks the enthusiasm and expertise her younger co-worker possesses. Further, she has shown signs of resenting the praise and attention Teacher 3A is receiving from other staff members and parents. Teacher 3B has become critical and negative toward her partner and seldom meets with her to plan lessons. She has also tried to get other staff members to find fault with Teacher 3A for introducing "new fangled" ideas and trying to change everything.

2. One of the English teachers on your staff has been teaching in Catholic schools for many years. She is considered something of a character by faculty, students, and parents because of her rather unorthodox teaching methods. But she is a master teacher who is well respected by parents and known as an institution in the community. Students look forward to having her in their senior year. Her programs have been extremely successful. She has a strong personality, is opinionated, and tends to intimidate others with lesser skills.

As principal, you are encouraging the English and social studies departments to develop interdisciplinary teaching units. This English teacher has no interest, and probably few skills, in pursuing this method of teaching. Therefore, whenever you have met with the departments, you have found her to be uncooperative and even rude to the others involved. The other team members have been so hurt by her remarks and lack of cooperation that they have begun to withdraw. You have noticed that even those who were initially enthusiastic about the new ideas have become disenchanted. While you see the teacher's gifts and recognize their importance to the total school program, you also see a need to move the curriculum in this new direction.

3. A distraught teacher comes to you after school and asks that a student be removed from class before the teacher does him bodily harm. It seems that, throughout the quarter, the student has been consistently rude to the teacher and disruptive in the class. When you talk with the student about his behavior, he says that the teacher always calls him by his older brother's name and never gives him a chance to participate in class. You remember that the older brother was asked to leave the school five years before because of academic and behavioral problems.

4. A parent comes to complain to you about his child's science teacher. The student received a D, but the parent received no notification of the student's lack of achievement before the report card. Further, the parent saw the student's science book at home regularly throughout the semester. With that much effort on the part of the student, the grade seems unjust. The parent asks you to have the grade changed and to put the student into a science section with another teacher.

Role: Principal as Managerial Leader

Area: Personnel Management

Competency: P6
Evaluating Staff

Whether informal or formal, the evaluation and assessment of teaching and non-teaching personnel is an important aspect of effective school management. According to Hind (1989), a performance review is an ideal time for a manager to express the desire to help a staff member succeed. The most effective evaluation is one in which the manager does much listening and communicates clearly with the person involved.

Evaluation has two purposes. First, it is formative, an ongoing developmental process supporting improvement, using a variety of styles of supervision, and incorporating instruments that correlate with the style of supervision selected (Glatthorn and Shields 1983). Second, it is summative, providing a record and objective evidence on which decisions about future employment are based (Daresh 1992).

Catholic school principals continually strive to bring out the best in others. Staff evaluation is a means of helping individuals achieve personal potential while providing the best possible educational experience for the students.

To support and give evidence of professional growth in evaluating staff, the learner will engage in the listed activities under the direction of the diocese (Model I) or through a self-directed program and/or with the guidance of a mentor (Model II).

The primary means of keeping a consistent record of activities is to keep an ongoing JOURNAL which would contain

1) a *Dated Log* section recording when activities were undertaken and completed,

2) a *Reading/Response* section in which notes from suggested readings and the response reactions are systematically organized, and

3) an *Experience (Activity)/Reflection* section in which one records ideas and insights gained through interacting with people or seeking out additional information in the course of completing the activities.

Learning Activities: P6
Evaluating Staff

1. Read the following and respond with reactions in a journal.* Ideally, you should discuss these readings and your reactions with a mentor. These integral readings are reprinted for your convenience on pages 111–118.

Glatthorn, A. A., and C. R. Shields. 1983. *Differentiated supervision for Catholic schools*. Washington, D.C.: National Catholic Educational Association, 2, 8–12.

Hind, J. F. 1989. Treat others with tough love and a tender touch. In *The heart and soul of effective management: A Christian approach to managing and motivating people*, 113–17. Wheaton, Ill.: Scripture Publications Press, Inc.

Shaughnessy, M. A. 1989. *School handbooks: Some legal considerations*. Washington, D.C.: National Catholic Educational Association, 19–20, 28–30.

Truitt, M. R. 1991. Preparation • presentation • follow-up: Keys to constructive criticism. In *The supervisor's handbook*, 46–49. Shawnee Mission, Kans.: National Press.

* In your journal, note insights concerning staff evaluation. Knowing your own style of leadership, which strategies seemed to hold the most promise? Which held the least? What questions do you have? What initial feelings do you have about the responsibility of judging the performance of others? Are there areas in your professional development that must be updated to make you proficient in evaluating others? If so, have you located materials or training that will help you develop the skills you need?

2. Reflect on your own experiences of being evaluated. Was the experience mainly formative or summative, or was it a combination of both? What was helpful or hurtful about the experiences? Pinpoint, if you can, the source of those feelings. What lessons do you take from those experiences to your own practice of evaluating teachers and other personnel, both formatively and summatively?

3. Discuss the issue of evaluation with one or two Catholic school principals. Here are some questions to ask:

   a. What types of evaluation are you using? If there is more than one type, when, where, and why do you use different methods? How satisfied are you with the system(s) used?

   b. Do you make any distinction between new teachers and veterans in the process of evaluation?

   c. How much time does each style require?

   d. How many formal or informal assessments are done for each staff member? Are there pre-observation and post-observation conferences?

   e. Are evaluation times scheduled or unscheduled?

   f. How do you provide for coaching or training in areas of growth?

   g. What strategies or documentation do you use in monitoring a less-than-effective staff member? What procedures are in place if the staff member must be dismissed or asked to resign?

   h. Is there due process or a grievance procedure for teachers who believe you have treated them unfairly? Do you feel this process is effective in mediating differences?

   i. Does the diocese have an established assessment program it requires you to follow? If so, what are the advantages and disadvantages of that system?

   j. If there are weaknesses in the program or tools for assessment, what do you do to compensate and evaluate your staff more effectively?

   k. What assistance is provided or required by the diocese in updating professional growth?

   l. What tools or instruments do you use to assess and monitor staff professional growth? Do you have opportunities to share your concerns with the diocesan office or with fellow principals in the diocese?

3. Inquire about the possibility of visiting a class with a principal. Afterward, discuss with the principal the strategies that might be used in a follow-up conference.

4. Request from the diocese a copy of the staff evaluation program. How do you evaluate the objectivity of the policies and process?

   a. Is there consistency between the teacher job description and the evaluation instruments used to document and rate performance?

   b. Are the instruments to document and report performance easy to use and understand? Are there separate instruments and processes for formative and summative evaluation?

   c. Is there a provision for differentiated supervision? If so, what determines who receives which style?

   d. What procedure is required to document ineffective performance?

   e. Is the highly effective teacher evaluated in a way that affirms yet challenges?

   f. Does the program hold the principal accountable for working with ineffective teachers to improve performance? What happens if performance does not improve?

   g. What is the procedure for requesting a teacher's resignation or for dismissing a teacher? What strategies does the principal use to keep the school board president informed; the pastor; the superintendent of schools? In the case of a dismissal, how is this information communicated to the various publics within the school?

   h. If a teacher or staff member must be replaced during the school year, what support and transition strategies are in place for the incoming replacement? for the students affected? for other staff members?

As a result of study, reflection, and interaction with knowledgeable individuals, the learner will be able to complete the following activities. The quality of response to these activities should give some indication of the level of expertise the learner is able to bring to the situation.

Outcome Activities: P6
Evaluating Staff

1. Write a critique of the diocesan procedure for evaluating staff members. Specify strengths and indicate ways the policy or process might be strengthened. Support your opinions with rationales gleaned from your readings and past experience.

2. Discuss the merits of the four models of evaluation presented by Glatthorn and Shields.
   a. What is the purpose of each?
   b. Which style of supervision would be used for the following teachers? Provide a rationale for the style selected, and suggest other provisions you might include to help each teacher reach a higher level of potential.
      - An experienced professional who is non-Catholic and new to Catholic schools. He holds additional certification in reading and is currently working toward his master's degree.

- A sister who has been teaching for 25 years and holds a master's degree, yet tends to teach from the same lesson plans year after year, rarely including new materials, and uses teacher-directed lecture-worksheet-test as the only mode of classroom instruction.
- An older beginning teacher, non-Catholic, eager and enthusiastic, very opinionated, with a strong personality.
- Four experienced professionals who have been teaching at your high school for 10 to 15 years. Three are extremely strong, while the fourth, who was once a master teacher, has declined in effectiveness over the past year. Two teach math and algebra; one teaches science; and the fourth, the weakest teacher, teaches history and French.
- A young, beginning teacher, a sister who has just completed her degree and is eager to begin her ministry.
- Three experienced professionals who have been on your staff for more than seven years and have earned excellent performance reviews each year. One teaches pre-kindergarten classes; another teaches kindergarten; the third teaches fourth grade. Specify the style and plan for each individual.

Personnel Management Bibliography

Role: Principal as Managerial Leader

Area of Responsibility: Personnel Management

Introduction

Guerra, M., R. Haney, and R. Kealey, eds. 1992. *National congress: Catholic schools for the 21st Century: Executive summary*. Washington, D.C.: National Catholic Educational Association.

P1. Recruits, interviews, selects, and provides an orientation for the school staff

Congregation for Catholic Education. 1982. *Lay Catholics in schools: Witnesses to faith*. Boston: Daughters of St. Paul.

Fuller, F. F. 1969. Concerns of teachers: A developmental conceptualization. *American Educational Research Journal* 6:207–26.

James, R., J. Perkowski, and M. Sesko. 1991. In the beginning: Orientation of the new teacher. In *Capital wisdom: Papers from the Principals Academy 1991*, 22–28. Washington, D.C.: National Catholic Educational Association.

John, R., and M. J. Wagner. 1991. Looking for saints: Hiring Catholic school teachers. In *Capital wisdom: Papers from the Principals Academy 1991*, 55–68. Washington, D.C.: National Catholic Educational Association.

Morvay, M., and C. von Buelow. 1990. *Show me the way: A teacher support program for beginning teachers*. Louisville, Ohio: Authors, 19–32.

Shea, M. 1986. Personnel selection. In *Personnel issues and the Catholic school administrator*, 13–15, 25–27, 29. Washington, D.C.: National Catholic School Educational Association.

Sheehan, L. 1990. Hiring the right person. *Momentum* 21(2):31–33.

Young, M. 1986. New wine in new wineskins: Challenge to administrators. In *Personnel issues and Catholic school organization*, 66–70. Washington, D.C.: National Catholic Educational Association.

P2. Knows and applies principles of adult learning and motivation

Belenky, M. F., B. M. Clinchy, N. R. Goldberger, and J. M. Tarule. 1986. *Women's ways of knowing*. New York: Basic Books, Inc., Publishers, 214–29.

Brookfield, S. 1986. *Understanding and facilitating adult learning*. San Francisco: Jossey-Bass.

Fielding, G., and H. D. Schalock. *Promoting the professional development of teachers and administrators*. School Management Digest Series. Eugene, Ore.: ERIC Clearinghouse on Educational Management, College of Education, University of Oregon, 7–9, 13–15.

Knowles, M. S. 1970. *The modern practice of adult education*. New York: Association Press.

———. 1984. *Andragogy in action*. San Francisco: Jossey-Bass, 9–13.

Knox, A. B. 1990. Understanding adult learners. In *Helping adults learn*, 15–31. San Francisco: Jossey-Bass.

Lewis, A. 1991. Turning theories into research and practice. In *Learning styles: Putting research and common sense into practice*, 19–32. Alexandria, Va.: American Association of School Administrators.

National Conference of Catholic Bishops. 1979. *National catechetical directory for Catholics of the United States*. Washington, D.C.: United States Catholic Conference, nos. 182–89.

Ristau, K. 1989. The role of the principal in the ongoing education of teachers. In *Reflections on the role of the Catholic school principal*, ed. R. J. Kealey, 60–65. Washington, D.C.: National Catholic Educational Association.

Silver, H. F., and J. R. Hanson. 1980. Understanding myself as a learner. In *Teacher self-assessment*, 63–81. Moorestown, N.J.: Hanson Silver and Associates, Inc.

———. 1980. Understanding myself as a teacher. In *Teacher self-assessment*, 95–110. Moorestown, N.J.: Hanson Silver and Associates, Inc.

P3. Knows and applies the skill of organizational management, delegation of responsibilities, and communication skills

Cappel, C. 1989 A reflection on the spirituality of the principal. In *Reflections on the role of the Catholic school principal*, ed. R. J. Kealey, 26–27. Washington, D.C.: National Catholic Educational Association.

Fielding, G., and H. D. Schalock. 1985. *Promoting the professional development of teachers and administrators*. School Management Digest Series. Eugene, Ore.: ERIC Clearinghouse on Educational Management, College of Education, University of Oregon, 66–67.

Libreria Editrice Vaticana. 1994. *Catechism of the Catholic Church*. Washington, D.C.: United States Catholic Conference, nos. 1897–1917.

McKinney. M. B. 1987. *Sharing wisdom: A process for group decision making*. Valencia, Calif.: Tabor Publishing.

Michelon, L. C. 1972. *The myths and realities of management*. Cleveland, Ohio: Republic Education Institute.

Smith, W. F., and R. L. Andrews. 1989. *Instructional leadership: How principals make a difference*. Alexandria, Va.: Association for Supervision and Curriculum Development, 46–48.

Sparks, G. J. 1986. The Catholic school administrator. In *The Catholic school administrator—A book of readings*, ed. E. M. Bushman and G. J. Sparks, 283–291. Portland, Ore.: Catholic Leadership Company.

Truitt, M. R. 1991. *The supervisor's handbook*. Shawnee Mission, Kans.: National Press, 55–57, 61–63.

Walker, J. E. 1990. The skills of exemplary principals. *NASSP Bulletin* 74:48–55.

P4. Uses group process skills effectively with various school committees

Glickman, C. D. 1990. *Supervision of instruction*. Boston: Allyn and Bacon, 372–88.

Libreria Editrice Vaticana. 1994. *Catechism of the Catholic Church*. Washington, D.C.: United States Catholic Conference, nos. 1724, 1738, 1886–88.

Lunenburg, F. C., and A. C. Ornstein. 1991. *Educational administration: Concepts and practices*. Belmont, Calif.: Wadsworth, 178–82.

Sheehan, L. 1990. *Building better boards: A handbook for board members in Catholic education*. Washington, D.C.: National Catholic Educational Association, 70–74.

Thomas, J. A., and B. Davis. 1989. The principal as part of the pastoral team. In *Reflections on the role of the Catholic school principal*, ed. R. J. Kealey, 45–54. Washington, D.C.: National Catholic Educational Association.

Truitt, M. R. 1991. *The supervisor's handbook*. Shawnee Mission, Kans.: National Press, 16–20.

Yukl, G. A. 1994. *Leadership in organizations*. Englewood Cliffs, N.J.: Prentice Hall, 412–33.

P5. Manages conflicts effectively

Drahmann, T. 1985. *Governance and administration in the Catholic school*. Washington, D.C.: National Catholic Educational Association, 21–30.

Hendricks, W. 1989. *How to manage conflict*. Leadership Success Series. Shawnee Mission, Kans.: National Press, 1–3, 6–14, 15–22.

Kambeitz, T. 1991. Teaching and stewardship. *The Living Light* 27(4):334–38.

Libreria Editrice Vaticana. 1994. *Catechism of the Catholic Church*. Washington, D.C.: United States Catholic Conference, nos. 1822–29, 2302–06.

Shaughnessy, M. A. 1989. *School handbooks: Some legal considerations*. Washington, D.C.: National Catholic Educational Association, 76.

Truitt, M. R. 1991. *The supervisor's handbook*. Shawnee Mission, Kans.: National Press, 16–18, 20–24.

P6. Evaluates staff

Barth, R. S. 1991. *Improving schools from within*. San Francisco: Jossey-Bass, 56–59.

Daresh, J. C. 1992. *Supervision, a proactive process*. New York: Longman.

Glatthorn, A. A., and C. R. Shields. 1983. *Differentiated supervision for Catholic schools*. Washington, D.C.: National Catholic Educational Association, 2, 8–12.

Hind, J. F. 1989. *The heart and soul of effective management: A Christian approach to managing and motivating people*. Wheaton, Ill.: Scripture Publications Press, Inc., 113–17.

Poplin, M. S. 1992. The leader's role: Looking to the growth of teachers. *Educational Leadership* 49(5):10–11.

Shaughnessy, M. A. 1989. *School handbooks: Some legal considerations*. Washington, D.C.: National Catholic Educational Association, 19–20, 28–30.

Truitt, M. R. 1991. *The supervisor's handbook*. Shawnee Mission, Kans.: National Press, 46–49.

Integral Readings for Personnel Management

In the Beginning: Orientation of the New Teacher

James, R., J. Perkowski, and M. Seski. 1991. In *Capital wisdom: Papers from the Principals Academy 1991*, 22–25. Washington, D.C.: National Catholic Educational Association.

In the beginning, new teachers are in darkness. The principal says, "Let there be light!" The principal then separates those whose feet are firmly fastened to the earth from those whose heads are wavering in the sky. Separating the new from the old, the principal calls the new teacher "novice," and the experienced teacher "mentor." Then the principal says, "Let us dialogue on how best to nurture the tiny seed of teaching, so that it will bring forth every hidden treasure from within." The principal sees that it is good.

The concept presented in this Genesis-like scenario is more formally stated in *The Pre-Service Formation of Teachers for Catholic Schools*: "The mission of Catholic education can be realized to the degree that competent educators are committed to striving toward Christian maturity and professional ministry in our Catholic school."

Educational research has shown that new teachers have expressed needs in several areas during their first years of teaching. These areas include: faith community, classroom management, classroom discipline, academic assessment of students, parent communication skills, and instructional skills.

This paper will offer suggestions for planning an orientation process for the new teachers' expressed needs and those perceived by the administration. In this process, experienced teachers may be used as mentors, based upon their recognized proficiencies. A mentor teacher is one who has shown mastery in one or more areas and acts as a resource person and guide for the new teacher.

This process may not be needed for every new teacher. The use of a needs assessment, such as the model provided in Appendix A, will indicate some direction to follow for each individual teacher. It is possible that needs other than those stated in the model may surface.

Purpose

A mentor program within a school serves many purposes. It enhances intrafaculty faith community by facilitating communication, developing personal relationships, and solidifying the Catholic identity of the school. As mentor and mentee [*sic*] work together, they share on various levels. They talk about how to deal with students, how to deal with parents and staff. They exchange information about the easiest ways to get materials, fill in forms, and perform the daily tasks of teaching.

Developing this everyday "task kind of sharing" builds a level of security and camaraderie. Once that level is achieved, the discussion of issues central to the identity of Catholic education can be discussed and implemented.

Through the mentor program, a new teacher develops proficiency with classroom skills, improves instructional techniques, and deepens interpersonal relationships with other staff members.

For the mentor teacher, the process allows for the recognition and use of his/her expertise and, further, provides for ownership by allowing the mentor to impact the instructional process throughout the school.

This process is also invaluable for the principal who tries to pursue the role of instructional leader. It will enable the principal to build the morale of returning staff by recognizing their strengths, and to provide a method of thorough and constant monitoring of new teachers. It gives the principal supportive documentation should need for it arise at a later date. Since persons from many different countries immigrate to the United States, a principal may use this process not only for a recent graduate of a teacher training program, but also for a person unfamiliar with the American educational system.

Initial process

The process begins with diocesan and local level orientations. This is followed by the distribution of surveys to new teachers and returning staff. (See Appendices A and B.) The new teacher indicates perceived needs, and returning staff identify strengths and/or proficiencies. The principal then reviews the surveys, adding input.

During the first two weeks of school, the principal makes three or four short informal observations of the new teacher, which adds further information to the new teacher's survey. The principal dialogues with the new teacher and together they reevaluate the initial needs assessment. The new teacher, in conjunction with the principal, fills in the form (Appendix C) outlining areas to be worked on. The principal then assigns the new teacher a mentor by matching needs with skills.

Ongoing process

The mentor works with the new teacher through classroom observation and scheduled meetings. The results of the observations and/or meetings are discussed, recommendations for improvement are made, a timeline is set, and a copy of this document is given to the principal. (See Appendix D.)

The new teacher practices the recommended skills or procedures which have been outlined in the plan. The mentor teacher and new teacher meet at scheduled times to evaluate progress in target areas. The principal also makes periodic informal observations of and confers with the new teacher. Monthly meetings are scheduled with principal, mentor, and new teacher to inform the principal of areas of progress. When the principal and mentor teacher, in conjunction with the new teacher, reach consensus that an area has been improved satisfactorily, another area is emphasized.

In some instances, the new teacher concentrates on more than one area at a time. For example, the new teacher's needs may require assistance in classroom management skills and parent communication skills. Classroom management skills might take a long time since it is a multifaceted topic. Parent communication skills cannot be postponed because parent-teacher conferences, letters home, and phone call communication with parents take place from the beginning of the school year. These areas, then, can be worked on simultaneously, perhaps using two different mentors.

Timeline

The timeline given below summarizes the beginnings of this mentoring process. The rest of the timeline should be worked out according to the goals, objectives, and areas defined in the appendices.

Upon hiring	Do needs assessment
August	Diocesan and local orientation of new teacher
	Administer strength/proficiency survey to returning teachers
September (1st & 2nd weeks)	Administrator does informal short observations and meets with teacher to reevaluate initial needs
September (3rd week)	New teacher pairs up with mentor teacher to outline goals and objectives
Set dates	To begin implementation of goals and objectives
	To evaluate progress with mentor and new teacher
	To meet with administrator, mentor, and new teacher

Central to the Catholic identity of our schools is an attitude of caring, concern, support, and praise within the school community. In keeping with this spirit, the principal and the mentor teacher(s) should take care to offer consistent encouragement and praise so that the new teacher will realize his/her value in the ministry of Catholic education.

Resources

Bercik, J.T. and S. Larsen, "A Survey of the Induction Year: Perceptions of the Experienced Educator," *Illinois School Research and Development*, Fall 1990, pp. 20–28.

The Pre-Service Formation of Teachers for Catholic Schools, Washington, DC, National Catholic Educational Association, 1982.

Teacher Evaluation Handbook, Department of Education, Diocese of San Jose, 1983.

Looking for Saints: Hiring Catholic School Teachers

John, R., and M. J. Wagner. 1991. In *Capital wisdom: Papers from the Principals Academy 1991*, 55–59. Washington, D.C.: National Catholic Educational Association.

At a session of the 1991 National Principals Academy, a principal lamented, "I lose sleep over hiring new teachers. I'm always looking for saints to do all a Catholic school teacher has to do." Well, saints just aren't available. However, many qualified and dedicated teachers are ready and willing to work in our schools.

Hiring teachers for a Catholic school is a serious responsibility. Our teachers need to be much more than people who impart curriculum. They need to be professionally and personally qualified men and women who have a vocation for teaching rather than individuals needing a job.

In 1972 the American bishops stated: "This integration of religious truths and values with the rest of life is brought about in the Catholic school not only by the presence of curriculum but, more important, by the presence of teachers who express an integrated approach to learning and living in their private and professional lives." (*To Teach as Jesus Did*)

In 1977, Rome reminded us again of the type of teacher needed for Catholic schools: "By their witness and their behavior teachers are of the first importance to impart a distinctive character to Catholic schools." (*The Catholic School*)

Finally, the Code of Canon Law guides the principal in hiring: "Formation and education programs in a Catholic school must be based on the principals of Catholic doctrine, and the teacher must be outstanding in true doctrine and uprightness of life."

Are we looking for saints? Not really. But the hiring principal must clearly search for teachers who can live and teach our faith. By their personal witness and behavior our teachers must be able and willing to pass on our faith tradition to their students. Following are some guidelines to assist principals with the hiring process.

Pre-interview process

The pre-interview process is as necessary as the interview itself. A principal must gather all available background on each candidate to be considered. Information, including academic credentials, previous employment, and personal experiences provides a clear backdrop. This backdrop highlights essential elements necessary in the selection of a quality candidate for the interview process.

The present assessment of the school with regard to returning teachers, letters of intent, formal appraisal outcomes, internal grade changes, enrollment, and other factors will have an effect on the hiring of teachers.

Another phase of the process is to use good teacher placement centers such as colleges, universities, religious communities, publications with educational listings, and local and diocesan education placement offices. The principal must identify the position and clearly indicate the needed preparation and skills. He or she must also request the applicant's portfolio of transcripts, various experiences, and letters of reference. Each applicant is prioritized according to his or her character and preparation and the needs of the school.

Interview process: diocesan level

The diocese can be of tremendous help to the local principal. A basic screening of applicants can ensure that all the schools have some preliminary information. This screening can be in the form of brief interviews or simple application packets. (See samples, Appendix A.)

The next step can be rewarding for both the diocese and the individual schools—a job fair. (See samples, Appendix B.) This annual event can be jointly run by the diocesan office and the hiring principals. The advantage is that principals get a brief (10-minute) interview with at least 10 candidates. This gives a school a first glance at many qualified candidates.

At the same time, the applicant has an opportunity to meet principals and get a sense of the spirit of our schools.

After a job fair, the principals can recall an applicant for more in-depth interviews. The preliminary work is done and the principal can spend the valuable interview time ensuring that the applicant truly desires to teach rather than just to have a job.

The diocesan office has one final responsibility. It is to make sure that all principals are constantly reminded of the critical importance of the hiring process, especially in light of the philosophy of Catholic education as stated in various church and episcopal documents.

Interview process: school site

There are many ways to interview. No one way is the right way. Again, it is important that the principal keep in mind the uniqueness of the Catholic school teacher and the demands of the position. We will demonstrate two methods: principal as sole interviewer and team interviewing.

Principal as sole interviewer. The principal selects an appropriate interview form or composes a set of questions so that comparative objectivity can be used among the applicants.

After this, the principal makes appointments for the initial interview. A 20-minute interview can determine the applicant's suitability.

During the interview, the principal makes sure the applicant is at ease. Remembering that the applicant needs to be professionally and personally qualified, the principal asks questions in both areas. Questions such as "Tell me about your present parish and your level of involvement" or "What are significant church issues today?" will quickly disclose the applicant's faith development. Questions such as "How would you develop a writing program for the third grade?" or "What would be your classroom management style?" will generate the professional qualifications of the person.

After reflection on the applicants, the principal will communicate the results to each individual and determine whether or not a second interview will be scheduled. For the second interview, use a standard in-depth instrument (i.e., SRI Teacher Perceiver) to look at specific educational themes or specific focuses. The principal reviews the outcomes and begins to formulate a decision.

Third interviews are scheduled with finalists. This interview is the practical one: review policies of the school, review mutual expectations, tour the premises, discuss open questions. After a discussion of the contract, the position can be offered.

The advantage of this process is that the school may not have hired a "saint," but the principal is assured that the strongest person, professionally and personally, is now a member of the ministry team.

Team interviewing. For this method, the principal is part of a team that interviews. Since the Catholic school has the responsibility to foster "community," members of the community should be a part of the hiring process. The principal asks for volunteers from the faculty. The process works well with as few as three or as many as seven faculty members.

The applicant meets the interviewing team, which has prepared questions to ascertain his or her personal and professional qualifications. Over a period of 30–40 minutes, the applicant responds to questions regarding religion, curriculum, teamwork, background, educational issues, and values. The principal acts as an observer and focuses on the interaction between the applicant and the faculty.

After the teachers have finished their questions, they ask the candidate to devise a teaching strategy from an object in the room, for example, a jar of jelly beans, a bouquet of flowers, a stack of business cards. A good question would be: "How would you use this item to teach math in the third grade?" The applicant takes a few minutes and then presents a short lesson.

Upon conclusion of the lesson, the principal takes part in the process. The principal asks a few questions for further clarity and information.

At this point the applicant is given time to make a concluding statement.

When the interview is over, the principal and faculty each write down a score from 1 to 5 (5 highest). For example, if there were six people in the room, an applicant with a 25 final score would have received something like: 4, 4, 5, 5, 3, 4 = 25. After a few interviews, it becomes very clear that one score is significantly higher than another. If two applicants are extremely close, they can come back for another round.

The advantage of this process is that it is extremely thorough and it gives the faculty ownership of the decision as well as a sense of support for a teacher they helped hire.

Conclusion

Like the administrator at the National Catholic Principals Academy, principals are always searching for the "saint." The above hints and ideas can effectively ensure that the best possible person is chosen for ministry in our Catholic school.

Resources

Sacred Congregation for Catholic Education, *The Catholic School*, Washington, DC, U.S. Catholic Conference, 1977.

The Canon Law Society of Great Britain and Ireland, *Code of Canon Law in English Translation*, Michigan, William B. Erdmann Publishing Company, 1983.

Diocese of Oakland, *School Department Interview Materials*, Oakland, CA, 1990.

Group Interview Process of St. Joseph Elementary School, Alameda, CA.

Sacred Congregation for Catholic Education, *Lay Catholics in School: Witnesses to Faith*, Daughters of St. Paul, Boston, MA, 1982.

SRI Selection Research Inc., Lincoln, NE.

National Council of Bishops, *Teach Them*, Washington, DC, U.S. Catholic Conference, 1976.

Teacher Selection Process of the Catholic School Services, Toledo, OH.

National Conference of Catholic Bishops, *To Teach as Jesus Did*, Washington, DC, U.S. Catholic Conference, 1972.

Personnel Selection

Shea, M. 1986. In *Personnel issues and the Catholic school administrator*, ed. J. S. O'Brien and M. McBrien, 25–27. Washington, D.C.: National Catholic Educational Association.

Hiring Procedure

The entire process is important, but how the applicant follows instructions is a valuable indication as to how the applicant will act in a working situation. In an emergency, where interview procedures must be bypassed, some form of temporary hiring should be used until credentials are properly checked.

A summary of an interview or screening process should include the following elements.

◆ professional and academic competence
◆ basic knowledge of the applicant's public and private life
◆ understanding of the philosophy of the school
◆ participation in religious activities of the school
◆ working conditions of this particular school
◆ knowledge that public violation of church teachings is grounds for dismissal
◆ demonstration lesson

A proper interview will go a long way toward the development of a workable, successful school operation.

Hiring Teachers: Practices and Precautions

Presuming that a supply of teacher candidates is available, the priority question becomes the hiring procedure. Casual or careless hiring procedures are a definite invitation to future headaches and problems. Firing rhymes with hiring and poor hiring inevitably leads to troublesome firing.

The NCEA recognized this situation and as early as 1973 set up a committee to develop guidelines. This committee quickly realized that it could not come up with absolute, infallible, and complete guidelines in this relatively unexplored new area. "Guidelines" became the key word as the committee developed a beginning framework (still valid) upon which different school systems in all parts of the nation could select and develop what was most useful to their particular aims and goals.

The basic framework for these guidelines covered three areas: selecting teachers from among a group of applicants; outlining basic principles which all teachers would be expected to believe in, follow, and practice; and setting up standards on growth and development of teachers in service in the schools.

The following is from the set of guidelines called *Procedures for Selection of Teachers for Catholic Schools*.

A) Application Process

1. Include questions on the role of teachers in the purposes and uniqueness of Catholic schools.
2. In the collection of factual data, be aware of limitations by the Equal Opportunity Commission on certain information.

3. Obtain information on academic background and credentials; accept only official transcripts.
4. Include a statement by the applicant as to the accuracy of the information, for example, "I understand that any misrepresentation of facts in this application will be considered just cause for dismissal at the discretion of the employer."
5. Ask permission to investigate any of the facts or statements submitted, for example, "I hereby grant _____ permission to investigate any of the facts or statements submitted by me, except where my written statement upon this form specifically requests that no investigation be made."
6. Indicate on the application the length of time you will file the application if the person is not hired.
7. Check with previous employers.
8. If the applicant is an ex-religious, contact the former congregation; let the applicant suggest one person and you select another.
9. Be sensitive to the problems caused by last minute or panic hiring procedures.

B) Interview Process

1. All documents and materials (references and transcripts) should be on file before the interview is conducted. Realize that it may not be possible to obtain information from present employer.
2. During the interview respect the confidentiality of information submitted regarding the applicant.
3. Interview questions and discussion should focus on "Guiding Principles for Teacher Commitment in Light of the pastoral *To Teach as Jesus Did* and "Guidelines for Teachers in Catholic Schools."
4. More than one person should interview the applicant (both at central office level and the local school level).
5. Make notes as soon after the interview as possible. Be honest; include both strengths and weaknesses of the applicant.
6. If possible, the interview process should provide for observation of the applicant in a classroom situation.

C) Orientation Program

1. In order to avoid conflicts between theory and practice, building the program around the "Guiding Principles for Teacher Commitment in Light of the Pastoral *To Teach as Jesus Did* and "Guidelines for Teachers in

Catholic Schools." Words and witness must be harmonized in order to avoid ambiguity.

These procedures are very basic but necessary. Certainly they are the minimum guidelines for teacher hiring. They present a set of positive steps to which each diocese or school might add or expand for its own specific conditions.

There are some negative factors or caution in hiring. If the applicant has previous teaching experience, it is mandatory that the principal contact the previous employer before making a commitment. The applicant may already be under contract or may have been terminated for cause by the previous employer. So-called "off the street" or "panic" hiring is always risky.

A substantial part of the interview should be concerned with the applicant's understanding and acceptance of the philosophy of the Catholic school and the public observance of the laws of the church. When a school has a stated philosophy which can actually be seen in practice in the day-to-day operation of the school, the administrator has an instrument upon which to base his or her judgments about the suitability of a prospective teacher to join the staff. This assumes that the prospective teacher has already been found competent and desirable in the academic framework of the school.

The last step in the process for selection of a teacher is the decision to hire or not to hire an individual. It need not be hurried and is best done in writing within an agreed upon, specified period. The administrator then has time to digest the interview, seek information, if such is needed, and come to a considered decision. If hired, the applicant should be requested or refused in writing.

Finally, the hiring decision from among professionally qualified and eligible candidates should make the Christian dimension of the individual a priority consideration. The candidate should clearly understand the minimum expectations as regards beliefs, attitudes, and behaviors. There should be no surprises on either side once the candidate reports for work.

Alfred McBride has written: "Hiring a believer does not guarantee the enduring commitment of the believer. The powers of secularization in the culture are sufficiently seductive and enchanting to the point that they may prevail over our Catholic educators and weaken their dedication to Christ . . . Catholic educators need the life-long possibilities of the grace of evangelization, the loving summons to a firm commitment of Jesus."

Promoting the Professional Development
of Teachers and Administrators

Fielding, G., and H. D. Schalock. 7–9, 13–15. School Management Digest Series. Eugene, Ore.: ERIC Clearinghouse on Educational Management, College of Education, University of Oregon.

The *cultural* aspect of schools has to do with the beliefs, values, and ideals that are shared among members of the school community. These include beliefs about the purposes of schooling, the roles of teachers and students, and the special "mission" or "character" of a school. Culture also refers to the forms through which common beliefs and values are expressed and communicated, such as stories told by a principal about special teachers or events that create desired images of the school. These forms of communication also include awards assemblies, honor rolls, pep rallies, and other public recognition of achievement or good conduct. The cultural norms and symbols of schools, in combination with the interpersonal and technical aspects of schools, define the context in which professional development efforts take place.

Participants

Besides paying attention to the context of a school, those designing inservice programs also must consider the kinds of concerns, expectations, and experience that participants are likely to bring to inservice events. Designs for staff development activities need to be sensitive, for example, to the differing concerns of elementary and secondary school teachers. As Lieberman and Miller (1984) point out, elementary teachers are likely to be concerned about such issues as how to teach more subjects than will fit in the mastery allotted, when to teach in large groups, or when to insist on mastery over content and when to be satisfied with mere "coverage." Secondary teachers typically have concerns about issues like packaging and pacing instruction to fit into set time periods, balancing loyalties to the faculty and loyalties to the student culture, and dealing with the school's organizational structures. These differing concerns need to be appreciated when plans for inservice programs are constructed.

Teachers at different stages of career development also may profit from different kinds of inservice activities. Whereas a new teacher, for example, might need assistance in understanding and internalizing a school's policies and norms, an experienced teacher might want assistance in becoming a department chair, a supervisor of student teachers, or an author of curriculum materials.

Finally, certain personal characteristics and attitudes of educators need to be appreciated when planning professional development activities since these factors influence teachers' receptivity to new practices or programs. In a widely cited experiment in inservice education, for example, Crawford and his colleagues (1978) found that teachers' verbal ability correlated positively and significantly with their use of recommended instructional practices. Several studies also have shown that teachers' attitudes toward themselves as teachers, toward inservice education, and toward educational change affect their response to inservice programs (Sparks 1983). For example, teachers who see themselves primarily as content experts who transmit basic knowledge to students might have a difficult time dealing with an inservice program on the use of simulations and role-playing in the classroom.

Objectives

The objectives of a professional development program refer to what participants are expected to gain from the program. Objectives can focus on a wide range of expected outcomes, from enhancing an individual's understanding of self or of a new academic specialty, to gaining proficiency in a new instructional model or program, to developing skills in group communication or decision-making.

It is sometimes helpful to describe objectives according to their degree of complexity and novelty. *Complexity* refers to the number of different attitudes, skills, or understandings participants are expected to develop or refine and the subtlety of relationships among them. Learning one or two separate techniques, for example, is less complex than learning how to use an integrated model of teaching. Novelty refers to the degree of familiarity participants already have with the content. Many teachers report that objectives of inservice activities typically deal with content with which they are already familiar. Inservice activities that focus on simple or familiar material need to be organized differently from inservice activities that address complex or novel material.

Finally, as Gall and his associates have pointed out (1982), objectives for staff development programs may be established that indicate desired changes in students as well as in teachers and administrators. Such programs frequently attempt to improve students' learning, attitudes, or behaviors. For example, inservice programs have been designed to help teachers reduce student discipline problems, or to increase the amount of class time students spend on academic tasks.

Procedures

Procedures are the methods used to accomplish the objectives of a professional development program. These may include lectures and discussions, microteaching, peer observations and "coaching," supervision and feedback from administrators, and informal colleague interactions. Distinctions often are made between procedures appropriate for developing *awareness* and knowledge of new practices and those appropriate for developing *skill* in using and adapting new practices. The appropriateness of a procedure obviously depends on its objectives and its clients.

Costs and Benefits

Costs of a professional development program include not only financial expenses but any opportunities or activities that participants forgo to participate in a program, such as giving up time for instructional planning. Also included are negative consequences linked to the program, for example, a decline in student interest in a particular subject area. Benefits of the program are gains in individual, program, or organizational effectiveness, feelings of personal satisfaction or growth, and other positive outcomes.

The anticipated costs and benefits of staff development, along with the other dimensions discussed earlier, need to be considered when planning professional development programs. All the dimensions introduced in this chapter will be treated in more depth in the chapters ahead.

Attitudes and Expectations

Research yields some useful conclusions about attitudes and expectations of teacher participants in inservice activities.

1. Teachers generally prefer inservice activities that deal with student motivation, affect, and attitude over those that deal with increasing student achievement (Schurr and others 1980). Hall and others (1973) found, however, that under supportive conditions, teachers may become less concerned about student affect and classroom management and more concerned about the issue of student achievement.

2. Teachers prefer inservice activities that permit them to work with other teachers (Holly 1982), particularly others with similar teaching responsibilities (Ngaiyaye and Hanley 1979).

3. Some evidence suggests that teachers appreciate having teachers from different schools represented in inservice activities (Gall and others 1982).

4. Several different sites for inservice are acceptable to most teachers (for example, a school district office or a university), but the most favorable site appears to be the teacher's school (Gall and others 1982).

5. Teachers have positive attitudes toward the participation of principals in inservice activities (Gall and others 1982).

6. As a group, teachers have positive attitudes toward inservice (Gall and others 1982). Krupp (1980) found, however, that teachers in their forties who had taught for twenty or more years consistently expressed negative attitudes toward staff development.

Less is known about the attitudes and expectations of principals toward professional development. On the basis of several surveys of principals' attitudes toward inservice, Wyant (1980) concluded that principals are most interested in inservice activities that deal with

◆ exercising leadership in educational improvement and change
◆ evaluating instructional programs and personnel
◆ maintaining good school-community relations
◆ providing staff development for teachers
◆ improving school climate
◆ developing specific skills in problem-solving, decision-making, and conflict resolution.

With respect to the "delivery" of inservice, Wyant suggested that principals had positive attitudes toward visiting other schools, participating in small group sessions to discuss common problems and share ideas, and attending inservice activities with teachers. They also expressed interest in credit courses offered on a regular basis.

Objectives

Available evidence indicates that inservice activity is fractionated over a wide variety of topics. Teachers interviewed in Gall's study participated in inservice activities that focused on basic skills instruction; general instruction-related topics, such as a lecture on effective schools research; specific subject areas; and personal and professional development generally, such as stress management for teachers. The objectives pursued within each of these areas were not clearly connected to each other.

Objectives for inservice activities usually involve simple, short-term learning. The focus of these activities typically is on enhancing teachers' routine practice rather than on bringing about broad improvement or shifts in basic approaches to instruction.

The conclusion that objectives for inservice activities are fractionated and rather unambitious seems to apply to inservice for administrators as well. Inservice training for principals has been characterized as a hodgepodge of "quick fix" sessions designed to deal with discrete topics like handling stress or using microcomputers. As McCurdy (1983) noted, such topics are not unimportant, but they seldom represent the type of comprehensive long-term professional development programs that are likely to increase substantially a principal's effectiveness.

Procedures

Traditional professional development procedures include university course work, presentations by experts during a school district's one or two yearly "inservice days," and workshops held during the school year.

These traditional procedures used to increase teachers' professional effectiveness have been faulted for failing to assist teachers in translating new ideas into day-to-day practice. They typically are one-time events that appear to have little impact on patterns of instructions.

Over the last decade, new and apparently more effective procedures have been developed, such as the Instructional Theory Into Practice (ITIP) program developed by Madeline Hunter (1976) and the Stallings Effective-Use-of-Time Program (Stallings and others 1978; Sparks 1983). Several promising procedures are described in detail in part 2.

References

Crawford, J. and others. (1978). *An experiment on teacher effectiveness and parent-assisted instruction in the third grade*, Vol. 1–3. Stanford, CA: Stanford University, Center for Educational Research. ED 160 148.

Gall, M.D.; Haisley, F. B.; Baker, R.; and Perez, M. (1982). *The relationship between inservice education practices and effectiveness of basic skills instruction*. Eugene, OR: University of Oregon, Center for Educational Policy and Management. ED 228 745.

Hall, G.; Wallace, R.; and Dossett, W. (1973). *A developmental conceptualization of the adoption process within educational institutions*. Austin, Texas: Research and Development Center for Teacher Education, The University of Texas.

Holly, M. L. (1982). Teachers' views on inservice training. *Phi Delta Kappan, 63,* 417–18.

Hunter, M. (1976). *Improved instruction*. E. Segundo, California. TIP Publications.

Krupp, J. A. (1980). *A phenomenological study of teacher perceptions of life development changes as related to inservice behaviors and needs*. Unpublished doctoral dissertation, University of Connecticut.

Lieberman, A.; and Miller, L. (1984). School improvement: themes and variations. *Teachers College Record, 86,* 4–19.

McCurdy, J. (1983). *The role of the principal in effective schools*. Arlington, VA: American Association of School Administrators.

Ngaiyaye, M. S. W.; and Hanley, J. L. (1978). What teachers want from inservice education. *North Central Association Quarterly, 53,* 305–311.

Schurr, K. T., and others. (1980, April). *Discrepancies in teacher and administrator preferences for inservice training topics*. Paper presented at the annual meeting of the American Educational Research Association, Boston, MA. ED 186 401.

Sparks, G. M. (1983). Synthesis of research on staff development for effective teaching. *Educational Leadership, 41* (3), 65–72.

Stallings, J.; Needles, M.; and Stayrook, N. (1978). *The teaching of basic reading skills in secondary schools, phase II. Final report*. Menlo Park, CA: SRI International.

Wyant, S. H.; Reinhard, D. L.; and Arends, R. I. (1980). *Of principals and projects*. Reston, VA: Association of Teacher Educators. ED 203 449.

Understanding Adult Learners

Knox, A. B. 1990. In *Helping adults learn*, 15–31. San Francisco: Jossey-Bass.

What do you know about adult learners that typically guides you in planning and conducting an educational program for adults? Many instructors recall their own experiences as learners, pertinent readings, and impressions of past participants in similar programs. Such recollections and impressions tend to blend together, and it may be difficult to extract implications for specific program decisions. The following generalizations about adults as learners may reinforce some of your current understandings and perhaps provide additional insights.

Adult learners have many characteristics related to past experience, current abilities and roles, and future aspirations that influence adult learning and teaching (Knox, 1977). You cannot take *all* these characteristics into account, even when assisting one learner, as in on-the-job training. Effective instructors recognize that there are some general characteristics associated with adult learning that enable them to be especially helpful to learners in each instance. Understanding such characteristics can enable you to *organize adult learners' activities around their backgrounds and aspirations*. This chapter presents some generalizations about characteristics of adults to take into account when helping adults learn. They are grouped in four sections: on enhancing proficiencies, development and learning, influences on participation, and the importance of active learner participation.

Enhancing Proficiencies

Adults engage in learning activities mainly to enhance their proficiencies. You can use information about proficiencies to assess educational needs, encourage persistence, and relate new learnings to old (Knox, 1980a; Knox, 1985). Proficiency is the capability to perform effectively if given the opportunity and typically entails a combination of knowledge, attitudes, and skills. In most adult life roles and tasks, actual performance reflects both the individual's proficiency and the influence of other people. As an instructor, you can help adults acquire desired proficiencies, but you cannot assure satisfactory performance.

Proficiency-oriented adult learning is similar to competency-based preparatory education for young people: both give attention to specific objectives, mastery learning, and evaluation of learner achievement of objectives. However, whereas competency-based preparatory education emphasizes achievement of minimal standards of performance in educational tasks, proficiency-oriented continuing education emphasizes achievement of optimal standards of proficiency related to adult life roles. This is especially apparent in continuing professional education.

An understanding of discrepancies between current and desired proficiencies is useful in several ways. Awareness of such a discrepancy can motivate an adult to engage in a learning activity. Specification of such a discrepancy is the main purpose of an educational needs assessment, whether performed by the learner or by someone else as part of the program development process. Program evaluation includes assessing the extent to which educational activity is enhancing current proficiencies so that they more closely approach desired ones (and sometimes assessing the extent to which even more desirable ones are recognized). Effective educational activities and materials help learners build on current proficiencies and progress toward desired proficiencies. Thus, an understanding of discrepancies between current and desired proficiencies helps to explain motives of adult learners and enables those who help adults learn to do so responsively and effectively.

As an instructor, you should understand that the impact of your program is affected by many influences on proficiency and on motivation to enhance proficiency. An adult's proficiencies change developmentally over the years. Unused proficiencies diminish. Adults who engage in work, family, and community activities in reflective ways gradually become more proficient in those activities. Evolving proficiencies result from personal and situational influences—past, current, and even prospective. Past influences include not only the individual's abilities, education, and experience but also opportunities and encouragement, which are sometimes related to social class. These past influences enter into an adult's general sense of being a proficient person, and this self-perception, along with current proficiencies, contributes to an individual's outlook regarding the risks and benefits of future efforts to enhance proficiency. This outlook interacts with current and evolving performance, as the adult and others who care about his or her performance form a sense of the adult's proficiency. Many personality-related characteristics, such as values, interests, self-concept, and attention to stability and change in the process of decision making, affect a person's striving to enhance proficiency. Especially for older adults, physical condition and health can modify an adult's efforts to enhance proficiency. Hopes and expectations for the future are major spurs to growth for some adults.

Gradual adjustments of proficiencies and tasks result in a fairly stable equilibrium for most adults most of the time. This stability tends to be interrupted by major role-change events, such as a job change, a family change, or a move to a new community, which require some adjustments and typically heighten readiness to learn. Rapid increases in proficiency can result, followed by periods of relative stability. Responsiveness to such teachable moments can increase the impact of your program.

An understanding of the transactional and developmental process by which proficiency evolves can be helpful in various ways to adult learners and to those who help them learn. The evolution of proficiency is developmental in that past characteristics influence current proficiencies, which influence future choices, and it is transactional in that it results from the individual's social interaction. An understanding of the process by which proficiency evolves can enable an engineer who confronts a new and different

assignment to anticipate the requisite proficiencies, select relevant learning activities, and thus apply what is learned to improve performance. Such understanding can enable a farmer engaged in an extension computer project on farm records to clarify agribusiness goals and related educational objectives. Hospital staff members can use concepts regarding proficiency to guide a practice audit comparing current practice with achievable standards of best practice in order to focus on needed improvements and monitor efforts to achieve them. Attention to participants' proficiencies can help an expert conducting a workshop relate new ideas to their current knowledge and encourage them to persist in the workshop and apply what they learn. A supervisor in a financial institution can use concepts regarding proficiencies to improve the annual performance review for employees so that supervisor and employee agree to growth goals for the employee to which both are committed.

A developmental understanding of current and desired proficiencies can also help individual adults in their self-directed learning efforts. Concepts about proficiencies can help individuals use their experience and aspirations to assess their educational needs, clarify their educational objectives, select educational materials, and evaluate their progress. The result should be challenging—but not overwhelming—learning projects that address the questions, problems, and opportunities that concern the learners, enhance their proficiency, and encourage them to apply what they learn to improve performance.

In some instances, such as self-directed learning projects on a leisure interest or learning activities on personal health and fitness, undertaken by adults with much experience with and leaning toward education, almost all of a learning project may be pursued on a self-directed basis. In other instances, such as orientation sessions for new entry-level employees with little understanding of procedures and expectations, most of the learning activity may be guided by the supervisor. Even so, self-directed learning can be a supplemental activity for some highly motivated new employees, and encouragement and assistance with self-directed learning during the coming months can be an objective of the orientation experience. In most instances (such as continuing professional education) direction of continuing education activities is a shared responsibility of the learner and others able and willing to help.

Use of ideas about proficiencies is illustrated by the experience of Tyler Springfield, a state library administrator.

Tyler Springfield conducted a five-day workshop for two dozen librarians who had recently assumed administrative responsibilities for staff development, cosponsored by a university library school and an association of librarians. Findings from a recent survey had alerted Tyler to the similarity of tasks and educational needs for most categories of library personnel, with the exception of administrators. The workshop participants' recent career transitions alerted Tyler to analyze gaps between current and desired proficiencies.

Tyler and the other workshop instructors were committed to help participants strengthen proficiencies that were new and important in their staff development roles. Because workshop registrations were confirmed a month ahead, Tyler was able to send a brief questionnaire to be completed for summary and use in the final planning process. Without this early preregistration, he would have distributed the questionnaire when participants arrived and had it summarized during the first session.

Because he and the other workshop planners were familiar with such participants, the staff development roles they were entering, and typical adjustments that people make in such career transitions, the questionnaire was quite selective. It requested information about pertinent experience, aspirations in the new role, self-confidence, major perceived barriers, and perceived sources of assistance.

Tyler used the summary of questionnaire findings and other background information to orient workshop instructors regarding the main gaps between participants' current and desired proficiencies. The summary was also used to select workshop materials and activities likely to connect new learnings to old and encourage persistence in learning activities during and after the workshop. After the workshop, participants were given their questionnaire statement of what they hoped to gain from the workshop as a basis for their evaluation of the extent to which those gains had occurred and for their planning of follow-up activities.

Development and Learning

Of course, adult development extends far beyond proficiencies—so far, in fact, that you may be tempted to throw up your hands and wonder why, as an instructor, you should pay attention to adult development at all. After all, even when you work individually with adult learners, you are not a counselor helping them cope with life crises. And when you work with groups of participants, they are so varied, how could you possibly have the time and expertise to comprehend their unique backgrounds and aspirations? You couldn't, of course.

But it is just that diversity that makes generalizations about adult development and learning so useful to you—not for individualizing your instruction to respond to all the differences but, rather, for helping you decide what options to provide: alternative materials and activities for groups of participants, specialized learning projects for individual participants.

Generalizations about various learning styles and interests that reflect developmental tasks and personality development warrant responsiveness and individualization. The highlights about adult development in this section suggest

dynamics that give rise to teachable moments in your participants' lives, moments that contribute to participation, motivation, and application. The concluding example of in-service teacher education suggests a few of the ways instructors can select and use developmental generalizations.

Learning Style. Adults vary in how they approach and use learning activities. The characteristic and preferred way in which an adult engages in learning activities is termed "learning style" (Claxton and Ralston, 1978; Cross, 1981; Dunn and Dunn, 1972; Gregorc, 1979; Holtzclaw, 1985; Kalamas, 1986a; Krupp, 1982). Intelligence, personality, age, formal education, and previous specialized experience all contribute to the great variety of learning styles within the adult population. These characteristics are associated with development generally. Thus, to understand and guide adult learning, it is important to understand adult development (Hultsch and Deutsch, 1981; Knox, 1977; Krupp, 1981; Merriam, 1983, 1984; Schaie and Geiwitz, 1982; Troll, 1982; Whitbourne and Weinstock, 1979).

A developmental perspective helps explain how adults acquire their learning style, what prompts learning activities, and how teaching style can both accommodate learning style and guide its further evolution. For example, change events, such as a job change, loss of a loved one, or even buying a new car, heighten readiness to learn and often trigger participation in educational activities (Aslanian and Brickell, 1980; Chiriboga, 1982; Glustrom, 1983). Understanding such events can enable you to offer educational activities that are responsive to those developmental tasks, publicize educational programs in ways that help potential participants recognize how the program is likely to aid in their developmental adjustment, and select relevant and helpful educational materials and activities.

Learning ability and style change gradually throughout life. Most adults can learn almost anything they want to if they are willing to devote enough time and attention and if they receive some assistance. However, the mix of learning abilities and interests evolves during adulthood, as some learning activities increase in attractiveness and ease of learning while others decline. The result is a stable plateau of general learning ability through most of adulthood, but with shifts in what seems important to learn and in how easy it is to master various types of learning tasks.

Regarding ability, for example, performance in learning tasks that benefit from accumulated experience, such as those that entail vocabulary, general information, and fluency in dealing with ideas, continues to improve during most of adulthood.

By contrast, performance in learning tasks such as rote memory, discovering figural and mathematical relations, and inductive reasoning steadily declines from young adulthood into old age. Consequently, as adults grow older, they tend to substitute wisdom for brilliance when dealing with intellectual tasks. These shifts in learning style reflect developmental trends in intelligence (Cattell, 1971; Horn, 1970).

Shifts in learning style also reflect developmental trends in personality during adulthood. Aspects of personality associated with learning style include cognitive style and growth, ego development, and moral development. Adults tend to evolve from unquestioning conformity to recognition of multiple viewpoints to deliberate commitment to application of universal principles and appreciation of relationships, both human and cognitive (Fowler, 1981; Kohlberg, 1973; Loevinger, 1976; Perry, 1970; Weathersby, 1981). However, people change in various directions, sometimes associated with differences in social class, gender, experience, and motives and perceptions (Baruch, Barnett, and Rivers, 1983; Gilligan, 1982; Loewenthal, Thurnher, Chiriboga, and Associates, 1975; Rubin, 1976; Weathersby, 1981). An appreciation of these trends and influences can enable you both to recognize major features of an adult's current learning style and to help adults enhance their learning style so that it will serve them even better in the future.

You can assess participants' preferred ways of learning in various ways. Informal ways include asking them on a registration form or in conversation to express their preferences. You can also provide a variety of methods and note choices and reactions, and you can ask them to share their reactions as a part of their program evaluation comments. Smith (1982, Appendix A) contains a review of learning-style inventories for those who want to use a more formal procedure. Providing participants with the results of any of these ways of assessing learning style helps them to clarify preferences and to make more informed choices in the future. Summaries of their preferences can guide your instructional decisions.

Various dimensions of cognitive style define characteristic modes of mental and creative functioning that people typically use for perceiving, remembering, thinking, and problem solving (Brown, 1978; Gubrium and Buckholdt, 1977; Steitz, 1985). One dimension is an analytic, impersonal approach to problem solving versus a more global, social orientation. Another dimension is cognitive complexity and abstraction (which enables people to view social behavior in ways that are highly differentiated, finely articulated, and flexibly integrated so as to accommodate diversity, conflict, and inconsistency) versus cognitive simplicity and concreteness (in which people function best when dealing with consistent information).

A third dimension is impulsivity (that is, using the first answer that comes to mind even if it is incorrect) versus reflection (pondering several alternatives before deciding). A fourth dimension is convergent thinking (which emphasizes logical conclusions and conventional best outcomes) versus divergent thinking (which emphasizes originality, variety, and quantity of relevant results).

Developmental Changes in Learning Style. The foregoing dimensions help characterize how an adult compares with other adults in typical cognitive style. By contrast, some dimensions, such as style of conceptualizing, seem to be developmentally ordered: Younger people have relational styles that rely on routine use of thematic or functional

relationships, and as they become older some of them develop more analytic ways of conceptualizing descriptive relationships, and with age and experience some go on to develop more categorical inferential styles (Messick, 1984).

If you understand these or other cognitive-style dimensions, you and the learners themselves can select and organize learning activities most likely to be useful (DeNovellis, 1984, 1985; Dixon, 1982, 1985; Holtzclaw, 1985; James and Galbraith, 1985; Myers and Myers, 1980; Schwen and others, 1979). Some of these dimensions contribute to more general cognitive development that sometimes occurs during late adolescence and young adulthood. For example, some college students progress from a simple dualism based on authority and division of meaning into two realms such as good versus bad, right versus wrong, and we versus they, through discovery of multiple perspectives and relativism, to the development of commitment within an awareness of relativism.

It is likely that cognitive style and development, with its focus on intellectual tasks such as perceiving, thinking, and problem solving, is related to the developing sense of self, with its focus on feelings about self, impulses, aspirations, and relations with other people. Like cognitive development, ego development continues into adulthood, and some adults continue to evolve in their sense of self and their approach to decision making.

Early stages of ego development tend to be impulsive, self-protective, and conformist, characterized by dependence, opportunism, manipulation, belonging, and stereotyping. Some adults never outgrow these stages of character development and interpersonal style and so experience difficulty when dealing with learning activities that entail dealing with complex patterns of ideas and making clear distinctions between process and outcomes. Several more advanced stages in the evolving sense of self entail increased awareness of one's own standards, appreciation of relationships between the self and others, and concern for communication and collaboration to deal with problems, opportunities, motives, and achievement. Cognitive styles at these stages of ego development are characterized by multiple perspectives and complex patterns of ideas. People who achieve individualistic, autonomous, and integrated stages of ego development become more attentive to relations between feelings and action, respect for individuality, interdependence, causation, self-fulfillment, inner peace, and identity. Their cognitive styles are typically characterized by conceptual complexity, recognition of distinctions between process and outcomes, tolerance for ambiguity, broad perspective, and objectivity.

There is ample and growing evidence that ego development continues well into adulthood (Bandura, 1982; Block, 1981; Hentges, 1983; Lasker and Moore, 1980; Weathersby, 1981; Wortley and Amatea, 1982). Furthermore, views of education shift with increasing levels of development, from an emphasis on practical benefits and occupational advancement, through broadened uses for personal coping and growth, to an intrinsic valuing of lifelong learning for self-fulfillment and social concern (Houle, 1984).

You can use an understanding of developmental orientations of adults to select appropriate learning activities. For example, prespecified objectives, packaged content and materials, and achievement testing, when they entail a passive learner role, and an educator role as transmitter of knowledge and judge of learner achievement may be comfortable for adults at a conformist stage of development or lower. However, such procedures may be dysfunctional for adults who have progressed to self-awareness or autonomous stages or beyond. For them, more active and self-directed learner roles (self-assessment, contract learning, discussion, simulation) may be more appropriate. Providing such options allows participants to select types of activities that seem best for them.

Learners prefer educational settings that fit their preferred learning style. However, in some instances the intent of continuing education is to help adults make transitions to higher levels of personal and cognitive functioning. The challenge is to help adults master an active process of praxis in which learners alternate between current proficiencies and a search for higher levels of understanding and mastery (Daloz, 1986; Flavel, 1976; Ford, 1981; Heffernan, 1983; Kolb, 1984; Richards and Perri, 1978). In such instances, teaching entails helping learners process ideas more deeply, confront discrepancies between current and desired proficiencies, recognize differing perspectives, examine assumptions and values, and consider higher-level reasoning. Such a transformation is more likely when adults gain a broad view of themselves as learners with goals to pursue and efficacy in the learning process. Their conviction that lifelong learning is essential to a continuous process of becoming helps them appreciate how their learning abilities (related to learning strategies and personal attributes) combine with their learning difficulties (related to content and task demands) to affect their learning performance.

A general instructional goal is self-actualization of learners. You encourage actualization and growth toward "what can be" when you take a holistic approach toward enhancing a range of proficiencies related to various life roles, in contrast with narrow skill training. Instructors' emphasis on creativity, excellence, and self-directed learning enables learners to gain mastery, self-esteem, and confident use of learning procedures (Connell, 1981; McAlindon, 1981; Rinke, 1985).

How do you think about such developmental transformations in your own instruction? Can your program contribute to longer-term participant goals such as career development, public leadership, or enrichment of family life? If so, progress seems more likely if you and the participants consider relations between program objectives and participant goals. Do you want to help participants progress to higher levels of understanding and problem solving? If so, explicit attention to learning how to learn may help.

A related aspect of personality is moral development. With age and experience, people expand moral judgments from a personal focus on their own needs and on demands from rules and people in authority to increasingly take other people into account: the group, the society, and finally all humanity. People vary in how fast and how far their moral development progresses. Those who achieve higher levels of moral development do so in part because of experience with adult choices and responsibilities. Such experience, and reflection about it, contributes to a commitment to principled justice that acknowledges various viewpoints and contexts. In this developmental process, a person can question assumptions and beliefs, and some people progress beyond problem solving to problem finding. In almost any content area, your teaching can assist adults with this type of transformation.

An understanding of learning style is useful in recognizing and selecting conditions under which adults with various characteristics are likely to learn effectively. In many instances this process entails matching educational activities to learning style. However, learning style evolves throughout life, and the effectiveness of learning strategies varies with the learning task. From adolescence through young adulthood, many people shift from *acquisition* of basic concepts and learning abilities to *specialization* (which is reflected both in the selection of an occupation and in the learning associated with that occupation) to *integration* in which ways of learning that were set aside during the earlier emphasis on specialization are now developed and combined with the dominant learning style to enhance career, lifestyle, and general creativity (Kolb, 1984; Schaie and Geiwitz, 1982).

In addition to these subtle shifts in learning style during adulthood, there are broad and sometimes dramatic changes in performance and personality that affect the learning activities in which adults engage. Understanding these developmental tasks can enable you to recognize emerging educational needs, select relevant materials, and encourage application of new learnings to improved role performance. Recognizing developmental tasks characteristic of each stage of adulthood can help explain the educational activities that adults voluntarily select (Darkenwald and Knox, 1984; Knox, 1979b; Okun, 1982; Snider and Houser, 1983). For the educational programs that employers provide for their employees, information about developmental tasks and work requirements can be combined to match organizational and individual needs (Schein, 1978).

Developmental tasks vary across the population, but for middle-class adults during the late teens and early twenties, typical developmental tasks include achieving emotional independence, developing an ethical system, preparing for marriage and family life, and choosing and preparing for an occupation. These concerns are reflected in the sizable enrollments of young people in educational activities related to work generally, career planning and preparation, assertiveness, personal development, consumer education, and human relations (Darkenwald and Knox, 1984).

Through the twenties and early thirties, the emphasis shifts to such tasks as starting a family, starting an occupation, managing a home, and assuming civic responsibilities. These developmental tasks are reflected in enrollments in educational activities related to occupational advancement and specialization, marriage and parenting, managing home finance, and volunteer leadership of youth groups.

Time perspectives change with the onset of middle age, and adults revise career plans and redefine family relationships. These developmental tasks are reflected in educational activities about career advancement, supervision, midcareer changes, parenting teenagers, relating to aging parents, marriage enrichment, and dealing with divorce (Knox, 1979b).

In middle adulthood, there is increasing attention to tasks associated with maintaining a career or developing a new one, restabilizing family relationships, making major civic contributions, and adjusting to biological change. Resulting educational activities include executive development, midcareer transition, human relations, social issues, stress management, and preparing for retirement.

Beyond retirement, there are tasks associated with adjusting to retirement, declining health, changing living arrangements, and the loss of loved ones. These concerns are reflected in educational activities related to finances, health, values, and leisure (Okun, 1982; Peterson, 1983).

How well do the foregoing generalizations fit your participants? If they are from families with average levels of formal education and above, the generalizations probably fit fairly well, because those are the adults most often studied. If not, what developmental tasks are most widespread and important for your participants? How could you use this information to increase program relevance?

Many continuing education activities are related to concurrent adult roles and responsibilities. This accumulating life experience both helps and hinders educational activity (Knox, 1985). It helps because such experience gives rise to the aspirations that motivate adults to participate and the current proficiencies on which they can build. It hinders because it creates competing time demands that can interfere with progress in educational activities. Examples include family health problems or major changes in work assignments that can cause adult learners to drop out or to interrupt their educational activity. Practitioners can provide responsive educational programs by being flexible in helping participants accommodate competing time demands (Brundage and Mackeracker, 1980).

Occasions for New Learning. Many adults experience major developmental changes from decade to decade. By contrast, from year to year, adult life is very stable as a result of personality, habit, role responsibilities, and other people's expectations.

However, this stability is periodically punctuated by role-change events. Examples related to occupation include starting a new type of work, job change, temporary unemployment, and retirement. Change events also occur in relation to family (marriage, children, loss of spouse) and other life roles (organizational leadership, move to new community). Such changes reflect both external influences and adults' own strivings.

Change events require adaptation, which produces teachable moments. These transitions trigger educative activity that may have been needed or desired for some time, because the change makes the discrepancy between current and desired proficiencies sufficiently apparent that the individual is ready to do something about it (Aslanian and Brickell, 1980).

In addition to widespread use of educational activities to adjust to external demands and to achieve educational objectives set by the situation, some adults use education to discover new objectives, to decide which proficiencies are desirable. Programs that seem interesting may be selected to explore what their topics actually entail. In such instances, the adult learner considers assumptions, alternatives, standards, implications, and influences related to desired proficiencies. For such purposes, the adult's aspirations become especially important. Practitioners with such a broad view of adult development help learners discover more important questions to pursue and problems to solve as well as resolve those they had earlier recognized (Argyris, 1982; Eble, 1983).

Responding to Learners' Diversity. As people grow older, they become both more similar and more different. They become more similar in that they confront more and more of the widespread dilemmas of society and in that their essential self becomes more apparent. They become more different in that their specialized circumstances, abilities, and experiences produce among all adults an increasing range of individual differences within each increasing age cohort (Knox, 1977).

Those who effectively help adults learn necessarily deal with this diversity. Because stereotypes about learners' backgrounds and interests tend to be quite inaccurate, effective practitioners find out about participants through such procedures as conversations, registration forms, organization records, and the initial sessions of an educational program. Recognition of pertinent individual differences can enable you to individualize materials, to provide alternative sections, and to encourage participants to share experiences and insights with other participants who have common concerns. The typical result is more specialized educational activities, materials, and self-directed study arrangements in an effort to maximize responsiveness and application. Sometimes, however, continuing education programs address common themes from diverse perspectives in an effort to promote a more comprehensive sense of self for the individual or greater solidarity for the organization. Humanistic approaches to general education for adults address the former goal, and organization development activities concerned with communication, conflict resolution, and team building address the latter.

Collaboration by school and university educators to provide in-service education for teachers illustrates uses of adult development concepts for helping adults learn (Knox, 1985; Steitz, 1985; Warnat, 1980). A key concept is the transactional and developmental nature of adult development in which personality and change events can combine to trigger motivational energy and educative activity for teachers to assume responsibility for dealing with boredom, challenge, coping, problem solving, and especially overload and stress. If you conduct such in-service programs, it would be helpful to understand and guide self-directed learning activities focused on discrepancies between current and desired proficiencies, in ways that enhance self-concept and self-esteem.

If you were helping to conduct in-service sessions for teachers on dealing with stress in classrooms, how might you use concepts about adult development to recognize and accommodate individual differences? You might begin by recognizing variations in the ways people deal with stress. Unlike reactive approaches to stress reduction, proactive mastery approaches to learning and problem solving under conditions of stress include investing energy, using resources, interpreting and formulating the problem, and responding constructively. Depending on optimal levels of stress for each participant, constructive responses might emphasize managing stress, changing a stressful environment, analyzing one's situation to identify alternatives to avoid stress, and channeling excess energy into constructive activities that can reduce tension. A developmental perspective could help distinguish such variations.

Perhaps instead of just discussing stress and burnout, you could help the participants make decisions about learning activities, which might encourage them to persist and to apply what they learn. You might do so by having them use their own classrooms as living laboratories for learning and problem solving related to stress. Their familiarity with their work settings would enable them to consider their current performance and proficiency in relation to expectations of people in related roles, standards, resources, and likely reactions to proposed changes. You and other resource persons from school and university might contribute by providing participants with perspectives on what might be, clarifying discrepancies between what is and what ought to be, identifying useful learning resources, and facilitating progress in dealing with stress and gaining a more positive sense of self and optimism about this aspect of professional practice. A developmental perspective could help in planning activities for growth during and after the program.

References

Argyris, C. *Reasoning, Learning, and Action: Individual and Organizational*. San Francisco: Jossey-Bass, 1982.

Aslanian, C. B., and Brickell, H. N. *Americans in Transition: Life Changes as Reasons for Learning*. New York: College Entrance Examination Board, 1980.

Bandura, A. "Self-Efficacy Mechanism in Human Agency." *American Psychologist*, Feb. 1982, pp. 122–147.

Baruch, G., Barnett, R., and Rivers, C. *Lifeprints*. New York: McGraw-Hill, 1983.

Block, J. "Some Enduring and Consequential Structures of Personality." In A. I. Rabin and others (eds.), *Further Explorations in Personality*. New York: Wiley-Interscience, 1981.

Brown, A. L. "Knowing When, Where, and How to Remember: A Problem of Metacognition." In R. Glaser (ed.), *Advances in Instructional Psychology*. Hillsdale, N.J.: Erlbaum, 1978.

Brundage, D. H., and Mackeracker, D. *Adult Learning Principles and Their Application to Program Planning*. Toronto: Ontario Institute for Studies in Education, Ontario Ministry of Education, 1980.

Cattell, R. B. *Abilities: Their Structure, Growth, and Action*. Boston: Houghton Mifflin, 1971.

Chiriboga, D. A. "An Examination of Life Events as Possible Antecedents to Change." *Journal of Gerontology*, Sept. 1982, pp. 595–601.

Claxton, C. S., and Ralston, Y. *Learning Styles: Their Impact on Teaching and Administration*. Washington, D.C.: American Association for Higher Education and ERIC Clearinghouse on Higher Education, 1978.

Connell, H. S. "Training Sales Managers on Motivation." *Training and Development Journal*, Nov. 1981, pp. 85–88.

Cross, K. P. *Adults as Learners: Increasing Participation and Facilitating Learning*. San Francisco: Jossey-Bass, 1981.

Daloz, L. *Teaching Adults*. San Francisco: Jossey-Bass, 1986.

Darkenwald, G. G., and Knox, A. B. (eds.). *Meeting Educational Needs of Young Adults*. New Directions for Continuing Education, no. 21. San Francisco: Jossey-Bass, 1984.

DeNovellis, R. "The Personality Type Preference Indicator (PTPI)." *Journal of Psychological Type*, 1984, 7, 29–31.

DeNovellis, R. "Understanding the Personality Type Preference Indicator." *Journal of Psychological Type*, 1985, 9, 34–40.

Dixon, N. M. "Incorporating Learning Style into Training Design." *Training and Development Journal*, July 1982, pp. 62–64.

Dixon, N. M. "The Implementation of Learning Style Information." *Lifelong Learning*, Nov. 1985, pp. 16–18, 26–27.

Dunn, R., and Dunn, K. *Educator's Self-Teaching Guide to Individualizing Instructional Programs*. New York: Parker, 1972.

Eble, K. E. *The Aims of College Teaching*. San Francisco: Jossey-Bass, 1983.

Flavel, J. H. "Metacognitive Aspects of Problem Solving." In L. B. Resnick (ed.), *The Nature of Intelligence*. Hillsdale, N.J.: Erlbaum, 1976.

Ford, N. "Recent Approaches to the Study and Teaching of 'Effective Teaching' in Higher Education." *Review of Educational Research*, 1981, 51 (3), 345–377.

Fowler, J. *Stages of Faith: The Psychology of Human Development and the Quest for Meaning*. New York: Harper & Row, 1981.

Gilligan, C. *In a Different Voice*. Cambridge, Mass.: Harvard University Press, 1982.

Glustrom, M. "Educational Needs and Motivations of Non High School Graduate Adults Not in Participating Programs." *Lifelong Learning*, Apr. 1983, pp. 19–21.

Gregorc, A. "Learning/Teaching Styles: Their Nature and Effects." In National Association of Secondary School Principals, *Student Learning Styles: Diagnosing and Prescribing Programs*. Reston, Va.: National Association of Secondary School Principals, 1979.

Gubrium, J. T., and Buckholdt, D. R. *Toward Maturity: The Social Processing of Human Development*. San Francisco: Jossey-Bass, 1977.

Heffernan, J. M. *Adult Development and the Workplace*. Columbus: National Center for Research in Vocational Education, Ohio State University, 1983.

Hentges, K. "The Holistic Life Cycle Curriculum in Adult Education: A Proposal." *Lifelong Learning*, Oct. 1983, pp. 7, 16–17, 28.

Holtzclaw, L. R. "Adult Learners' Preferred Learning Styles, Choice of Courses and Subject Areas for Prior Experiential Learning Credit." *Lifelong Learning*, Apr. 1985, pp. 23–27.

Horn, J. L. "Organization of Data on Life-Span Development of Human Abilities." In L. R. Goulet and P. B. Baltes (eds.), *Life-Span Developmental Psychology: Research and Theory*. Orlando, Fla.: Academic Press, 1970.

Houle, C. O. *Patterns of Learning: New Perspectives on Life-Span Education*. San Francisco: Jossey-Bass, 1984.

Hultsch, D. F., and Deutsch, F. *Adult Development and Aging: A Life-Span Perspective*. New York: McGraw-Hill, 1981.

James, W. B., and Galbraith, M. W. "Perceptual Learning Styles: Implications and Techniques for the Practitioner." *Lifelong Learning*, Jan. 1985, pp. 20–23.

Kalamas, D. J. *Prepare to Work with Adult Learners*. Teaching Adults, module N-1. Prepublication copy. Columbus, Ohio: Center for Research in Vocational Education, 1986a.

Knox, A. B. *Adult Development and Learning: A Handbook on Individual Growth and Competence in the Adult Years*. San Francisco: Jossey-Bass, 1977.

Knox, A. B. (ed.). *Programming for Adults Facing Mid-Life Change*. New Directions for Continuing Education, no. 2. San Francisco: Jossey-Bass, 1979b.

Knox, A. B. "Proficiency Theory of Adult Learning." *Contemporary Educational Psychology*, 1980a, 5 (3), 378–404.

Knox, A. B. "Adult Learning and Proficiency." In D. Kleiber and M. Maehr (eds.), *Advances in Motivation and Achievement*. Vol. 5: *Motivation in Adulthood*. Greenwich, Conn.: JAI Press, 1985.

Kohlberg, L. "Continuities in Childhood and Adult Moral Development Revisited." In P. Baltes and K. Schaie (eds.), *Developmental Psychology: Personality and Socialization*. Orlando, Fla.: Academic Press, 1973.

Kolb, D. *Experiential Learning: Experience as the Source of Learning and Development*. Englewood Cliffs, N.J.: Prentice-Hall, 1984.

Krupp, J. *Adult Development: Implications for Staff Development*. Manchester, Conn.: Adult Development and Learning, 1981.

Krupp, J. *The Adult Learner*. Manchester, Conn.: Adult Development and Learning, 1982.

Lasker, H. M., and Moore, J. F. "Current Studies of Adult Development: Implications for Education." In H. M. Lasker, J. F. Moore, and E. Simpson, *Adult Education and Approaches to Learning*. Washington, D.C.: National Institute for Community Development, 1980.

Loevinger, J. *Ego Development: Conceptions and Theories*. San Francisco: Jossey-Bass, 1976.

Loewenthal, M. F., Thurnher, M., Chiriboga, D. and Associates. *Four Stages of Life: A Comparative Study of Women and Men Facing Transitions*. San Francisco: Jossey-Bass, 1975.

McAlindon, H. R. "Education for Self-Actualization." *Training and Development Journal*, Oct. 1981, pp. 85–91.

Merriam, S. B. *Themes of Adulthood Through Literature*. New York: Teachers College Press, Columbia University, 1983.

Merriam, S. B. *Adult Development: Implications for Adult Education*. Information Series, no. 282. Columbus, Ohio: ERIC Clearinghouse on Adult, Career, and Vocational Education, 1984.

Messick, S. "The Nature of Cognitive Styles: Problems and Promise in Educational Practice." *Educational Psychologist*, 1984, 19 (2), 59–74.

Myers, I. B., and Myers, P. B. *Gifts Differing*. Palo Alto, Calif.: Consulting Psychologists Press, 1980.

Okun, M. A. (ed.). *Programs for Older Adults*. New Directions for Continuing Education, no. 14. San Francisco: Jossey-Bass, 1982.

Perry, W. *Forms of Intellectual and Ethical Development in the College Years: A Scheme*. New York: Holt, Rinehart and Winston, 1970.

Peterson, D. A. *Facilitating Education for Older Learners*. San Francisco: Jossey-Bass, 1983.

Richards, C. S., and Perri, M. G. "Do Self-Control Treatments Last? An Evaluation of Behavioral Problem Solving and Faded Counselor Contact as Treatment Maintenance Strategies." *Journal of Counseling Psychology*, 1978, 25, 376–383.

Rinke, W. J. "Holistic Education: An Answer?" *Training and Development Journal*, Aug. 1985, pp. 67–68.

Rubin, L. B. *Worlds of Pain: Life in the Working-Class Family*. New York: Basic Books, 1976.

Schaie, W. K., and Geiwitz, J. *Adult Development and Aging*. Boston: Little, Brown, 1982.

Schein, E. H. *Career Dynamics: Matching Individual and Organizational Needs*. Reading, Mass.: Addison-Wesley, 1978.

Schwen, T. M., and others. "Cognitive Styles: Boon or Bane?" *Viewpoints in Teaching and Learning*, Fall 1979, pp. 49–65.

Smith, R. M. *Learning How to Learn*. Chicago: Follett, 1982.

Snider, J. C., and Houser, N. P. "Guides to Growth in the Gray Classroom." *Lifelong Learning*, Jan. 1983, pp. 18–20.

Steitz, J. A. "Issues of Adult Development Within the Academic Environment." *Lifelong Learning*, Apr. 1985, pp. 15–18, 27–28.

Troll, L. E. *Continuations: Adult Development and Aging*. Monterey, Calif.: Brooks/Cole, 1982.

Warnat, W. I. *Adult Learning in Inservice Training and Staff Development*. Washington, D.C.: Adult Learning Potential Institute, American University, 1980.

Weathersby, R. P. "Ego Development as an Aim of Higher Education." In A. W. Chickering and Associates, *The Modern American College: Responding to the New Realities of Diverse Students and a Changing Society*. San Francisco: Jossey-Bass, 1981.

Whitbourne, S. K., and Weinstock, C. S. *Adult Development*. New York: Holt, Rinehart and Winston, 1979.

Wortley, D. B., and Amatea, E. S. "Mapping Adult Life Changes: A Conceptual Framework for Organizing Adult Development Theory." *Personal and Guidance Journal*, Apr. 1982, pp. 476–482.

Turning Theories into Research and Practice

Lewis, A. 1991. In *Learning styles: Putting research and common sense into practice*, 19–32.
Arlington, Va.: American Association of School Administrators.

In his seminal book, *The Structure of Scientific Revolutions*, T.S. Kuhn notes that when a new field is being investigated or undergoes a new interest, everything that is known about it has equal weight. At first no single approach or idea is strong enough to develop a paradigm. After awhile, many paradigms may develop; finally, one emerges as the accepted view.

Learning styles theorists, researchers, and practitioners have not necessarily followed this traditional paradigm-building process. Because early research seemed so applicable to common-sense instruction in the classroom, many educators immediately accepted it as validating practice. As a result, learning styles research became a popular component of staff development programs before being subjected to the rigorous competition of other approaches or the intense scrutiny of prolonged investigation.

Further analysis and research on learning styles has prompted a renewed interest in the area. A number of fresh research ventures are being considered. In fact, it is apparent that learning styles will remain an open research book for some time to come because of constantly accumulating knowledge about physiological, cultural, cognitive, and other processes that affect learning. On the one hand, that makes it an exciting field. On the other, it begs for caution.

Reviewing the research on learning styles, Lynn Curry, a researcher in Ottawa, Canada, found several weaknesses. Although much has been promised from the research, she says, in general "the learning style conceptualizations, and the claims made on their behalf, remain to be systematically and comparatively evaluated in practice."[1]

Nonetheless, some theories have been tested enough to yield results with enough substance to at least intrigue, if not persuade, educators of their potential importance for the classroom.

Dissecting Brain Research

In the late 1970s, educators—and many who read the current "pop" literature—were busy trying to decide if they were "left" brain or "right" brain. Analysis of one's "brain" proclivity, in many respects, prompted an interest in the identification of one's learning styles. The Yearbook of the National Society for the Study of Education in 1978 published *Education and the Brain,* which focused primarily on the implications of neurological research which portrayed the brain as having different regions for different functions.

Roger Sperry, in his groundbreaking research of the 1950s, postulated that humans basically have two brains, with each one processing information differently and both serving equally important functions. The right hemisphere uses information in a non-verbal and holistic manner; the left hemisphere, by contrast, absorbs information in a more linear, sequential, and logical fashion. In recent years, researchers have added an "integrated" mode of thinking on a par with left- and right-brain dominance, positing that the two functions depend upon each other.

Another field of research on the brain, based primarily on observations of the effect of different kinds of environments on rats, contends that stimulation actually increases the weight and density of the neocortex of the brain. This has led to theories and research about the malleability of human intelligence—and the idea that stimulation can increase brain activity.

Long before these theories earned Nobel prizes, Reuven Feuerstein of Israel demonstrated that intelligence can be developed through experience (stimuli) guided by a "mediator" (parents, teachers, other adults) who provides meaning to the experience. Intelligence is not fixed, according to Feuerstein, but rather can be changed through structured cognitive development. Feuerstein's most dramatic experiments have been with young people with Down's Syndrome who gained enough skills through his Instrumental Enrichment Program to become caretakers of the elderly.

Mediated Learning in Detroit

For many special education teachers in the Detroit public schools, their students are not handicapped. Rather, they are "functioning at a lower level"—and the teachers definitely believe they can help the students learn at a higher level.

Using "mediated learning" approaches, these teachers, in a pilot program of the school district, reported early on significant changes in the social behaviors of their students. "They are more engaged with others, they seem to value themselves better, they have moved from impulsive learning to more thoughtful, active learning," says Janet Jones, coordinator of the Mediated Learning Experience Center.

The center and the teachers are integrating the teaching methods of Reuven Feuerstein, a psychologist, educator, and director of the Hadassah-Wizo-Canada Research Institute in Jerusalem. Beginning his work with seriously traumatized children who survived the Holocaust, Feuerstein developed a theory that low-performing young people (and adults), including the underachieving gifted, do not suffer from deficiencies that are irremediable or inherited. Rather, they never were exposed to certain attitudes, habits, and patterns of learning, he believes.

Feuerstein says that intelligence can be developed (he dismisses an immutable IQ) and that this comes about through "mediated learning." In fact, he proposes that the main goal of culture and of education should be to enable people to change, to "modify" themselves. Skills and strategies are not important, he says, because they change too frequently, but "teaching people to learn and modify themselves by learning new processes, new ways of doing things," will enable them to be lifelong learners.

The application of Feuerstein's methods to special education populations has received the most notice. He has documented, for example, the progress of Down's Syndrome youngsters from passive, rote-oriented learners to young people capable of taking care of the elderly. A few of his early special education students are now college professors.

Through extensive training in Feuerstein's methods, teachers, first of all, develop a new value system about their students—"a belief that all students can change," says Jones. The training then provides "strong, visible" instructional methods based on this belief. For example, teachers use teaching materials that are much more interactive than is customary, they ask more questions and more probing ones, and they allow students to express themselves more fully, according to Jones.

Feuerstein believes that human beings are changed in two ways—by direct exposure to stimuli and by the interaction with a mediator, e.g., parents and teachers. It is this latter influence which is unique to the human psyche, as compared to others in the animal kingdom. It is the mediator who shapes stimuli so that it makes sense to children and young people, who makes sure that the goal is not just "survival" but a life of quality, and who imposes a meaning on what is learned. The parent and teacher, says Feuerstein, should say, "I want you to see this because . . ." or "There is a goal in what you should do."

Unfortunately, he has observed that too many children are not receiving these "mediated learning experiences."

Parents who are poor, for example, are concerned only with survival, not with quality. Their goal is food on the table, not whether it is good or looks appetizing, he notes. However, wealthier families also have stopped "mediating to their children," he says. They assume school will do it, but "a child who has come to school without the kinds of change abilities produced by mediated learning experiences will not be affected by school," he believes.

Detroit is using Feuerstein's intervention methods, primarily the "Learning Potential Assessment Device." This consists of about 400 hours of exercises, such as creating different pictures out of dots, aimed at developing habits of thinking. The exercises, however, are not endless repetitions; rather, they require "rediscovery" of the goals of learning.

The methods are being applied to younger children through a Cognitive Enrichment Network of early childhood educators in Detroit, says Jones. And a new mentoring program for special education children will provide well-trained "mediators" as case managers for the students. Her center now offers training in Feuerstein's methods, rather than having to depend upon outside consultants.

"We are learning that much of what has been the model for handicapped education is based on a belief system that some children have intelligence, and some do not," Jones explains. "Our new paradigm accepts the idea that all human beings are born with the capacity to change and be changed."

Generally, early brain research seemed to be a breakthrough in attempts to understand the different ways students approach learning. Since then, additional research has gone beyond what now has come to be considered a very simplistic view of the brain. Educators are learning—and the research is still so fluid as to not have developed a paradigm—that right- and left-brain tendencies are only part of a very complex process within the brain for dealing with stimuli. In other words, the split brain is not as important to one's capacity for learning as the sum of the parts.

For example, Nobel laureate Gerald Edelman, director of the Neurosciences Institute at Rockefeller University, contends that ascribing localized functions of the brain to strengths or weaknesses in ability to learn is too simple. Reviewing Edelman's research, Douglas Carnine, a professor in teacher education at the University of Oregon, explains that the neuroscientist believes the special centers are part of a larger procedure which he describes as categorization and recategorization.[2] How humans carry out categorization and recategorization affects how they perceive, recognize and store information.

For educators, Edelman's views are important because of their explanation of a learner's ability to detect "sameness." It is the research on "sameness" that can help provide equal opportunity to learn in school because it explains how students make mistakes, Carnine says. The research is pretty solid on how learners make mistakes through "unintended samenesses," he says. For example, young children know that when a chair is turned in the opposite direction, it remains a chair. Similarly, when a "b" is turned,

they often assume that it remains a "b" instead of becoming a "d." Making this mistake does not mean that a child has a weak visual brain function; rather, research shows that children "are more likely to confuse objects and symbols that share visual or auditory samenesses, such as 'b' and 'd'."

Using this kind of research, Carnine says, educators can develop activities that help students learn samenesses that are appropriate and point out when they are mislearning:

> To reduce confusion between "b" and "d," for example, the curriculum designer can separate the introduction of these letters over time. When "d" is introduced some time later, a teacher could stress the differences between "b" and "d," using visual discrimination tasks before introducing auditory discrimination tasks.

Confusing Intelligence and Style

Psychologist Robert Sternberg of Yale University has described how his theories about thinking styles have been developed through research and how they help teachers decide which students are "smart." Unless teachers take students' favored styles into account, they will confuse styles with quality of mind and unfairly label students' abilities, he cautions.

Sternberg says there are three major ways of being smart—analytic, synthetic, and practical—but only the first is typically recognized in schools.[3] Those who are analytic often are test-smart, he says. They are rewarded by the current mode of schooling, but they are not good at coming up with their own ideas.

"The result is that our schools essentially mislead students," Sternberg says. "They develop and reward them for skills that later on will be important, but much less important than they are in school. The IQ-smart children often simply disappear into the woodwork. If we look at the people who make the greatest difference to our society, they are often not the people with the highest IQs."

Test criteria tend to mislead teachers, says Sternberg. Tests are not good at measuring practical intelligence because the intelligence is embedded in context—the cultural conditioning around children. People are not all of one style of intelligence, says Sternberg, and schools need to foster all aspects of intelligence:

> . . . (W)e need to recognize people who are smart in their lives are people who figure out what it is they are good at, and what it is they are not good at, and then make the most of their strengths while compensating for or remediating for their weaknesses. In other words, the most practically intelligent people are not necessarily the ones who are the highest in any of these three styles, but rather, people who figure out what it is that they are good at, and then capitalize on it: Being smart in the real world means making the most of what you have, not conforming to any preset stereotypical pattern of what others may consider smart.

Research reveals a rich source of evidence on child development that suggests the interests, perspectives, and patterns unique to each child begin very early and persist to adult life.

The Prospect Archive, at the Prospect School and Center in North Bennington, Vermont, includes a collection of school work from 350 students over a 20-year period. The samples were taken from the portfolios of "ordinary" students and included math papers, poems, stories, essays, and various forms of art work.

According to Patricia Carini, the founder of the archive, the archive collections show that not only do patterns of learning and interests develop early, but children deal with concepts, such as time, space, motion, people, and danger, very differently. Each has a characteristic style of joining his or her inner world with the outer "action" world, Carini says.

Just as the works of artists are continuous, analysis of individual student work in the archive shows that each piece created is part of one's whole way of doing things. Carini explains that an individual's work is so unmistakably that person's that it has changed her way of looking at those generalizations that refer to the child only as an instance of normative development. "It is unmistakably continuous," she says.

The archive is available for study by educators. For more information, contact Prospect Archive and Center for Education and Research, North Bennington, Vermont 05257.

Developing New Assessment Tools

Howard Gardner's theories on different intelligences led him to focus his research on one aspect—that of developing new forms of assessment that can adapt to more than the verbal and mathematical skills traditionally measured by current paper-and-pencil tests. This work is being conducted by Project Zero, a Harvard University center, and includes such projects as:

◆ Arts PROPEL, a collaboration of the Educational Testing Service and the Pittsburgh Public Schools to assess learning in music, imaginative writing, visual arts, and other areas neglected by most standard measures.

◆ The use of videotapes to study student exhibitions based on a theme over time, assessing such dimensions as the conceptualizing of a project, originality, technical quality, effectiveness of presentation, and collaborative skills (the "laboratory" is the Key Elementary School in Indianapolis, where the curriculum and environment are based on Gardner's ideas about multiple intelligences).

◆ Project Spectrum, a Boston-based research project to provide multiple stimuli in preschools and kindergartens with materials that encourage children to use different kinds of intelligences.

◆ Only Project Spectrum has produced sufficient data for analysis, according to Gardner and Thomas Hatch.[4] The results are "reasonably consistent" with the claims of multiple intelligence theory, they reported, with children showing relative strengths and weaknesses and with their exhibition of intelligences independent of each other.

Intervention, Inventories, and Instruction

The hemispheric line of reasoning to explain learning preferences has resulted in several inventories and in research on intervention strategies. For example, the tendency to use a particular hemisphere of the brain, according to some experiments, can be influenced by changing the reinforcement used in instruction or through extensive and very specialized training. Paul Torrance, who has conducted research with gifted children, claims that a child's preferred style of learning can be changed through specific intervention techniques as quickly as in six to 10 weeks.

However, the 4MAT model developed by Bernice McCarthy is the only major one being used in instruction. She used learning style inventories developed by Torrance and Kolb to determine four learning style quadrants—innovative, dynamic, analytic, and common sense. Her 4MAT model superimposes right and left hemispheric tendencies on each of the four quadrants, forming an eight-step cycle.

In a presentation to a New York State Board of Regents forum on learning styles, McCarthy and Marcus Lieberman summarized research conclusions on the right-, left-, and whole-brained effects upon students and their relationship to the 4MAT model.[6] They found that:

◆ Approximately equal percentages of boys and girls fall into each of the four learning style groups.

◆ During formal schooling years, students tend to favor the concrete experience dimension over the abstract dimension.

◆ More students were right-mode dominant than left-mode dominant.

◆ Each of the four learning style quadrants had right-mode, left-mode, and whole-brained students.

◆ These brain dominance characteristics are related to sex in some as yet undetermined way.

◆ These brain dominance characteristics are related to age and educational experience in some complex interaction with the dimensions of concreteness and abstractness in some as yet undetermined way.

◆ There is a strong tendency toward left-mode in quadrants two and three and a strong tendency toward right-mode in quadrants one and four. So, the relationship between the concrete and the right mode and the abstract and the left mode is a strong one.

They describe several research studies (Fairfax County, Virginia; Kirkwood, Missouri; and North Carolina) which

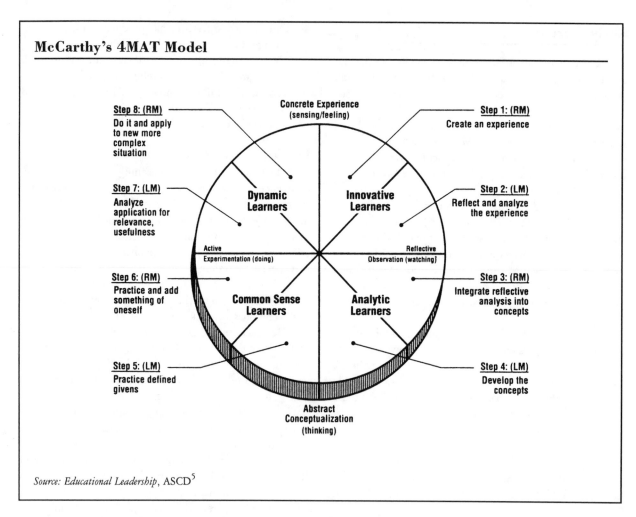

Step 8: (RM)
Do it and apply to new more complex situation

Step 7: (LM)
Analyze application for relevance, usefulness

Step 6: (RM)
Practice and add something of oneself

Step 5: (LM)
Practice defined givens

Concrete Experience
(sensing/feeling)

Step 1: (RM)
Create an experience

Step 2: (LM)
Reflect and analyze the experience

Step 3: (RM)
Integrate reflective analysis into concepts

Step 4: (LM)
Develop the concepts

Dynamic Learners

Innovative Learners

Common Sense Learners

Analytic Learners

Active Experimentation (doing)

Reflective Observation (watching)

Abstract Conceptualization (thinking)

Source: Educational Leadership, ASCD[5]

found positive effects by using the 4MAT model to help teachers understand students' learning styles.

Understanding Differences

Learning styles is one of five strands of the staff development program at the Millard School District in Omaha, Nebraska. The emphasis on learning styles is paying off in the classroom, reports Penny Kowal, director of instructional improvement for the district.

She describes a recent graduate class on learning styles where teachers began sharing results of using the approach with their students. One teacher implemented the 4MAT system in a middle-level social studies class and described his decision to deviate from his usual lecture and use instead analogies and empathic understanding of differences with his eighth graders. He commented that his students "had never been involved in a discussion to the level that they were on that day." The difference, he said, was due to his decision to begin the lesson on a "feeling" level.

Recognizing that she was an "analyzer," a high school English teacher began to construct lessons that involved feelings as well as critical thinking. According to Kowal, the response among her students was "overwhelmingly favorable." She continued with the changes because so many more of her students remarked how much they enjoyed her class. Other teachers in the class reported that

when they began to purposely teach to kinesthetic styles, as well as to auditory and visual, there was a noticeable increase in participation by many students.

The most detailed research on 4MAT, described in an article in *The Elementary School Journal* on a controlled group study, indicates partial success with teaching to the learning styles preferences indicated by the 4MAT approach, contrasted with traditional textbook-centered instruction.[7] The 4MAT lessons used a number of strategies—visuals, collaboration, hands-on activities and lectures, with two lessons each devoted to the four learning style preferences.

Based on a science unit with third graders from different socio-economic groups, the 4MAT instruction appeared to be superior with regard to content knowledge, comprehension, application, and analysis. Likewise, students in the 4MAT instruction had more positive attitudes toward instruction. However, according to co-authors Rhonda Wilkerson and Kinnard White of the University of North Carolina, these students did not perform any better on synthesis and evaluation than did those taught by the textbook approach.

Developing a Student Assessment

Different fields of research contributed to the development of a learning styles assessment by the National Association of Secondary School Principals (NASSP). The association long has been interested in learning styles, launching a network in 1979 in cooperation with St. John's University.

Through conferences, guidebooks, and a task force, NASSP, under the guidance of its director of research, James W. Keefe, used diagnosis as the focus of its interest in learning styles. Learning style assessment, Keefe wrote in 1988, "opens the door to a more personalized approach to schooling, to student advisement and placement, to improvement of student skills, to successful instructional strategy, and to meaningful evaluation of teaching and learning."[8]

Its national task force on learning styles adopted an "umbrella" research model, first proposed by Kolb, which incorporated cognitive, affective, and physiological/environmental research areas. It borrowed from the fields of personality theory, cognitive style research, and aptitude-treatment interaction research, according to Keefe. After reviewing research on about 40 broad characteristics, the Task Force selected 24 for further research. These included:

- **Perceptual responses**—how do you get a student's attention: visually, auditorily, or kinesthetically;

- **Field dependence-independence**—how a student experiences the environment, either with visual cues (field dependence) or without (field independent);

- **Successive-simultaneous processing**—preference between two forms of information processing: step-by-step (successive) or all at once (simultaneous);

- **Focusing-scanning**—ability to zero in on what's important to a problem;

- **Narrow-broad categorizing**—ability to create discrete categories to remember information;

- **Sharpening-leveling**—how a student merges new experiences, either by over-generalizing or by over-discriminating;

- **Thinking judgment-feeling judgment**—how a student reaches a conclusion, either through intellectual factors or emotional factors;

- **Achievement motivation**—striving for excellence for its own sake rather than an external reward;

- **Risk-taking-cautiousness**—a learner's willingness to take chances to reach a goal;

- **Persistence**—a learner's willingness to work beyond the minimum time, experience discomfort, and face the chance of failure;

- **Time of day preferences**—a learner's response depends on the time of day, owing to the body's heat cycle;

- **Need for mobility**—the learner's need for a change in posture and location.

These became the basis of further review of the literature, concept papers, and a three-year pilot study that tried out learning styles profiles with thousands of students, modifying the instrument at least three times. This research, says Keefe, determined a model that includes three groups of factors:

- **Perceptual responses**—visual, emotive, and auditory.

- **Cognitive skills**—spatial, analytic, sequential processing, memory, simultaneous processing, discrimination, and verbal-spatial.

- **Study/instructional preferences**—mobility, posture, persistence, sound, time of day, lighting, verbal risk, manipulative, grouping, and temperature.

Although the model resembles a gestalt of several elements, Keefe believes that learning style "emerges from this paradigm as an important and stable construct with a meaningful place in contemporary learning theory and practice."

Addressing Cognitive Needs, Strengths

The impact does not happen "overnight," but integrating the results of the NASSP Learning Style Profile into instruction and student support results in improved achievement, Jack Jenkins, director of the P.E. Yonge Laboratory School in Gainesville, Florida, reports.

Students in the University of Florida laboratory school are given the LSP in the sixth and ninth grades, as are students who are new enrollees in the secondary grades. The results are given to the individual student's adviser, who then makes them available to the student's teachers, upon request. In addition, all sixth graders attend a group session where the LSP's purpose and interpretation are explained; their advisers discuss the results with students individually.

Of the three areas covered by the LSP—cognitive, perceptual, and instructional study preferences—the cognitive one gets the first and most prominent attention, according to Jenkins. "When we help students strengthen their cognitive skills weaknesses, they start doing better academically over time," he says. Students spend one to two hours a week in a cognitive skills center, and "we help transfer how and what students are learning in the center back to their classrooms," he explains.

A history teacher, for example, may discover that a student has weak skills in analysis. The student might be given brief passages to read in the center, then given analytical questions that are asked and answered cooperatively—in a group setting.

Using knowledge about one of his advisee's perceptual preferences, Jenkins recalls helping a student who was failing a course pull his grades up to a C. "I looked at his LSP and found out that this student preferred an auditory response," he says. The student said that he studied for tests by reading over his notes, so Jenkins advised him to read his notes aloud and to read test questions softly to himself before trying to answer them. The student showed immediate improvement.

Using the LSP, teachers also adjust students' schedules to fit the "best time of day" for particular subjects, according to Jenkins. This information is revealed in the profile's section on instructional study preferences.

A 57-year-old tradition in the university community, the Yonge Laboratory School has many long-time teachers who are not interested in using the LSP, but other teachers and Jenkins have become experts in administering and interpreting the profile. They conduct workshops for other teachers throughout the state. The school is working on a system to put the LSP individual student information in computer files for more immediate access by teachers.

An Early Instrument

One of the first inventories of learning styles to be used in classrooms is that developed by Joseph Renzulli of the University of Connecticut and Linda Smith, a consultant on gifted and talented programs in Clayton, Missouri.

Their work is based on student self-selection of learning style preferences.

A number of studies, they reported in an article in *Theory Into Practice*, found "a significant difference in student achievement and/or attitude toward subject matter when students were allowed to learn in their preferred mode of instruction."[9]

Their Learning Styles Inventory, developed in the late 1970s, consists of 65 items that give information to teachers about student attitudes toward different teaching strategies, including lecture, projects, drill and recitation, peer teaching, discussion, teaching games, independent study, simulation, and programmed instruction.

Several research studies have been conducted on the inventory, particularly its use with gifted students. The general conclusion is that matching learning style preferences can have a positive effect and is a factor that can be manipulated, unlike IQ and prior achievement.

There is no definitive teaching approach, say Renzulli and Smith, but teachers who recognize the value of using a broad range of instructional strategies will more likely improve learning than teachers with a limited scope.

What's an Inventory?

A learning styles inventory is a self-report or scale that allows individual students to indicate their preferences and dislikes about specific approaches to learning.

At least a half dozen instruments available to educators are strictly inventories, or assessment tools, according to James Keefe, director of research at the National Association of Secondary School Principals. The best known is the Learning Style inventory developed by Rita Dunn of St. John's University.

Without referring to the latter or any specific inventories, Keefe suggested school leaders be cautious when considering the purchase of an inventory or learning styles program.

"A lot of people in the field are 'dog and pony show artists.' They are making a living from learning styles and you make a living not by giving general presentations on the trends in the field but by talking about your own model and the wonderful things it's going to do," he said.

An Integrative Approach

Using Anthony Gregorc's four "mindstyles," Kathleen A. Butler, head of a Connecticut educational consulting firm, The Learner's Dimension, has developed a map of learning style categories and terms. Her Style Differentiated Instruction looks like this:

Mindmapping Student Styles

Kathleen Butler observed each of Gregorc's four mindstyles in a classroom.[11]

Marcy, a concrete sequential learner, requires structure. She strives for accuracy and completes work on schedule. She likes hands-on activities. However, Marcy is uncomfortable in new situations, hesitates to try new things, and walks away when frustrated.

Rob, an abstract sequential learner, performs best when left alone to read and think. He likes to arrive at his own conclusions, based on research and expert opinions. Yet in striving to be head of the class, Rob does not accept criticism well and gets angry when he receives a poor mark.

Liz, an abstract random learner, performs at her best when permitted to express feelings, especially in a group. She responds to questions at length. However, Liz has trouble working independently and finds it difficult to focus on detailed instructions.

David, a concrete random learner, succeeds best when he can experiment and generates a wellspring of creative ideas. Yet David has little patience for fine details and has trouble offering reasons for the conclusions he has reached.

Butler contends teachers find the mindstyles guide very helpful in putting a framework around their own intuition about good teaching. Children and teachers combine aspects of all four styles, she says, but most work naturally with one or two of them. Some children show a dominant style early; others may take a long time to reveal preferences.

The "Environmental" Approach

A group of researchers affiliated primarily with the Center for the Study of Learning and Teaching Styles at St. John's University in Jamaica, New York, early on promoted the importance of responding to students' individual learning styles in order to improve achievement and behavior. The researchers include Rita Dunn, director of the center; Kenneth Dunn, professor at Queens College, Flushing, New York; Shirley Griggs; Marie Carbo, who has specialized in students' reading styles; and other faculty and doctoral students at St. John's University.

The Dunns published *Teaching Students Through Their Individual Learning Styles* in 1978. With Carbo, they wrote *Teaching Students to Read Through Their Individual Learning Styles* in 1986. Their research also has been published extensively by NASSP and Association for Supervision and Curriculum Development.

Citing results from almost 20 research studies, Rita Dunn and others define learning style as "a biologically and developmentally imposed set of personal characteristics that make the same teaching method effective for some and ineffective for others."[12] Their citations lean heavily on physiological, sociological, and environmental factors related to learning styles. For example, research by Dunn contends that four elements affect from 10 percent to 40 percent of students (depending on age, gender, hemisphericity, and achievement)—quiet versus sound, bright or soft lighting, warm or cool temperature, and formal versus informal seating designs.

Griggs and Dunn and V.J. Tappenden found that vocational students tend to not be "morning people." Generally, their studies on time preferences found most students are not alert in the mornings, the researchers suggest.[13]

They also note that more than 70 percent of school-age children are affected by perceptual preferences. Even high school teachers, they say, find that using manipulatives, visuals, and other resources that can match individual preferences increases student achievement and interest.

Conflicting Claims

The validity and conclusions of some research cited by Dunn and others has come into question, however. In an exchange with Dunn in *Exceptional Children*,[14] Kenneth Kavale of University of Iowa and Steven Forness of UCLA contend that research on types of preferences, leading to determination of individual learning styles, "for the most part . . . has not yielded the promised results."

Analyzing 39 research studies of learning styles, Kavale and Forness concluded that the evidence "indicates essentially no effect for modality (based on types of preferences) teaching. . . . Any attempt to make it appear as such (effective) by suggesting constricted instances where it

---

Matching Your Teaching Style to Your Student's Learning Style

Styles	Characteristics	Need an instructional focus that supports	Prefer strategies such as	Styles are matched when asked to	Types of products
CONCRETE SEQUENTIAL	organized factual efficient task-oriented detailed	structure & pattern direction, details practical problems realistic situations hands-on learning	hands-on approaches workbooks data-gathering how-to projects computers	sort, label, list collect, chart make, construct class, measure prepare, build	time-line graph diorama model exhibit
ABSTRACT SEQUENTIAL	intellectual analytical theoretical critical convergent	reason & logic ideas & information theory & concepts analysis & evaluation independent study	lecture, text content mastery extensive reading reporting conceptual problems	outline, report devise, speculate infer, hypothesize summarize, verify critique	debate document theory lecture research
ABSTRACT RANDOM	imaginative emotional interpretative holistic flexible	interpretation explanation communication illustration peer-teaching	group work webbing, mapping media, music personalized examples role-playing	associate, connect relate, express share, present interpret, perform imagine, counsel	writing arts, music interview helping project journal
CONCRETE RANDOM	divergent experiential inventive independent risk-taking	open-ended activity exploration investigation experimentation options	brainstorming simulations, games problem-solving experiments finding alternatives	explore, consider reorganize forecast, process predict, create recommend	invention editorial solutions games experiments

Source: Learning88.[10] Copyright © 1988. All rights reserved.

---

might be effective is a disservice because of the potential waste of valuable instructional time."

Similarly, Carbo's research on the relationship of learning styles to reading achievement was criticized by Steven Stahl of Western Illinois University for flawed methodology in the December 1988 *Phi Delta Kappan*.[15] Carbo, on the other hand, accuses Stahl of bias toward phonics instruction in the same issue and cites numerous research studies using her Reading Style Inventory, which found that matching students' reading styles "results in significant gains in reading comprehension, better attitudes toward reading, and more reading for pleasure, particularly for at-risk students."

Putting Research into Practice

Reviewing the controversy over research results, education journalist John O'Neil concludes that "allegations and countercharges of shoddy scholarship and vested interests have clouded the issue and made it all the more difficult for practitioners to decide what's worth pursuing."[16]

How are educators actually using learning styles? This question was asked of Pat Guild, director of graduate education programs at Antioch University in Seattle and the author of *Marching to Different Drummers*, and her explanation categorizes much of the research threads:

Broadly there are three different approaches. There's a focus on the individual: know thyself. And know the other person you're interacting with. It's very important for an educator when working with another person to understand in depth what both are like. Personal awareness is an aspect of all learning style treatments, but some advocates emphasize it more than others —Tony Gregorc, for example, and to a certain extent the Myers-Briggs people [developers of an instrument to assess personality types].

Another aspect of learning styles is application to curriculum design and to an instructional process. Knowing that people learn in different ways, you use a comprehensive model that provides for the major differences. That's the approach taken by Bernice McCarthy, Kathy Butler, and several others.

The third approach is diagnostic/prescriptive. You identify key elements of the individual's learning style, and as much as possible, match your instruction to those individual differences. That's the method espoused by Rita and Ken Dunn and by Marie Carbo.[17]

Notes

1. Curry, Lynn, "A Critique of the Research on Learning Style," *Educational Leadership*, October 1990, p. 54
2. Carnine, Douglas, "New Research on the Brain: Implications for Instruction," *Phi Delta Kappan*, January 1990, pp. 372-377.
3. Sternberg, Robert J., "Styles of the Mind," paper prepared for the 1990 Summer Institute of the Council of Chief State School Officers.
4. Gardner, Howard and Hatch, Thomas, "Multiple Intelligences Go To School," *Educational Researcher*, November 1989, pp. 4-9.
5. Reprinted from *Educational Leadership*, October 1990, p. 33, with permission by the Association for Supervision and Curriculum Development, Alexandria, Va.
6. McCarthy, Bernice and Lieberman, Marcus, "Learning Styles Dialogue," EXCEL Inc., Barrington, Ill., 1988.
7. Wilkerson, Rhonda and White, Kinnard, "Effects of the 4MAT System of Instruction on Students' Achievement, Retention, and Attitudes," *The Elementary School Journal*, March 1988, pp. 357-368.
8. Keefe, James W., *Profiling and Utilizing Learning Style*, National Association of Secondary School Principals, Reston, Va., 1988.
9. Smith, Linda and Renzulli, Joseph, "Learning Style Preferences: A Practical Approach for Teachers," *Theory Into Practice*, Volume 23, No. 1, pp. 44-50.
10. Reprinted from *Learning88*, November/December 1988, pp. 30-34, with permission of the Springhouse Corporation, Springhouse, Pa.
11. Butler, Kathleen A., "Learning Styles," *Learning88*, November/December 1988, pp. 30-34.
12. Dunn, Rita, Beaudry, Jeffrey and Klavas, Angela, "Survey of Research on Learning Styles," *Educational Leadership*, March 1989, pp. 50-58.
13. ibid., p. 55.
14. Kavale, Kenneth and Forness, Steven, "Substance Over Style: Assessing the Efficacy of Modality Testing and Teaching," *Exceptional Children*, November 1987, pp. 228-239; and "Substance Over Style: A Rejoinder to Dunn's Animadversions," *Exceptional Children*, January 1988, pp. 357-361.
15. Stahl, Steven A., "Is There Evidence to Support Matching Reading Styles and Initial Reading Methods?" *Phi Delta Kappan*, December 1988, pp. 317-322.
16. O'Neil, John, "Findings of Styles Research Murky at Best," *Educational Leadership*, October 1990, p. 7.
17. Brandt, Ron, "On Learning Styles: A Conversation with Pat Guild," *Educational Leadership*, October 1990, p. 10.

Sharing the Light of Faith:
National Catechetical Directory for Catholics of the United States

National Conference of Catholic Bishops. 1979. Nos. 182–89.
Washington, D.C.: United States Catholic Conference.

Chapter VIII.*
Catechesis Toward Maturity in Faith

Part B: Catechesis and Human Development

Section I: The Stages of Human Development

182. Early adulthood

The point of transition from adolescence to early adulthood varies considerably from one individual to another. Here we are considering young adults as those between the ages of 18 and 35, although not everyone has reached psychological, emotional, and spiritual maturity even by the latter age.

There are many subgroups with overlapping membership with the young adult population (e.g., high school students; members of the military; veterans; college, university, and technical school students; blue-collar workers and professionals; unemployed persons; members of particular cultural, racial, and ethnic groups). Young adults may be single, married with children, unmarried with children, married without children, separated, divorced, or widowed. Some are physically handicapped, emotionally disturbed, or mentally retarded. Obviously, no single catechetical approach will suffice for all.

Young adults are among the most likely to sever contact with organized religion.[14] This is unfortunate for many reasons, not the least because this is the period during which critical decisions are generally made concerning state of life, choice or partner, and career.[15] It must be recognized that many in this age group are alienated from the institutional Church and may be lost if greater emphasis is not placed on their evangelization and catechesis.

183. The making of life decisions

Near the end of adolescence or in early adulthood it becomes necessary to translate one's ideals into a personal way of life. Long-term choices and decisions must be made concerning vocation, career, and even religious affiliation. Such choices condition future growth. Prolonged unwillingness to make any choices of this kind prevents continued growth and is usually a sign that, regardless of age, the individual is still at an earlier stage of maturity.

Catechesis seeks to help people make the crucial decisions of this period in accord with God's will. It invites young adults to commit themselves to the living of full Christian lives and to engage in ministry within and for the Church community.

Catechesis also continues to present scripture and encourage reflection on it. While experience and personal interaction remain helpful for learning, reading and disciplined study are even more important than before. Catechesis seeks to encourage faith-inspired decisions and close identification with the adult faith community, including its liturgical life and mission. At this age level, catechesis, particularly of those continuing their education in college, will include courses in Christian philosophy and theology.

184. Middle adulthood

At present there is no generally accepted theory of life stages in adulthood that satisfies stringent scientific criteria. The middle years seem to resist categories. In fact, middle age itself is a relatively new concept: before 1900, when average life expectancy in the United States was less than 50, old age was thought to set in around 40. Catechists, nevertheless, will find many helpful insights in the new and increasingly numerous studies on the stages of adult life.

Typically, an individual enters the adult years with optimism and enthusiasm. Ideals are dominant. High goals are set. Ambition is strong. Challenges are eagerly accepted. Self-confidence is undimmed.

Crises of limits arise when people are defeated and disappointed in their efforts to achieve major goals in life: for example, through the experience of incompatibility and disillusionment in marriage; divorce; job dissatisfaction or job loss; the uncertainties associated with deciding on a second career; severe financial problems; difficulty in maintaining friendships; inability to undertake or sustain commitments; severe illness; the death of a loved one and its consequences; serious problems with offspring; inability to express deep emotions; profound loss of self-esteem; fear of failure; fear of success.

As a result, many people experience increasing boredom and loneliness, a sense of routine, fatigue, discouragement in facing decisions and their consequences. Ideals suffer in confrontation with hard reality. Hopes for ultimate success are dimmed by failure and the experience of personal weakness. The first signs of physical aging begin to appear. Eventually, a kind of spiritual crisis is likely. Before, the limitations of being human were to a great extent either not apparent or not part of one's personal experience; now they are inescapable realities in one's own life.

Several options are possible: escape—literal, physical flight or retreat into fantasies; change—new life decisions which may or may not succeed; rebellion, resentment, and

---

* Editor's note: Chapter notation refers to this excerpt.

hostility; or acceptance of one's limitations and, thereby, of one's humanity. Escape delays or prevents further growth; change may further growth or be another kind of escape; hostility is generally self-destructive. Positive acceptance means moving to a new stage of maturity, which can be a basis for spiritual growth. With grace and the use of Christian wisdom,[16] it is possible to deepen one's relationship with God and other people. One can also exercise a more truly personal freedom, for many obstacles to the exercise of responsible freedom have been removed and one is better able to place oneself wholly at God's disposal and to love without expecting anything in return, either from God or other people.

Catechesis can help adults live out their life decisions, prepare them for the crises of life, and assist them through these crises.

185. Some guidelines for the catechesis of adults

A number of catechetical norms and guidelines for adult catechesis have already been mentioned in this chapter. Others are noted elsewhere. What follows is intended to offer further assistance with regard to the Christian message as it pertains to adults, as well as to methodology.

a) The Christian message

The content of adult catechesis is as comprehensive and diverse as the Church's mission. It should include those universally relevant elements which are basic to the formation of an intelligent and active Catholic Christian and also catechesis pertaining to the particular needs which adults identify themselves as having.

The following description of content is not exhaustive.[17] Its elements have been selected either because of their relationship to the fundamental objectives of catechesis or their relevance to the present social scene in the United States.

Adult catechesis includes the study of scripture, tradition, liturgy, theology, morality, and the Church's teaching authority and life.[18] Church history is important for placing events in proper perspective.

Adult catechesis seeks to present the Church in all its dimensions, including its missionary nature, its role as sign or sacrament of Christ's presence in the world, its ecumenical commitment, and its mandate to communicate the whole truth of Christ to all persons in all times. (Cf. Mt 28,20)

Because Christ commissioned the apostles to teach people to observe everything He had commanded (cf. Mt 28,20), catechesis includes "not only those things which are to be believed, but also those things which are to be done."[19] Adult catechesis seeks to make adults keenly aware that an authentically Christian moral life is one guided and informed by the grace and gifts of the Holy Spirit, and that decisions of conscience should be based on study, consultation, prayer, and understanding of the Church's teaching.

Adult catechesis gives parents and guardians additional instruction to help them in carrying out their particular responsibilities. It also provides similar instruction, at least of a general kind, to all adults, since the entire community has obligations toward the young.

It addresses the Church's mission to promote justice, mercy, and peace, including the vindication of religious, human, and civil rights which are violated.

Adult catechesis offers education for change, including the skills essential for dealing with the rapid changes typical of life today.

b) The methods

Adults should play a central role in their own education. They should identify their needs, plan ways to meet them, and take part in the evaluation of programs and activities.

Catechesis for adults respects and makes use of their experiences, their cultural, racial, and ethnic heritages, their personal skills, and the other resources they bring to catechetical programs. Whenever possible, adults should teach and learn from one another.

Much effective learning comes from reflecting upon one's experiences in the light of faith. Adults must be helped to translate such reflection into practical steps to meet their responsibilities in a Christian manner. Where appropriate experiences have not been part of a person's life, the catechetical process attempts to provide them, to the extent possible. This suggests the use of discussion techniques, especially in small groups, and the cultivation of communication skills.

Other methods of adult catechesis include reading, lectures, workshops, seminars, the use of media, the Catholic press and other publications, and audio-visuals: in fact, all methods available to sound secular education. Specifically religious experiences—retreats, prayer meetings, and the like—provide extremely valuable opportunities for people to pause and reflect on their lives.

All catechetical programs, including those for adults, should be evaluated periodically.

186. Later adulthood

As people mature, their increased knowledge and proper love of self make it possible for them to enter more readily into self-giving relationships with others. Their courage, honesty, and concern increase. Their practical experiences grows. They come to enjoy higher levels of personal freedom. Properly use, these can be the most creative and fruitful years. The attitudes, example, and experience of mature persons make them invaluable educators in and of the faith community.

It would be a mistake, however, to suppose that as people grow older they automatically grow more religious or more mature in their faith. Generally speaking, pastoral ministry has paid too little attention to old age.[20] The needs of this age group have seldom been addressed by catechesis. Everyone needs to be confirmed in supernatural hope and prepared for the coming passage from this life to eternal happiness with God.

Death should be depicted for what it is, the final opportunity to assent to the divine will and give oneself freely to God. Several stages have been identified in the process by which and individual typically comes to terms with the fact he or she will die: denial, anger, bargaining with God, depression, and finally acceptance. Impending or anticipated death provides an opportunity to catechize the elderly and their families on the meaning of Christian death as a sharing in the paschal mystery, a personal sharing in Christ's death so that one may share also in His resurrection, as well as on the steps by which one prepares one spiritually for death. So the aged become signs of God's presence, of the sacredness of earthly life, of eternal life, and of the resurrection to come.[21]

187. Some recommendations for catechesis in later adulthood

Aging is a natural process with positive and negative aspects. Besides continuing the emphases of adult catechesis, catechesis for the aging seeks to give them physical, emotional, intellectual, and spiritual support so that they can make fruitful use of leisure time, understand and accept the increasing limitations imposed by age, and grow in faith even as they grow in years.

Catechesis notes the significant contributions with the aged make to the entire community through their shared work and witness.

Catechesis and all others who deal with the aged should make use of the growing body of research in geriatrics and related subjects. This area, relatively unexplored, is one where the Church could usefully initiate research, develop creative new programs, and disseminate information about effective programs which already exist.

Elderly people themselves can provide some of the most effective catechesis for the aged. They should receive preparation for this work and should have the opportunity not only to participate in programs but direct them.

188. The importance of adult catechesis

The act of faith is a free response to God's grace; and maximum human freedom only comes with the self-possession and responsibility of adulthood. This is one of the principal reasons for regarding adult catechesis as the chief form of catechesis. To assign primacy to adult catechesis does not mean sacrificing catechesis at other age levels; it means making sure that what is done earlier is carried to its culmination in adulthood.

Rapid changes in society and the Church make adult catechesis especially important today. Adults need help in dealing with their problems and communicating their faith to the young. Adult catechesis is also relevant to the Church's mission on behalf of justice, mercy, peace, and respect for human life—a mission which depends heavily upon informed and motivated lay people.[22] Adults need to learn and practice the gospel demands of stewardship: God gives everyone a measure of personal time, talent, and treasure to use for His glory and the service of neighbor.

Because of its importance and because of all other forms of catechesis are oriented in some way to it, the catechesis of adults must have high priority at all levels of the Church. The success of programs for children and youth depends to a significant extent upon the words, attitudes, and actions of the adult community, especially parents, family, and guardians.

189. Motivation for adult catechesis

There are many ways of motivating people to become involved in adult catechesis; here we shall mention only a few. Today, when perhaps more adults than ever before are participating in continuing education courses of all kinds, there is every reason to think many can be attracted to appealing catechetical programs.

The best inducement to participate is an excellent program. People are drawn by the testimony of satisfied participants, as well as personal invitations from friends and Church leaders.

The total environment of the parish is also an important factor in motivating adults. This includes the quality of the liturgies, the extent of shared decision making, the priorities in the parish budget, the degree of commitment to social justice, the quality of the other catechetical programs. Programs for adults should confront people's real questions and problems honestly and openly. As far as possible, they should offer positive reinforcements and rewards; the learning environment should be attractive and comfortable; adults should be encouraged to realize their potential for becoming religiously mature—or more mature—persons. Good publicity in the media, religious and secular, is also very helpful.

Notes

14. Cf. *Catholic Schools in a Declining Church* (1976), p. 148.
15. Cf. GCD, 83, which invites study of the stage of young adulthood.
16. Cf. *Ibid.*, 94.
17. Cf. *Ibid.*, 97, for a treatment of the special functions of catechesis for adults.
18. Cf. Church, 14.
19. GCD, 63.
20. *Ibid.*, 95.
21. Cf. *Ibid.*
22. Cf. Laity 2, 7.

The Role of the Principal in the Ongoing Education of Teachers

Ristau, K. 1989. In *Reflections on the role of the Catholic school principal*, ed. R. J. Kealey, 60–65. Washington, D.C.: National Catholic Educational Association.

Principals of Adult Learning

Leaders have available to them a wealth of information concerning growth and development of the human person. Russell (1985) has presented helpful ideas for understanding the adult learner and planning the learning process for teachers. Principals need to use these generally accepted precepts about adult learning in planning for good staff development.

Ego-Involvement

The first point to consider in adult learning is ego-involvement. Learning a new skill, technique, or concept may promote a positive or negative view of self. There is always fear of external judgment that we as adults are less than adequate. Adults will resist learning situations they believe are an attack on their competence or are viewed as an insult to what they are presently doing. Many attempts at inservice or staff development fail because planners do not pay attention to this point.

Self-Planning

Adults want to be the originators of their own learning; that is involved in the selection of objectives, content, activities, and assessment of those activities. Faculty development prescribed by others and spoon-fed to passive adults rarely has any lasting effects and is more likely to be met with resistance. Therefore, it stands to reason, teachers themselves must be included in the planning and design of any staff development. The principal's role in the planning process is one of empowering the teachers to take charge of their own development.

The recent literature on businesses that succeed (Kantor, 1983 and Peters, 1982) describes employees working with leaders who allow people to have their own power instead of with leaders who control and tell others what to do. Bennis (1985) talks about a style of leadership that pulls rather than pushes, attracts and energizes people to an exciting vision of the future. The principal is the person who can articulate and embody the ideal toward which the school is striving.

Prior Learning

Adults come to any learning experience with a wide range of previous experiences, knowledge, skills, self-direction, interests, and competence. The design of education for adults needs to be very respectful of the attributes the person brings to the learning situation. Educators of children and young adults spend a good deal of time planning for teaching, including in each lesson discussion, reading activities, media experiences, and concluding work. New knowledge not only builds upon what is already known but fits the developmental level of the students.

Learning Styles

Effective teachers plan for the learning style of the student and include activities matched to the needs of the learner. However, when it comes to education for teachers we seem to throw good teaching/learning principles out. Teachers are asked to sit and absorb a forty-five minute lecture on a topic not of their own choosing at a time when most of them are weary from the work of the day. The activities, the reading, the critical thinking, the opportunity to practice the skills are missing.

Teachers would never present to children or young adults a topic totally disconnected from what went on before or what will come tomorrow. No high school class assembles for a period to consider linear regression statistics when the course addresses English literature for a semester. Yet, we offer to teachers scattered topics and then, perhaps only once. It is no wonder a peek into an inservice or staff development session often reveals a teacher checking papers, another grading student work, and usually someone knitting. It is a vision of passive learners.

Adult learning is enhanced by behaviors that demonstrate respect, trust, and concern for the learner. Well-planned sessions that consider who the learners are and the gifts and background the learners bring with them display a respectfulness to the person of the teacher.

Relevant to Personal Needs

Several other points about adult learners that principals should keep in mind include the realization adults will commit to learning something when the goals and objectives of the learning are considered realistic and important to the learner. In other words, adults will learn, retain, and use what they perceive is relevant to their personal and professional needs. Another vote should be cast here for involvement of the teachers in the selection of the staff development activities.

Adult Interaction

Adults also prefer to learn in informal situations where social interaction can take place among the learners. This would speak again to the avoidance of the lecture-only approach.

Motivation

The most difficult aspect of adult learning for principals to wrestle with is motivation. Adult motivation for learning and doing one's job has two levels. One is to participate and do an adequate job. This first level comes as the result of good salary, benefits, and fair treatment. But the second and more important is to become deeply involved, going beyond the minimum or norm. The second builds on the first, but comes from recognition, achievement, and increased responsibility—the result of behavior, the leader's behavior, and not more dollars. While the need to supply recognition and share responsibility must be designed by the principal, it is comforting to realize that true motivation is produced by the learner. The principal can encourage and create conditions which nurture what already exists in the adult.

Sponsorship

The craft of learning and teaching, an integral part of the journey of our lives, can also be supported by understanding the educational tradition offered by the church. Many rituals include a model of sponsorship. Both the sacraments of Baptism and Confirmation include sponsors. The sacrament of Matrimony asks for others to witness and support the promises of the couple. The revised ritual in the rite of Christian Initiation of Adults (RCIA) offers an effective model of sponsorship. My colleague Dr. Katherine Egan, CSJ, first drew the parallel between the RCIA and staff development in a talk at the NCEA 1987 Convention in New Orleans.

The RCIA asks us to welcome new members, to encourage and challenge one another through a process of sharing experiences, ritual, and service. The RCIA speaks of initiation, invitation, questioning, and support. From the very beginning sponsorship is included. The sponsorship that is part of our religious heritage is the same idea the recent literature on supervision and staff development addresses.

Coaching and collegial learning focus on the same things as the responsibility of the sponsor. The sponsor stands beside, next to, the other rather than above. The sponsor invites the other to try a fresh way. The sponsor is a sympathetic colleague with whom the new teacher can share doubts and frustrations as well as successes. There is a spirit of interdependence not dependence.

The role of the coach in staff development as described in the literature is to encourage and give consistent support as one learns new teaching methods and explores other levels of curriculum development. The coach, as the sponsor, can supply knowledge, teaching credibility, facilitation, and availability. The RCIA, though focusing on the reception of new members into the church, also establishes the ongoing cycle of deeper and deeper belonging to the faith community. Staff development, too, addresses the cycle of learning, the beginning, the middle and the end, which becomes a new beginning.

Framework for Staff Development

The process of journey and a model of sponsorship provide the conceptual framework for thinking about staff development. The framework becomes the shaper, the support structure for what we hope to do. If we think in terms of cooking it makes a great difference in what kind of pan or dish something is baked. Similar ingredients will become a cake or muffins depending on which pan the chef chooses. Without the pan, there is no shape or structure, no foundation in form. Similarly, once time is given to carefully thinking through what the finished item should look like, using the framework of our traditions as a guide,

the principal and faculty can move on to the planning of specific details. The planning will include the principles of adult learning as a main ingredient.

Suggestions

I would like to include a few other random suggestions.

Invest in human capital.

The school budget should include monies for ongoing education of everyone who is involved in the school. When there are limited budgets, spend the money on people first. People are far more important than things. People will also reward the whole endeavor of schooling in return for the investment. Explore some of industry's ideas about pay incentives. Many schools reward people financially for their efforts to continue to learn. If you are going to spend money, spend it on your own faculty.

Use the talent of your faculty.

Your own faculty members can teach other faculty members about new ideas and methods. Get teachers to visit other places and report that experience to everybody else. Urge teachers to attend a class and come back and teach what they learned to the rest of the staff. What the teachers are learning and what the staff are practicing are certainly material for a publicity campaign which keeps before the parents the image of the whole school as a community of learners.

Model self-development processes.

And a last admonition: lead as never before—by example. People in organizations are all boss-watchers. For better or worse, what you spend your time on (not what you sermonize about) and what visions you share will become the faculty's preoccupation. The final confirmation about "what really counts around here" is all the things to which you give time. Albert Schweitzer often said "example is leadership." You must pursue your own scholarship right along with the teachers and set the example by paying attention to the skills and knowledge you need to be an educational leader.

Conclusion

Catholic schools are grounded in the faith and traditions of the whole church and have wisely used those traditions as the framework for what goes on in the schools. Catholic schools have always been very creative places, often out of necessity. School leaders who reflect upon the traditions the larger church presents, being respectful to adults, and using a bit of creativity will be able to lead a faculty which is excited about learning for themselves and for the students they teach.

References

Bennis, Warren & Burt Nannis. *Leaders: The Strategies for Taking Charge*. New York: Harper and Row, 1985.

Kantor, Rosabeth Moss. *The Change Masters*. New York: Simon and Schuster, 1983.

Peters, Thomas. *Thriving on Chaos*. New York: A. Knopf, 1982.

Robinson, Russell D. *An Introduction to Helping Adults Learn and Change*. Milwaukee: Omnibook, 1983.

Understanding Myself as a Learner
The TLC Learning Style Inventory

A self-diagnostic tool for adults to assess learning styles preferences.

Silver, H. F., and J. R. Hanson. 1980. In *Teacher self-assessment*, 63–81.
Moorestown, N.J.: Hanson Silver and Associates, Inc.

Purpose

The Learning Style Inventory (LSI) is a self-descriptive test based on Carl Gustav Jung's Theory of Psychological Types (1921). The instrument is designed to help you identify your own learning profile based on preferences for how information is collected and judgments are made about its significance.

Directions

Below are twenty sets of four behaviors. Rank the behaviors in each set based upon your own preferences, i.e., those behaviors pertinent to the way you learn. Assign a 5 to the term which best characterizes your learning style preferences, a 3 to the term which next best characterizes your learning style preferences, a 1 to the next most characteristic behavior, and a 0 to the behavior which you feel *least* characterizes your learning processes.

As you read through the list of behaviors in each set, you may find it hard to choose the behavior that best characterizes your learning style preferences. This is predictable. Every learner operates in a variety of ways in different situations. Yet each of us does have preferences for some behaviors over others. Keep in mind that there are no right or wrong answers. All the choices are equally acceptable. The aim of the inventory is to describe how you learn, not to evaluate your learning ability.

If you get stuck on an item, go on to the next.

❖ ❖ ❖ ❖ ❖ ❖ ❖ ❖ ❖ ❖ ❖ ❖ ❖ ❖

I. Choosing Self Descriptors

In each of the following twenty horizontal sets, rank the four behavioral descriptors in order of: first preference (5), second preference (3), third preference (1), fourth preference (0).

Be sure to assign a different weighted number (5, 3, 1, 0) to each of the four descriptors in each set. Do not make ties. Rank the descriptors according to those which best describe you, i.e., your learning preferences.

Descriptors are to be analyzed *horizontally* as sets of four across the four lettered columns. *Do not* compare descriptors vertically.

	A	B	C	D
1.	Creative	Personal	Organized	Analytical
2.	Facts	Theories	Values	Feelings
3.	Emotional	Spontaneous	Literal	Interpretive
4.	Harmonizing	Questioning	Utilizing	Imagining
5.	Speculative	Competitive	Cooperative	Independent
6.	Developing	Relating	Searching	Practicing
7.	Planning	Implementing	Conversing	Innovating
8.	Patterns	Human Interactions	Details	Possibilities
9.	Doing	Pondering	Collaborating	Debating
10.	Abstract	Personal	Concrete	Ideal
11.	Sharing	Strategizing	Eureka!!!	Trial and Error
12.	Humanistic	Realistic	Aesthetic	Theoretical
13.	Concepts	People	Insights	Specifics
14.	Logic	Products	Empathy	Understanding
15.	Romanticize	Socialize	Routinize	Systematize
16.	Sensible	Mystical	Emotional	Logical
17.	Products	Ideas	Images	Sentiments
18.	Roles	Laws	Loyalties	Principles
19.	Memorize	Emulate	Divergent Expression	Discovery Method
20.	Hypothetical	Inspirational	Methodical	Experiential

II. Self-Analysis Profile

In each of the twenty sets of behavioral descriptors the words/terms correspond to four distinct learning styles. The learning styles are based on the different ways people collect information (their perceptions) and make decisions about the significance of that information (their judgments). The two ways we collect information are "sensing" and "intuiting." The two ways we judge information are "thinking" and "feeling."

The preference for sensing or intuition is independent of the preference for thinking or feeling. As a result, four distinct combinations occur.

Functions
1. Sensing/Thinking (S-T)
2. Sensing/Feeling (S-F)
3. Intuitive/Thinking (N-T)
4. Intuitive/Feeling (N-F)

Each of these combinations produces a different kind of learning style characterized by whatever interests, values, needs, habits of mind, surface traits and learning behavior naturally result from those combinations.

Subjective Ranking

Before scoring your learning preference profile please rank order the styles based upon your own immediate perceptions of your learning preferences. Please carefully read the style descriptions which follow and determine which description is "most characteristic," next most characteristic, third most, and least characteristic.

Learning Style Descriptions

SENSING-FEELERS (S-F)

Overview*

The Sensing-Feeling learner can be characterized as sociable, friendly, and interpersonally oriented. This type of learner is very sensitive to people's feelings: his own and others. He prefers to learn about things that directly affect people's lives rather than impersonal facts or theories.

Approach to Learning

The S-F's approach to learning is a personal one. He works best when he is emotionally involved in what he is being asked to learn. The S-F learner tends to be spontaneous and often acts on impulse, i.e., in terms of what "feels right." He is interested in people and likes to listen to and talk about people and their feelings. He likes to be helpful to others and needs to be recognized for his efforts.

The S-F learner, more than any other type, enjoys personal attention. He is very involved in his own personal and emotional development, and believes that without human relationships life has little meaning. He often needs reassurance that what he is doing is correct and will be approved. He is greatly influenced by the likes and dislikes of others.

The S-F enjoys working with others and is particularly warmed by their approval. He is equally sensitive to indifference. He is often influenced more by his peers than by authority figures, and sometimes may lose sight of his own ideas while trying to go along with the group. He likes to think out loud, to work with others, to share his ideas, and to get responses from his friends. He prefers cooperation to competition.

The S-F learner views content mastery as secondary to achieving harmonious relationships with others. He enjoys learning through encounters, group process, personal friendships, and tender (if not loving) attention.

Learns Best

The S-F learns best in a warm, friendly, supportive and interactive environment in which students are encouraged to share their personal thoughts, feelings, and experiences, and to interact with one another. He benefits most when the instructional process emphasizes collaborative approaches in which students share ideas and materials and work in small groups.

The S-F enjoys group activities, games with lots of action in which everyone can participate and no one loses, discussions, reading stories about people and their feelings, writing and talking about things he likes to do, group process activities, and art and music which allow him to express his feelings.

The S-F student needs to participate in group activities to develop his powers of empathy. He needs to have time and resources to learn about himself. He needs to have an opportunity to explore, change, and develop attitudes and values in reference to others.

(Preference ranking_____)

SENSING-THINKERS (S-T)

Overview

The S-T learner can be characterized as realistic, practical, and matter-of-fact. This type of learner is efficient and results-oriented. He has a high energy level for doing things which are pragmatic, logical, and useful.

Approach to Learning

The S-T learner likes to complete his work rapidly and in an organized and efficient manner. He tends to be neat, well-organized, and precise in his work. His appetite for work and his need for immediate feedback is often a challenge for the instructor. The S-T learner enjoys work and needs to be kept busy. He would prefer to do almost anything rather than remain in his seat listening to someone speak. He needs to be active, to be doing, to see tangible results from his efforts, and to be in control of the task.

---

*The feminine pronoun is used to refer to the teacher, the masculine pronoun for the student.

The S-T learner prefers step-by-step directions when assigned a task; he becomes impatient if the instructions become long and involved. This type of learner more than any other wants to know exactly what is expected of him. He needs to know what he is to do, how he is to do it, and when it is to be done. The S-T learner will often lose interest in an activity if it moves too slowly, or if he can see no practical use for what is expected.

The S-T learner needs clearly structured environments. The main focus of this environment is on factual mastery of some set of skills, and an opportunity to apply them to something practical, or to demonstrate proficiency in the skill. He prefers assignments which have right or wrong responses rather than open-ended or interpretive ones. He is highly motivated by competition, learning games, and awards, etc.

Learns Best

The S-T learns best in an organized systematic activity-oriented, instructor-directed atmosphere. He needs to be actively engaged in purposeful work. The instructional environment requires well-defined procedures and content. This content needs to be presented in an orderly and systematic manner. The instructional emphases for the S-T are on competitive and independent approaches to learning.

The S-T learns best when he can directly experience with his five senses what he is expected to learn. Motivation comes from being able to see the practicality of what he has learned and putting the new learning into immediate use. Thus the S-T learns best when he can see the utility for what he is being asked to learn. Sometimes the need for utility can be transferred to alternative reward systems such as merit, recognition, awards, etc.

The S-T learner has little tolerance for ambiguous situations. He wants to know what is expected of him before he begins. He needs clearly stated ground rules. He works best when there are clearly stated objectives, and when achievement is quickly recognized and rewarded. The S-T learner likes games that are competitive, have clear rules, and lots of action.

The S-T learner needs a clearly defined instructional approach with the focus on content mastery, the mastery of basic skills, or the immediate opportunity to employ what's been learned. In short, he needs well-defined action activities with immediate tangible results. He learns best from repetition, drill, memorization, programmed instruction, workbooks, demonstration, field trips, and direct actual experience.

The S-T learner retains more from first hand experience than from reading or studying. He enjoys repeating skills already mastered over learning new skills. Action, repetition, and feedback are his preferred methods for learning.

(Preference ranking _____)

Overview

The Intuitive-Thinking learner can be characterized as theoretical, intellectually-curious, and knowledge-oriented. This type of learner prefers to be challenged intellectually and to think things out for himself. The N-T is curious about ideas, has a tolerance for theory, a taste for complex problems, and a concern for long-range consequences.

Approach to Learning

The N-T approaches learning in a logical, organized, and systematic fashion. The N-T brings organization and structure to both people and things. He takes time to plan and to think things through before beginning work on an assignment. He organizes ideas and determines what resources are necessary to complete required tasks.

The N-T prefers to work independently or with other thinking types. He requires little feedback until his work is completed. He does not like to be pressed for time. When working on something of interest, time is meaningless. He displays a great deal of patience and persistence in completing difficult assignments if they have captured his interest.

The N-T is interested in theoretical models, constructs, and ideas. His interest in facts is only in relation to the proving or disproving of theory. Otherwise, facts or details hold little interest for him.

The N-T learner's approach to understanding things and ideas is by breaking them down into their component parts. He likes to reason things out, and to look for logical relationships. His thought processes follow a cause-and-effect line of reasoning. He is constantly asking "Why?" His questions tend to be provocative as contrasted with questions requiring information or facts.

The N-T is an avid reader. His learning is vicarious. He enjoys the use of abstract symbols, formulae, the written word and technical illustrations as a preferred way of collecting data.

Learns Best

The N-T learns best in an intellectually stimulating atmosphere, in which he is challenged to think critically, analytically, and to be "stretched" to increase his reasoning abilities. The instructional emphasis for the N-T is placed on independent and creative approaches to learning. He prefers to learn by discovery and experimentation.

The N-T learner needs the freedom to identify his own interests, to participate in selecting his own learning activities, and to be given the time and resources to develop his own ideas. The N-T learner enjoys independent research projects, reading on a topic of current interest, theorizing, lectures, games of strategy, expression of ideas, debates, and projects which call for the use of intuition and thinking.

The N-T enjoys solving problems, and talking with others about great ideas. He enjoys argument as a way of clarifying ideas. Nearly everything of interest to the N-T turns into oral or written words, or symbol systems. The N-T is interested in seeing things synoptically, in gathering as much information as possible about a subject, and following a cause-and-effect process in his thinking. The N-T always wants to know "Why?", and "Where is the evidence?"

(Preference ranking _____)

INTUITIVE-FEELERS (N-F)

Overview

The Intuitive-Feeler can be characterized as curious, insightful, imaginative, and creative. The N-F is one who dares to dream, is committed to his values, is open to alternatives, and constantly searches for new and unusual ways to express himself.

Approach to Learning

The N-F approaches learning eager to explore ideas, generate new solutions to problems, and discuss moral dilemmas. The N-F's interests are varied and unpredictable. He enjoys a wide variety of things. He prefers activities which allow him to use his imagination and to do things in new and different ways. He is turned off by routine or rote assignments and prefers questions which are open ended, such as "What would happen if . . . ?"

The N-F student is highly motivated by his own interests. Things of interest will be done inventively and well. Things which he does not like may be done poorly or be neglected altogether. When engaged in a project which intrigues him, time is meaningless. The N-F operates by an "internal clock" and therefore often feels constrained or frustrated by external rules or schedules.

The N-F learner is independent and non-conforming. He does not fear being different and is unusually aware of his own and other people's impulses. He is open to the irrational and not confined by convention. He is sensitive to beauty and symmetry and will comment on the aesthetic characteristics of things.

The N-F learner prefers not to follow step-by-step procedures, but rather to move where his intuition takes him. He prefers to find his own solutions to challenges or problems rather than being told what to do or how to do it. He is able to take intuitive leaps. He trusts his insights.

He often looks for new and different ways to solve problems. He often takes circuitous routes to get where he wants to go. He may solve a problem but not be able to explain how he arrived at his solution.

Learns Best

The N-F learns best in a flexible and innovative atmosphere where there are a minimum number of restrictions, many alternative activities, and where a premium is placed on creating their own learning activities or solutions to problems. The N-F's instructional emphases are on curiosity, creativity, and a clarification of his personal values.

The N-F enjoys activities allowing for personal self-expression through artistic forms. The N-F enjoys creating things, designing projects around his own interests, reading, "messy" activities (e.g., sculpture, potting, mixing paints, etc.), meditation, contemplation, fantasizing, and projects allowing him to employ his intuition and feeling.

The N-F needs to explore his creative potential, to find ways to express his ideas and beliefs, and to share his inspirations with others. He has an acute need to develop his own unique style of being. He has a keen interest in other belief systems, new projects, and possibilities for what "might be." He has a futures orientation. He is interested in things that might happen, but have not yet happened.

(Preference ranking _____)

Subjective Ranking of Preferences

1. Most characteristic_____

2. Next most characteristic_____

3. Third most characteristic_____

4. Least characteristic_____

Now that the styles have been entered based on your personal judgments, go to the next page (Scoring Self-Descriptors) and follow the directions for computing the Learning Preference Scores. Then complete the Learning Preference Profile. You are now in a position to compare the subjective or personal analysis of your learning styles preference with the identification of style from the Learning Preference Profile.

III. Scoring Self-Descriptors

To compute your Learning Preference Score for each of the four learning styles:

1. Remove insert sheet.
2. Transfer the numbers from your answer sheet to the scoring sheet. For example, if in the first set of behaviors, you ranked the behaviors:

1. ___0___ Creative   ___5___ Personal   ___3___ Organized   ___1___ Analytical

transfer these numbers to the appropriate behavior on the scoring sheet, as follows:

1. ___5___ Personal   ___3___ Organized   ___1___ Analytical   ___0___ Creative

Compute your score by adding the numbers for each column vertically.

	S-F Sensing/Feeling Rank	S-T Sensing/Thinking Rank	N-T Intuitive/Thinking Rank	N-F Intuitive/Feeling Rank
1.	Personal	Organized	Analytical	Creative
2.	Feelings	Facts	Theories	Values
3.	Emotional	Literal	Interpretive	Spontaneous
4.	Harmonizing	Utilizing	Questioning	Imagining
5.	Cooperative	Competitive	Independent	Speculative
6.	Relating	Practicing	Developing	Searching
7.	Conversing	Implementing	Planning	Innovating
8.	Human Interactions	Details	Patterns	Possibilities
9.	Collaborating	Doing	Debating	Pondering
10.	Personal	Concrete	Abstract	Ideal
11.	Sharing	Trial and Error	Strategizing	Eureka!!!
12.	Humanistic	Realistic	Theoretical	Aesthetic
13.	People	Specifics	Concepts	Insights
14.	Empathy	Products	Logic	Understanding
15.	Socialize	Routinize	Systematize	Romanticize
16.	Emotional	Sensible	Logical	Mystical
17.	Sentiments	Products	Ideas	Images
18.	Loyalties	Roles	Laws	Principles
19.	Emulate	Memorize	Discovery Method	Divergent Expression
20.	Experiential	Methodical	Hypothetical	Inspirational
Totals	___	___	___	___

❖ ❖ ❖ ❖ ❖ ❖ ❖ ❖ ❖ ❖ ❖ ❖ ❖ ❖

IV. Analyzing Your Learning Preferences

Strengths of the Preferences

STRENGTHS	STYLE SCORE
Very strong preference	80–100
Strong preference	60–79
Moderate preference	40–59
Low preference	20–39
Very low preference	0–19

Learning Profile

No one learning style adequately represents the complexity of one's learning behavior. We all operate in a variety of ways in different situations. In reality, we often use a combination of styles at any one time. Therefore, it is important to identify not just one's learning style, but one's learning profile. One's Learning Profile consists of a "dominant style" (the highest score), the one most preferred and most often used; an "auxiliary style" (second highest score), the next most likely to be used; your "back-up style" (third highest score); and your "least-used style" (the lowest score).

DIRECTIONS FOR PLOTTING YOUR LEARNING PROFILE

Having completed the scoring of your learning preferences, plot your profile below. To plot your profile, enter the scores by style in the spaces provided. Enter the scores from the highest number (dominant) to the lowest (least used). Then enter a point (dot) in the appropriate column for each of the four scores. Finally, connect the points with straight lines. This plotting provides a visual estimate of the relative strengths of each style.

1 MODE	2 SCORE	3 STYLE	PLOT PROFILE					
			0	20	40	60	80	100
Dominant								
Auxiliary								
Back-up								
Least Used								

Interpreting the Learning Style Inventory

Profile plots take varying forms but all follow a pattern. The first pattern is called a "graduated profile."

In the graduated profile, each of the successive choices consumes a majority of the remaining available points. In other words, the four preferences are clearly distinguished, and each preference receives the greatest spread or range of points possible.

Graduated Profile

1 MODE	2 SCORE	3 STYLE	PLOT PROFILE					
			0	20	40	60	80	100
Dominant								
Auxiliary								
Back-up								
Least Used								

A second profile is called the "double dominant." A double dominant preference means that the respondent has chosen preferred descriptors equally from two separate styles. It is reflected on the bar chart as follows:

Double Dominant Profile

1 MODE	2 SCORE	3 STYLE	PLOT PROFILE					
			0	20	40	60	80	100
Dominant								
Auxiliary								
Back-up								
Least Used								

A third variation, the "balanced styles," indicates that the respondent has chosen the behaviors across all four styles, i.e., that according to type, he has no clear preferences or he operates with some flexibility across all the styles. This profile looks as follows:

Balanced Styles Profile

1 MODE	2 SCORE	3 STYLE	PLOT PROFILE					
			0	20	40	60	80	100
Dominant								
Auxiliary								
Back-up								
Least Used								

A fourth variation points to the selection of a dominant style, but also to the pairing of the supportive and auxiliary styles. This means that while there is a clearly preferred dominant, there is also a paring or equivalent comfort level between the second and third choices of styles. The chart reflects these preferences as follows:

Dominant and Pairs Profile

1 MODE	2 SCORE	3 STYLE	PLOT PROFILE					
			0	20	40	60	80	100
Dominant								
Auxiliary								
Back-up								
Least Used								

Still another way to interpret the LSI's findings is to look at the dominant and auxiliary choices in terms of either the judgment or perception functions. The chances are that either the perception or the judgment functions will be the same for both the first and second choices. For example, if your dominant was Sensing-Thinking and your auxiliary was Intuitive-Thinking, then in both cases you prefer thinking as the judgment mode. This choice also means that feeling is the least preferred and falls therefore in the "supportive" and "least used" categories. Or, conversely, if both perception functions fall in the dominant and auxiliary choices, then the opposite perception function is clearly relegated to the supportive and least used categories, e.g., where dominant Sensing-Feeling is paired with auxiliary Sensing-Thinking, the clear preference is for sensing as the perception mechanism. Intuition is, therefore, the third and last choice.

Characterizations of Learning Styles

Having completed and analyzed your learning profile, you will be asked to rank the descriptions of the four basic learning styles. Read through each of the four descriptions and rank them according to the one which is most characteristic of you as a learner (dominant learning style), second most characteristic (auxiliary learning style), third most characteristic (supporting learning style), and least like you (least-used learning style). Before you read the descriptions and perform the ranking task some interpretive or precautionary notes are in order.

First, the following descriptions are characterizations. They are written in generalities to provide mental pictures of the four learning styles. As such, they are stereotypes, and no one is exactly like the learner described.

As you read the descriptions, you will find that one style may be "right on target" except for a few words or a phrase. We suggest that you focus on the appropriateness of the description in its totality as a self-indicator rather than on the points that may be atypical.

Second, each learning style reflects aspects of your behavior. Certainly some styles are more reflective of your perceived behaviors than others.

There may be one style with which you have little or no compatibility.

Third, no one style or combination of styles is better than any other. Each style has its own assets and liabilities.

Fourth, learning preferences are heavily influenced by environment. Thus, our styles may be influenced as the environment changes.

Last, for some of us it is easier to find our dominant style, and for others it is easier to identify the least-used style. In either event, you will now have some new verbal pegs on which to "hang" a better understanding of how you function as a learner. In addition, these sensitivities will assist you in more accurately assessing how others may learn.

THE SENSING-FEELING LEARNER

Overview*

The Sensing-Feeling learner can be characterized as sociable, friendly, and interpersonally oriented. This type of learner is very sensitive to people's feelings: his own and others'. He prefers to learn about things that directly affect people's lives rather than impersonal facts or theories.

Approach to Learning

The Sensing-Feeler's approach to learning is a personal one. He works best when he is emotionally involved in what he is being asked to learn. The Sensing-Feeling learner tends to be spontaneous and often acts on impulse, i.e., in terms of what "feels right." He is interested in people and likes to listen to and talk about people and their feelings. He likes to be helpful to others and needs to be recognized for his efforts.

The Sensing-Feeling learner, more than any other type, enjoys personal attention. He needs to feel relaxed,

comfortable, and to enjoy himself while he learns. He likes to think out loud, to work with other students, to share his ideas, and to get the reactions of his friends. He much prefers cooperation to competition and needs reassurance or praise that he is doing well. He is greatly influenced by the likes and dislikes of others. On occasion, he may complete an assignment as much to please someone else than because of any interest he has in the task itself.

Approach to Problem-Solving

The Sensing-Feeler's approach to problem-solving activities is greatly influenced by his own values and life experiences. He may disregard or reject information that does not conform to his own life experiences. He likes harmony and prefers to work in group situations as a way to draw out pertinent facts for problem-solving. He is comfortable working with interpersonal type problems because of his sensitivity to people's feelings.

Assets and Liabilities

The Sensing-Feeling learner's strength is his interest in other people. He is sensitive to his own and others' concerns and will listen to many different points of view. He works best in group situations and knows what it takes to facilitate group movement and growth. He is trusted by others because he is spontaneous, shows emotion, and is honest about his feelings.

On the other hand, the Sensing-Feeling learner has liabilities. Because he is so involved with his feelings, he is easily hurt by others and may be overemotional. He finds it difficult to separate himself from his work and takes constructive criticism as an attack on his personal self-worth. He may be so concerned with what other people think and feel that he is unable to assert himself, to express his own opinions, to stand firm for what he believes, to take charge, or to lead. He often finds it difficult to plan ahead and to be objective, or to weigh the evidence around him before he takes action on his feelings.

Learns Best

The Sensing-Feeler learns best in a warm, friendly, supportive, and interactive environment in which students are encouraged to share their personal thoughts, feelings, and experiences, and to interact with one another.

He benefits most when the instructional process emphasizes collaborative approaches in which students share ideas and materials and work in small groups.

The Sensing-Feeler thinks best when talking and/or listening to other people. It is often difficult for him to sit down and begin work, especially when it does not relate to him personally, or when it has to be done alone.

The Sensing-Feeler enjoys group activities, games with lots of action in which everyone can participate and no one loses, discussions, reading stories about people and their feelings, writing and talking about things he likes to do,

---

*For the purposes of describing behaviors, we are following the convention of referring to teachers using the female pronoun, and to students using the male pronoun.

group process activities, and art and music which allow him to express his feelings.

The Sensing-Feeling student needs to participate in group activities to develop his power of empathy. He needs to have time and resources to learn about himself. He needs to have an opportunity to explore, change, and develop attitudes and values in reference to others.

The Sensing-Feeling student learns best from first-hand experiences that relate to him personally and help him to understand who he is and how he functions.

The Sensing-Feeling student enjoys working with others and is particularly sensitive to their approval or disapproval. He is equally sensitive to indifference. He is influenced more by his peers than by authority figures and may lose sight of his own ideas while trying to cooperate with the group.

The Sensing-Feeling learner views content mastery as secondary to achieving harmonious relationships with others. He enjoys learning through group process, personal friendships, and tender (if not loving) attention.

THE SENSING-THINKING LEARNER

Overview

The Sensing-Thinking learner can be characterized as realistic, practical, and matter-of-fact. This type of learner is efficient and results-oriented.

He prefers action to words and involvement to theory. He has a high energy level for doing things which are pragmatic, logical, and useful.

Approach to Learning

The Sensing-Thinking learner likes to complete his work in an organized and efficient manner. He tends to be neat, well-organized, and precise in his work. His appetite for work and his need for immediate feedback is often a challenge for the teacher. The Sensing-Thinking learner enjoys work and needs to be kept busy. He would rather do almost anything than remain in his seat, listening to someone speak. He needs to be active, to do, to see tangible results from his efforts, and to be in control of the task.

The Sensing-Thinking learner prefers step-by-step directions when assigned a task and becomes impatient if the instructions become long and involved.

More than any other learner, this type wants to know exactly what is expected of him. He needs to know what he is to do, how he is to do it, and when it is to be done. The Sensing-Thinking learner will often lose interest in an activity if it moves too slowly or if he can see no practical use for it.

The Sensing-Thinking learner needs clearly structured environments with the main focus on factual mastery of skills and an opportunity to apply them to something practical or to demonstrate proficiency in the skill. He prefers assignments which have right or wrong responses rather than open-ended or interpretive ones. He is highly motivated by competition, learning games, grades, gold stars, etc.

Approach to Problem-Solving

The Sensing-Thinker's approach to problem-solving emphasizes specific facts, trial-and-error, and pragmatic solutions. Problems are seen as puzzles that require constant manipulation of the pieces until the correct solution is discovered. The Sensing-Thinker works best with problems that require concrete exploration and manipulation rather than the analysis of abstractions. When confronted with a problem, he looks for solutions from past experiences and relies on previously tested procedures rather than looking for new solutions. If the first attempt at solution doesn't work, he will try another—as long as time and resources permit. Sensing-Thinkers are people of action searching for practical solutions to their immediate problems.

Assets and Liabilities

The Sensing-Thinker's strengths are in his ability to apply himself to the task at hand. He is concerned with action and tangible results. He is highly task-oriented and a good person to have on a committee concerned about getting work done. He is organized, adept at collecting the facts, and attentive to detail. He is pragmatic and able to apply past experience to problems. He searches for simple yet workable solutions and is able to face difficulty with realism. He is able to write and speak directly to the point. He is efficient and tends not to procrastinate.

On the other hand, the Sensing-Thinking learner's liabilities are that he may be inflexible and unable to adapt to change. He may be dogmatic and headstrong. He has a limited tolerance for ambiguity and thus may take action before he has considered all the consequences. The Sensing-Thinking learner may oversimplify complex issues or fail to see the possibilities beyond the immediate facts. He is overly concerned about what is right and wrong so that he overlooks the gray areas where truth tends to lurk. He distrusts those things which can't be quickly verified by the senses. Furthermore, because of his task orientation, he may overlook the feelings of the people with whom he is working.

Learns Best

The Sensing-Thinker learns best in an organized, systematic, activity-oriented, instructor-directed atmosphere. He needs to be actively engaged in purposeful work. The instructional environment requires well-defined procedures and content. This content needs to be presented in an orderly and systematic manner. The instructional emphases for the Sensing-Thinker are on convergent, competitive, and independent approaches to learning.

The Sensing-Thinker learns best when he can directly experience with his five senses what he is expected to learn. Motivation comes from being able to see the practicality of what he has learned and from putting the new learning into immediate use. Thus, the Sensing-Thinker learns best when he can see the utility of what he is asked to learn. (Sometimes the need for utility can be alternatively satisfied by good grades or other tangible forms of recognition.)

The Sensing-Thinking learner has little tolerance for ambiguous situations. He wants to know what is expected of him before be begins. He needs clearly stated ground rules. He works best when there are clearly stated objectives and when achievement is quickly recognized and rewarded.

The Sensing-Thinking learner likes games that have competition, clear rules, and lots of action.

The Sensing-Thinking learner needs a clearly defined instructional approach with the focus on content mastery, the mastery of basic skills, or the immediate opportunity to employ what has been learned. He learns best from repetition, drill, memorization, programmed instruction, workbooks, demonstration, field trips, and direct actual experience. In short, he needs well-defined action activities and immediate tangible results.

THE INTUITIVE-THINKING LEARNER

Overview

The Intuitive-Thinking learner can be characterized as theoretical, intellectual, and knowledge-oriented. This type of learner prefers to be challenged intellectually and to think things through for himself. The Intuitive-Thinker is curious about ideas, has a tolerance for theory, a taste for complex problems, and a concern for long-range consequences.

Approach to Learning

The Intuitive-Thinking learner approaches school-work in a logical, organized, systematic fashion. The Intuitive-Thinker brings organization and structure to both people and things. He takes time to plan and think things through before beginning work on an assignment. He organizes his ideas and determines what sources are necessary to complete required tasks.

The Intuitive-Thinker prefers to work independently or with other thinking types. He requires little feedback until his work is completed. He does not like to be pressed for time. When working on something of interest, time is meaningless. He displays a great deal of patience and persistence in completing difficult assignments if they have captured his interest.

The Intuitive-Thinker is interested in theoretical models, constructs, and ideas. His interest in facts is only in relation to the proving or disproving of theory.

The Intuitive-Thinking learner's approach to understanding things and ideas is by breaking them down into their component parts. He likes to reason things out and to look for logical relationships. His thought processes follow a cause-and-effect line of reasoning. He is constantly asking "Why?" His questions tend to be provocative as compared to questions about information or facts.

The Intuitive-Thinker is an avid reader. His learning is vicarious, and therefore abstract symbols, formulae, the written word, and technical illustrations are preferred sources of collecting data.

The Intuitive-Thinker usually displays a facility for language and expresses his ideas in detail. Everything the Intuitive-Thinker touches turns into words, spoken or written. He enjoys arguing a point based on logical analysis. In discussion, he often enjoys the role of "devil's advocate" or purposefully arguing an opposite point of view.

The Intuitive-Thinking learner is also concerned about being correct. He strives toward perfection, is self-critical, and is upset by mistakes—his own or other people's.

Approach to Problem-Solving

The Intuitive-Thinker approaches problem-solving situations with relish. He enjoys looking at the problem from as many perspectives as possible. He is precise in his formulation of the problem statement. He then looks for as many alternative solutions as are feasible in resolving the situation. He is not bothered by the complexities of the problem, and generally does not become too invested in the details. His main concern is to properly conceptualize the problem issues so that he can postulate probable solutions. He especially enjoys the thought process that goes with looking at the cause-and-effect relationships for each proposed solution.

Assets and Liabilities

The Intuitive-Thinking learner sets high standards for himself and for those with whom he works. At his best, he is adept at analyzing complex ideas and theories and at discovering principles and relationships among ideas. He is objective, able to organize information, forecast consequences, weigh the law and evidence, and apply previously learned ideas to new situations. His ideas are well thought out, and he is able to stand firm against opposition. He is patient, persistent, enjoys research, and is comfortable addressing intellectually challenging problems.

On the other hand, at his worst, he may be overly critical of himself and others. When making a point, he may show lack of concern for the feelings of others. When explaining what he knows, he will monopolize conversations by rambling on in abstractions which no one else is following. His conversations may turn into theoretical lectures. He talks above people rather than with them. He may have little tolerance for other people's ideas especially if they disagree with his own positions. He may be so involved with his own reasoning that he fails to see the reasoning of others. He may have difficulty working with others.

Learns Best

The Intuitive-Thinker learns best in an intellectually stimulating atmosphere in which he is challenged to think critically and analytically and in which he is "stretched" to increase his reasoning abilities. The instructional emphasis for the Intuitive-Thinker is placed on independent and creative approaches to learning. He prefers to learn by discovery and experimentation.

The Intuitive-Thinking learner needs to have the freedom to identify his own interests, to participate in selecting his own learning activities, and to have the time and resources to develop his own ideas. The Intuitive-Thinking learner enjoys independent research projects, reading on topics of current interest, theorizing, lectures, games of strategy, expression of ideas, debates, and projects which call for the use of intuition and thinking.

THE INTUITIVE-FEELING LEARNER

Overview

The Intuitive-Feeling learner can be characterized as curious, insightful, and imaginative. The Intuitive-Feeler is one who dares to dream, is committed to his values, is open to alternatives and is constantly searching for new and unusual ways to express himself.

Approach to Learning

The Intuitive-Feeling student approaches learning eager to explore ideas, to generate new solutions to problems, and to discuss moral dilemmas. The Intuitive-Feeler's interests are varied and unpredictable. He enjoys a wide variety of things. He prefers activities which allow him to use his imagination and to do things in new and different ways. He is turned off by routine or rote assignments and prefers questions which are open ended, such as "What would happen if . . . ?"

The Intuitive-Feeling student is highly motivated by his own interests. Things of interest will be done inventively and well. Things which he does not like may be done poorly or forgotten altogether. When engaged in a project which intrigues him, time is meaningless. The Intuitive-Feeler operates by an "internal clock" and, therefore, often feels constrained or frustrated by external rules or schedules.

The Intuitive-Feeling learner is independent and non-conforming. He does not fear being different and is usually aware of his own and other people's impulses. He is open to the irrational and not confined by convention. He is sensitive to beauty and symmetry and will comment on the aesthetic characteristics of things.

The Intuitive-Feeling learner prefers not to follow step-by-step procedures but rather to move where his intuition takes him. He prefers to find his own solutions to challenges or problems rather than being told what to do or how to do it. He is able to take intuitive leaps. He trusts his insights. He often looks for new and different ways to solve problems. He often takes circuitous routes to get where he wants to go. He may solve a problem but not be able to explain how he arrived at his answer.

The Intuitive-Feeling learner is able to adapt to new situations. He is flexible in thought and action. He prefers changing environments with many resources and materials. The Intuitive-Feeler, more than any other type, is less likely to be disturbed by changes in routine. The Intuitive-Feeler is comfortable working with a minimum of directions. His work is sometimes scattered and may look chaotic to thinking types. The Intuitive-Feeling learner is often engaged in a number of activities at the same time and moves from one to the other according to where his interests take him. He starts more projects than he finishes.

Approach to Problem-Solving

The Intuitive-Feeler enjoys solving new problems. He is particularly interested in problems of human welfare. He is adept at thinking divergently and searching for alternative solutions. He often offers unusual, unique, inventive, or "way out" responses. He sometimes is more concerned about generating possible solutions to a problem than choosing one and carrying it out. The Intuitive-Feeler is interested in the future, "what might be," and "what could happen." He looks beyond the facts and details to see the broad perspective or the "big picture." He needs to look at a problem from many different perspectives and searches for unique and unexpected solutions.

Assets and Liabilities

The Intuitive-Feeling learner is not constrained by convention and is open to new ideas and approaches. He is able to think divergently, is idealistic, and is willing to tackle difficult problems with zest. He is able to arouse enthusiasm and commitment on the part of others to achieve a goal. He is creative and adept at reading the signs of coming change, is able to supply ingenuity to problem-solving, and is able to generate new and unusual possibilities for addressing issues of human welfare.

On the other hand, his approach to problems, though creative, is sometimes unrealistic and lacks pragmatic judgment. The Intuitive-Feeler, at his worst, has difficulty facing problems with realism. He is never satisfied with what is and always wants to change something. He moves from one good idea to another but may be unable to put any of the ideas into action. He is enthusiastic about what he is doing one day and bored the next. He is over-committed and involves himself in many more projects than he can complete. He has difficulty planning and organizing his time. He often overlooks essential details and fails to take action on what needs to be done at the moment.

Learns Best

The Intuitive-Feeler learns best in a flexible and innovative atmosphere where there are a minimum number of restrictions, many alternative activities, and where a premium is placed on creating his own learning activities or solutions to problems. The Intuitive-Feeler's instructional emphases are on curiosity, creativity, and a clarification of his personal values. He enjoys self-expressive activities, creating things, projects designed around his own interests, reading, messy activities, meditation, contemplation, daydreaming, and fantasizing. He enjoys projects which allow him to use his intuition and to express his feelings.

This type of learner needs to explore his creative abilities to find ways to self-expression, to share his enthusiasm and his inspirations with others. He has an acute need to develop his own unique style of being. He has a keen interest in alternative belief systems, possibilities, and new projects. Things which may not have happened but may be made to happen are a source of continuing interest.

Thinking About Your Learning Style

The next phase of the self-assessment process is to look at yourself as a learner in terms of your strengths and needs for improvement.

The first part of this process is to analyze your responses from the Learning Style Inventory with your own subjective responses. Then, respond to the questions which follow as a way of putting the differences or distinctions into clearer focus.

Having now read the descriptions of the four learning styles and ranked them, compare your subjective responses with your responses to the Learning Style Inventory.

My Responses		LSI Responses
_____	Dominant	_____
_____	Auxiliary	_____
_____	Supportive	_____
_____	Least Used	_____

Understanding Myself as a Teacher
The TLC Teaching Style Inventory
A self-diagnostic tool to identify one's preferred teaching style.

Silver, H. F., and J. R. Hanson. 1980. In *Teacher self-assessment*, 95–110.
Moorestown, N.J.: Hanson Silver and Associates, Inc.

Purpose

The Teaching Style Inventory (TSI) is a simple self-description test based on Carl Gustav Jung's Theory of Psychological Types (1921). The instrument is designed to help you identify your own teaching profile based on your preferences for particular behaviors. The behaviors fall into the following ten categories: classroom atmosphere, teaching techniques, planning, what one values in students, teacher-student interactions, classroom management, student behaviors, teaching behaviors, evaluation, and goals.

Directions

Based upon your conscious preferences and pertinent to the way you teach, rank in order the behavior descriptions in each category by assigning a 5 to the behavior which best characterizes your teaching style, a 3 to the behavior which next best characterizes your teaching style, a 1 to the next most characteristic behavior, and a 0 to the behavior which least characterizes you as a teacher.

As you read through the list of behaviors in each category, you may find it difficult to choose the behavior that best characterizes your teaching style. This is understandable since every teacher operates in a variety of ways in different situations, yet each of us does have preferences for some behaviors over others. Keep in mind that there are no right or wrong answers. All the choices are equally acceptable. The aim of the inventory is to describe how you teach, not to evaluate your teaching ability.

I. Choosing Teaching Preferences

In each of the following ten (10) sets of behaviors rank the four responses in order of

First preference	5 Points
Second preference	3 Points
Third preference	1 Point
Fourth preference	No Points

Be sure to assign a different weighted number (5, 3, 1, or 0) to each of the four descriptors in the set. Do not make ties.

I.   Classroom Atmosphere
The classroom atmosphere I feel best about emphasizes the following:

___ 1.   A warm, friendly supportive atmosphere in which students are encouraged to work collaboratively, and to share their personal thoughts, feelings, and experiences; to interact with one another.

___ 2.   An organized, systematic, activity-oriented, teacher-directed atmosphere in which students are actively engaged in purposeful work.

___ 3.   An intellectually stimulating atmosphere in which students are provided with a variety of resources and activities designed to develop their critical thinking skills, and to stretch their limits of performance.

___ 4.   A flexible, innovative atmosphere with a minimum of restrictions in which students are encouraged to create their own activities for learning. A classroom with many resources chosen or designed to stimulate curiosity.

II.   Teaching Techniques
My teaching techniques often provide for activities:

___ 5.   which usually have right or wrong answers and require students to draw upon recall, memory, and comprehension. My instructional strategies may include drill, lecture, programmed instruction, seatwork, homework, questions and answer sessions, practice, worksheets, workbooks, hands on activities, demonstrations, field trips, and competitive games.

___ 6.   in which students are personally and emotionally involved in their learning, and in which they work collaboratively and cooperatively with others. My instructional strategies may include small group discussions, sharing personal feelings and experiences, social problem-solving, role plays, simulations, peer tutoring, small and large group projects, team games, sensitivity training, team-building, and consensus decision-making.

___ 7.   in which students can explore their creative abilities, find ways for self-expression, gain inspiration, and explore personal values. My instructional strategies may include open-ended discussions, discussing moral dilemmas, values clarification, creative and artistic activities, personal contracts, creative writing, divergent expression, synectics, guided fantasy, inventing, imagining, writing poetry, using analogies, and exploring alternative belief systems.

___ 8.   in which students are challenged to think critically, to deduce consequences, to compare and contrast, to analyze, synthesize, and evaluate alternatives. My instructional strategies may include independent research, reading assignments, written essays, debating issues, brainstorming, problem-solving, divergent thinking, the Socratic method of questioning, lecture, systems analysis, theorizing, and research methods.

III. Planning
I am most comfortable and do my best teaching when my plans:

___ 9. account for the students' personal, social, and survival skills, rather than following a curriculum guide or text book. I tend to respond to the "here and now" class needs in order to capitalize on spontaneous events for instruction. My plans may be well developed but not followed.

___ 10. follow prescribed curriculum guides or text chapters, which are translated into specific weekly or daily plans. Any variation in activity is thought out in detail and schedule changes are rarely made.

___ 11. are based on the interests and curiosities of the students. Curriculum guides, texts, and materials are used as resources for a constantly changing program rather than as the program itself.

___ 12. follow a broad outline in which the main concepts or themes are identified and looked at from several directions and disciplines; focus on conceptual objectives rather than measured results. Units are organized around key open-ended question or themes, with details left to emerge during instruction.

IV. Preferred Qualities of Students
I especially like young persons who:

___ 13. are honest with their feelings, are sensitive to the rights and feelings of others, and place a high value on relationships with significant adults, friends, and getting along with people.

___ 14. are clear about what they like and don't like, have well defined goals, are task oriented, organized, neat, complete their work on time, are respectful and well prepared in class.

___ 15. have insights and original ideas, who are concerned with larger issues, sometimes question the way things are done, and may have artistic interests and abilities.

___ 16. are relatively mature and knowledgeable, are excited by ideas, able to articulate their thoughts and can work well independently.

V. Teacher/Student Interaction
I am at my best when teaching students who:

___ 17. are interested in ideas and theories behind the facts, like to work independently, display patience and persistence in completing difficult tasks and strive for perfection.

___ 18. have strong personal interests, look beyond facts and details to see broader perspectives; are open to the unusual; are not confined by convention;

are interested in solving problems with particular reference to human welfare.

___ 19. are comfortable sharing their personal thoughts and feelings; like to work cooperatively with another student or in small groups; are interested in other people and act on their behalf; relates to me positively and cooperatively.

___ 20. like to take action on their ideas, who learn best from direct experience and step-by-step procedures, have a high energy level for completing tasks, and want to have clear answers/products which tell them then-and-there how well they are doing.

VI. Classroom Management
I manage my class by:

___ 21. establishing well-defined rules and procedures, and covering content in an orderly, prescribed manner, by sticking to a good lesson plan.

___ 22. responding to and being sensitive to my student needs; by allowing students to work cooperatively in an informal setting.

___ 23. providing a flexible structure which allows students to choose learning activities from a variety of alternatives. The work environment may include projects or questions which are offered more for the stimulation of ideas and for the richness of the experience than for attaining and measuring specific outcomes.

___ 24. constructing learning situations where students are challenged to think for themselves, to discover and apply new knowledge and concepts, and to work through and find solutions to problems.

VII. Appropriate Behaviors
In working with students to achieve appropriate behavior, I prefer to:

___ 25. assist students to think/feel through the consequences and the significance of their behavior in order to enable them to acquire an internal sense of discipline and morality.

___ 26. establish clear standards and expectations for correct behavior, preferably in a written form, such as policy. Punitive consequences for infractions of rules are consistent and predictable—"Firm but Fair."

___ 27. arrange a person-to-person conference, enlist the help of a small group of students, or even to bring up the issue with the whole class in order to help the student to behave in a socially acceptable manner.

___ 28. examine the basis and justification for the rules, in order to make sense to students and to me. At times, I am a bit annoyed when students don't use self discipline to behave in an obviously sensible and prudent way.

VIII. Teaching Behavior

As a teacher I tend to be:

___ 29. insightful, chaotic, creative. I try to inspire my students to explore possibilities and to find ways of self expression.

___ 30. intellectual and knowledge oriented. I try to serve as a resource person to my students and assist them in their inquiries. I try to stimulate my students' intellectual development, asking "why" questions which require independent thought.

___ 31. pragmatic, work- and efficiency-oriented. I tend to be the primary source of information and tasks and spend the majority of my time communicating information and directing students as to what to do and how to do it.

___ 32. warm, friendly, and empathetic. My main focus is to stimulate students to work cooperatively, to feel good about themselves, to participate in open-ended discussions, and to share their personal thoughts and feelings.

IX. Evaluation

In considering the evaluation of student work (assignments, grades, etc.), I am inclined to emphasize the following factors:

___ 33. what is observable, measurable, and quantifiable. The focus is on what students know and can demonstrate.

___ 34. the student's abilities to reason, to conceptualize, to understand, and the ability to apply what has been learned to new situations.

___ 35. each student's achievement in light of his efforts, individual abilities, and personal problems or needs.

___ 36. opportunities for students to evaluate their own work, and to establish their own aesthetic and performance criteria.

X. Educational Goals

In summary, my educational goals generally center around:

___ 37. providing support for the development of a positive self concept, the acquisition of survival skills, and teaching skills which enable one to communicate and interact better with students.

___ 38. the mastery of specific content and skills by being able to read, doing basic arithmetic, finding and collecting information, presenting data, and organizing facts.

___ 39. understanding of concepts, interpreting ideas, hypothesizing, research methods, and critical thinking.

___ 40. the development of a student's personal potential and competence, creative abilities, and the clarity of personal beliefs in relation to themselves and the human community.

Categorizing Behaviors

In each of the ten categories the behaviors correspond to four different teaching styles. The teaching styles are based on the different ways people prefer to use their perception (sensing and intuition) and their judgment (thinking and feeling). The preference for either type of perception function is independent of the preference for either type of judgment function. As a result, four distinct combinations occur.

1. Sensing/Thinking (S-T)
2. Sensing/Feeling (S-F)
3. Intuitive/Thinking (N-T)
4. Intuitive/Feeling (N-F)

Scoring

I. SUBJECTIVE RANKING

Before scoring your Teaching Style Inventory please rank order the styles based upon your own immediate perceptions of your teaching preferences. Please carefully read the style descriptions which follow and then determine which description is most characteristic, next most characteristic, third most, and least characteristic. Remember that everyone operates in all four styles but that we tend to choose one particular style more often than the others.

Teaching Domains

SENSING/THINKING TEACHERS—are primarily outcomes-oriented (skills learned, projects completed). They maintain highly structured, well-organized classroom environments. Work is purposeful, emphasizing the acquisition of skills and information. Plans are clear and concise. Discipline is firm but fair. Teachers serve as the primary information source and give detailed directions for student learning.

(Preference _____)

SENSING/FEELING TEACHERS—are empathetic and people-oriented. Emphasis is placed on the students' feelings of positive self-worth. The teacher shares personal dealings and experiences with students and attempts to become personally involved in students' learning. The teacher believes that school should be fun and introduces much learning through games and activities that involve the students actively and physically. Plans are changed frequently to meet the mood of the class.

(Preference _____)

INTUITIVE/THINKING TEACHERS—are intellectually oriented. The teacher places primary importance on students' intellectual development. The teacher provides the time and the intellectual challenges to encourage students to develop skills in critical thinking, problem solving, logic, research techniques, and independent study. Curriculum planning is developed around concepts frequently centering around a series of questions or themes. Evaluation is often based on open-ended questions, debates, essays, or position papers.

(Preference _____)

INTUITIVE/FEELING TEACHERS—are innovatively oriented. The teacher encourages students to explore their creative abilities. Insights and innovative ideas are highly valued. Discussions revolve around generating possibilities and new relationships. The classroom environment is often full of creative clutter. The teacher encourages students to develop their own unique styles. Curriculum emphasizes focus on creative thinking, moral development, values, and flexible, imaginative approaches to learning. Curiosity, insight, and artistic self expression are welcomed.

(Preference _____)

Teaching Styles Self Profile

1. Most characteristic_____

2. Next most characteristic_____

3. Third most characteristic_____

4. Least characteristic_____

Now that your teaching styles have been entered based on your personal judgments, turn to the directions for computing your Teaching Style Inventory scores; then complete the Teaching Styles Profile. You are now in a position to compare the subjective or personal analysis of your teaching style preference with the identification of style from the Teaching Style Inventory.

❖ ❖ ❖ ❖ ❖ ❖ ❖ ❖ ❖ ❖ ❖ ❖ ❖ ❖ ❖

II. Scoring Teaching Preferences

To complete your teaching preference score for each of the four teaching styles, transfer your rank numbers from the answer sheets to the scoring sheet below for each of the behaviors. Compute your score by adding the rank numbers for each column.

		COLUMN 1 S-F Item No., Rank No.	COLUMN 2 S-T Item No., Rank No.	COLUMN 3 N-T Item No., Rank No.	COLUMN 4 N-F Item No., Rank No.
I	Classroom Atmosphere	1 _____	2 _____	3 _____	4 _____
II	Teaching Techniques	6 _____	5 _____	8 _____	7 _____
III	Planning	9 _____	10 _____	12 _____	11 _____
IV	Preferred Qualities of Students	13 _____	14 _____	16 _____	15 _____
V	Teacher/Student Interaction	19 _____	20 _____	17 _____	18 _____
VI	Classroom Management	22 _____	21 _____	24 _____	23 _____
VII	Appropriate Behaviors	27 _____	26 _____	28 _____	25 _____
VIII	Teacher Behavior	32 _____	31 _____	30 _____	29 _____
IX	Evaluation	35 _____	33 _____	34 _____	36 _____
X	Educational Goals	37 _____	38 _____	39 _____	40 _____
		TOTAL _____	TOTAL _____	TOTAL _____	TOTAL _____

Another way to interpret your Teaching Style Inventory findings is to look at your preferences in terms of their cognitive, affective, concrete, or abstract content. There are two cognitive teaching styles which are the dominant thinking processes. These are the Sensing-Thinking and the Intuitive-Thinking styles. There are also two primarily affective teaching styles emphasizing the feeling component: i.e., Sensing-Feeling and Intuitive-Feeling. These same domains may also be interpreted as emphasizing degrees of abstraction or concreteness, i.e., concreteness as the Sensing-Thinking and Sensing-Feeling orientations and abstraction as the Intuitive-Thinking and Intuitive-Feeling orientations. Hence, the style depends on which function is the dominant in the top two pairings, i.e., your dominant and auxiliary choices. Thus the four possible sets of emphases may be pictured as follows:

COGNITIVE STYLES (T)		CONCRETE STYLES (S)	
S-T	N-T	S-F	S-T
AFFECTIVE STYLES (F)		ABSTRACT STYLES (N)	
S-F	N-F	N-F	N-T

In looking at your dominant and auxiliary preferences the chances are that there will be a single choice or function for either perception or judgment. For example, a profile might look as follows:

Dominant S-F

Auxiliary S-T

Supportive N-F

Least Used N-T

In the above example the functional preference for both the dominant and auxiliary choices is sensing, hence this teacher's style choices may be characterized as concrete in orientation.

Another way to interpret the Teaching Style Inventory scoring is to examine your preferences against each one of the ten decision categories or variables. For each of these ten categories you may wish to identify the teaching styles you selected and then list them as first, second, third, and last choices. The sample worksheet below may be helpful to you in this listing. Example:

Category	Choice Ranking			
	1st	**2nd**	**3rd**	**Last**
1. Classroom Atmosphere				
2. Teaching Techniques				
3. Planning				
4. Preferred Qualities of Students				
5. Teacher/Student Interaction				
6. Classroom Management				
7. Appropriate Behaviors				
8. Teacher Behavior				
9. Evaluation				
10. Educational Goals				

Characterizations of Teaching Styles

Having now completed an analysis of your teaching profile (your first, second, third, and last choices of styles) an opportunity is presented to rank order the four teaching styles based on detailed descriptions of each of the styles. These descriptions identify the recurring and most observable behaviors for each of the styles. By choosing a first, second, third, and last preference you have still more data for self-knowledge and the analysis of your teaching style.

As with learning styles, some precautionary notes are in order. First, the descriptions are inevitably stereotypic and general. No one teacher is precisely like the style described. Still, as a general picture the description identifies major behaviors and beliefs that may clarify the style for your own thinking. Second, teaching styles can only be described in terms of what is observable. Those observations always take place within a particular context or environment. Environments change and have an impact on behaviors. The descriptions, therefore, must be seen as generalizations without regard to context. Third, the teaching style used may not be the same as the teacher's personality type or learning style. Teachers must continually change their teaching styles to meet the needs of students and the objectives to be achieved. Fourth, no one style or profile is superior, in and of itself, to any other. Each style has its own strengths and weaknesses based upon context, content, and external pressures. What the descriptions or characterizations provide, therefore, is simply a sketch, an overview, of the dominant behaviors of each teaching style. Your own teaching style is discovered by filling in the sketch and by continually seeking to match your instructional intents with your observable behaviors.

THE SENSING-FEELING TEACHER

Overview

The Sensing-Feeling teacher is characterized by qualities of personal warmth, friendliness, empathy, concern for others, and interpersonal relationships. She concentrates on the social and emotional adjustments of her students. She works in the "here and now" and often uses pupil interactions as the "content" for her teaching activities.

Approach to Teaching

The Sensing-Feeling teacher strives to establish a classroom atmosphere which supports student social interaction. She encourages her students to share their personal thoughts, feelings, and experiences. She manages her classroom according to what "feels best." She may change a well-planned lesson on the spot if it does not feel right or if it is not responsive to the needs of her students. She believes that learning should and can be enjoyable because as the student learns and is confirmed in the learning he feels better. The Sensing-Feeling teacher also believes that school should be a place where students learn about themselves, develop constructive and rewarding relationships,

and learn the necessary skills to get along and work cooperatively with others.

The Sensing-Feeling teacher wants to be liked by her students, peers, and significant others. She is sensitive to her students' personal needs both in and out of school. She enjoys personal contact with her students and outwardly expresses her affection for them.

The Sensing-Feeling teacher particularly values students who attempt to be honest with their feelings, are sensitive to the rights and feelings of others, and can work cooperatively.

The Sensing-Feeling teacher prefers to evaluate her students' achievement in light of the effort expended, individual abilities, personal problems, and needs. She often relies on her own value judgments rather than on objective data. She is often influenced more by her own personal likes and dislikes than by external rules, procedures, or standards.

Issues of class conduct are handled by personal conferences and small group discussions. Class meetings are held as a way to establish socially acceptable behavior. Her approach to problems of discipline includes consideration of extenuating circumstances, her own appraisal of the personal significance of the infraction, and an attempt to understand the "intent" in contrast to the result of the infraction.

Her approach to teaching is one in which students can become personally involved in their learning. She tends to introduce new content by asking her students how they are personally related to the facts, ideas, objects, or places in question.

Commitment to learning is facilitated by demonstrating to the student his existing knowledge of what is being taught, i.e., the new content. Toward these ends she relies a great deal on discussions, group discovery projects, group awareness activities, exercises in clarifying communications, role-playing, acting out stories, participatory games in which no one loses, "show and tell," sharing personal feelings, and other kinds of interactive group process learning activities.

Assets and Liabilities

The Sensing-Feeling teacher is responsive to the social and emotional needs of her students. She recognizes each child as a person with his own unique potential. She develops a classroom atmosphere that is warm, friendly, and interactive. She encourages her students to value other people's feelings and to respect the rights of others. She attempts to utilize the experiences and interactions of her students to bring understanding to the content she is teaching. She helps her pupils understand and accept their feelings and to deal with their feelings more openly. Her classroom activities are creative mixtures of physical activity, i.e., active rather than passive learning, and they focus on drama, service projects, discussions, and activities in which students are encouraged to express their feelings.

The Sensing-Feeling teacher's liabilities are that she may be overly involved in the personal problems of her pupils or peers. She may tend to overlook important content that has no feeling orientation. Science and math may end up short-changed in contrast to social studies, language arts, and history. She so needs to be appreciated that negative criticism or a lack of responsiveness from her students may sometimes be interpreted as a personal rejection. Her feelings are easily hurt. She may have an overly strong need for support and approval from those around her. She may also become easily discouraged or upset when things do not go as she had hoped. Her need to be liked or appreciated may thwart her ability to be objective, constructively critical, or firm in her decisions.

Teaches Best

The Sensing-Feeling teacher is at her best when teaching to her students' personal, social, and survival (coping) skills. She emphasizes process rather than product, i.e., how to work with people rather than final results. She prefers to respond to the here-and-now rather than to the there-and-then, whether past or future. She capitalizes on spontaneous events for instructional insights.

She works best in cooperative situations with students and peers. She works best when content can be handled in small group instruction and interactions. She encourages peer tutoring. Her primary goals are reflected in activities providing for student feelings of self-worth, improved communication skills through self-expression, and the acquisition of social skills.

THE SENSING-THINKING TEACHER

Overview

The Sensing-Thinking teacher is characterized by an orientation to hard work, efficiency, neatness, tasks, skills development, and the covering of the required content of the course or class. Her interests are with skills mastered and projects completed. Her emphasis is on product rather than process. She teaches in the here-and-now but makes continual reference to previously learned skills. She is pragmatic, realistic, and industrious. She plans her work and works her plan.

Approach to Teaching

The Sensing-Thinking teacher maintains a well structured and highly organized classroom environment. There is a place for everything, and everything is in its place.

Students are encouraged to work in externally observable and purposeful ways; i.e., effort in and of itself is a value. There is a concentration on learning activities that are individually focused since the purpose of learning is skills mastery. Thus her teaching techniques focus on drill, demonstration, competitions, and workbook activities. The acquisition of information for its own sake is a value since learning is looked upon as work.

In class the Sensing-Thinking teacher spends most of her "talk time" giving directions and providing information. The information flow tends to be teacher-to-learner with students called on to provide the correct answers or to demonstrate the proper skills in response.

The Sensing-Thinking teacher's plans are clear and concise. She covers content in an orderly and prescribed manner and generally does not vary appreciably from approved curricula.

The Sensing-Thinking teacher sets down, in advance, clearly defined classroom rules and procedures. She establishes clear expectations for student behavior. Such disciplinary procedures are usually in written form, e.g., class policies or rules or a class constitution. Student infractions of rules are met quickly, consistently, impersonally, and predictably. Sensing-Thinking teachers address discipline in a "firm but fair" manner.

Sensing-Thinking teachers value students who are task-oriented, well-organized, neat, respectful, prompt, and prepared.

In evaluating her students' skill mastery she makes extensive use of objective tests, quizzes, homework, recitation, and demonstrations. Her focus is on desired outcomes, i.e., on what is measurable, observable, testable, and justifiable. Classroom time is provided for students to demonstrate skills mastered or information learned.

The Sensing-Thinking teacher's instructional techniques make use of seat work, question and answer periods, practice, immediate responses to answers, worksheets, workbooks, hands-on activities, demonstrations, competitive games, lectures, audio-visual presentations, field trips, and craft projects.

Assets and Liabilities

The Sensing-Thinking teacher believes in hard work and the completion of required tasks. She is thorough and good at working with details. She covers all required course content within a classroom management system that is efficient and effective. She knows that required skills can only be learned by practice and repetition. She enjoys a full day of activities, in which everyone is involved and doing something. As students complete their work, she provides immediate feedback on its acceptability or correctness. She uses the energies that learners have in task-focused games. She reflects the outside world's concern for the acquisition of specific knowledge and skills. She rewards the hard workers and admonishes the slower students to achievement through greater effort. She is generally predictable, not easily flustered, and a reliable source of information. She assists students in learning self-discipline, competing for the best scores and grades, and learning the fundamentals for academic success. She tends to be methodical, concerned with clarity in providing instructions, and businesslike in establishing the learning environment.

The liabilities of the Sensing-Thinking teacher are that she may overlook the individual learner's needs in the push for content or skills mastery. She may overemphasize detail to the point where the students become bored or discouraged. Her concern with rules may make her appear rigid or unfeeling. The concern for order and organization may result in such regimentation that students get "turned off." Her dependency on lesson plans and fixed curriculum guides may mean that she overlooks the spontaneous instructional content of the classroom. Her overreliance on pat procedures may make it difficult for her to adapt to an ever-changing classroom environment. She may tend to become set in her ways.

As the primary information giver she may discourage students from searching for answers from other sources. Her thrust toward convergent teaching strategies may distract students from looking for other alternatives. As the giver of directions, she may end up suppressing any natural leadership tendencies on the part of students.

Teaches Best

The Sensing-Thinking teacher is at her best when instructing in skills mastery or information recall through drill and repetition. She teaches best from well-defined objectives and specific resource materials. She excels in teaching those content areas that are linear and cumulative. Organization, planning, outlining, cataloging, rule-making, and planning procedures are second nature for her. She teaches best where students can see the practicality and utility of what's expected. For students who need or want immediate responses to their work she is pleased to comply.

The Sensing-Thinking teacher is less comfortable working in open-ended, interactive situations without well-defined objectives, rules, resources, or procedures. She tends not to choose work of a hypothetical or abstract nature. She wants and needs to know what the end results of her labors are to be. She has identical expectations for her students.

THE INTUITIVE-THINKING TEACHER

Overview

The Intuitive-Thinking teacher is characterized by an orientation to ideas, theories, concepts, and rational thought. She emphasizes the ability to think critically and independently. She emphasizes the need to discover and apply knowledge to solving problems and thinking in terms of cause and effect. Her goal is to develop her students' intellectual abilities. She seeks knowledge and understanding.

Approach to Teaching

The Intuitive-Thinking teacher's approach to teaching emphasizes the posing of intellectual questions, making available extensive resources and materials, and providing for learning through discovery. Lessons are designed to be intellectually stimulating; to emphasize the development of critical thinking skills; and to present students with opportunities to deduce consequences, to compare and contrast, to analyze, to synthesize, and to evaluate. Her instructional strategies rely heavily on widebased reading, the attainment of concepts, divergent thinking, games of strategy, debate, open-ended questioning, problem-solving, brainstorming, and independent study projects that have a research orientation. Her verbal teaching behaviors make extensive use of the Socratic method in which the student, through questions and answers, discovers the truths within

his own experience. She lectures frequently, makes extensive use of existing theory, and constantly asks her students to hypothesize about relationships. These hypotheses, hers or her students', become the basis for the assignment of independent study projects.

The Intuitive-Thinking teacher appreciates students who demonstrate intellectual maturity for their age group, can make defensible analyses, are excited by ideas, can handle symbol systems (language, math, logic, etc.) and can work well independently.

The Intuitive-Thinking teacher prefers to manage her classroom and questions of discipline by having open discussions on the need for rules, seeking responses to what might happen if there were no rules or authorities, and having the class prepare their own conventions for acceptable behavior. Classroom problems are presented to the students as issues to be analyzed and worked through. School rules that are not defensible in terms of reasoning or logic tend to be overlooked. She looks for good judgment and common sense on the part of her students and is sometimes annoyed by her students' immature behavior.

The Intuitive-Thinking teacher's teaching behavior emphasizes the acquisition of knowledge and the development of intelligence. She serves as a resource person to her students and assists them in their personal intellectual inquiries. Her verbal behaviors stress the search for causes, hence she constantly asks "Why?", "What are the reasons?", and "What would happen if . . . ?"

In evaluating her students' performance, she is more concerned about their understanding the general idea, principle or formula than about precise, detailed answers. As a result she makes extensive use of essay questions, open-ended test questions, research projects, knowledge of pertinent resources, the writing of position papers, debates, and demonstrations of the students' mastery and integration of concepts and rules.

Assets and Liabilities

The Intuitive-Thinking teacher's assets are in presenting ideas and concepts. She brings enthusiasm and commitment to the teaching of the great ideas and to assisting students in learning to think critically and independently. She is a superb organizer of resource materials and can stimulate high levels of student involvement in discussing controversial questions. She is expert at turning problem situations into opportunities for problem-solving by looking dispassionately at causes and their probable effects. She has a unique ability for translating ideas into learning experiences appropriate to the age group of her class. She encourages an open attitude of exploration—both to assist the pupil in learning what is within himself, as well as to incorporate the knowledge of the larger world outside himself. She provides an atmosphere of challenging opportunities, innovativeness, and learner independence.

The Intuitive-Thinking teacher's liabilities are often reflected in an absence of commitment to pertinent detail. She may overlook the need for the mastery of certain basic skills in students who speak well and think logically.

In providing a stimulating learning atmosphere she may fail to specify precisely what is to be learned, or completely frustrate the learner who needs detailed instruction. Her concern about teaching ideas may baffle the student who needs to be addressed in the "here-and-now" and her disposition for independent study projects may genuinely frustrate those students who need to work in small groups or tutorial relationships.

Her emphasis on cognitive growth may be to the detriment of how the pupils may be feeling. The open-endedness of her questions may frustrate those sensing students that need to have limits set.

In her relationships with her peers, she may appear aloof or overly intellectual. Her apparent lack of concern over school rules may frustrate central office personnel. On school committees she may frustrate other members by being more concerned about doing something conceptually sound than by trying out something and staying on schedule.

The Intuitive-Thinking teacher may tend to speak over the heads of her students, to be too critical (especially for the Sensing-Feeling student), and to withhold praise or approval when it is really called for.

Teaches Best

The Intuitive-Thinking teacher is at her best when presenting broad concepts and themes. She is uncomfortable when required to follow a predetermined "who," "what," and "when" outline.

She teaches best when the desired learning comes from student responses to ideas and theories, and when her students can secure pertinent detail on their own. She works best when questioning students and leading them to their own conclusions rather than telling them what the answers are or precisely how to arrive at solutions. She works best in developing her own goals and objectives rather than being responsible for predigested materials. She teaches best when she has a wide array of materials and resources and can pursue her students' interests in making her points rather than being confined to workbooks, practices, or drills.

The Intuitive-Feeling Teacher

Overview

The Intuitive-Feeling teacher is characterized as enthusiastic, insightful, and innovative. She tends to be a creative and aesthetically motivated person. She tries to inspire her students to explore possibilities and to find ways to better express themselves. Innovation and creativity are highly valued. The Intuitive-Feeling teacher's students generally discover that they have gifts and talents of which they were previously unaware.

The Intuitive-Feeling teacher tends to be morally sensitive and alert. She has a keen sense of her own personal beliefs. She tends to be a practitioner of one or more of the arts. She pays particular attention to beauty, symmetry, harmony, and the aesthetic qualities of things or ideas.

Approaches to Teaching

The Intuitive-Feeling teacher emphasizes the abilities and processes involved in thinking creatively, imaginatively, and aesthetically. She places a heavy premium on assisting students in exploring their inner world of possibilities.

In her classroom she provides for a flexible, innovative atmosphere with myriad resources to stimulate the learner's creative and thinking abilities. There are few restrictions in her classroom. To the passer-by the room seems like a place of chaotic yet purposeful work. A major objective is to stimulate the learner's curiosity.

The Intuitive-Feeling teacher most appreciates those students who have original insights and ideas, who are concerned with the larger issues of justice and morality, who question the way things are done, and who can express themselves in creative and artistic ways.

The Intuitive-Feeling teacher arranges her class day so that students are challenged and so that these challenges can be responded to in a flexible way. In providing learning experiences for her students, she concentrates more on the richness and personal investedness of the student than in specific measurable outcomes. The purpose of these enrichment activities is to assist students in feeling and thinking through the consequences of their knowledge and behavior in order to help them think more clearly about who they are, as well as what they wish to become. The Intuitive-Feeling teacher assists her students in looking for their individual and unique potentials and in expressing those potentials in creative ways.

The Intuitive-Feeling teacher's teaching behavior tends to be marked by spurts of insight, a high energy level, a tolerance for confusion and clutter, and an openness to alternative means of expression. She is also very concerned about her students as persons, and relates to them as co-searcher and friend rather than as an authority figure.

In evaluating her students, the Intuitive-Feeling teacher is very aware of the personal circumstances surrounding each student's work. She brings high levels of empathy to bear in assessing student outcomes and evaluates those outcomes in light of the student's own needs. A student's creative work is judged for its artistic merit, its theme and subject matter, and the degree to which it represents the learner's maturity and aesthetic sense. Intuitive-Feeling teachers are committed to assisting students in becoming increasingly self-reliant, articulate, and independent.

Assets and Liabilities

The Intuitive-Feeling teacher's assets include the ability to stimulate curiosity, to challenge the imagination, and to think about values in personal terms. She can empathize and establish close personal relationships with students and peers. She is a fountain of good ideas and is open to the ideas of others. She elicits responses from her students as a preferred way of communicating content. She is typically enthusiastic because she can relate what she is doing in class to her own and her students' values. Her acute interpersonal perception and judgment make her alert to what is happening in the class and to using class situations as learning experiences. She is a role model for solving problems openly and creatively.

On the other hand, her liabilities may be that her creative approach to learning sometimes leaves unexamined the need for detailed planning and for the identification of required resources for ambitious tasks. Her need to improve things may sometimes result in routine chores being overlooked or underdeveloped. Intuitive-Feeling teachers may put off paper work until it reaches a crisis level. Students who need continual reinforcement in learning the basics may feel they have been offered too much too soon when they are still grasping after the specifics of what is to be learned. By the same token, there may sometimes be confusion over precisely what it is that students are required to learn since so much time and energy is committed to getting a broader, global picture of life and its values. In other words, her liabilities may suggest that she is more interested in the future than the present. She may overlook the need to rehearse students in the basic skills and be disappointed when students need extensive individual instruction or can't seem to relate to the intellectual and creative challenges of the classroom. Her concern with the larger issues of justice and morality may be too abstract for some of the more sensing-based learners. She may become so involved in the non-directive approaches to learning that students become confused about precisely what it is they are to learn or what they are to be held accountable for. She may become so involved with the articulate and creative students that she ignores or overlooks those struggling to keep up. Students who have difficulty in sharing their feelings, talking about their goals, or becoming involved in service projects may not get the time they need to develop their own skills and value systems. Her enthusiasm may be seen by some as an effort to impose her own values on her students and peers. Her peers sometimes see her as impulsive, subjective, and somewhat unpredictable. She is disappointed when her class does not match her enthusiasm and commitment to a task.

Teaches Best

The Intuitive-Feeling teacher is at her best when stimulating her students to respond creatively to problem situations. She is most effective when establishing rich learning experiences based on personal trust. The exploration of new possibilities and unusual or creative solutions to pupil-identified problems is a favored area for discussion. She is frustrated by classroom work requiring extensive drill, memorization, and repetition.

She is at her best when identifying resource materials and working environments that result in pupil interactions on social issues. She is most comfortable as an orchestrater of dramatic productions, role-plays, artistic exhibits, and debates on social issues. She is less comfortable in the areas of discipline or requirements that her classroom be traditionally organized. She is at her best in making the learning situation exciting, creative, stimulating, and personally relevant to her students.

She is at her best when classroom activities can be channeled to address student needs and interests. She works best with students who have strong personal interests and who demonstrate concern over aesthetic and moral issues. Her educational goals focus on assisting students in clarifying their personal beliefs, achieving more of their own unique potentials, and describing those beliefs in imaginative and artistic ways. Her classroom is a chaotic clutter of animated learners, rich in resources and meaningful human relationships. She works to develop student competencies, creative abilities, and interpersonal skills founded on well-articulated moral thought and discussion.

❖ ❖ ❖ ❖ ❖ ❖ ❖ ❖ ❖ ❖ ❖ ❖ ❖ ❖ ❖

Thinking About Your Teaching Style

The next phase of the self-assessment process is to look at yourself as a teacher in terms of your strengths and needs for improvement.

The first part of this process is to analyze your responses from the Teaching Style Inventory with your subjective responses; then, to respond to the questions which follow as a way to put the differences or distinctions into clearer relief.

As with the ranking of your learning styles in the chapter with the Learning Styles Inventory, you are encouraged to rank and then to compare your subjective responses with your responses to the Teaching Style Inventory.

My Responses		TSI Responses
_____	Dominant	_____
_____	Auxiliary	_____
_____	Supportive	_____
_____	Least Used	_____

Analyzing your teaching styles and preferences requires the same careful reflection as did the consideration of your learning styles. A step in the direction of conducting such an analysis is the thoughtful completion of the questions which follow.

1. Do your subjective responses agree with your Teaching Style Inventory profile? If not, where do the differences occur?

2. If there are disagreements, what might some of the possible explanations be?

3. How does your teaching style profile compare with your learning style profile? Are they the same? If not, on what levels are they different, i.e., dominant, auxiliary, supportive, or least used? What are some of the possible reasons for the differences?

4. List at least two examples of your teaching behavior that represent your dominant style or superior functions.

5. In what ways has your dominant style served as an asset in the classroom? Give two or three examples.

6. In what ways has your dominant style served as a liability in the classroom? With whom? Give examples. Think of students who could have been better served if you had used other teaching styles.

7. List two examples of times when a lack of skills in your least used style have led to problems in your classroom.

8. What style(s) were you using when answering questions 7 and 8?

Having completed these eight self-diagnostic questions, read the descriptions of teacher abilities by styles. Identify those abilities in which you feel you need improvement with a check (✓). Identify your strongest abilities with a plus sign (+).

SENSING-FEELING TEACHING ABILITIES

_____ establishes a warm, friendly, supportive atmosphere in which students are encouraged to interact with one another, work cooperatively, and share their personal thoughts, feelings, and experiences

_____ comfortable with shifting from prescribed plans in order to respond to the here-and-now class needs and moods; capitalizes on spontaneous events for instruction

_____ encourages students to be involved personally and emotionally in their learning

_____ adept at working with students who are sensitive, need to be nurtured, and prefer to work interactively and collaboratively with others

_____ establishes appropriate student behavior by developing positive relationships with students, face-to-face communications, and small group meetings

_____ encourages students to be honest with their feelings, sensitive to the rights and feelings of others, and work cooperatively

_____ comfortable with interactive and collaborative teaching techniques emphasizing fun, student interactions, and personal experiences as content

_____ evaluates student achievement in light of effort made, ability, need, and personal problems

INTUITIVE-THINKING TEACHING ABILITIES

_____ establishes an intellectually stimulating atmosphere in which students are provided with a variety of resources and activities designed to challenge their thinking abilities, develop their analytical skills, and stretch their limits of performance

_____ comfortable planning in broad outlines around key open-ended questions or themes in which main concepts or ideas are identified and looked at from several directions and disciplines

_____ encourages students to think for themselves, to discover and apply knowledge and concepts to new problems

_____ adept at working with students who are mature and knowledgeable, excited by ideas, and prefer research projects and independent work assignments

_____ establishes appropriate student behavior by helping students to examine the basis of and justification for rules

_____ encourages students to think for themselves, to ask "Why?", to use their reasoning skills, to be logical, and to strive for perfection

_____ comfortable with teaching strategies that encourage critical thinking emphasizing planning, independent research projects, inductive and deductive reasoning, and problem-solving techniques

_____ evaluates students' ability to reason and apply what has been learned through the use of open-ended questions, real life problems, and through their demonstration of abilities to apply, analyze, synthesize, and evaluate ideas

SENSING-THINKING TEACHING ABILITIES

_____ establishes an organized, systematic, activity-oriented, teacher-directed atmosphere in which students are engaged in purposeful work

_____ able to follow prescribed guides or texts which are translated into weekly or daily plans

_____ adept at working with students who are competitive, action-oriented, and who learn best from direct experience and step-by-step procedures

_____ establishes well-defined rules and procedures for covering content in an orderly and prescribed manner

_____ establishes appropriate behavior by setting clear standards and expectations set for students

_____ encourages students to be goal-oriented, to apply themselves to the task at hand, to be neat, organized, and punctual, and to follow rules and procedures

_____ utilizes programmed instruction, behavioral objectives, demonstrations, and teacher-directed activities to help students acquire mastery of specific content and skills

_____ evaluates student skills using precise behavioral measures (true-or-false tests), observations, student demonstrations, frequent tests or quizzes, and criterion referenced measures

INTUITIVE-FEELING TEACHING ABILITIES

_____ establishes a flexible, innovative atmosphere with a minimum of restrictions in which students are encouraged to express their creative abilities and to design their own activities for learning

_____ able to use curriculum guides, texts, and materials as resources for a constantly changing curriculum based on the interests and curiosities of the students

_____ adept at working with students who have strong personal interests, insights, original ideas and who question the way things are done

_____ utilizes open-ended discussions, moral dilemmas, creative and artistic activities to enable students to explore their creative abilities, to find ways of self-expression, to gain inspiration, and to explore personal values

_____ evaluates student skills by judging creativity, flexibility, fluency, and originality of responses; uses observations, peer juries, personal aesthetic criteria, and creative artistic products

_____ establishes opportunities for students to choose learning activities from a variety of alternatives

_____ establishes appropriate behavior by assisting students to think/feel through the consequences and the significance of their actions in order to enable them to acquire an internal sense of discipline

_____ encourages students to look for new ways of doing things, to follow their inspirations, to be open to the unusual, and not to be confined by convention

On the basis of the strengths and needs you identified, which are your strongest and least used styles? How do these styles match up with your own subjective analyses? Your Learning Style Inventory results? Your Teaching Style Inventory results?

List below the teaching abilities that you want to develop based on your own ranking.

❖ ❖ ❖ ❖ ❖ ❖ ❖ ❖ ❖ ❖ ❖ ❖ ❖ ❖

Teaching Abilities I Need To Develop

As a final step in the identification of your teaching behaviors answer the questions which follow.

1. How might I use all four styles in my classroom? In my school committee work? In my goals for personal and professional growth?

2. How does my preferred teaching style affect the unsuccessful students in my class?

3. How does my preferred teaching style affect the gifted and talented students in my class? The artists? The dreamers?

4. What do I want my students to know about me in terms of my learning and teaching preferences?

A Reflection on the Spirituality of the Principal

Cappel, C. 1989. In *Reflections on the role of the Catholic school principal*, ed. R. J. Kealey, 26–27. Washington, D.C.: National Catholic Educational Association.

Conclusion

"See, I am doing something new! Now it springs forth, do you not perceive it? (Isaiah 43:19)"

When I ponder and pray that word of God as it interacts with my own life experiences, this is what I perceive as new in the theology of my ministry, the holy ground ahead:

1. **Empower.** I must decrease and they must increase. More and more the ideas, the ways of implementation, the management, the leadership should be coming from the teachers, students, and parents. There must be greater community involvement in the discernment process. I must deliberately put myself in need.

2. **Risk.** Take the risks together as a community. The greater the risk, the more likely that the Lord's intervention will be recognized for what it is: His doings!

3. **Think servant.** Be available for the Lord's work of the moment.

4. **Historicize.** Keep the community in touch with the history of its journey.

5. **Affirm! Affirm! Affirm!** Look for new ways to validate that which is good. High tech can make high touch possible! My word processor allows me to be personal for more, if not more personal.

6. **Celebrate.** The storage shed converted to a classroom is an accomplishment.

7. **Remember whose image is terribly important.** Superimpose His image and the image of this church on your blueprints for action.

There is joy in the journey

. . . searching the soul of our school for hints of its new direction

. . . searching my own for the newness He wants me to perceive in my leadership role

. . . anticipating those moments of illumination when I will recognize that the sufficiency of grace was there, like manna, for the moment's need and

. . . Finding the Lord in it all.

Promoting the Professional Development of Teachers and Administrators

Fielding, F., and H. D. Schalock. 1985. 66–67. School Management Digest Series. Eugene, Ore.: ERIC Clearinghouse on Educational Management, College of Education, University of Oregon.

Utilizing the Talents of Lead Teachers

Effective principals capitalize on the strengths of staff members when organizing and implementing staff development programs. They recognize that principals alone cannot carry out all the functions necessary to ensure the success of a program. In addition to using resources and services from the central office, they are apt to rely heavily on a "lead" or "master" teacher within the building to assist in planning inservice activity; providing training, support, and technical assistance; and informally monitoring the progress of an improvement effort (Hord, Stiegelbauer, and Hall 1984). Principals also may use the services of lead teachers within a district at large or from neighboring schools, as

was described in the section in chapter 4 on the Valley Education Consortium's work in school improvement.

Principals of course must take care not to delegate so much responsibility to lead teachers that they effectively become assistant principals or members of the administration. Lead teachers function best as facilitators, not policy makers or supervisors.

Principals need to establish a clear framework within which lead teachers are to operate. They also need to ensure that lead teachers receive special training and support to prepare them for their roles, particularly if they are called upon to foster fundamental changes in classrooms or the school as a whole. The need for special training was amply documented in Showers' studies of peer coaching. It also is reflected in the efforts that have been made to train teachers in the role of OD [Organizational Developer] trainer and facilitator, and in the design and operation of the Valley Education Consortium's program implementation and improvement teams.

Establishing Collaborative Structures

It is commonly observed that teachers work in relative isolation from each other and know little about what their colleagues believe or do. This professional isolation needs to be reduced to achieve the goals of most professional development programs. As Little (1984) has observed, collaboration among staff implementing new practices is essential for several reasons. First, it may reduce the fear of risk taking. It is less frightening to try a new idea and risk failure when one's peers are also taking the risk. An implementation team may offer moral support to its members and show tolerance for error. Second, understanding and implementing complex innovations typically require a great deal of thought and preparation. Teachers' ideas and plans invariably are enhanced when they have the opportunity for group discussion, shared work in preparing materials, and collective problem-solving around implementation issues. Finally, some innovations are not effective unless implemented on a large enough scale to alter the entire pattern of teaching and learning in a building. Put differently, by their very nature, inservice programs designed to make changes at the program or organizational level require teachers to work together toward common or complementary goals.

Collaborative structures can take a variety of forms. These include the kind of informal teams of peer observers described by Glatthorn (1984), the weekly inservice and curriculum planning sessions observed by Little (1984), the monthly meetings of lead teachers in the Valley Education Consortium, and the quarterly cadre meetings held in the Keele district. In one form or another, collaborative structures are necessary to support large-scale changes in teaching and schooling.

References

Glatthorn, A. A. (1984). *Differentiated supervision*. Alexandria, VA: Association for Supervision and Curriculum Development. ED 245 401.

Hord, S.; Stiegelbauer, S.; and Hall, G. (1984). Principals don't do it alone: researchers discover second change facilitator active in school improvement efforts. *R & DCE Review, 2,* (3), pp. 1, 2, 5.

Little, J. W. (1984). Seductive images and organizational realities in professional development. *Teachers College Record, 86,* 84–102.

Instructional Leadership: How Principals Make a Difference

Smith, W. F., and R. L. Andrews. 1989. 46–48.
Alexandria, Va.: Association for Supervision and Curriculum Development.

Expectations of an Instructional Leader

Communicator

Communicating effectively in an organization requires skills beyond the interpersonal level. As instructional leader, the principal must be able to develop a sound and trusting relationship with the staff by behaving consistently, objectively, and fairly over time. Rules for communicating must be made explicit regarding the content and the processes that are acceptable within the culture of that school. What topics, for example, may be discussed openly by the entire staff? By parent-staff advisory groups? By students and staff? By supervisor-teacher dyads? What structures and process will be used by what groups to make which decisions about governance of the school? To what degree will autonomy be given to the staff in the decision-making process? Which decisions will be made by the principal after asking for staff input and advice? How do building decisions fit into the scheme of the school district's processes? All of these questions should be answered through the principal's leadership and communication with the staff (Smith 1989).

Processes are all-important. The principal models commitment to those processes in establishing school goals together with staff, parents, and students. Resources are committed to the goals, and evaluation systems are established. Frequent reference is made to the goals, and classroom observations, inservice topics, and faculty meetings focus on those priorities.

A clear vision for the school is articulated by the principal to the point of redundancy. Through slogans, themes, logos, and reminders, the principal makes it known that everyone in this school is headed in the same general direction. Individual teachers may choose different means of achieving this, emphasizing different strengths and interests, but the overarching direction supersedes individual whim.

Frequent feedback is given to teachers after classroom visits, to custodians and secretaries after performance observations or special contributions, to students for achievements of all kinds, and to parents for their support and efforts. Further, the principal employs a consistent "feedback loop" to tell those involved in the decision-making processes how their input or involvement affected the final outcome or decision. Regular bulletins and newsletters are published for the staff, parents, and students.

Each year, the principal reviews the expectations for staff performance and the system to be employed for clinical supervision and evaluation. Roles of peer observers and coaches are clarified. Staff members are involved in establishing priorities for inservice training and staff development activities. Faculty meetings are well-organized "instructional episodes." The principal has clear objectives, involves participants to promote learning of the objectives, adjusts the time or process to meet needs that arise during the meeting, and has methods for closing the meeting to be sure everyone understands what was discussed. Careful planning for all meetings ensures they are worthwhile and do not waste time on items that can be handled elsewhere.

Data that may be used to assess the principal's performance as communicator include:

1. Written procedures for making school decisions delineate clearly what content will be discussed by what groups to what outcome.

2. Staff meetings are well organized and reflect careful planning with regard to objectives, activities, participation, and closure.

3. School goals are publicized in a variety of ways. They are referenced by the principal in budget allocations, newsletters, and reports to the supervisor. Teachers and parents can verbalize the school's goals.

4. The school's vision is publicized overtly through themes, logos, or statements.

5. Written messages are given to the staff, parents, and students by the principal as recognition for their accomplishments.

6. Individual staff members can describe the evaluation system and the principal's expectations for their performance.

Visible Presence

The principal who is visible in the school truly seems to be everywhere: in hallways, staff rooms, classrooms, the boiler room, the cafeteria; at the bus loading area at strategic times; at school plays, sporting events, concerts, and other special programs. Always there at assemblies, the principal helps to reinforce standards of behavior and supports faculty and student participation.

Visible principals do many things at once. On the way down the hall to visit a classroom, she talks with several students, a teacher, and a custodian. A handy note pad may be used en route to jot down things to do or remember.

The principal's secretary is polite but firm when parents or others appear in the office and ask to see the principal. The response might be, "Ms. Johnson is observing in a classroom for the next hour. May I schedule an appointment for you when she returns?" Never does the secretary remark, "Oh, she isn't at her desk now."

The day begins early for the principal, who makes a quick walkthrough to greet custodians and the kitchen staff. Special events or jobs of the day can be described to staff members ahead of time.

Drop-in classroom visits are frequent, and the principal enjoys talking with students about their work, assisting some, or participating in a class activity. Because such visits are a familiar occurrence, the teacher and students seldom vary their routine to acknowledge the principal's presence. Clearly, the principal belongs in this setting.

Frequently the principal participates in staff development or inservice courses. In fact, the principal attempts to learn new curriculum content or a teaching skill by practicing in staff meetings or classrooms and talking about those experiences with staff. During classroom observations, the principal may ask to see the teacher use one of the skills from a workshop or to teach some aspect of content being emphasized.

A number of examples illustrate ways in which the supervisor can evaluate the principal's skills at being a visible presence:

1. Drop-in visits to the school find the principal "out walking around the campus" or visiting classrooms.

2. Attending student assemblies on occasion, the supervisor notes how the principal interacts with students and the staff.

3. Shadowing the principal for a day reveals the methods by which several things are accomplished at once.

4. The secretary often tells the supervisor that the principal is "out in the classrooms" or "in the cafeteria."

5. When dropping in classrooms with the principal, the supervisor notes that students and the staff go about their business as usual.

6. The principal makes a staff development activity one performance goal for the year. He demonstrates a new skill for the supervisor.

In this chapter we've seen the kinds of behaviors that can be expected of principals who are instructional leaders. In the next chapter, we take a closer look at seven real principals who are living up to those expectations in their daily routines.

Reference

Smith, W. F. (1989). *School-Based Management: Metaphor for Motivation*. Olympia: Association of Washington School Principals.

The Catholic School Administrator

Sparks, G. J. 1986. In *The Catholic school administrator—A book of readings*, ed. E. M. Bushman and G. J. Sparks, 283–91. Portland, Ore.: Catholic Leadership Company.

Individuals and organizations must clarify the role of principals and diocesan supervisors and find ways for them to be accountable for the improvement of instruction. This is a complex undertaking which Castetter (1982) states should involve local educators, local boards of education, diocesan boards of education, diocesan personnel, and the administrators involved. Diocesan superintendents and school boards should make it clear that they expect the administrators involved to be responsible for instructional leadership and that they incorporate their expectations into the accountability system of the school or diocese.

Revised job descriptions are helpful in this, emphasizing a focus on instructional concerns and allocating clerical and similar functions to others. Graduate preparation programs should also be modified. Too often such programs focus primarily on the management role of school leaders and not enough on their instructional improvement responsibilities. Administrators cannot provide instructional leadership if they have not been trained for it.

Working with Staff

Supervision

Providing instructional leadership implies that supervision is a joint effort where collegiality and team work provide the necessary structure for mutual goal attainment; that is, the teachers' objectives are met and the school's purpose is fulfilled. The following duties and responsibilities of the principal, proposed by Wiles and Bondi (1980), belong in this supervisory category:

1. To work with the staff in the formulation and execution of an adequate philosophy of education consistent with the diocesan-wide philosophy.

2. To assume leadership for providing a continuous program of curriculum improvement which will at the same time contribute to diocesan-wide curriculum improvement.

3. To work with the staff in the development of instructional goals consistent with diocesan goals for the various levels and curriculum areas.

4. To work with the staff in the development and implementation of a diocesan-wide program of evaluation and appraisal.

5. To work with the staff in the development, application, and supervision of programs for atypical students.

6. To work with the staff in the formulation and execution of diocesan-wide policies relative to pupil classification, marking, reporting and promoting.

7. To ascertain the need for instructional staff specialists and to direct and supervise their work.

8. To assume responsibility for a continuous program of supervision within the unit.

9. To assume responsibility, within the framework of the diocesan plan, for a continuous program of inservice education for the staff members.

10. To keep abreast of new educational developments on the local, state, and national levels and to inform the staff concerning them.

11. To provide for the interchange of information and ideas among teachers and other staff personnel.

12. To see that the necessary facilities, equipment, books, and supplies are available when required.

To Delegate or Not?

Thus far this work has treated the role of the principal —qualifications, leadership, organization, and curriculum. Since the purpose is to inform and not overwhelm this seems to be a good time to discuss the topic of delegation. Often the cry is heard that administrators need to delegate more and thus help prevent burnout. Nevertheless this area is one of controversy and must be tailored to the individual style of the person delegating according to Drucker (1983). Delegation is a management technique which increases the effectiveness of the administration in the Catholic school. Delegation is the assignment of meaningful tasks or responsibilities, either operational or managerial, to one or more subordinates. Drucker (1983) reaffirms the traditional five functions of management have been considered to be planning, organizing, coordinating, directing, and controlling; and that delegation fits into all of these functions, and any of these functions, or parts of them, may be delegated. To be an effective leader, the Catholic school administrator must decide whether or not to delegate, when to delegate, what to delegate, and to whom to delegate.

There is a great deal of uncertainty surrounding the question of what to delegate. Sergiovanni (1984) provides some general principles which may serve as useful guidelines for making delegation decisions.

1. Delegate things that will benefit the school. If delegation does not create benefits that are greater than the possible disadvantages (inherent risks, time required, etc.), it is to be questioned. Delegation is often an act of faith, since it may be difficult to measure possible long-range disadvantages, and the Catholic School Administrator must rely on personal experience,

knowledge, and judgment to determine if there will be benefits to the school.

2. Delegate things that will improve your own performance. Every administrator has strengths and weaknesses: delegating work to another staff member whose strength lies in that area can be a good management decision. The main concern of the Catholic school administrator is not to do the job, but to get the job done.

3. Delegate things that will improve your "quality of worklife." Catholic school administrators frequently spend time in trying to improve the quality of life for students and teachers. But what about the administrator's quality of life? Many staff members would like to be included in the administrative burdens of the school, provided they are recognized and in some way eventually rewarded for their efforts. Developing a team spirit and delegating to other members of the team can relieve a great deal of pressure and improve the quality of work life for many Catholic school administrators.

4. Delegate things that enrich the work lives of staff members. Delegation not only relieves the Catholic School Administrator of overwhelming responsibilities, but also enriches the staff members' jobs. This makes each job more attractive and challenging to the person who performs it. Simply delegating more and more responsibilities to an individual may not be seen as job enrichment, however. Changes must be interesting, challenging, and involve a reasonable work load.

Some good candidates for delegation include routine tasks and responsibilities, jobs that demand a great deal of time, details you don't like, things that must be done immediately—when you just don't have the time.

Tasks to Delegate

Principals wisely delegate some administrative responsibility to their staff. Ordinarily, except for a few routine tasks, such as general student supervision, most principals don't delegate work to their staff. Why? Some principals just don't think of delegation as one of their responsibilities. Some principals are so busy themselves that they don't look around to see that their teachers are not too busy to take responsibility for some project. Or, principals may feel that it would be unworthy of them to pass on their jobs to someone else. Other principals have managed; they will manage somehow. However, today, delegation does not consist in merely passing out miscellaneous jobs to staff members; there is a whole new philosophy of delegation.

Principals should look over the duties they perform in a day, or a week, and organize these responsibilities into three categories or levels (Castetter, 1982):

1. Tasks which a school clerk or custodian could do equally well

2. Tasks which a teacher could do, or could be trained to do

3. Tasks which administrators must do themselves.

Level One—the most mechanical or routine type—could be done by a nonprofessional person. Counting money collections is in this category; so are passing out supplies, answering the telephone, typing letters, dusting shelves, and unpacking cartons. Some principals have confessed that they actually spend one-third of their time on such picayune tasks. Most schools could arrange for at least a part-time secretary, even if only on a volunteer basis. Janitorial jobs should be delegated to nonprofessional workers and should not be done by a trained school administrator.

Level Two—jobs which a teacher could do—requires some professional background, but teachers have enough training, or could be trained, to carry them out. For example, the job of orienting new teachers could be taken over by an experienced teacher acting as an adviser. Preparing for home and school association meetings might be largely delegated to staff members working under the direction of the principal. Ordering, distributing, and inventorying supplies could be done by a clerk, under the direction of a staff member. Directing practice for First Holy Communion, preparing assembly programs, conducting the testing program—all of these responsibilities might be shared with faculty members acting under the principal's leadership.

Level Three—jobs which principals must reserve to themselves—involves responsibilities which the principal must discharge personally as responsible head of the school. One of these duties is directing the program of inservice growth. Another is acting as liaison person with outside individuals and groups such as the pastor, the diocesan superintendent, public school officials, and health agencies. Another administrative responsibility is to formulate school rules and to see that board policies are carried out. The final responsibility for the educational program of the school is of course the principal's. All that is strong, and weak, in the school program reflects not on an individual staff member, but on the principal as the responsible head of the school. Final responsibility is always the principal's!

The principal should be sure that the delegated work is important and needs to be done. It may seem almost too obvious to say that delegated work must never be mere busy work, masquerading as democratic procedures. Nothing kills interest and initiative more surely than the realization that the project isn't necessary and won't be used.

Also, the teacher's work load should be taken into consideration. The teacher's first duty is to the class: semiadministrative duties are in second place. If teachers are to devote themselves to both class work and delegated duties with energy and originality, their work load must be reasonable.

Further, the principal should make clear the limits of authority and responsibility. The teacher, or clerk, should know exactly what is expected of them, how much authority they have, and how their work is to be coordinated with the work of the entire staff. Once the teacher has begun the project, principals should assist as needed but should not hover about as if they doubted the teacher's ability to carry out the assignment. Recognition should of course be given for delegated work well done.

Problem Solving

Closely aligned with delegation is the area of problem solving. This is another example of an area where the principal is not, or should not, be expected to have the expertise to solve all problems. Certainly the solution may be articulated by the principal, or supported by the principal, but no one can rightly expect all answers to flow from one source. Once administrators sense that something is wrong within the organization, they must discover the specific causes of the problem. The personnel affected by the difficulty should be involved in the situation.

Once the administrators have identified the problem, they must determine what—if anything—should be done about it.

Surfacing, or the identification of the specific causes of the problem, requires the input of those persons involved in the problem. While it is impractical to directly involve all affected individuals, a communication network or "grapevine" can be established which allows indirect involvement.

The grapevine can be used to solve the problem.

The informal communication network serves as a model for the formal organizational communication network. This formal network must include certain key elements that make the grapevine effective: credibility of the sender, willingness of the sender to transmit the message, and the manner in which the sender transmits the message.

In organizing a formal grapevine the administrator must tap the informal leadership. Such leaders must be identified by their peers and asked by the administrator to serve on a formal planning committee, which becomes the central core for the formal "grapevine"—the central linking committee. In solving an organizational problem, this committee acts as follows (Campbell, 1982):

Step 1: Hierarchy of Needs: Prior to the first meeting, the linking committee members will have surveyed their constituents about their major areas of concern, and concerns are arranged in a hierarchical order so that major concerns can be identified. Linking committee members then communicate the hierarchical order of concern to their constituents for acceptance. It is vital to the communication network that the entire staff be aware of both content and procedure. Such involvement promotes commitment. It follows, then, that linking committee members must be able to communicate accurately. They must be representative of not only their constituents but also of their committee.

Step 2: Goals and Objectives: Once a hierarchy of needs has been established and verified, tentative goals and objectives are developed by the central linking committee using the same linking process that was used in the identification, specification, and verification of organizational needs. The information acquired by the committee concerning tentative goals and objectives is now used to form definite goals and objectives for the total organization.

Step 3: Strategies: Using the accepted goals and objectives, the central linking committee can now brainstorm possible strategies. The linking process—committee member to linking committee to committee member to constituent—is used to determine advantages, disadvantages, strengths, and weaknesses of the proposed strategies and to provide a broad data base for determining the effect of the strategies.

Turning the grapevine, or informal communication network, into a formal communications network for organizational problem solving requires administrative commitment and utilization of the informal organizational leadership as well as the effective functioning of the linking process. Such a communication network, using the informal leader to indirectly involve all those affected by the problem, results in the effective sensing, surfacing, and solving of organizational problems.

Public Relations
The Administrator's Role

The prior information on delegation and problem solving centered around involving others in a mutually beneficial relationship and establishing a listening process through both formal and informal networks. This work demands that the administrator recognizes the importance of the individual in the school program. Catholic school administrators know that personal contact with students, teachers, parents, and community members is in part their response to the Gospel message. Working on a one-to-one basis provides an opportunity to deepen a relationship and reaffirm service in the church. The foundation for a solid public relations program often depends upon the actions of the administrator in establishing quality Catholic education.

References

Campbell, R. F. *Administrative Theory as a Guide to Action*. Chicago: University of Chicago Press, 1983.

Castetter, William B. *The Personnel Function in Educational Administration*. New York: Macmillan, 1982.

Drucker, Peter F. *Technology, Management and Society*. New York: Harper and Row, 1983.

Sergiovanni, Thomas J. *Supervision*. New York: McGraw-Hill, 1985.

Wiles, Jon and Joseph C. Bondi. *Curriculum Development: A Guide to Practice*. Columbus: Merrill, 1980.

Time Management

Truitt, M. R. 1991. In *The supervisor's handbook*, 55–57, 61–63. Shawnee Mission, Kans.: National Press.

United Airlines makes a clever handout available to its staff called "A Round Tuit." It is a single sheet of paper which has a large circle on it. Inside the circle is the following message:

"This is a Round Tuit. Guard it with your life! Tuits are hard to come by—especially the round ones. It will help you to become a much more efficient worker. For years you have heard people say, 'I'll do this when I get a Round Tuit.' So, now that you have one, you can accomplish all those things you have put aside because now you have a Round Tuit."

Create your own Round Tuit and give it to someone who has put off doing something important. It will convey your message in a humorous way.

How to Be an Effective Delegator

Many supervisors are promoted into their positions from "the trenches." Often they are more used to (and more comfortable with) performing the technical functions required to get the work done. As supervisors, though, their success is dependent on the work of others—the people they supervise.

Successful delegation includes three basic steps:

1. Assigning the work to the appropriate team member.

2. Gaining the agreement and commitment of the worker to perform the duties satisfactorily for the supervisor.

3. Granting the appropriate authority to the worker to take the actions necessary to complete the task.

Overcoming the most common obstacles to delegation

1. **Fear of making a subordinate look too good.** The measure of a supervisor is almost entirely based upon the performance of those supervised. It's not what you do that counts, it is what you get done. The only way to get the most done is by making sure that your employees are encouraged, challenged, and equipped with everything they need to be as effective and productive as they can be.

2. **"I'd better do it myself."** Many managers and supervisors short-circuit their supervisory potential by taking on work that should be done by their employees. Their excuse is, "If I want it done right, I'd better do it myself." It may be true. There may be many jobs that you actually can do better than anyone you could delegate to, but that is not the point. You can't be effective as a supervisor and do your employees' work, too. And, beyond that, you can't expect your people to get as good at a task as you until they've had the chance to learn by making their own mistakes—probably the same way you learned.

3. **Wanting to look busy.** Some supervisors hoard work that should have been delegated in order to be (or appear to be) constantly busy. Their desire is to set a good example for the workers. A better example would be set by a supervisor who shows good self-management skills by working on what's really the most important and appropriate task at hand.

4. **Working on what "feels good."** Supervisors often are promoted into their positions because of their effectiveness at various jobs in their department or company. New supervisors, in particular, may find themselves chained to the old tasks that they can perform with more confidence and comfort.

5. **Preconceived ideas about employee abilities.** Supervisors should avoid preconceptions about the abilities (or lack of abilities) of their employees. Even a worker who has not been successful in the past may perform very well with a new task under new circumstances.

Managing Time Wisely

Many supervisors feel they do not have enough time in their workday to do all they have to do. However, the problem usually isn't the amount of time available, but the use to which that available time is being put. A number of time management problems are common among supervisors . . . and fortunately, solutions exist for minimizing them.

Time-Wasters

Here are some items that cause supervisors to lose precious workday time. Check those that apply to you.

____ 1. Telephone interruptions that disrupt work progress.

____ 2. Visitors who drop by unexpectedly.

____ 3. Meetings that accomplish little.

____ 4. Crisis situations for which no contingency planning has been done.

____ 5. Putting effort into small things while high priority matters go unattended.

____ 6. Personal disorganization requiring time to find things when they are needed.

____ 7. Doing routine tasks that others could do equally well.

____ 8. Trying to do too much at once and underestimating the time things will take.

____ 9. Work "falling between the cracks" or being duplicated unnecessarily due to confusion about lines of authority and responsibility.

____ 10. An inability to say "no" to others.

Research indicates that most supervisors fall prey to at least half of these things. Thankfully, the effect of each can be reduced with specific time management techniques.

A Different Kind of Communication

Working to Survive

For many businesses, especially those in highly competitive markets, survival cannot be taken for granted. Supervisors know that only maximum efficiency and effort on everyone's part will enable that company to survive. But how can they convey that same sense of urgency to their employees without frightening or discouraging them?

Harwood Cochran, chairman of Overnite Transportation Co. (OTC), uses an effective method. *Forbes* magazine reports that every time a competitor goes bankrupt, Cochran puts the failed trucker's logo up on his red brick wall underneath a sign that reads, "deregulation done 'em in." He has mounted 47 company logos with room for plenty more.

"I want my employees to know that we're not guaranteed to be here," Cochran explains. His employees have cooperated with OTC's economy measures and, as a result, Cochran's business is profitable in an industry racked with closings and red ink.

If you need to alert employees to stressful conditions in your industry, keep them vividly aware of competitors' problems and they'll draw the needed inferences about your firm.

How to Communicate More Powerfully

The 5-Step Formula for Clear Work Instructions

1. **Be friendly.** Instructions given in a friendly way are more likely to be met with friendly and willing cooperation.

2. **Keep it simple.** Your instructions should be clear and concise. Make sure you have organized your thoughts and have a clear idea of the outcome you want.

3. **Not just what, but why.** Explain not just what is going to be done, but why the action is being taken.

4. **Get feedback.** Ask employees if they have any questions or suggestions. Ask them to tell you what they are going to do. Do not ask them if they understand.

5. **Follow-up.** Monitor the activity of your employees to see if instructions are being followed. Even better—ask them to report their progress periodically.

Giving Directions

Beverly Potter, management consultant, suggests using the DAD system when giving orders. DAD stands for Describe, Ask for clarification, and Direct.

DESCRIBE the problem situation objectively, specifically, simply, and without accusations to the employee. ("Jim, your district is lagging behind the others in sales. We need at least a 10% increase in the next six months.")

ASK the employee how s/he feels about the situation and for suggestions. This clarifies the problem and gives you added perspective. ("What's your view of the sales problem? How might we best achieve that goal?")

DIRECT the employee in simple, concrete terms, considering his/her suggestions when possible. Ask for further clarification if you think the directive might be misunderstood. ("I agree that a promotional campaign should be launched. Do you foresee any obstacles to doing that?")

The DAD system is especially appropriate with an employee whose opinion is important and whose actions must be directed.

Key Points for Improving Oral and Written Communication

Helpful hints for one-on-one conversations . . .

1. Decide in advance the outcome you want from the conversation.

2. Take a minute to organize your thoughts before you begin. It may help you to jot down some key points. In most situations there is absolutely nothing wrong with referring to your notes. It can even strengthen the impression you make.

3. Listen to what the other party is saying—really listen. Don't think about what you are going to say next.

4. Solicit feedback from friends about your one-on-one oral skills. Be prepared to hear some criticism.

5. Tape record yourself. You might be amazed at some sloppy speech habits you are unaware of. Uhs, ands and you-knows are the most common.

Communicating in Letters, Memos, and Reports

1. **Make an outline of your thoughts.** Look particularly at the organization of your material. Do you cover each point before moving on? Do your thoughts flow logically? Do you make a smooth transition between major points?

2. **Get feedback on your written skills.** Again, don't take the criticism personally.

3. **Don't avoid writing.** You can only get better at what you practice.

4. **Analyze material you read.** Whether it's a well-written memo or a magazine article that you like, examine what made the material clear, concise, and interesting to read.

Decision-Making

Sheehan, L. 1990. In *Building better boards: A handbook for board members in Catholic education*, 70–74.
Washington, D.C.: National Catholic Educational Association.

According to Peter Drucker, "a decision is a judgment: a choice between alternatives." As a judgment, a decision is the best possible choice under given conditions. It is not always the optimal choice, but one on which the group agrees to act at the given time. The decision may be incremental progress rather than a final or complete solution, because the "right solution" may be unknowable or illusory.

Step One

A problem-solving process usually has three phases. The first is defining the problem. This step assumes a recognition on the part of the leader or some members, and then subsequently the group, that there is a decision which must be made. However, the question should be asked, is a decision necessary, or should we do nothing? These are the first questions the group must consider before any definition can be achieved. The board may want to consider the consequences of these stands. If we act, we may be better off. If we do not act, we probably will survive. The board should compare the effort and risk of action to the risk of inaction. Act if, on the balance, the benefits outweigh the costs and risks. Act, or do not act, but do not hedge or compromise at this stage.

The goal, therefore, in problem definition, is finding the right question, not the right answer. The board must identify the real problem, not the symptoms.

Step Two

The second step in problem-solving is solving and deciding. Once the problem has been identified, then it should be analyzed. Facts should be gathered by asking the following questions: What information is needed? How valid is the information we have? What more do we need to know? What information can we not get? At this point it is also appropriate to ask who must make the decision, who must be consulted, and who must be informed.

After analyzing the problem, the board should generate alternative solutions. There are three reasons to consider alternatives: 1) to safeguard the decision-maker from being held captive by a single idea; 2) to provide fallback positions, should initial position not be successful; 3) to stimulate the imagination and provide new and different ways of perceiving and understanding. Discussion and dissent are means to consensus.

In deciding which of the alternatives to choose, the board should begin with the alternatives which most clearly meet objective elements of the situation, recognizing that the best decision involves approximation and risk, and the compromise will probably occur.

Step Three

The third step in the problem-solving process is action. The action plan should recognize that action must be effected through other people, and therefore the plan should consider who these people are and how they can be helped to understand actions/changes that are expected. The board should ask who must know what action should be taken, who must take it, and what does the action have to be, so that those who must do it can do it. The last step of the action plan outlines the steps to be followed.

After the action or implementation has occurred, adequate means for evaluation should be provided. The evaluation should test the actual events against the expected results.

Benefits and Costs of Group Decision-Making

Decisions here are being made by a group, not an individual. This brings some particular dynamics to bear on the process of deciding. Awareness of some of these pluses and minuses could help one be more effective in making decisions.

Benefits

- Pooling of resources, both cognitive and experiential —usually two heads are better than one, or at least they can be.
- Number of alternatives increases, which means greater ability to handle more complex issues.
- Opportunity to utilize special talents and devise tasks.
- Presence of others increases motivation levels.
- Potential for unique solutions emerges, which no one member had.
- Potential for synergy makes group solution better than any individual solution.
- All understand the decision better.
- Increase acceptance of the decision because of participation in its creation.
- Individual and group development is enhanced.

Potential Costs

- More time and energy of members required.
- Consensus is difficult to reach.
- Potential for domination by strong individual, reducing contribution of others.

◆ Potential for shifting attention from decision-making to social relations (may become embroiled in personalities or external concerns).

Ambiguities

◆ Disagreement is likely, but may be constructive depending on the leader's or group's skill in dealing with it.

◆ It takes longer to make a decision, but it may be a better one or a decision may be avoided altogether.

Ways Groups Make Decisions

Groups have the potential to make better decisions than individuals do. Some behaviors and decision modes, however, may not work well for groups, or may inhibit building a consensus decision. At times these modes may happen or may be useful in moving the group forward, but in general, it is presumed that consensus decision-making is preferable to any one of these.

Some decision modes which may not always work are:

◆ **Majority Rule Voting**
This is useful in routine procedural decisions, but in major policy decisions it may leave a minority who cannot agree and may have difficulty supporting the majority decision. This would impede the effectiveness of the decision.

◆ **Polling the Membership**
This may be useful to determine a prevailing opinion, but is not definite, nor does it always indicate the group has decided. It is a technique on the road to decision-making at best.

◆ **Averaging**
This is an attempt to bring together the least common denominators in all perspectives under the guise of consensus. It may, however, not allow members to heartily agree or buy into the decision.

◆ **Railroading**
A sub-group with an organized, unified agenda is able to maneuver the majority.

◆ **Handclasping**
One member supports the suggestion of another and these two make a decision before the group has considered the situation. Example: One, "I think we should appoint a committee to investigate the possibility of a new gym." Two, "I agree and will serve on the committee." A decision is made by less than the total group.

◆ **Self-authorization**
An individual makes a decision, may announce it, and carries it out without the consent of the group. The person may be a leader or well-respected member. The decision does not, however, represent the will of the group.

◆ **The Plop**
A member makes a contribution and receives no response or recognition. This may represent a lost opportunity or a disorganized group.

◆ **Satisfying**
The group makes a so-called acceptable decision, but avoids dealing with the real issue.

Decision modes which usually do produce better group decisions are:

◆ **Consensus**
All members understand the decision and recognize it as the best possible, given the group and the situation. Everyone is willing to accept the decision and at least go along with it and support it. It is best that each person in the group articulate aloud his or her positive consent to the decision.

◆ **Genuine Unanimity**
This is rare and should only be accepted after a complete review of the alternatives.

Group Decision Behaviors

Consensus is a decision process for making full use of available resources and for resolving conflicts creatively. Consensus is difficult to reach, so not every decision will meet with everyone's complete approval. Complete unanimity is not the goal—it is rarely achieved. But each individual should be able to accept the group judgment on the basis of logic and feasibility. When all group members feel this way, you have reached consensus as defined here and the judgment may be entered as a group decision. This means, in effect, that a single person can block the group if she or he thinks it necessary; at the same time, she or he should use this option in the best sense of reciprocity. Here are some guidelines to use in achieving consensus:

◆ Avoid arguing for your own rankings. Present your position as lucidly and logically as possible, but listen to the other members' reactions and consider them carefully before you press your point.

◆ Do not assume that someone must win and someone must lose when discussion reaches a stalemate. Instead, look for the next most acceptable alternative for all parties.

◆ Do not change your mind simply to avoid conflict and to reach agreement and harmony. When agreement seems to come quickly and easily, be suspicious. Explore the reasons and be sure everyone accepts the solutions for basically similar or complementary reasons. Yield only to positions that have objective and logically sound foundations.

◆ Avoid conflict-reducing techniques such as majority vote, averages, coin-flips, and bargaining. When a dissenting member finally agrees, don't feel that she or he must be rewarded by having his or her own way on some later point.

- Differences of opinion are natural and expected. Seek them out and try to involve everyone in the decision process. Disagreement can help the group's decision because with a wide range of information and options, there is a greater chance that the group will hit upon more adequate solutions.

- Be willing to accept a decision which may not be its first choice, but may be the best the group can make after weighing alternatives and the concerns of members.
- If consensus is not achievable, the leader must determine whether to continue the discussion at the next meeting or bring the matter to majority vote.

The Principal as Part of the Pastoral Team

Thomas, J. A., and B. Davis. 1989. In *Reflections on the role of the Catholic school principal*, ed. R. J. Kealey, 45–54. Washington, D.C.: National Catholic Educational Association.

"The times, they are a changin'." This statement is true for practically every aspect of our lives, including the church. Within the structure of the Catholic Church, a different focus in regard to leadership and ministry has evolved since the Second Vatican Council.

Changing Context of Ministry

Those who were involved in the administration of a parish elementary school prior to Vatican Council II remember well that the pastor was boss! There seemed to be little limit to his absolute authority except perhaps a bishop, often in a far away city. If the pope in Rome was infallible, then, as these writers saw it as Catholic grade school students, the pastor was nearly infallible in his parish. The assistant priests were just that, assistants, not associates; and the pastor felt perfectly free to grant a free day to the school children on his feast day, birthday, or the parish patron saint's day. In short, the pastor needed no help nor much advice in running his parish. He was after all, with a little help from the bishop, called by God to his post.

The Second Vatican Council did much to alter this approach in parish leadership. The pastor was challenged to share his responsibilities and work cooperatively with associates, deacons, and laity in the parish community. Canon 519 of the Revised Code of Canon Law (1983) clearly affirms this position:

> The pastor is the proper shepherd exercising pastoral care in the community entrusted to him under the authority of the diocesan bishop in whose ministry of Christ he has been called to share; in accord with the norm of law he carries out for his community the duties of teaching, sanctifying, and governing, with the cooperation of other presbyters or deacons and the assistance of lay members of the Christian faithful.

Within this framework the principal/minister in a parish school is called to share in a collaborative approach. This is a basic premise in which we firmly believe.

Reiterating the importance of the ministry of the Catholic school, Vatican II's Declaration on Christian Education emphasizes the principal/minister's role as witness of the Gospel. As such, the educational leader must be willing to recognize that responsibilities extend beyond the school to the total parish. Collaboration with the parish team is proper and fitting, not accidental or easily dispensed with. A view which sees the principal's role as only school-related violates this premise.

The role of the principal is multi-faceted. Manno (1985) described three aspects of the principal/minister's responsibilities: spiritual leader, educational leader, and manager of the school community. This model recognizes well that principals in Catholic schools have duties which extend beyond those of their public school counterparts. Public school principals, functioning within a district with a board of education, are building persons; they carry out an educational program in a given building.

Rarely are the Catholic schools of a diocese modeled on the public school system, however. The Catholic school principals/ministers are more than building educational leaders; they are also spiritual leaders called to a ministry of service in the Christian community. Moreover, since the Catholic school principals/ministers cannot turn elsewhere for the management aspect of their schools, these principals/ministers are also managers.

Members of Parish Teams

All of these responsibilities are carried out within the context of the total ministry which occurs within the parish. Thus it is a necessity that the principal/minister serve as a member of the parish pastoral team.

Teaming with other leaders on the parish staff will involve all aspects of the principal's ministry—teaming in spiritual leadership, teaming in educational leadership, and teaming in management. While the principal/minister remains the person chiefly responsible for the school, under the pastor, the school administrator will fund tremendous resources available from other team members and will be aided greatly in carrying out the educational duties. The principal no longer needs to be perceived as the only person concerned about the school ministry.

In addition to the call of Vatican II for a collaborative approach to ministry, there are a number of other reasons why the principal/minister should serve as a member of the parish pastoral team.

The parish school is an integral part of the ministry that occurs in each parish community. One of the basic goals of every parish community is to pass on the faith to succeeding generations. The parish school enables this goal to be accomplished in an effective manner. This ministry affects not only the students in the schools but also their families, immediate and extended.

The school serves as a natural community builder within the parish setting. Parents are closely involved with school activities and often, through encouragement from the principal/minister, become active in the broader parish community. Frequently, it is observed that parents of children in the parish school are the leaders in many parish activities. In order for the principal/minister to encourage parental and family involvement in the parish, the educational leader must be keenly aware of what is happening at the parish level. The principal/minister is in a prime position to foster a sense of bondedness between the school families and the parish community.

In addition, the school provides a vital means of perpetuating the vision and goals of the parish. The principal/minister and school staff need to know clearly the parish vision, and the school vision should flow naturally from this broader parish vision.

Bishop Thomas Costello from the Diocese of Syracuse summarized this point well in a 1983 address to pastors and principals in the Diocese of Toledo, Ohio:

> I think that the school helps us to integrate Church life, faith life, and the rest of human life through the togetherness we experience in academics, athletics, problem solving, fund raising, working, praying, playing, and socializing. I think the school is a fantastic evidence of pastoral care. If you want to know what you can do to help your parents, help them educate their children. Nothing is more important to them or to the Church.

When the principal/minister serves as a member of the pastoral team, a requirement is participation in all scheduled meetings of this group. Some may respond by saying that this adds one more responsibility to the already long list of duties for the principal/minister. However, this affiliation with the pastoral team is one of the most important relationships that the principal must maintain and it must be a top priority. Why is this so?

In the parish setting, one does not want to isolate the school from the rest of the parish. An "us" versus "them" situation is harmful to all involved. Isolation often breeds an unhealthy competition, and the school can easily be perceived as that group of people which absorbs the majority of the parish finances and which gives little in return. Perhaps you have experienced this situation and know the divisiveness which can exist.

When the principal/minister is part of the pastoral team, a valuable source of communication is created. The principal/minister is able to have knowledge and understanding of the total parish picture. The danger of harboring a "school-only" mentality quickly becomes removed. This is true for all members of the pastoral team. They can easily challenge fellow team members who limit their vision to only their particular areas of ministry.

Members of the pastoral team form a support system for one another. Though staff members cannot, and more than likely should not, participate in every parish activity, the fact that they are knowledgeable about what is happening is an important means of support. Often, friendships that extend beyond the work environment are developed among team members.

Relations between Principal and Pastor

While the principal/minister serves as a member of the pastoral team, this in no way should lessen the vital relationship which needs to exist between the pastor and the principal/minister.

The principal/minister must take time to meet with the pastor on a regularly scheduled basis. Pastoral team meetings cannot replace this one-on-one time spent together. Unless the pastor and the principal make a concerted effort to schedule meeting times, a "catch as catch can" pattern seems to emerge. This situation is the least desirable if meaningful dialogue is to occur. Both pastor and principal/minister need to prepare for their meeting time. The principal/minister should be able to tell the pastor what is happening in the school and to share concerns. This is also a time when the pastor may want to share some of his concerns, not only in relation to the school but also in relation to the parish.

It is not necessary that the principal/minister and pastor be "best friends," but it is essential that they be able to work together. Spending time in the one-on-one meeting situation enables the pastor and principal/minister to know one another better and to develop a mutual respect. A pastor or principal/minister who tears the other down because of a lack of understanding can quickly destroy any sense of community. In order to be supportive of one another, pastor and principal/minister need to know each other's thinking, reasoning for specific decisions, statements, etc. Also, the pastor and principal/minister need to take time to share their beliefs and values in regard to Catholic education. The principal/minister needs to know clearly what the pastor's expectations are concerning the principal's ministry in the school and in the larger parish setting. None of this can occur unless the principal/minister and the pastor are communicating frequently with one another.

Another plus for frequent communication between pastor and principal/minister deals with their relationship with the school advisory council or school board. As important issues are raised, the pastor and the principal/minister are asked to share their thoughts. If both know one another's thinking and have prepared for the meeting with council members, "surprises" will be avoided, surprises which would be a source of embarrassment or upset for either the pastor or the principal/minister. Again, this does not mean that the principal/minister and the pastor will always have similar opinions. However, understanding enables them to be respectful of differences of opinion and also facilitates reaching a decision that both can accept.

Pastor's Involvement in the School

Still another important issue which must be raised is the pastor's involvement in the school ministry. With so much emphasis on the principal/minister serving as a member of the pastoral team and on the frequent communication between principal/minister and pastor, a pastor may feel that this suffices and actually fulfills his responsibility to be actively involved in the school ministry. This is a sensitive issue and one that needs to be addressed with clarity since it can create tensions between the pastor, the principal, and the school staff.

School staff members at times have unrealistic expectations of the pastor in terms of his presence in the school and his interaction with the pupils. Often, too, staff members lack understanding of Father's strengths and automatically assume, for example, that every pastor feels at ease in teaching students at all grade levels. The reality may be that Father is not a teacher and would be much more effective in a less formal situation with the students.

The main point is that the principal and the pastor need to discuss this issue thoroughly. The principal/minister may end up challenging Father to review the amount of time he is willing to spend in school or at school-related activities. The principal/minister, in turn, needs to communicate to the school staff the results of these discussions. Better yet would be the pastor discussing his views with the school staff.

This is a major area where discontent can exist and it extends also to the involvement of associate pastors. Thus the importance of reaching a consensus cannot be stressed enough.

We have spent a lot of time reflecting on this relationship between the principal and the pastor because we see this as a key factor in the effectiveness of the ministry of the school within the parish setting.

Relations with Other Members of the Parish Team

Now we would like to turn our thoughts to the relationship between the principal/minister and other members of the pastoral team.

Directors of Religious Education

The principal/minister as a religious leader must interface with the Director of Religious Education (DRE). While most principals are charged with the responsibility of the religion program within the school setting, the parish DRE can assist greatly. Cooperative planning for the sacramental preparation programs with parents is a prime example. Also, school staff and parish catechists can come together for days of retreat and inservice. The principal/minister can be instrumental in helping to bridge the gap between the school program and the C.C.D. program. Such action helps stem negative feelings which sometimes occur from school

staff and students concerning the use of the school facilities for the parish C.C.D. program.

Parish Liturgist

Liturgy is another area of constant collaboration. The principal/minister can ask the assistance of the parish liturgist in providing workshops for teachers to assist them with the planning of children's liturgies. The parish liturgist is a valuable resource for teachers as they instruct and prepare the students to take an active role in liturgy as readers, commentators, and servers. These celebrations of Eucharist with the school community can be very positive experiences for the students and surely serve as a basis for preparing them for their adult lives as worshipers in a parish community. Students also have opportunities to experience paraliturgical celebrations. Again, the parish liturgist can provide assistance to the school staff in preparation of these celebrations.

Often the parish liturgist is in charge of music for worship. Again, whoever works in this area can assist teachers as they strive to choose music appropriate for the specific liturgical or paraliturgical experience. The principal/minister is instrumental in coordinating schedules when the music minister can practice with the students. Sometimes these practices will involve the entire student body; at other times a school choir will have been formed.

Business Manager

A parish business manager is being hired in more and more parishes throughout the country. The business manager can take many of the responsibilities that formerly were given to the principal in relation to the general maintenance of the facility and in assigning duties to maintenance personnel. Often, too, the business manager will work with the principal in the area of finance. Being relieved of major responsibilities in these areas allows the principal/minister to devote more time to other aspects of the ministry. A close working relationship between the principal/minister and the business manager is essential. Obviously, the principal must have an ongoing knowledge of the financial situation, as well as other areas of concern in relation to the facility.

All of the above examples detail practical aspects of collaboration between members of a parish pastoral team. Hopefully, these examples have also deepened the reader's conviction that such collaboration enhances the ministry of the principal in the parish school.

Collaboration

This latter point raises a question in regard to people's readiness for a collaborative ministry. There are certain prerequisites as noted by Loughlan Sofield and Carroll Juliano in their book, *Collaborative Ministry* (1987). Collaboration is based on the ability to relate to others in a trusting manner, assuming that others intend good and not harm. Also, one must have the ability to function both independently and cooperatively. This implies that one can take initiative and assume personal responsibility for choices. On the other hand, one is also able to work with others in a "give and take" manner. Lastly, one has a strong self-identity and is willing to move beyond simply performing tasks with others. He or she is ready to share faith with others as well. It has been noted that when people are able to share faith, they usually experience a corresponding ability to work in closer collaboration with one another. It takes time to develop such a climate among pastoral team members.

It is our experience in working with principals that this collaborative approach to parish ministry is strongly desired. Sometimes we find that principals are frustrated because they feel that their efforts in such an approach are stymied because pastors are not quite ready to change their styles of leadership. On the other hand, pastors sometimes experience this same frustration because principals maintain a "school only" mentality in regard to their ministry and are not willing to see the broader vision in terms of total parish ministry.

The transition from the former style of leadership where the pastor was the "boss" to a collaborative approach will take time. However, we firmly believe that it is this latter approach to which we are called and we have every confidence that the many faith-filled men and women who are committed to extending God's kingdom will continue to struggle together to make this approach a reality.

References

Canon Law Society of America. Code of Canon Law. Washington, DC: Canon Law Society of America, 1983.

Loughlan, Sofield, S.T., and Carroll Juliano, S.H.J.C. Collaborative Ministry. Notre Dame, IN: Ave Maria Press, 1987, pp. 47–55.

Manno, Bruno V. Those who Would be Catholic School Principals. Washington, DC: National Catholic Educational Association, 1985.

The Supervisor's Handbook

Truitt, M. R. 1991. 16–20. Shawnee Mission, Kans.: National Press.

Most Quality Circle Sessions Have Several Standard Components:

1. At the beginning of the meeting, the previous issues considered by the group are summarized. The members need to know that the decisions made at earlier meetings are being acted upon so they feel that their time and effort actually have been making a difference. They also need to know specific performance results of past actions they have taken so both they and the company learn the extent to which changes instituted from their recommendations have positively affected the company.

2. The group then identifies new problems that need consideration. These are listed and the most important or urgent one is selected by the group for concentrated attention.

3. The group decides what information is needed to fully understand the problem at hand. They may have to devise a record-keeping system for the upcoming week to learn just how frequently the problem arises or how costly it is. Or, they may need to invite someone from outside the group to discuss problems that come from or subsequently affect other units.

4. When essential information is gathered, possible solutions are thrown out by group members. After alternative solutions are listed, the group decides upon criteria to use in identifying the best way to handle the problem. Finally, they select the solution that seems most likely to result in improving their performance and/or making work more satisfying for them.

5. The supervisor usually agrees to present the proposed solution to higher-ups who need to be kept informed and/or who must approve the solutions.

When these procedures are followed consistently and skillfully, quality circles are a valued and cost-effective use of employees' time.

Improving Relations between Groups

Groups working for the same organization often act toward each other as if they were with competing companies. You may find that the supervisor and members of another group are obstructing, rather than helping, your group do its job. If this happens, it will be helpful for you to know why groups tend to conflict and how to reconcile their differences.

Reasons for Inter-Group Conflict

What causes groups to compete?

◆ **Interdependency**—When groups depend on each other to get their work done they get frustrated when things go wrong and tend to blame the other group for the problems that exist.

◆ **Limited resources**—When groups don't have enough equipment or material to get their work done, competition between them for those scarce resources becomes likely.

◆ **Interdependent rewards**—When groups are rewarded only on the basis of their own work, the organization is reinforcing them for struggling against each other rather than for cooperating.

◆ **Different goals**—When groups' goals differ—for example, one group (such as sales) is most concerned with the amount of business generated and another group (such as manufacturing) wants to make only flawless products—their inharmonious goals will generate conflict.

◆ **Different time periods**—When one group is concerned with meeting short-term deadlines and another group pays more attention to long-range achievements, they are each likely to see the other as ignoring or obstructing their own efforts

◆ **Status incongruity**—When one group gets partial and distorted information about what another group does, it will often misunderstand and misjudge the other group's actions.

Remember: Knowing what causes inter-group conflict is the first step in alleviating it.

Solutions for Inter-Group Conflict

When your group and other groups in your organization begin to develop negative stereotypes about each other and feel pleased when the other groups fail, you and the supervisors of the other groups need to intervene. How can you rebuild harmony and cooperation? By decreasing competition:

Decreasing Competition between Two Groups—People who feel they are working on the same side of the line are less likely to feel competitive. Unity is built by:

1. **Emphasizing the common enemy**—Opposing groups unite when they recognize that they are facing a threat bigger than each other. When employees realize that they face the danger of losing contracts to a competing company or of losing their jobs altogether, they are motivated to rally together and to compromise their differences—which usually seem minor in the big picture.

2. **Increasing cooperative rewards**—When management provides recognition to both groups equally and when it rewards each group somewhat on the basis of how well they mesh their work with the work of the other group, both groups are encouraged to cooperate.

3. **Task force meetings**—Representatives from each group should meet periodically to plan and to discuss progress made on specific projects involving the two groups.

4. **Reducing inter-group distance**—Arrangements are made for groups that are interdependent to work as nearby each other as possible so members can readily communicate during work breaks and can reach each other immediately when problems arise.

Every opportunity taken to emphasize that the two groups have more to gain by cooperating than by competing and to help them get to know each other will help in resolving inter-group conflict.

How to Build Teamwork

In order for a group of people to attain their maximum potential as a team, these conditions must be met:

1. The group must have a common goal.

2. The members must have a mutual trust for one another.

3. Each member must have a thorough understanding and acceptance of the system of rewards, discipline, and work sharing.

The 4 Steps to Building a Team

1. **The supervisor must see to it that the work environment is (and is perceived by the team members as) fair, reasonable, and friendly.** Unfortunately, the supervisor cannot do this alone. All levels of management have an impact. But, if the supervisor doesn't actively see that this environment is established with the work unit, all the efforts of upper management will be to no avail.

2. **The supervisor must demonstrate an ability to see things from the workers' point of view.** Not from the negative attitude of, "It's us against upper management," but from the perspective that the supervisor has the empathy to understand the issues from the employees' side of things.

3. **The supervisor must strive to gain acceptance as the group's leader.** While the supervisor has formal authority that has been delegated down from upper management levels, his or her effectiveness will be greatly enhanced by the willing support of the team members.

4. **Encouraging employee contribution to working out problems, participating in decision-making and so forth also boosts commitment and team spirit.** Similarly, team members also value being kept up-to-date about things that will affect them, the work unit or the company.

5 Steps to Increased Team Productivity

1. **Set a specific, attainable improvement goal.** Improvement should first be sought in those areas where volume or quality of work is below par. Compare this with what the supervisor and team members believe should be accomplished. Mutual agreement is reached on where to start. There should also be general agreement on how the improvement will be accomplished.

2. **Remove the roadblocks to success.** Make a list of the obstacles blocking progress toward the goal. All team members should participate in determining ways to remove or work around the obstacles.

3. **Make certain all team members are aware of and committed to the accomplishment of sought-after goals.** Everyone must know what is going to be done, how it is going to be done and why it is important to them.

4. **Groom the team.** Each team member's contribution is important to the accomplishment of the unit's objectives. Recognizing this fact, assess each member's abilities. Give extra training or instruction to those who need it. If necessary, transfer the employee to a position where she or he can contribute appropriately.

5. **Keep them informed.** A winning team always wants to know the score. Information on how, when, why, and where the team members are in relation to achieving their goals has positive effects. It tells them where the team stands and gives them recognition for what they are doing. This information should be frequent and complete.

Teamwork

Share this paragraph with staff members who believe that "doing your own thing" is all that matters:

My supervisxr txld me that teamwxrk depends xn the perfxrmance xf every single persxn xn the team. I ignxred that idea until my supervisxr shxwed hxw the xffice typewriter perfxrms when just xne single key is xut xf xrder. All the xther keys xn xur typewriter wxrk just fine except xne, but that xne destrxys the effectiveness xf the typewriter. Nxw I knxw that even thxugh I am xnly xne persxn, I am needed if the team is tx wxrk as a successful team shxuld.

Kill the Umpire

Drahmann, T. 1985. In *Governance and administration in the Catholic school*, 27–30.
Washington, D.C.: National Catholic Educational Association.

Conflict Resolution and Due Process

It is easy to imagine ourselves at a baseball park on a pleasant sunny afternoon, enjoying ourselves as we root for the home team. It has been an exciting afternoon as the teams held each other to an even score. Now, late in the game, one of "our" players has reached third base, and on a long ground ball hit by a teammate, attempts to reach home base to score what may be the winning run. The throw is to the catcher, and both ball and runner seem to arrive at the same time. The umpire's signal, as seen when the dust clears, is "out!"

The stands, filled with fans of the local team, erupt with protest, and we hear the familiar cry: "Kill the umpire!" It takes some time for the uproar to calm down so the game may proceed. Obviously, there was a definite difference of opinion, and many felt that an injustice had been done.

The circumstances may be less striking in a Catholic school, but it is true that conflict may occur and grievances may be present. Disputes may come up between teachers and students, teachers and parents, between teachers and the school administration, and among teachers themselves. They may arise from conflicts over grading, instructional methods, work assignments, school events, salaries and working conditions, or any number of other causes, including personality conflicts.

A number of methods are in place in Catholic schools for settling the minor conflicts which inevitably arise in any institution, as well as the occasional major disputes. They range from informal conciliation to legally-structured steps for the settlement of grievances. Many times they are indicated in the faculty handbook, or are available in other school publications. Many conflicts could be avoided or easily settled if all personnel in Catholic schools would keep in mind two essential concepts. The first is that Catholic schools, like all other church enterprises, must be built upon total respect for the dignity and worth of every human person. Decisions and processes, if we are to carry out Christ's command to "Love thy neighbor as thyself," must proceed with respect and love of persons as their basis. Vatican II, in its foundation document, *Pastoral Constitution on the Church in the Modern World*, has emphasized this as a fundamental characteristic and ideal of the contemporary church.[19]

Secondly, as has been pointed out in Chapter 6, Catholic schools strive to build a "community of faith," according to whichever effort is made to have the school personnel, including board, parents, and students, model the unity that Jesus prayed for at the Last Supper: "That they may be one as you, Father, and I are one" (John 17:11). The American bishops, in *To Teach as Jesus Did*, stated that "all those involved in a Catholic school—parents, pastors, teachers, administrators, and students—must earnestly desire to make it a community of faith which is indeed living, conscious and active."[20]

However, in spite of these lofty ideals, it remains true that conflict arises in Catholic schools. People of faith and good will see things differently. Resources are limited, and hard decisions must be made in their allocation. Administrators often are faced with the necessity of deciding questions when there seem to be contradictory facts alleged by the disputing parties. Emotions can be aroused; sides are chosen; and "win-lose" situations easily develop. It often seems that even Solomon's decision to split the child as related in *I Kings* (Chapter 3) would not be an adequate solution.

What is a teacher to do if a dispute arises with the principal, a parent, a fellow teacher, or a student? It is always possible to follow the biblical injunction found in St. Matthew's Gospel (18:15) to attempt to do so on a one-to-one basis. To try honestly to discuss the point of contention with the other party, along with a sincere attempt to understand the other's position may suffice to resolve the matter. This applies to an assignment dispute with the principal, a disciplinary misunderstanding with a student, or grading problem raised by a parent. Sometimes, the first attempt at such conflict resolution fails, and a teacher may find it necessary to ask for another conference.

If the problem persists, it is helpful to call on a third party for help. The school principal wants to assist in conflicts with parents and students, and would be the ordinary recourse when individual attempts at conciliation have failed. Informal conferences, involving the administration, are able to settle most disputes, and the latter's decision is usually accepted as final.

When a resolution of the matter still does not take place, more formal processes may have to come into play. In many Catholic schools, a structured appeal process is available for use by students, parents, and teachers. (Where unions or organized teacher associations are present, these organizations provide processes for disputes involving teachers.) Commonly there is a procedure for due process. It may involve the board or the diocesan education office. It may be a form of *conciliation*, whereby a third party tries to bring about a mutual agreement, or *arbitration*, by which the matter is settled by decision of a third party.

Due process, that is, the means by which a person may get a fair hearing when a grievance is present, is the right of everyone in Catholic schools. It essentially consists of the opportunity to present one's case to someone in authority and to confront the accuser if there is such. Elaborate procedures which resemble a courtroom process are not required. Since elements of the judicial process may at times be helpful, they may be stipulated in the formal due process procedures of some schools and dioceses.

The ideal procedure for settling conflicts in Catholic schools, as in all groups and organizations, is one which is simple, fair to all, and prompt. The "family atmosphere" of most Catholic schools is conducive to this ideal, and it is hoped that all teachers in these schools make a sincere attempt to use existing procedures, when necessary, with great good will and sincere, deep desire to keep the welfare and growth of the students as the paramount consideration.

Catholic school personnel are urged to constantly strive to go beyond themselves in working for the great overall purposes of Catholic education. *The Catholic School* reminds us that:

The cooperation required for the realization of this aim (building up the Kingdom of God) is a duty of conscience for all members of the community, teachers, parents, pupils, administrative personnel. Each has his or her own part to play. Cooperation of all, given in the spirit of the Gospel, is by its very nature a witness not only to Christ as the cornerstone of the community, but also to the light who shines beyond it.[21]

Summary

1. As in any group of human beings, conflicts arise within Catholic school settings.
2. Teachers, administrators, parents, and students are encouraged to settle disputes with the spirit and principles of the Christian community to which Catholic schools aspire.
3. Catholic schools commonly provide informal and formal methods of conflict resolution and the settlement of grievances.

Notes

19. *Pastoral Constitution on the Church in the Modern World,* #12–17.
20. *To Teach as Jesus Did,* #106.
21. *The Catholic School,* #60, 61.

How to Manage Conflict

Hendricks, W. 1989. 1–3, 6–14, 15–22. Leadership Success Series. Shawnee Mission, Kans.: National Press.

Understanding Conflict

Conflict, A Fact of Life

Conflict is inevitable! There is a passionate pull inherent in the relationships of life. Humankind always struggles with conflict. Wars have been waged throughout the centuries with little lasting effect, and in the business world, one can scarcely imagine a day without conflict and the stress it causes.

This ever-present conflict demands attention. We need a way to diffuse our fear of conflict. Our business, family, and social contacts can be enhanced when conflict is understood. In this chapter, we will define conflict and identify prevailing myths that have restricted our efforts to manage it.

Naming the Territory

Map makers of days gone by labeled unknown territory as the place where dragons existed. For businesses today, conflict is that unknown territory. However, businesses and individuals can't afford to have an unknown territory like conflict. Psychological security is gained when we name the territory of our fears. Therefore, our first step toward effectiveness in managing conflict is to name the territory—become familiar with the unknown.

The Chinese symbol for conflict is a product of two Chinese words: danger and opportunity. Conflict is neither positive nor negative. Resolution can move in either direction. This symbol provides a label for conflict, removing it from the world of the unknown. Conflict does not necessarily mean impending disaster, but includes an opportunity. The territory is manageable!

Myths About Conflict

Myths arise when we lack understanding. They cause us to operate under misconceptions and biased perspectives. It's possible that some myths have invaded your thoughts about conflict. Below are five common myths about conflict.

Five Myths That Inhibit Positive Conflict Management:
1. The presence of conflict is a sign of a poor manager.
2. Conflict is a sign of low concern for the organization.
3. Anger is negative and destructive.
4. Conflict, if left alone, will take care of itself.
5. Conflict must be resolved.

Myth #1: The presence of conflict is the sign of a poor manager. This myth plays on both low self-esteem and insecurity, and pulls a manager into a fear cycle of worry and scurry. The fact is, conflict happens! An effective manager anticipates conflict when possible, deals with conflict when it arises, and enjoys its absence when possible. Relationships are too diverse to effectively judge the quality of a manager on the presence or absence of conflict.

One quality that made Willie Shoemaker an extraordinary jockey was his excellent control. The horse, often unaware of his presence, never felt his hand on the rein unless it was needed. A good manager has this "soft set of hands" during conflict.

Tension will naturally arise as your business relationships are stretched to their limit. Your ability as a manager rises when you respond with the "soft hands" of conflict management, neither judging nor being judged by the presence of conflict.

You will be judged by what you do with the conflict, not by the presence of it!

Myth #2: Conflict is a sign of low concern for the organization. This implies that people expend enormous amounts of time and energy on things that matter little. Generally, people defend and protect those areas where deep concern exists, so conflict indicates genuine concern.

Conflict can help clarify your emotions, and serves as a tool for identifying your underlying values.

Myth #3: Anger is negative and destructive. This myth ignores anger as an emotion, neither positive nor negative, like the wide array of human emotions experienced daily. The energy needed to move in a positive direction comes from the emotions generated by those who care enough to get involved. Anger is only one letter away from danger, but it also can lead to satisfaction when dealt with appropriately.

Myth #4: Conflict, if left alone, will take care of itself. This is a half-truth. You can avoid conflict—it is a valid coping strategy, but not the only strategy. The intensity of conflict varies. Left unchecked, conflict can escalate as easily as dissipate.

Myth #5: Conflict must be resolved. This myth stifles creativity, causing the manager to become solution-oriented. Some conflict is best managed by endurance, while other events require multiple solutions. Quick movement toward resolution can limit success.

This excessive focus on a solution can be counter-productive. Single-focused thinking that sometimes happens when we believe we must find a solution can cause a loss of perspective. Failure to see the big picture while coping with a particular problem, even a major one, can become a major pitfall during conflict.

Summary

Competent business people often become ineffective during conflict, held captive by the power of such myths. The goal is to explore the territory known as conflict, name
it, and weaken the control of exaggerated emotions (myths) that surround it. We are now ready to take the next step in conflict management: assessment.

Three Stages of Conflict

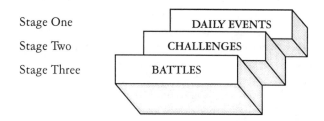

Stage One
Stage Two
Stage Three

DAILY EVENTS
CHALLENGES
BATTLES

Stage One conflict is the least threatening and easiest to manage. As conflict escalates to stages two and three, it becomes more difficult to manage and the potential for harm increases.

Conflict moves between stages, but it does not necessarily follow a linear pattern. A Stage One conflict on Monday morning, left unattended, can escalate to Stage Three by the end of the day. Conversely, high levels of conflict may dissipate with time, quite unexpectedly. Given this fickle nature, the following list of a conflict's underlying characteristics can provide you with additional insight.

Characteristics of Conflict

1. As conflict escalates, concern for self increases.
2. The desire to win increases with a rise in self-interest. Saving face takes on increased importance at higher levels of conflict.
3. Nice people can become harmful to others as conflict increases.
4. Conflict management strategies that work at low levels of conflict are often ineffective, and at times are counter-productive at higher levels of conflict.
5. Conflict may skip levels.
6. People are likely to be at different individual levels during conflict, but an overall organizational level of conflict can be identified.

Looking for Solutions

A one-alarm fire does not require full gear and every truck in the house. The intensity of a fire determines the response of a fire department. Conflict and the intensity it presents determines the strategy you should use.

The three stages of conflict require different management strategies.

◆ A Stage One conflict and the accompanying emotions can best be addressed with coping strategies
◆ Stage Two requires more training and specific management skills
◆ At Stage Three, intervention is necessary.

Characteristics of Stage One

Stage One conflict is ongoing and generally requires little action. Most individuals employ coping strategies unconsciously, and these coping skills are an excellent tool at this level. But coping strategies, like tolerating the actions of co-workers, are most effective when they are deliberate rather than unconscious.

This stage is characterized by day-to-day irritations. These irritations can be passed off, sometimes indefinitely. But an irritation can become a problem. A conflict management strategy at this level should notice if and when this shift from irritation to problem occurs.

The variable that causes irritation to become a problem is people. Different personalities, coping mechanisms and ever-changing life events make it impossible to predict when an individual has had enough. When the shift occurs an alarm should sound, alerting the individuals to bring out the "conflict squad."

Avoidance is one effective coping strategy for day-to-day irritations. We pass things off rather than deal with them because they're minor. You employ avoidance with your boss when you decide that silence might be a better tactic than discussion. The deliberate coping strategy of avoidance happens when you determine there is neither time nor motivation to alter the idiosyncrasies of another. If your contact with the person is minimal, the chances are good that you have managed the irritation appropriately. At this stage a "live and let live" attitude works pretty well.

Think back to your grade school playground, when teams were picked and friends paired off. Instantly, a coping strategy was initiated by those doing the choosing and those chosen last. The games went on, but feelings of alienation were sometimes generated. Similar feelings are produced during daily contacts with other people. One too many irritations can cause problems that must be solved.

Obliging is a slightly stronger form of avoidance, where an individual "gives in" to another. Obliging involves one's desire to "fit in" and belong. This desire to belong is usually strong, and overrides lower levels of conflict. This strategy uses a give-in attitude so things can keep moving. Deliberate obliging can be beneficial to team effort, but there is no way to predict how long an individual will oblige.

Conflict at Stage One is real, although low in intensity. When people work together, differences exist in goals, values, and individual needs. At Stage One, parties feel discomfort and possibly anger, but are quick to "pass off" these emotions. Individuals are usually willing to work toward a solution during Stage One conflict, often with a sense of optimism that things can be worked out.

This optimism might be detected as a "no big deal" attitude. Facts and opinions are shared openly with one another once the problem has surfaced. Communication is usually clear, specific, and oriented to the present because the people and the problem are not intertwined as they are in more intense conflict.

This distinction is significant. The easiest way to discern whether you are in a Stage One conflict or a more intense level is to observe participants' ability to separate people from the problem. Brainstorming and creative problem-solving work well at Stage One because participants are willing to discuss problems rather than personalities.

Listening and participation are essential at this level. As a conflict manager, initiate joint listening and exploration ventures with an emphasis on teamwork and shared responsibility. This strategy focuses all the participants in a common direction and allows everyone to contribute.

Ways to Handle Stage One Conflict

1. Initiate a process that examines both sides. Can a framework be built that encourages understanding of one another?
2. Ask if the reaction is proportional to the situation. Is either party carrying residual emotions from another event? (Example: Ask each party to consider if this event is isolated or whether the feelings reflect previous disagreements.)
3. Identify points of agreement and work from these points first, then identify the points of disagreement. Is it possible to leap the hurdle of conflict by seeing the whole picture?

Characteristics of Stage Two

Conflict takes on the element of competition at Stage Two, typified by a "win-lose" attitude. Losses seem greater at this stage because people are tied to the problems. Self-interest and "how one looks" become very important. A "cover your hind-end" attitude can also be observed. At Stage Two people keep track of verbal victories and record mistakes, witnesses take sides, and an imaginary debate develops with scores being tallied. The level of commitment required to work through conflict also increases.

Volunteer organizations have difficulty managing conflict at Stage Two because it is easier to walk away rather than maintain the commitment necessary to manage conflict. In private industry alliances and cliques form.

Because the conflict is more complex at Stage Two, problems can no longer be managed with coping strategies. At this stage, the people are the problem. A discussion of issues and answers often proves futile because the people and the problem have become so entangled. You'll also notice resistance when attempts are made to address the issues. To manage conflict effectively at Stage Two, you must implement a people management strategy.

As you work with people, notice the words that are selected to describe conflict or disagreement. At Stage Two conflict, the language is less specific; people talk in generalizations. You'll hear references to the phantom "they" and comments like "everyone believes." Words of exaggeration like "always" and "never" increase in frequency during Stage Two conflict.

Competing parties are less likely to provide accurate facts to one another because the trust level has declined. Questions of "How will you use this information?" become a major concern.

It's important to note that the atmosphere is not necessarily hostile at Stage Two. But it is cautious! Put-downs, sarcasm, and innuendoes are survival tactics (but ineffective management tactics) used during Stage Two conflict. Coping strategies like avoidance and obliging that worked so well at Stage One now become ineffective. A "wait-and-see" attitude degenerates into a "you-prove-yourself-to-me" attitude at Stage Two.

You must separate the people from the problem as a first step to managing the conflict at this stage. Here are some ideas:

Ways to Handle Stage Two Conflict

1. Create a safe atmosphere. Provide an environment where everyone is secure:
   - Make the setting informal
   - Establish neutral turf
   - Have an agenda
   - Be in control
   - Set the tone, be slightly vulnerable

2. Be hard on the facts, soft on the people. Take an extended amount of time to get every detail. Clarify generalizations. Who are "they"? Is "always" an accurate statement? Question whether any fact was missed.

3. Do the initial work as a team, sharing in the responsibility for finding an alternative everyone can live with. Stress the necessity of equal responsibility. Do not carry this load for the group, which is a tendency of conflict managers.

4. Look for middle ground but do not suggest compromise. Compromise implies "giving up" cherished points. Instead, creatively look for the middle ground by focusing on points of agreement.

5. Allow time to pull competing parties toward acceptable ground without forcing issues or concessions.

6. Remember, it is much harder to compete sitting next to someone than across the table. Or sit in a circle.

Stage Two conflict left unchecked will delude thinking and magnify the problems. Conflicting parties see themselves as more benevolent and others as more evil than is actually the case. When you notice comments that focus on either/or, black and white thinking, conflict has escalated into Stage Three.

Characteristics of Stage Three

At Stage Three, the objective shifts from wanting to win toward wanting to hurt. The motivation is to "get rid" of the other party. Conflict has escalated; something must give! Changing the situation and problem-solving are no longer satisfactory for those locked into Stage Three conflict. Being right and punishing wrong become consuming motivations.

Insiders and outsiders are identified by the competing parties as people choose sides on "the issues that matter." Self interest and the "good of the organization" are equated in the thinking of individuals holding a position in Stage Three conflict.

Leaders emerge from the group and act as spokespersons. Outsiders are enlisted toward the cause, giving little room for middle ground. Small factions evolve, and group cohesiveness is more important than organizational unity.

The merits of an argument and the strength with which positions are held are greatly exaggerated at this stage. A loss of perspective is quite likely on the part of all participants. One tactic you should consider once you observe Stage Three attitudes is the initiation of an intervention team that is neutral to the groups in conflict. For example, members from a disinterested department could be formed to address the concerns and issues of each party. The role of such an intervention team could take the form of mediation or arbitration. During mediation, both sides present their case to the intervention team and the team facilitates discussion and encourages movement toward a mutually acceptable solution. Usually, the opposing parties remain responsible for finding common ground and solutions in mediation.

If consensus cannot be reached, arbitration can be used as a next stage. Each party would present its best case, and one side is selected over the other. There is obviously a great deal to be lost by both sides once this tactic is used, but it can bring an end to high level conflict. Arbitration, especially binding arbitration, demands enforcement. All parties must follow and accept the conclusions of the intervention team or leave!

The members of an intervention team must be perceived as totally impartial, able to provide a fair hearing for everyone. This intervention team will be required to sift through many emotions in search of facts, and they must also provide clear-cut direction at the conclusion of the fact-finding process.

Individuals locked into a Stage Three conflict will likely prolong the conflict, consumed by the event and the energy it provides. Even after management has made its conclusions, some will continue the fight, pursuing their "holy mission."

Negotiation and arbitration are the tools you'll need to bring an end to Stage Three conflict. Negotiation requires parties to sit across from one another and work through the conflict in the presence of an outside agent. This process, once begun, can produce solutions to the problem, but is not likely to produce harmony, because at Stage Three parties have decided that someone must go. At Stage Three, every party loses some ground looking for something workable.

Arbitration takes the negotiation process one step further. Each side presents their best case. The outside agent then selects one or the other. The benefit of this process is that one side is clearly a winner. The disadvantage, of course, is that few companies can afford to have a group of losers!

When conflict escalates to Stage Three, the best strategy you can employ is to minimize the losses and prepare to refocus those who remain.

What do you do with the losers? Possibly replacement or out-placement can be tried. A cooling off period for the losers might also be initiated once a decision is made. It is vital that you have a complete grasp of the negotiation/arbitration process, or you may find you have nothing left to manage.

Ways to Handle Stage Three Conflict

1. Details are important. The outside intervention team must be willing to pay attention to every detail, wading through a considerable amount of negative emotion.

2. Company time must be expended to interview every possible participant.

3. Logic and reason are not effective in dissuading others at this stage. Because everyone will not hold Stage Three intensity in the conflict, identify those individuals who are at the lower stages of conflict and begin redirecting these individuals, providing an alternative source for their energy.

4. Clear corporate goals and a sense of direction will be necessary for individuals to walk away from Stage Three conflict as winners. The good conflict manager delegates tasks to people and redirects events, encouraging the skills of everyone. This is not the time to cover up the event, but it need not be the all-consuming issue individuals have made it out to be!

Summary

The Boy Scout motto, "Be prepared," is excellent advice for conflict management. The following chart can be used as a checklist for assessing conflict.

Conflict Assessment Checklist

Stage One

	Yes	No
1. Are individuals willing to meet and discuss facts?		
2. Is there a sense of optimism?		
3. Is there a cooperative spirit?		
4. Does a "live and let live" attitude typify the atmosphere?		
5. Can individuals discuss issues without involving personalities?		
6. Are the parties able to stay in the present tense?		
7. Is the language specific?		
8. Do solutions dominate the management efforts?		

Stage Two

	Yes	No
1. Is there a competitive attitude?		
2. Is there an emphasis on winners and losers?		
3. Is it hard to talk about problems without including people?		
4. Is the language generalized?		
5. Can you identify these statements: "They" "Everyone is . . ."		

Stage Two (continued)

	Yes	No
"You always . . ." "He never . . ."		
6. Is there a cautious nature when issues are discussed?		
7. Can you detect a "cover-your-hindend" attitude?		
8. Do the parties make efforts to look good?		

Stage Three

	Yes	No
1. Are attempts being made to get rid of others?		
2. Is there an intention to hurt?		
3. Have obvious leaders or spokespersons emerged?		
4. Is there a choosing up of sides?		
5. Has corporate good become identified with a set of special interests?		
6. Is there a sense of "holy mission" on the part of certain parties?		
7. Is there a sense that things will never stop?		
8. Has there been a loss of middle ground, allowing only black or white options?		

Constructive Conflict Action

Overview

The story of Pinocchio is an excellent reminder about the nature of relationships. Geppetto, the wood-carver, wanted a son; so he carved a "wooden boy." But Pinocchio, being wooden, was incapable of making effective decisions; feelings and emotions got in the way. Pinocchio made error after error; his nose growing longer; ineffective in the real world of decisions.

Pinocchio became a real decision maker. The journey was long and painful, but the end result was life. The business manager who begins the journey of conflict management can bring this "life" to any corporation.

Perhaps you've been bogged down by circumstances? Do you often find yourself overwhelmed as you try and keep things together? Like Pinocchio, we need a personal transformation that leads to effective management and powerful decision-making, especially in the face of conflict.

Decision-making is the task of management. A wrong or hasty decision can produce conflict. In addition, the rapid pace of modern business naturally produces conflict. Like Pinocchio, a busy executive must discover a resource for effective decision-making.

If you are going to make the best decisions during conflict, you'll need a healthy understanding of human relationships. Here are seven principles for maintaining positive relationships during conflict.

1. Build Winners; Voting Builds Losers

The power of positive relationships comes through a management style that builds winners. Voting is a technique used to decide between options, but unfortunately options tend to represent individual desires, especially at higher levels of conflict. A decision to vote can begin a political process where winners and losers begin to keep score.

Should voting be used? Yes, but you should assess the decision being made and consider the ramifications of a choice made by the voting method. How will the losers participate with the new majority? Can a vote be tabled long enough to meet and discuss alternatives with representatives of competing views?

Voting is most effective during lower intensity conflict because the people are problem focused and have less of themselves invested. But voting is too frequently chosen during Stage Two and Three conflict because sides and opinions are easy to count. The "either/or" thinking of Stages Two and Three often promotes the conflict rather than leading to its resolution. One question you should ask is, "Have we exhausted all the options?"

2. Declare a Moratorium

The declaration of a moratorium is a valuable tool. Relationships are more important than a decision. Roger Fisher, in *Getting Together* says, "If we want a relationship that can deal with serious differences, we have to improve the process itself, independent of the particular substantive problems involved." Time taken to ensure this principle builds a healthy foundation that can tolerate intense conflict.

A moratorium can be declared over issues, problems, or decisions. The manager uses time as a resource, deliberately stating intentions and working behind the scenes to ensure the greatest possible outcome. These suggestions could be used to introduce a moratorium . . .

- ◆ "We have some time; let's meet in small groups and look for alternatives."
- ◆ "No decision is worth hurt feelings. There are several people who have spent company time and proposed quality ideas. I want to find out why there is such diversity of opinion."
- ◆ "The amount of time and energy that have been spent on this issue is significant. We're not ready to decide. A little more time invested now that we've seen the issues might help everyone."

3. Encourage Equal Participation

Shared responsibility increases ownership. Higher stages of conflict cause individuals to become destructive and lose sight of the organization in favor of personal issues. Opportunities for participation increase the likelihood that individuals will see Level Three conflict as risky—too great a loss.

A simple reminder that "we" are a team can often encourage the desired ownership. You can also share the leadership responsibility by expecting team members to think like a manager in the situation, asking for creative responses to the events that promote cooperation rather than split decisions.

Other examples of shared responsibility include subdividing tasks that generate deliberate barriers of responsibility, and then expecting team leaders to cross the barriers by providing assignments that require cooperative efforts. The importance of shared responsibility is to make the point, emphatically, that no one person owns a problem and everyone shares in the responsibility for solving sticky issues.

Author Thomas Peters' fever about the need for a service-oriented management style applies during conflict: "We must fundamentally shift our managerial philosophy from adversarial to cooperative." Peters continues, "It is vital to engage in multi-function problem-solving and to target business systems that cross several functional boundaries. Ford and IBM both say they wasted years before realizing that most quality improvement opportunities lie outside the natural work group."

4. Actively Listen

Listening skills cost very little. They are the easiest to learn and can be implemented through sheer desire. People are constantly talking, but too often never stop and listen.

All a manager has to do is stop speaking! Listening affirms others in several ways:

1. Listening says you are important, and I'll take time to hear what you have to say.
2. Listening provides quick access to a perspective on conflict.
3. Listening provides data for the manager to make decisions.
4. Listening builds relationships.

Many people are uncomfortable with silence. The effective manager knows that taking time to listen, even if there are periods of silence, is an investment in the relationship. Here are just a few things you can do to fill the silence while tending to the other person:

◆ Watch the individual's eyes—notice the color.
◆ Learn to read body language.
◆ Test yourself after visiting with others. Did you gain as much information as you gave out?

5. Separate Fact From Opinion

It is easy to believe your position is the truth. At best, an opinion only represents the truth, and far too often opinion reflects perception rather than reality. If you challenge categorical statements and encourage "conditional truth," you will be more effective during higher levels of conflict because the very issues of Stage Two and Stage Three deal with perceptions.

Conditional truth is a philosophical acceptance that the position any person takes is accurate and in the best interest of the company. When we develop a "conditional truth" orientation, it grants every participant the opportunity to be correct and the right to be heard before conclusions are drawn or decisions made.

If you take strong leadership at this point, conflict becomes a matter of separating perspectives rather than challenging liars, a difficult task with adults. But be cautious. Stage Two conflict escalates quickly. Your staff will be ready to blame and accuse rather than work toward resolution, causing a distortion of facts. Conditional thinking will make it harder for individuals to "own" positions.

An additional benefit when you separate fact from opinion is a rise in creativity. Individuals conditioned to consider alternative perspectives are less likely to settle for easy answers. And during confrontation they are more likely to look for options as standard procedure.

Conditional truth is more of an attitude than a process. The effective manager instills a questioning attitude that looks for alternatives rather than debate.

6. Separate People From the Problem

This is a strategy necessary to manage conflict at any stage. Once the people and the problem are tangled together, a problem becomes unmanageable! Personality problems include a multitude of variables, and many are hard to change.

During conflict it is easy to forget due-process practices. During the higher stages people tend to forget these details. This can result in the early termination of an employee. In business, we must find ways to ensure that details are noticed.

Some may find it difficult to separate the people from the problem, but as a manager you must! Some ideas that can help you separate people from the problem include:

1. Talk in specific rather than general terms.
2. When dealing with Stage Two or Three conflict, use concrete terms and ask for facts.
3. Address conflicting parties as if they have no information. This provides opportunity for them to hear a perspective without having to defend their territory, separating them from the event for a moment.
4. Create a safe environment. The "flight/fight" response is activated during high stages of conflict. Safety enhances the possibilities that individuals will move away from protracted positions.

7. Divide and Conquer

A great deal of energy is consumed through debate and persuasive tactics. The destructive power that is present during the higher stages of conflict comes when coalitions are formed. Another interesting factor is that as conflict increases, the people involved have a greater need for support. An effective manager has built a team concept and refers to the team at every turn. It is harder for coalitions to form when there is a larger identity. Comments that can point out a team orientation could include, "Superstars make headlines, but are not always easy to work with," "There is one team in this company."

During conflict it is easy to focus on the negatives. So easy that we tend to act and react in counter-productive ways. Here are five major don'ts:

Five Don'ts During Conflict

1. Don't Get in a Power Struggle. There is a significant relationship between power and authority. Most sociologists acknowledge the fact that as power increases, authority decreases and vice versa. Well-known sociologist Erik Erikson noted that children become emotionally disturbed when they possess power they cannot responsibly handle. Psychologist Emile Durkheim discovered that clearly defined norms and rules are needed to govern life, or people become self-destructive.

One creative response you can bring to conflict is an ability to give away power, allowing others to take control of their feelings and the event in question.

Your authority increases when you empower others instead of getting into power struggles. Power tends to be coercive; authority involves a sense of respect. If you can find a way to turn aside power struggles, you'll be more effective during conflict. Once a power struggle begins, three results are possible:

1. The other person is stopped or possibly killed.
2. The other person quits.
3. An ongoing jockeying for position begins.

The end result of power struggles is usually not worth the payoff. Here are some things you can do to avoid power struggles:

◆ Don't argue unless you are prepared to waste time. Reason won't work.

◆ Don't engage in a battle unless you are prepared to lose because you already have.

◆ Don't take total responsibility for others' emotions. As the one in control, share the responsibility.

2. Don't Become Detached From the Conflict. At first, this may seem contradictory, but it is actually a way to monitor conflict and keep it under control. It is important that you have passionate concern for both the people and the problem. Business will not operate without people, and it cannot operate effectively until substantive conflict is managed. Concern is one motivation that drives us to find opportunity in conflict.

A macho image of detached leadership provides a distorted perspective too easily imitated and too frequently used. Who wouldn't like to be in charge and have the physical and mental skills to dominate a business situation? Business images of strong-willed Lee Iacocca or free-swinging Donald Trump are just two examples of the "macho businessman" who has complete control and is able to leap tall buildings in a single bound.

The super-power image works in the movies! It works in isolated business dealings and it usually works when we have extreme control of the events and the dollars. Rarely do we have a tailor-made script of power and ability that the movie heroes possess. The tendency to imitate this macho image can deprive you of the natural passion for both your people and your product.

3. Don't Let Conflict Establish Your Agenda. Time management specialists suggest it is important for a manager to "do the important and delegate the urgent." This principle is often distorted under the pressure of conflict, and managers are found ignoring many important business matters in an attempt to deal with the conflict.

Perspective is the key. In conflict, as with any management issue, the executive must know both the goals and direction the company is moving. Decisions and responses to conflict should match this overall direction. But sometimes urgent needs interfere with daily schedules. A time study should reveal that you have spent time managing the priorities and not managing conflict unendingly.

Here are some handy tips that can help you manage the urgent:

◆ Don't spend all your time and energy on one issue.

◆ Watch time traps. Are there tasks that always seem to consume your time before you're aware it's gone?

◆ Identify urgent issues, especially negative or conflict issues. If you notice one consistent time offender, manage that offender.

❖ Are your people delegating up to you, getting you to do their work?

❖ Are they bringing solutions along with concerns?

❖ Do they feed you moan-and-groan needs? It's easy to get caught in a negative cycle, and there are always people and events that can feed a "poor me" syndrome.

4. Don't Be Caught "AWFULIZING." Joan Borysenko, author of *Minding the Body, Mending the Mind,* defines awfulizing as "the tendency to escalate a situation into its worst possible conclusion." It is easy to be pushed to worst-case scenarios when faced with Stage Two or Three conflict. Those locked into higher levels of conflict lose their ability to quantify the intensity of the problem.

Reminders to Avoid Awfulizing

◆ People are rarely as benevolent as they perceive themselves to be.

◆ People are rarely as evil as their opponents perceive them to be.

◆ Individuals rarely spend as much time thinking about the issues as believed.

◆ The motivations of others are rarely as planned or thought out as presented. Most aspects of conflict spin off other events and are not the result of coldhearted calculation.

◆ Every conflict has a history that extends beyond the present. The people and their previous patterns of relating taint the present perception.

5. Don't Be Fooled by Projection. Projection is an emotional release. Individuals unconsciously project their own flaws and weaknesses onto others. To be effective during conflict, you should notice the generalizations and accusations being made about others, especially comments about someone's motivations. We may understand others and we may be able to predict their actions accurately, but it is dangerous to believe anyone can read the mind of others.

Summary

Geppetto had a great love for his creation, Pinocchio. According to the fairytale, he traveled far and wide seeking his lost son. When the story ended, there was a miracle —Pinocchio was alive, a real person! The "Seven Principles of Positive Relationships in Conflict Management" and the "Five Don'ts of Conflict Management" mentioned in this chapter are best attempted by those who have a love for their job, their company, and its people. The kind of love a wood-carver has for his work.

It's your relationships with people that will determine your success in managing conflict because it will take a "fairytale" type of love to stay on course as you steer through the pain of conflict. But there's also a "fairytale" ending waiting for you!

School Handbooks: Some Legal Considerations

Shaughnessy, M. A. 1989. 76. Washington, D.C.: National Catholic Educational Association.

Administrative decisions are the day-to-day management choices of the principal. It is important for everyone to understand these distinctions from the beginning.

Generally, boards will set policies in these major areas: administration, personnel, students/parents, plant, and finances.

The board is responsible to ensure that the administration is implementing policies. The board probably also has some responsibility in evaluating the principal's job performance, at least in relationship to the board. Recently, many experts are suggesting that evaluation of the principal can best be done by other educational experts with the board giving appropriate input. In any case, the board should ensure that evaluation of the principal is being conducted according to policy.

Personnel policies concerning hiring and dismissal procedures, as well as grievance procedures, are the province of the board. It is important to note that the board should not be concerned with *who* is hired and *who* is dismissed, but rather that hiring and terminating are conducted according to policy. If the board functions at any level as part of an appeals process, the board should understand that it is to determine whether policies and procedures were fairly followed, not whether it agrees with the final decision.

A board meets its obligations to students and parents by approving program goals, handbooks, and other policies.

If a parish council or other body does not have the responsibility for the school plant, the school board may have that duty. The board must ensure that building safety is a priority and that all civil codes are met.

The board also will have either advisory or policy-making input regarding tuition setting, salary scales, and budget approval.

Differentiated Supervision for Catholic Schools

Glatthorn, A. A., and C. R. Shields. 1983. 2, 8–12.
Washington, D.C.: National Catholic Educational Association.

Figure 1: Credo for Supervision in Catholic Schools

A Special View of and Relationship with the Child

We see the pupil as a child of God, one who needs the nurture of Christ-like caring. We value teachers who share that view and can respond to His Spirit that dwells within those children.

A Special Vision of the School

We hold a vision of the school as a Christian community, where Christian values are made manifest. We value teachers who work together to create that sense of community.

A Special Kind of Classroom

We believe that the classroom should be a caring community, a special learning environment where the unique personhood of the child is respected and nurtured. We value teachers who strive to create that kind of classroom community.

A Special View of the Curriculum

We believe that a major goal of education is the development of the ability to make their ethical decisions and take moral action. We value teachers who see that goal as an important outcome of their teaching and shape their curricula accordingly.

A Special View of the Teacher

We believe that, with God's help, all teachers can grow professionally and personally, finding ways to contribute their special talents to the education of God's children. We value supervisors who can create professional environments where such growth is fostered and such contributions are rewarded.

A Special View of the Supervisory Relationship

We believe that such professional growth can best come about through helping relationships that are authentic, mutual, and individualized. We will do all in our power to develop such relationships, so that Catholic schools can become the best they can be.

Chapter 2.*
A Rationale for and Overview of Differentiated Supervision

We have suggested in the first chapter that teachers are special people with special needs—who need some options in the type of supervision which they experience. We would like in this chapter to provide a more explicit rationale for supervisory options and describe briefly how the differentiated model responds to that need for choice.

For years, of course, there has been widespread dissatisfaction about the standard supervision offered in most schools. The causes of this dissatisfaction are multiple. First, supervision tends to be unsystematic. Good and Brophy (1978) report that, since teachers are seldom observed in any systematic way, they do not receive the feedback they need to improve their effectiveness. At best, it is often sporadic in nature. Both Goodlad (1976) and Blumberg (1974) report teachers experience little meaningful interaction with those in supervisory positions, and it is too often negative in its orientation. As a consequence, teachers rather generally perceive supervision as a threat. (See, for example, Denham, 1977; and Withall, 1979.)

These obvious inadequacies of what is usually termed "traditional supervision" have led many in the profession to advocate the use of clinical supervision, a more systematic and intensive process of conferring, observing, analyzing, and debriefing. Those advocating clinical supervision have stressed the importance of providing the teacher with objective feedback about the lesson, rather than making negative evaluations. Recent evidence suggests that clinical supervision, effectively implemented, can make a difference in teacher performance and attitude. (See Sullivan, 1980, for an excellent review of the research on clinical supervision.)

However, there are two reasons why it seems unwise to provide clinical supervision to all teachers. The first is a practical one; there is just not enough time. Principals in Catholic schools are generally very busy individuals with many administrative tasks competing for their attention. As Delahanty (1976) discovered, principals feel that the greatest problem in providing supervision is the lack of time for classroom visitation and conference. A recent study (Shields, 1982) of Catholic elementary school principals cites the pressure of other duties as a factor that negatively influences supervisory practices in Catholic schools.

The second reason is that all teachers do not need clinical supervision. It has been most widely used in the

---

* Editor's note: Chapter notation refers to this excerpt.

preservice education of teachers, where its emphasis upon the basic skills of teaching seems most appropriate. However, the need for the close attention of clinical supervision is less apparent in working with experienced and competent teachers. While we believe that all teachers can profit from feedback, we are not convinced that a successful teacher requires the intensive help of clinical supervision. We concur with Barth's (1979) observation that when a teacher becomes "self-critical, self-motivating, self-evaluative, and self-confident, there may be little need for formal education and supervision" (p. 77).

Since principals are too busy to provide clinical supervision to all teachers, and since experienced and competent teachers do not need it, then it makes sense for the supervisor to limit clinical supervision to those who need it or request it. It seems to be administratively more efficient and effective to give good supervision to the few teachers who need it than to give only cursory attention to all. But those who do not need clinical supervision can use some feedback and want to be more actively involved in some supervisory process, as Shields (1982) discovered.

The answer for them is not to be ignored—but to give some options. Teachers are unique individuals who need the individualization we think students should have. They bring to the teaching-learning environment a diversity of talents, experience, and expectations. Some teachers have a substantial knowledge of their subject matter yet lack the technical skill to impart this knowledge; others are rich in techniques but have only a superficial grasp of content. Some prefer to work together; others prefer to work on their own. To treat all teachers alike, ignoring special strengths and weaknesses and being insensitive to particular predilections, reflects a failure to recognize human diversity.

Because of these differences we have developed an approach which we call "differentiated supervision for Catholic schools." Differentiated supervision is simply a way of providing different kinds of supervisory support for teachers with different needs. Some teachers need the intensive support of clinical supervision. Others can profit from working with colleagues in a process we call collaborative professional development. Still others can work on their own in a self-directed mode, and some can grow from the less formal "administrative monitoring" that goes on in every good Catholic school.

At this point it might be useful to elaborate somewhat on the options offered to teachers. We think the best way of doing this is to summarize the salient features in a form that might be easily copied and shared with teachers. Accordingly, we present in Figure 2, the "what, why, who, and how" of the four modes.

We would stress again here that we do not wish to impose the total system on a school. In fact, as we shall explain later, we have had most success in describing and explaining the four processes to principals and teachers and helping each school develop its own version. One thing we have discovered in the process is that schools will vary in the options chosen. In the Shields (1982) study the six participating facilities reflected different option patterns. The other interesting development that surprised us is that many teachers chose more than one option. A typical reaction was, "I like the idea of getting some clinical supervision—but I also would like to get involved in that collaborative development."

We do not have convincing evidence that the differentiated program will make radical changes in behavior. We do know that it is feasible—and that teachers in general feel very positive about it, because they have a choice. One of the special advantages is illustrated in this true anecdote about a teacher whom we shall identify as Miss Anton.

Miss Anton had taught many years in departmentalized intermediate grades. In finding a new position, she agreed to teach in a self-contained eighth grade classroom. She felt a sense of panic because she had never taught reading and did not know where to begin. Since the school was involved in a pilot test of differentiated supervision, she requested collaborative professional development and chose the first grade teacher as her development teacher. The first grade teacher taught her how to use the instructor's manual in developing a reading lesson, gave a demonstration lesson in the eighth grade room, and coached the teacher in her planning and presentations. Miss Anton felt she had learned a great deal.

And what of the first grade teacher? She had asked to be involved in both collaborative and self-directed development. In the self-directed component, she wanted to work on making more effective use of classroom time. Her personal analysis indicated that she wasted too much time at the beginning of class. So in conjunction with her principal, she developed and implemented a series of strategies to get class off to a more efficient start.

References

Barth, R. S. Teacher evaluation and staff development. *The National Elementary Principal*, 1979, 58 (2), 74–77.

Blumberg, A. *Supervisors and Teachers: A Private Cold War*. Berkeley: McCutchan, 1974.

Delahanty, Brother D. *Helping Teachers Grow Through Instructional Leadership and Supervision*. Winona, Minnesota: St. Mary's College Press, 1976.

Denham, A. Clinical supervision: What we need to know about its potential for improving instruction. *Contemporary Education*, 1977, 49 (1), 33–37.

Good, T. L. & Brophy, J. E. *Looking into Classrooms* (2nd Ed.), New York: Harper & Row, 1978.

Goodlad, J. I., Klien, M. F. & Assoc. *Looking Behind the Classroom Door*. Worthington, Ohio: Charles A. James Publishing Co., 1974.

Shields, S. C. R. *A feasibility study of differentiated supervision for Catholic schools*, Ed.D. dissertation, University of Pennsylvania, 1982.

Sullivan, C. G. *Clinical supervision a state of the art review*. Washington, D.C.: Association for Supervision and Curriculum Development, 1980.

Withall, J. Classroom observation and feedback. *Journal of Teacher Education*, 1979, 30 (1), 55–58.

Figure 2. Four Options for Supervision

Clinical Supervision

What? Clinical supervision is a systematic and carefully planned program of supervision in which the supervisor works with the teacher to assist him or her in professional growth. Typically clinical supervision incorporates several cycles of preobservation planning, observation, analysis of observational data, and debriefing, concluding with the evaluation of the cycle.

Why? The purpose of clinical supervision is to help the teacher improve professional skills—by planning and reflecting about plans, by getting feedback about performance, and by analyzing the significance of that feedback with a trained supervisor.

Who? Three types of teachers seem to find clinical supervision desirable. Beginning teachers seem to need its intensive assistance. Experienced teachers new to a given school understand the usefulness of close attention from the supervisor. And all teachers who care about their professional growth will from time to time wish to be involved in this mode of supervision.

How? The supervisor confers with the teacher to review plans and clarify objectives; the supervisor visits the class and makes close observations of teacher and pupil behavior; the supervisor analyzes those data to identify recurring patterns suggesting success and difficulty; the supervisor and teacher confer to examine together the observational data.

Collaborative Professional Development

What? This is a process in which a small group of teachers work together for their own improvement, observing, discussing, and analyzing.

Why? While there are some teachers who need the help of trained supervisors in dealing with instructional problems, and other teachers prefer to work alone, most experienced teachers will welcome the chance to work together with colleagues.

Who? Teachers who are experienced and competent—who are interested in working with colleagues.

How? Through cooperative sharing, teachers will assess needs, set goals, develop together appropriate strategies, hold observation sessions, and discuss those observations together.

Self-Directed Professional Development

What? Self-directed professional development is a process by which a teacher systematically plans his or her professional growth and conscientiously carries out this plan over a period of time. The teacher is primarily responsible for his or her own professional growth.

Why? Some teachers have the autonomy to direct their own growth, and they prefer to work independently, rather than working with colleagues or a supervisor.

Who? Experienced and competent teachers who are self-directing and prefer not to work with colleagues.

How? The teacher assesses needs, sets goals, plans and carries out strategies, with the supervisor serving as a supportive resource.

Administrative Monitoring

What? Administrative monitoring is a process in which the principal makes brief yet systematic visits to classrooms, in order to monitor performance and gather tentative impressions about teaching and learning.

Why? The monitoring assists the principal in assessing the educational climate, provides him or her with many opportunities to interact with teachers and students, and serves as a means for making informal evaluations of programs.

Who? Experienced and competent teachers who do not choose collaborative or self-directed professional development.

How? The principal makes brief visits daily, notes significant behaviors, and confers informally as needed.

Treat Others with Tough Love and a Tender Touch

Hind, J. F. 1989. In *The heart and soul of effective management: A Christian approach to managing and motivating people*, 113–17. Wheaton, Ill: Scripture Press Publications, Inc.

It is not enough that every person understands that business must make a profit to survive. As Waterman states in *The Renewal Factor*, "Pursuit of profit is hardly a cause that inspires loyalty or makes life meaningful for most people, unless company survival is at issue, and even then it may not be enough."

Every person must identify with what is trying to be accomplished in their area of work to achieve that profit, i.e., how he or she belongs with and contributes to it. And a person must get the feeling he or she makes a meaningful difference. They must get the feeling their manager is saying: "I want you, I need you. I will help you succeed."

The Tender Touch

There is no better time for a manager to drive home this feeling than during a performance review. But remember this is a sensitive moment of truth for that person, and it has to be done with care, warmth, and patience. It won't work if you are stern, forceful, and distant. Much training and practice is required for a manager to be effective. Here are some of the basic "caring" ingredients that need to be included in a performance review:

1. First, get the feelings and inputs of the person as to how the responsibilities of the job are viewed. Check to see that there is a clear and mutual understanding of the job definition. This helps both parties to focus on what the job is specifically about.

   Most importantly, though, it sets the stage for discovering what the person is specifically doing to support people reporting to him or her. This important part of the opening discussion emphasizes that accountability involves a measure of effectiveness in supporting and developing others.

2. Then you must secure the person's evaluation of his or her work experience. Find out how you can help them perform better. What can the company do to help them perform better? What are their strengths and weaknesses? Where do they think their job is taking them?

   This starts the self-evaluation process which is the essence of a good performance review. It creates a positive atmosphere and provides a basis for your comments.

3. Next, as a manager who has been heavily involved with this person, you should know the person's skills and be able to tell her the opportunities to be provided to help her grow. You must though, get individual input and agreement to these self-development plans and programs.

4. Finally, identify the person's expectations for the next accountability period. In other words, develop goals the person will commit to putting in place quarter by quarter. This becomes the basis for developing and amending a set of projects with objectives that mesh between the individual and the company.

The most effective evaluation is one where the manager does a lot of listening. Above all, the manager must communicate understanding. Often people don't really say what they mean, but rather say what they feel. Managers must be able to understand those feelings. We need to ask what the person is really feeling. As managers we need to understand the language of emotion behind the language of intellect. We must involve our intuitive natures. To do this, we must be "listening with the third ear." Only then can we be more responsive to people's developmental needs and in turn motivate them for greater productivity.

There is another crucial aspect to this management approach to understanding. As you listen you must put aside your own importance, opinions, and biases. Managers must learn to empathize with employees and share in their emotions. It is only in this way that you will be able to relate and respond to the real concerns of people.

Tough Love

During the performance review focus your constructive comments on the specific issues, projects, or behavior; never attack the employee personally. As Mary Kay Ash says, "Sandwich every bit of criticism between two layers of praise."

Caring for the developmental needs of others means not only saying the job has to be done better, but explaining that this is the way to do it. It means recognizing the strengths of a person may be better applied to a different type of job and getting that person to consider a transfer within the organization.

Never let unethical conduct go unchecked, poor performance unnoticed, or accountability unanswered. Address them directly and openly but always encourage a change of attitude in that person to do better. There will always be those who selfishly push themselves ahead at the expense of others. No matter what results they achieve in the short term, they will in the long term do harm to a company. If it is allowed to go unchecked, it either demoralizes others or becomes an acceptable way of managing among others. Animosity festers, political infighting accelerates, and productivity suffers.

There will be those who put profit before principle. They need to learn business ethics. Others will have a scorpion-like character whose nature can't be nurtured. And you will face those who, for one reason or another, cannot achieve the realistic results mutually agreed upon for the job.

Tough love means saying, as painful as it may be, "No more of this, enough time has been invested, enough patience has been applied, enough training has been expended. You are dragging yourself and others down with your poor attitude and performance." Sometimes drastic changes have to be made. It may even require dismissal.

Every situation varies with the individual and the circumstances. Only you as a manager know if your feelings are truly objective, if the evidence for your action is based on positive knowledge and proof, and if you have faithfully applied the "commandments of caring." Only you can answer if you have provided the opportunities for the person to become all she was created to be. Only you can judge if this person has failed or if you have failed this person.

If you are passing over someone for promotion or terminating an associate's employment, the amount of care you take will make all the difference. If you keep self-esteem intact, make the adjustment easier, it will go a long way in determining the individual's acceptance of the situation. Most people immediately get defensive and upset when informed of such unfavorable decisions. But it is also the nature of most people to respond to genuine concern and care and eventually admit that the action taken is understandable, sometimes even in their best interests.

Jesus Christ: Tough and Tender

Jesus managed His disciples with tough love. He affirmed and promoted the Law (the Ten Commandments) with them. He insisted that they maintain standards of conduct. Christ challenged and encouraged them to strive after obedience and excellence in carrying out His kingdom mission. He never let a poor performance go unanswered—whether it was Peter's untimely sleeping, James' and John's selfish aspiring for power, Matthew's greedy money-worshipping, or Judas' fateful betrayal. But at the same time, His management style stressed a tender touch. For all of His demands upon the disciples, He also expressed deep concern and sensitive caring for their needs. He desired to help them be all that God created them to be.

Christ's development of His disciples is a guiding example of how you can bring together tough love with a tender touch when managing and motivating people. He successfully demonstrated how to integrate softness, feeling, and generosity with tough-minded, realistic thought. From His example you learn to combine a corporate mind and servant heart and bring out the best in people. You can follow in the master manager's footsteps and help your people to reach their fullest potential—to be all that God created them to be.

School Handbooks: Some Legal Considerations

Shaughnessy, M. A. 1989. 19–20, 28–30.
Washington, D.C.: National Catholic Educational Association.

The best models for policy development are ones that either have the principal write the first draft of policy and bring it to the board or a committee for discussion and revision or have the principal serve as a member of a committee developing policy in a given area or areas. It is important that both pastor and board recognize the principal as the educational expert in the school and utilize that expertise to the fullest extent possible. Principals also communicate the policy and provide for its implementation.

One of the principal's most serious responsibilities is the supervision of teachers. It is crucial that administrators, teachers, and board members understand that the supervision and evaluation of teachers are the principal's responsibility. The principal is supposed to ensure that the best possible educational experience is given to students. In reality, supervision is quality control for the school.

Supervision of personnel is not just determining that persons are performing their tasks in a satisfactory manner; it is also job protection for the teacher. If a principal does not supervise a teacher, and allegations are later made against the teacher, the principal will have no evidence to use in support of the teacher. If a teacher is faced with a malpractice suit charging failure to teach or inadequate teaching, the principal is the person best-equipped to assist the teacher in meeting those charges. One would hope that

the principal's supervisory data show that the teacher was doing an adequate job in the classroom.

Teachers

The duties of teachers can also be classified under two headings: (1) implementing school rules and policies and (2) supervising the safety and learning of students.

It is important that teachers understand that their job is to implement rules, even if they do not personally agree with them. Lack of agreement is not a reason to fail to enforce a rule. If a teacher cannot support a given rule or policy, that teacher can use whatever channels exist to modify the rule, but until a change is made, the teacher is obligated to follow the directive. If a person cannot, in conscience, support the action required and change cannot be effected, then that person's only real choice is to leave the situation and seek other employment.

Supervision of children's safety and learning has both mental and physical implications. It is not enough for a teacher to be bodily present; the teacher must concentrate on the students. There have been a number of student accidents and injuries that could have been avoided if the teacher had been paying closer attention to the students. The concepts of mental and physical supervision will be discussed in greater detail in the last chapter.

The following chapters will deal with faculty, parent/student, and board handbooks. The last chapter will discuss some specific areas of tort liability concern.

Supervision and Evaluation of Teachers

Supervision and evaluation of teachers certainly involve matters of personnel policy. Since these activities are the most important for both faculty and administration, a separate section is devoted to their consideration.

Frequency and format

Administrators have a responsibility to supervise and evaluate teachers. But teachers have the right to know approximately how often they can expect to be supervised and what format the report of the supervisory visit will take. Therefore, "Supervision and Evaluation of Teachers" is a fourth area that should be included in faculty handbooks.

Supervision can be problematic for both the principal and the teacher. A principal who never taught any grade lower than the sixth may feel inadequate in a first grade teacher's classroom; a high school principal who taught English may feel less than competent in a physics classroom. However, administrators and all effective educators should be able to recognize good teaching within five to ten minutes after entering a classroom. If supervision is an ongoing, formative process, then both the principal and the teacher can grow together and help each other to improve the learning environment of the school. If supervision is seen as punitive—as something that is only engaged in if the principal is "out to get a teacher," then it will hardly be successful.

Evaluation is summative: an administrator sums up all the available data and makes a decision regarding contract renewal. Evaluation of teaching performance, then, should be based on more than supervisory data. A principal will seek to answer such questions as, "Does this teacher support the rules of the school?" "Does he or she look after the safety of the children?" as well as "Is he or she a good subject matter teacher?" Evaluation then is a more encompassing concept than supervision, but both should be present in a good school. The demands placed upon administrators make it too easy to defer supervision; to state that "I wish I could observe teachers' classrooms, but I just don't have time" or "Mrs. Smith probably isn't doing a very good job, but she is a nice person, and I don't have the heart to fire her. Besides, who needs the hassle anyway?" is unacceptable.

All school administrators must understand that teachers and administrators are in schools for the students; the students are not there for the teachers' employment. Surely, there is no more sacred responsibility than ensuring that students are being taught by capable, competent, caring professionals and that all teachers are encouraged and given the means to become the best professionals they can be.

Ultimately, it is the principal who is responsible for the supervision and evaluation of teachers even if someone else,

such as the pastor, signs the contract—because the principal is the chief executive officer of the school. Supervision and evaluation enable a principal to make wise decisions about contract renewal. It is not just for a principal to decide not to renew a teacher's contract if the principal has never observed the teacher at work. Unfortunately, most educators can recall one or more situations in which a person lost a teaching position because he or she couldn't keep order or was considered incompetent, even though the person's principal had never been in the classroom. Written observations that have been shared with the teachers involved provide some of the best data available in making employment decisions. A principal can use the data to ask questions at the end of the year. For example, "We have discussed some of the difficulties you have had with keeping the other children on task while you are working with the reading groups. I know that you have tried thus and such a strategy, and when I last visited your classroom, it seemed to be working fairly well. Have you tried any other strategies or had any other thoughts about how to better the learning environment for the students when your attention necessarily can't be on the total group?"

The handbook should state the school policy on supervision of teachers. Who is responsible for supervising teachers/visiting classrooms? Is it the principal's sole responsibility, or are other persons, such as vice-principals, department heads, or level coordinators, involved? How often will the teacher be supervised? What format will be used?

Scheduled vs. unscheduled visits

Will the supervisor's visits be scheduled or unscheduled? If the visits are normally scheduled (for example, twice a semester or three times a year), does the principal/other administrator reserve the right to observe classes at unscheduled times?

The teacher also has a right to know how he or she will be evaluated. How will the supervisory visits be incorporated into the end-of-the-year evaluation? Who will see this evaluation? Will the evaluation become part of the teacher's permanent file? Does the teacher have an opportunity to respond in writing to the evaluation? Will the teacher's response become part of the evaluation record? Considering these questions and developing policies to answer them will help an administrator operate on fairly solid legal ground.

Although most educators would agree that supervision is a formative experience and evaluation is a summative one, the distinction becomes blurred in many Catholic schools where the principal serves as both supervisor and evaluator. These dual responsibilities can present very real problems. A teacher may be reluctant to discuss problems with a principal if he or she thinks that information could be used against him or her in an evaluation. Catholic school principals who wear both hats need to be especially knowledgeable of human relations and of sound legal practice.

Preparation • Presentation • Follow-up: Keys to Constructive Criticism

Truitt, M. R. 1991. In *The supervisor's handbook*, 46–49. Shawnee Mission, Kans.: National Press.

Preparation for Constructive Criticism

Reprimanding a person works best when you give it some forethought. The next time you must administer some criticism, take these steps:

◆ **Set an appropriate time and place.** Talk with the person as soon as possible after the event, but do so in private. Don't criticize someone in front of people—especially those people whose opinion that person values. The reaction you get will be for the onlookers' benefit and will distort your interaction.

◆ **Think through your opening comments in advance.** If possible, rehearse your initial statements aloud with someone you trust—perhaps a friend, your spouse, or a fellow supervisor. If irritation has built up in your mind, you may find your initial comments loaded with anger. Venting some feelings can defuse your hostility.

◆ **Think about the other person's view of the situation.** Ask your rehearsal partner to imagine both how the other person probably saw the incident and how that person might hear your criticism. Remember, people usually do what they think is best, so the behavior you are criticizing somehow made sense to that person at the time.

Presenting the Criticism

When reprimanding someone:

◆ **Get to the point immediately.** Don't spend more than a minute or two in small talk—aimless chatter leaves the other person guessing and he or she will probably misinterpret the purpose of the meeting. Instead, first identify the incident you are addressing, next describe how you saw it, then explain why you think the individual's behavior was not what it should have been.

◆ **Ask whether the other person understands** the points you've made so far. Then, get his or her perspective. Ask for the reasoning behind the actions. (Be prepared to learn from that—you may have misinterpreted something.)

◆ **Focus on the future.** What's happened is "water under the bridge." Concentrate on what can be learned from this incident. Emphasize that your concern is not to scold or punish, but to make the organization work more effectively in the future. Be specific about what behavior you would prefer from that individual the next time a similar situation arises and explain why you believe that that alternative would yield a better

outcome. Check whether the other person understands and agrees to do what you are proposing. Genuine agreement is better than forced compliance.

Following Up On Criticism

No matter how considerate you attempt to be, a confrontation is still experienced as a put down unless you follow it up properly.

◆ **Be positive about the individual** even though you are being negative about that person's specific behavior. Mention the things he or she does that you value and appreciate. Position yourself on the person's side—say that above all you want things to work out well for the individual in your organization and you know they can.

◆ **Emphasize that, for you, the past is past and you are expecting good things to occur in the future.** If appropriate, set a meeting for a time after a few actions of the kind you criticized are likely to happen again. When you meet, you can assess how things are going. This follow-up meeting will give you a chance to check on progress, nip any new problems in the bud, and catch the person doing things right!

Concerning Performance Appraisals

William Scherkenbach, Ford Motor Company's Director of Statistical Methods, points out a serious drawback in most performance appraisal systems. He maintains that they reduce initiative and risk-taking. They encourage what he calls the Alexiev Mentality.

You may recall that Vassily Alexiev was a Russian super heavyweight weightlifter. He was paid a sum of money for each world record he broke. Being a disciplined athlete, he broke a lot of world records. But, being a smart person too, he broke them only a few grams at a time.

The Alexiev Mentality is encouraged by performance appraisal systems that are based on whether or not employees achieve their objectives. Because of the penalty for failing to make objectives and because objectives typically are negotiated, employees end up with goals that don't have much "stretch" or are relatively easy to achieve.

Another factor contributing to the Alexiev Mentality is fear of the unknown. A person may know of ways to achieve an 8% savings in one year. However, he is required by his objectives to attain only a 5% savings each year. What happens by the end of the year? He shows a 5% savings. He banks the additional 3% for the next year so that the objective for that year can be met.

What's the alternative? Scherkenbach believes it is appraising people on broader criteria than specific individual objectives. He recommends evaluating employees on all of their contributions "to the continuous improvement of the company."

How to Conduct Performance Appraisals

On the surface it would seem that evaluating employee performance ought to be fairly easy. After all, performance appraisals should be tied directly to job success. The hang-up comes in creating realistic and appropriate measures for determining job success.

There are a number of pitfalls you'll want to avoid as you evaluate employee performance:

◆ Avoid the "halo" effect where a high rating on a favored trait adds unmerited points in other areas.

◆ Be sure to rate the worker only for performance on the current job. Don't let work on a previous job color your evaluation either positively or negatively.

◆ Rate the employee through the entire period covered by the evaluation. Don't let the performance of the last two weeks unduly influence you. Don't let a months-old incident weigh too heavily, either.

◆ Avoid the tendency to give an "average" rating on each point. Part of the objective for performance appraisals is to point out "soft spots" for further development. Across-the-board average marks hide these.

◆ Try to hold separate sessions for performance appraisal and salary review. The appraisal interview should focus on performance considerations only.

Questions the supervisor should answer before the interview:

1. What specific points can you praise the employee for?
2. What are the specific areas in which you want the employee to improve?
3. Can you support your evaluation of the employee's performance with hard facts?
4. What specific improvement(s) do you want to see?
5. What kind of help or training can you offer?
6. What kind of follow-up do you have planned?

The goals of the performance appraisal interview:

1. To provide the worker with a precise understanding of how the supervisor feels the worker is performing.
2. To provide the worker with a clear understanding about what performance is expected on the job.
3. To establish a mutually agreed-upon program of performance improvement.
4. To develop a stronger working relationship between the supervisor and the worker.

Institutional Management

The Catholic School Principal's Role: Church Governance and Structures

Lourdes Sheehan, RSM

Introduction

Because Catholic schools are an integral part of the Church's mission, it is essential for the principal to understand how the school relates to the parish(es), diocese, and/or religious congregation that sponsor it. Each of the four types of Catholic schools—parish, interparish (also called regional or consolidated), diocesan, and private—has differing funding sources and governance structures within which it operates. There is no one set of policies, much less practices, that operates in all Catholic schools. In spite of its image as a hierarchical organization with universally enforced norms, the Church's policies and practices of educational governance and accountability are neither uniformly defined nor universally practiced in Catholic schools.

There is a great deal of local autonomy at both the diocesan and parish levels so that what really happens in a school depends on local personalities, policies, and politics. The information and suggestions which follow are based on commonly understood principles and church law. It is essential for the principal to be well-informed about the diocese's and/or religious community's educational policies and to apply these general comments to her/his specific situation.

Definitions

A *parish school* is defined as an institution (elementary or secondary) that is associated with only one parish. This parish community provides spiritual, communal, and financial support (sometimes called subsidy).

Those schools that serve and are supported by more than one parish are called *interparish, regional*, or *consolidated* schools. The terms "interparish" and "regional" are often used interchangeably, but use of the term "consolidated" is usually reserved to describe the merger of two or more existing schools that may be located at more than one site. In practice, however, the responsibilities of the principal are the same. Usually the financial support flows directly from the parishes to the school, and all parishes share responsibility for spiritual and communal support.

A *diocesan school* is one that is not identified with any one parish or group of parishes and ordinarily the subsidy goes directly from the diocese to the school. Principals of diocesan schools need to ensure spiritual and communal support from those parishes that send students to the school.

Traditionally, *private schools* are those that are owned, operated, and sponsored by a religious congregation that is responsible for the school's support. Recently, some religious congregations have established boards of trustees and charged them with the responsibility for operating the schools. In these instances, usually the congregation maintains a sponsorship relationship with the institution. Some private schools have been started by lay boards of trustees which must work out the school's formal relationship with the diocesan bishop in order to call the school Catholic.

Parish schools

Approximately 74 percent of the Catholic elementary (6,052) and secondary (141) schools in the

United States are operated as a single parish school (Brigham 1993). Ultimately, each is the responsibility of the pastor of the parish who according to church law is the canonical administrator of the entire parish including the school. Ordinarily, the pastor is assisted by the active participation of parishioners on a finance council (*Code of Canon Law* Book V, Title II), pastoral council, and school board/committee. These collegial bodies are constituted as consultative to the pastor.

In practice, it is the school principal who functions as the actual administrator of the school. The principal is the parish staff member who works most closely with the school board/committee and/or other school parent groups. The key to the effective operation of the school and ultimately the parish is a compatible working relationship between the pastor and principal marked by frequent communication and mutual respect and trust.

Hiring Practices

When the majority of principals were appointed by the religious congregations, hiring was not the issue it is today. The question of who hires is basic to the understanding of accountability. The parish is obligated to follow diocesan policy in this and all other education matters. However, because of differing practices and the emerging role of boards, it is necessary for the principal to understand hiring practices as well as roles and relationships among parish leaders.

Recognizing that the pastor has the final word and is, as a matter of fact, the "employer" of the principal, Father John Gilbert (1983), an experienced educator and pastor, believes that the pastor should make it an absolute practice that no principal is hired without the involvement and consent of both the board and the staff with whom the principal works. There are many ways to ensure this involvement. The most common is to establish a search/interview committee whose members include those individuals and groups whose relationship with the principal affects the running of the school.

While the pastor should be in close communication with this committee, it does not seem essential that he attend each and every meeting. It would be unfortunate, however, if he were never involved and simply received the final recommendations from the committee without the benefit of prior

discussion. Somewhere between no involvement and running the committee there is a middle ground which will ensure agreement on the job description or role of the principal and on the specific needs of the parish and school.

Ordinarily, the principal is responsible for hiring faculty and staff. Some policies require that the diocese approve applicants for teaching positions prior to their being hired. Others state that the pastor, and sometimes the diocese, must approve all contracts before they are binding.

Evaluation Practices

Standard personnel practice recognizes that the person who hires is the one ultimately responsible for evaluation and continuation of the contract. The principal will want to ensure regular discussions with the pastor to provide a good basis for the more formal evaluation carried out at least every three years. This process usually involves those other groups with which the principal relates. Most dioceses have well-established processes and procedures for evaluation and offer the services of the education staff to assist both the principal and pastor. In those infrequent instances where a dispute arises over the principal's contract, both parties have the opportunity to appeal to the diocesan arbitration and conciliation process.

The principal is primarily responsible for regular written evaluations of faculty and staff according to diocesan policies and procedures.

Accountability Issues

The relationship of the parish school board and the principal is influenced by the way other consultative bodies are established and function in the parish. If the parish school board/committee has the understanding that it is "policy-making" and has actually hired the principal, then in a very real sense the principal is the "employee" of the board. In the more common practice, the board has been consulted in the hiring process and the pastor actually signs the contract. In any case the question of all relationships needs clarification. Regardless of the accountability structure, honest and collaborative discussion among the principal, board, and pastor is always the ideal when considering the welfare of the school.

In a very real sense, the principal is accountable to the parents who have entrusted their children to the faculty and staff of the school. While this relationship cannot, strictly speaking, be put under the category of governance, it is very real and demands that the principal possess a commitment to availability and communication with all parents. All of the effectiveness research, especially that reported in the *Effective Catholic School Study* (Bryk et al. 1984), reports that one of the most significant indicators of an effective school is that faculty, parents, and students share a common vision and commitment to the mission of the school. There is no way in which this important factor can be achieved without time and effort being spent on communication.

Interparish schools

Because the number of interparish schools, including regional and consolidated ones, is growing, the principal of such a school needs to pay special attention to questions of governance and accountability. At the present time they constitute 10 percent (855) of all Catholic schools; 9.7 percent, or 703, are elementary and 12 percent, or 152, are secondary (Brigham 1993). The challenges facing the principal of this type of school are unique.

Governance and Management

In the other three types of schools, the lines of accountability within which the principal functions are clear: in a parish school, the principal is directly accountable to the pastor; in a private school, to the major superior of the religious congregation or board of trustees; and in a diocesan school, to the bishop through the superintendent. However, because an interparish school serves equally a number of parishes, its principal is directly accountable to more than one pastor. When a school board is involved, the issue of accountability becomes more complicated.

Dioceses are establishing new types of governance structures to address these schools. Some call for the bishop to appoint, from among the supporting pastors, one who will serve as the "school pastor." In this instance, the principal relates to this pastor in a manner similar to that of a parish school principal. Other dioceses are rethinking the role of the board in an interparish school and giving it delegated authority to operate the school within diocesan guidelines. Often all of the pastors and representatives of supporting parishes are members of the board. In this latter case, the relationship of the principal and such a board differs from that of the parish school principal and board. Principals of such schools will need to meet with diocesan education staff to clarify and understand the governance structure.

Other Issues

There are two issues important to the principal which are common to all Catholic schools.

Relationship of school to diocese

The diocesan superintendent of schools has the responsibility to see that diocesan educational policies are implemented in each school. The superintendent and staff usually schedule regular meetings with principals to discuss diocesan policies and procedures and are available to visit individual schools and provide direct assistance to the principal.

New principals, in particular, should obtain and study the diocesan education manual which will provide specific information about such matters as curriculum, personnel policies, lines of accountability, and various policies which affect students, health and safety regulations, and state and federal regulations.

Local, state, and federal education programs

The individual principal may have limited contact with the local, state, and federal education agencies, but has the responsibility, nevertheless, to know applicable statutes and regulations which affect non-governmental schools (also referred to as private schools). The Department of Education of the United States Catholic Conference regularly forwards information regarding federal issues, and state Catholic conferences send material from the state to the superintendent, who in turn gives these and appropriate local information to the principals.

Diocesan schools

Diocesan schools (581) comprise 35.5 percent, or 444, of the secondary and 2 percent, or 137, of the elementary Catholic schools in this country

(Brigham 1993). A principal of a diocesan school is directly accountable to the diocese. In practice, this usually means that the responsibility is to the bishop through the superintendent of schools and some type of board structure at either the school or diocesan level.

Governance and Management

Since the practice of designating elementary schools as diocesan seems to be relatively new, there is no traditional pattern to cite. However, at the secondary level the past practice in many dioceses was to have a diocesan priest serve as the principal of the school. In those instances where a woman religious or lay person was appointed principal, the usual practice was for the bishop to appoint a priest as director, coordinator, or school pastor. The intent of such a practice was to establish clear lines of accountability between the school and diocese. In many dioceses, this is no longer the practice with the result that the issue of the principal's accountability is not as clear.

Finances

Most diocesan secondary school principals relate to some type of board. In some instances, the diocesan school board is responsible to the bishop for recommending policies, especially financial ones. While individual principals are not usually members of such a board, they are often invited to make presentations and may be called in as consultants. The diocesan superintendent of schools is the educational staff person to whom the board relates. Some diocesan principals establish local advisory boards with whom they consult on local matters. More recently, such boards are assuming responsibilities in the area of development, including public relations and marketing.

Private schools

While much of what has already been noted about principals of parish schools also applies to private schools, it is important to acknowledge that those who serve as administrators of private schools have unique relationships to the religious congregations and/or boards of trustees responsible for the schools.

Schools operated by religious congregations are the largest percentage of Catholic secondary schools at 35.5 percent, or 512. At the elementary level, private schools are the smallest group at 3.5 percent, or 282 (Brigham 1993). Traditionally, Catholic private schools (794 total) have enjoyed the clearest lines of authority and accountability. For years, the principal was a member of the religious congregation and was appointed by the superior to serve a specific term. In practice, the principal enjoyed almost total autonomy in the daily administration of the school and the evaluation of personnel. When that practice changes, all parties need clarity and understanding regarding roles and relationships.

Governance and Management

As more religious congregations establish boards that include non-congregational members, the issues of governance and management need clarification. More often than not, the key point of discussion is the hiring of the principal and, therefore, the relation of that person to the religious congregation and to the board. When the administrator is a member of the congregation, that issue is not as complicated as it is when a lay person assumes that position. As fewer religious assume such roles, a person considering working as principal in a private school needs to understand existing relationships and expectations of both the congregation and board. Often the congregation will appoint one of its members to work with the lay principal and board during such a transition.

Finances

Most private schools operate without significant financial support from either the diocese or the religious congregation. The board usually has the responsibility for operating the school with a balanced budget. The principal is charged with operating the school within that approved amount.

Principals of private schools should be aware that the relationship between some congregations and their board are in the development stage. Therefore there may be some unresolved issues. An example of such an issue is who has responsibility for capital improvements and repairs to the school facilities. One approach may be for the congregation to recognize its role as "landlord" and function in this manner with regard to major repairs and renovations. This model assumes that the board of trustees will function as a "tenant" and may allocate a percentage of the operating budget as either rent or contingency for upkeep. Since the principal will be ultimately responsible for the administration of the budget, it is important that he or she has a solid understanding of all related issues.

Relationship with the Diocese

Traditionally, private schools have operated in dioceses as a significant part of the congregation's mission. The bishop has ordinarily related to the school through the major superior of the congregation. Most private schools cooperate with the diocesan schools office and are subject to follow diocesan policies in the areas of religious education. This recognizes the authority of the bishop as the chief catechist.

When private schools are not directly related with a religious congregation, both the principal and board need to be clear about how the formal relationship with the bishop is both established and maintained.

Conclusion and reflection

In order to function effectively, the local Catholic school principal needs to know how the Catholic Church is organized.

The general descriptions of how the four major types of schools are organized and function will help potential and new principals understand terminology and, perhaps, ask the right questions.

The principal should remember what was said earlier in this article about what really influences the governance and accountability of Catholic schools—personalities, politics, and policies present at the local level. This is the real situation; however, this comment need not be construed in a negative manner. It remains true that local autonomy is one of the best-kept secrets in Catholic schools, and, I believe, contributes to the school's effectiveness. The effective principal will observe the local scene and determine in consultation with a mentor and the diocesan education staff how to function most effectively.

The challenges facing the Catholic school principal in the areas of governance and structure should be seen as neither overwhelming nor insurmountable. The most effective principal will understand and be committed to the type of school she/he is called to lead; will clarify roles and relations among principal, pastor, and board; and will analyze the personalities, politics, and policies of the local situation.

Reflection Questions

1. Define the types of Catholic schools you might some day administer.

2. Develop a chart listing the different types of schools. For *each* type of school—parish, inter-parish, diocesan, private—specify:

   ■ To whom is the principal directly accountable?

   ■ What type of school board/committee would be part of this type of school's governance? What would be the board's responsibilities?

   ■ What responsibilities would the principal assume for school finances?

   ■ What would be the process for evaluating the principal's performance? Who would participate? How often?

■ What would be the responsibilities of the pastor(s), diocese, and religious congregation for the school?

■ What would be the major administrative and governance challenges to the principal?

3. As a principal what is your relationship with the diocese? What services are provided to you?

4. What responsibility and process would the principal use to hire teachers and staff?

Resources

Brigham, F. H. 1993. *United States Catholic elementary and secondary schools 1992–93*. Washington, D.C.: National Catholic Educational Association.

Bryk, A. S., P. B. Holland, V. E. Lee, and R. A. Carriedo. 1984. *Effective Catholic schools: An exploration*. Washington, D.C.: National Catholic Educational Association.

Canon Law Society of America. 1983. *Code of canon law: Latin-English edition*. Washington, D.C.: Canon Law Society of America.

Gilbert, J. 1983. *Pastor as shepherd of the school community*. Washington, D.C.: National Catholic Educational Association.

O'Brien, J. S., ed. 1987. *A primer on educational governance in the Catholic Church*. CACE/NABE Governance Task Force. Washington, D.C.: National Catholic Educational Association.

Sheehan, L. 1990. *Building better boards*. Washington, D.C.: National Catholic Educational Association.

Area of Responsibility: Institutional Management

Kay Alewine and Maria Ciriello, OP, Ph.D.

Catholic schools were among the first institutions founded by Catholics in the new world. From colonial times to the present, the Catholic school system in the United States has no comparable model in the world. The foundation of these institutions stands as a glorious achievement, a monument to the hard work, support, and dedication of countless men and women. The tradition of Catholic schools is a result of "both an active engagement with the world and, at times, strong reaction to it" (Bryk 1993, p. 15).

Bryk (1993) divides the historical development of Catholic schools into three periods. The first period, from the early 1700s through 1830, coincides with the establishment of the Catholic Church in the new nation and parallels similar educational efforts of Protestant groups. "The provision of education was an informal matter" (p. 18). The second period spans from 1830 to 1960, during which Catholic schools followed the waves of immigrants and developed into a formal system separate from the tax-supported system of public schools. In the present period, since 1960, Catholic schools have responded to increasingly complex social and economic factors within both the Church and American social life.

Historically, the Catholic school in the United States has been more a systematic way of schooling than a tightly knit school system. As a result, schools were established and continue to be sponsored in several ways. Before 1960 Catholic schools were generally sponsored by a parish, a religious congregation, or the diocese. Since 1960, other types of Catholic schools have evolved. Interparish and regional schools may be sponsored by two or more parishes or directly by the diocese. Other schools, established by independent lay boards, have sought affiliation with the Catholic Church.

Presently three out of four Catholic elementary schools in the country are associated with and sponsored by an individual parish. About a third of Catholic secondary schools are sponsored by and operated under the auspices of religious communities. These are often called "private" schools because their governance is distinct from that of the local diocese. Another third of secondary schools are sponsored by dioceses and thus called "diocesan" schools. About one in ten Catholic schools is an elementary or secondary interparochial regional or independent Catholic (board-operated) private school (Brigham 1993).

Regardless of the sponsorship of a school, each is an institution that interacts with other institutions and agencies as it goes about the business of providing educational experiences within an integral religious perspective. Institutional management involves knowledge and understanding of relationships within the school and between the school and other groups. Providing a safe environment within the school promotes the effectiveness of the school program. Understanding the intricacies of the school governance structure, school law, and canon law—along with recognizing the importance of the relationship of the school to the local Catholic school board, the diocesan office, the religious congregation, and the local public school districts—enhances the purposes and work of the school. Being alert to the opportunities afforded by participation in federally funded education programs might help return to parents a portion of their tax dollars. The use of technology in school administration and the integration of technology into the curriculum demonstrate the potential to bring the school into the twenty-first century.

Directional statements and beliefs adopted by the participants of the National Congress: Catholic Schools for the 21st Century (*Executive Summary*, Guerra, Haney, and Kealey 1992) reinforce the concept of the school as an institution:

- "Catholic schools are an integral part of education in the United States and a valuable asset to the nation" (p. 21).

- "Effective Catholic school governance requires the preparation, empowerment and collaboration of the community which it serves" (p. 25).

- "Governance with the full participation of the laity is the key to the future of Catholic Schools" (p. 25).

The principal as institutional manager in a Catholic school is called to the following expectations:

I1. To provide an orderly school *environment* and promote *student self-discipline*

I2. To understand Catholic school *governance structures* and work effectively with *school boards*

I3. To recognize the importance of the *relationship* between the school and the *diocesan office*

I4. To recognize the importance of the *relationship* between the school and *religious congregation(s)*

I5. To know *civil and canon law* as it applies to *Catholic schools*

I6. To understand *state requirements* and *government-funded programs*

I7. To understand the usefulness of *current technologies*

The following pages address each expectation concerning institutional management separately. In an introduction, a rationale is presented to clarify the importance of the expectation as a basic competency for the Catholic school administrator. Learning activities, including readings and interactions with experienced professionals, are prescribed. To foster optimum growth and insight, the learner is encouraged to seek a mentor and to make every effort to interact with personnel actively involved in the day-to-day functioning of Catholic educational institutions. A written record (journal) of all related readings and activities is integrated to enhance personal development and to provide a systematic chronicle of professional experiences. Finally, outcome activities are listed to give the learner opportunities to demonstrate mastery of the specific competency.

Role: Principal as Managerial Leader

Area: Institutional Management

Competency: I1
Environment and Student Self-Discipline

One of the assumptions of the effective school research study (Purkey and Smith 1985) is that "the school is responsible for providing the overall environment in which teaching and learning occur" (p. 355). A safe, orderly environment and student self-discipline are two aspects of school culture that contribute to an effective school. Purkey and Smith (1985) discuss the components of school culture and emphasize its importance:

> The most persuasive research suggests that student academic performance is strongly affected by school culture. This culture is composed of values, norms, and roles existing within institutionally distinct structures of governance, communication, educational practices, and policies. . . . Successful schools are found to have cultures that produce a climate or "ethos" conducive to teaching and learning. . . (p. 357).

The Catholic school's educational mission of message, community, and service (*To Teach as Jesus Did* 1973) along with worship mandates that the school strive conscientiously to develop a school culture characterized as "communal school organization." According to Bryk and Driscoll (1988), a communal school organization has three core elements:

- a system of values that is shared and commonly understood among the members of the school;

- a common agenda of activities that signifies membership in the school;

- a distinctive pattern of social relationships that embody an ethic of caring (Convey 1992, p. 95).

The shared values and social relationships that demonstrate an ethic of mutual caring give the Catholic school principal a solid foundation on which to build an effective philosophy of discipline, including a constructive code of conduct.

As part of the implementation of this philosophy, the principal will be scrupulous in documentation of the school code of conduct and discipline policy in school handbooks. Shaughnessy (1989) stresses that the development and writing of the school handbooks is an important aspect of school management. Handbooks for teachers, students, and parents are important references, containing policies and procedures for which school community members are responsible.

To support and give evidence of professional growth in understanding what is entailed in providing an orderly school environment and promoting student self-discipline, the learner will engage in the listed activities under the direction of the diocese (Model I) or through a self-directed program and/or with the guidance of a mentor (Model II).

The primary means of keeping a consistent record of activities is to keep an ongoing JOURNAL which would contain

1) a *Dated Log* section recording when activities were undertaken and completed,

2) a *Reading/Response* section in which notes from suggested readings and the response reactions are systematically organized, and

3) an *Experience(Activity)/Reflection* section in which one records ideas and insights gained through interacting with people or seeking out additional information in the course of completing the activities.

Learning Activities: I1
Environment and Student Self-Discipline

1. Read the following and respond with reactions in a journal.* Ideally, you should discuss these readings and your reactions with a mentor. These integral readings are reprinted for your convenience on pages 154–81.

Doyle, R., N. Kinate, A. Langan, and M. Swanson. 1991. Evaluation of the school's Catholicity. In *Capital wisdom: Papers from the Principals Academy 1991*, 1–6. Washington, D.C.: National Catholic Educational Association.

Drahmann, T., and A. Stenger. 1989. *The Catholic school principal: An outline for action.* Rev. ed. Washington, D.C.: National Catholic Educational Association, 25–26.

Governal, M. A. 1986. Effective principaling in the Catholic school. In *The Catholic school administrator—A book of readings*, ed. E. M. Bushman and G. J. Sparks, 161–64. Portland, Ore.: Catholic Leadership Company.

Saphier, J., and R. Gower. 1997. Classroom climate: Community and mutual support, risk taking and confidence, influence. In *The Skillful Teacher: Building Your Teaching Skills*, 357–394. 5th ed. Carlisle, Massachusetts: Research for Better Teaching, Inc.

Shaughnessy, M. A. 1989. *School handbooks: Some legal considerations.* Washington, D.C.: National Catholic Educational Association, 24–27, 62–68.

Also, read the following section from the *Catechism*.

Libreria Editrice Vaticana. 1994. *Catechism of the Catholic Church.* Washington, D.C.: United States Catholic Conference.

No. 2030: The Church is the vehicle through which the Christian fulfills his/her vocation. It is where one receives the word of God containing the teachings of Christ.

* In your journal, note insights concerning the importance of providing an orderly school environment and promoting student self-discipline. What ideas concerning discipline do you want to incorporate into your philosophy? What strategies appear to be the most effective in establishing and maintaining an orderly school environment? What responsibilities do students and staff members have in maintaining an orderly environment? What are some of the legal issues that concern you? What ramifications do legal concerns have for handbook policy? What is the role of the school board in developing handbook policy? What is the role of the school board in discipline and the orderly environment of the school? What questions do you have regarding this competency?

2. Visit one or two Catholic schools to learn about measures taken by the administration to create a safe and orderly environment that promotes student self-discipline.
    a. What security and safety measures are taken on school grounds and within the building while school is in session? Ask whether any civil laws or diocesan policies apply to the precautions taken.
    b. What directives are given to visitors to the school?
    c. What procedures are in place for dropping off and picking up students?
    d. What procedures are followed when someone other than a parent calls for a student?
    e. How and to what extent do the principal, teachers, and other staff members work together to foster a caring environment that motivates the students to be responsible for their actions, do their best, and be concerned about the rights of others?
    f. What is the school's philosophy regarding student discipline? How are discipline policies decided on? What are the roles of parents and students in this process?
    g. How are security procedures and discipline policies communicated to the staff, students, and parents?
    h. What measures are in place to allow for due process?
    i. What inservice training informs staff and school board members about current legal issues regarding security and discipline in Catholic schools?

3. Obtain copies of the Catholic school handbooks for teachers and staff, students, and parents. Look for the sections dealing with safety, security, and discipline.
    a. Are policies clearly explained?
    b. Are expectations clearly spelled out?
    c. Is there a description of desired behaviors, as well as undesirable behaviors?
    d. How are the consequences of behavior listed?
    e. What are the procedures for reward and punishment?
    f. To what extent are parents encouraged to be involved in the management of students' behaviors?

How do you assess the tone of this material (authoritarian, collaborative, punitive, motivational, coercive, positive, negative)? Is the tone consistent with the mission and philosophy of Catholic education? What evidence do you see that the current discipline program promotes student self-discipline? Evaluate the thoroughness of the material. What assumptions are made? What comments or suggestions would you offer?

4. Seek out one or more teachers, students, parents, or school board members who have current, personal familiarity with Catholic school security measures and discipline codes.
   a. How extensive is each person's personal knowledge of these aspects of the school?
   b. What part, if any, does each have in formulating policies or procedures pertaining to security and discipline in the school?
   c. What responsibility has each had in implementing the directives?
   d. How does each person assess the reasonableness and fairness of the policies and procedures?
   e. What suggestions for change or improvement might these people have? What rationale do they give for their opinions?

What conclusions can you draw from the interviews? How do the accounts of those interviewed mesh with the information you received from the school administration and handbooks? What insights have you gleaned? What are your concerns? What recommendations would you make?

As a result of study, reflection, and interaction with knowledgeable individuals, the learner will be able to complete the following activities. The quality of response to these activities should give some indication of the level of expertise the learner is able to bring to the situation.

Outcome Activities: II
Environment and Student Self-Discipline

1. Develop a comprehensive checklist to evaluate security measures employed by a school. What influence, if any, would the age of the students attending the school have on the measures?

2. Develop a list of standards to be used to evaluate a school discipline code consistent with the goals and objectives of a Catholic school.

3. Design a hearing process that would model for schools how to ensure a student's rights in a serious matter.

4. *Elementary School Scenario*

You have just been hired as principal of a Catholic elementary school. At an early August meeting attended by the pastor and the chair of the school board, you sign your contract. The board member comments that she hopes you "do something" immediately about classroom discipline. She says that when she visited the school last year, the classrooms frequently seemed noisy and unruly. The pastor chimes in, "While you're at it, see what you can do to make sure the children pay better attention at the liturgies."
   a. What is your assessment of the real issues alluded to here? What are the assumptions of each person about you, the school, and the children?
   b. Outline the steps you will take to respond to the expectations of the pastor and the board member.
   c. How you will gather further information? Whom will you involve? What eventual actions will you take?
   d. By what standards will you evaluate the proposed plan of action? the consequences of the plan?

5. *Secondary School Scenario*

You are in your first year as principal of a Catholic high school of 700 students. You have an assistant principal in charge of discipline who has been at the school for five years.

One February morning, you receive a call from the manager of a fast food restaurant in the neighborhood. He complains that the previous evening four boys, two of whom were wearing the school's athletic jacket, were involved in an incident at the establishment. The manager says the boys' behavior was loud, boisterous, and rude. They pushed in front of waiting customers. When the manager intervened, one of the boys responded sarcastically with vulgar language that included a racial epithet. The boys left immediately, continuing to make vulgar remarks as they exited.

The manager followed them outside, where he noticed several beer cans close to where the boys' car was parked. The manager mentions that one of the jackets had the number 75 on it. You realize that the second-highest scorer of your number 3-ranked basketball team is implicated.

a. Specify the issues involved and the publics to be considered in this situation.
b. What are the ramifications for the school, the basketball team, the students involved, and the student body in general? Who else is affected by this incident?
c. Outline the steps you will take to respond to this situation.
d. What information will you gather, how will you gather it, and whom will you involve?
e. Specify the process you will use to decide on a course of action to resolve this problem.
f. By what standards will you evaluate the proposed plan of action? the consequences of the plan?

Role: Principal as Managerial Leader

Area: Institutional Management

Competency: I2
Governance Structures and School Boards

At its best, the board serves as a "lifeline" or "pulse," facilitating communication to and from the principal, the family, and the parish, as well as the broader community, and facilitating effective school management. The board brings together committed people, including lay, religious, and clergy, to participate in the educational ministry of the Church.

The functions of the board include planning, policy formation and enactment, financial management, selection and appointment of the principal, public relations, marketing, and evaluation. The support of an effective board enables the principal to be a more focused educational leader. The board also provides an opportunity for parents to become more active in their children's education (Sheehan 1990).

Sometimes, because of role confusion, Catholic school boards may be perceived by Catholic school principals, staff members, and parents as more of a hindrance than an asset to the productive functioning of the school. However, when formed thoughtfully and operated within the guidelines established by the National Catholic Educational Association (NCEA) and within the context of diocesan governance policies, the school board can be one of the most effective vehicles of the school's mission. The keys to effectiveness are a board that thoroughly understands its role and a principal who forges a partnership that cultivates and furthers the well-being of the school. The principal has the responsibility of educating board members about their role and responsibilities. In addition, the principal provides the board with relevant school information to expedite decisions and enhance its performance.

Sheehan (1990) notes that boards and commissions have been an integral part of Catholic education for many years. Approximately 68 percent of U.S. Catholic schools have some form of educational governance structure.

Because our society is increasingly litigious, boards and principals are aware of the need to be completely professional and alert to issues that affect Catholic schools: due process, tort liability, the duties and rights of students and employees, and the duties and responsibilities of board members (Shaughnessy 1988).

By taking the time to develop the gifts and aptitudes of the board, the Catholic school principal will reap long-lasting blessings, as the potential of dedicated people will be harnessed to work for the welfare of the school.

To support and give evidence of professional growth in demonstrating a knowledge of Catholic school governance structures and the skills necessary to work effectively with school boards, the learner will engage in the listed activities under the direction of the diocese (Model I) or through a self-directed program and/or with the guidance of a mentor (Model II).

The primary means of keeping a consistent record of activities is to keep an ongoing JOURNAL which would contain

1) a *Dated Log* section recording when activities were undertaken and completed,

2) a *Reading/Response* section in which notes from suggested readings and the response reactions are systematically organized, and

3) an *Experience(Activity)/Reflection* section in which one records ideas and insights gained through interacting with people or seeking out additional information in the course of completing the activities.

Learning Activities: I2
Governance Structures and School Boards

1. Read the following and respond with reactions in a journal.* Ideally, you should discuss these readings and your reactions with a mentor. These integral readings are reprinted for your convenience on pages 182–99.

Bailey, R., U. Butler, and M. Kearney. 1991. Development of the Catholic school board. In *Capital wisdom: Papers from the Principals Academy 1991*, 39–44. Washington, D.C.: National Catholic Educational Association.

National Conference of Catholic Bishops. 1979. *Sharing the light of faith: National catechetical directory for Catholics of the United States*. Washington, D.C.: United States Catholic Conference, Chapter X.

Shaughnessy, M. A. 1991. *A primer on school law: A guide for board members in Catholic schools*. Washington, D.C.: National Catholic Educational Association, 29–34.

Sheehan, L. 1990. What is a Catholic school board? In *Building better boards: A handbook for board members in Catholic education*, 1–5. Washington, D.C.: National Catholic Educational Association.[1]

Sparks, G. J. 1986. Preparing a presentation for the board of education. In *The Catholic school administrator—A book of readings*, ed. E. M. Bushman and G. J. Sparks, 293–95. Portland, Ore.: Catholic School Leadership Company.

* In your journal, note insights concerning Catholic school governance structures and how principals work effectively with school boards. What are the strengths of the principal-board relationship? How does a pastor impact a school board? How are the operations of the board affected when leadership from the principal or pastor is lacking? What differences are there when the school is sponsored by a religious community rather than the parish or the diocese? What questions do you have regarding board formation and operations?

2. Contact the Office of Catholic Schools to ascertain what the diocesan guidelines for school boards and educational commissions are and which schools in the diocese have them. If there are none, try to interview the superintendent to learn the governance structure of the schools of the diocese.

   a. Who makes decisions for a school?

   b. Are there any structures in the parishes that have influence over schools (e.g., education committee, finance committee, etc.)?

   c. Does the board set goals for itself? If not, how are goals formulated? If so, when and how are these goals evaluated?

   d. With whom do principals consult, and to whom do they answer?

3. If school boards exist, request permission to attend board meetings at one or two institutions. Also meet with a board member, possibly the chair, and the principal.

   a. Summarize the business of the meeting. What issues were discussed?

   b. What was the tone of the meeting? How were decisions reached? Was anyone present besides the board members?

   c. What are the board's responsibilities? Are they articulated in bylaws or a constitution?

   d. How is the agenda developed?

   e. Is there a yearly calendar? When do financial planning and budgeting get attention?

   f. What is the role of the board in the evaluation of the school head?

   g. Does the board have a committee structure? Who is eligible to be a committee member?

   h. What strategies are used to select members of the board? For those elected, are there any screening processes in place? What education do aspiring board candidates receive about the role and responsibilities of Catholic boards (especially in comparison to serving on a public school board)?

   i. If applicable, what role does the pastor play with the board? How does he impact the board? OR What is the jurisdiction of the board, in the case of a private non-parish-related school?

   j. What is the role of the principal in relation to the board?

   k. How does the board see its function? Is this, in fact, what is needed to best support the school?

   l. What inservice training is provided to new board members? Who conducts these sessions? What professional growth opportunities are provided to board members?

---

1   Editor's note: *Building Better Boards* is an essential reference for every Catholic school administrator. The book should be part of the administrator's library.

m. What strategies are in place to deal with ineffective board members?

n. Are policy manuals in place? How are policies from the board promulgated?

o. What assistance does the diocese provide to individual school boards? Does it differ depending on the sponsorship of the school?

p. What are the outstanding accomplishments of the board? How has the board been most effective?

q. What measures might the board take to increase its effectiveness? What are the roles of the principal and, if applicable, the pastor in that improvement?

What conclusions have you drawn about the principal's responsibility toward the board? What aspects of the principal's relationship with the board will be most challenging for you?

As a result of study, reflection, and interaction with knowledgeable individuals, the learner will be able to complete the following activities. The quality of response to these activities should give some indication of the level of expertise the learner is able to bring to the situation.

Outcome Activities: I2
Governance Structures and School Boards

1. As principal, you are called upon to facilitate an information night for people interested in learning about the governance of the school. Some people are new to the school or parish community and are simply curious. Others are seriously aspiring to become part of the school board in the near future.

a. What are your objectives for this group?

b. How will you meet the needs of all those who attend the meeting? What considerations must you keep in mind to satisfy both groups?

c. What is the core of information you want this group to learn and understand? Outline your presentation in detail. Include copies of handouts or transparencies you might use.

d. What process will you use to get this information across?

e. What assumptions would you make about this group of people? How can you capitalize on the interest of this group?

f. What means will you use to get feedback from this group?

g. How will you evaluate the effectiveness of the evening?

h. Whom might you invite to be part of the program? Why?

2. You are the first lay principal of a diocesan high school. There has been no separate board for the school. Rather, the issues of the school have been dealt with by a committee of the diocesan board of education, which oversees this high school, two middle schools, and ten elementary schools sponsored by the diocese.

You have had several meetings with the diocesan superintendent and the chair of the diocesan school committee and have convinced them that the size and complexity of issues emanating from the high school merit a separate school board to attend specifically to these issues. The superintendent has finally agreed to take up the matter with the bishop and wants you to prepare the proposal, including

a. the rationale, with the advantages and disadvantages a separate board would have for the school and the diocese;

b. the details of organizing such a board (committees, etc.);

c. its relationship to the diocesan board; and

d. the criteria, qualifications, and recruitment strategies for future members.

Prepare a proposal that makes a strong case on behalf of the school.

Role: Principal as Managerial Leader

Area: Institutional Management

Competency: I3
Relationship with the Diocesan Office

Although it is common to speak of the "Catholic school system," in essence the individual Catholic school enjoys considerable autonomy in areas that are often centralized in public school systems. The vast majority of Catholic schools have virtually complete control over income and expenditures, hiring of personnel, and internal policies. Indeed, public school administrators are often amazed at the autonomy inherent in the position of Catholic school principal.

Historically, Catholics have been proud of the success of the site-based management model. It is complementary to the principles of subsidiarity and collegiality promulgated by the Second Vatican Council. Some public school researchers are looking at Catholic school management practices in their quest for public school restructuring.

But today few individual Catholic schools have the resources to address adequately all the critical educational and administrative issues that routinely face the school. It is neither productive nor feasible for individual schools to duplicate efforts in responding to state mandates and federal guidelines. The diocesan Office of Catholic Schools generally supplies the expertise and support needed for the individual schools.

More important, the Catholic school is both a civil and an ecclesiastical institution. Therefore, the school is subject to both state and church laws. The bishop, by virtue of canon law, has special responsibility and authority to set direction for schools and to be vigilant regarding the religious aspects of the school (O'Brien 1987). The central diocesan Office of Catholic Schools functions as the arm of the bishop in providing leadership and support services. All diocesan education offices provide guidance, expertise, and policy pertaining to religious education, curriculum, personnel development, pupil services, administration of state and federal programs, and legal issues. In addition, some dioceses provide services in public relations, marketing, and development.

The sponsorship of the school determines the extent and form of the relationship with the central diocesan office. Schools sponsored by parishes and schools directly sponsored by the diocese are bound by all educational policies and guidelines developed by the diocesan office. Schools sponsored by religious communities or independent lay-Catholic groups have relationships that are not as clearly defined. Regardless of sponsorship, there are ample opportunities for the Catholic school principal to interact with and benefit from the assistance of the central diocesan schools office.

To support and give evidence of professional growth in understanding the importance of the relationship between the school and the diocesan office and knowledge of the services and support available to schools, the learner will engage in the listed activities under the direction of the diocese (Model I) or through a self-directed program and/or with the guidance of a mentor (Model II).

The primary means of keeping a consistent record of activities is to keep an ongoing JOURNAL which would contain

1) a *Dated Log* section recording when activities were undertaken and completed,

2) a *Reading/Response* section in which notes from suggested readings and the response reactions are systematically organized, and

3) an *Experience(Activity)/Reflection* section in which one records ideas and insights gained through interacting with people or seeking out additional information in the course of completing the activities.

Learning Activities: I3
Relationship with the Diocesan Office

1. Read the following and respond with reactions in a journal.* Ideally, you should discuss these readings and your reactions with a mentor. These integral readings are reprinted for your convenience on pages 200–07.

   Drahmann, T. 1985. *Governance and administration in the Catholic school.* Washington, D.C.: National Catholic Educational Association, 15–16.

Hennessey, C., C. A. Solomon, K. Mitchell, S. Plasek, D. A. Clifford, and T. Bogar. 1992, 1988. *Administrator's handbook of regulations.* Houston, Tex.: Catholic School Office, Diocese of Galveston-Houston, 7–10.

Sheehan, L. 1986. Policies and practices of governance and accountability. In *Personnel issues and the Catholic school administrator*, ed. J. S. O'Brien and M. McBrien, 1–11. Washington, D.C.: National Catholic Educational Association.

* In your journal, note insights concerning the relationship between the diocesan office and the local school. What advantages are there in having the support and guidance of a central office? Compare and contrast the typical public school office and the diocesan central office. What advantages do you see in site-based management as practiced by Catholic schools, especially when compared to central-office control in public school systems? Do you see any disadvantages? What questions do you have about the services offered by the diocesan office?

2. Visit one or two diocesan office consultants to learn about the support offered to schools.
   a. How do they envision their part in the total picture of educational ministry?
   b. What do they bring to their offices, professionally and experientially?
   c. What are their major responsibilities? What is a typical day like?
   d. What kinds of services are provided to the schools? How often do they visit the schools?
   e. What system is in place for communication between the central office and local schools?
   f. Do teams of principals meet regularly with central office staff to exchange ideas and receive direction and guidelines for school operation?
   g. What kinds of training are offered annually to administrators, school staff, new principals, school boards, etc.?
   h. Does the diocese provide a mentoring program for new principals?
   i. Are school principals and staff members ever included in policy or program formation? If so, how?

3. Visit one or two Catholic school principals, and ask about their perspectives on services provided by the diocesan office. If possible, try to visit at least one new principal. What assistance has been provided to make the first year as effective as possible? What services or training are provided by the diocese to ensure that accreditation requirements are met by individual schools?
   a. How often does the principal directly contact the central office? What are the reasons for contact?
   b. How often and under what circumstances do central office personnel visit the schools?
   c. What service provided by the diocesan office is most valuable to the principal?
   d. What additional services does the principal request or need from the diocesan office?

As a result of study, reflection, and interaction with knowledgeable individuals, the learner will be able to complete the following activities. The quality of response to these activities should give some indication of the level of expertise the learner is able to bring to the situation.

Outcome Activities: I3
Relationship with the Diocesan Office

1. Contrast and compare the management responsibilities of the Catholic school administrator with those of the typical public school administrator in your part of the country. Enumerate and discuss the advantages and disadvantages you find in each system. What lessons can be learned from the public school style of administration to improve Catholic schools?

2. Develop an organizational chart of your diocesan office. Specify the role and responsibility of and service rendered by each position on the chart. What questions would a principal refer to each position? Specify the information each position might require from the school. How might the requirements differ depending on the sponsorship of the school?

3. As a new principal, what services provided by the diocesan office do you feel will be the most beneficial? Take into consideration your personal strengths and areas of growth in school management, and match them with a corresponding diocesan service. What specific services does the diocese provide in each area that would increase your strengths and supplement your knowledge or build your skills?

Role: Principal as Managerial Leader

Area: Institutional Management

Competency: I4
Relationship with Religious Congregation(s)

Until 1950, 90 percent of Catholic school teachers were members of religious congregations. In 1990, the situation has almost completely reversed, with over 85 percent of full-time faculty in Catholic schools being lay teachers (Convey 1992). Today, a Catholic elementary school with a lay Catholic principal and a totally lay faculty is the norm in many parts of the country.

In those cases, remnants of the charism of the religious community that formerly staffed the school are part of the history and heritage of the school. Some vestiges may still be present in the school traditions. If so, the principal may want to perpetuate the tradition when it contributes to the mission and quality of the school.

When members of religious communities are still among the staff of the school, the principal must be aware of contractual agreements between the school and the congregation. These arrangements, by nature, may differ from those in place for lay personnel. Besides the basic salary, other benefits, such as housing, automobiles, transportation costs, and insurance, may be part of the agreement. Ordinarily, dioceses have policies that offer guidance about these matters. In other cases, negotiations occur directly with the religious on staff or with someone representing the congregation. Aside from financial matters, regular communication with religious community leaders concerning staffing and evaluation is in order.

To support and give evidence of professional growth in understanding the importance of the relationship between the school and the religious congregation(s) and knowledge of the arrangements necessary for working with religious as staff members, the learner will engage in the listed activities under the direction of the diocese (Model I) or through a self-directed program and/or with the guidance of a mentor (Model II).

The primary means of keeping a consistent record of activities is to keep an ongoing JOURNAL which would contain
1) a *Dated Log* section recording when activities were undertaken and completed,
2) a *Reading/Response* section in which notes from suggested readings and the response reactions are systematically organized, and
3) an *Experience(Activity)/Reflection* section in which one records ideas and insights gained through interacting with people or seeking out additional information in the course of completing the activities.

Learning Activities: I4
Relationship with Religious Congregation(s)

1. Read the following and respond with reactions in a journal.* Ideally, you should discuss these readings and your reactions with a mentor. These integral readings are reprinted for your convenience on pages 208–09.

   Drahmann, T. 1985. *Governance and administration in the Catholic school.* Washington, D.C.: National Catholic Educational Association, 16–18.

   Drahmann, T., and A. Stenger. 1989. *The Catholic school principal: An outline for action.* Rev. ed. Washington, D.C.: National Catholic Educational Association, 17.

   * In your journal, note insights concerning the relationship between the school and the religious congregation. What questions do you have about their personnel policies? What questions do you have about the contributions of the religious to our schools? Does the congregation offer other educational or spiritual services to the school? How could you strengthen the relationship between the school and the congregation?

2. Visit a school that still has religious on the staff. Determine from your interview to what extent Catholic schools might expect to include

---

religious as personnel in the future. What roles have the religious played in that school's history? In what ways and how frequently does the school recognize the community that serves or has served the school? What issues might arise for a lay principal who has religious on staff? How do salaries and benefits for religious compare with those of lay staff? How does the school highlight and encourage religious vocations in their students? What strategies are used to teach about vocations?

3. Visit a school that was once associated with a religious community. How is the relationship that existed between the school and the congregation still evident? How many alumni from the school or members of the parish have entered the priesthood or the religious life?

4. Become familiar with the role religious have played in the schools in the history of your diocese. Learn whether there are any policies regarding employment for religious in the schools. Are there any congregations of religious who have their main or provincial house within the diocese or nearby? If it is feasible, visit the religious congregation personally to inquire about the future of the group's involvement in Catholic education.

As a result of study, reflection, and interaction with knowledgeable individuals, the learner will be able to complete the following activities. The quality of response to these activities should give some indication of the level of expertise the learner is able to bring to the situation.

Outcome Activities: I4
Relationship with Religious Congregation(s)

1. *Scenario*

You are the principal of a school that was staffed by a religious order for several years. One retired sister remains, who volunteers to serve the school in a myriad of ways. List ways you could recognize her efforts and the service of the order in the history of the school.
   a. What events could you acknowledge?
   b. What feast days are particularly meaningful to the order?
   c. How would the children be involved in the recognition?
   d. What involvement from school groups (alumni, parents, and school board) and parish groups could be included?
When the sister is no longer able to be part of the school community, what procedure will you follow to bring closure to her work? Whom should you contact?

You are the principal of a school that was once staffed by a religious community. The sisters have been gone from the school for ten years. Older parishioners and some parents often make references to the work of the sisters in the school and parish, but the current students have no experience with sisters. Develop some strategies to acquaint the student body with the history of the school and the contributions of the sisters.

a. How would you personally become acquainted with the congregation and its works?

b. Where could you learn about the founder or foundress (characteristics and qualities, goals, and mission)?

c. Whom in the parish might you consult? How would you get in touch with the congregation?

d. How you would present this information to the students?

e. How would you continue to keep the contribution and spirit of the sisters alive in the school?

You have recently been offered a position as the principal of a high school owned by a religious community. The school also has a board of trustees. Before you decide whether to accept the position, several issues need to be explored.

a. Specify the process you will use to answer the following questions:
   i) What specific issues of governance and management should be addressed?
   ii) To whom will you be accountable?
   iii) What is the jurisdiction of the board?
   iv) Who determines your job description, and who will evaluate your performance?

b. List the other questions you have about the responsibilities of the position.

c. If you accept the position, how will you become familiar with:
   i) the history and spirit of the sponsoring religious congregation?
   ii) the role the school plays in the congregation's mission to the Church?

d. Outline the measures you will take with the faculty and student body to keep the spirit of the congregation vibrant.

Role: Principal as Managerial Leader

Area: Institutional Management

Competency: I5
Civil and Canon Law for Catholic Schools

Catholic schools are both civil and ecclesiastical institutions. That means that the school is governed by both civil and canon (church) law. Shaughnessy (1989) specifies four types of civil laws that affect education in the United States:

■ constitutional law (both state and federal),

■ statutes and regulations,

■ common-law principles, and

■ contract law.

"In the Catholic school and in any private school, contract law is the predominant governing (civil) law" (Shaughnessy 1989).

Catholic schools are also obliged to observe church law. But in a situation where both types of law must be considered in a courtroom, although the court will make whatever allowances it can for canon law, contract law will take precedence (Shaughnessy 1991).

Knowledge of school law, particularly private school law, is crucial to the Catholic school principal. There have been more suits filed against the Church since 1980 than in all the years prior. Because school boards and pastors automatically become part of legal actions taken against the school, they too must be kept informed (Shaughnessy 1991). The principal will be expected to take the initiative in informing the board of the legal ramifications of its work.

In resolving conflicts between parents and the school, between staff members, between administration and staff, and so forth, the principle of subsidiarity ought to be the norm. In other words, every attempt should be made to address and resolve problems at the lowest level possible. Many dioceses have established policies and procedures to hear grievances, whether brought by students, parents, staff members, or administration. When both parties adhere to these policies, many problems can be mediated and solved outside the courtroom (Shaughnessy 1991).

Regardless of the way conflict is resolved, the principal must keep systematic, conscientious documentation, including accurate, ongoing records of situations involving violations of contract, policy, procedure, or other civil law. This documentation may be called as evidence in the case. Principals must also see that staff members receive regular training in procedures and strategies for obtaining and keeping accurate, concise documentation.

Since the school falls under contract law, the school handbooks become extremely important, for they are the contract between the school and the parent (or the administration and the staff). Great care should be taken when compiling the school handbooks. When problems reach the grievance level or the courtroom, both the school and the parent or staff member will be held accountable to what the handbook says (Shaughnessy 1989).

The principal must also see that staff and board are apprised of canon law. A brief review of the major issues in canon law that concern schools is appropriate at the initial faculty and board meeting. In addition, the faculty should be kept current about general church issues. A consistent annual review of selected church documents by the staff and school board should be planned by the principal. Principals are responsible for timely promulgation of diocesan policies to staff, students, and parents.

To support and give evidence of professional growth in knowledge of canon and civil law as it applies to Catholic schools, the learner will engage in the listed activities under the direction of the diocese (Model I) or through a self-directed program and/or with the guidance of a mentor (Model II).

The primary means of keeping a consistent record of activities is to keep an ongoing JOURNAL which would contain

1) a *Dated Log* section recording when activities were undertaken and completed,

2) a *Reading/Response* section in which notes from suggested readings and the response reactions are systematically organized, and

3) an *Experience (Activity)/Reflection* section in which one records ideas and insights gained through

interacting with people or seeking out additional information in the course of completing the activities.

Learning Activities: I5
Civil and Canon Law for Catholic Schools

1. Read the following and respond with reactions in a journal.* Ideally, you should discuss these readings and your reactions with a mentor. These integral readings are reprinted for your convenience on pages 210–23.

   CACE/NABE Governance Task Force. 1987. *A primer on educational governance in the Catholic Church*, ed. J. S. O'Brien. Washington, D.C.: National Catholic Educational Association, 7–16.

   Shaughnessy, M. A. 1991. *A primer on school law: A guide for board members in Catholic schools*. Washington, D.C.: National Catholic Educational Association, 5–13, 16–22.

   ———. 1989. *School handbooks: Some legal considerations*. Washington, D.C.: National Catholic Educational Association, 1–3, 11–15.

   Also, read the following sections from the *Catechism*.
   Libreria Editrice Vaticana. 1994. *Catechism of the Catholic Church*. Washington, D.C.: United States Catholic Conference.

   Nos. 707–10: God teaches us through law, which is the sign of God's promise and covenant.
   Nos. 2104–06: All people are bound to seek truth and to embrace it as a manifestation of God.

   * In your journal, note insights concerning civil and canon law as it applies to Catholic schools. What questions do you have about keeping abreast of changes in civil law as it affects Catholic schools? Do you need clarification about constitutional law and civil law as they pertain to Catholic schools?

2. Visit one or two Catholic schools to gauge the general level of legal knowledge and awareness among the administration and employees.
   a. How do the principals keep themselves and their staff members and boards abreast of the latest legal concerns for Catholic schools?
   b. What strategies ensure that staff and board members know how to organize careful, accurate records and documentation?

   c. Have the principals had to use the grievance process? If so, did they find it useful, and comprehensive enough to meet their needs during deliberations?
   d. What support is provided by the diocese to apprise principals of the legal and canonical obligations of the school and its employees?

3. Obtain a copy of the teacher assessment program and the guidelines for termination of a teacher used by the school or diocese. How are the processes related? Discuss the consistencies, or lack thereof, between the process for assessing teacher performance and that for termination. What strengths and weaknesses do you see? Accompany your opinions with rationales.

4. Obtain student and faculty handbooks from a school. Evaluate them for thoroughness in complying with civil and canon law. What recommendations would you make for revising these documents?

   As a result of study, reflection, and interaction with knowledgeable individuals, the learner will be able to complete the following activities. The quality of response to these activities should give some indication of the level of expertise the learner is able to bring to the situation.

Outcome Activities: I5
Civil and Canon Law for Catholic Schools

1. *Scenario*

   You have just been hired as the principal of an established school. For various reasons, neither the board nor staff have had any training regarding legal issues for Catholic schools.
   a. What is your plan of action to see that training begins as soon as possible?
   b. Plan the first year's staff and board development.
   c. Use a timeline to schedule training.
   d. List materials to be used. When possible, provide copies of handouts or transparencies to be used in presentations.
   e. What other resources would you use: local, diocesan, religious, secular?

2. *Scenario*

You have just been hired as the principal of an established school. In preparing to open school, you go through the files to find the record of student attendance and the fire drill schedule from the previous year. You cannot locate either. Thinking that they must be misplaced, you begin a systematic search through the files. As you proceed, you find some things, but to your dismay, you realize that systematic record keeping must have been neither a strong point nor a priority of your predecessor.

a. What are the potential legal problems of this situation?

b. What immediate and long-range steps will you take to remedy the situation? Who should be informed of this predicament? How will you involve your part-time secretary in this process?

c. What rationale and education will you present to the professional staff to impress upon them the need for systematic records? What follow-up will you do in this regard?

d. How could you recover some of the missing data?

Role: Principal as Managerial Leader

Area: Institutional Management

Competency: 16
State Requirements and Government-Funded Programs

Every state has a school code that contains legal requirements that apply to schools. The length of the school day and school year, compulsory school attendance age, required immunizations before attendance, teacher certification requirements, and credit requirements for high school graduation are a few areas regulated by the state. However, because of their tax-exempt status, some laws may apply differently to Catholic schools than to public schools.

It is the principal's responsibility to learn how specific state laws apply to Catholic schools and to ensure that the school is in full compliance with these laws. The diocesan Office of Catholic Schools is the best resource for information regarding state law.

Some federal laws also apply to Catholic schools, because they are public institutions. Non-discriminatory employment practices and health regulations are examples. In ordinary circumstances, the diocesan Office of Catholic Schools will provide competent guidance to the principal. (Should a special need arise, the USCC Department of Education will act as a resource to any parish or school.) The most current information about pending legislation and subsequent regulations is provided regularly to the dioceses by the USCC Department of Education.

The principal of a non-public school is responsible for administering state and federal aid programs available to non-public students. Many dioceses have a consultant who specializes in federal program assistance to principals. Because federal programs are subject to change, the principal needs to stay alert. In 1988, Hennessey delineated four types of federal programs in which Catholic schools typically participate:

- Title I, Chapter 1: Low-Income Supplemental Compensatory Programs

- Title I, Chapter 2: Education Block Grants and Library Aid

- Title II: Critical Skills Improvement (Eisenhower Mathematics and Science Education Act)

- Title V: Drug-Free Schools and Communities Acts of 1986

Dioceses can also advise the principal of the availability of special education services for students who need diagnosis and intervention. With the rising cost of Catholic school tuition, parents have less discretionary money for remedial services needed by their children. Principals, concerned about the welfare of the students and wishing to obtain justice for parents, will work hard to participate in any program that assists the parents in realizing a return benefit from their tax dollars.

To support and give evidence of professional growth in understanding state requirements and government-funded programs, the learner will engage in the listed activities under the direction of the diocese (Model I) or through a self-directed program and/or with the guidance of a mentor (Model II).

The primary means of keeping a consistent record of activities is to keep an ongoing JOURNAL which would contain

1) a *Dated Log* section recording when activities were undertaken and completed,

2) a *Reading/Response* section in which notes from suggested readings and the response reactions are systematically organized, and

3) an *Experience(Activity)/Reflection* section in which one records ideas and insights gained through interacting with people or seeking out additional information in the course of completing the activities.

Learning Activities: I6
State Requirements and Government-Funded Programs

1. Read the following and respond with reactions in a journal.* Ideally, you should discuss these readings and your responses with a mentor. These integral readings are reprinted for your convenience on pages 224–33.

   Hennessey, C., C. A. Solomon, K. Mitchell, S. Plasek, D. A. Clifford, and T. Bogar. 1997. *Administrator's handbook of regulations.* Houston, Tex.: Catholic School Office, Diocese of Galveston-Houston. [Federal Programs Section 1–4, Special Education Section 1–4.]

   McLaughlin, T. 1985. *Catholic school finance and Church-State relations.* Washington, D.C.: National Catholic Educational Association, 34–37, 44–52.

   United States Department of Education, Office of Private Education. 1992. Government programs. In *Handbook on serving private school children with federal education programs*, 12–13, 78–80. Washington, D.C.

   * In your journal, note insights concerning government-funded programs and corresponding requirements. Do you understand the grant-writing process and the manner in which public schools must notify local Catholic schools regarding grant applications? Do you know the rights of Catholic schools and students to apply for such services? (Experience has shown that public schools may or may not know or wish to reveal all that Catholic schools and students are entitled to.) What questions do you have regarding referral services provided by public school districts to private school students? Under what circumstances can Catholic schools use federal programs and services from more than one public school district simultaneously? What questions do you have regarding the acquisition of programs, services, or materials for your school?

2. Visit one or two Catholic schools to learn about their level of participation in government-funded programs.

   a. What problems, if any, have principals encountered in gaining cooperation from the public school districts to make programs and services available to their students?

   b. What strategies do principals use to monitor services and materials provided by these agencies?

   c. How are parents involved in program planning, and how is this documented?

   d. Are there any efforts to train parents of children who are "learning-different" to become advocates for their children to guarantee continuation of services if they must enter the public school system? (This becomes a painful decision when the Catholic school cannot provide the educational programs or therapies necessary.)

   e. Are there parent support groups for those who have children who are learning differently?

   f. What assistance is provided to principals from the diocesan school office?

3. Request an appointment with the person in the diocesan office who works with state and federal aid programs.

   a. What are the major responsibilities of the office?

   b. What are the typical programs available to the Catholic schools of the diocese?

   c. What information does the person provide to new principals?

   d. What resources are available to assist with awareness of programs for Catholic school children?

   e. What other questions would you like this person to answer?

As a result of study, reflection and interaction with knowledgeable individuals, the learner will be able to complete the following activities. The quality of response to these activities should give some indication of the level of expertise the learner is able to bring to the situation.

Outcome Activities: I6
State Requirements and Government-Funded Programs

1. Discuss the four major government-funded programs (Title I, Chapter 1; Title I, Chapter 2; Title II; and Title V). What services and materials are available through the programs? What are the concurrent regulations for usage? What procedure is required for program application?

2. Discuss the basic rights of students enrolled in Catholic schools and their families. List resources available through the diocesan office and state regulating agencies that can be used when these rights are denied to private school students.

3. Devise outlines and visual materials for staff information-update sessions on
   a. laws and programs applicable to employees and
   b. staff responsibility with regard to state and federal aid programs and services available to students.

Role: Principal as Managerial Leader

Area: Institutional Management

Competency: I7
Current Technologies

Participation in the knowledge explosion made possible by advancing technologies for communicating, accessing, and storing information is important to the future of our students. Systems that supplement every aspect of classroom teaching exist to augment and reinforce the curriculum. It is important for the principal to keep abreast of developments and provide the equipment necessary to make technology available to students. Inservice training and development programs for the entire staff are integral to a successful program integrating technology into the classroom.

Similarly, programs exist that expand and simplify the management and administrative responsibilities of the school office. Technology can enhance the capacity and productivity of the school office. Efforts by the principal and administrative staff to become knowledgeable and proficient will reap incredible benefits in terms of time saved and increased quality of service.

To support and give evidence of professional growth in understanding the use of current technologies, the learner will engage in the listed activities under the direction of the diocese (Model I) or through a self-directed program and/or with the guidance of a mentor (Model II).

The primary means of keeping a consistent record of activities is to keep an ongoing JOURNAL which would contain

1) a *Dated Log* section recording when activities were undertaken and completed,

2) a *Reading/Response* section in which notes from suggested readings and the response reactions are systematically organized, and

3) an *Experience (Activity)/Reflection* section in which one records ideas and insights gained through interacting with people or seeking out additional information in the course of completing the activities.

Learning Activities: I7
Current Technologies

1. Read the following and respond with reaction in a journal.* Ideally, you should discuss these readings and your reactions with a mentor. These integral readings are reprinted for your convenience on pages 234–42.

   Brigham, F. H. 1993. *Technology and Chapter 1: Solutions for Catholic school participation.* Washington, D.C.: National Catholic Educational Association, 7, 10, 18, 19.

   Gettys, D. J. 1994. Integrating technology in education: The principal's role. *Principal* 73(4): 52–53.

   Kabat, M., M. C. Valenteen, and W. Langley. 1991. Computers in the school: Working hard or hardly working? In *Capital wisdom: Papers from the Principals Academy 1991*, 45–47. Washington, D.C.: National Catholic Educational Association.

   National Conference of Catholic Bishops. 1979. *Sharing the light of faith: National catechetical directory for Catholics of the United States.* Washington, D.C.: United States Catholic Conference, nos. 17, 20, 22.

   Schuster, J. 1993. The managing principal: Using technology to share the power. *Electronic Learning* 12(8):26–28, 30.

   * In your journal, note insights concerning the growing use of technology in schools—with a special focus on assistance to administrators as managerial leaders. What questions do you have regarding administrative technology? What are the major programs you have discovered, and how can you foresee their use to you as a principal? What training is available locally to assist you in learning how to use them? What are the characteristics of a quality technology program in the classroom?

2. Visit one or two Catholic schools that use technology for school management.
   a. List the adaptations that were needed to introduce technology into daily school operations.

b. What problems have arisen, and how have the principals met the challenges?

c. How did the principals acquire the training necessary to use the equipment and programs?

d. What training opportunities for staff are available to expand their use of technology?

e. Does the diocese provide assistance through the central office—in the form of either a consultant or inservice training for administrators or staff?

f. Does the diocese have a parish or school data system? If so, how does the principal use the school management system? What networking opportunities are available to the schools?

g. What sources of funding have principals used to furnish equipment, programs, and training to their schools?

h. How do principals keep up-to-date on the latest advances? Are there provisions for technological expansion in the school's long-range plan?

3. Research school management software packages, through computer magazines or by attending an educational conference that features such programs.

a. Develop a checklist of features offered.

b. Justify the need for and practicality of each program feature for
   i) a small elementary parish school, grades K–8, serving 150 families,
   ii) a private high school of 900 students, and
   iii) an interparochial school serving four parishes and 300 families.

c. Specify the pros and cons of each program.

d. How can technology be integrated into the school's operation to enhance teaching and learning?

As a result of study, reflection, and interaction with knowledgeable individuals, the learner will be able to complete the following activities. The quality of response to these activities should give some indication of the level of expertise the learner is able to bring to the situation.

Outcome Activities: I7
Current Technologies

1. Develop a philosophy and rationale for implementing meaningful technology instruction in both an elementary and a secondary school. What leadership is needed to enable the teachers to integrate technology into teaching and learning throughout the school?

For *both* school levels:

a. List goals of technology instruction in all facets of the curriculum.

b. At the elementary level: at what grade and in which subjects should computer instruction be introduced? At the secondary level: how can the technology supplement the library resources available to the students within and beyond the school?

c. What efforts should be made to develop or upgrade the media center?

d. How should equipment be distributed (clustered in one room, spread out in various classrooms, etc.)?

e. Who should be responsible for computer instruction?

f. What inservice training will help the faculty become computer- and technology-literate?

g. Who will be expected to incorporate computer instruction into classes?

h. How will you help the faculty overcome its resistance to this change?

i. How will the school utilize the resources of the local business community to enhance its technology?

j. What other aspects need attention in order to provide students with a meaningful, technologically literate education?

2. *Scenario*

You have just accepted a position at a school that uses little or no technology. Equipment for a few classrooms has been earned through a supermarket promotion. The school has just purchased a computer for the office, but the secretary, who has been with the school for 15 years, has never used a computer and is frightened at the prospect of learning. You have very little computer experience, except for some word processing during graduate study. Clearly, a plan must be devised to introduce technology into the school office. It is June, and school is set to begin in mid-August.

Local resources are available, if somewhat limited. There are two nearby community colleges and a large branch campus of a major state university within 30 minutes' drive of your community. Library facilities are excellent.

The budget set by the previous principal allows $750 for instructional staff development and $350 for continuing education for the administrator. No funds were set aside for clerical staff inservice training.

A number of parishioners are experienced with technology; two are parents of students who graduated from your school recently.

Your community is small, but many businesses and some offices of major industries are located there. Many business owners and employees are parishioners. There is a local chamber of commerce, but the school is not yet a member.

The parish office has purchased the components of the parish data system used by the diocese. The school management component costs $900, which includes inservice training of staff, but no funds are budgeted for that purchase.

Design the first year of a five-year plan that will bring the school office up to date in the use of technology.

Institutional Management Bibliography

Role: Principal as Managerial Leader

Area of Responsibility:
Institutional Management

Introduction

Brigham, F. H. 1993b. *United States Catholic elementary and secondary schools 1992–93*. Washington, D.C.: National Catholic Educational Association.

Bryk, A. S., V. E. Lee, and P. B. Holland. 1993. *Catholic schools and the common good*. Cambridge, Mass.: Harvard University Press.

I1. Provides for an orderly school environment and promotes student self-discipline

Bryk, A. S., and M. E. Driscoll. 1988. *The high school as community: Contextual influences and consequences for students and teachers*. Madison, Wis.: Wisconsin Center for Educational Research.

Convey, J. J. 1992. *Catholic schools make a difference*. Washington, D.C..: National Catholic Educational Association.

Dombart, P. 1992. A job to suit up for. *Educational Leadership* 49(5):83.

Doyle, R., N. Kniate, A. Langan, and M. Swanson. 1991. Evaluation of the school's Catholicity. In *Capital wisdom: Papers from the Principals Academy 1991*, 1–6. Washington D.C.: National Catholic Educational Association.

Drahmann, T., and A. Stenger. 1989. *The Catholic school principal: An outline for action*. Rev. ed. Washington D.C.: National Catholic Educational Association, 25–26.

Governal, M. A. 1986. Effective principaling in the Catholic school. In *The Catholic school administrator—A book of readings*, ed. E. M. Bushman and G. J. Sparks, 161–64. Portland, Ore.: Catholic Leadership Company.

Libreria Editrice Vaticana. 1994. *Catechism of the Catholic Church*. Washington, D.C.: United States Catholic Conference, no. 2030.

MacNaughton, R. H., and F. A. Johns. 1991. Developing a successful schoolwide discipline program. *NASSP Bulletin* 75(536):52–56.

National Conference of Catholic Bishops. 1973. *To teach as Jesus did*. Washington, D.C.: United States Catholic Conference.

Purkey, S. C., and M. S. Smith. 1985. School reform: The district policy implications of the effective schools literature. *Elementary School Journal* 85:353-89.

Reck, C. 1988. *The small Catholic elementary school: Advantages and opportunities*. Washington, D.C.: National Catholic Educational Association, 28–43, 76–77.

Saphier, J., and R. Gower. 1997. Classroom climate: Community and mutual support, risk taking and confidence, influence. In *The Skillful Teacher: Building Your Teaching Skills*, 357–394. 5th ed. Carlisle, Massachusetts: Research for Better Teaching, Inc.

Sergiovanni, T. J. 1992. *Moral leadership*. San Francisco: Jossey-Bass, 72–81.

Shaughnessy, M. A. 1989. *School handbooks: Some legal considerations*. Washington, D.C.: National Catholic Educational Association, 24–27, 62–68.

I2. Understands Catholic school governance structures and works effectively with school boards

Bailey, R., U. Butler, and M. Kearney. 1991. Development of the Catholic school board. In *Capital wisdom: Papers from the Principals Academy 1991*, 39–44. Washington, D.C.: National Catholic Educational Association.

Drahmann, T. 1985. *Governance and administration in the Catholic school*. Washington, D.C.: National Catholic Educational Association, 1–20.

Gilbert, J. 1983. *Pastor as shepherd of the school community*. Washington, D.C.: National Catholic Educational Association, 9–10, 17–20.

National Conference of Catholic Bishops. 1979. *National catechetical directory for Catholics of the United States*. Washington, D.C.: United States Catholic Conference, Chapter 10.

O'Brien, J. S., ed. 1987. *A primer on educational governance in the Catholic Church*. CACE/NABE Governance Task Force. Washington, D.C.: National Catholic Educational Association, 21–45.

Shaughnessy, M. A. 1989. *School handbooks: Some legal considerations*. Washington, D.C.: National Catholic Educational Association.

———. 1991. *A primer on school law: A guide for board members in Catholic schools*. Washington, D.C.: National Catholic Educational Association, 29–34.

Sheehan, L. 1986. Policies and practices of governance and accountability. In *Personnel issues and the Catholic school administrator*, 1–9. Washington, D.C.: National Catholic Educational Association.

———. 1990. *Building better boards: A handbook for board members in Catholic education*. Washington, D.C.: National Catholic Educational Association, 1–5.

Sparks, G. J. 1986. The Catholic school administrator. In *The Catholic school administrator—A book of readings*, ed. E. M. Bushman and G. J. Sparks, 293–95. Portland, OR: Catholic Leadership Company.

I3. Recognizes the importance of the relationship between the school and the diocesan office

Drahmann, T. 1985. *Governance and administration in the Catholic school*. Washington, D.C.: National Catholic Educational Association, 15–16.

Hennessey, C., C. A. Solomon, K. Mitchell, S. Plasek, D. A. Clifford, and T. Bogar. 1992, 1988. *Administrator's handbook of regulations*. Houston, Tex.: Catholic School Office, Diocese of Galveston-Houston, 7–10.

O'Brien, J. S., ed. 1987. *A primer on educational governance in the Catholic Church*. CACE/NABE Governance Task Force. Washington, D.C.: National Catholic Educational Association.

Sheehan, L. 1986. Policies and practices of governance and accountability. In *Personnel issues and the Catholic school administrator*, ed. J. S. O'Brien and M. McBrien, 1–11. Washington, D.C.: National Catholic Educational Association.

I4. Recognizes the importance of the relationship between the school and religious congregation(s)

Convey, J. J. 1992. *Catholic schools make a difference*. Washington, D.C.: National Catholic Educational Association.

Drahmann, T. 1985. *Governance and administration in the Catholic school*. Washington, D.C.: National Catholic Educational Association, 16–18.

Drahmann, T., and A. Stenger. 1989. *The Catholic school principal: An outline for action*. Rev. ed. Washington, D.C.: National Catholic Educational Association, 17.

I5. Knows civil and canon law as it applies to Catholic schools

Corr, M. A. 1986. Justice in teacher termination. In *Personnel issues and the Catholic school administrator*, 128–31, 133–39. Washington, D.C.: National Catholic Educational Association.

Libreria Editrice Vaticana. 1994. *Catechism of the Catholic Church*. Washington, D.C.: United States Catholic Conference, nos. 707–10, 2104–06.

McLaughlin, T. 1985. *Catholic school finance and Church-State relations*. Washington, D.C.: National Catholic Educational Association, 55–67.

O'Brien, J.S., ed. 1987. *A primer on educational governance in the Catholic Church*. CACE/NABE Governance Task Force. Washington, D.C.: National Catholic Educational Association, 7–16.

Shaughnessy, M. A. 1989. *School handbooks: Some legal considerations*. Washington, D.C.: National Catholic Educational Association, 1–3, 11–15.

———. 1990. *Catholic schools and the law*. Mahwah, N.J.: Paulist Press, 22–23.

———. 1991. *A primer on school law: A guide for board members in Catholic Schools*. Washington, D.C.: National Catholic Educational Association, 5–13, 16–22.

I6. Understands state requirements and government-funded programs

Hennessey, C., C. A. Solomon, K. Mitchell, S. Plasek, D. A. Clifford, and T. Bogar. 1997. A*dministrator's handbook of regulations*. Houston, Tex.: Diocese of Galveston-Houston. [Federal Programs Section, 1–4; Special Education Section, 1–4.]

McLaughlin, T. 1985. *Catholic school finance and Church-state relations*. Washington, D.C.: National Catholic Educational Association, 29–54.

Monahan, F. J. 1991. Non-public schools and public policy. In *Political action, public policy and Catholic schools*, 21–23, 26–27. Washington, D.C.: National Catholic Educational Association.

United States Catholic Conference. 1991. *Political responsibility: Revitalizing American democracy*. Washington, D.C.: United States Catholic Conference.

United States Department of Education, Office of Private Education. 1992. Government programs. In *Handbook on serving private school children with federal education programs*, 12–13, 78–80. Washington, D.C.

Williams, L. P., ed. 1994. *State laws affecting private schools*. Washington, D.C.: U.S. Department of Education Office of Private Education.

I7. Understand the use of current technologies

Brigham, F. H. 1993. *Technology and Chapter 1: Solutions for Catholic school participation*. Washington, D.C.: National Catholic Educational Association, 7, 10, 18–19.

Gettys, D. J. 1994. Integrating technology in education: The principal's role. *Principal* 73(4):52–53.

Goodman, D. 1992. Strategies for staying up-to-date. *Inc.: The Office Technology Advisor* 14(12):8–11, 14–15.

Hunter, J. O. 1992. Technological literacy: Defining a new concept for general education. *Educational Technology* March: 28–29.

Kabat, M., M. C. Valenteen, and W. Langley. 1991. Computers in the school: Working hard or hardly working? In *Capital wisdom: Papers from the Principals Academy*

1991, 45–47. Washington, D.C.: National Catholic Educational Association.

National Conference of Catholic Bishops. 1979. *National catechetical directory for Catholics of the United States*. Washington, D.C.: United States Catholic Conference, nos. 17, 20, 22.

Schuster, J. 1993. The managing principal: Using technology to share the power. *Electronic Learning* 12(8):26–30.

Watts, G. D., and S. Castle. 1992. Electronic networking and the construction of professional knowledge. *Phi Delta Kappan* 73(9):684–89.

Integral Readings for Institutional Management

Evaluation of the School's Catholicity

Doyle, R., N. Kinate, A. Langan, and M. Swanson. 1991. In *Capital wisdom: Papers from the Principals Academy 1991*, 1–6. Washington, D.C.: National Catholic Educational Association.

To Teach as Jesus Did, the American bishops' pastoral, is pivotal to any meaningful consideration of the catholicity of a Catholic school. What is unique and distinctive about a Catholic school can easily be blurred. For a Catholic school to be true to its mission as an agent of change in this world, its Catholic identity must be evident and operative.

At the heart of this Catholic identity is the love of God and others that motivates and permeates relationships and daily activities. Beyond this core reality, *To Teach as Jesus Did* and subsequent church documents describe characteristics that identify the four essential and interrelated concepts of message, worship, community, and service.

These concepts form an evaluative instrument in enabling leadership to get a perspective on the catholicity of a school.

Objectives:

1. To assist local school leadership with a means of accountability for the catholicity of its school
2. To contribute to the continuance of Catholic schools, not only as communities of academic excellence, but also as viable and credible communities of faith
3. To provide an instrument for evaluation, reflection and growth

Process:

Phase 1: Administrator evaluation
Phase 2: Review of results
Phase 3: Follow-up

Indicators of Catholic Identity

Principals, teachers, staff, students, parents and parishioners view each other as brothers and sisters in Christ.

The truths of the Gospel as proclaimed by the Catholic Church are taught with conviction.

Gospel values are incorporated into all aspects of school life.

A supportive environment enables the young to mature in the faith.

Students are challenged to live the gospel message.

An excellent and comprehensive program is provided by ministers of Catholic education.

Source: *The Religious Dimension of Education in a Catholic School*, Congregation for Catholic Education, Rome, 1988.

Phase 1: Administrator evaluation
Directions: Circle the response that best describes your school.
1. Consistently
2. Often
3. Sometimes
4. Seldom
5. Never

Message
There is evidence of systematic religious education.

    1   2   3   4   5

Updated theological and liturgical materials are used.

    1   2   3   4   5

Teachers are involved in ongoing religious formation and theological studies.

    1   2   3   4   5

The life and values of Jesus are consciously integrated into the curriculum.

    1   2   3   4   5

There is a definite effort between school and home to share faith activities.

    1   2   3   4   5

Visible signs and symbols of Catholic faith are displayed.

    1   2   3   4   5

The Bible is used as a primary source of religious education.

    1   2   3   4   5

Worship

Daily prayer experiences for children and staff are provided to nourish a personal relationship with Christ.

      1   2   3   4   5

Sacramental preparation and celebration hold high priority in the curriculum.

      1   2   3   4   5

Liturgical celebrations and the liturgical feasts are opportunities for integrating life and prayer on a regular basis.

      1   2   3   4   5

Faith stories and experience are shared.

      1   2   3   4   5

Time is scheduled for retreats and/or days of reflection.

      1   2   3   4   5

Community

Specific means are provided for developing the Catholic lifestyle and spirituality of staff, students and parents.

      1   2   3   4   5

The atmosphere is Christian and caring.

      1   2   3   4   5

There is good morale.

      1   2   3   4   5

Parents are an integral part of this faith and learning community.

      1   2   3   4   5

Actions reflect what is stated in the school philosophy.

      1   2   3   4   5

Students and their opinions are respected.

      1   2   3   4   5

A cooperative relationship with the clergy is evident.

      1   2   3   4   5

Service

Students are taught habits of heart and mind for service.

      1   2   3   4   5

Students are involved in activities that reflect global awareness and environmental sensitivity.

      1   2   3   4   5

Special consideration is given to those in need.

      1   2   3   4   5

Specific outreach projects are done.

      1   2   3   4   5

Phase II: Review of results

The entire staff reviews the results, identifies the weakest area and plans strategies.

Phase III: Follow-up

Worship	Strategies	Responsible Person	Timeline
Prayer	Whole school praying	Principal/ student	Weekly/ ongoing
	Home room prayer	Home room teacher	Daily in classroom
	Faculty prayer	Principal	Every Friday before class
Sacraments			
Eucharist:	Teachers involve parents and children	Sacramental team	One meeting per month
Reconciliation:	Teachers involve parents and children	Sacramental team	One meeting per month
Confirmation: (if in 7th or 8th grades)	Teachers involve parents and children	Sacramental team	One meeting per month
Liturgy	Student involvement in preparation and participation	Principal/ teachers/ music ministers/ clergy	Once a month minimum
Faith Experiences	Two retreats outside school	Planning committee	Present to end of year
Theological Update	Each faculty member attends one program	Principal and faculty	Present to end of year

Resources

National Conference of Catholic Bishops, *To Teach as Jesus Did*, Washington, DC, 1972.

The Catholic Identity of Catholic Schools, Washington, DC, National Catholic Educational Association (NCEA), 1991.

Congregation for Catholic Education, *The Religious Dimension of Education in a Catholic School*, Rome, 1988.

Congregation for Catholic Education, *The Catholic School*, Rome, 1977.

Congregation for Catholic Education, *Lay Catholics in Schools: Witnesses to Faith*, Rome, 1982.

National Conference of Catholic Bishops, *Sharing the Light of Faith* (National Catechetical Directory for Catholics of the United States), 1979.

About the Authors

Robert Doyle, St. Mary's School, Melrose, Minnesota

Nancy Kinate, OSF, St. Joseph School, Green Bay, Wisconsin

Aideen Langan, CP, Msgr. Matthew F. Clarke School, Wakefield, Rhode Island

Marcian Swanson, SSSF, St. Matthias School, Chicago, Illinois

The Catholic School Principal: An Outline for Action

Drahmann, T., and A. Stenger. 1989. 25–26. Rev. ed.
Washington, D.C.: National Catholic Educational Association.

Chapter 8.[*]
The Principal as Pupil Manager

The principal has overall responsibility for the life of the school and for the general welfare of the students who attend it. These responsibilities include traditional matters such as attendance, discipline, health, safety, and playground supervision, as well as more contemporary problems resulting from family disorders, drug abuse, and growing legal restrictions.

1. Administrative Actions

____ 1. Observes, assists, and is present to students in their daily activities
____ 2. Sets absence and tardy procedures
____ 3. Establishes and reviews a discipline policy
____ 4. Establishes and reviews a homework policy
____ 5. Selects grading and reporting procedures
____ 6. Establishes and maintains dress guidelines
____ 7. Provides for hallway, lunchroom, and playground supervision
____ 8. Provides a policy on drug abuse and smoking
____ 9. Provides counseling and guidance services
____ 10. Provides health services and procedures
____ 11. Knows and uses referral agencies for problems which the school cannot solve
____ 12. Maintains adequate records
____ 13. Establishes procedures for suspension, expulsion, promotion, and non-promotion which follow diocesan guidelines

2. Policies and Decisions of Supervisory Body

____ 1. Sets age of admission
____ 2. Adopts a policy of non-discrimination in admission
____ 3. Sets policy on dress guidelines
____ 4. Approves a grievance procedure for students
____ 5. Sets policy for students and teachers who may contract AIDS, or confirms diocesan policies

3. Faculty Handbook

____ 1. Discipline policy and procedures
____ 2. Homework policy
____ 3. Tardiness and absence procedures
____ 4. Playground and lunchroom duties
____ 5. Policy on drugs, alcohol, and smoking
____ 6. Dress regulations, enforcement
____ 7. State regulations affecting students

4. Parent/Student Handbook

____ 1. Attendance procedures
____ 2. Discipline policy and procedures
____ 3. Homework expectations
____ 4. Special regulations: drugs, alcohol, smoking, AIDS
____ 5. Dress regulations
____ 6. Promotion and non-promotion policies

5. Resources

____ 1. *Fostering Discipline and Discipleship Within the Catholic Educational Community.* Washington, DC: National Catholic Educational Association, 1985.
____ 2. "The Healing Ministries of Catholic Education" *Momentum.* September, 1987. (Topics covered in this issue include drug and alcohol abuse, suicide prevention, health problems, death, AIDS education, and child abuse.) Washington, DC: National Catholic Educational Association.
____ 3. *The Media Mirror: A Study Guide on Christian Values and Television.* Three levels, elementary, junior high, and high school. Washington, DC: National Catholic Educational Association, 1984.
____ 4. Traviss, Mary Peter, O.P. *Student Moral Development in the Catholic School.* Washington, DC: National Catholic Educational Association, 1985.

6. Issues

____ 1. What is a fair and effective policy on:
____ a. homework
____ b. attendance
____ 2. How should a Catholic school retain students who are serious discipline problems?
____ 3. When should conduct outside the school affect a student's status in a Catholic school?
____ 4. How can students with drug and alcohol problems be best helped?
____ 5. Should the teacher or the principal handle discipline problems?
____ 6. Is corporal punishment suitable in Catholic schools?
____ 7. How can teachers with poor control over their classrooms be aided?
____ 8. How can a principal ensure the enforcement of school rules by all teachers?

---

[*] Editor's note: Chapter notation refers to this excerpt.

Effective Principaling in the Catholic School

Governal, M. A. 1986. In *The Catholic school administrator—A book of readings*,
ed. E. M. Bushman and G. J. Sparks, 161–64. Portland, Ore.: Catholic Leadership Company.

Principals are effective to the extent that they provide teachers with coaching, guidance, and the rewards necessary for satisfaction and performance.

Principals are also effective to the degree that they moderate their leader behaviors in reference to the task structure. For example, if the goal of the school is ambiguous, the subordinates desire highly directive behavior on the part of the leader. In contrast, if the goal or task is easily structured, the subordinates expect highly supportive and participative behavior on the part of the leader. In the latter case, highly directive behavior may be an irritant.

According to this plan, then, effective principals need to study the teachers' characteristics as well as the environmental pressures or demands in the school to decide if they need to be directive, supportive, or both in their administrative practices.

Climate

Researchers of school effectiveness have consistently pointed out the importance of an orderly environment in a school. It is rather difficult to imagine anyone learning in chaotic surroundings.

Climate, unfortunately, seems to be a loosely-defined construct, and there seems to be considerable variation in its measurement in the different research studies. Thus, it is somewhat difficult to draw definitive conclusions from the available data. Researchers, nonetheless, have demonstrated that school climate and student achievement are positively associated (Anderson, 1982; Bossert, Dwyer, Rowan, and Lee, 1982).

Climate Conceptualizations

Probably the most well-known conceptualization of the organizational climate in school is the study of elementary schools by Halpin and Croft (Hoy and Miskel, 1982). They developed a descriptive questionnaire to identify important aspects of teacher-teacher and teacher-principal interactions. It is commonly called the *Organizational Climate Description Questionnaire* (OCDQ). It measures school climates somewhere along an open-closed continuum. Openness refers to genuineness and authenticity in interactions. It also refers to the effective blending of personal needs with task accomplishment. Closedness, by contrast, refers to artificiality and inauthenticity. It also refers to the predominance of task accomplishment at the expense of personal needs or vice versa.

In all, there are six distinctive patterns of interaction along the continuum. Using the OCDQ instrument, researchers were easily able to identify schools with either the open or closed climate, but they found it difficult to define precisely the ones in between.

Although this model is limited in terms of its theoretical foundations, its common sense descriptions are noteworthy. The key administrative behavior pattern described was thrust, or the energy and drive the principals exhibit as role models for teachers. It seems straightforward to project that if principals are in evidence in the buildings, observing what transpires, offering suggestions, monitoring progress, and suggesting new techniques, then teachers will more than likely focus on their tasks and become more genuine in their interactions with others. Another key administrative behavior identified was consideration, or the ability to assist teachers when there is interference with the teaching process. If principals demonstrate considerateness and thrust to their teachers, they would effectively blend personal needs with task accomplishment and create an open environment.

The key teacher behavior pattern described was *esprit*, or the energy, loyalty, and mutual supportiveness that teachers bring to the school. It also seems very sensible to project that if teachers worked together as a team, school problems would be less burdensome. Imagine a school in which the principal's thrust and considerateness along with the teachers' *esprit* were high.

Another way to conceptualize the climate of the school is in terms of the dominant patterns that teachers and principals use to control students. Donald J. Willower and Ronald G. Jones (1967) described pupil control as the "dominant motif" within the school social system, the integrative theme that gives meaning to patterns of teacher-student and teacher-principal relations.

Within this framework, pupil control can be conceptualized along a continuum from custodial to humanistic. These two contrasting types refer to one's individual ideology and corresponding types of school organizations. Thus, pupil control ideology is the view that school personnel have of the students.

The custodial orientation is usually found in the traditional school, which provides a very rigid and highly controlled environment. Maintenance of order is primary, and students are usually stereotyped in terms of their appearance, behavior, and social status. Teachers who have a custodial orientation very often conceive of the school mainly as an autocratic organization with a rigid pupil-teacher status hierarchy. Students are told what to believe and do. Teachers do not attempt to understand student behavior, but instead view misbehavior as a personal affront. Often these teachers are more concerned about what others will say about them if their students seem out of control than with the causes of the children's misbehavior.

The humanistic orientation usually leads to a more open environment in which students learn through cooperative interaction and experience. Teachers try to understand why children misbehave and realize that misbehavior is not always a personal affront. Today many children come to school trying to deal with an overload of personal and familial problems, and very often the students do not cope very well.

Using the Pupil-Control Ideology Form (PCI) to measure schools along a custodial-humanistic orientation, researchers have found that they can generate predictions about the nature of the school. For instance, custodial schools will probably have more alienated students, more goal displacement, and less communication than humanistic schools.

The custodial orientation seems to be inconsistent with the philosophy of Catholic education, which holds a special view of the child and values a special caring relationship that grows from the view. Students are seen and treated as God's children, and the faculty and principal are called upon to respond to His Spirit that dwells within the children.

The humanistic viewpoint of the student is more compatible with the philosophy of Catholic education. Yet, humanism is limited as a philosophy. For example, children are unique, not only because they are human beings, but more importantly because they are God's children.

Principals of Catholic schools need to know how to sense and read the climate of their schools. They and their faculties need to reflect on their views of the students and examine themselves to see if their behaviors towards the students and each other flow from the philosophy of Catholic education.

References

Anderson, C. S. "The Search for School Climate: A Review of Research." *Review of Educational Research,* 52, 368–420, 1982.

Bossert, S.; Dwyer, D.; Rowan, R.; and Lee, G. "The Instructional Management Role of the Principal." *Educational Administration Quarterly,* 18, 34–64, 1982.

Hoy, W. and Miskel, C. *Educational Administration, Theory, Research and Practice.* New York: Random House, 1982.

Willower, D. and Jones, R. "Control in an Educational Organization." In J. D. Raths et. al. (Ed.), *Studying Teaching* (424–448). N.J.: Prentice-Hall, 1967.

Classroom Climate:
Community and Mutual Support, Risk Taking and Confidence, Influence

Saphier, J., and R. Gower. 1997. In *The skillful teacher: Building your teaching skills*, 357–394. 5th ed. Carlisle, Mass.: Research for Better Teaching, Inc.

The research on classroom climate is thin but clear: thin because the volume of studies is much smaller than in the cognitive areas, clear because the findings are consistent across populations, ages of students, and subjects. Whenever students feel empowerment, acceptance, and safety to take risks and try things that are hard for them, they like school better and learn more (Moos and Moos 1978; Haertel, Walberg, and Haertel 1981; Fraser and Fisher 1983; Fraser 1986, 1989; Nunnery, Butler, and Bhaireddy 1993).

That sounds like common sense, and it is, but the research in this area is approximately where research on clarity was thirty years ago. At that time we knew that teachers who were rated as clear on a Likert scale got better results with students. We did not know, however, what they did in their practice to earn those ratings. We did not have a construct for the elements of clarity and how they were related to one another, an operational model for how they worked in interrelationship, or a sense of whether some of the elements were more important than others. We know a great deal more about clarity now. We can at least profile essential elements and have data to support their individual contribution to successful teaching and learning. The same is not true for classroom climate. Here we are at the Likert scale stage.

Although the tradition of research on classroom climate has roots in the 1920s, Withall (1949) was the first to formulate a definition of the group phenomenon known as social-emotional climate. He noted

> a general emotional factor which appears to be present in interactions occurring between individuals in face to face groups. It seems to have some relationship to the degree of acceptance expressed by members of a group regarding each other's needs or goals. Operationally defined, it is considered to influence: (1) the inner private world of each individual; (2) the *esprit de corps* of the group; (3) the sense of meaningfulness of group and individual goals and activities; (4) the objectivity with which a problem is tackled; (5) the kind and extent of interpersonal interaction in the group.

Studies since then have examined "high-inference" variables and found better student achievement when the class is rated high on measures such as cohesiveness and satisfaction and low on measures such as friction, difficulty, and competitiveness (Fraser and O'Brien 1985).

Overall, these studies show that "students' cognitive, affective, and behavioral outcomes are related to students' perceptions of psychosocial characteristics in classrooms" (Chavez 1984; Battistich et al. 1995).[1]

The following four propositions speak to the importance of classroom climate:

1. The basic psychological needs of all humans make up an acknowledged and universal list: safety, self-control, affection, inclusion, self-esteem, recognition, self-actualization and freedom and fun (see Maslow 1962; Dreikurs and Gray 1968; Schutz 1967; Glasser 1965, 1994).

2. The degree to which one's psychological needs are met determines how much of one's energy and attention is available for learning. If an individual is hurt and severely wanting in any of these needs, learning slows to a crawl or a halt. If these needs are adequately met, learning proceeds normally. And if they are met at a high level and nourished, learning flourishes.

3. Classroom climate directly influences how students do in school. It influences individually how their thermometers read on each of the basic psychological needs. It is not the only variable, but it is a major variable shaping the degree to which each student's psychological needs are met during class time.

4. When the climate goes beyond meeting safety and security needs and develops strength on the important dimensions of climate—community, risk taking, and influence—learning accelerates.

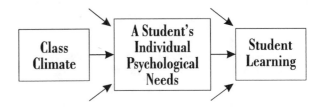

___

1   In recognition of the importance of these characteristics, major staff development programs such as Dimensions of Learning (Marzano and Pickering 1992) have begun to include components on students' feelings of acceptance, ability, and safety. Educators for Social Responsibility, a nonprofit corporation, offers workshops throughout the country for teachers on conflict-resolution strategies and community building. It is located at 23 Garden Street, Cambridge, MA 02138; 800-370-2515. The Northeast Foundation for Children offers similar high-quality workshops. It is located at 71 Montague City Road, Greenfield, MA 01301; 800-360-6332.

Classroom Climate: What Is It?

Our operational definition of classroom climate will be "the feelings and beliefs students have and the cumulative patterns of behavior that result from those feelings and beliefs regarding community and mutual support, risk taking and confidence, and influence and control." *Community and mutual support* are defined as an individual's feelings in relation to a group—feelings of acceptance, inclusion, membership, and maybe beyond into friendship and affection. *Risk taking and confidence* represent an internal, personal dimension that is influenced significantly by the reactions of others to one's behaviors. Put-downs and sarcasm, however subtle they may be, reduce one's confidence that it is safe to risk thinking and trying. A classroom climate that rewards effort and persistence will deemphasize speed and help students learn that errors are merely opportunities for learning, not signs of personal deficiency. *Influence and control* represent the dimension of class climate that pertains to personal efficacy, defined as one's power to produce effects. It answers the following questions: To what degree do I as an individual get to make my presence felt legitimately in helping things function in here? How am I empowered to be a player, an influencer, someone who matters as opposed to a silent cipher whose existence makes no observable difference in the flow of life in the room, to say nothing of making choices about how I spend my own time? All three of these dimensions of class climate matter for student learning.

These three major strands of classroom climate are summarized in Figure 13.1, which treats each as a developmental aspect of climate—developmental in that there are stages of sophistication and maturity for each of the three strands, so a teacher planning to strengthen any of

---

Figure 13.1 Three Major Strands of Classroom Climate
Each strand can be broken down into discrete stages of development.

Climate for High Achievement for All Students

COMMUNITY AND MUTUAL SUPPORT	CONFIDENCE AND RISK TAKING	INFLUENCE AND CONTROL
"I feel accepted and included in this group. People are on my side and want me to do well. I can help others and they will help me."	"It's safe to take a risk. If I try hard, learn from errors, and persist, I can succeed here."	"I can have some influence on the way things go here. I can have some say. I matter."

Inclusion and Affiliation	5 Student Beliefs That Liberate or Limit Learning		Personal Efficacy
Knowing others	Mistakes help one learn.	vs Mistakes are a sign of weakness.	Empowering students to influence the pace of class
↓	↓	↓	↓
Greeting, acknowledging, listening, responding, and affirming	You are not expected to understand everything the first time around. Care, perseverance, and quality are what count.	vs Speed is what counts. Faster is smarter.	Negotiating the rules of the classroom game
↓	↓	↓	↓
Group Identity, responsibility, and interdependence	Good students solicit help and lots of feedback on their work.	vs Good students can do it by themselves.	Teaching kids to use the principles of learning and other strategies
↓	↓	↓	↓
Cooperative learning, social skills, class meetings, and group dynamics	Consistent effort and effective strategies are the main determinants of success.	vs Inborn intelligence is the main determinant of success.	Students' using knowledge of learning style and making choices
↓	↓	↓	↓
Problem solving and conflict resolution	Everyone is capable of high achievement, not just the fastest.	vs Only the few who are bright can achieve at a high level.	Students and their communities as sources of knowledge

---

them would do well to plan activities and new practices with the stages in mind. The stages for the first strand, community and mutual support, are well treated in the developmental literature (Aspy 1977; Wood 1994; Johnson and Johnson 1995). The stages in the other two strands are more hypothetical, though their elements are supported individually by research.

The sections that follow examine each strand separately and describe the meaning of each element in it (e.g., what does "knowing others" in the community strand mean, and why is it important to classroom climate?). Before leaving each element, we will describe specific strategies and practices teachers can use to develop it.

Community and Mutual Support

This dimension of climate describes the degree of inclusion, affiliation, and mutual support students feel with one another. When it is well developed, the student can say, "I feel accepted and included here. People are on my side. I can help others, and they will help me."

Within this dimension are five levels of development, each paired with a characteristic statement:

1. *Knowing others:* "I know these people and they know me."

2. *Greeting, acknowledging, listening, responding, and affirming:* "I feel accepted and included. People respect me, and I respect them."

3. *Group identity, responsibility, and interdependence:* "I'm a member of this group. We need each other and want each other to succeed."

4. *Cooperative learning, social skills, group meetings, and group dynamics:* "I can help others and they will help me."

5. *Problem solving and conflict resolution:* "We can solve problems that arise between us."

These relationships of warmth and inclusion don't get built by accident or by themselves. Teachers contribute to the strength and texture of the climate of inclusion and affiliation that students experience through their behaviors (Cabello and Terrell 1993): their verbal interaction patterns with individual students, their means of handling conflicts between students, the cooperative structures they introduce for interaction among students, and their explicit teaching of social skills.

Knowing Others

Gene Stanford, a high school English teacher, identified this strand of classroom climate as a developmental continuum in his 1977 book, *Developing Effective Classroom Groups*. He realized that the foundation of being a group member was knowing something about the others in the group. As a result, he regularly did brief get-acquainted activities (twenty-one listed in his book) in the early months of the school year with students in his classes.

Teachers who periodically take a few minutes several times each week to do these activities do not report time problems keeping up with the curriculum or studying what is required. These modest front-end investments in building community increase efficiency and time on task in the long run. (The same can be said for the other levels of community building in this strand.)

Dozens of books are available with excellent get-acquainted activities (Stanford 1977; Shaw 1992; Seigle and Macklem 1993; Bennett and Smilanich 1994) that are active and enjoyable. In People Bingo or the version called Find a Person Who, students mingle and try to get signatures in boxes of a grid where facts are listed about unknown people in the group, for example, "Spent a year in France." Each student has to find the person matched to that fact and get his or her signature in that box. Some activities are more lengthy, like structured interviews of partners. After the interview, each partner introduces the other to the class or to a small group based on the interview.

One of our favorites has always been Artifact Bags, which is just as popular among groups of adults as it is among fifth graders. Participants bring in unlabeled shopping bags containing five items that represent something about their lives or their interests. At each session, one participant chooses a bag at random and displays the items in it one at a time to the other participants, who are sitting in a circle. Participants try to guess who the owner is. After the fifth item is shown and described by the person who has been picking from the bag (some items may be too small for all to see thoroughly when just held up), the group makes a collective guess. Then the real owner reveals himself or herself and explains the significance of each item. There may be time to do two or three people at each session.

The popularity of this activity with adults signals how little opportunity there is in schools and school districts as workplaces to come to know one's colleagues. One doesn't have to take the whole faculty away on a retreat to pay attention to group building and relationship building.

Community-building strategies gain importance in the overall picture of classroom climate building for students as the forces of scheduling and course structures assume more importance starting in grade 6. These forces depersonalize and fractionate the sense of community for students.

Greeting, Listening, Responding, Acknowledging, and Affirming

Have you ever noticed that in some settings (sometimes in whole towns) people look you in the eye, smile, and greet you when you walk by or enter their space? Beyond simply getting students information about each other, we might work on creating the conditions and teaching the skills of acknowledging and responding to one another. People who are greeted and acknowledged regularly feel affirmed and tend to be more available for learning. In the Morning Meeting structure at the Greenfield Center School in Greenfield, Mass., the first activity uses one of the dozens of formats available for having the children greet one other around the circle. This is not a practice confined to the primary grades. Positive greeting is a form of acknowledgment worth fostering at any age. Wood (1994) writes, "It is important for students [of grades 4, 5, 6] to not only greet each other in the morning, but to learn to greet any member of the class in a friendly and interested way. Issues of gender, cliques, and best friends are developmental milestones for 9–13 year olds. Greetings help students to work on these issues in a safe structure every morning. It is the entry point for the teacher in her social curriculum each morning."

A sample greeting activity appropriate for the elementary grades is a ball toss greeting, which can be varied so that it will be challenging and build cooperation for older children. It begins with the children standing in a circle and greeting each other one at a time by tossing a ball. For example, Leslie starts the greeting by saying, "Good morning, John!" and then tosses the ball to John. He returns Leslie's greeting, then chooses another child in the circle to greet and toss the ball to. When the ball has been tossed to everyone except Leslie, it finishes by returning to her with a greeting. In a variation, the ball goes around one more time silently (with no greeting or talking) repeating the pattern it just made. Children will enjoy doing it several times this way and competing against the clock (Stephenson and Watrous 1994).

Acknowledging and affirming one another can be structured into group meeting times. The Social Competency Curriculum (Seigle and Macklem 1993) uses Spotlight as an activity to affirm positive attributes and behaviors. One child is picked by the teacher (a different one each time) to be in the spotlight. The others then take turns giving the selected child compliments with specific examples: "Tim, it's nice the way you are considerate of other kids, like when you made room for me to get into the circle." Each child may speak only once and must address the child selected, not the teacher. The child in the Spotlight just listens.

Good listening can be taught explicitly. Students can be warmed up to the qualities of good listening by doing a mirroring exercise. Two partners stand and decide who will be the leader (person A) and who the follower (person B). Partner A puts his or her hands up and moves them around, palms facing partner B, who has to make his or her hands exactly mirror A's hands. After about 45 seconds the facilitator calls "time," and partners switch roles. A becomes the follower and B the leader. To do this activity well, both partners need to focus intently on each other. That sets the stage for direct teaching and practice of social skills, especially listening.

Direct teaching of children to listen involves role playing and practice. It can begin by asking students, "Think of someone who really listens to you. Why do you think that person does it?" Role-play listening attentively with the class, and have them tell you what they saw and heard. Record their answers. Next have students describe someone they know who doesn't listen. Do a role-play with

someone, and record what students say about these behaviors they heard and saw. Students are now ready to practice listening in trios: one listener, one speaker, and one observer.

Many teachers embed practice in listening in classroom routines—for example, by asking a student who wants to speak to summarize what the previous students said in a discussion. This request is thrown out randomly so students can't predict when they'll have to summarize the previous student.

Group Identity, Responsibility, and Interdependence

Cooperative learning structures (see Kagan 1992) and cooperative models (Johnson and Johnson 1987; Slavin 1986) encourage team building because they form natural groups where individuals are allied with one another. Thus, creating a team name, a logo, or a banner becomes a natural way for getting the kids involved with one another. On a higher level, students start depending on one another and see how they need one another. Jigsaw structures (Aronson 1978) force interdependence because students must rely on their peers to learn certain material so they can present it to the others on the team.

Broken Squares is an activity often used to introduce students to interdependence. Five perfect squares, each 6 inches on a side, are cut into pieces, mixed up into five piles, and put in five envelopes (see Figure 13.2). Each team of five gets one envelope each. Their job, *without talking or signaling*, is to make five perfect squares. Individuals may not take pieces from anyone else; they can only give pieces away. When they give a piece to a team member, individuals may not put the piece in place in the persons puzzle: they can just give it to the person. Debriefing this activity with the questions listed in Figure 13.2 provides a fine entry point for discussing what happens if a person is ignored or withdraws or if a person tries to dominate the task.

Regular academic tasks can be adapted to the Broken Squares structure. An oaktag sheet with spelling words (or technical words or foreign language or English vocabulary words) can be cut up into a pile of individual letters. The letters are sorted randomly into five envelopes. Each of five team members gets one envelope. Their job as a group, *without talking or taking pieces from another*, is to build the words, spelled correctly. A poster of the words spelled correctly should be available for the group to consult while doing the task.

Social Skills and Group Dynamics

The fourth level of community building focuses more explicitly on developing the skills to work effectively in groups. Social skills are taught in the manner of the Listening example already described. Class meetings become a common framework for teaching and exercising these social skills, which are often posted by name around the classroom.

Figure 13.2 Broken Squares Activity

This activity is often used to introduce students to interdependence.

Reproduced from *A Handbook of Structured Experiences for Human Relations Training, Volume 1*
J. William Pfeiffer and John E. Jones, Editors. La Jolla: University Associates Publishers, Inc., 1974.

DIRECTIONS FOR MAKING A SET OF BROKEN SQUARES

A set consists of five envelopes containing pieces of cardboard cut into different patterns which, when properly arranged, will form five squares of equal size. One set should be provided for each group of five persons.

To prepare a set, cut out five cardboard squares, each exactly 6" X 6". Place the squares in a row and mark them as below, penciling the letters lightly so they can be erased.

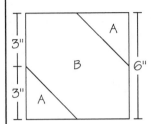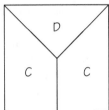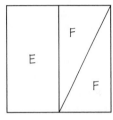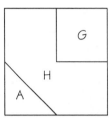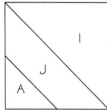

The lines should be so drawn that, when the pieces are cut out, those marked A will be exactly the same size, all pieces marked C the same size, etc. Several combinations are possible that will form one or two squares, but only one combination will form all five squares, each 6" X 6". After drawing the lines on the squares and labeling the sections with letters, cut each square along the lines into smaller pieces to make the parts of the puzzle.

Label the five envelopes 1, 2, 3, 4, and 5. Distribute the cardboard pieces into the five envelopes as follows: envelope 1 has pieces I, H, E; 2 has A, A, A, C; 3 has A, J; 4 has D, F; and 5 has G, B, F, C.

Erase the penciled letter from each piece and write, instead, the number of the envelope it is in. This makes it easy to return the pieces to the proper envelope, for subsequent use, after a group has completed the task.

Each set may be made from a different color or cardboard.

Broken Squares

Directions

Each of you has an envelope which contains pieces of oaktag for forming squares. When the signal is given, the task of your group is to form *five squares of equal size*. Each square will measure 6" X 6". The task will not be completed until five perfect squares have been completed.

Rules

1. No member may speak.

2. No member may ask another member for a piece or in any way signal that another person is to give him or her a piece. (Members may voluntarily give pieces to other members.)

(The letters on the pieces are irrelevant to the task; they are just for getting pieces back into the right envelope at the end of the exercise.)

Processing "Broken Squares"

1. What happened first? What strategies were in use at the beginning?

2. What were you (each individual) thinking about the first few minutes?

3. What happened next? Did strategies shift? Were there different phases to how you functioned as a group?

4. Did someone make a move that shifted the group's approach or in some way broke a long jam?

5. Did anyone feel left out or appear to be left out?

6. What role did each individual play in the group?

7. What did you become aware of about yourself about cooperation and competition?

8. What insight/awareness did you get about *groups* in cooperative tasks?

(Three excellent sources on how to run classroom meetings for social skill development are Glasser 1969, Seigle and Macklem 1993, and Wood 1994.)

Consensus-seeking exercises with an analysis of behavior and results afterward are useful. Tasks such as Lost in Space and Arctic Survival (Lafferty 1987) give problems to teams from fifth grade on up that require prioritizing a list of items; for example, which ten of twenty potential items should be taken from a crashed plane if the group has to survive in subarctic conditions until rescued? Individuals do the task alone first, then redo it with team members by sharing information and the rationales they used. The group choices almost always turn out to he closer to the expert's best answer than any individual's answer alone. Thus, the point is made about the benefits of pooling expertise and using consensus. After the activity, groups follow directions to examine the roles various members of the group played when they were working together. Valuable learning emerges about what behaviors individuals can do to make groups effective. Information emerges about blocking behaviors and what each individual could do to be a more potent group contributor next time.

Mysteries (Stanford 1977) is another such structure. The clues necessary to solve a mystery are put on 3 x 5 index cards and one clue is given to each student. The task is to identify the culprit with deductive logic by a process of elimination if all the information from all the clues is available. The students who sit in a circle can read their card aloud but cannot give it to anyone else, nor can any student read another student's card. This structure forces students to share information, organize it, and develop organization and leadership skills. As with all such tasks, the analytical discussion afterward (called *processing*) is the most important part of the activity. It is here that students reflect on what helped and what obstructed the group's progress, and they make commitments about what they'll try to do better next time.

In Mysteries, the class is asked to make an accusation only when they all agree. If they are wrong, the teacher doesn't give the right answer but sends them back into the group to reexamine the evidence. In any event, after 20 minutes, the activity ends if the guilty party hasn't been identified, and the class returns to the task on another day.

The things students learn about successful group processes and about individual social and task skills from these activities do not necessarily transfer into their everyday behavior unless teachers specifically plan for that transfer. Successful teaching of social skills requires (1) naming the skill, (2) creating an understanding of the utility of the skill in life, (3) modeling it, (4) having students practice it, and (5) giving students direct feedback on how they're doing. In addition to feedback from their teacher, having students process their own level of functioning in a group (that is, discuss it and self-assess) consistently correlates with better skill development and better academic learning (Yager et al. 1986). The explicit teaching of social skills and the frequent debriefing or processing by students of how they did builds an expectation through repetition that the skills will be used generally in the classroom. Transfer to settings outside school is more likely to happen if we follow the guidelines of the principle of learning Teach for Transfer found in Chapter 9.

Conflict Resolution

The final stage of development for a healthy classroom (or school) community is building the capacity of its members to solve their own conflicts. This work includes acknowledgment that conflicts are normal and that controversy, which is not the same as conflict, is actually good for learning.

Conflict is defined as a situation where the needs of two people are at odds, and the current course of behavior or action appears to make one the winner at the expense of the other. *Conflict resolution* means coming up with a solution that meets the needs of both parties or a compromise that both can live with.

Most conflict-resolution models have similar steps and teach similar skills. For example, Thomas Gordon's (1974) model includes the skills of active listening and "I" messages, which are vital communication skills for enabling people to work through classic conflict-resolution steps.

The following steps occur in variations in most programs:

1. Recognize your anger, calm down, and collect yourself. Some programs teach relaxation or self-imposed time-out techniques for this stage.

2. Identify the real problem. Johnson and Johnson (1995, pp. 5–6) break down the second step into valuable components:
   ❖ Jointly define the problem as small and specific.
   ❖ Determine what each person wants.
   ❖ Determine how each person feels.
   ❖ Exchange reasons and rationale for positions.
   ❖ Reverse perspectives.

This stage can take some time. Many models advocate teaching students to identify their *needs*, not to speak in terms of actions or the solutions they want. Probing questions, clarifying questions, and considerable active listening are often required here. That is why a neutral mediator is often introduced into the process.

3. Decide on a positive goal. State a desired outcome in positive terms—for example, "We will both get enough time at the computer to rewrite our drafts."

4. Think of several solutions. Brainstorming techniques are often taught to students in this stage.

5. Evaluate the solutions, and pick one to try.

6. Make a plan. Often just picking a solution—"Share the computer time after lunch fifty-fifty"—isn't enough. A specific plan is needed designating who will do what, when, and where. The plan may need to be written and agreed to in writing.

7. Evaluate the plan to see if both parties are keeping their part of the bargain, if the plan is good, or if it needs to be revised. (For details and elaboration of these steps see Johnson and Johnson 1995, pp. 5:1–5:30.)

We are convinced that Johnson and Johnson (1995) are right: *every* student, not just some, should be trained as a mediator. It is in being a mediator that students learn and internalize the skills of conflict resolution. Only then will they have the skills available for their own autonomous use when they get into conflicts themselves. The implication is that mediation training for *all* students is the most powerful model for teaching effective conflict-resolution skills and getting students to transfer them into daily practice.

Social Problem Solving meetings as described in William Glasser's *Schools Without Failure* (1969) are an ideal forum for developing these steps and the skills to go with them.

In the only classroom climate study to investigate differential effects of climate variables by gander and race, Deng (1992) found that the achievement gap between Blacks, Hispanics, and Whites in mathematics and the achievement gap between boys and girls in mathematics widened when community was weak and tension was high. This finding underlines the importance of community as a variable in academic achievement for girls in math and perhaps for students of color in all subjects when classes are integrated.

Risk Taking and Confidence

As we move from community building to the domain of risk taking, we examine what teachers can do to promote confidence and a safe atmosphere to "go for it." The five levels of this dimension of classroom climate are not as clearly developmental as they were in community because each level here is really a belief rather than a set of steps. We believe that the foundation of intellectual risk taking in classrooms is built on internal beliefs about errors and what they mean, about speed of learning and what it signifies, about the need to "get it" on your own as opposed to working with others and getting help.[2] Productive beliefs about errors, speed, and getting help may be derived from one's basic belief about intelligence (namely, that intelligence can be developed, and everyone can do well if they put in the time and use good strategies to learn). Whatever the relationships between these beliefs turn out to be, it is clear that we can identify a repertoire of teacher behaviors associated with strengthening each belief.

Figure 13.3 shows the five beliefs that underline risk taking in their negative and positive forms. The positive beliefs are life liberating, the negative ones life limiting.

This risk-taking dimension of climate has to do with the amount of confidence a student has and the amount of social and academic risk taking the student will do. If it is well developed, a student might be able to say, "It's safe to take a risk here. If I try hard, learn from errors, and persist, I can succeed."

There is a need to collect specific strategies and approaches for nourishing student risk taking, a need that has been suggested but thus far unfulfilled. Others often acknowledge the importance of risk taking but seldom explain how to cultivate it. For example, one author writes, "A big piece of teaching for understanding is setting up social norms that promote respect for other people's ideas. You don't get that to happen by telling. You have to change the social norms—which takes time and consistency" (Lampert 1994).

---

2   Thanks to John D'Auria for his creative thinking in helping to work out this framework.

Figure 13.3: Five Beliefs That Underlie Risk Taking
Positive beliefs are life liberating, the negative ones life limiting.

POSITIVE BELIEFS	NEGATIVE BELIEFS
On errors:	*On errors:*
Mistakes help one learn.	Mistakes are a sign of weakness.
On speed:	*On speed:*
You are not expected to understand everything the first time around. Care, quality, and perseverance are what count.	Speed is what counts. Faster is smarter.
On getting help:	*On getting help:*
Good students solicit help and lots of feedback on their work.	Good students can do it by themselves.
On effort and ability:	*On effort and ability:*
Consistent effort and effective strategies are the main determinants of success.	Inborn intelligence is the main determinant of success.
On effort and ability:	*On effort and ability:*
Everyone is capable of high achievement, not just the fastest.	Only the few who are bright can achieve at a high level.

But how to do this, one wonders.

Here is another example. In a wonderful exposition on the practices of exemplary teachers who use cognitive strategies to move students from novice to expert in their problem solving in various disciplines, Bruer (1993) writes:

> The benchmark lesson on gravity begins 6 weeks into the course. By this time Minstrell [the teacher] has established a rapport with his class. He has created an environment conducive to developing understanding, a climate where questioning and respect for diverse opinions prevail, a climate where the process of scientific reasoning can be made explicit and self-conscious. Even veteran teachers marvel at how uninhibited Minstrell's students are in expressing ideas, suggesting hypotheses, and arguing positions. (p. 42)

How does Mr. Minstrell get his students to be so uninhibited?

> A few days later, Minstrell and the class analyze their reasoning about the time it would take a 1-kilogram and a 5-kilogram object to fall the same distance. They run the crucial experiment—a miniature replay of Galileo's apocryphal experiment at Pisa. After both balls hit the floor simultaneously, Minstrell returns to the board where he had written the quiz answers. "Some of you were probably feeling pretty dumb with these kind of answers. Don't feel dumb," he counsels. "Let's see what's valuable about each of these answers, because each one's valuable. Why would you think heavier things fall faster?"* (pp. 43–44)

Now we are beginning to get clues about creating this uninhibited atmosphere.

Here is a final example acknowledging the importance of risk taking:

> Inquiry teaching is difficult for teachers and requires skills that must be developed through intensive staff development. If a student whose answer is challenged does not trust the teacher, or the other students, the follow-up question, intended to cause the student to think more deeply about the subject, may have the opposite effect. The student may interpret the follow-up question as a clue that the initial response was wrong and that he or she is about to be made to feel foolish in front of the rest of the class. Threat seems to reduce our ability to think at higher levels, and what could be more threatening than public failure and ridicule?

> For this type of instruction to be effective, a teacher must create a classroom environment where students *feel safe to express their thinking*, where they trust their teacher and fellow students, and where they understand the difference between criticizing ideas and criticizing people. (italics added) (Ellsworth and Sindt 1994)[†]

This interpretation of the effect of removing threat—the threat of being laughed at, of feeling foolish, or of being wrong—is resoundingly confirmed by current trends in research on brain function (Sylvester 1994). What then can we say about specific ways to strengthen a climate for risk taking?

Errors

In this country we tend to believe in the fixed, innate, and unalterable nature of intelligence. Most children learn early in school that mistakes are signs of weakness instead of data to use and an opportunity for learning. Cultivating the latter belief about mistakes is the very foundation for confidence and risk taking in the classroom. Thirty years ago Jerome Bruner represented this idea when he said that our goal should be to help students "experience success and failure not as reward and punishment, but as information." People who succeed in building this element of climate do so explicitly. Beverly Hollis, a seventh-grade English teacher in Lincoln, Mass., writes:

> At the beginning of the year, when students are reticent to answer and wait time has been exhausted, I ask, "Is this a life-or-death situation? No, well, so what if you're wrong then? This is one answer out of the trillion you will give in your life, so what if it's wrong? If it is wrong, I guarantee I won't let you leave until you've heard the right answer, and you'll probably remember it longer for having missed it. But most importantly, you will have risked giving the answer. So many insightful answers and comments are never made because you, as students, are afraid to be wrong. I don't want that to be the case in this room."

> I talk about risks in my personal life—my month-long wilderness canoeing trip—and risks I'm taking by teaching a unit in a particular way. I'll say, "I want to try something new I've learned in my class, and I need your feedback." I do ask for their feedback after every unit. I tell them they can say they disliked a particular approach I used on the material covered as long as they offer positive criticism in pointing out what they didn't like and why, and if they offer alternatives or suggestions

---

* Reprinted with permission from the Summer 1993 issue of the *American Educator*, the quarterly journal of the American Federation of Teachers. Bruer, John T. "The Mind's Journey from Novice to Expert." *American Educator* 38 (Summer 1993): 6–15.

† Ellsworth, P. C., and V. G. Sindt. "Helping 'Aha' to Happen: The Contributions of Irving Sigel." *Educational Leadership* 51 (May 1994): 40–44. Copyright © 1994 by ASCD. Reprinted by permission. All rights reserved.

of what else I could have done to make it better. [Notice that in letting students critique her units, Ms. Hollis is giving them power.] I also give them choices about how they want to learn a particular unit and ask them to tell me why this would be the best approach to take. They love having the power; they have been incredibly perceptive, and as a consequence, they have been very accepting of my high expectations and my criticism when they fall short of the mark. I have students earn extra credit points to improve their grades on tests by listing what they were mixed up about or how they "messed up" on a test answer. And I openly and readily admit my own mistakes. Hopefully, this climate of honesty and risk taking allows me to correct students and myself without any of us feeling guilty or stupid for having made a mistake.

Anna Shine of the New England School of English in Boston says:

> One of the behaviors I encourage is making mistakes or guessing. I tell my students that I don't care if they are wrong, but I do care if they don't try, that there is no shame in trying and making a mistake or in falling short of their goals, but there is shame in not trying. And worse than shame, a learning opportunity is not maximized. Again and again, I say to them, "Mistakes are not important; understanding is."

> Obviously students will not take risks unless it is safe to do so. So, in my classroom, I try to create this environment, to make it safe to make mistakes because students can learn from mistakes. In fact, I reward students with big (2 inches in diameter) gold stars in two situations. One is if they produce great work, and the other is if they produce great mistakes.

> On the first day of class, when I show them my gold stars, they look at me as if I'm crazy. "A gold star for a mistake?" they think. "She doesn't know what she's doing." However, they soon learn that a gold star mistake is a mistake from which every student in the class can learn something. By making this great mistake, the student has provided everyone with a new learning opportunity, and the student himself has learned that it is safe to take a risk. By taking that risk, he grew (his knowledge and his confidence), the class learned, and he received one of the coveted gold stars.

In a similar vein, Terry McCarthy of the North Pole Elementary School in Fairbanks, Alaska, gives "Bravery Points" to kids who have the courage to try hard questions or problems even if they're not sure they can get them. In these and other ways invented by thoughtful teachers, climates of risk taking and safety to make errors are deliberately created and nurtured.

Speed

A second belief about learning that children bring to school in this country is that faster is better instead of believing that care, quality, and perseverance are what matter. What do teachers do to disabuse students of the life-limiting belief in the virtue of speed versus care and perseverance?

In Chapter 11, we described a policy on retakes of tests that would grant students as a final grade the highest score they got on a test or its retake no matter how many tries they took (assuming alternate forms of tests are available). This practice would replace averaging the test and its retake. Beyond that practice, giving only A, B, and Not Yet as grades signals that ultimate performance at high standards is what we're after, and nothing less will do. Getting there after suffering through a period of "Not Yet" does not make one's A any less valuable—just longer in coming.[3]

Use of wait time, with an explanation of it to the class, is an everyday practice that reinforces thoughtfulness and perseverance rather than quickness. Mary Ann Pilat of the Wellesley Middle School uses a related practice, called the Level Playing Field:

> I explain to students that linear thinkers can come up with prompt answers to class discussion questions, but that gestalt, divergent thinkers, an equally legitimate learning style, often are stimulated onto side connections and thoughts by questions in class. So while following those interesting thoughts, the speedster linear thinkers have answered the question and appear to be getting all the answers. Divergent thinkers tend to participate less in class. So to make the playing field level for them in getting ready for a class discussion, I put the major questions we're going to discuss on the board and give everyone five minutes to think about them first before starting the discussion. I've been getting much greater participation from lots more kids, including some who never spoke in class before.

The final strategy for valuing care and perseverance above speed is the routine practice of Reteaching Loops

---

3   Innovative school schedules can support this grading policy. Trimesters can be scheduled instead of two semesters. In between each trimester, a week can be reserved for two purposes: students who have completed all course requirements at a high level can take enrichment or extension courses; students who have not yet completed course requirements at a high level can have one extra focused week with teacher support to finish their "Not Yets."

described in Chapter 11. To make Reteaching Loops do what they can for classroom climate, nominating oneself for inclusion in a loop must be a behavior of high esteem and status in the class.

Getting Feedback and Help

Another factor that obstructs learning and contaminates most classroom climates is the belief that "good students do it by themselves," instead of the belief that what makes good students is that they solicit help and lots of feedback on their work.

Teachers support the development of this belief by explicitly modeling and encouraging it and by creating structures that manifest it. For example, the peer editing process in place in many writing programs can be applied to reports in other subjects; students would be expected to have peers critique their drafts according to commonly understood criteria and to do final drafts with their input in mind.

Other structures for mutual help can be structured into classroom routines:

◆ Students can take turns taking notes for the "absentee folder," which sits on a desk in the back of the room as a resource for absent students. When students come back after an absence, the notes help them catch up on what they missed, and the student who took the notes is available for personal help to the student who was absent.

◆ Teachers can organize students in groups or pairs of "study buddies" who are expected to help each other interpret assignments and prepare for tests.

◆ Various models of cooperative learning build in incentives for all team members that each member does well. Improvement of any individual's score on a quiz over that person's previous average earns points for the whole team. Team study time is provided so the members can help each other out. (See Slavin 1986.)

Many other activity structures, such as Teammates Consult, Four Corners, Pairs Check, and Learning Buddies (Kagan 1992), are available for helping students get committed to asking for appropriate help.

Effort and Ability

To the degree that students believe intelligence is innate, fixed, measurable, and unevenly distributed, they will probably also believe that whatever quantity of intelligence they have is the main determinant of how they will do in school and elsewhere in life (Howard 1993). It is difficult to be brought up in this country believing anything else, for the concept of intelligence as an entity that regulates our possibilities is more developed and more influential in the United States than in any other nation. In fact, the concept of intelligence as a fixed and measurable entity was created on our very own shores at a particular time in history, between approximately 1890 and 1920 (Gould 1982; Oakes 1985).

In this section we move on to the consequence of this belief, to the sweet fruits of its opposite, and how to transform students' belief into that opposite image. The opposite belief—the life-liberating one that fuels motivation and accelerates learning when it replaces the belief that innate intelligence is the main determinant of success—is this: Consistent effort and effective strategies are the main determinants of success (Howard 1993). With these two things in place, everyone is capable of high achievement, not just the fastest and most confident.

Attribution theory explains the dynamics at work in the two different belief systems (Weiner 1970). The theory posits that the reasons we give to ourselves (the attributions we make) for our success when we succeed and for our failure when we fail have a dramatic impact on our future behavior. In fact, these internal explanations account for our future behavior. Teachers who want to help students change their beliefs about the value of effort and the importance of good strategies versus innate intelligence pursue positive behaviors in the ten arenas of classroom life described in Chapter 11. For example, they stick with students who don't answer quickly; they give cues and use wait time. Here the chapter on Classroom Climate overlaps with Chapter 11 (the study of teaching behaviors that convince students they are able and that effort is what matters). The arenas through which the three messages— "This is important," "You can do it," "I won't give up on you"—are sent are also the vehicles on hand for convincing students they already have enough intelligence to do rigorous material well. What they need to do is work long enough, be resourceful, and learn strategies that will help them. Teachers' responsibility is to teach them strategies explicitly.

Influence

"Effective teachers know that to become engaged, students must have some feelings of ownership—of the class or the task—and personal power—a belief that what they do will make a difference" (Dodd 1995). This belief is echoed in two bodies of literature of the 1980s and 1990s. First, many frameworks for understanding thinking and personality style (e.g., Myers and McCaulley 1985; Harrison and Bramson 1982) find large percentages of people who have the need to be in charge or in control of at least certain aspects of their environment in order to function well. Second, the literature on constructivist learning and teaching posits that learning for true understanding requires students to construct their own meaning (Brooks and Brooks 1993). This involves owning their own questions and pursuing their own lines of inquiry with teacher guidance. These two literatures support the same proposition: Successful teachers find ways for students to have some ownership and influence over the flow of events and the intellectual life of the classroom.

There are many ways to offer students choice and influence over their lives in school. One pertains to the social system of the classroom—the rules of the classroom game as opposed to the rules for interpersonal behavior one often sees posted on walls. The rules of the classroom game pertain to social norms and procedures for conducting class discourse. They are often undiscussed and unwritten, though that is something we would recommend changing. The teacher asks a question, the student responds, and the teacher evaluates is a typical cycle of discourse reflecting the "rule" that the teacher will control the talk in the room. Without losing control of the class or the curriculum, a teacher can permit students to participate in shaping and operating these procedural systems for discourse and business.

Another route to ownership and influence goes through learning style and choices. Many authors (e.g., Mamchur 1990) urge giving students choices whenever possible about how to work on learning new concepts or carry out assignments. Student choice making can be improved and empowered by knowledge about their own learning styles.

Finally, in addition to having some control over the rules of the classroom game and the shape of the learning activities they pursue, students can have some joint ownership of the intellectual life of the classroom through the way in which questions are posed and meaning is generated.

The five sections that follow might be thought of as levels of depth and sophistication in our strategic approach to giving students authentic influence in classroom life. Whereas you could work on them in any order or even simultaneously, it is useful to understand which ones are more complex and why. Then you can avoid biting off more than you can chew in developing this strand of classroom climate. You need not address the five issues sequentially and wait for a certain level of "development" before beginning practices aimed at another level. For example, there is no need to wait until students are stopping a class to ask for clarification before teaching students about their own learning style and how to use that knowledge to influence assignments. But it might be worth bearing in mind that the five approaches described below do increase progressively in complexity. Therefore, if you are interested in developing student ownership and influence you might start with the simpler and then move slowly to the more complex forms of student ownership.

Stop My Teaching

"Stop my teaching" refers to empowering the students to use signals to tell a teacher when the instruction is leaving them behind. Lilian Katz (1992) talks about giving her son, a beginning teacher, some basic principles of practice for successful teaching:

> One of the things you always want to do as a teacher . . . teaching children old or young, doesn't matter who, you always want to teach the children

to say to you things like: "Hold it; I'm lost." "Can you go over this one more time?" "Is this what you mean?" "Can you show me again?" "Have I got it right?" . . . ways in which you empower the learner to keep you posted on where they need help. If the children are very young you just say, "Pull my sleeve." . . . whatever, as long as the child has the strategy to say to you "I don't get it." "I'm lost." "You're going too fast." "Hold it." and so on. (ASCD Conference 1992)

Teachers who take this injunction seriously develop signal systems where students can indicate on their own initiative that they are lost and want the teacher to stop and explain again. Hand signals like thumbs down held tight against one's chest could be such a signal. Or students could put red, yellow, or green cards on the corner of their desks like traffic light signals. Thus, teachers could get a quick visual read on how well students were understanding a discussion.

When the idea of stopping the teaching becomes part of classroom culture, other symbols or phrases come to represent the practice. One teacher told her class the story of a family vacation where she and her husband and six children stopped at McDonalds for lunch. Loading up hurriedly in the tightly packed van after their quick meal, they didn't do a head count and were four miles down the road before Mom said, "Where's Bobby?!?" Bobby was back at McDonalds.

The teacher now uses that phrase frequently in class as a coded signal: "Have I left you at McDonalds?" and the children also use the code to signal when they're getting lost. "Ms. Swift, I think I'm back at McDonalds!" The humorous shared code serves to authorize the practice of stopping the teacher's teaching, and the teacher's affirming reaction shows the practice to be a valued one that earns kudos for the child rather than a frown or a veiled accusation of inadequacy.

Negotiating the Rules of the Classroom Game

Negotiating the rules of the classroom game means involving students in creating the routines and procedures of classroom discourse and class business. These rules are different from the rules of behavior that teachers and students commonly work out at the beginning of the year. The rules we are talking about here are usually tacit, underground, and unstated. They pertain to teacher-student and student-student interaction around such issues as questions and answers, class dialogue, and procedures and protocols for taking turns. Recitation lessons of teacher questions and student answers do indeed often turn out to be a game, where students try to win by getting the right answers and avoid losing by shrinking into invisibility when they don't know the answers.

Once in one of our courses, Dick Adams, a housemaster at Newton North High School in Newton, Mass., asked his students if he had ever played Guess-What's-On-the-Teacher's-Mind with them. The concept had come up when we studied questioning techniques under clarity. Recall that teachers who play Guess-What's-On-the-Teacher's-Mind (GWOTM) ask inexplicit questions when they have a particular answer in mind but the way they ask the question allows for a universe of possible answers. "I don't ever do that, do I?" asked Dick. A number of slow, knowing affirmative nods came back at him from the students. "No . . . Really? Give me some examples."

They did. And from that opening there proceeded a class discussion of how to conduct class discourse in such a way as to eliminate student pet peeves and increase productive participation. For example, they decided together that a student who couldn't answer a question could refer it to another student, whom they named. If three students in a row couldn't answer the question, Dick would conclude he had asked a bad question; then he had to ask it in a different way or ask students where the gap was.

His students became so excited over the way the class was going that they asked one of us to videotape the class. We realized that the students were not just happy over the new dynamics and improved clarity of class discussions, but elated over having been a force that influenced the shape of the class itself. Students had changed the rules of the classroom game in collaboration with their teacher and emerged from the traditional nether region of passive ciphers to active and authorized players in determining how things go.

The point of this story is to raise the question: What opportunities do students have to influence the rules of the classroom game, to shape the form and dynamics of interaction and operation? How can we give them ownership in these rules?

Teaching Students to Use Principles of Learning and Other Strategies

A third way to give students influence in classroom life is to share with them teaching and learning strategies we use ourselves. By including them in the secret knowledge of teaching and learning strategies, we give students choices, power, and license to control their learning.

Many of the Principles of Learning set out in Chapter 9 should be taught to students directly so they can use them themselves to be more powerful learners. The same is true for a number of techniques in Chapter 8. This is a good moment to review those principles to decide which ones you think would be most beneficial to turn over to your students as tools for learning. The more we are interested in empowering students and giving them choices, the more we will explicitly put learning tools at their disposal and urge them to use them autonomously.

Here are some of our nominees for principles to teach to students:

◆ *Sequence:* Students can use this principle to sequence their own lists when studying vocabulary words (or anything else that is sequential in nature) so the items hardest for them are in the optimal first and last positions.

◆ *Practice:* Students can use knowledge of this principle to optimize their personal practice schedules.

◆ *Goal setting:* Students can use this principle to set realistic academic and behavioral targets for improvement and make effective plans of action to meet them.

◆ *Explanatory devices:* Visual imagery and especially graphic organizers can become regular tools for students. Imagery can be used to pause during study and construct meaning in a visual way. Graphic organizers can become a habit as a note-taking technology through which students assimilate information as they read, hear, or see it. Teachers can integrate the use of these devices into assignments and work toward having students choose when and how to use them.

While passing these strategies on to students, teachers who are aware of attribution theory and who are committed to conveying the three expectations messages—"This is important," "You can do it," and "I won't give up on you"—will see they have a special opening. They will seize frequent opportunities to connect the use of these strategies with student success rather than let students attribute successful performance to intelligence. "Well, José, did you use any graphic organizers when you reviewed that chapter? No? Well, look—you're a strong visual learner. You and I both know that. Let's go over how to use that strategy with material like this. I know you can make it work for you!"

Learning Style and Choices

"Students using knowledge of learning style" means teachers are not just using their knowledge of learning style to adapt lessons for the styles of their students; they are teaching the students about their own learning styles and the implications of those styles for what kinds of assignments will be difficult and what will be easier. Furthermore, they encourage students to use knowledge of their own styles to guide their study routines and even to ask for modifications in assignments that allow them to use their strengths. These steps set the stage for a more complex level of empowerment, that is, giving students explicit choices over assignments, forms of tests, and forms of projects. The "Nonreport Report" is a practice that invites these choices.

Many readers will have been to a workshop on learning style in their careers, and some may be thoroughly trained in one or more of the learning style frameworks. These frameworks help us understand the similarities and differences in the ways humans take in, process, and express their learning. They also help us understand the features of the learning environment and the different kinds of activities that work best for individuals. For example, some people learn best when they can talk and interact with others as they deal with new concepts. Others like to read, listen, view, and assimilate alone before interacting with other people. This body of knowledge about learning style preferences can be a powerful vehicle for giving students ownership in classroom life.

Helping students understand their own learning style sets the stage for some important forms of empowerment. First, students can predict (and teachers can help them predict and prepare for) the difficulty of certain assignments or tasks that do not match their preferred learning style. If we have set the stage properly and taught about learning style, the value system associated with learning style frameworks enables students to see their difficulty in certain tasks as attributable to differences, not deficiencies. Second, the capacity to predict learning style match or mismatch to tasks enables students to mobilize extra effort and to seek help when appropriate. When we encourage students to use knowledge of their own learning style to do either of these two things, we are empowering them in significant ways.

The simplest place to start teaching students about learning style is with modality preference: visual, auditory, kinesthetic, or combinations of them. Simple modality preference tests (see Barbe and Milone 1980) can be used to have students identify their preferences. Then we must look for (and share out loud with students that we are looking for) ways to vary our teaching to address different modalities.[4]

Another framework for learning style differences that students can use in the same way is the left-brain–right brain or global-analytic framework. Rita Dunn (1990) provides another useful set for students to know about and for them to use to empower their learning effectiveness. Anthony Gregorc's (1985) framework provides a fourth and more complicated but highly useful cut at style difference. Bernice McCarthy's 4MAT System (1987) is a fifth, and Gardner's Multiple Intelligences (1983) frameworks provides a sixth. Finally the sophisticated Myers-Briggs provides a seventh.

All of these frameworks are worthy of study, and we believe they are an important part of teachers' professional knowledge. But for the sake of classroom climate and this particular dimension of influence, the point is to choose one of them and work overtly on giving the framework to students, that is, teaching them to use it not to label themselves but to modulate their effort, seek help when appropriate, and sometimes take initiative to alter assignments based on their self-knowledge from a learning style perspective. Giving students license and encouragement to speak up in this way to ask for modifications of assignments brings us to the topic of choices.

What kinds of choices do students get to make about their academic work and how they do it? Carolyn Mamchur (1990) writes: "Giving students choices may seem like a complex issue. But actually, it is dead simple. The rule is

this: whenever you can give a student a choice of any kind, do it."

A Nonreport is a good example of students' influencing assignments and the shape of products. There is nothing particularly unique about Nonreports. They are simply outside assignments—but with several major differences. A Nonreport is anything that does not fall into the category of straight written information. The task is to convince students accustomed to the way school is supposed to be that their teacher will accept and value their ideas. Their first question is usually "What do you want?" since they know that pleasing the teacher is the quickest way to a good grade. Here is how a Nonreport works:

1. Impress on them that a standard written report will receive no credit, since it does not meet the requirements of the assignment.

2. Make the assignment worth enough points so that not doing it will result in a substantial drop in grade. At first, there is a great risk in doing something not completely spelled out, so the risk of losing credit must be greater.

3. Create a grading scale that gives equal merit to content and to creativity (more loosely, to the effort the student has to make to personalize the knowledge he or she conveys).

4. Keep the topic very general, giving the students ample opportunity to select from among a wide variety of ideas. For example, if you are studying a unit on measurement, allow them to select anything at all dealing with measurement. Point out to them that there are few occupations (hobbies, sports, etc.) that do not contain measurement of some kind. Give them examples. Challenge them to name something that apparently has nothing to do with measurement—but be quick enough on your feet to find the measurement involved.

5. If they insist, and they may at first, give them a couple of examples of Nonreport-type formats (they are endless and limited only by imagination). For example, they could create a game, write a song, role-play a game show, do a slide or tape presentation, make a scrapbook, or build a model. But warn them that they will receive more credit for doing something you haven't thought of than copying something you have. And stick by that statement!

6. Perhaps most important, don't do this assignment unless you are willing to truly value the students' ideas. If you can't suspend your own idea of what is right or good and try to see the product from their point of view, they will never believe you again. But neither

---

4   Useful resources for thinking about including multiple modalities in instruction are David Lazear, *Multiple Intelligence Approaches to Assessment* and *Seven Pathways to Learning*, published by Zephyr Press.

should you give credit for hastily conceived and executed junk. I once received a shoebox with a hole punched in one end that was labeled "Working model of a black hole." Hah!

I have found that giving 10 points for the idea, 10 points for the execution, and 10 points for the content, plus 5 for effort, works out well—a total of 35 points. The effort points come in when a person has had three weeks to do a project that might be reasonably well done but obviously took only 15 minutes compared to someone else who spent several hours. You can tell by looking.

The first time you do this, you will probably receive the usual assortment of collages, collections, and posters copied from books. But when these students see the more adventurous, creative, and "fun" projects getting all the praise, they will be more willing to let go a little the next time.

By the end of the first year that I had students do these projects, I turned them loose on a topic we had not covered in class: solar energy. They researched the topic, did their Nonreports—including a working parabolic solar cooker and a miniature solar greenhouse complete with Trombe walls made of plastic soft drink bottles—and presented them to the class, thus covering almost all the important aspects of solar energy—with no effort on the part of the teacher. One of the most rewarding aspects of these assignments is that, frequently, the students who usually get C's or D's in regular assignments really come into their own on Nonreports.

Nonreports allow students to plan, research, and execute. It evokes their creative potential and forces interaction with the content. Many students sought "experts" to help them and learned the intricacies of carpentry, photography, sound, and art—because they wanted to. And it is tremendously exciting to see projects come into the classroom that are far beyond anything the teacher would have assigned or expected. (Anonymous, *Mindsight*, New Lenox, Ill., 1989)

We would add specific criteria for success that make clear to students exactly what the attributes of quality work in the Nonreport will be. For example, in the Nonreport on solar energy, the criteria could be: (1) explains three different ways of converting solar energy, (2) discusses costs and efficiencies of various forms of solar energy, and (3) uses data to compare the efficiency of solar, fossil fuel, and nuclear energy. Students using these criteria could create dozens of different kinds of products to represent their learning, from radio shows to models to hypercard assemblies.

Randolf and Evertson (1995) give a simple example of student choice that suggests how plentiful are the opportunities for giving them:

Ms. Cooper often delegated tasks that would typically be assigned [by her] to students. We have already described students as providing the text for writing class through Sharing Models/Generating Characteristics. In this activity, students also took on the task of controlling the floor, which would traditionally be a teacher task. Areas of student control include deciding how to participate, getting the class's attention and leading the discussion by calling on peers . . . student readers usually stood in the front of the room, but Ms. Cooper gave students the option of reading from their desks. Students were given the same choice when they shared their rough drafts with the class. The fact that Ms. Cooper did not define this aspect of appropriate participation gave students choice in how to manage this aspect of controlling the floor.

The ability of students to make choices and control the activity flow and the discourse within the group is partially responsible for the success of cooperative learning. In all cooperative learning models, students work in groups in which they control the dialogue, who speaks, when, and for how long.

Students and Their Communities as Sources of Knowledge

Constructivist Teaching

Constructivist pedagogy brings student influence to the intellectual life of the classroom and may be the most advanced level of student ownership. It is also the most complex and requires the largest paradigm shift for teachers; most of us, after all, were educated in schools where other people's constructions of knowledge were handed to us for consumption and digestion. Brooks and Brooks (1993) provide five overarching principles of constructivist pedagogy:

1. Posing problems of emerging relevance to learners.

2. Structuring learning around "big ideas" or primary concepts.

3. Seeking and valuing students' points of view.

4. Adapting curriculum to address students' suppositions.

5. Assessing student learning in the context of teaching. (p. 33)

There is still a place in good education for "active reception learning" as Ausubel (1963) puts it. But there is also a large place for carefully designed teaching that allows students to construct meaning for themselves.

Randolf and Evertson (1995) in their analysis of interactive discourse in a writing class describe this kind of pedagogy: "The construction of knowledge, which takes

The Principal as Managerial Leader

place through negotiation, depends on the redistribution of power from teachers to students. The fact that knowledge is presumed to come from students defines students as knowledge-holders, an identity usually retained by the teacher."

Constructivist teaching puts students in the legitimate role of knowledge generators and knowledge editors, whether in science, social studies, language arts, or any other academic discipline (Brooks and Brooks 1993). The examples in the Randolf and Evertson study describe a series of lessons on literary genre. They show how teachers' conscious regulation of dialogue and interaction with students can make students genuinely empowered knowledge generators. For example, one teacher, Ms. Cooper, asked students to bring in examples of fables to share and discuss in class so they could extract the characteristics of fables from analyzing these examples. At one point she asked the class to look for generalizations they could make about the morals of fables:

Teacher: What can we say about the characteristics of morals? [Students offer some suggestions.]

Maybe we need to explain what a lesson or moral is—how to be a better person. I'm going to put that up, unless you have objections.

Laurie: They're trying to prevent you from making mistakes. [Teacher writes, "Stories are used to help you become a better person and not make mistakes."]

Tim: I disagree. Sometimes some of the things are wrong.

Hillary: Can be [used to help you]. [Teacher changes "are" to "can be" in the sentence on the board: "Stories can be used to help you become a better person and not make mistakes."]

Onika: But everybody makes mistakes.

Teacher: You're right [Adds to the sentence on the board: "or learn from characters' mistakes in the story."], but the purpose of the fable is to help you not to make so many mistakes.

In analyzing this episode Randolf and Evertson (1995) comment:[*]

The discussion begins with Ms. Cooper's question. The answers she receives do not give her the information she wants, so Ms. Cooper supplies her own answer: a moral teaches how to be a better person. In stating her answer, Ms. Cooper clarifies

her question: she is asking about the purpose of a moral. With this new information, Laurie is able to supply a response that Ms. Cooper validates by incorporating it into the characteristic she is writing on the chalkboard. So far Ms. Cooper is in the position of authority in the classroom, initiates the topic, students respond with possible answers, and she evaluates them, rejecting all responses until she hears one that fits her expectations.

The nature of the interaction changes, however, as Tim questions the characteristic that is the joint construction of Ms. Cooper and Laurie. In effect, Tim takes on the role of evaluator of the response, moving Ms. Cooper into the role of co-collaborator with Laurie. Ms. Cooper's response is thus demonstrated to be as open to evaluation as any other participant's response.

Onika and Susan then join the deliberation, questioning the need for morals as they have defined them in class more than they are questioning the definition itself. Why, they argue, should morals try to keep you from making mistakes, when you're going to make them anyway, and they help you learn? These contributions are initiations of a new topic, which Ms. Cooper responds to and evaluates by treating them as negotiations of meaning, signaling her acceptance by incorporating the new contribution into the statement on the board. Thus, the characteristic as it is finally stated is the joint construction of Ms. Cooper, Laurie, Tim, Hillary, Onika, and Susan.

Similar scenarios can be found in the literature for helping students construct knowledge in science and mathematics. This kind of teaching requires a role shift for some teachers of significant proportions away from being dispensers of knowledge to facilitating negotiation of meaning by students.

The role of the teacher in constructivist science teaching is often to involve students in predicting phenomena, then reacting to observed phenomena and constructing hypotheses, which they then test to account for their observations. For example, most students predict that heavy objects fall faster then lighter ones—which is incorrect. The hypothesis making and dialogue about subsequent experiments and explanations that constructivist teachers facilitate have similar qualities to the dialogue in the Randolf and Evertson example.

The changes that take place when teachers move to include more constructivist teaching in their repertoire are subtle but significant. The classroom does not look any different, and the assignments and topics may not seem much different. Where the changes show up is in dialogue

---

[*]   Reprinted with permission. Randolf, Catherine H., and Carolyn M. Evertson. "Managing for Learning: Rules, Roles, and Meanings in a Writing Class." *Journal of Classroom Interaction* 30 (Summer 1995): 17–25.

Integral Readings for Institutional Management: II   **173**

with students and in the roles teachers and students are playing in the conversations they have in class. Though surface changes may appear small, the role shift is large, and the evidence is strong that the effect is large in student motivation, effort, and understanding (Newmann and Wehlage 1995).

Culturally Relevant Teaching

As we move toward the year 2020, when fully half of all children in the United States will be people of color,[5] it is especially important to be creating schools that acknowledge and value the culture of all students. Excluding these children's cultures from school artifacts, customs, arts, and curriculum not only demotivates but alienates significant numbers of students (Cummins 1986). Ladson-Billings (1995) brings this argument into the more immediate domain of curriculum by pointing out that using the community as a source of curriculum experiences makes learning meaningful and active and also culturally relevant:

> Early in the school year, one teacher asked the students to identify one area in which they believed they had expertise. She then compiled a list of "classroom experts" for distribution to the class. Later, she developed a calendar and asked students to select a date that they would like to make a presentation in their area of expertise. When students made their presentations, their knowledge and expertise was a given. Their classmates were expected to be an attentive audience and to take seriously the knowledge that was being shared by taking notes and/or asking relevant questions. The variety of topics the students offered included rap-music, basketball, gospel singing, cooking, hair braiding, and baby sitting. Other students listed more school-like areas of expertise such as reading, writing, and mathematics. However, all students were required to share their expertise. (Ladson-Billings 1995)

Some may wonder how such open-ended assignments can be congruent with a school curriculum that contains specific skills the students are supposed to be mastering.

By using practices described in Chapter 16, teachers can weave skill objectives for research, organization, and reading, writing, and speaking skills (or any other skills that are in the curriculum) into the criteria for good presentations by student experts. The point that Ladson-Billings makes is that the students own the knowledge they present, and the knowledge is acknowledged to have value. The "classroom experts" assignment is a practice that is congruent with augmenting student ownership and influence because the knowledge of students and the culture from which that knowledge comes—namely, the students' own culture—is explicitly validated by a school learning activity.

"Culturally relevant teaching" is the topic of the article from which the Ladson-Billings excerpt comes. Culturally relevant teaching does not mean teaching about other cultures, though that can have value. It means validating the culture of students by including in-school learning experiences, topics, scenes, and knowledge that derive from the culture of the students themselves. It looks not only to individual students but also to the community from which the students come as a source of curriculum experiences.

> One teacher used the community as a basis of her curriculum. Her students searched the county historical archives, interviewed long-term residents, constructed and administered surveys and a questionnaire, and invited and listened to guest speakers to get a sense of the historical development of their community. Their ultimate goal was to develop a land use proposal for an abandoned shopping center that was a magnet for illegal drug use and other dangerous activities. The project ended with the students making a presentation before the City Council and Urban Planning Commission. One of the students remarked to me, "This [community] is not such a bad place. There are a lot of good things that happened here, and some of that is still going on." The teacher told me that she was concerned that too many of the students believed that the only option for success involved moving out of the community, rather than participating in its reclamation. (Ladson-Billings, 1995, p. 479)[6]

---

5   Hodgkinson, H. Presentation to Phi Delta Kappan Annual Conference, 1993.
6   In other parts of her report, Ladson-Billings (1995) argues extensively for building class community and an atmosphere of mutual support and help.

Classroom Climate Survey

This is a good point for readers to assess where they are in their thinking and practices with regard to classroom climate. We encourage readers to fill in the following survey for each of the three strands and compare answers in groups with colleagues.

Community and Mutual Support
How are students encouraged to get to know one another and to get to know other people?

When are students listened to, acknowledged, and affirmed as worthwhile, important, and cared-for people?

When do students learn group responsibility and interdependence?

What opportunities are there for learning social skills and cooperative learning?

How are conflict-resolution strategies being learned and practiced in the classroom and around the school?

Risk Taking and Confidence
What are the times when students are encouraged to take risks and find out it's okay to do so?

What do I do to disabuse students of the life-limiting belief in the virtue of speed versus care and perseverance?

When does the belief "good students solicit help and lots of feedback on their work" get communicated in the classroom?

In what ways do students learn that effort makes the difference?

Influence
What are the times when students are in a controlling or influencing role?

What principles of learning are students knowledgeable about and encouraged to use?

What are the opportunities for giving control to students within the models of teaching being used?

What opportunities are there to have students be authentic knowledge producers and structure classroom discourse from the constructivist perspective?

What opportunities are there for students to be experts?

What are the ways in which the local community culture is viewed as a source of "authorized" curriculum and thus as a worthwhile source of knowledge?

Source Materials on Classroom Climate

Anonymous. *Mindsight*. New Lenox, Ill., 1989.

Aronson, E. *The Jigsaw Classroom*. Beverly Hills, Calif.: Sage Publications, 1978.

Aspy, David, and F. N. Roebuck. *Kids Don't Learn from People They Don't Like*. Amherst, Mass.: Human Resource Development Press, 1977.

Ausubel, D. P. *The Psychology of Meaningful Verbal Learning*. New York: Grune & Stratton, 1963.

Barbe, Walter B., and Michael N. Milone, Jr. "Modality." *Instructor Magazine* (January 1980).

Battistich, Victor, Daniel Solomon, Dong-il Kim, Marilyn Watson, and Eric Schaps. "Schools as Communities, Poverty Levels of Student Populations, and Students' Attitudes, Motives, and Performance: A Multilevel Analysis" *American Educational Research Journal* 32 (Fall 1995).

Battistich, Victor, Daniel Solomon, Marilyn Watson, Judith Solomon, and Eric Schaps. "Effects of an Elementary School Program to Enhance Prosocial Behavior on Children's Cognitive-Social Problem-Solving Skills and Strategies." *Journal of Applied Developmental Psychology* 10 (1989): 147–169.

Bennett, Barrie, and Peter Smilanich. *Classroom Management*. Ontario, Canada: VISUTRONIX, Bookation, 1994.

Berger, Ron. "Building a School Culture of High Standards." Unpublished paper. Shutesbury, Mass.: Shutesbury Schools, 1990.

Berman, Sheldon. "Educating for Social Responsibility." *Educational Leadership* (November 1990): 75–80.

Brooks, Jacqueline Grennon, and Martin G. Brooks. *The Case for Constructivist Classrooms*. Alexandria, Va.: ASCD, 1993.

Bruer, John T. "The Mind's Journey from Novice to Expert." *American Educator* 38 (Summer 1993): 6–15.

Cabello, Beverly, and Raymond Terell. "Making Students Feel Like Family: How Teachers Create Warm and Caring Classroom Climates." *Journal of Classroom Interaction* 29 (1993): 17–23.

Charney, Ruth Sidney. *Teaching to Care: Management in the Responsive Classroom*. Greenfield, Mass.: Northeast Foundation for Children, 1992.

Chavez Chavez, Rudolpho. "The Use of High-Inference Measures to Study Classroom Climates: A Review." *Review of Educational Research* 54 (Summer 1984): 237–261.

Crocker, Robert K., and Gwen M. Brooker. "Classroom Control and Student Outcomes in Grades 2 and 5." *American Educational Research Journal* 23 (Spring 1986): 1–11.

Cummins, James. "Empowering Minority Students: A Framework for Intervention." *Harvard Educational Review* 56 (February 1986): 18–36.

Curran, Lorna. *Cooperative Lessons for Little Ones*. San Juan Capistrano, Calif.: Resources for Teachers, 1991.

Deng, Bing. *A Multilevel Analysis of Classroom Climate Effects on Mathematics Achievement of Fourth-Grade Students*. Paper based on Ed.D. dissertation at Memphis State University, February 1992. ED 348 222.

Dodd, Anne Wescott. "Engaging Students: What I Learned Along the Way." *Educational Leadership* (September 1995).

Dreikurs, R. *Psychology in the Classroom*. New York: Harper & Row, 1957.

Dreikurs, R., and L. A. Grey. *A New Approach to Classroom Discipline: Logical Consequences*. New York: Harper & Row, 1968.

Dunn, Rita, and Kenneth Dunn. *Teaching Students Through Their Individual Learning Styles: A Practical Approach*. Reston, Va.: Prentice-Hall, 1978.

Ellsworth, P. C., and Vincent G. Sindt. "Helping 'Aha' to Happen: The Contributions of Irving Sigel." *Educational Leadership* (February 1994).

Fraser, B. J. "Two Decades of Research on Perceptions of Classroom Environment." In B. J. Fraser (ed.), *The Study of Learning Environments* (pp. 1–33). Salem, Ore.: Assessment Research, 1986.

Fraser, B. J., and D. L. Fisher. "Student Achievement as a Function of Person-Environment Fit: A Regression Surface Analysis." *British Journal of Educational Psychology* 53 (1983): 89–99.

Fraser, Barry J., John A. Malone, and Jillian M. Neale. "Assessing and Improving the Psychosocial Environment of Mathematics Classrooms." *Journal of Research in Mathematics Education* 20 (1989): 191–201.

Fraser, Barry J., and Peter O'Brien. "Student and Teacher Perceptions of the Environment of Elementary School Classrooms." *Elementary School Journal* 20 (1985): 567–580.

Gardner, Howard. *Frames of Mind: The Theory of Multiple Intelligences*. New York: Basic Books, 1983.

Gibbs, Jeanne. *Tribes: A Process for Social Development and Cooperative Learning*. 2d ed. Santa Rosa, Calif.: Center Source Publications, 1989.

Glasser, W. *Reality Therapy*. New York: Harper & Row, 1965.

———. *Schools without Failure*. New York: Harper Colophon Books, 1969.

———. *The Total Quality School*. 1994.

Gordon, Thomas. *T.E.T.: Teacher Effectiveness Training*. New York: Peter H. Wyden, 1974.

Gould, Stephen J. *The Mismeasure of Man*. New York: W. W. Norton, 1982.

Gregorc, Anthony F. *Inside Styles: Beyond the Basics*. Maynard, Mass.: Gabriel Systems, Inc., 1985.

Haertel, G. D., H. J. Walberg, and E. H. Haertel. "Socio-psychological Environments and Learning: A Quantitative Synthesis." *British Educational Research Journal* 7 (1981): 27–36.

Harrison, Allen F., and Robert M. Bramson. *The Art of Thinking*. New York. Berkeley Books, 1982.

Hodgkinson, H. Presentation to Phi Delta Kappan Annual Conference, 1993.

Howard, Jeffrey. *The Social Construction of Intelligence*. Lexington, Mass.: Efficacy Inc., 1993.

Johnson, David W., and Roger T. Johnson. *Learning Together and Alone: Cooperative, Competitive, and Individualistic Learning*. 2d ed. Englewood Cliffs, N.J.: Prentice-Hall, 1987.

Johnson, David W., and Roger T. Johnson. *Teaching Students to Be Peacemakers*. Edina, Minn.: Interaction Book Co., 1995.

———. "Why Violence Prevention Programs Don't Work—What Does." *Educational Leadership* (February 1995): 63–68.

———. *Learning Together and Alone*. 2d ed. Englewood Cliffs, N.J.: Prentice-Hall, 1987.

Kagan, S. *Cooperative Learning*. San Juan Capistrano, Calif.: Kagan Cooperative Learning, 1992.

Katz, Lilian. "Five Keys to Successful Implementation of the Whole." Presentation to Association for Supervision and Curriculum Development, 1992. Audiotape 612–92123.

Kreidler, William J. *Creative Conflict Resolution*. Glenview, Ill.: Scott Foresman, 1984.

Ladson-Billings, G. "Toward a Theory of Culturally Relevant Pedagogy." *American Educational Research Journal* 32 (Fall 1995).

Lampert, Magdalena. "When the Problem is Not the Question and the Solution Not the Answer: Mathematical Knowing and Teaching." *American Educational Research Journal* 27, no. 1 (1990): 29–63.

Lafferty, J. Clayton. *The Subarctic Survival Situation*. Plymouth, Mich.: Human Synergistics, 1974, 1992.

Lazear, David. *Multiple Intelligence Approaches to Assessment: Solving the Assessment Conundrum*. Tucson: Zephyr Press, 1994.

———. *Seven Pathways of Learning: Teaching Students and Parents about Multiple Intelligences*. Tucson: Zephyr Press, 1994.

Mamchur, Caroline. "But the Curriculum." *Phi Delta Kappan* (April 1990).

Maslow, A. *Toward a Psychology of Being*. Princeton, N.J.: Van Nostrand, 1962.

McCabe, Margaret E., and Jaquelline Rhoades. *The Nurturing Classroom*. Willits, Calif.: ITA Publications, 1989.

McCarthy, Bernice. *The 4MAT System: Teaching to Learning Styles with Right/Left Mode Techniques*. Barrington, Ill., 1987.

Moos, R. H., and B. S. Moos. "Classroom Social Climate and Students' Absences and Grades." *Journal of Educational Psychology* 70 (1978): 263–269.

Myers, Isabel B., and Mary H. McCaulley. *Manual: A Guide to the Development and Use of the Myers-Briggs Type Indicator*. Palo Alto, Calif.: Consulting Psychologists Press, 1985.

Nelson, Jane, Lynn Lott, and H. Stephen Glenn. *Positive Discipline in the Classroom*. Rocklin, Calif.: Prima Publishing, 1993.

Newmann, Fred M., and Gary G. Wehlage. *Successful School Restructuring*. Madison, Wis.: University of Wisconsin, 1995.

Nunnery, John A., E. Dean Butler, and Venkata N. Bhaireddy. "Relationships between Classroom Climate, Student Characteristics, and Language Achievement in the Elementary Classroom: An Exploratory Investigation." Paper presented at the Annual Meeting of the American Educational Research Association, Atlanta, April 1993.

Oakes, Jeananie. *Keeping Track*. New Haven, Conn.: Yale University Press, 1985.

Pfeiffer, J. William, and John E. Jones. *A Handbook of Structured Experiences for Human Relations Training*. Vol. 1–8. La Jolla, Calif.: University Associates, 1974.

Poplin, Mary, and Joseph Weeres. *Voices from the Inside*. Claremont, Calif.: Institute for Education in Transformation, Claremont Graduate School, 1992.

Randolf, Catherine H., and Carolyn M. Evertson. "Managing for Learning: Rules, Roles, and Meanings in a Writing Class." *Journal of Classroom Interaction* 30 (Summer 1995): 17–25.

Scearce, Carol. *100 Ways to Build Teams*. Palatine, Ill.: IRI/Skylight Publishing, 1992.

Schutz, W. J. *Expanding Human Awareness*. New York: Grove Press, 1967.

Seigle, Pamela, and Gayle Macklem. *Social Competency Program*. Wellesley, Mass.: Stone Center, 1993.

Sharan, Yael, and Shlomo Sharan. *Expanding Cooperative Learning through Group Investigation*. New York: Teachers College Press, 1992.

Shaw, Vanston. *Community Building in the Classroom*. San Juan Capistrano, Calif.: Kagan Cooperative Learning, 1992.

Slavin, R. *Using Student Team Learning*. Baltimore: Center for Research on Elementary and Middle Schools, John Hopkins University, 1986.

Solomon, D., M. Watson, K. Delucchi, E. Schaps, and V. Battistich. "Enhancing Children's Prosocial Behavior in the Classroom." *American Educational Research Journal* 25 (1988): 527–554.

Stanford, Gene. *Developing Effective Classroom Groups*. New York: Hart Publishing Co., 1977.

Stephenson, James, and Beth Watrous. "The Morning Meeting Repertoire: A Collection of Ideas That Work." *The Responsive Classroom* 5, no. 2 (Fall/Winter 1993): 8.

Sylvester, Robert. *A Celebration of Neurons: An Educator's Guide to the Human Brain*. Alexandria, Va.: Association for Supervision and Curriculum Development, 1994.

Vernon, D. Sue, Jean B. Schumaker, and Donald D. Deshler. *The SCORE Skills: Social Skills for Cooperative Groups*. Lawrence, Kansas: Edge Enterprises, 1993.

Wade, Rahima C. "Encouraging Student Initiative in a Fourth Grade Classroom." *Elementary School Journal* 95 (March 1995): 339–354.

Weiner, B. *Theories of Motivation: From Mechanism to Cognition*. Chicago: Markham, 1972.

Wentzel, Kathryn R. "Social Competence at School: Relation Between Social Responsibility and Academic Achievement." *Review of Educational Research* 61 (Spring 1991): 1–24.

Withall, John. "The Development of a Technique for Measuring the Social Emotional Climate of the Classroom." *Journal of Experimental Education* 17 (1949): 347–361.

Wood, Chip. *Yardsticks*. Greenfield, Mass.: Northeast Foundation for Children, 1994.

———. *The Responsive Classroom*. Greenfield, Mass.: Northeast Foundation for Children, 1994.

Yager, Stuart, Roger Johnson, David Johnson, and Bill Snider. "The Impact of Group Processing on Achievement in Cooperative Learning Groups." *Journal of Social Psychology* 125 (1986): 389–397.

School Handbooks: Some Legal Considerations

Shaughnessy, M. A. 1989. 24–27, 62–68.
Washington, D.C.: National Catholic Educational Association.

Faculty Handbooks

When administrators are writing or revising handbooks, there are at least three main areas of teaching duties to include.

Instruction of students

The first area might be entitled "Instruction of Students." Teachers should be clearly told what they are expected to do in the instruction of students. It is not necessary to dictate *how* teachers are to do everything, but it is necessary to delineate some broad guidelines as to what they are to accomplish.

For example, a handbook might contain some directives as to whether textbooks are to be "covered" in their entirety; there should be some designation of the persons to be consulted for help and direction (principal, department head, grade level coordinator, etc.). Appropriate methods of teaching might be discussed. Amounts of time given for seatwork or independent study should be indicated.

Minimum and maximum times for homework assignments should be stated.

Supervision of students

A second area might be called "Supervision of Students" within the learning situation. Supervision outside the regular classroom should be thoroughly discussed. The fact that supervision is mental (the person has to be paying attention to the students) as well as physical (the teacher is bodily present) should be stressed.

Procedures for leaving students unattended should be discussed. There are situations, such as emergencies, that could require a teacher to leave a classroom unattended. Courts recognize this fact; however, courts do expect that students will not be left without directions as to their behavior. The standard courts use is: the younger the children chronologically or mentally, the greater the standard of care. If a teacher must leave the students, what procedures should be followed? How should the teacher ensure that students know what to do in the absence of a teacher?

Grading and Record-keeping

A third area involving teaching duties would be that of "Grading and Record-keeping." The school should clearly state what factors are to be considered in the determination of grades. Letter grades and numerical equivalents should be defined.

Teachers should know what their responsibilities are in regard to record-keeping. How long should attendance records be kept? States have different requirements, but, at the minimum, attendance records should be kept for five years after the student graduates or leaves the school. There have been cases in which the police and courts have asked for the school to verify a student's attendance on a particular day, even several years after an alleged incident occurred. If it is possible to keep the attendance records indefinitely, a school should do so.

Teachers or the school office staff should keep grade books on file, in the event that a student challenges a grade or brings a lawsuit necessitating verification of a grade. Conflicts regarding grades can be avoided if there is a policy in place stating that any request for consideration of a grade change must be made within a given number of days after the reception of the report card.

Teachers should keep their plan books on file either in the school office or in their home in case an educational malpractice suit should be filed against them. The plan book will indicate that the teacher did follow the curriculum and did teach whatever concepts were required.

Professionalism

Teachers are professionals, and all educators need to be periodically reminded of the expectations of the profession and of their duties to the institution which employs them. Hence, a principal may wish to include some statement about professionalism and loyalty in the faculty handbook.

Non-Teaching Duties

Non-teaching duties comprise a significant portion of teacher responsibility. An administrator might want to utilize the index card method and begin writing down everything a teacher is expected to do that is not, strictly speaking, an instructional duty. Even if the school has a handbook, an administrator might find that a week or so of keeping "non-teaching duties" in mind is a worthwhile exercise.

Cafeteria, playground, study hall supervision

Some non-teaching duties come immediately to mind. In the elementary school, teachers are very often assigned to supervise the playground and the cafeteria. What exactly is a playground supervisor supposed to do? If he or she is expected to be present on the playground from one bell to the next, that expectation should be stated in the handbook. Procedures for accidents and reporting fighting and/or other disciplinary problems should be included.

For teachers assigned to cafeteria or study hall supervision, the same types of questions should be answered. If teachers are not to leave the students they are supervising except in case of an emergency, then the handbook should state that rule.

Student discipline

Teachers are expected to enforce student discipline. The student disciplinary code should be included in the faculty handbook, even if it is printed in a separate handbook for parents and/or students, so that teachers have all policies and procedures readily accessible in one place. The disciplinary actions that are reserved to the principal or other administrative personnel should be outlined.

Field trip policies and procedures

The area of field trips has been largely problematic for schools, yet almost all teachers would agree that field trips can be very worthwhile parts of the teaching/learning experience. All steps which should be followed before taking a field trip should be cited in detail.

Extra-curricular activities

Teachers are almost always expected to sponsor some sort of extra-curricular activity. These activities can range from candy drives and Christmas plays to coaching sports.

The faculty handbook should state the school's expectations regarding teachers' sponsorship for extra-curricular activities. Can each teacher be required to moderate one or more activities? Will the more time-consuming activities carry compensation and, if so, what is the scale of compensation?

The responsibilities of extra-curricular moderators should be presented, perhaps in outline form. Activities such as dances might benefit from a checklist-type approach so that teachers can easily see if they have met their responsibilities.

Attendance at meetings and other school events

A final area of non-teaching duties consists of meetings. What meetings are teachers expected to attend? Parent/Teacher conferences? PTA meetings? School drama presentations? It might be helpful to publish a yearly list of meetings that teachers will be responsible for attending. Administrators might wish to reserve the right to require attendance at other meetings in the course of the year. Perhaps a statement that, as far as possible, a certain number of days' notice will be given, would be helpful.

Parent/Student Handbooks

If a parent is reluctant to confront a teacher alone, the administrator might offer to be present at a conference. Requiring persons to attempt to work out their difficulties mutually is certainly consistent with the demands of the Gospel and makes good legal sense as well.

If a parent wishes to communicate with a teacher, how should contact be made? Spontaneous visits to a classroom ought to be discouraged, but a parent could be directed to make an appointment by telephone or letter. If the teacher wishes to contact the parent, how might the parent expect that his contact will be made? Parents need such information.

How should a parent contact an administrator? If an appointment is necessary, how should it be made? Obviously,

there are times when informal contacts will occur. There are also times when everyone will profit if people have an opportunity to distance themselves from the situation before discussing it. Thus, the existence of a procedure for communication can be helpful.

Discipline Code

Rules/penalties/exceptions

As this work has indicated, the school should strive for simplicity and clarity in rule construction; long lists of rules should probably be avoided. Phrases such as "other inappropriate behavior" or "conduct unbecoming a Christian student" cover many types of misbehavior. Examples of infractions could be provided.

The principal or other administrator should retain the right to make exceptions. There may be a case in which mitigating circumstances call for a different response than has been the norm in the past. A phrase such as, "the principal is the final recourse in all disciplinary situations and may waive any disciplinary rule for just cause at his or her discretion" may be in order. It is true that this may appear to be inviting everyone to seek to be an exception; however, this author believes it is better to take that risk than to "box" one's self [*sic*] into a corner with rules that offer no flexibility.

Phrases such as "must" or "will result in a certain penalty" can result in little or no leeway. Phrases such as "can" or "may" give a disciplinarian room to allow for individual circumstances.

Generally, diocesan handbooks will offer guidance in the area of student discipline and rules' development and promulgation.

Due process/appeals

While considering the development of procedural due process guidelines, educators should be aware that there is a time investment involved. If a teacher allows a student to tell his or her story instead of summarily imposing punishment ("All students whose names are on the board will remain after school"), the teacher makes a commitment to spending time with a student who faces discipline. The principal or disciplinarian makes a commitment to listening to the student's side of the story as well as to the teacher's, and the benefit should be obvious: students perceive teachers and administrators as trying to be fair and, one hopes, will internalize the values thus modeled.

All Catholic schools, then, should commit themselves, to notice and a hearing in any disciplinary situation; in this way, the school is meeting the minimum requirements of due process. This commitment would mean that this student is told what he or she did that was wrong and is given a chance to be heard.

Somewhat more extensive procedures should be developed if the penalty is suspension. One-day suspensions, at minimum, should require that the principal be involved and that the parents be notified. Longer suspensions should involve the same notification but should also include a written notice of the charges and an indication of the time and place of the hearing. Cases in which the possibility of expulsion exists require a more formal notification and hearing at which the student should be able to confront accusers. Careful documentation must be kept in all major disciplinary proceedings.

Public schools may be required to grant a student facing expulsion the right to bring legal counsel to the hearing. Catholic schools, however, should avoid the presence of legal counsel. To allow a student to bring an attorney could be setting a precedent. The presence of attorneys often results in an adversarial situation, which can make the achievement of any sort of pastoral reconciliation very difficult.

This discussion of discipline should be helpful to Catholic school principals and faculties as they attempt to develop and modify rules and policies. The guiding principle in any discussion of discipline and due process should be the desire to act in a Christian manner characterized by fairness and compassion.

Maternity/paternity policies

Catholic schools, elementary as well as secondary, are faced with the situations of unwed mothers and fathers. This issue is certainly an emotionally charged one. School officials need to consider carefully the consequences of any policies that are adopted. At the very minimum, students should be allowed to finish their work and receive grades and diplomas.

Although some parents and teachers may believe that pregnant students do not belong in school, school officials should ponder what kind of messages students receive if unwed parents are excluded from school. Is a real, if unintended, message being sent that abortion is an answer that will help the student to save face and continue in the Catholic school? Is a situation such as the *Dolter* case being constructed in which the young woman is discriminated against because she is the one who becomes pregnant while the young man can deny his involvement?

Whether the unwed parent is allowed to participate in such activities as commencement is a difficult question. At the very least a school should consider a statement such as, "Pregnancy is not a reason for dismissal from school." To do otherwise seems to indicate an unwillingness to support a student who has made a choice to give life, rather than to end it.

Extra-curricular Activities

All extra-curricular activities sponsored by the Catholic school should be listed, along with the requirements for participation. If certain academic and conduct standards must be maintained for participation, these should be noted.

Any other policies that may be in effect should also be stated. If, for example, a student must be in school in order to participate in a sport or other activity on a given day, that fact should be clarified.

As far as possible, the same standards for all extra-curricular activities should be set and maintained. It does not seem fair for a football player to be denied participation because of low grades if a drama club member with similar academic standing can continue in the club simply because state or diocesan standards govern only participation in athletics.

Field Trip Policies/Forms

Privilege not a right

Field trips are privileges afforded to students; no student has an absolute right to a field trip. The school handbook should state that field trips are privileges and that students can be denied participation if they fail to meet academic or behavioral requirements.

Standard permission form

It is an excellent practice to include a copy of the school's permission form in the handbook. Then, if a student forgets to bring the form home, a parent can copy the proper form from the book and fill in the appropriate date and place. Schools should not accept forms other than the one the school has adopted.

Letters stating, "John can go with you today," simply provide no legal protection for the school.

The handbook should state that students who fail to submit a proper form will not be allowed to participate in the field trip. The handbook should also state that telephone calls will not be accepted in lieu of proper forms.

The right of parents to refuse to allow their child to participate in a field trip might also be mentioned.

Liability of school

Although no parent can sign away a child's right to safety, a handbook should state that the parents are expected to sign the permission form which releases the school from liability. School officials must understand, of course, that there is no such protection from the consequences of negligent behavior on the part of school staff; however, a proper form offers a school as much protection as can be had.

Parent Service Requirement

Many Catholic schools today find that they cannot operate without support beyond that provided by tuition. It is perfectly legitimate to require parents to give some sort of service in addition to the payment of tuition. However, parents must be told of this requirement when enrolling their children.

The handbook should define what is expected. Is the parent required to give a certain number of hours of service to the school? What sorts of activities meet these requirements? Is the parent or student expected to participate in fund-raising? Is there any alternative? (For example, can a parent pay an additional fee and thus avoid service?) What is the penalty for non-participation?

Parent organizations

The names and functions of all school or school-related organizations to which parents may belong should be listed, along with requirements for participation.

The role of the school board, if there is one, should be defined and the method for making contact with the board should be stated.

Use of School Grounds

Case law indicates that schools can be held responsible for accidents on playgrounds or school property before or after school. Some schools have a policy stating that children are not to arrive before a specified time and are to leave by a certain hour. But it is a policy or rule that is often not enforced. No school official wants to be insensitive to the problems of working parents; however, it is not fair for parents to assume that it is permissible to drop children at school very early in the morning and/or to pick them up very late in the afternoon. It is also not fair to assume that teachers or principals who arrive at school early or who stay late will be responsible for children. If a child is injured while on school property during an unsupervised time, a court will look to the parent/student handbook to see if a policy is in place, and if it has been enforced.

Athletic practices and other activities, such as parish-sponsored programs, pose problems as well. The question of supervision must be addressed in the handbook, and parents must know what the school will and will not do.

There are several approaches to this supervision problem. One is to post "no trespassing" signs and enforce a policy of no student presence on school grounds outside specified times. If a student is on the grounds at a time when no supervision is provided, the parents should be notified. Appropriate warnings and penalties should be given. The school and the school board might want to consider a policy that would require parents to withdraw a child from school after repeated offenses.

Another approach would be to provide funds to pay someone to supervise before and after school. With more and more schools adding day care and after school care programs, another solution is possible. A policy could be developed stating that any child who is present in the school building or on the grounds at prescribed times will be placed in day care and the parents will be billed for the service.

There are, of course, other options; the important thing is to do something. Do not take refuge in the belief that since nothing has ever happened, nothing will. One lawsuit could be extremely costly and could perhaps be avoided if rules, policies, and procedures had been developed and enforced.

School/Principal's Right to Amend Handbook

It is advisable to add a clause stating that the school or the principal retains the right to amend the handbook for just cause and that parents will be given prompt notification if changes are made.

Agreements Signed by Parents and Students

For everyone's protection, parents and students should be asked to sign a statement such as, "We have read and agree to be governed by this handbook." Such a statement avoids many of the problems that can arise when parents or students state that they did not know such a rule existed.

A school would be well advised not to admit a student to classes until such a signed agreement is submitted. Since courts construe handbooks as part of the contract existing between the school and the parents/students, it is both legally and ethically wise to ensure that all parties to the contract have read it and agree to be ruled by it.

Development of the Catholic School Board

Bailey, R., U. Butler, and M. Kearney. 1991. In *Capital wisdom: Papers from the Principals Academy 1991*, 39–44. Washington, D.C.: National Catholic Educational Association.

The principal is the educational and spiritual leader of the board. In this leadership capacity, the principal needs to be aware of and sensitive to the uniqueness of the Catholic school board. The principal should help the board members to understand the nature of the church's shared decision-making process, as well as their need to develop a faith life.

Principals must lead the board to share in the teaching mission of the church by helping the membership to use their gifts and talents for the benefit of the school community.

Fostering faith life

Each Catholic school must be an example of a living faith community. Catholic schools are called upon to make faith real in the world. Board members too are challenged to witness to the presence and reality of the risen Lord in the community where the school is located.

Board members represent a variety of constituencies but their ministry calls them to put aside personal interest and work for the greater good.

A primary way to foster the faith life of the board is by facilitating liturgical and prayer experiences for members. The principal can integrate faith community experiences into board life by developing a prayer and liturgy planning committee as a board subcommittee. This group can assist with:

◆ planning prayer services and retreats, as well as prayers to begin each meeting
◆ planning a liturgy for board intentions
◆ commissioning board members in a public ceremony, i.e., on Catechetical Sunday
◆ planning a board appreciation Mass
◆ organizing a hospitality committee to provide a positive climate for board meetings
◆ providing social interaction between board members and faculty
◆ involving board members in Catholic Schools Week
◆ inviting board members into the school during special events
◆ recognizing birthdays and other special occasions for board members

In-service training

The principal needs to challenge the board to a higher level of skill development through in-service training. Many resources are available to help a board became more skilled in board work and in understanding the issues confronting Catholic education today. In-service training is a primary time for reviewing pertinent church documents such as *To Teach as Jesus Did* and the bishops' pastorals. In-service time can also be used to explore issues concerning liturgy, sacraments, and religious education.

Following are suggestions for board development.

◆ A 15–20 minute segment at the beginning of each meeting provides an in-service experience such as the discussion of a pertinent educational issue.
◆ Two or three hours several times a year allows for activities such as watching a video and following-up with discussion.
◆ A full day in-service one time during the board year can be used for a retreat day away from school or for training conducted by a consultant.

Shared decision making

In the pre-Vatican II church, laity were not actively involved in the decision-making processes for Catholic education. Vatican Council II called for the involvement of the laity and for a sense of shared decision making that involves pastor, principal, and board.

In today's church, board members are called and chosen to be ministers by participating fully in the decision-making process. A minister is one who is called to service—one who serves in his or her own name at the request of or in the name of someone else. In this sense of call and response, the church recognizes the ministry of the educational board.

The ministry of shared decision making is a theological principle. Vatican II states that each member of the church has a right and obligation to assist the church by offering time and talent so that its mission may become more effective. An important share of the responsibility for this mission lies with the school board as the policy makers who work with the principal in a spirit of cooperation and interdependence.

Our model of shared decision making is Jesus, who used apostles and disciples to teach the concept of shared ministry. He could have brought the good news of salvation alone but he chose to work though the gifts and talents of others. His criteria were not riches or fame. Rather, he chose individuals who were open, capable of growth, and capable of being human.

To make shared decision making a reality rather than just a theoretical idea, the board must have good communication skills and a positive relationship with the principal. The principal's report is an important tool for building good communication between principal and board.

Report to the board

The report serves to inform the board about the school so that board members can make knowledgeable decisions and act as a positive public relations agent within the community. The principal will want to share student, staff, and school management information in reports to the board.

Student information. Board members are interested in the students' experience of school and the principal wants the board to be informed about school events. Therefore, the principal should regularly update the board on important aspects of student life in the school. Some items of interest may be:

◆ changes in school enrollment
◆ awards and honors given to the school or particular students
◆ field trips for students
◆ recruitment of new students
◆ special programs, assemblies, speakers and/or programs on topics such as substance abuse, career awareness, family life education, and safety

Staff information. Although the staff works for the principal, the board is interested in the staff's welfare. The principal should keep the board informed of events such as:

◆ in-service training attended by the teachers and/or principal
◆ opportunities for parental involvement in the school
◆ awards and honors given to faculty members
◆ creative projects instituted by staff

School management information. Another key area about which boards need information is the management of the school. The board needs to be informed about changes and opportunities that may impact their work, such as budget and policy formation. The principal makes sure the board has current information so that they can make informed choices and decisions. Some items of information are:

◆ administrative implementation of board policy
◆ financial management, including a monthly budget update, development activities, fund-raising activities/calendar, and tuition collection/book fees
◆ results of standardized tests, health screening
◆ curriculum development and new textbook implementation
◆ technology implementation and plans for future expansion

Board mailings

Another effective method of fostering positive communication between the school and the board is a monthly mailing. This will give board members the opportunity to be tied into board work more than one evening per month. Providing members with ongoing information will better prepare them for board meetings and help to establish good relationships between the board and the school community. Following are some items to be included in board mailings:

◆ community-building information such as birthdays and special events of board members
◆ prayer assignments for each meeting
◆ minutes from the last meeting and agendas for the upcoming meeting
◆ any in-service information to be read ahead of time
◆ any memos or notices sent out to the school community, school newsletters, or school papers

Effective Catholic schools of the future will have active boards who are informed about the school's mission, goals, and programs. These boards will be in a position to set a vision for the future of their schools. Informed boards must also be models of a gospel community with a highly developed faith life that can serve as a foundation for their work.

Resources

Mary Benet McKinney, *Sharing Wisdom: A Process for Group Decision Making*, Valencia, CA, Tabor Publishing, 1987.

Debra Hintz, *Prayer Services for Parish Meetings*, Twenty-Third Publications, P.O. Box 180, Mystic, CT.

Debra Hintz, *Gathering Prayers*, Twenty-Third Publications.

Edward Hays, *Prayers for the Domestic Church*, Forest of Peace, Inc., Rt. One, Box 248, Easton, KS 66020.

Code of Ethics for Catholic School Board Members, Washington, DC, National Catholic Educational Association (NCEA).

Partners in Catholic Education, NCEA.

Distinctive Qualities of the Catholic School, NCEA.

The Board Member's Prayer, NCEA.

Building Better Boards Handbook and Video program, NCEA.

School Board Study Programs I and II, NCEA.

Issue-Gram, a newsletter for National Association of Catholic Boards of Education members, NCEA.

The following are from the United States Catholic Conference, 3211 Fourth Street, NE, Washington, DC 20017-1194

To Teach as Jesus Did

The Challenge of Peace: God's Promise and Our Response

Economic Justice for All

Sharing the Light of Faith (National Catechetical Directory)

Teach Them

The Religious Dimension of Education in a Catholic School

Sharing the Light of Faith:
National Catechetical Directory for Catholics of the United States

National Conference of Catholic Bishops. 1979. Chapter 10.
Washington, D.C.: United States Catholic Conference.

Chapter X.[*]
Organization for Catechesis

220. Introduction

One can hardly emphasize too strongly the catechetical importance of the witness to faith given by individuals living according to their Christian beliefs and values. But organizational structures are also needed to achieve the goals and ideals set forth in this NCD. Appropriate structures can help ensure opportunities for the entire Christian community to grow in faith.

Some topics treated in this chapter have already been discussed in Chapter VIII in relation to faith and human development; here they are examined from the point of view of organization.

Part A. General Organizational Guidelines

221. Organizational principles

The following principles are important to catechetical organization.

a) Effective planning is person-centered. It does not propose structures without reference to the people involved. It sets growth in faith as the goal and recognizes the Christian family as the basic community within which faith is nurtured.

b) Each of its members has a responsibility for the whole Church. Each has a duty to foster a living, conscious, active faith community. Laity, religious, and clergy alike are called to participate in those aspects of catechetics—organization, implementation, evaluation—with respect to which they are interested and qualified. Recognizing that they are stewards of God's gifts, they should be generous in supporting the catechetical effort. Shared responsibilities implies the development and use of such structures as councils and boards.

c) Planning groups should make a clear statement of their philosophy, their goals, and the basic beliefs underlying the goals. (Cf. next article.)

d) Higher-level planning groups should not try to do what can be done as well, or better, by groups at lower levels. For example, diocesan bodies ought not to set policies or make decisions which deprive parishes of authority concerning matters they are able to handle. Respect for local decision making encourages initiative, while freeing larger units to concentrate on needs which only they can meet, or which require coordination or a common approach. Groups should seek outside help only when needs clearly exceed local capabilities.

e) At all levels it is essential that overall plans make provision for communication and accountability.

f) Administrators in each local community are responsible for equitable allocation of available services, opportunities, and resources. Strong central leadership is needed to ensure that resources are used for the good of all. Communities in need should have opportunities equal to those enjoyed by more favored communities.

g) Structures should flow from need and be suited to the achievement of the stated goals.

h) Goal setting, planning, implementation, accountability, and evaluation are continuing processes.

222. Planning and evaluation

a) Planning

Planning is an essential part of any serious organizational effort. There are many planning processes; catechists involved in organization should be exposed to several and familiar with at least one.

Certain elements are common to all planning systems:
i)   a clear understanding of the essential mission and major objectives;
ii) assessment of needs, as well as current and potential resources;
iii) identification of long- and short-range goals;
iv) identification of concrete activities to reach the goals, rated according to priority;
v)   establishment of a budget which reflects available resources;
vi) establishment of favorable conditions for carrying out the activities which have been decided upon;
vii) periodic review and evaluation; and
viii) restatement of goals and activities when necessary.

It is important that planning for catechetical programs at the parish, diocesan, and national levels be part of a total pastoral plan. Such a plan, which takes into consideration the Church's entire mission, is best developed by representation of the various ministries of the Church.[1] Urgent demands upon limited resources require cooperation among all pastoral ministries.

Planning is a continuous process. The associated skills develop with experience. Good planning enriches decision making and forestalls crisis-oriented decisions.

b) Evaluation

Catechetical programs should be subjected to regular evaluation. The evaluation should be made in light of established goals and objectives, which themselves should be evaluated periodically.

---

* Editor's note: Chapter notation refers to this excerpt.

There is a need to develop instruments for evaluating catechetical programs. The United States Catholic Conference (USCC), National Conference of Diocesan Directors of Religious Education-CCD, National Catholic Educational Association, and other representative agencies should collaborate in meeting this need. The norms and guidelines set forth throughout this NCD provide criteria for evaluation.

223. Research

Rapid developments in the Church, society, and education underlie the great need for research related to catechesis. Wherever possible, dioceses and parishes ought to examine themselves in order to ascertain their requirements and make plans for meeting them.

Diocesan, regional, and national groups are responsible for developing research instruments and projecting and testing models for local use. It is the responsibility of the religious education representative of the USCC Department of Education to coordinate efforts on the various levels and disseminate the results of research to diocesan offices and other interested parties. The other offices of the Department of Education, the departments of the United States Catholic Conference, and the agencies of the National Conference of Catholic Bishops provide the same services to their constituents, with regard to the catechetical components of their ministries.

The Office of Research, Policy and Program Development of the USCC Department of Education has the following functions: to maintain a listing of current and completed research in Catholic education, including catechetics; to help identify present and future research needs; to make a continuing study of trends in Catholic education, including projections for the immediate and distant futures. The staff works closely with Catholic colleges, universities, learned societies, and research groups in performing these functions.

Associated with the Office of Research, Policy and Program Development is the United States Center for the Catholic Biblical Apostolate. In relation to catechesis its pastoral purpose is to ascertain the needs of the dioceses with respect to Bible study programs, especially in adult education, and to promote popular biblical publications as well as wide distribution of the scriptures.[2]

It is highly desirable that catechists at all levels know and use the results of research. Useful research at any level should be shared as widely as possible with the rest of the Church.

Part B. The Parish

224. The parish community

The parish is the basic structure within which most Catholics express and experience faith. Ordinarily, a parish is made up of the people within a defined territorial area, for whose care and service a priest has been assigned by the bishop. There are other parishes for Catholics of a particular ethnic group or particular rite; and there are some parishes which do not have fixed boundaries but are made up of persons linked by common social bonds.[3]

Catholics have a right to look to their parishes to carry out Christ's mission by being centers of worship, preaching, witness, community, and service. At the same time, parishioners have reciprocal duties of involvement and support toward their parishes. Maturity of faith obviously rules out the neglect of one's duties as a parish member.

Every parish needs a coherent, well-integrated catechetical plan which provides opportunities for all parishioners to encounter the gospel message and respond by fostering community and giving service.

The parish and its catechetical program take into account that the whole Church is missionary and that evangelization is a basic duty of God's people.[4]

A single representative board, responsible for the total educational program, should be involved in catechetical planning in every parish. Different circumstances will require different organizational forms. The board can be a separate body, a committee of the parish council, or some other entity, elected or appointed. Its members should receive training and pastoral formation to help them share a vision of the Church's global mission, of the overall parish goals, and of catechetical priorities in the context of those goals.

As far as possible, parish catechetical programs are to be established, financed, staffed, and evaluated in light of the goal of meeting the needs of everyone in the parish. Particular concern will be directed to the handicapped, the neglected, those unable to speak up effectively on behalf of their own rights and interests, and minority cultural, racial, and ethnic groups.

Parish catechetical efforts should be related to the catechetical undertakings of neighboring parishes and other religious groups. They should take into account the schedules and programs of public and parochial schools. Interparochial cooperation is particularly necessary to make resources available to poor or otherwise disadvantaged communities.

Parish bulletins and other publications should be utilized in catechesis.

225. Adults

Through a parish catechetical board, a committee, or a chairperson of adult catechesis, the pastor should see to it that catechetical programs are available for adults as part of the total catechetical program.

The form adult catechesis takes will depend on a variety of factors: size and makeup of parish, community stability, cultural and educational background of parishioners, etc. There are a number of appropriate models: small group discussions, lectures with questions and discussion, retreat programs, sacramental programs, dialogues between adults and young people, adult catechumenate.

Parish planning groups should be creative in designing ways to reach and motivate adults to participate.

Priests should be mindful that the Sunday homily, based on the scriptures of the day, is a notable opportunity to nurture the faith of the adult community through the ministry of the word.

226. Family ministry

Family ministry involves announcing the good news to those within the immediate family circle first of all. However, family members should in turn be aware of the Christian family's authentic mission to evangelize the wider community. "In a family which is conscious of this mission, all the members evangelize and are evangelized. The parents not only communicate the Gospel to their children, but from their children they can themselves receive the same Gospel as deeply lived by them. And such a family becomes the evangelizer of many other families, and of the neighborhood of which it forms part."[5]

As the Church in miniature, the family is called to serve the needs of its own members, other persons and families, and the larger community. In it evangelization, worship, catechesis, and Christian service are vitally present.

Many parishes offer family-centered catechetical programs. These are intended to bring families together—to learn, experience, and celebrate some aspect of Catholic belief or living—and help them carry out their responsibilities in and to the Church's catechetical mission.

Some family programs center upon the liturgy, using themes of the liturgical year as the starting point. Participants separate according to age (preschool, primary, intermediate, junior and senior high school, and adult levels) to discuss the theme and then come back together for a common activity and celebration. Suggestions for home activities may also be given. Other programs, such as "family evenings," focus on the family in the home setting. Each family examines the designated theme in relation to its own circumstances, in order better to understand and carry out its mission in the world. Some family programs have a more elaborate design and aim at total catechesis.

While family-centered catechesis is to be encouraged, peer group catechetical experience should also be part of a total catechetical program.

Within families there is need and opportunity for spouses to catechize each other and for parents to catechize children. There are several possibilities: e.g., parents can catechize their children directly, which is the ideal; they can participate in parish catechetical programs which serve their children; spouses can catechize each other by trustingly and openly sharing their insights concerning the gospel's relevance to their lives.

Since the Christian family is a "domestic Church," prayer and worship are central to it. Christian family life involves prayerful celebration within the family, as well as liturgical celebration in the parish community of which it is an integral, active part.

Another component of authentic family ministry and an important goal of family catechesis is the rendering of Christlike service. Sensitized to others' needs by the imperatives of Christian love and justice, the individual family seeks, according to its ability and opportunities, to minister to the spiritual, psychological, and physical needs of the whole human family.

Family ministry is a vital source of strength for the catechetical process in the home and in the parish.

More research is needed concerning the influence of the home on family members. This would help catechists and people engaged in family ministries to develop more effective forms of home- and family-oriented catechesis.

227. Young adult ministry

This is a "catechetical moment of the gospel" with respect to young adults (18–35), for all practical purposes a newly identified population in U.S. society, many of whose members are engaged in an intense search for spirituality and values.

Church-sponsored young adult programs should respond to the expressed needs of participants while reflecting the four interrelated purposes of catechesis: to proclaim the mysteries of the faith; to foster community; to encourage worship and prayer; and to motivate service to others.

The gradual manner of God's self-revelation, manifested in scripture, provides a model for catechetical efforts directed to young adults, as does the catechesis recommended in the revised *Rite of Christian Initiation of Adults*. Program content includes psychological and sociological matters considered in the light of faith, questions of faith and moral issues, and similar matters pertaining to human experience.

Catechists not only instruct young adults but learn from them; they will be heard by young adults only if they listen to them. Young adult ministries must be developed and conducted in ways which emphasize self-direction, dialogue, and mutual responsibility. The Church should encourage young adults to minister to one another, to listen to God's word in community, and to serve other members of the faith community and the world community. It should offer leadership in developing new ministries, alternative community experiences, and instruments of effective catechesis, for this purpose using the talents of young adults who are willing to collaborate.

228. Youth ministry

a) Description of youth ministry

Youth catechesis is most effective within a total youth ministry. Such ministry requires the collaboration of many people with different kinds of expertise.

It is *to* youth that it seeks to respond to adolescents' unique needs. It is *with* youth in that it is shared. It is *by* youth in that they participate in directing it. It is *for* youth in that it attempts to interpret the concerns of youth and be an advocate for them.

Total ministry to youth includes catechetical activities in which the message is proclaimed, community is fostered, service is offered, and worship is celebrated. There is need for a variety of models integrating message, community, service, and worship and corresponding to the stages of development and levels of perception of the young. Guidance and healing, involvement of youth in ministry, and interpretation and advocacy of their legitimate interests and concerns also have catechetical dimensions.

The need for a variety of approaches should be taken into consideration in preparing social, recreational, and apostolic programs, as well as retreats and other spiritual development activities.

b) Parish catechetical programs for youth

Parish and community programs designed to meet the needs of Catholic students who do not attend Catholic high schools provide settings for formal catechesis for many Catholic young people in the United States. Participation in such programs is voluntary, and they are usually less structured than school programs and open to a number of alternative models.

Professional advice, local initiative, and consultation with young people themselves should all go into the planning of these programs. Local circumstances should determine such decisions as whether to make them parish- or home-centered, whether they should have a formal "classroom" or informal "group" format, whether they should be scheduled weekly over an extended period of time or concentrated in a shorter time span, or whether some particular mixture of formats and schedules should be employed.

Catechetical planners should know the number of young people of high school age in the community and how many are not being reached by the catechetical ministry of school or parish.

Adequate personnel, professional services, and budget are essential. Programs broad enough to appeal to all the young people of a community are usually most effective.

The study of scripture, the Church, the sacraments, and morality should be part of the overall program. In a comprehensive ministerial program such instruction will flow from and lead to service, liturgy, and community.

The community dimension will usually be expressed in a preference for small groups within which relationships can develop. Weekend prayer, "search," encounter, or retreat experiences provide liturgical experiences in a communal setting of acceptance and exchange.

Service opportunities (e.g., visiting the aged or shut-ins, assisting catechists who teach handicapped children, working with community action programs) should also be part of programs for youth. They help develop lasting motivation for service to others.

Catechesis consistently speaks of the Church's missionary nature and the obligation of all its members to share in some way in its missionary activity. It discusses religious vocations (priesthood, diaconate, brotherhood, and sisterhood) and encourages students to be open to the call of the Holy Spirit. Lay ministries are also presented as a form of direct involvement in the mission of the Church. In particular, catechesis should remind parents of the need to extend a prudent but positive invitation to their children to consider a religious vocation as a way of living out their Christian commitment.

229. Catechetical programs for children

While giving increased emphasis to adult catechesis, the faith community must also strive continually to provide parish programs of high quality for children.

Primary, intermediate, and junior high school catechesis are specialized fields requiring specialized training. They are grouped here to emphasize the need for sequence and coordination.

Though the influence of peers and of adult catechists is important, catechetical programs are not intended to supplant parents as the primary educators of their children. Parental involvement in catechetical programs is essential.

Adequately staffed and budgeted parish catechetical programs at every level should be provided for children who do not attend Catholic schools. The limited time available for these programs makes it absolutely necessary to set priorities and to give them active support.

Curricula should be properly sequenced, presenting essential truths in a manner appropriate to the abilities of the age group. Whether a curriculum's content is sufficiently comprehensive is determined by judging the curriculum as a whole. As the ability to understand develops, more important truths should be reinforced and treated in greater depth. Religious learning should relate to the child's general experience of learning.

It is essential that a parish elementary catechetical program include opportunities for participants to experience community. Children grow in their understanding and appreciation of what a worshipping community is through participating in class or group prayer and in liturgies which have been carefully planned together by students and teachers.

The concept of service has limited application on the elementary level, especially in the early years. Parents play an important role in its development by sensitively prompting their children to perform acts of kindness and compassion in the home and neighborhood. Service-oriented class projects can be introduced in the intermediate grades. By junior high school, service projects similar to those mentioned above in the discussion of youth ministry are appropriate.

Catechesis introduces children to the idea that the Church's mission is the mission of Jesus and of the Holy Spirit. It describes this work of the Church and explains the notion of vocation.

230. Catechesis for preschool children

Preschool programs should focus mainly on parents, providing them with opportunities to deepen their faith and become more adept at helping their children "form a foundation of that life of faith which will gradually develop and manifest itself."[6] However, programs for preschool children themselves are also desirable, in accordance with the guidance given in article 177.

231. Special catechesis

Catechetical programs for people with mental, emotional, or physical handicaps should be provided on the parochial, regional, or diocesan level. Each handicap requires its own approach, and separate programs are therefore required for each category of handicapped persons. Those involved in special catechetical programs should receive the training needed to perform their particular duties.

The parish community should be informed about the needs of its handicapped members and encouraged to support them with love and concern. The faith witness of handicapped persons can be a model and stimulus to growth in faith on the part of parishioners generally.

The families of the handicapped also need care and concern, including assistance directed to helping them participate with competence and confidence in the catechesis of their handicapped members.

232. Catholic schools

Catholic schools are unique expressions of the Church's effort to achieve the purposes of Catholic education among the young. They "are the most effective means available to the Church for the education of children and young people."[7]

Catholic schools may be part of the parish structure, interparochial or regional, diocesan or private. Growth in faith is central to their purpose.

As a community and an institution, the school necessarily has an independent life of its own. But a parochial school is also a community within the wider community, contributing to the parish upon which it depends and integrated into its life. Integration and interdependence are major matters of parish concern; each program in a total catechetical effort should complement the others.[8]

Similarly, regional, diocesan, and private schools should work in close collaboration with neighboring parishes. The experience of community in the schools can benefit and be benefited by the parishes.

Teachers in Catholic schools are expected to accept and live the Christian message and to strive to instill a Christian spirit in their students. As catechists, they will meet standards equivalent to those set for other disciplines and possess the qualities described in Chapter IX, Part A [nos. 205–211].

The school should have a set religion curriculum, with established goals and objectives, open to review and evaluation by parish boards and diocesan supervisory teams. It is recommended that an integrated curriculum provide options for catechists and students by offering electives along with the core curriculum.

It is desirable that Catholic high schools in a diocese work together to share resources, provide opportunities for teacher training and development, and cooperate in establishing program guidelines.

The school's principal and faculty are responsible for making clear the importance of religion. The quality of the catechetical experience in the school and the importance attached to religious instruction, including the amount of time spent on it, can influence students to perceive religion as either highly important or of little importance.

Its nature as a Christian educational community, the scope of its teaching, and the effort to integrate all learning with faith distinguish the Catholic school from other forms of the Church's educational ministry to youth and give it special impact. In Catholic schools children and young people "can experience learning and living fully integrated in the light of faith,"[9] because such schools strive "to relate all human culture eventually to the news of salvation, so that the life of faith will illumine the knowledge which students gradually gain of the world, of life, and of mankind."[10] Cooperative teaching which cuts across the lines of particular disciplines, interdisciplinary curricula, team teaching, and the like help to foster these goals of Catholic education.

"Building and living community must be prime, explicit goals of the contemporary Catholic school."[11] Principal and faculty members have a responsibility to help foster community among themselves and the students. Creative paraliturgies and sacramental celebrations for particular age groups can strengthen the faith community within the school.

Catholic school students should be introduced gradually to the idea and practice of Christian service. In early years, efforts to instill a sense of mission and concern for others help lay a foundation for later service projects, as does study of the lives of the saints and outstanding contemporaries.

Junior and senior high school programs should foster a social conscience sensitive to the needs of all. Familiarity with the Church's social encyclicals and its teaching on respect for human life will be part of this formation. (Cf. Chapter VII) Opportunities for field and community experiences are highly desirable. Teachers, administrators, parents, and students should be involved in planning service projects. One measure of a school's success is its ability to foster a sense of vocation, of eagerness to live out the basic baptismal commitment to service, whether this is done as a lay person, religious, deacon, or priest.

Catechesis speaks of the missionary nature of the Church. It points out that all Christians are responsible for missionary activity by reason of the love of God, which prompts in them a desire to share with everyone the spiritual goods of this life and the life to come. Catholic schools provide opportunities for participation in missionary projects through the Holy Childhood Association, the Society for the Propagation of the Faith, etc. They also provide students with opportunities to search for the gifts that the Holy Spirit offers them for this ministry.

Through a carefully planned process, the entire school community—parents, students, faculty, administrators, pastors, and others—needs to be involved in the development of its goals, philosophy, and programs.

233. Catholic schools and the disadvantaged

The Second Vatican Council urged bishops and all Catholics to "spare no sacrifice" in helping Catholic schools to fulfill their functions more perfectly, and especially to care for "the needs of those who are poor in the goods of this world or who are deprived of the assistance and affection of a family or who are strangers to the gift of faith."[12]

In many places in the United States the Church has responded with an extremely large human and economic investment in schools whose pupils are for the most part disadvantaged children in the poverty areas of large cities. An increasing number of parents in poverty areas are making heroic personal sacrifices to send their children to Catholic schools, convinced that the education provided there affords a realistic and hopeful opportunity for breaking out of "the hellish cycle of poverty"[13] and moving into the social and economic mainstream. These schools serve a critical human and social need, while also providing a complete education which includes catechesis and guidance. In urban areas the Catholic school has a special role of giving witness and fostering evangelization.

234. Religion and public education

In a series of decisions concerning prayer and Bible reading during the 1960s, the United States Supreme Court in effect excluded specific efforts to inculcate religious values from the public schools.[14]

Efforts have been made to fill the vacuum created by these decisions by introducing into public schools courses and programs which in one way or another bear upon religion and values. The objective study of religion, whatever form it takes, seeks to convey information about religion or to foster appreciation of its nonreligious contributions, but not to advocate religious belief and values; while courses in sex education, psychology, and sociology, along with "sensitivity" and value clarification programs, deal directly with values.

Many believe it is not possible to produce neutral textbooks on religion and values, much less to teach in a truly neutral way about such matters. Some ask whether "neutrality" about religion and values is appropriate, even supposing it were possible. Many, particularly parents and Church leaders, believe so-called neutrality of this kind weakens young people's religious and moral beliefs and leads to relativism and indifference.

In order to remedy the situation, parents and community leaders, including representatives of churches and synagogues, should become involved in the planning, development, implementation, and evaluation of courses and programs dealing with religion and values. Issues of a highly controversial nature should be treated with extreme sensitivity. Teachers and administrators should be conscious of their responsibility to deal respectfully with pupils from diverse backgrounds and value systems, and should be adequately trained to do so. When young people or their parents object to a program on religious or moral grounds, the public schools should exempt such pupils from participation without embarrassing them.

It is important that parish planners be aware of such courses and programs in public schools and be prepared to address the issues and questions they raise in parish catechetical programs.

235. Released time

The laws of some states provide for releasing students from public school during regular school hours so that they can attend catechetical programs off the school premises.[15]

Some states make an hour or more available each week for catechetical instruction. Others provide for "staggered" time, releasing students on an individual or group basis at different hours and days throughout the week. While a number of places have reported good success with these forms of released time, others have complained that scheduling and transportation present serious practical difficulties; they have also noted the bad effect of compartmentalizing religion and relegating catechesis to a small and inadequate portion of the child's or youth's total school time.

More satisfactory results have been reported in a few places which make available a block of time for catechesis —several hours, a whole day, or even several consecutive days.

Good results have been achieved in both released time programs and after-school catechesis by catechetical centers established adjacent to public schools.

Released time programs are more effective when part of a broader parish catechetical program.

Dioceses and state Catholic conferences will find it helpful to appraise the local situation and seek viable released time programs, if these are desired. As this is an issue that interests many, a cooperative approach with other churches is advantageous.

Parishes, individually or collectively, should seek out viable alternatives to released time in cooperation with educational administrators in the public sector.

236. Ethnic parishes

Revived interest in ethnicity, based on recognition of the major contributions made by ethnic groups to the nation's cultural richness, has stimulated interest in ethnic parishes. They provide significant liturgical and cultural experiences for many people. While "ethnic" forms of religious expression are to be encouraged, means should also be sought for sharing their values with the Church at large, including neighboring geographical parishes.

Representatives of national parishes and of cultural and ethnic groups should be the prime movers in planning and organizing catechetical programs for themselves.

237. Military parishes

The special needs of military personnel and their families must be recognized by both diocesan and military chaplaincy administrators. Military and diocesan parishes should cooperate. Diocesan catechetical offices should relate to and serve military parishes.

Because of the mobility and, at times, the isolation of military life, it is important to give priority to standard procedures for procuring catechetical materials, and to the development of parental and lay leadership. The need for professional catechists and coordinators, especially on large bases or posts, is as urgent as in any civilian parish.

Military parishes provide good opportunities for ecumenical efforts, since places of worship and educational facilities are frequently shared by all denominations.

Part C: The Diocese

238. Diocesan structures

The chief elements of the diocesan administrative structure directly related to catechesis are as follows:

a) Diocesan pastoral council

In fulfilling his duties as pastor and chief teacher of the diocese, the bishop consults with the diocesan pastoral council where one exists.[16] Its consultative function extends to everything which is part of the bishop's pastoral responsibility.

The council assists in establishing a broad pastoral plan for the diocese. In relation to catechesis, it works with the bishop to identify the values, philosophy, needs, and goals of the Christian community, both in general and with specific reference to catechesis. It also consults with other diocesan bodies, such as the diocesan council of the laity, priests' senate, sisters' council, etc.

b) Diocesan catechetical/education board

The diocesan board has the responsibility of developing policy, thus giving unified leadership to the various concerns reflected in the total catechetical ministry.

Its tasks are to identify, define, and set priorities among catechetical/educational objectives related to the goals specified by the pastoral council; to specify broad programs to achieve the goals; and to make decisions concerning implementation. Periodically the board should evaluate itself and its performance. A diocesan board is most effective when it is broadly representative of all the people of the diocese. In choosing members, cultural, racial, and ethnic groups, geographic regions, and the like should be considered. Its members should include people of faith active in catechesis and related educational and pastoral fields. When possible, it is advantageous for the membership to include specialists of various kinds, parents, youth, and public educators. The board should seek advice from other boards and similar bodies in the local Church and from individuals who can assist the catechetical ministry.

c) Diocesan catechetical office

The *General Catechetical Directory* refers to the "Catechetical Office" which is "part of the diocesan curia" and the "means which the bishop as head of the community and teacher of doctrine utilizes to direct and moderate all of the catechetical activities of the diocese."[17]

No single model can be recommended here for a diocesan administrative structure to direct catechetical activities. The size, needs, administrative style, and resources of a particular diocese affect this decision. However, a number of workable models or structures have been developed during the past decade.

In large dioceses with complex problems, a chief diocesan administrator of Catholic education, representing the bishop, is responsible for and coordinates the entire catechetical/educational mission through a Department of Education. All offices—which may include a School Office, Office of Religious Education (CCD), Adult Education Office, Campus and Young Adult Ministry Office, and Family Life Ministry Office—report directly to this chief administrator. Frequent collaboration among staff of the various offices fosters the coordination of catechetical efforts and facilitates interdisciplinary projects and programs.

In some dioceses, the Office of Religious Education is responsible for administering diocesan catechetical policy. Where this structure exists as the "catechetical office," personnel should be available to administer and service adult, youth, elementary, preschool, and special catechetical programs.

In other dioceses there is an Office for Christian Formation, with a vicar or secretary responsible for administering catechetical policy and coordinating the catechetical functions with other aspects of pastoral ministry: education, liturgy, ecumenism, etc.

Whatever its structure, the Diocesan Catechetical Office should have sufficient professional personnel to serve as resources to parishes, areas, or regions in relation to all aspects of catechesis. It should engage in regular collaboration and cooperation with other diocesan offices which have a catechetical dimension: i.e., offices for continuing education of the clergy, liturgy, ecumenism, communications, social justice, etc.

Part D: Provinces, Regions, The National Office

239. Regional and provincial cooperation

Regional and provincial cooperation is desirable to coordinate diocesan efforts, provide a common voice in consultation, and broaden the insights and experiences of all involved. Such cooperation should involve bishops, diocesan catechetical personnel, pastors, priests, deacons, religious, and laity, especially parents. Planned coordination promotes mutual assistance and the sharing of programs and personnel, and fosters people's growth in faith through action. Liaison should be established and maintained with state Catholic conferences, where they exist, and with ecumenical groups involved in catechetical or religious education work.

240. National catechetical office

The *General Catechetical Directory* states that a conference of bishops should have a permanent structure to promote catechetics on the national level.[18] The Department of Education of the United States Catholic Conference, through its religious education component, has the mission of carrying out the catechetical policies of the bishops of the United States.

Through its coordinator and specialists in catechetics, the department is to keep informed of catechetical developments, evaluate them, identify needs, specify directions for the future, and determine strategies of implementation. It is to disseminate information and provide consultation, especially with regional groupings, while undertaking only those activities that cannot be done, or done as well, at the local, diocesan, or regional levels. The department also is to collaborate with national professional associations.

It is desirable that the United States Catholic Conference include specialists from the Eastern Churches on the staff of its Department of Education or, at least, establish liaison with the corresponding entities of the Eastern Churches in order to insure catholicity in catechetical programs.

Before national policy decisions are made, the department is to consult with various advocacy groups and with the USCC Committee on Education, which is a representative group responsible for formulating and recommending policy. Policy itself is established by the USCC Administrative Board and the General Assembly of Bishops.

To the extent possible, the Department of Education is to maintain liaison and exchange information with the national catechetical offices of other countries.

Part E: Higher Education

241. Seminaries

Seminarians in college or the theologate need a clear understanding of the roles they will have in the catechetical programs of the parishes and institutions to which they will be assigned as priests.

"In addition to having an accurate knowledge of Sacred Scripture and systematic theology, the seminarian should learn those special skills of pedagogy needed to communicate the Gospel message in a clear, precise and well-organized way."[19] It is also necessary that seminarians come to understand the process of human growth and development so that they can give catechesis adapted to the age and ability of those being catechized. They should have an opportunity to acquire the skills necessary to organize and direct a catechetical program on the parish level.

The catechetical preparation of seminarians should be carried on in collaboration with the personnel of the diocesan catechetical office. Training includes in-service experiences, catechetical workshops, and congresses.

Seminaries serve the local Church by making their faculties and facilities as available as far as possible to the diocese and the community-at-large.

242. Colleges and universities

a) Graduate programs in religious studies

Graduate departments of religious education offer a variety of programs for people preparing for professional careers in catechetical ministry. Such programs establish academic qualifications for professional leadership, serve as centers for research and development, and convene appropriate seminars. They should be interdisciplinary, offering advanced courses in theology, scripture, liturgy, catechetics, communications, parish administration, and related sacred and human sciences.

Graduate schools of religious studies, through their own national organizations and in cooperation with the USCC Department of Education, are invited to establish uniform standards for candidates for advanced degrees in catechetics.

Graduate programs should make special provisions to meet the needs of cultural, racial, and ethnic groups or individuals with special catechetical requirements: for example, through research, placement of student catechists, and pilot programs directed to such groups.

Graduate schools are encouraged to offer courses and programs in the theologies, liturgies, and forms of spirituality of the Eastern Churches. In doing so, they will be taking advantage of and helping to make more widely known an often neglected source of enrichment for the Church.

Within their financial means, graduate schools can meet a great need by providing scholarships to poor but talented persons, representatives of minority groups, and those who wish to dedicate themselves to some aspect of special education but are unable to pay for their training.

Graduate departments should seek to know and collaborate with local pastoral personnel. Whenever possible, they should cooperate with diocesan catechetical offices in arranging field experiences for their students in local pastoral settings (parishes, schools, institutions, etc.). Catechetical offices and graduate schools can also serve the Church by cooperating in other training efforts related to adult catechesis.

b) Undergraduate programs

Catholic colleges are encouraged to offer undergraduate degree programs in catechetics and theology, both for those who wish to pursue graduate studies and become full-time catechetical workers and for those who may assume other leadership roles in the Church. The requirements for such degrees should be as demanding as those for any other academic discipline.

It is important that Catholic institutions of higher learning maintain strong programs in theology and religious studies. Besides being centers of authentic Catholic theology, they should, as far as possible, offer courses in other theologies to meet the needs of an ecumenical age.

The cooperation of Catholic colleges with diocesan catechetical offices, neighboring parishes, and other institutions which require the services of catechists is highly desirable. The college faculty should be available to help ascertain local pastoral needs and provide supervised in-service training in catechetics or theology programs.

243. Campus ministry

Campus ministry is the Church's presence on the college and university campus. It views the milieu of post-secondary education as a creative center of society, where ideas germinate and are tested, leadership is formed, and the future of society is often determined.

Campus ministry involves pastoral service to the entire campus community: students, administrators, faculty, and staff. In every institution, regardless of size and character, campus ministry confronts a range of concerns which reflect in microcosm the catechetical concerns facing the entire Church.

Especially on the nonsectarian, non-Catholic campus, today's student often receives uncritical exposure to modern ideologies and philosophies, to crucial questions concerning faith, ethical behavior, and human life, and to a multiplicity of cults and new religious movements. Campus ministry must create, in an atmosphere of freedom and reverence, an alternative forum for theological and philosophical inquiry. This includes classes on Catholic thought, scripture seminars, opportunities for different forms of prayer, workshops or lectures in social justice, and opportunities to share on various levels with other recognized religious groups. Formal and informal counseling relating to spiritual, social; and psychological concerns should also be offered to help people integrate the gospel into their lives.

Pastoral service on the campus is to emphasize worship, community, and tradition through the development of a community of faith. It should offer enriching exposure to modern and traditional liturgical forms, not only in the liturgy itself but through paraliturgical services emphasizing the communal aspects of sacramental life.

Finally, campus ministry should seek to serve the university institution itself. It should work for responsible governance on the part of the academic institution and for the maintenance of high standards and values. Campus ministers must be concerned with the institution's programs, policies, and research, and with how these promote or hinder human development. This affords them opportunities to deepen understanding of social justice and be of service to the broader community.

Since these various modes of service are expanding and becoming more complex, campus ministry must have adequate personnel. Today's ministry staff is, typically, composed not only of priests, but increasingly of religious and lay persons, faculty, and graduate students, each with special areas of concern and often working as a team to develop a community of faith. As part of the diocese's mission and responsibility, campus ministry should be carried on in cooperation with local parish communities.

Part F: Other Catechetical Settings

244. Residential facilities

Catechesis takes place in a variety of comprehensive but specialized settings, such as convalescent or nursing homes, child-care institutions, residential facilities for the mentally handicapped, and schools for the deaf. People in such facilities have a right to live as normally as possible.

Chaplains in such facilities should be trained for their specific tasks, including catechetical approaches suited to particular groups.

Professional or nonprofessional catechists with appropriate experience work with chaplains by visiting the residents regularly and catechizing, either formally or informally.

Parish, diocesan, and other Church structures and agencies must take the needs of persons in residential facilities into consideration in their planning. As far as possible, they should be incorporated into the life of the parish community, with steps taken to accommodate their special needs.

245. Specialized groupings

A number of movements in the United States bring together men and women who are seeking to deepen their faith. Groups which join for prayer, worship, and the sharing of insights provide catechetical settings. Their members should be encouraged to participate actively in their parishes. Priests, religious, and lay people need to become involved with such groups, and diocesan and parish catechetical offices should assist them as much as possible.

246. Chaplaincies

Hospitals, professional groups, police and fire departments, fraternities, prisons, and juvenile homes provide settings for adult catechesis and reflection. Chaplains to such groups and institutions should take advantage of these opportunities. Diocesan and parish catechetical personnel should assist the chaplains as much as possible, particularly by offering standards for catechesis in these settings.

247. Other ministerial training centers

Ministerial training centers, such as formation centers for religious men and women or lay people, should provide quality programs in catechesis, appropriate to the particular ministry for which the students are preparing.

Catechesis encourages the development of new ministries in and for the life of the Church. The concept of the priesthood of the laity calls for the development of new ministries to supplement the pastoral office in the Church. This would include ministries in the liturgical, catechetical, teaching, service, and administrative fields.

248. Conclusion

At all levels high priority must be given to providing structures within and through which the total catechesis of God's people can be accomplished. In providing such structures, national, regional, diocesan, and parish planning groups should apply the principles set forth in this chapter. Next we turn to the resources which catechists have available for their work.

Notes

1. Cf. GCD, 129; TJD, 142.
2. Cf. Revelation, 22.
3. Cf. *Directory on the Pastoral Ministry of Bishops*, Sacred Congregation for Bishops, February 22, 1973. Publications Service, Canadian Catholic Conference, 174.
4. Cf. Missionary Activity, 35–38; Church, chapters I and II.
5. *On Evangelization* (Paul VI, 1975), 71.

6. GCD, 78.
7. TJD, 118; cf. also, *The Catholic School*, Sacred Congregation for Catholic Education. United States Catholic Conference, 1977.
8. Cf. TJD, 92.
9. *Ibid.*, 103.
10. Christian Education, 8.
11. TJD, 108.
12. Christian Education, 9.
13. Letter of Pope Paul VI to French social action groups meeting in France, July 1, 1970.
14. *Engel v. Vitale*, 370. U.S. 421 (1961); *School District of Abington Township v. Schempp, Murray v. Curlett*, 374 U.S. 203 (1963).
15. Cf. *Illinois ex. rel. McCallum, Board of Education*, 333 U.S. 203, 227 (1948); and *Zorach v. Clauson*, 343 U.S. 306 (1952).
16. Cf. Bishops, 27; for the desirability of such councils, cf. *Directory on the Pastoral Ministry of Bishops, op. cit.*, 204.
17. GCD, 126.
18. Cf. *Ibid.*, 128.
19. *Program of Priestly Formation*, National Conference of Catholic Bishops. United States Catholic Conference, 1976,151.

A Primer on School Law: A Guide for Board Members in Catholic Schools

Shaughnessy, M. A. 1991. 29–34. Washington, D.C.: National Catholic Educational Association.

Chapter 5.*
Duties and Responsibilities of Board Members

The preceding chapters have attempted to discuss the civil law principles affecting Catholic schools. This chapter will consider specific duties and responsibilities of board members in Catholic schools.

Obviously, board members have responsibilities to the body that owns and/or operates the school. Those duties will usually be found in the Constitution or by-laws of the board.

Generally, a board would approve the budget, endorse programs, set tuition, and establish hiring and dismissal procedures. Depending on whether the board was a consultative board or a board with limited jurisdiction, another party such as a parish council, a pastor, or an official of the religious congregation may have final approval of all policies suggested by a board.

The board would monitor the programs, the budget, and the implementation of policy. The principal, who is the board's chief executive officer, would certainly suggest policies and would perhaps write the first drafts of policies. The board would approve the policies (passing them to another party for final approval, as appropriate) and holds the principal accountable for their implementation. The board should, therefore, develop a plan for the evaluation of the principal's job performance.

Duties to Diocese/Church

The school board has definite duties to the diocese and to the larger church. If the school is a parish school or one owned by the diocese, the school board must ensure that the policies it develops are consistent with ones already established by the diocese. If, for example, diocesan policy states that only Catholics who actively practice their religion in accordance with the teaching of the church may be hired in schools owned and operated by the diocese or parishes within the diocese, the local school board must ensure that its policies are consistent with those of the

diocese. Practically speaking, this would mean that divorced Catholics who have contracted a second marriage without the church's approval are not hired or rehired. (Boards may be very reluctant to terminate the contract of someone in such a situation; however, board members must realize that many injustices are wrought when policies and rules are applied inconsistently or when a local board attempts to act at variance with diocesan policy.)

If the board or specific members of the board cannot agree with a given diocesan policy, then change must be sought through the appropriate channels; a board is not free to adopt a policy at variance with established diocesan policy. The board's responsibility is clear: to uphold the policies of the diocese and to develop local policies which are in harmony with those of the diocese.

The same principles would be true if the school is sponsored by a religious congregation. The board must be ruled by the philosophy and goals of the sponsoring group. However, the relationship between a Catholic school not owned by the diocese and the diocese is not always clearly defined or understood. Such a school would probably be free to have a salary scale that is lower or higher than the diocesan scale. The one non-negotiable area would be that of faith and morals. Any Catholic school exists under the primary authority of the bishop and so is subject to him in the area of faith and morals. As stated in Chapter 2, a school that wishes to be truly Catholic can never be completely independent of the bishop.

Cases involving faith and morals can be very complex and very emotional. For example, it can be very difficult to terminate the contract of a person who has taught effectively in a Catholic school for ten years because that person enters into a marriage that the church does not recognize as lawful. But if a school board retains such an individual in contradiction of existing diocesan policy, it is unfair to expect diocesan support if problems result from the board action. When tensions arise, board members must keep their responsibilities to the diocese and to the church in view. If a board member cannot support a policy (and support does not necessarily mean agreement; it does mean a willingness to live with and not criticize the decision),

---

* Editor's note: Chapter notation refers to this excerpt.

then the board member's only real choice is to resign from the board.

Duties to the Principal

School boards have responsibilities to the principal. Today many school boards appoint the principal. If the board does not appoint the principal, it probably has a significant part in the selection process. The board's first responsibility is to ensure that the person selected meets the qualifications set by the diocese or sponsoring party.

Since the principal is responsible to the school board (as well as to other appropriate parties, such as the pastor or a religious superior), the principal should report to the board how he or she is ensuring that policies are implemented. The board should annually review the criteria and procedures for the evaluation of the principal's job performance. It should further ensure that evaluation (at least the board's part of the process) is, in fact, being conducted according to policy. If evaluation is omitted or done casually, problems can result when a board later attempts to call a principal to accountability and/or begins to consider non-renewal of contract. It is certainly not moral, and it may well be a breach of contract for a board to vote for non-renewal or recommendation of non-renewal of a principal's contract without the principal's having had some evaluative feedback and a chance to correct any deficiencies.

Just as supervision and evaluation of faculty is job protection for teachers, so evaluation of the administrator should be viewed as job protection for the principal as well as assurance that the principal is functioning satisfactorily in the position.

If the principal is found to be deficient in job performance and performance improvement plans are not effective, it is the board's responsibility to move into dismissal proceedings unless some other party clearly has that responsibility. It is usually advisable to offer an opportunity for resignation to a principal (or to any other employee who is found professionally deficient). This procedure makes good legal sense and allows the departing employee to retain a measure of dignity.

The principal has the right to expect that the administration of the school is his or her responsibility and that board members will not interfere in the day-to-day running of the school. It is often easy for a board member to succumb to the temptation to get involved in disciplinary matters, academic disputes, and/or faculty/principal problems. The board member has to remember that his or her responsibilities are really twofold: (1) to develop policies and (2) to support the persons and activities that implement those policies.

If the school board really cannot support the principal's decision, the board should call an executive session (one in which no one other than board members and the principal are in attendance). In that session, board members can state their views and listen to those of the principal. The principal might be asked to develop different policy implementation plans. Goals and objectives are ways of implementing policies; the principal may be able to make modifications that would be acceptable to the board. Ideally, the board and the principal can come to some understanding and/or compromise. If no compromise can be reached that both parties can support, the board may have to call in an outside facilitator or arbitrator.

Disagreements should be left in the board room. Board members must constantly remember that their power is that of the board when it is in session; there is no power vested in individual board members. Becoming involved in administrative/parent or teacher/parent or administrative/teacher disputes only weakens the authority of both the administrator and the board. The principal, however, should keep board members informed about problem or potential problem situations so that board members will be able to respond in an intelligent manner if they are questioned.

In the end, if the board and/or the pastor or other appropriate party cannot support the principal's administration, the principal will have to leave the situation. There is no more crucial relationship for the success of the educational ministry than that of the board and the principal. That relationship should foster a sound academic experience in a Christian community. When the principal and the board function in an atmosphere in which each respects the rights of the other and in which healthy dialogue and the resolution of differences are promoted, the teaching ministry of the Church should thrive.

As the board has responsibility for the evaluation of the job performance of the principal, the principal has responsibility for the hiring, supervision, and evaluation of teachers. As stated in Chapter 4, teacher evaluation is not the board's role. The development of personnel policies is. The board should set policies that call for regular supervision and evaluation of teachers. How the principal implements the policies is his or her responsibility.

Duties to Teachers

The board does have responsibilities to teachers. All schools should have faculty handbooks. The principal is the person who is probably best equipped to make recommendations about what should be in the handbook. Board members should be familiar with all school handbooks. The principal should keep the board informed of any changes in handbooks. This kind of reporting helps to ensure that board members are well-equipped to support the school and its administration. Faculty handbooks range in size from a few pages stapled together to books of 100 or more pages. At the very minimum, faculty handbooks should contain the following: an outline of expectations regarding teaching duties should be included; these expectations should involve such areas as the construction of lesson plans, homework policies, and grading standards. Non-teaching duties should be addressed. Generally, these duties are more controversial than teaching duties. Such requirements as cafeteria, playground, and study hall supervision should be discussed. The procedures to be followed for field trips should be detailed. If an unfortunate accident were to occur on a field trip and no specific policies were in place, a teacher could rightfully claim that the school board was at fault for failing to ensure that proper procedures were followed.

The high school has long been home to many extra-curricular activities. Today more and more such activities are found in the elementary school. Student councils, drama clubs, and musical productions are very much a part of some elementary schools. Athletic programs are growing in the elementary school as well as the high school. Staff members must be found to moderate and coach these activities. The board must ensure that whatever is expected of teachers in regard to extra-curricular activities is stated before contracts are signed so that the chances for dispute are minimized.

Job protection for teachers in Catholic schools is a legitimate concern. Although a 1979 case, *National Labor Relations Board v. the Catholic Bishop of Chicago, et al.* (440 U.S. 490), rendered the creation of new unions in Catholic schools somewhat unlikely, there are unions in some Catholic school systems that existed prior to 1979. If a legitimate union exists, the board must work through it. However, most Catholic schools, particularly our grade schools, are not unionized. Although our schools may not have formal tenure systems, and, indeed, many contracts across the country are year-to-year contracts, the situation of *de facto* tenure as discussed in Chapter 4 may exist. In fact, a Catholic school can create an expectation of continuing employment. If a Catholic school dismissed a teacher who had been working in the school for ten years, the court would look at the policies, procedures, and past practices of the school or school system. If teachers are usually retained in the system after three or four years and rarely, if ever, face non-renewal of contract, *de facto* tenure may be found to exist. As discussed earlier in this book, Catholic schools are not bound by Constitutional due process; however, they are bound by common law considerations of fairness.

In the public sector, due process demands that an accused person be given notice and a hearing before an impartial tribunal. Further, the person has the right to question accusers, provide witnesses on his or her own behalf, and the right to have an attorney present. The person has the right to appeal the decision. At the minimum, Catholic school boards should develop policies requiring that a teacher facing suspension or dismissal be told of the charges and be given an opportunity to refute them. Some process of appeal should be in place. In most dioceses, the bishop will be the last "court of appeal." The important point is that there be some avenue of appeal for a teacher who has been in the Catholic system for a period of time that would have resulted in tenure if he or she had been in the public system.

If the school or the diocese does not have a grievance procedure, the pastor (or religious superior in a school owned by a religious congregation) should initiate a plan to develop one to ensure that teachers are treated fairly. What constitutes matter for a grievance should be clearly stated. Every disagreement a teacher has with a principal is not a potential grievance. Only serious situations which cannot be solved through other channels should be brought to a grievance procedure. The local board has a responsibility to respect the grievance procedure and to encourage persons to utilize the procedure when appropriate.

Duties to Parent/Student Community

A fourth group to which the board has specific responsibilities is the parent/student community. All schools should have a parent/student handbook in which the policies that affect parents and students are explained. Some areas that should be included are: admission policies, academic policies, the procedure for communication between parents and teachers and/or administration, the discipline code, rules concerning extra-curricular activities, field trip policies and forms, emergency procedures, parent service and fund-raising requirements, and the role of the school board.

Parents should be informed about the function of the school board and about the policies governing attendance at school board meetings, speaking at school board meetings, and bringing matters to the attention of the school board. School boards must guard against becoming a "dumping ground" for complaints. Only serious matters which appropriately belong to the school board should be considered and then, only after all other channels have been exhausted. School boards should not become involved in matters which are the province of principals or teachers.

Board members have serious responsibilities to the church, to the diocese, to the parish or parishes that sponsor the school, to the sponsoring religious congregation, to the principal, to teachers and staff, and to parents and students. The role of the board member is to oversee good school operation and effective ministry through the development of sound policy.

Board members must understand that they can be held personally liable if they knew or should have known that a certain policy or action violated a person's rights. In these days of increasing litigation, board members need liability insurance. As a matter of simple justice, those owning schools should make every attempt to obtain liability insurance for those who serve on boards. However, if the school, parish, or diocese cannot provide the insurance, board members should obtain their own coverage.

What Is a Catholic School Board?

Sheehan, L. 1990. In *Building better boards: A handbook for board members in Catholic education*, 1–5. Washington, D.C.: National Catholic Educational Association.

A Catholic school board is a body whose members are selected and/or elected to participate in decision-making in designated areas of responsibility. Usually these areas include planning, policy formulation/enactment, finances, the selection or appointment of the principal, development including public relations and marketing, and evaluation. Board members also include the administrator (principal/superintendent) and canonical administrator (pastor/bishop).

Types of Catholic Schools

The organizational structure of the school will almost always dictate how the school board is constituted. For example, models which are appropriate for the parish elementary school may not be appropriate for the diocesan secondary school or regional school, and are usually not appropriate for most private schools.

Most Catholic schools function within the traditional organization of parish, diocese, or religious congregation.

A **parish school** is part of the educational mission of the parish for which the pastor is the canonical administrator. He delegates, according to diocesan policy, administrative responsibilities to the school principal, who is accountable to him.

Diocesan schools function as part of the diocese and the principal is usually accountable to the bishop through the superintendent of schools.

Private Catholic schools are part of the mission of the religious congregation and the principal is responsible to the elected/appointed community administrators. Some private Catholic schools are owned and operated by lay boards of trustees. In order to call themselves Catholic, these institutions receive formal approval from the diocesan bishop and commit themselves to follow diocesan norms regarding religious education programs and the Catholicity of the school.

An exception to this traditional organizational pattern is the regional or interparish school, that is, a school supported by more than one parish. Some dioceses appoint one of the pastors of a contributing parish as the school's canonical administrator. This person, representing the other pastors, is the one to whom the principal is accountable. Some dioceses constitute boards of regional schools with limited jurisdiction. Board constitutions clearly state the canonical leadership between these schools and the parishes and/or dioceses. Other dioceses formally erect this type of school as a separate juridic person and appoint the principal as the canonical administrator.

Types of Boards

Four types of school boards are often referred to in governance literature. They are jurisdictional boards, boards with limited jurisdiction, consultative boards, and regulatory boards. In A *Primer on Educational Governance in the Catholic Church*, these types are defined as follows:

Jurisdictional—a board which not only legislates but also controls. It has final authority and total jurisdiction for all areas of educational policy and administration, as well as the legislative power to enact policy. There are no jurisdictional boards in the Catholic Church.

Board with Limited Jurisdiction—a board which has power limited to certain areas of educational concern. It has final but not total jurisdiction, since the diocesan bishop has jurisdiction over the religious education and Catholicity of all schools including private schools, and most religious congregations have canonically reserved powers.

Consultative—a board which operates in the policy-making process by formulating and adapting, but never enacting policy. This type of board is more in keeping with shared decision-making in the Catholic Church because of the consultative status of the diocesan presbyteral council and the diocesan finance council. The constituting authority established those areas where the board is to be consulted. Such action is usually made effective by the board's constitution.

Regulatory—a board which enacts or uses existing rules and regulations to govern the operation of its institutions. This type of board is considered administrative rather than policy-making or consultative. Public school boards are usually designated as regulatory.

Only consultative boards and boards with limited jurisdiction are appropriate models of Catholic school boards.

In order to appreciate the role of these boards, it is necessary to understand the nature of consultation within the church.

Consultative Bodies in the Church

The 1983 Code of Canon Law requires several consultative bodies in each diocese and parish. Each diocese has a presbyteral council and college of consultors (cc. 495, 502), and a finance council (c. 492), and every parish has a finance council (c. 537). Other consultative bodies, such as a diocesan pastoral council and parish pastoral councils, are recommended by the Code. Although not specifically mentioned, education boards, councils, and commissions are certainly within the spirit of the Code and should be constituted within the norms given for the mandated consultative bodies.

Consultation implies that the administrator(s) will listen to the advice of the properly convened body in certain designated matters prior to a decision being made. The operating principle is that the administrator(s) will not act contrary to the advice which has been given, especially when there is a consensus, unless the administrator(s) has an overriding reason. It is customary for the administrator(s) to communicate this reason to the consultative body.

Civil Incorporation

Catholic school boards may or may not be incorporated according to the civil laws of the state and the policies of the diocese or religious congregation. Board members should know and understand the status of the civil corporation with which the board is affiliated.

A diocesan bishop exercises his authority in accord with Canon Law and in accord with all applicable civil law —federal, state, and local. In regard to church property, there are three major systems which states use to legislate ownership. They are: the bishop-as-trustee, the bishop-as-corporation-sole, and the corporation aggregate. In the bishop-as-trustee method, the title to the property is vested in the bishop-as-trustee and the equitable title is vested in the members of the parish. (The state statutes that apply in this case are the ones that govern nonprofit or religious corporations.) The bishop-as-trustee holds the title for the benefit of the parish. Although he retains the right of supervision and the right to govern in accord with church law, the trustee can delegate the control of the property to the administrator of the parish.

In the bishop-as-corporation-sole method, the bishop holds absolute title to the church's property until he is transferred, retires, or dies. In civil law, the bishop can do anything he wishes with the property as long as it is in compliance with church law. The person who is appointed the new bishop becomes the corporation sole.

In the corporation aggregate method, there are two different ways the property may be owned. In the first, legal title is vested in incorporated trustees with equitable title vested in the non-incorporated parish. In the second, legal title is vested directly in the corporate officers of the parish who are elected and act as a board of directors or trustees. In this case, they are the agents of the corporation. The state statutes that apply here are the ones which govern a charitable trust or an aggregation of charitable trusts.

Religious congregations hold property in their own right according to laws of the state. The articles of incorporation define the role and authority of the agents of the corporation. According to church law (Canon 1290), all administrators are bound to observe the civil laws of any given territory "with the same effects in a matter which is subject to the governing power of the Church, unless the civil regulations are contrary to divine law or canon law makes some other provision . . ." (*A Primer on Educational Governance in the Catholic Church*, NCEA, 1987).

Most diocesan and parish school boards are not separately incorporated while many boards of private and diocesan/regional schools are. The preferred model for private schools is the two-tiered board composed of both corporate members and boards of directors (cf. Appendix for model).

Consultative Boards

A consultative board is one which cooperates in the policy-making process by formulating and adapting, but never enacting policy. To call a group "consultative" does not diminish its importance; rather it indicates that the body is inserted into the governance structure of the organization in a significant way.

The pastor or canonical administrator related to the school enacts policy developed by a consultative board before it can be promulgated and implemented.

Boards with Limited Jurisdiction

A board with limited jurisdiction has authority limited to certain areas of educational concern. It has final, but not total jurisdiction. The constitutions of boards with limited jurisdiction should clearly state the areas in which the board has authority and those which are reserved to the bishop and/or to the religious congregation. For example, these boards have no authority to change the diocesan philosophy of education or to formulate local policies which are not in concert with diocesan policies in religious education. Most religious congregations reserve such powers as approval to change the philosophy and mission of the school, approval of debts over a certain amount, ownership of property, and others (cf. Appendix for sample constitutions).

Diocesan Boards

Diocesan school boards are usually constituted as consultative to the diocesan bishop. The policies which they develop are enacted/approved by the bishop and promulgated by him for implementation in the diocese.

Areas of Board Responsibility

Those areas in which all Catholic school boards should be involved are:

Planning—establishing a mission statement and a strategic plan.

Policy Formulation/Enactment—to give general direction for administrative action.

Finances—developing plans and means to finance ongoing educational programs including setting tuition, negotiating subsidy, and developing the annual budget.

Selection/appointment of the principal—participating according to its constitution and the policies of the diocese and/or religious congregation in determining the principal.

Development, including public relations and marketing—includes understanding the school's mission, a commitment to that vision, the involvement of people, the formulation of a plan, the development and presentation of a case statement to the public, and finally the acquisition of funds to bring the plan to fruition.

Evaluation—determining whether goals and plans are being met, not evaluating individual staff members, administrators or students, except the principal's relationship with the board, and determining the board's own effectiveness.

Chapters two through seven detail these responsibilities.

Decision-Making

Consensus-building is the appropriate mode of decision-making for a Catholic school board. Consensus means that all board members agree to support the decision which appears to be the best, under the present circumstances, for the greatest number of people. In those cases where a vote needs to be recorded for legal purposes, *Roberts Rules of Order Revised* should be followed.

Preparing a Presentation for the Board of Education

Sparks, G. J. 1986. In *The Catholic school administrator—A book of readings*,
ed. E. M. Bushman and G. J. Sparks, 293–95. Portland, Ore.: Catholic Leadership Company.

The board of education meeting is a useful, necessary forum for the Catholic school administrator to present methods and philosophies to both the board members and to interested parents and other parishioners present. A significant amount of presentation time may be devoted to defending school programs and interpreting school practices in light of the Gospel. An effective presentation will contain many of the following elements:

1. Always prepare data carefully and recheck for accuracy prior to releasing them orally or in a visual form. Inaccuracies will surely return to haunt the careless administrator.

2. Arrange materials well physically. Such seemingly minor items as seating, public address systems, electrical connections, availability and location of screens, access to preplanned supplementary handouts, and the like carry with them the minimal essentials of a well-received delivery.

3. Understand the concept of "timing"—when to begin, when to reveal the central themes of your message, how to expose material for maximal impact, when to "detour" from your main topic, when and how to close effectively.

4. Be aware of the "instant boredom" which can afflict boards of education—they perhaps have heard it all before. Conscious closure on their parts must be avoided and such verbal or visual pyrotechnics as necessary must be used without turning the delivery into a circus.

5. Keep your deliveries free from technical language, hackneyed phraseology, and obnoxious educational jargon. Failure to do this will lose the more educated, frequently supportive elements of the audience and serves largely to obfuscate issues, creating resentment and misunderstanding.

6. Maintain an "antiseptic" tone to your remarks. Avalanches of defensive or apologetic remarks heighten whatever inadequacies people perceive in the school in the first place. On the other hand, never be so confident about your stance that an audience sees you as unapproachable, distant, and arrogant. A fine line exists here, and it is largely personal style which controls and governs that sensitive middle ground.

7. If other professional personnel (e.g., a panel of faculty) are to be used in a presentation, be sure they are rehearsed to an extent deemed prudent. Be sure that each member is briefed on timing, political implications, and the potentially incendiary nature of "unwise" commentary.

8. Always avoid "preaching" to sophisticated audiences. Diatribes, polemics, or hysterical outbursts are elements of public speaking which smother what might otherwise have been well-received remarks.

9. Never become involved in verbal warfare or exchange intellectual artillery fire (even if baited) with board members, parents, or other parishioners at such meetings. Even if you win the intellectual argument, you lose the emotional one. Refer to earlier comments on the ABC's of Administration.

10. Be sure all visual and handout materials are prepared well in advance, proofread carefully, and that final versions are scrupulously accurate and attractive. Never settle for even questionable crispness, let alone marginal sloppiness.

11. Compress all presentations in both time and content as much as possible, however charismatic your speaking or journalistic style. Verbal virtuosity has its place; it does not happen to be at board meetings, however.

12. Keep deliveries simple, direct, uncluttered, and above all, clear. Remember, a misunderstood message will always get increasingly distorted, and such inaccuracies and manglings can never really be explained away.

13. Never mask or attempt to perfume the truth. Do not shock needlessly, but do not euphemize the obvious either.

14. Review your intended remarks with the pastor prior to making them final, so that an internal "surprise-free" climate exists. Such prudent caution salvages beforehand what might otherwise prove to be a political holocaust from which the school may find it difficult, if not impossible, to disentangle itself.

15. Styles of delivery will and should vary considerably. Catholic school administrators may not all be gifted orators; they need not be. Their presentations, however, need intelligent planning, recognition of the nature of the audience, and a sound sensing of what needs to be said and how best to say it.

Governance and Administration in the Catholic School

Drahmann, T. 1985. 15–16. Washington, D.C.: National Catholic Educational Association.

Chapter 4.*
Major or Minor League?

The Central Office, Diocesan and Congregational Relationships with Schools

For a major league baseball player, the ultimate disgrace is to be sent back to the minors. He has lost status as well as salary; it is seen as a clear indication of failure; he now will be performing in a second-class setting.

Many teachers in both public and private school systems may wonder if the superintendents and those associated as staff of that office are the "major league" players in a school system, whereas the principals and teachers are in the "minor leagues." The central office administrators seem to get the headlines; those in the schools receive little public recognition.

This may apply to a certain extent to public school systems, which usually are highly centralized, but it is rarely the case in Catholic schools. Because the important decisions regarding personnel and finances are largely made at each individual school, the diocesan superintendent of schools plays a lesser role than the public school counterpart in that position.

There is interesting historical background for the role of the Catholic school office. Formerly, there were dioceses where there was strong direction and control, but more often, each school was largely independent of the office. In the latter instances, superiors and supervisors from the religious order which staffed the school were likely to be quite influential. They often determined policies and procedures, even the selection of textbooks.

At the present time, because of the diminished number of religious in the school, a Catholic school is more likely to receive direction, supervision, evaluation, and assistance from the diocesan office, rather than from a religious order. The decisions of the diocesan board of education and the superintendent's office may deal with teacher qualifications, fund-raising activities, administration, hiring, curriculum and textbooks, inservice activities, and special areas of instruction such as the religion programs and human sexuality instruction.

Why are Catholic schools organized on a diocesan basis? This stems from the fact that the Catholic Church is organizationally divided into regional units (dioceses), each headed by a bishop (or archbishop). The bishop, as a successor of the Apostles, is selected to lead what is theologically considered to be the *local church*—more than an administrative unit, rather it is a living cell of Christ's Body, which together with others, form the entire church under the pope.

A special function of the bishop is to be the chief teacher in the diocese. Others who exercise this function in the educational work of the church do so as sharers in the bishop's teaching ministry. This is the broad base for the authority of the diocesan education office, which also acts as a means of support and assistance for each school.

Present church law states that the local bishop has authority over all Catholic schools located in his diocese, including those which are directed by religious orders (Canon 806, #1).[11]

In some areas, diocesan funds to assist the schools are disbursed from the central office.

How do religious orders presently affect the schools? As is well known, religious communities in times past supplied the majority of teaching and administrative personnel for Catholic schools (and financed both preliminary and continuing education for their members). As stated above, religious order supervisors worked with school personnel to give assistance and assure quality. At present, members of religious communities are in a minority in most schools, but they still are able to be an influence in preserving the valued traditions of the school.

Note

11. *Canon Law*, 303.

---

* Editor's note: Chapter notation refers to this excerpt.

Administrator's Handbook of Regulations

Hennessey, C., C. A. Solomon, K. Mitchell, S. Plasek, D.A. Clifford, and T. Bogar. 1992, 1988. 7–10.
Houston, Tex.: Catholic School Office, Diocese of Galveston-Houston.

Sample Organization of Diocesan Structure and Policies Relating to Schools

1110 Bishop

The bishop as the ordinary of the diocese is the chief representative of the Church's teaching authority. Diocesan structure includes 4 Vicariates which represent all parishes and 5 Secretariats which represent all Departments within the diocese.

The bishop, as the chief representative of the church's teaching authority, is the head of the Diocesan System of Schools. The administration of the schools is carried out by the Superintendent. Religious Education is under the guidance of the Director of the Office of Continuing Christian Education.

1120 Vicariate

Four vicars who represent the Bishop within the respective vicariate to the priest, deacons, and laity. The vicars coordinate the functions of the deans, attend deanery meetings, and perform all other duties given to them.

1130 Secretariat Directors

Five persons form a cabinet overseeing, under the Bishop, the operations of Chancery Services. The Directors coordinate the departments in their division through joint planning and sharing information. They also conduct periodic evaluations to determine if the goals of each department are being met.

1130.1 Secretariat for Christian Formation

This secretariat is part of the diocesan structure that coordinates the five offices which deal directly with Christian Formation.

The Catholic School Office is included in the Secretariat for Christian Formation.

1210 Texas Catholic Conference Education Department (TCCED)

TCCED is the designated coordinator of all activities related to state accreditation. As such it shall establish standards which a diocesan system of schools must satisfy to be accredited and shall adopt an accreditation process to be used in Catholic Schools.

1210.1 Texas Catholic Conference Education Department Accreditation Commission (TCCAC)

Membership consists of all superintendents of the 14 dioceses, other experts in the field of education, and two bishop members who serve as episcopal liaison. The Commission through committees is responsible for setting up the operations, ongoing planning of the accreditation process, review of school compliance, and reporting of accreditation status.

1310 Diocesan Board of Education

The Diocesan Board of Education is an advisory organization delegated by the Bishop and responsible to the diocese for diocesan sponsored educational programs.

1320 Superintendent

The superintendent of schools is the organizational and instructional leader in the system of Catholic schools —Diocese of Galveston-Houston.

1320.1 Specific Responsibilities

◆ Directs and coordinates the Catholic School Office.
◆ Coordinates and supervises the central administrative services for the efficient operation of all Catholic Schools.
◆ Implements all policies of the Diocesan Board of Education.
◆ Implements the principles and standards for accreditation. (Texas Catholic Conference Education Department)

1330 Diocesan Consultants

Consultants, in respective educational areas, are responsible to the Superintendent and provide assistance in central administration, service, and planning to the schools. A job description and explanation of services is shared with the principals in August and January.

1340 Continuing Christian Education

The Continuing Christian Education Office develops programs, provides consultation and services for curriculum and personnel development to Catholic schools, parish schools of religion, and adult religious education programs in the diocese.

1350 Diocesan Media Center

The Diocesan Media Center offers a rental library for films, filmstrips, kits, cassettes, slides, records, and videos in the areas of religion, teacher training, affective education, and general curriculum. Workshops on the care and maintenance of audiovisual equipment and materials as well as film festivals are also available.

1410 Pastor

The pastor is the spiritual leader of the parish and ex officio, the chief administrative officer of the parish school. It is his duty to see that the teachings of the church are clearly and accurately presented. The immediate direction of the school and its instructional program is, however, to be delegated to the principal. Satisfactory and effective administration depend on the cooperation and mutual support of both pastor and principal in matters of local educational policy.

1420   Local Board of Education

The local board of education assists the pastor and principal with policymaking, budgets, and financing. The local board of education is charged with the responsibility of implementing Diocesan Board of Education policies. (Refer to Diocesan Board of Education Policy 110, 120)

1420.1   Guidelines Policy #120

"Every parish shall have an education board (body)."

The principal of each school is encouraged to give support to the parish in the inauguration of a policy-making board. Where a board is already established, the principal is the educational professional to guide and assist the board members in their role as board members.

Policy #120 also sets up three models for education boards:

1. Parish with a religious education program and a school—one board of education would be formed for all education programs. This is considered as the ideal model.

2. School Board—formed when there is a regional school serving many parishes; or where the school and religious education programs are not ready to form a joint board of education.

3. Religious Education Board—for a parish where there is no school.

All education boards are policy-making boards and function for the good of the persons they serve. To ensure their proper structure and function, guidelines have been established for board members, executive officers, and pastors. Workshops are held several times a year for proper involvement in the education process.

1420.2   Board Inservice

The Diocesan Board of Education has established a policy that assists members of a board to become knowledgeable about their duties and responsibilities

The Diocesan Board of Education sponsors at least three workshops a year for the specific purpose of training board members, principals, DREs, and pastors in the roles and responsibilities each has to each other and to the board as a whole.

The principal should avail himself/herself of these workshops and encourage the board members and the pastors to attend.

The Diocesan Board will give assistance to local boards whenever possible. The Board Consultant is available to all boards. Her role is one of, not limited to, training and informing boards of proper procedures. She offers assistance in writing constitutions, bylaws, and mission statements.

1430   Regional Board of Education

Those schools which represent a number of parishes in a specific region are Regional Schools. The Regional School is administered by a principal who is directly responsible to the Superintendent of Catholic Schools.

The Regional Board of Education is composed of representation of lay persons (nonprofessional educators) within the Region. A Regional Board is accountable to the Diocesan Board of Education.

1440   Principal

The principal is the educational leader of the school, possessing full administrative responsibility for the instructional program of the school, and the local Board of Education or school committee.

1440.1   Principal Qualifications

The principal must hold a master's degree in Administration and have 5 years of teaching experience; 3 years must have been in a Catholic School. This experience must be in the respective grade level for which he/she is applying, i.e., Elementary, Junior High, Secondary.

1440.2   Principal Responsibilities

As the educational head of the school, the principal is held accountable for school policies outlined in the Texas Catholic Conference Education Department Accreditation Principles and Standards, Diocesan School Goals, the Diocesan Board of Education Policies, State Rules for Curriculum, and the Catholic School Office Administrators Handbook of Regulations.

1440.3   Specific Responsibilities

◆ Maintains a Christian atmosphere in the Catholic School.

◆ Communicates the directives of the superintendent to the staff, community, and students.

◆ Plans, leads, implements, and directs the school's curricular and extracurricular programs in compliance with TCCED and Catholic School Office regulations.

◆ Observes and evaluates the school's total program, works with teachers to improve the learning process, and participates with School Office personnel in determining major program revisions or undertaking new programs.

◆ Maintains good communications with the pastor and local education board on matters pertaining to the Catholic school.

◆ Interviews staff applicants, issues contract of employment, and has the responsibility to employ and dismiss the school staff personnel.

Policies and Practices of Governance and Accountability

Sheehan, M. L., RSM. 1986. In *Personnel issues and the Catholic school administrator*, ed. J. S. O'Brien and M. McBrien, 1–11. Washington, D.C.: National Catholic Educational Association.

People are always searching for a perfect model which would settle the matter of the governance of Catholic schools. This chapter will not settle that question. The fact is there is no one set of policies, much less practices, that operates in all Catholic schools. In spite of its image as a hierarchical organization with universally enforced norms, the church's policies and practices of governance and accountability are neither uniformly defined nor universally practiced in Catholic schools.

What really happens in schools depends on personalities, policies, and politics at the local level. Given a high degree of autonomy and significant differences in governance models among the various types of schools, it follows that no single set of policies and practices is possible or desirable. Within this context, this chapter will address the topic of governance under the four typical organizational structures for Catholic schools: parish, interparish, diocesan, and private.

A parish school is defined as an institution (elementary or secondary) which is associated with only one parish from which it receives some subsidy. Those schools are designated interparish which are supported by more than one parish. Usually the subsidy flows directly from the parishes to the school. A diocesan school is one which is not identified with any one parish or group of parishes; ordinarily the subsidy goes directly from the diocese to the school. Traditionally, private schools are those which are owned, operated, and sponsored by a religious congregation which receives no parish or diocesan subsidy.

Parish Schools

Approximately 75 percent of the Catholic elementary and secondary schools in the United States are operated as single-parish schools.[1] Ultimately, each is the responsibility of the pastor of the parish and is subject to the same church laws that govern parishes. These state that the pastor has the exclusive right to act on behalf of the parish in all juridic affairs, is responsible for the administration of all parish goods, and within the limits of the law has the ultimate authority in the parish and therefore in the parish school. The pastor must have a finance council which functions in accordance with diocesan norms and, if the bishop requires it, a pastoral council.[2] The *Code of Canon Law* does not mention education boards or commissions; however, one should presume that where they exist the collegial body must be constituted in a manner which is consistent with existing canons, diocesan legislation, and other collegial bodies.

In practice, it is the school principal who functions as the administrator of the school and the member of the parish staff who works with the school board/committee and/or other parent groups. There is obvious accountability to the parish administrator, the pastor. A good working relationship between pastor and principal, including mutual respect and trust, is key to the effective operation of the school and ultimately the parish.

When the majority of principals were appointed by the religious congregation, hiring was not the issue it is today. The question of who hires is basic to the understanding of accountability. The parish is obligated to follow diocesan policy in this and all other education matters. However, because of differing practices and the emerging role of boards it is necessary to consider hiring practices as well as roles and relationships among parish leaders.

Recognizing that the pastor has the final word and is as a matter of fact the "employer" of the principal, Father John Gilbert believes that the pastor should make it an absolute practice that no one is hired without the involvement and consent of both the board with whom the principal works and the staff.[3] There are many ways to insure this involvement. The most common is to establish a search/interview committee. Membership includes those individuals and groups whose relationship with the principal affects the running of the school.

While the pastor should be in close communication with this committee, it does not seem essential that he attend each and every meeting. It would be unfortunate if he were never involved and just received the final recommendations from the committee without the benefit of prior discussion. Somewhere between no involvement and running the committee there is a middle ground which will ensure agreement on the job description and on the specific needs of the parish and school.

Standard personnel practice recognizes that the person who hires is the one ultimately responsible for evaluation and continuation of the contract. Regular discussions and a commitment to keep one another informed will provide a good basis for the more formal annual evaluation carried out at least every three years. This process should involve those other groups with which the principal relates. Most dioceses have well established processes and procedures for evaluation and offer the services of the education staff to assist both the principal and pastor. In those instances where a dispute arises over contracts, both parties have the opportunity to appeal to the diocesan arbitration and conciliation process.

How the other collegial bodies in the diocese are constituted will determine to a large extent the relationship between the principal and the school board. If the board has the understanding that it is "policy-making" and has actually hired the principal, then in a very real sense the principal is the "employee" of the board. The more common practice is where the board is constituted as consultative or advisory. There the question of relationship needs clarification, but the issue of authority need not cloud the discussion. What is crucial is that the diocese state clearly its understanding of the role of collegial group, as expressed in the canons and the documents of Vatican II.

In a very real sense, the principal is accountable to the parents who have entrusted their children to the faculty and staff of the school. While this relationship cannot strictly be put under the category of governance, it is very real and demands that the principal possess a commitment to availability and communication with all parents. If good common sense is not sufficient to bring people to this conclusion, perhaps the findings of the *Effective Catholic Schools*[4] study are. One of the most significant conclusions of this research is that one of the main characteristics of an effective school is that faculty, parents, and students share a common vision and commitment to the mission of the school. There is no way in which this goal can be achieved without time and effort being spent on communications.

The individual principal may have limited contact with either the federal, state, or local education agency, but has the responsibility to know those statutes and regulations which affect non-governmental schools. The services of the Department of Education of the United States Catholic Conference are readily available to assist in governmental matters. Regular updated communications are sent to diocesan offices regarding pending federal legislation.

Most dioceses promulgate education policies which affect parish schools directly. Technically there is a distinction between legislative statements which have the force of policy and those guidelines designated as administrative. In practice they are implemented at the parish level with the same commitment.

Depending on the size and organizational structure of the diocese, the superintendent of schools reports directly to the bishop or functions as part of an office of education and is directly accountable to the secretary or vicar for education. The impact that the diocesan arrangement has on the parish school is usually not significant. The principal needs to know such practical matters as where the responsibility for religious education rests both at the diocesan level and in the parish. Given that the principal is the administrator of the total school program, it seems advisable for that person to have the responsibility for the religious education as well. This allocation of responsibility does not in any way minimize the need for the principal and the parish director of religious education to work together as members of the parish staff for the good of all. This same principle applies at the diocesan level where the superintendent of schools should have the administrative control of the entire curriculum in the diocese. As the chief catechist the bishop has final authority for the religious education in his diocese; the clarification of accountability in this matter is especially helpful to ensure the effective functioning of the school.

Private Schools

Constituting 38.5 percent of Catholic secondary schools, schools operated by religious congregations are the largest percentage of Catholic secondary schools. At the elementary level, private schools are the smallest group at 5 percent.[5] Traditionally, private schools have enjoyed the clearest lines of authority and accountability. The major superior and council of the religious community have the authority for the administration of the congregation and its works. They ordinarily appoint the principal of the school who is also a member of the congregation and in practice enjoys almost total autonomy in the daily administration of the institution.

The authority of the bishop in the areas of religious education and the Catholicity of the school is recognized, but for all practical purposes never exercised. Relations with the diocesan school office are usually cordial but distant, probably because there is no involvement in either finances or personnel. While the lines of authority remain clear as far as ownership and sponsorship of private Catholic schools are concerned, there seems to be a changing climate regarding the schools' operations.

As more religious congregations establish boards with non-congregational members, the issues of governance and management need clarification. More often than not, the key point of discussion is the hiring of the principal and therefore the relation of that person to the religious congregation and to the board. When the administrator is a member of the congregation that issue is not as complicated as it is when a lay person assumes that position. There are many models which seem to be working; what is essential is that there be a clear understanding between the congregational leadership and the board of directors of the school.

Finances are always an area of concern. Most statements of relations with boards of directors give the responsibility for the operations of the school to the local board with the understanding that the operating budget will be a balanced one. An unresolved issue for most congregations and their schools is the question of responsibility for capital improvements and repairs. One approach may be for the congregation to recognize its role as "landlord" and function in this way in regard to major repairs and renovations. This model assumes that the board of directors will function as a "tenant" and may allocate a percentage of the operating budget as either rent or contingency for upkeep.

The person who most needs clarity in the question of roles and relationships is the principal. It does not seem wise to rely on either membership or chance to ensure that the school will be administered in accordance with clear policies and guidelines. The question of the principal's accountability in the private school is different in those instances where there is another person designated as the president of the school. Where both of the individuals are members of the same congregation, they probably enjoy the same understanding as to the traditional role definitions in this arrangement. Where a member of the congregation serves as president and a lay person functions as principal, much time and energy should be given to clarifying responsibilities. Perhaps there are some analogies between this model and the functioning relationship between the pastor and principal at the parish school.

Diocesan Schools

Diocesan schools comprise 35.5 percent of the secondary and 4.2 percent of the elementary Catholic schools in this country.[6] Organizationally, the diocesan school is directly accountable to the diocese; practically, this usually means that the responsibility is to the bishop through the superintendent of schools and some type of board structure. Since the practice of designating elementary schools as diocesan seems to be relatively new, there is no traditional pattern to cite. However, at the secondary level the past practice in many dioceses was to have a diocesan priest serve as the principal of the school. In those instances where a woman religious was appointed principal, the usual practice was for the bishop to appoint a priest as director, coordinator, or school pastor. The intent of that practice was to provide clear lines of canonical authority. In many dioceses, this is no longer the practice with the result that the issue of authority is not as clear. In some instances, boards have been constituted as, or have assumed the position of being, jurisdictional or policy-making. In other schools, the principal functions almost autonomously. Neither of these extremes is desirable. If diocesan schools are to remain tied to the diocese canonically, there have to be clear lines of accountability and responsibility. Before attempting to determine these lines, it is important for the diocese to state how it wants to relate to these schools. For instance if the bishop through the school office wishes to establish or maintain a close tie in with the principal of each school and the size of the diocese permits it, the superintendent of schools could be designated as that person to whom the principal is directly responsible. In this instance the principal would be hired by the superintendent in much the same way that the pastor hires the principal of the parish school.

The same guidelines and norms governing roles and relationships would apply. On the other hand, in complex situations, the diocesan school could be erected as a juridic person in its own right. In those cases the principal would become the canonical administrator of the school and accountable to the bishop for the administration of the goods and services of the school. The advantage of this model is that the school functions as a separate juridic person with specific rights and responsibilities as given in the *Code of Canon Law*.

Regardless of which model the diocese uses, the role of the school board remains an issue. Recognizing that boards are currently functioning with differing understandings and differing degrees of "authority," the challenge of sharing responsibility for the operations of the diocesan school remains. Whether school boards have been operating for a number of years, are relatively new, or are nonexistent, diocesan officials need to ask themselves as well as the people in the field: Why should we have school boards? What can they do that is not or cannot be done by the professional educators? Without clarity about these basic questions, no organizational model will make sense in the long run. After the initial enthusiasm wears off, the group itself will spend time trying to answer these very same questions. Although it may be appropriate for each group to define itself in terms of specific long-range goals, it is not the responsibility of each board to determine its authority and/or how it will relate to the diocese.

Perhaps the most commonly asked question regarding the constitution of boards is: Are they policy-making? What is meant by this term varies. For some dioceses, the practice is for the boards to meet, make decisions, and have them either ratified or vetoed by someone in authority. Because the practice of veto is rarely used, the boards appear to have the final authority. As long as all is going well, no one has problems. However, when there is disagreement about direction, personnel, and finances, then the issue of authority arises with resulting hostility and animosity. For an institution which has the building of community as one of its prime purposes to allow this kind of situation to develop or continue is, at best, inappropriate. Unless the bishop is willing to allow the school to function as a separate incorporation with a board of trustees which has jurisdiction over the operation of the school (with the understanding that the bishop retains authority over the religious education and catholicity), then the diocese must clarify the issue of who in fact has authority in what areas in diocesan schools. A case could be made for a number of approaches. However, it does not seem realistic to attempt to constitute a school board for a diocesan school in a manner which does not recognize the already defined and operative authority structure of the Church. Boards can be organized in a manner which recognizes that fact and gives parents and other concerned parties a responsible voice in the operation of Catholic schools.

Interparish Schools

Because the trend toward the formation of an increasing number of interparish/regional/consolidated schools is growing, the governance and accountability practices regarding these schools need particular attention. At the present time, they constitute 17.8 percent of the Catholic schools; 6.4 percent are elementary and 11.4 percent are secondary.[7] Whatever challenges face the Catholic educational community regarding parish, diocesan, and private schools, they pale in comparison to the problems of interparish schools.

Even if in practice the governance issues of other schools lack clarity, at least it is clear who has the authority. How that individual chooses to exercise the authority is not the issue here. In a parish school, the principal is accountable to the pastor; in a private school, to the major superior and council of the religious congregation through whatever structure they have established; in a diocesan school to the bishop usually through the superintendent of schools. Given the organization of those schools which are designated as interparish, a major problem occurs when there is no one who has the canonical authority for the school. Some of these schools attempt to function with the pastors of the contributing parishes assuming this position. Ordinarily this approach is workable as long as the individuals who were involved in the original reorganization remain. Because this arrangement is largely dependent on personalities rather than sound organizational principles, it does not provide a firm foundation for the future.

The vacuum created when the locus of authority is absent is frequently filled by a strong principal who more often than not operates in an independent and often quite successful manner. In the absence of such a leader, the board finds itself in the position of having to function in a manner which can blur the distinctions between policy and administration and often creates problems regarding responsibilities for policies. In this situation the person who has to deal with the everyday realities of this situation is the principal.

Often it is not clear to whom the principal is formally accountable and as a result, she or he ends up answering to many different individuals and groups as if they had formal authority. Even if an individual principal with special fortitude could sustain this ambivalent situation, the lack of clarity serves as a deterrent to the future of the school. For instance, in many of these schools, responsibility for the property which is used by the school is not clearly defined. Probably the site is one which formerly functioned as a parish school and technically is still "owned" by that parish. Now that the responsibility for the school is shared with other parishes, who assumes this role? Often the interparish school board finds itself functioning as if it were the group responsible or the founding parish finds itself maintaining the buildings without a systematic means of sharing this burden with the other contributing parishes.

While more and more dioceses are developing guidelines in this regard, there seems to be a pressing need to clarify the status of these schools. This governance issue is current because the number of these schools is increasing. More and more dioceses are working with parishes toward mergers and consolidations necessitated by population shifts. If the "new" schools are supported by more than one parish, they are indeed regional schools. It is important to discover some method of organizing this type of school so that the relationship with the institutional church is clear. If a school is going to call itself Catholic, the bishop has responsibility to ensure his relationship with and commitment to the future strength of the school. One model already functioning in practice if not by policy is that of the school's being erected as a juridic person.

There are interparish schools with boards which have begun to assume a role similar to that of the juridic person. Many have assumed debts in the name of the interparish school or board; others have sued or been sued in a court of law. Often the school's relationships are not formalized and in some instances the school seems to have all of the responsibilities and none of the rights of a juridic person in church law.

At the beginning of this chapter, it was suggested that what really happens in the governance and accountability of Catholic schools is largely dependent on the personalities, politics, and policies present at the local level. This is the real situation. However, this comment need not be construed in a negative manner. There is a tremendous amount of goodwill, leadership, and conviction regarding the value and potential of Catholic schools today. Those in leadership positions have the obligation to address the issues involved in governance and accountability in some systematic manner. Principals of Catholic schools and board members are competent, dedicated individuals who share a vision of what Catholic schools are for the church and society. They alone cannot resolve these issues. The real tragedy will occur if people of goodwill who share responsibility for the post-Vatican II church allow local politics to prevent their addressing these issues. Years ago, a wise statesman reminded us that often evil prevails when good people do nothing. This statement should not be true of Catholic educational leaders today.

Summary

1. Catholic schools are usually organized under four structures: parish, interparish, diocesan, and private. The policies and practices of governance and accountability in them are varied and unique to local circumstances.

2. Parish schools, at least in theory, have clear lines of authority. The key to successful administration is for the principal to determine how to work with the pastor, the canonical authority of the parish and the parish council, as well as with the numerous school communities to which the principal owes accountability. A key issue in these relations is who hires the principal.

3. While the lines of authority remain clear as far as ownership and sponsorship of private Catholic schools are concerned, there seems to be a changing climate regarding the schools' operations. Religious congregations need to be clear in establishing expectations and relationships with the school's board of directors/trustees.

4. A diocese needs to determine its relationship with those schools designated as diocesan. Regardless of the organizational model in place, the role of the school board remains an issue. Recognizing that boards are currently functioning with differing understandings and degrees of "authority," the challenge of sharing responsibility for the operations of the diocesan school remains.

5. Given the organization of those schools which are designated as interparish, a major problem occurs when there is no one who has the canonical authority for the school. Because the number of interparish schools is increasing, this governance issue is critical and some means of organizing this type of school so that the relationship with the institutional church is clear must be determined.

6. Catholic school personnel, especially those in leadership positions, must address the current issues involved in governance and accountability in some systematic manner.

Notes

1. *United States Catholic Elementary and Secondary Schools, 1984-1985* (Washington, D.C.: National Catholic Educational Association, 1985), p. 10.
2. *Code of Canon Law* (Grand Rapids, Michigan: Wm. B. Eerdmans Publishing Company, 1983), Book V, Title II.
3. Rev. John A. Gilbert, *Pastor As Shepherd of the School Community* (Washington, D.C.: National Catholic Educational Association, 1983).
4. *Effective Catholic Schools: An Exploration* (Washington, D.C.: National Center for Research in Total Catholic Education, 1984).
5. *United States Catholic Elementary and Secondary Schools 1984-1985*, op. cit.
6. *Ibid.*
7. *Ibid.*

Suggested Readings

Mallett, Rev. James K. "Reflections on the Application of the New Code of Canon Law to the Governance of Catholic Educational Institutions." A clear and concise presentation to the 1985 St. Louis NCEA Convention which offers, among other topics, suggestions to Catholic education leaders regarding board models.

Sheehan, Sr. Lourdes. "Catholic Boards Must Recognize the Authority Structure," *Momentum*. Washington, D.C.: National Catholic Educational Association, February, 1985, pp. 32-33. Offers suggestions as to reasons why some boards have experienced difficulty functioning.

Governance and Administration in the Catholic School

Drahmann, T. 1985. 16–18. Washington, D.C.: National Catholic Educational Association.

Chapter 4.*
Major or Minor League?

The Central Office, Diocesan and Congregational Relationships with Schools

At the present time, because of the diminished number of religious in the school, a Catholic school is more likely to receive direction, supervision, evaluation, and assistance from the diocesan office, rather than from a religious order. The decisions of the diocesan board of education and the superintendent's office may deal with teacher qualifications, fund-raising activities, administration, hiring, curriculum and textbooks, inservice activities, and special areas of instruction such as the religion programs and human sexuality instruction.

Why are Catholic schools organized on a diocesan basis? This stems from the fact that the Catholic Church is organizationally divided into regional units (dioceses), each headed by a bishop (or archbishop). The bishop, as a successor of the Apostles, is selected to lead what is theologically considered to be the *local church*—more than an administrative unit, rather it is a living cell of Christ's Body, which together with others, form the entire church under the pope.

A special function of the bishop is to be the chief teacher in the diocese. Others who exercise this function in the educational work of the church do so as sharers in the bishop's teaching ministry. This is the broad base for the authority of the diocesan education office, which also acts as a means of support and assistance for each school.

Present church law states that the local bishop has authority over all Catholic schools located in his diocese, including those which are directed by religious orders (Canon 806, #1).[11]

In some areas, diocesan funds to assist the schools are disbursed from the central office.

How do religious orders presently affect the schools? As is well known, religious communities in the times past supplied the majority of teaching and administrative personnel for Catholic schools (and financed both preliminary and continuing education for their members). As stated above, religious order supervisors worked with school personnel to give assistance and to assure quality. At present, members of religious communities are in a minority in most schools, but they still are able to be an influence in preserving the valued traditions of the school, especially its religious character. New teachers in schools, which have long been served by a particular order, are well advised to learn the special traditions of that community, to what extent these are remembered and esteemed by parents and graduates, and how these have shaped the present character of the school.

There are many Catholic schools which are owned and controlled by religious orders, largely on the secondary level. These exist in a diocese with the permission of the bishop and are subject to his authority, but in practice they operate independently of the diocesan Catholic school system. The head of the school is appointed by the religious order, and major decisions are subject to the authority of the superiors and/or the councils of the order. The order maintains a commitment to supply personnel to the school, and often gives it substantial financial assistance for its operating budget, for maintenance and repairs, and for new construction. The schools operated by an individual order often maintain their unique traditions as "Mercy schools," "Christian Brothers schools," "Jesuit schools," etc.

Religious orders more and more are sharing the governance with the schools they own with boards which have been formed for each school. These boards have varying degrees of influence and/or authority. Some are advisory only. Others are decision-making boards whose major actions require approval by the order. Some religious have leased their schools to a corporate board, who are free to direct them almost totally, subject to general church authority. To a greater or lesser degree, parents, clergy, and the laity in general are in this way brought to share in the direction of the school.

Religious orders provide an important complement to the diocesan organization. The sisters and brothers and priests are groups with far-flung regional, national, and even international membership. They work in a diocese with the approval of the bishop, but they bring a broad view of the church to their schools, a sense of mission and dedication, and a flexibility whereby members can easily change both location and occupation in order to meet new needs. Religious orders are responsible for the growth of the Catholic parochial school system in the United States, and their contribution can never be forgotten.

A teacher in a Catholic school will find that administrators and fellow staff members may be priests who belong to the diocesan clergy (i.e., are directly subject to the local bishop) or priests who are members of religious orders, (e.g., Franciscans, Benedictines, Dominicans). Or, they may be the colleagues of members of one or more of the

---

*   Editor's note: Chapter notation refers to this excerpt.

many sisterhoods and brotherhoods, who have been working in American Catholic schools since the Ursuline Sisters arrived in New Orleans and began their school in 1727. It is both interesting and helpful to learn about the history and nature of the religious "families" who are present in the school; they represent centuries of accumulated religious and educational wisdom.

It is easy to see that Catholic school teachers need to know the source of governing directives which come from outside the local school or parish. Principals and boards may be subject to directives from the diocesan office and teachers should be aware of these. To the extent that, in some schools, a religious community carries responsibility for direction and assistance, teachers should know this also. Understanding and cooperation should be the hallmark of their response, as both the "major league" and the "minor league" players work together to advance the cause of Catholic education.

Summary

1. Formerly, religious orders furnished extensive direction and supervision to Catholic schools, along with numerous personnel. Today they are still an important influence in most schools, but with fewer personnel and less overall involvement.

2. Diocesan education offices have replaced the religious orders as sources of direction and assistance.

Note

11. *Canon Law*, 303.

The Catholic School Principal: An Outline for Action

Drahmann T., and A. Stenger. 1989. 17. Rev. ed.
Washington, D.C.: National Catholic Educational Association.

Most Catholic schools include members of religious orders among their staff and/or in administrative positions. The continuing value of religious teachers, as well as the unique contributions they make to Catholic schools, should be recognized by the principal, whether he/she be religious or lay. There should be an awareness of the responsibility of the principal regarding the members of religious orders who serve on the staff of the school.

1. Administrative Actions

____ 1. Clarifies the contractual agreements and/or the placement policies of religious communities

____ 2. Communicates with religious community leaders regularly

____ 3. Invites community leaders/supervisors to visit the school

____ 4. Plans recruiting efforts to obtain religious

____ 5. Publicly recognizes the contribution (past and present) of the religious community(ies) of the school

2. Policies and Actions of Supervisory Body

____ 1. Clarifies contractual arrangements with the religious community or with the individual religious

____ 2. Approves job conditions for religious personnel (salary, benefits, housing, auto, insurance, etc.)

3. Faculty Handbook

____ 1. Recognizes the history, charism, and traditions of the religious community(ies) serving in the school

4. Parent/Student Handbook

____ 1. Describes the history and tradition of the religious community

5. Resources

____ 1. Religious community newsletter and publications

6. Issues

____ 1. To what degree can Catholic schools plan on religious personnel in the future?

____ 2. What are the distinctive contributions made by religious to Catholic schools?

____ 3. What is the special challenge facing a lay principal of a school where there are religious on the staff?

____ 4. Should religious receive salaries equivalent to those of lay teachers?

____ 5. How can a Catholic school play a significant role in fostering religious vocations?

____ 6. Should the tradition and charism of the religious community first staffing the school be retained? How?

A Primer on Educational Governance in the Catholic Church

CACE/NABE Governance Task Force. 1987. Ed. J. S. O'Brien, 7–16.
Washington, D.C.: National Catholic Educational Association.

Governance and Law

There are two basic systems in the church's approach to governance. The first is the executive system. Here the responsibility is placed in the hands of an individual who is supposed to work with other people in a collaborative or consultative manner. The individual, however, is responsible to take the initiative, come to the final decision, order the implementation, and hold people accountable for carrying out the decision.

The second is the collegial system. Here the same responsibilities are vested in a group, for example, the chapter of a religious congregation or board of trustees, which counts on individuals to carry out tasks. Educational governance by the diocese and parish generally functions out of the executive system (Provost, 1985).

Catechetics

Although in the United States the word "catechetics" is often associated with religious education, the Code of Canon Law views catechetics in a much broader perspective, that is, as being an activity of the entire people of God under the direction of the bishop in the diocese and the pastor in the parish. The distinction is described in Canon 773:

> There is a proper and serious duty, especially on the part of pastors of souls, to provide for the catechesis of the Christian people so that the faith of the faithful becomes living, explicit and productive through formation in doctrine and the experience of Christian living.

Catechetics, therefore, is a pastoral activity. It is part of the ministry of the word. It is a ministry that is done under the direction of the bishop or pastor. It is also something that should involve all members of the parish community. It is certainly not limited to specialists, even though specially trained catechists do have a significant role to play in this ministry. In the code, "ministry of the word" is seen as the general framework for preaching, catechetics, and Catholic schools.

Catholic Schools

Canon 795 introduces the section of the code that deals with Catholic schools, a distinct enterprise from the catechetical effort of the church:

> Since a true education must strive for the integral formation of the human person, a formation which looks toward the person's final end, and at the same time toward the common good of societies, children and young people are to be so reared that they can develop harmoniously their physical, moral and intellectual talents, that they acquire a more perfect sense of responsibility and a correct use of freedom, and that they be educated for active participation in social life (Canon 795).

Although the Code of Canon Law makes a clear distinction between catechetics and Catholic schools, it is important to bear in mind the particular context of the American Catholic church. Catechetics in the broad sense of the term is the responsibility of the entire church community. Religious education as it has evolved in more formal settings requires specially trained catechetical personnel. Because of these special needs, dioceses have taken on a larger role in the direction and support of parish religious education programs.

Catholic schooling is a professional activity which is done in service of parents. It is under a dual direction. First it is under the direction of the hierarchy; and second it is under the direction of the authorities in the school who have the professional competence to do so. Unlike catechetics, it is not something done by all members of the church. The great percentage of Catholic schools in this nation are parish based and are more directly the responsibility of the local pastor. Thus, in its direction and support of Catholic schools, the diocese must carefully recognize the role of the local pastor.

The Code of Canon Law highlights the role of the bishop in regard to Catholic schools. The bishop has a special responsibility and authority over Catholic schools within his diocese. As Provost (1985) writes:

> The bishop is to set the direction for education in the diocese within general norms that may or may not be established by the conference of bishops. He is also to exercise vigilance over faith and morals and have a quality control over teachers of religion in all schools in his diocese. These include those that are run by religious. The only exception would be a school run by religious only for its members like a novitiate. But any school whatsoever that professes itself to be Catholic school is subject to the vigilance of the bishop.

Although the educational mission of the diocese is determined in part by its connection with the universal church, it is also more clearly refined in its direction by the bishop and his direct involvement in those efforts.

Diocesan Governance

The Code of Canon Law describes the authority of the diocesan bishop as legislative, judicial, and executive in nature. The authority must be exercised either by the bishop himself or by someone with vicarious or delegated power. In the case of executive authority, the diocesan bishop depends greatly on others to exercise his leadership, such as vicars, pastors, or individuals especially delegated for a particular task, for example, superintendents of schools.

Legislative

In the case of legislative authority, the diocesan bishop cannot delegate his power to legislate. The bishop is the only legislator in the diocese. He cannot entrust any person or groups with the authority to enact legislation. Even a diocesan synod convoked to consider new legislation for the local church does not have the authority to legislate:

> The diocesan bishop is the sole legislator at a diocesan synod while the remaining members of the synod possess only a consultative vote; he alone signs the synodal declarations and decrees which can be published only through his authority (Canon 466).

When this prescription of Canon Law is applied to governance in the education structures of the church, it becomes clear that no individual (other than the diocesan bishop) and no board or commission can be given the authority to legislate. All education or school boards and commissions are therefore by reason of the law consultative in nature. (Even boards with limited jurisdiction are consultative at least in the area of religious education.) Boards and commissions may certainly propose and recommend legislation, but they cannot enact it.

Judicial

Mallett (1985) states that judicial governance is concerned with resolving disputes through canonical procedures. The bishop exercises judicial governance through the diocesan tribunal or other judicial processes which he initiates personally. A judge appointed by the bishop has the power by law to resolve disputes and impose penalties (Canons 1419 and 1364–1369). Although in the past judicial processes were rarely used except in matrimonial questions, bishops have begun to employ them in special circumstances. In many cases, penalties have been incurred.

Most disputes in the United States church are resolved through procedures established by executive governance. In conciliation, the bishop's conciliator tries to help the parties resolve the dispute. In arbitration, the parties bind themselves to a resolution by investing the arbitrator with the power to mandate a solution. Disputes arising from the exercise of executive authority are not subject to resolution by judicial process (Canon 1400.2).

Executive

Executive governance is exercised by the bishop both personally and through vicars, namely the vicar general and the episcopal vicars. A vicar general enjoys most of the rights and the duties of executive governance, which the Code of Canon Law recognizes as the bishop's governing authority. An episcopal vicar enjoys the same authority as a vicar general for a "determined section of the diocese or in a certain type of business or over the faithful of a determined rite or over certain groups of persons" (Canon 476).

Of course the bishop must decide which rights and duties of executive governance are to be exercised by an episcopal vicar. For example, an episcopal vicar for education should automatically have the competence to exercise the bishop's authority as given in the law, as should the vicar general. As Mallett (1985) points out, "The law itself attaches certain rights and duties to the office of vicar. Therefore, when someone is appointed to this office, he automatically has the authority attached to the office."

Executive governance is also exercised by the bishop through delegation. As was noted above, the diocesan bishop possesses ordinary power in Christ's name. He is able to delegate part of that power to an individual in order to carry out his executive governance. Mallett (1985) sums it up this way:

> Some governance officers are not appointed as episcopal vicars. These officers, such as the superintendent of schools, might be understood as delegates of the bishop. The bishop has the right to delegate someone with certain rights and duties. In this case he must specify exactly what competence he wishes to give his delegate. It is not sufficient simply to provide the person with a title. Without a specific act of delegation, a superintendent of schools would not be able to exercise any juridic authority whatsoever, unless such authority came from the state by virtue, perhaps, of state accreditation.

The executive governance of a diocese can also be achieved through the bishop's consulting various members of the Christian faithful, especially consultative bodies established within the diocese. As Provost (1980) wrote, "The teaching of the Church is quite clear: there are to be consultative bodies, and bishops or others in charge of dioceses are to use them." Three consultative bodies seem to be of special importance for the executive governance of a diocese: the diocesan finance council (Canon 492), the presbyterial council (Canons 495–502), and the diocesan pastoral council (Canons 511–514). Mallett (1985) writes:

> Each of these three diocesan groups may have some impact on Catholic education. The pastoral council will likely understand Catholic schools as an important component of pastoral work. The

presbyterial council may be involved in recommending diocesan legislation which would affect Catholic schools. Finally, the financial administration of schools is monitored by the diocesan finance council, and permission for some acts of extraordinary administration require its involvement. Yet, none of these groups is primarily concerned about Catholic schools and would not likely be competent to develop regulations or policies for the governance of a Catholic school system. Although the code does not propose a consultative body for educational purposes, it seems advisable that such diocesan bodies be constituted by bishops.

Additionally, the diocesan bishop may delegate to a board or a commission authority to enact diocesan policies (as distinct from diocesan laws) which direct education programs.

In writing about the different boards or commissions, Mallett (1985) makes a proper distinction between law and policy:

> In my judgment, binding norms or law should be issued by the bishop only in special cases where it is necessary to protect rights and promote the common good. This understanding of the limited nature of law is incorporated in the revised code. . . . Where it is a question of rights, laws may be necessary. To give one example: If a diocese instituted a retirement program for all school teachers, it would not suffice merely to exhort pastors and principals to cooperate with this program. The demands of justice would require the cooperation of all administrators so that equitable retirement benefits can be provided for all teachers.

I understand a policy to be a statement which limits the administrative discretion proper to administrators. Arbitrariness in administration should be eliminated, but administrators need to exercise a certain flexibility in the application of standard criteria and procedures. Policies provide limitations to this administrative discretion. . . . I do not believe that policies should be understood as laws, since laws completely eliminate discretionary application unless the administrator obtains a dispensation from higher authority. Educational policies promulgated by competent diocesan authorities are often recognized as binding by civil courts.

Parish Governance

The revised Code of Canon Law greatly emphasized the exercise of the leadership role of the pastor to whom the pastoral care of the parish is entrusted. The law restates the conciliar teaching that in exercising the care of souls parish priests and their assistants should carry out their work of teaching, sanctifying, and governing in such a way that the faithful and the parish communities may understand that they are truly members both of the diocese and of the universal church (Decree, 30).

Among the duties of the pastor, then, is that of "governing, with the cooperation of other presbyters or deacons and the assistance of lay members of the Christian faithful" (Canon 519). Part of the pastor's governing role is to be administrator of the ecclesiastical goods of the parish. In his administration of these goods, the pastor must follow the regulations established by the Code of Canon Law as well as any diocesan legislation. Such administration becomes particularly noteworthy in the areas of finance and the observance of "civil laws pertaining to labor and social policy" (Canon 1286).

Mallett (1985) is particularly insistent that the pastor's role in the administration of a parish school must be respected as to the rights he enjoys and the duties to which he is obliged. As Mallett (1985) writes:

> I strongly suggest that diocesan legislation is necessary to clarify the relationship between the pastor and the parish school principal. Such legislation could identify those responsibilities which the principal should be empowered to fulfill, such as the employment of teachers, the supervision and evaluation of teachers and other school employees, the formulation of policies for consideration by the school board or the budget and financial reporting and accounting of school operations. . . . The pastor would clearly have certain rights and duties in addition to the ultimate financial control. These rights and duties would involve the employment, supervision and evaluation of the principal, supervision of religious education and formation programs, and the approval of school disbursements in accordance with policies which he establishes.

As with the diocese, the governance of a parish can also be achieved through the pastor's consulting various members of the Christian faithful, especially consultative bodies within the parish. Three consultative bodies are of special importance for the executive governance of a parish.

Canon 537 requires the establishment of a finance council in every parish. Where a parish school exists, the need for ongoing consultation with the finance council becomes obvious and its relationship to the school is extremely important.

A second consultative body suggested by the code and described in Canon 536 is the pastoral council at the parish level. Its role is to give assistance in fostering pastoral activity. Certainly the education mission of the parish is involved in this pastoral activity.

Parish pastoral councils often establish an education committee as part of the larger parish pastoral council in order to provide ongoing communication between the parish school and the catechetical program, and the parish pastoral council.

Schools and Ecclesiastical Structure

Just as American society includes both individuals and corporations which are established under civil law, so the church includes individuals and corporations established under Canon Law. The term "juridic person" is the term given to the church corporation.

The parish school is part of the juridic person of the parish. A regional school may be part of the juridic person of one of the sponsoring parishes or of the diocese. A diocesan school may be a part of the juridic person of the diocese and a religious congregation's school a part of the juridic person of the religious order. All these types of schools may be established as separate juridic persons. Other schools not part of a juridic person may be called Catholic if approved by competent church authority.

Canon Law requires that all juridic persons have administrators who are responsible for the material welfare of their institutions in accordance with Canons 1281-1288. Where the school is part of an existing juridic person, the responsibility of the canonical administrator must be respected as the ultimate authority. That person does not need to be a priest. Where the school is a separate juridic person, the canonical administrator is most often the principal of the school.

There are people who govern and those who cooperate with these ministers of governance, as well as those who receive within and from the governance system that capability and freedom to carry out rights and responsibilities. Governance in itself is a means of exercising rights and responsibilities in the service of others—and in service of one's own growth as a member of Christ.

Those who exercise governance have a responsibility to see that the rights and duties of people are affirmed within this institution and community called church. These rights and duties remain inviolable and inalienable. Thus the person who exercises governance is one who frees up and orchestrates the talents of others to promote the gospel message. Governance is not and cannot be an end in itself; rather, it is in service of persons (Canon Law, 1986).

Civil Law and Church Property

A diocesan bishop exercises his authority in accord with Canon Law and in accord with all applicable civil law—federal, state, and local. In regard to church property, there are three major systems which states use to legislate ownership. They are: the bishop-as-trustee, the bishop-as-corporation-sole, and the corporation aggregate.

In the bishop-as-trustee method, the title to the property is vested in the bishop as trustee and the equitable title is vested in the members of the parish. (The state statutes that apply in this case are the ones that govern nonprofit or religious corporations.) The bishop-as-trustee holds the title for the benefit of the parish. Although he retains the right of supervision and the right to govern in accord with church law, the trustee can delegate the control of the property to the administrator of the parish.

In the bishop-as-corporation-sole method, the bishop holds absolute title to the church's property until he is transferred, retires, or dies. In civil law, the bishop can do anything he wishes with the property as long as it is in compliance with church law. The person who is appointed the new bishop becomes the corporation sole.

In the corporation aggregate method, there are two different ways the property may be owned. In the first, legal title is vested in incorporated trustees with equitable title vested in the non-incorporated parish. In the second, legal title is vested directly in the corporate officers of the parish who are elected and act as a board of directors or trustees. In this case, they are the agents of the corporation. The state statutes that apply here are the ones which govern a charitable trust or an aggregation of charitable trusts (Sheehan, 1981, pp. 10–13).

Religious congregations hold property in their own right according to the laws of the state. The articles of incorporation define the role and authority of the agents of the corporation. According to the church law (Canon 1290), all administrators are bound to observe the civil laws of any given territory "with the same effects in a matter which is subject to the governing power of the Church, unless the civil regulations are contrary to divine law or canon law makes some other provision. . . ."

Contracts and Employee Relations

In another place (Canon 1286), church law states the administrators should "observe meticulously the civil laws pertaining to labor and social policy according to Church principles in the employment of workers . . . [and] are to pay employees a just and decent wage so that they may provide appropriately for their needs and those of their family."

Thus every diocese should have policies regarding contracts for all employees, both diocesan and parish, which clearly state the terms of the contract and the rights and responsibilities of the employee. These contracts are signed by an authorized agent of the corporation as recognized by the state. It is important to remember that only authorized agents of the corporation may enter into contracts on behalf of the corporation.

Dioceses also need policies in other personnel areas to protect both employer and employee rights. These policies would cover such areas as compensation and benefits, leaves and absences, grievance, and administration review procedures.

Diocesan administrators should make parishes and schools aware of the laws governing the operation of private (including Catholic) schools within the state and should be familiar with diocesan laws and policies. Board members especially need to know the broad parameters of the law as it affects Catholic education. The courts would expect that a person who accepts membership on a board would have some basic understanding of the laws that apply to that school. (Dioceses and religious congregations need to provide liability insurance for officers, agents, and board members.)

Unlike public schools, which are governed primarily by state statute and constitution, Catholic schools operate out of contract law. With the exception of an allegation of discrimination, the court will look at the provisions of the contract rather than at the protections of the constitution when Catholic schools are involved in litigation (Shaughnessy, 1987). A good source for this kind of information is the diocesan or religious congregation attorney.

School Boards

Catholic and public schools have very different board structures, so different in fact that a comparison of the two is necessarily limited. The main similarity between public school boards and Catholic boards is that both are in some way involved in policy development. The differences include both the purposes of each board and the way in which the boards function. Public schools are governed by elected or appointed boards whose source of authority comes from the citizens through American democratic processes. Public education is a function of the fifty separate states. The general assembly of each state (by whatever name) has jurisdictional authority for public schools within the state in accord with its constitution and court rulings.

In contrast, the authority for Catholic schools is vested in the various corporations, for example, the diocesan bishop, the parish corporation, the religious congregation, which are responsible for ensuring that Catholic schools are organized and administered in accord with church and civil laws. Thus Catholic educational boards are not jurisdictional as are public school boards. However, as will be explained later, not being jurisdictional does not lessen their importance.

References

Code of canon law. (1983). Washington, D.C.: Canon Law Society of America.

Decree on the pastoral office of bishops in the church. (1965). In A. Flannery (Ed.), *Vatican Council II.* Northport, NY: Costello.

Mallett, J. K. (1985). *Educational governance in the Catholic church.* Unpublished manuscript.

Provost, J. H. (1985). *Concepts of governance from church law of interest to education.* Unpublished manuscript.

Provost, J. H. (1980). The working together of consultative bodies —great expectations. *The Jurist* 40, 257–281.

Shaughnessy, M. A. (1987). *Legal ramifications of school board membership: A look at responsibilities and liabilities.* Unpublished manuscript.

Sheehan, M. L. (1981). *A study of the functions of school boards in the educational system of the Roman Catholic church in the United States.* (Doctoral dissertation, Virginia Polytechnic Institute and State University).

A Primer on School Law:
A Guide for Board Members in Catholic Schools

Shaughnessy, M. A. 1991. 5–13, 16–22. Washington, D.C.: National Catholic Educational Association.

Chapter 2.* The Laws Affecting Catholic Education in the United States

The laws affecting education in the United States today can generally be classified in four categories: (1) constitutional law (both state and federal constitutions); (2) statutes and regulations; (3) common law principles; and (4) contract law.

It must be kept in mind from the outset that the law is not the same in the public and private sectors. Federal Constitutional law protects individuals against the arbitrary deprivation of their constitutional freedoms by government and government officials. Students and teachers in public schools are protected by Constitutional law since public schools are governmental agencies and the administrators of public schools are public officials.

Practically, this means that Catholic schools can have regulations and procedures that would not be permissible in a public school. Students can be required to wear uniforms. The expression of free speech can be limited. For example, students and teachers would probably not be allowed to wear buttons criticizing the pope or promoting abortion. Catholic schools have a legal right to make these regulations. If public schools attempted to impose similar rules, they could be guilty of violating the right to free speech as guaranteed by the first amendment.

School board members need this information. A parent or student or teacher might claim that some Constitutional right, such as that of free speech, had been violated. It is important for school board members (and, indeed, for all involved with the school) to understand that a person does not have the same rights in a private setting that one would have in a similar public setting. One can always choose to leave the private setting, of course; but, as long as one chooses to stay, the exercise of certain freedoms can be restricted. This does not mean that a board can be arbitrary in developing policies. But Catholic schools do not have to accept all the behaviors that the public school has no choice but to accept.

Constitutional Law

There are only two situations in which Catholic or other private schools can be required to grant Constitutional protections: (1) if state action can be found to be so pervasive within the school that the schools can be considered a state agent and/or (2) if a compelling state interest, loosely defined as an overwhelming need for an action, can be shown.

Some of the main arguments advanced to prove the presence of state action in private educational institutions are: (1) an institution's acceptance of government monies; (2) the tax-exempt status of the private institution; (3)

---

* Editor's note: Chapter notation refers to this excerpt.

education as a quasi state function (sometimes called a "public benefit theory" since schools, particularly elementary and secondary ones, perform a public service); and (4) state involvement with the school through accreditation or similar procedures and/or statutory requirements with which the school complies.

A relevant case is *Rendell-Baker v. Kohn,* 102 S. Ct. 2764 (1982). This situation involved a dismissed teacher in a private school which received 90–99% of its funding from the government. The Supreme Court ruled that, despite the level of funding, there was no state action in the school. Since the government had no role in dismissal decisions, the school was not required to grant any Constitutional protections to its teachers and, one might assume, to its students. No student or teacher using a state action argument has prevailed in a lawsuit against a private school to date.

Given that private schools have the right to exist and since they are not bound to grant Constitutional protections unless significant state action is found, litigations alleging a denial of Constitutional rights will have to prove the existence of significant state action within the institution before the court will grant relief.

Private school cases indicate that without a finding of state action or compelling state interest, the courts will not hold private schools to the requirements of Constitutional protections. The case law should not be interpreted to mean that private schools can do anything they wish and the courts will not intervene. Case law is constantly being developed and so it is difficult to state hard and fast rules. The fact that no case involving student discipline in the private school has ever reached the United States Supreme Court indicates perhaps the reluctance of the court to intervene in the private sector.

State constitutional law may apply to private as well as public schools. It is not unusual to find a statement such as, "Anyone owning and operating an educational institution in this state shall . . . ." As long as whatever is required does not unfairly impinge upon the rights of the private educational institutions and can be shown to have some legitimate educational purpose, private schools can be compelled to comply with the state constitutional requirements.

Statutes and Regulations

Federal and state statutes and regulations govern the public school and may govern the private school as well. Failure to comply with reasonable regulations can result in the imposition of sanctions. The case of *Bob Jones University v. United States* 103 S. Ct. 2017 (1983) illustrates this point. Because of a religious belief, Bob Jones University's admissions and disciplinary policies were racially discriminatory. The Internal Revenue Service withdrew the university's tax-exempt status based on a 1970 regulation proscribing the granting of tax-exempt status to any institution which discriminated on the basis of race. Before a private school will be forced to comply with a law or regulation, the state's compelling interest in the enforcement of the regulation will have to be shown.

In the *Bob Jones* case, the government's compelling interest in racial equality was sufficient for the court to order Bob Jones University to comply with the antidiscrimination legislation or lose its tax-exempt status. In effect, the court said, "We cannot compel you to change your religious belief, but the government will not give you support in the form of tax-exempt status in order to advance this discriminatory belief."

A similar case in a Catholic school is *Dolter v. Walhert* 483 F. Supp. 266 (N.D. Iowa 1980). The Catholic school was found guilty of sex discrimination when it did not renew the contract of an unmarried, pregnant teacher since the evidence clearly indicated that unmarried male teachers who were known to have engaged in premarital sex were evaluated by a different standard.

Federal law prohibits discrimination on the basis of race, sex, handicap, age, and national origin. Although it also prohibits discrimination on the basis of religion or creed, the right of religious organizations to give preference to its own members is upheld. Practically, this means that Catholic schools may give preference to Catholic students and may give hiring preference to Catholic teachers and other employees.

The government cannot pass laws so restrictive that a school's existence is placed in jeopardy. The right of the Catholic school to exist was firmly established by the Supreme Court in 1925 when a religious order operating a private school brought suit challenging an Oregon statute which would have made public education compulsory. In this landmark case, *Pierce v. the Society of Sisters* 268 U.S. 510 (1925), the Supreme Court declared the statute unconstitutional not only because it interfered with the rights of the school owner, but also because it interfered with the right of parents to choose the education of their children.

Common Law

The third type of law which applies to both the public and private sectors (and, indeed, to all cases, whether school cases or not) is the common law. *Black's Law Dictionary* (1979) defines common law:

> "Common law" consists of those principles, usage and rules of action applicable to government and security of persons and property which do not rest for their authority upon any express and positive declaration of the will of the legislature (p. 251).

Common law principles may also be considered to be derived from God's law, especially by persons in religious schools. Many common law principles are founded in basic morality such as those in the Bible and in other religious writings. Due process or fairness considerations can be considered part of the common law.

In order to discuss common law considerations of fairness, one must understand the meaning of Constitutional due process/fairness. There are two kinds of Constitutional due process: procedural and substantive.

Much has been written about due process, but one of its simplest definitions is that of "fairness." We expect that parties to a suit in court will be treated fairly by the judge and/or the jury. We expect that a person accused of a crime will be told what it is he or she is accused of having done (notice); that he or she will be given a hearing or trial by an impartial party or parties; that the accused will be able to confront the accusers (cross-examination) and call witnesses on his or her own behalf. These expectations are the definition of procedural due process. In a court case, we would also expect that an accused person would be represented by an attorney.

Substantive due process has been defined as meaning that "If a state is going to deprive a person of his life, liberty or property, the state must have a valid objective and the means used must be reasonably calculated to achieve the objective" (Alexander, 1980, p. 343). Substantive due process involves moral as well as legal ramifications: is this action fair and reasonable? In the public sector, substantive due process is present whenever a person has property (anything that can be owned, whether tangible or not) or liberty (freedom and/or reputation) interests.

In public school due process cases, justices have called for actions based on morality, a sense of fair play, as much as on what the Constitution does and does not demand. Courts rely on a belief that educators are trying to do what is right. Since educators are assumed to be behavioral models for students, courts hold educators, whether in the public or private schools, to strict standards of "fairness."

While Catholic schools are not held to the Constitution, courts have indicated that they can be held to standards of fairness in accordance with the school's own principles and commonly accepted standards of the behavior of reasonable people. In a case involving a dismissed Catholic school student, the court states:

> A private school's disciplinary proceedings are not controlled by the due process clause, and accordingly such schools have broad discretion in making rules and setting up procedures for [their] enforcement, nevertheless, under its broad equitable powers a court will intervene where such discretion is abused or the proceedings do not comport with fundamental fairness (Geraci v. St. Xavier High School, 13 Ohio Op. 3d 146 Ohio 1978).

The court suggests that, even if state action does not exist in private schools, the schools may still be held to a standard or what it called "fundamental fairness." Fundamental fairness is sometimes used as a synonym for due process, although Constitutional due process requires specific protections as stated in law and interpreted by the courts. Fundamental fairness in a private school, though similar to Constitutional due process, should not be equated with it.

In a private school case similar to *Geraci, Wisch v. Sanford School, Inc.*, 420 F. Supp. 1310 (1976), the court scrutinized the school's rules and dissemination of its code of conduct to determine that what it called "contractual procedural fairness" had been given the student. The court specifically addressed the basic fairness provision in a private school-student relationship and stated that such fairness would have been better met if the school had had a written disciplinary code.

Contract Law

In the Catholic school and in any private school, contract law is the predominant governing law. A contract may be defined as: "An agreement between two or more persons which creates an obligation to do or not to do a particular thing" (Black, 1979, pp. 291-92). Generally, the five basic elements of a contract are: (1) mutual assent (2) by legally competent parties for (3) consideration (4) to subject matter that is legal and (5) in a form of agreement which is legal.

Mutual assent implies that two parties entering into a contract agree to its provisions. A Catholic school agrees to provide an education to a student and, in return, his or her parents accept that offer. A Catholic school offers a teacher a contract and the teacher accepts. If one party does not or cannot agree to the terms of the contract, then no valid contract exists.

Legally competent parties implies that the parties entering into the contract are lawfully qualified to make the agreement. A school is legally qualified to enter into contracts to educate students and to employ teachers. Parents are legally competent to agree to pay tuition and meet other obligations (minor students are not legally competent, and so parents or legal guardians must sign contracts on their behalf). A properly qualified teacher is a legally competent party; a person who does not possess the qualifications needed to perform as a teacher would not be a legally competent party to enter into a teaching contract.

Consideration is what the first party agrees to do for the other party in exchange for something from the second party. The Catholic school agrees to provide educational services to a student in return for payment of tuition and adherence to the rules. The school agrees to pay the teacher a salary in return for teaching services.

Legal subject matter assumes that the provisions of the contract are legal. An agreement (as condition of employment) that a female teacher would resign if she became pregnant would probably not be legal, as such a condition would probably be construed as a violation of antidiscrimination laws and Constitutional freedoms as well.

Legal form may vary from state to state. If a contract calls for witnesses and no witnesses' signatures are found on the contract, then the contract is probably not in legal form.

If any one of the five elements of a contract is missing, the contract very often may be held null and void.

Excluding allegations of negligence, cases against Catholic schools are very often breach of contract cases:

> A breach of contract occurs when a party does not perform that which he or she was under an absolute duty to perform and the circumstances are such that his or her failure was neither justified or excused (Gatti and Gatti, 1983, p. 124).

Breach of contract can be committed by any party to the contract (the school/administrator or the teacher or student). It is generally conceded, however, that it is futile for a Catholic school to bring breach of contract charges against a teacher who wants to terminate his or her contract; it is highly unlikely that a judge will compel a person to teach against his or her wishes.

While teachers can usually break their contracts without severe consequences, a school can incur serious penalties if it either terminates a teacher's employment or terminates a student's enrollment without just cause during a contract term. Two cases involving breach of contract in the Catholic school illustrate.

In the breach of contract of a Catholic school teacher, *Weithoff v. St. Veronica School* 210 N.W. 2d 108 (Mich. 1973), the court considered the case of a teacher who had been dismissed from her position because of her marriage to a priest before he was free, according to church law, to marry. The court was careful to note that a church-sponsored school could contractually require teachers and other employees to observe the tenets of its faith. The testimony shows that a new regulation requiring teachers to be practicing Catholics was never promulgated but was simply placed in a file drawer. Since the teaching contract bound the employee to "promulgated" policies, the court held that the school could not legally dismiss the teacher. Obviously, if the regulation had been promulgated, the case might have had a different ending.

Another conclusion was reached in the similar case of *Steeber v. Benilde-St. Margaret's High School* (No. D.C. 739 378, Hennepin County, Minnesota, (1978)) in which a teacher protested the nonrenewal of her contract following her remarriage after a civil divorce. The court upheld the right of the school to terminate the teacher's contract since she was no longer a member in good standing of the Catholic Church.

In the first case, the school breached its contract with the teacher because it failed to promulgate the rule to which it sought to hold the teacher. In the second case in a very similar situation, the court ruled in the school's favor because the school had properly proceeded according to the provisions of its contract.

William D. Valente (1980, p. 464) offers this advice to teachers in private schools who think that their rights are being violated:

> Thus, a teacher who is offended by private school orders that suppress speech, invade privacy, or impose disciplinary sanctions without notice or hearing must look elsewhere than to constitutional doctrines for legal relief, except in the unusual situation where the private school is considered to be engaged in official government action.

The "elsewhere" to which a Catholic school teacher must look is generally contract law.

Three private school student discipline cases illustrate that contract law places obligations on the school as well as on the parents and students.

The 1981 case of *Block v. Hillel Torah North Suburban Day School* 438 N.E. 2d 976 involved a first grader expelled in midyear for excessive absence and tardiness. The parents alleged that the expulsion was in retaliation for the mother's actions. The parents charged that, according to usage and custom, the first year's contract bound the school to providing eight years of education. The court ruled that the school was not bound to continue educating the child because of the highly personalized nature of the educational services. Relying on the principle that the remedy for breach of contract is damages not performance of the contract, the court ruled that the parents could seek money damages from the school.

This case demonstrates the fact that a private school, whether Catholic or any other kind of private school, will not be forced to reinstate a wrongfully dismissed teacher or student. It is important for everyone in the Catholic school to understand this fact. A court could order the reinstatement of a wrongfully terminated public school student or teacher because of the requirements of the Constitution.

At first glance, this ability to employ and to admit whom one wills might seem unfair. Our American system of private enterprise operates on a doctrine of "employ at will." No one can be compelled to remain in a private relationship that is repugnant to him or her. If terminating the relationship violates contractual agreements or basic fairness, the terminating party may have to pay damages in compensation but, at least to date, no private school has been ordered by a court to reinstate a student or teacher, regardless of the reason for dismissal.

Two previously cited cases also illustrate breach of contract. In the *Wisch* case, the court ruled that the school did not breach its contract by expelling the student who had violated school rules. In the *Geraci* case, which involved a student who helped a boy not a student at the school to obtain entrance to the school and throw a pie in the face of a teacher, the court ruled that the student, not the school, had breached the contract.

The importance courts rightfully place on the development, promulgation, and implementation of rules is enormous. Since handbooks and other written agreements can be construed as part of the contract existing between the school and students and parents or between the school and its teachers, it is important that as far as possible and practical, rules be in writing.

Courts will look for evidence of good faith: did the institution have a rule? Was the rule promulgated—did the parties concerned—students, parents, and teachers—know of the rule? Courts will generally not concern themselves with the wisdom of the rule—or even with the rightness or wrongness of the rule. The court is only concerned with the existence of a properly promulgated rule or policy and with evidence that the institution acted in good faith according to the procedures it stated would be followed. Courts will look for basic fairness in the execution of the contract between the Catholic school and the student/parent or the teacher when it is alleged that the school acted improperly and so breached the contract.

Catholic school board members, then, should have at least a minimal understanding of civil law and its application to the private sector. At this point in time, the only occasion in which Constitutional protections may be invoked is in the area of discrimination. All other cases alleging deprivation of rights will be judged by contract law and the provisions of the contract existing between the disputing parties.

Tort Liability of Schools

Tort suits generally can be classified along four categories in the schools: (1) those resulting from negligence; (2) corporal punishment; (3) search and seizure; and (4) defamation. Students will most often bring suit under the first three categories; although anyone injured on school grounds may also bring negligence suits. Defamation suits may be brought by students who seek to show wrongful expulsion or other disciplinary measures; but it seems more likely that teachers who are disciplined or have their contracts terminated or not renewed will bring defamation suits.

Negligence

Negligence is the most common of all lawsuits filed against teachers and administrators (Gatti and Gatti, 1983). Even though negligence is the "fault" against which schools must most constantly guard, it is also the most difficult type of case about which to predict an accurate judicial outcome. What may be considered negligence in one court may not be considered negligence in another. It is much better, obviously, to avoid being accused of negligence in the first place than to take one's chances on the outcome of a lawsuit.

Gatti and Gatti (1983) have defined negligence as "the unintentional doing or not doing of something which wrongfully causes injury to another" (p. 246). There are four elements which must be present before negligence, in the legal sense, can be said to exist. These elements, which have been defined by many legal writers, are duty, violation of duty, proximate cause, and injury. If any one of the four elements is missing, no negligence and hence, no tort, can be found to exist. Since negligence is an unintentional act which results in an injury, a person charged with negligence is generally not going to face criminal charges or spend time in prison.

An examination of each of the four elements necessary to constitute a finding of negligence should be helpful. First, the person charged with negligence must have had a duty in the situation. Students have a right to safety, and teachers and school officials have a responsibility to protect the safety of all those entrusted to their care. It is expected that boards have developed policies and administrators have developed rules and regulations which provide for the safety of all.

Board members and school administrators should be aware of the fact that courts may hold them responsible for student behavior and its consequences occurring on school property before or after school. William Valente (1980, p. 358) comments: "Beyond the duty to supervise school grounds during normal operating hours, supervision may be required before and after class hours when students are known to congregate on school grounds." It is important, then, that policies be in place that provide for adequate supervision.

In one case, *Titus v. Lindberg*, 228 A. 2d 65 (N.J., 1967), an administrator was found to be liable for a student injury occurring on school grounds before school hours because: he knew that students arrived on the grounds before the doors were opened; he was present on the campus when they were; he had established no rules for school conduct outside the building, nor had he provided for supervision of the students. The court found that he had a reasonable duty to provide supervision when he knew students were on the property and that students were there as a regular practice. Although there was no school board involved in this case, it is relatively easy to see how board members could be involved if a similar situation were to occur today.

The second element involved in negligence is violation of duty. Negligence cannot exist if the person charged with negligence has not violated a duty. If a teacher is properly supervising a playground and one child picks up a rock and throws it and so injures another child, the teacher cannot be held liable. However, if a teacher who is responsible for the supervision of the playground were to ignore rock-throwing or were to allow it to continue and injury resulted, the teacher would probably be held liable.

If a school board knew that a dangerous situation existed in a school and made no attempt to develop policy to govern the situation, it is very likely that board members could be found to have violated their duties.

The third requirement of negligence is that the violation of duty must be the proximate cause of injury. The action or inaction of the person must have been a contributing factor to the injury. Simply put, if the person had acted as a reasonable person should act, the injury would not have occurred. In other words, would the injury have occurred if proper supervision had been present? The court or jury has to determine whether or not proper supervision could have prevented the injury and, in so deciding, the court has to look at the facts of each individual case.

The case of *Smith v. Archbishop of St. Louis* 632 S.W. 2d 516 (Mo. Ct. App. 1982), which involves a Catholic school, illustrates the concept of proximate cause. In this case, a second grade teacher had kept a lighted candle on her desk every morning during the month of May. She gave no special instructions to the students regarding the danger of a lighted candle. On the morning of a school play, the plaintiff (one who brings a lawsuit) was dressed in a costume partially composed of crepe paper. While the teacher was helping students in another part of the room, the plaintiff's costume caught fire. The teacher had difficulty putting out the flames and the child sustained serious facial and upper body burns, necessitating several operations and painful treatments. The court awarded substantial damages to the child.

The *Smith* case illustrates the concept of foreseeability. The plaintiff did not have to prove that the defendant could foresee that a particular injury (child's catching fire) had to occur; the plaintiff had to establish that a reasonable person could have foreseen that injuries could result from having an unattended lighted candle in a second grade classroom when no safety instructions were given to students.

In cases involving Catholic schools, board members are sometimes sued both individually and in their capacities as board members. In a case such as *Smith*, the court would look for the existence of appropriate policy and of appropriate supervision of the person charged with the implementation of that policy—the principal.

Negligence is a difficult concept to understand fully and it is often difficult to predict what a court will determine to be proximate cause in any particular allegation of negligence. Spontaneous injuries that would have occurred whether or not a supervisor had been present may result in a court's deciding that the institution and the teacher cannot be charged with negligence. The importance of safety procedures and supervisory policies being in place (whether or not an institution is charged with negligence) is obvious.

The fourth element necessary for a finding of negligence is injury. No matter how irresponsible the behavior of the person in authority, there is no negligence if there is no injury. If a teacher leaves twenty first graders unsupervised near a lake and no one is injured, there can be no finding of negligence and, hence no tort. Any reasonable person, though, can see that no one in authority should take the risks that may result in injury.

Most negligence cases occur in classrooms because that is where students and teachers spend most of their time. However, there are other areas that are potentially more dangerous than the classroom and, hence, a greater standard of care will be expected from teachers and administrators.

Shop, lab, and physical education classes contain greater potential for injury, and cases indicate that courts expect teachers to exercise greater caution than they would in ordinary classrooms. Schools are expected to keep equipment in working order and to keep the area free of unnecessary hazards. It is also expected that students will be given safety instructions regarding the use of potentially dangerous equipment.

Athletics presents another hazard, probably one of the most serious. Clear and Bagley state the nature of the problem (1982):

> First, it must be assumed that litigation can and will arise from each and every [athletic] injury that occurs. This creates an awareness that much is at stake. Second, it must be believed that the only way to avoid liability for injury is to be completely free from cause relating to it. Third, no [school] action can ever be taken or not taken which results in injury to a student (p. 185).

Even if every possible precaution were taken, the possibility for student injury during athletics is very high. Boards and administrators (who very often are content to let athletic directors and coaches worry about athletic programs) have very real duties to ensure that competent, properly trained personnel serve as coaches for teams; that clear procedures, including documentation, are followed when accidents occur and that there is no delay in seeking medical attention when even the slightest possibility exists that medical help might be needed; and in ensuring that

equipment and playing areas are as hazard-free as possible.

A common legal standard judging supervision cases, "The younger the child chronologically or mentally, the greater the standard of care expected." It might be acceptable to leave a group of high school seniors alone for ten minutes in a math class when it would not be acceptable to leave a group of first graders alone. It is reasonable to expect that fifteen-year-olds of average intelligence could observe traffic signals when crossing a street. But it would not be reasonable to expect mentally handicapped fifteen-year-olds to be responsible for crossing the street.

Board members will not, of course, be responsible for actual supervision. But boards are responsible for seeing that appropriate policies and procedures for supervision are in place and are being implemented.

In developing and implementing policies for supervision, the educator and/or board member must keep in mind the reasonableness standard and ask, "Is this what one would expect a reasonable person in a similar situation to do?" No one is expected to think of every possible situation that might occur. A court would not necessarily consider it unreasonable if a school did not have a rule prohibiting throwing chairs; the court would expect, though, that there would be some sort of rule encompassing the possibility of such an activity, for example, "Students are not to throw objects." No one can foresee everything that might happen; but reasonable persons can assume that certain situations might be potentially dangerous. The teacher in the *Smith* case should have foreseen that second graders might be injured by an open flame.

The best defense for school boards and administrators in a negligence suit is a reasonable attempt to provide for the safety of those entrusted to their care by the development and implementation of rules and policies. The reasonable board is one that ensures that administrators supervise teachers in their implementation of rules and policies.

Corporal Punishment

Corporal punishment is perhaps one of the most controversial topics in education today. The laws of most states allow corporal punishment in public schools under certain conditions and say nothing about the private school.

The private school is not governed by the same rules in regard to corporal punishment as is the public school. Unless corporal punishment is prohibited in all schools by state law, Catholic schools may use it. Because of growing awareness of child abuse concerns as well as psychological considerations, the use of corporal punishment is a legal risk. Private schools are not immune to civil tort cases or criminal charges of assault and battery if corporal punishment results in injuries to the student.

If corporal punishment is to be used in a school, definite policies and procedures governing its administration should be in place. Generally, the following guidelines should be considered in developing such a policy: (1) punishment should be for the correction of the child; (2) no permanent injury should result; (3) only the principal and/or the principal's designate should administer the punishment; (4) punishment must be administered with an appropriate instrument; (5) the maximum number of blows should not exceed three; (6) a witness should be present; and (7) written documentation of the punishment should be kept.

All disciplinary policies, but especially those concerning corporal punishment, should be reviewed by the board annually. Private schools, like public schools, might be well advised to devise other means of discipline than physical ones, both from the standpoint of avoiding lawsuits and from the standpoint of one's school philosophy and good psychology.

Search and Seizure

The 1985 case, *New Jersey v. T.L.O.* 105 S. Ct. 733 recognized the right of public school officials to conduct searches if reasonable suspicion (rather than the stricter standard of probable cause) exists.

Private schools, although not bound to observe even the reasonable cause standard, should, nonetheless, have some kind of policy for searching students and/or seizing their possessions. Searching a student should require "more" cause than searching a locker.

Private schools could be subject to tort suits if harm is alleged to have been done to a student because of an unreasonable search: "Searches of students will have to be conducted according to the 'reasonable person' doctrine of tort law; that test includes not only the manner of the search, but the justification for the search in the first place" (Permuth *et al.*, 1981, p. 65). Catholic school officials could be charged with the torts of assault and battery and/or invasion of privacy.

Defamation

Defamation is the violation of a person's liberty interest or right to reputation. *Black's Law Dictionary* defines defamation as:

Includes both libel [what is written] and slander [what is spoken]. Defamation is that which tends to injure the reputation; to diminish the esteem, respect, goodwill or confidence in which the plaintiff is held, or to excite adverse, derogatory or unpleasant feelings or opinions against him. . . . A communication is defamatory if it tends so to harm the reputation of another as to lower him in the estimation of the community or to deter third persons from associating or dealing with him.

The potential for defamation to be alleged certainly exists in Catholic schools. It is important that school officials be factual in their comments, whether written or oral, about the conduct of students or employees. The same cautions exist whether one is dealing with students *or* teachers.

Several authors have pointed out that the truth is not always the best defense, since truthful statements can be defamatory (Gatti and Gatti, 1983). Generally, the truth is a valid defense only if the statement was made without malice and to someone with a legitimate right to hear the statement. If a school board member knows that a teacher some years ago obtained an illegal abortion or completed a drug or alcohol rehabilitation program, he or she has no right to communicate that knowledge to a third party who has no legitimate reason for receiving that information.

When making statements or writing entries in records, a person should restrict statements to pertinent facts. The Family Educational Rights and Privacy Act of 1974 changed the rules on record-keeping so that students and parents would be protected, but many schools, including Catholic ones, still place potentially damaging information in school folders. Catholic schools boards should ensure that there are record-keeping policies in place that: (1) limit contents of records to what is absolutely necessary; (2) provide for periodic culling of older records; and (3) limit access to records to appropriate persons (only administrators and professional staff who have legitimate reasons for reading files should have access to them).

In regard to teachers, it is generally held that teachers have legal as well as moral rights to see whatever is in their files. Only school administrators should have access to teacher files. School board members have no legal right of access to student or teacher records.

This chapter on tort liability has discussed several areas of legal concern for Catholic schools and, hence, for persons serving on Catholic school boards.

It is important for board members to understand that they are not responsible for deciding which actions an administrator will take, but for developing the policies that guide the administrator in making decisions.

References

Alexander, Kern. (1980). *School law*. St. Paul: West.

Black, Henry Campbell. (1979). *Black's law dictionary*. (5th ed.). St. Paul: West.

Bloch v. Hillel Torah North Suburban Day School, 438 N.E. 2d 976 (1981).

Clear, Delbert and Bagley, Martha. (1982). Coaching athletics: a tort just waiting for a judgment? *NOLPE School Law Journal*, 10 (2), 184–192.

Dolter v. Wahlert, 483 F. Supp. 266 (N.D. Iowa 1980).

Gatti, Richard D. and Gatti, Daniel J. (1983). *New encyclopedic dictionary of school law*. West Nyack, NY: Parker.

Geraci v. St. Xavier High School, 13 Ohio Op. 3d 146 (Ohio 1978).

New Jersey v. T.L.O., 105 S. Ct. 733 (1985).

Permuth, Steve, *et. al.*, The law, the student and the Catholic school. Washington: NCEA.

Pierce v. the Society of Sisters, 268 U.S. 510 (1925).

Rendell-Baker v. Kohn, 102 S. Ct. 2764 (1982).

Smith v. Archbishop of St. Louis, 632 S.W. 2d 516 (Mo. Ct. App. 1982).

Steeber v. Benilde—St. Margaret's High School, (No. D.C. 739 378, Hennepin County, Minnesota, 1978).

Titus v. Lindberg, 228 A. 2d 65 (N.J., 1967).

Valente, William D. (1980). *Law in the schools*. Columbus: Merrill.

Weithoff v. St. Veronica School, 210 N. W. 2d 108 (Mich. 1973).

Wisch v. Sanford School, Inc., 420 F. Supp. 1310 (1976).

School Handbooks: Some Legal Considerations

Shaughnessy, M. A. 1989. Washington, D.C.: National Catholic Educational Association, 1–3, 11–15.

The Laws Affecting Catholic Education in the United States

The laws affecting education in the United States today can generally be classified according to four categories: (1) constitutional law (both state and federal); (2) administrative law: statues and regulations; (3) common law principles; and (4) contract law. It must be kept in mind from the outset that public school law and nonpublic school law (in this case, Catholic school) differ greatly in many respects, primarily because the two school systems evolved from opposite sources.

Constitutional Law

Federal constitutional law

Federal constitutional law protects individuals against arbitrary deprivation of their constitutional freedoms by government and government officials. Students and teachers in public schools are protected by constitutional law since public schools are governmental agencies and the administrators of public schools are public officials. Students and teachers in nonpublic schools are not protected by federal constitutional law because private schools are private agencies. When a student enrolls in a Catholic school, that students and/or the parents voluntarily surrender certain constitutional protections while in the Catholic school. Of course, a person in a private institution can always voluntarily leave that institution and enter the public sector where constitutional rights are protected, but as long as the person remains in the private sector, the Constitution offers no protection.

Therefore, what cannot lawfully be done in a public school may be done in a Catholic school, e.g., the First Amendment to the Constitution protects an individual's right to free speech. Therefore, administrators in public schools may not make rules prohibiting the expression of unpopular viewpoints. Since no such constitutional protection exists in the Catholic school, administrators may restrict the speech of both students and teachers.

State constitutional Law

On the other hand, however, state constitutional law may apply to private as well as public schools. It is not unusual to find a statement such as, "Anyone operating an educational institution in this state shall be required to. . . ." So long as whatever is required does not unfairly impinge on the rights of the private educational institution and can be shown to have some legitimate educational purpose, private schools can be compelled to comply with the state constitutional requirements which normally are not as restrictive as those of the federal Constitution.

Mix of federal and state constitutional law

The only situation in which a private school can be required to grant federal constitutional protections is if

state action can be found to be so pervasive within the school that the school can fairly be said to be acting as an agent of an individual state. State action can be defined as:

> In general, term used in connection with claims under due process clause and Civil Rights Act for which a private citizen is seeking damages or redress because of improper governmental intrusion into his life. In determining whether an action complained of constitutes "state action" within the purview of the Fourteenth Amendment, court must determine whether sufficiently close nexus exists between state and challenged action so that the action may fairly be treated as that of the state itself (Black, p. 1262).

Therefore, if state action can be demonstrated to exist in an institution or a specific program or activity of an institution, constitutional protections (of which due process is a major one) must be provided.

As Black's definition points out, the factor which determines the existence of state action is the nexus (relationship) between the state and the challenged action.

Given that nonpublic schools have the right to exist, *Pierce v. Society of Sisters* (1925), and since they are not bound to grant constitutional protections, unless significant state action is found, litigants alleging a denial of constitutional rights will have to prove the existence of significant state action within the institution before the court will grant relief. It is very important for Catholic school officials to keep these facts in mind. It is not uncommon for parents, students, or teachers to claim that their federal constitutional rights have been violated in the Catholic school, when, in fact, no constitutional rights ever existed.

Some of the main arguments advanced to prove the presence of state action in private educational institutions are (1) an institution's acceptance of government monies; (2) the tax-exempt status of the private institution; (3) education as a quasi state function (sometimes called a "public benefit theory" since schools, particularly elementary and secondary ones, perform a public service); and (4) state involvement with the school through accreditation or similar procedures and/or statutory requirements with which the school complies.

Administrative Law: Statutes and Regulations

Administrative law, which encompasses federal and state statues and regulations, governs the public school and may govern the private school as well. Failure to comply with reasonable regulations can result in the imposition of sanctions. The relatively recent case of *Bob Jones University v. United States* 103 S. Ct. 2017 (1983) illustrates this point. When Bob Jones University, a nonpublic institution, was found to use racially discriminatory admissions policies, the Internal Revenue Service withdrew the university's tax-exempt status based on a 1970 regulation proscribing the granting of tax-exempt status to any institution which discriminated on the basis of race. Before a private school will be forced to comply with a law or regulation, the state will have to demonstrate a *compelling interest* in the enforcement of the regulation. Black (1979) defines compelling state interest as a: "Term used to uphold state action in the face of attack, grounded on Equal Protection of First Amendment rights because of serious need for such state action" (p. 256).

In the *Bob Jones* case, the government's compelling interest in racial equality was sufficient for the court to order Bob Jones University to comply with the anti-discrimination regulation or lose its tax-exempt status.

Other examples of compelling state interests in educational concerns might be curriculum or graduation requirements, teacher certification and school certification regulations. In these cases the state could very possibly prove a compelling state interest in the proper education of the public.

The state cannot pass laws so restrictive that a school's existence is placed in jeopardy. The right of the private school to exist was firmly established by the Supreme Court in 1925 when two agencies operating private schools brought suit challenging an Oregon statue which would have made public education compulsory. In this landmark case, *Pierce v. the Society of Sisters* 268 U.S. 510 (1925), the Supreme Court declared that statue unconstitutional not only because it interfered with the rights of the school owners, but also because it interfered with the right of parents to choose the education of their children.

Common Law

The third type of law which applies to both public and private sectors (and, indeed, to all cases, whether school cases or not) is the common law. *Black's Law Dictionary* (1979) defines common law:

> As distinguished from law created by the enactment of legislatures, the common law comprises the body of those principles and rules of action, relating to the government and security of persons and property, which derive their authority solely from the usages and customs of immemorial, antiquity, or from the judgments and decrees of the courts recognizing, affirming, and enforcing such usages and customs; . . . "Common law" consists of those principles, usage and rules of action applicable to government and security of persons and property which do not rest for their authority upon any express and positive declaration of the will of the legislature (p. 251).

Sometimes called judge-made law, common law principles may also be considered to be derived from God's law, especially by persons in religious schools. Many common

law principles are founded in basic morality, such as that contained in the Bible. Therefore, it is not uncommon for a court to discuss basic fairness or common law standards of decency in a decision, even without reference to a specific state or federal law.

Contract Law

The fourth kind of law which governs both public and private schools is contract law. Public schools are governed by contract law in some instances, especially in the area of teacher contracts. However, most cases involving public school teacher contracts also allege violation of constitutionally protected interests as well, so contract law is not the only applicable law.

In the nonpublic school and, therefore, in the Catholic school, contract law is the predominant governing law. A contract may be defined as: "An agreement between two or more persons which creates an obligation to do or not to do a particular thing" (Black, 1979, pp. 291–92). Generally, the five basic elements of a contract are (1) mutual assent (2) by legally competent parties for (3) consideration (4) to subject matter that is legal and (5) in a form of agreement which is legal.

Mutual assent implies that two parties entering into a contract agree to its provisions. A Catholic school agrees to provide an education to a student, and the parents accept that arrangement, or a Catholic school offers a teacher a contract which the teacher accepts. "To be binding a contract must have both a legal 'offer' and 'acceptance' " (Mawdsley and Permuth, unpublished manuscript, p. 5).

Consideration is what the first party agrees to do for the other party in exchange for something from the second party. The private school agrees to provide educational services to a student in return for payment of tuition and adherence to school rules. The school agrees to pay the teacher a salary in return for teaching services.

Legally competent parties implies that the parties entering into the contract are lawfully qualified to make the agreement. A school is legally qualified to enter into contracts to educate students and to employ teachers. Parents are legally competent to agree to pay tuition and meet other obligations (minor students are not legally competent, and so parents or legal guardians must sign contracts on their behalf). A properly qualified teacher is a legally competent party; a person who does not possess the qualifications or skills needed to perform as a teacher would not be a legally competent party to enter into a teaching contract.

Legal subject matter assumes that the provisions of the contract are legal. An agreement that a teacher would not marry a person of another race as a condition of employment might not be legal, as such a condition would probably be construed as a violation of anti-discrimination laws.

Legal form may vary from state to state. If a contract calls for witnesses and no witnesses' signatures are found on the contract, then the contract is probably not in proper legal form. If any one of the five elements of a contract is missing, the contract may be held to be null and void.

Cases involving student and teacher discipline (particularly, dismissal) in Catholic schools often allege breach of contract:

> A breach of contract occurs when a party does not perform that which he or she was under an absolute duty to perform and the circumstances are such that his or her failure was neither justified nor excused (Gatti and Gatti, 1983, p. 24).

Breach of contract can be committed by either party to the contract (the school/administrator or the teacher or student). It is generally conceded, however, that it is futile for a school to seek to bring breach of contract charges against a teacher who wants to terminate a contract; it is highly unlikely that a judge will compel a person to teach against his or her wishes. Historically, courts will not compel performance of a contract, since a contractual arrangement is seen as a private arrangement, and courts will not force persons to associate with each other against their will. The remedy for breach of contract is damages. In order for a school to collect damages, it would have to show that it had been damaged. Generally, a court will rule that it is not very difficult to replace a teacher, and so damages are not appropriate.

While teachers can usually break their contracts without severe consequences, schools and administrators who terminate a teacher's employment during a contract term without just cause or who terminate a student's enrollment without just cause can ordinarily expect to pay damages if a lawsuit is filed. Two cases involving breach of contract in Catholic schools will illustrate the concept.

In the breach of contract case of a teacher in a Roman Catholic school, *Weithoff v. St. Veronica School* 210 N.W. 2d 108 Michigan (1973), the court concerned itself with the case of a woman who had been dismissed from her position because of her marriage to an ex-priest. The court was careful to note that a church-sponsored school could contractually require teachers and other employees to observe the tenets of its faith. The testimony shows that new regulations requiring teachers to be practicing Catholics had been adopted by the school board but had never been promulgated. Therefore, the court held that the school could not legally dismiss the teacher without being liable for damages. Obviously, if the principal and/or school board had been careful to disseminate its regulations, this case might have had a different ending.

An opposite conclusion was reached in the similar case of *Steeber v. Benilde-St. Margaret's High School* No. D.C. 739 378, Hennepin County, Minnesota (1978), in which a teacher protested the non-renewal of her contract following her remarriage after a civil divorce. The court upheld the right of the school to terminate the teacher's contract since she was no longer a member in good standing of the Catholic Church.

In the first case, the school breached its contract with the teacher because it failed to promulgate the rule to which it sought to hold the teacher. In the second case, though, in a very similar situation, the court ruled in the school's favor because the school had properly proceeded according to its contract.

William D. Valente (1980) offers this advice to teachers in private schools who think that their rights are being violated.

> Thus, a teacher who is offended by private school orders that suppress speech, invade privacy, or impose disciplinary sanctions without notice or hearing must look elsewhere than to constitutional doctrines for legal relief, except in the unusual situation where the private school is considered to be engaged in official government action. (p. 464)

The "elsewhere" to which a Catholic school teacher must look is, generally, contract law. Mr. Valente's words are a timely admonition to faculty in Catholic schools as they consider their rights and responsibilities and to administrators as they develop, revise, and implement contracts and handbooks.

The relationship of both public and private institutions to students has been compared to that of a fiduciary. Professor Warren Seavey first applied this theory to public institutions in 1957, three years before the landmark *Dixon vs. Alabama State B.O.E.*, 294 F. 2d 150, cert. den. 368 U.S. 930 (1961) case. Seavey maintained that because an educational institution was subject to the duties of a fiduciary in dealing with its students, it should at least have to explain to students what rights they are waiving when they (or their parents) sign a form. Writing in the *Harvard Law Review*, Professor Seavey takes a strong stand:

> It is shocking that the officials of a state educational institution, which can function properly only if our freedoms are preserved, should not understand the elementary principles of fair play. It is equally shocking to find that a court supports them in denying to a student the protection given to a pickpocket. (p. 1407)

"The protection given to a pickpocket" became an oft-quoted phrase and illustrated the apparent injustice in giving more protections to common criminals than to students. A little more than a decade later, Professor Charles Wright (1969), in the *Vanderbilt Law Review*, would seem to apply Professor Seavey's sentiments to the private sector:

> [It] seems ... unthinkable ... that the faculty and administration of any private institution would consider recognizing fewer rights in their students than the minimum the Constitution exacts of the state universities, or that their students would long remain quiescent if a private college were to embark on such a benighted course. (pp. 1027, 35)

References

Black, Henry Campbell. *Black's law dictionary*. (5th ed.). St. Paul: West.

Gatti, Richard D. and Daniel J. Gatti. *New Encyclopedic Dictionary of School Law*. West Nyack, NY: Parker, 1983.

Seavey, Warren A. "Dismissal of students: due process." *Harvard Law Review*, 70, 1406–1410, 1957.

Valente, William D. *Law in the schools*. Columbus: Merrill, 1980.

Wright, Charles A. "The constitution on the campus." *Vanderbilt Law Review*, 22, 1027–1088, 1969.

Administrator's Handbook of Regulations

Hennessey, C., C. A. Solomon, K. Mitchell, S. Plasek, D. A. Clifford, and T. Bogar. 1997.
[Federal Programs Section 1–4, Special Education Section 1–4].
Houston, Tex.: Catholic School Office, Diocese of Galveston-Houston.

Federal Programs Information

Catholic Schools in the Diocese of Galveston-Houston participate in the following federal program opportunities under the Elementary and Secondary Education Act of 1965 (ESEA) as amended by the Improving America's School Act of 1994 (public law 103-382).

TITLE I

Part A of Title I of ESEA, Improving Basic Programs Operated by Local Educational Agencies, is designed to help disadvantaged children meet challenging content and student performance standards. Section 1120 of Title I requires that a local education agency (LEA) provide eligible private school children Title I educational services or other benefits that are equitable to those provided to eligible public school children. Title I services for eligible private school children must be developed in consultation with private school officials. The location of instructional services under Part A of Title I for private school children is limited by the U.S. Supreme Court's decision in *Aguilar v. Felton.*

> *In Aguilar v. Felton, 473 U.S. 402 (1985), the Supreme Court ruled that the provision of Chapter I (the current Title I, Part A program) instructional services by private school teachers to religious school children in religious school buildings constituted "excessive entanglement."*

Funding is determined by the number and/or percentages of students living in poverty within LEA boundary.

TITLE II

The Dwight D. Eisenhower Professional Development Program supports local, state, and federal efforts to stimulate and provide the sustained and intensive high-quality professional development in the core academic subjects that is needed to help students meet high academic standards and thus achieve the National Education Goals. To ensure the continuity of professional development that was supported by the program's predecessor in math and science, the first $250 million in appropriated funds must be devoted to professional development in these subjects. The participation of private school students under Title II is governed by the Uniform Provisions contained in Sections 14503-14509 of Part E of Title XIV of IASA.*

TITLE III

Technology for All Students represents a commitment on the part of Congress and the Department of Education to promote the use of educational technology to support school reform and to assist schools in adopting educational uses of technology to enhance curricula, instruction, and administrative support to improve the delivery of educational services and to help achieve the National Education Goals. *Technology for All Students* provides for the equitable participation of private school students. The specifics for the equitable participation of private school students are governed by Section 14503-14509 of Part E of Title XIV of IASA.*

TITLE IV

The Safe and Drug-Free Schools and Communities Act provides assistance to establish, operate, and improve comprehensive safe and drug-free school programs. Title IV adds violence prevention as a key element of the program and broadens the types of prevention programs that LEAs can support. Examples of programs that can be supported by the *Safe and Drug-Free Schools Program* include mentoring, comprehensive health education, community service and service learning projects, conflict resolution, peer mediation, and character education. The uniform provision of Sections 14503-14509 of Part E of Title XIV govern the participation of private school students in the *Safe and Drug-Free Schools and Communities Program.**

TITLE VI

Innovative Education Program Strategies (formerly Chapter 2), supports projects to encourage systematic reform and improve student achievement. Title VI supports a broad range of local activities in eight primary areas: technology related to implementing reform; acquisition and use of instructional and educational materials, including library materials and computer software; promising education reform projects such as magnet schools; programs for disadvantaged and at-risk children; literacy programs for students and their parents; programs for gifted and talented children; school reform efforts linked to Goals 2000; and school improvement programs or activities authorized under Title I.

Title VI contains language for the equitable participation of private school students. Section 6402 (a) (1) of Part D of Title VI requires that LEAs provide, for the benefit of students within the LEA who are enrolled in private, non-profit elementary and secondary schools, secular neutral and non-ideological services, materials, and equipment. In determining what Title VI services to provide for the benefit of private school students, an LEA must consult with appropriate private school officials. Expenditures for Title VI services for private school students must be equal to expenditures for Title VI services for public school students with LEA, taking into account the needs of children and other factors.

* Part E of Title XIV-Uniform Provisions for the Participation of Private School Students

Sections 14503–14509 of Part E of Title XIV contain the Uniform Provisions that govern the participation of private school students, teachers, and other personnel in programs covered by this section. Under Title XIV, the LEA is required to provide services to eligible private school children, teachers, and other personnel consistent with the number of eligible children enrolled in private elementary and secondary schools in the LEA. This same language is used in Title VI to define the LEA's responsibility to provide service to eligible private school children. This differs from the Title I requirement that requires the LEA to service private school children who **reside in the LEA. Title VI and XIV require that the LEA serve eligible private school children enrolled in private schools located in the LEA.**

Title XIV contains requirements for timely and meaningful consultation. This consultation between public and private school officials must occur before any decision is made that could adversely affect the ability of private school students to participate and must continue through all phases of the program. The consultation must include how children's needs will be identified, what services will be offered, how and where the services will be provided, how the services will be assessed, and the amount of funds to be used for those services.

The goal of the consultation process is to design and implement a program that will provide equitable services to eligible private school students. This includes equal per pupil expenditures for public and private school students, an equal opportunity to participate in the benefits of the program, and an offer of service that is equitable.

Federal Program Local Procedures

The Catholic School Office works with twenty local education agencies in providing federal program opportunities for Catholic school students and teachers in the Diocese of Galveston-Houston. The local education agency is responsible for administering federal programs. Services and procedures differ among the local agencies.

The federal program director at the Catholic School Office works directly with the federal program personnel at the Houston Independent School District (HISD) in planning and implementing programs.

Principals outside of the HISD boundary are asked to meet with federal program personnel in their respective districts each year to familiarize themselves with district opportunities and local procedures. The diocesan federal program director is available to work with principals, coordinators, and local education agencies in planning and implementing programs.

General Information and Record Keeping

◆ Federal funds used must **supplement** and in no case **supplant** funds made available from non-federal sources.
◆ Maintain a separate file for each federal program.
◆ Document all communications.
◆ Keep copies of all documents, forms, letters, inventories, packing slips, etc.
◆ Annual family income surveys are required to be kept **by the principal in a confidential file** for all students.
◆ Parents must be notified by letter that their children are eligible for **Title I** services, and a signed parent consent form must be on file at the school before a student receives services.
◆ Complete and return all LEA and Catholic School Office requests and forms promptly.
◆ If you have any questions, call the federal program director at the Catholic School Office.

Special Education Information

Skills Center

Teachers in the Skills Center shall be degreed in Special Education in the area of Generic Special Education or Learning Disabilities (LD). They may teach in the Skills Center, if they are degreed and have 15 hours in Special Education to teach the Educable Mentally Handicapped (EMH) or Learning Disabled (LD). If they are degreed and are qualified for EMH, they must obtain credits in the area of learning disabilities.

Due Process

This process here outlined is approved for the Catholic Diocese of Galveston-Houston in accord with Teacher Education Association (TEA) Special Education Guidelines, and is in compliance with Individuals With Disabilities Act of 1990 (IDEA).

Referral Committee consists of, but is not limited to:
1. Director of Special Education (or representative as designated)
2. Principal of school
3. Regular classroom teacher(s)

Responsibilities of Referral Committee:
1. Attendance at a scheduled meeting of the committee members
2. Identification of student as having learning problems
3. Staffing of student to make recommendations

Each student must have a comprehensive education evaluation

This includes (but is not limited to):

1. Intelligence test
2. Educational Achievement test
3. Speech and Hearing Screening
4. Medical History

Diocesan Director of Special Education will make a final decision for approval of a child into the Skills Center. The local Admission, Review, and Dismissal Committee (ARD) needs to meet regarding the children accepted in a Skills Center.

Local ARD Committee consists of:

1. Director of Special Education or designated representative
2. Principal of the school or Administrative Representative
3. Special Education Teacher - Skills Center Teacher
4. Classroom Teacher(s)
5. Parents
6. Anyone else who may have worked with the child

Responsibilities of ARD Committee:

1. Category of the learning problem and is the child eligible for special resource assistance
2. Appropriate placement of the students
3. The Individualized Educational Program (IEP) is written by the ARD committee with long-range goals and short-range goals

Each child must have an IEP that was developed by the ARD Committee. The Committee develops the IEP with the parent present in consultation. The completed IEP must be approved by the Director of Special Education. The IEP is further developed in detail by the teacher in planning the student's educational program.

Each Special Skills Center student will have on file in the principal's office the following:

1. Data sheet of referral committee
2. Report of the comprehensive testing
3. Report of the ARD Committee decision
4. Permit with parent(s) signature to receive services
5. Copy of health record and cumulative card
6. A copy of IEP will be in the principal's office and in the office of the Director of Special Education

Explanation of Services

In the ARD meeting, special services are explained to parents. Parents decide if they want services. The IEP is developed and signed. A copy is given to the parent. The permit to attend classes in Special Education must be signed by parent(s). The teacher will meet with parents at least four (4) times a year (October, January, March, and May).

Teachers in a local school must be informed that a Special Education Skills Center Class is beginning. They will be involved with Special Education Teacher(s) to give pertinent information before the development of the IEP. *The teacher and the Special Education Teacher have periodic conferences, planned in accord with the school's report card schedule.*

In the Skills Center, where children receive assistance for part of the day, the student-teacher ratio is 18 to 20 students per teacher. The student-teacher ratio for a self-contained Skills Center, a classroom where children spend the entire day, is 12 to 15 pupils per teacher. In a school where a half-day Skills Center is financed, the student-teacher ratio is 8 to 10 students per teacher. In the Skills Center during a class period, the students may range within a three-year age span.

In the secondary level of education, the student-teacher ratio is 40 to 60 students per teacher for a Skills Center where students receive assistance for part of the day.

All children are accepted in the Skills Center on a nine-week trial basis in order to observe and confirm that the child is in the appropriate educational placement.

The Diocese has a central ARD Committee, as needed for special meetings.

Members:
- ❖ Director of Special Education
- ❖ Director of Health Services
- ❖ Director of Guidance and Counseling

Superintendent of Schools has final approval in the Process of Special Education Services.

MODIFICATIONS IN THE REGULAR CLASSROOM

School _____ Year _____ Student's Name _____

Grade _____

Modifications required to ensure success in regular, remedial, and supportive programs (including eligibility for participation in extra-curricular activities) are suggested.

1. Changes in the pace of instruction
2. Oral tests
3. Short answer tests
4. Modified tests
5. Taped texts
6. Highlighted texts
7. Taping lectures
8. Note-taking assistance
9. Extended time for assignment completion
10. Shortened assignments
11. Assignment notebooks
12. Study sheets
13. Repeated review/drill
14. Reduce pencil/paper tasks
15. Calculators
16. Preferential seating
17. Interpreter for the deaf
18. Frequent breaks

19. Defined physical spaces
20. Cooling-off period
21. Concrete reinforcers
22. Positive reinforcers
23. Behavior management systems
24. Special instructional or adaptive equipment:_____
25. Oral directives
26. Changes in requirements of essential elements in Diocesan Curriculum
27. Changes in project or report requirements

_____

MODIFICATIONS USED:

SUBJECT	NUMBER
_____	_____
_____	_____
_____	_____

If times vary from accreditation requirements, give justification: _____

_____

_____

Teacher _____ Date _____

Perceptual Learning Style:
The best learning style for the student is

_____ Auditory _____ Visual _____ Multisensory _____ Tactile

Learning Characteristics:
Strengths (+) Weaknesses (−)

_____ spatial relations _____ coordination _____ speed of writing/copying

_____ handwriting _____ oral reading _____ organizational skills

_____ silent reading comprehension _____ vocabulary skills _____ attending to task

_____ other: _____

COMMENTS:

Catholic School Finance and Church-State Relations

McLaughlin, T. 1985. 34–37, 44–52. Washington, D.C.: National Catholic Educational Association.

A tax deduction is an *indirect* reduction.

A tax credit is a *direct* reduction in the amount of tax parents would pay on their federal income tax. The reduction would be decided by the specifics of a tax credit law. The credit is computed by subtracting an amount from the total tax that the parents would otherwise pay. Suppose, again, that the parents earn $25,000 and, based upon standard deductions for the size of that particular family, had a tax due of $2800. If, also, the parents were entitled to tax credits for two children totaling $1650, they would subtract that from the tax figure of $2800 and pay a tax of $1150.

The tax deduction is a very modest savings to parents. In the one state (Minnesota) where it is operative, the average deduction per child is less than $30. Other states soon may move toward debating the issue of tax deductions in their legislatures. Of course, the states must have a state income tax or some other tax which would permit a reduction, and possess a receptive group of legislators. Private school parents, and other leaders, also must be willing to enter the public arena to speak strongly for such a return on their tax investment.

Federal Assistance to Catholic School Students

The participation of the federal government in elementary and secondary education historically has been minor. The degree of federal financial aid to public education might be pegged at around six percent of total funding. The private sector cannot generally expect much financial assistance from federal programs.

The National Defense Education Act (NDEA), which became law in 1958, included a provision of 10-year loans to private schools for science, math, and foreign language equipment. The Elementary and Secondary Act (ESEA) of 1965 redefined the federal role in education and became the first federal program to contain provisions requiring federally-funded services for private school students. The breakthrough, which allowed congressional approval of ESEA, came in the form of an agreement on a child-benefit approach to federal aid between interest groups representing both public and religious school organizations. This aid was to focus on educationally disadvantaged children in both public and private schools. It was not considered aid to the school itself. The result of this agreement was that local school districts were required to make available to private school students educational services paid for by the federal government.[22]

The delivery system for federal aid to students in private schools was the local public school district, called in legislation the local education agency (LEA). The only exception was that where state law prohibited involvement in programs for private schools, the U.S. Commissioner of Education was responsible for providing these program benefits directly. This procedure has become known as the "Title I by-pass."

However, despite the intention that private school students were to receive service under ESEA Title I, the extent of private school participation really depended upon the willingness of state and local education agencies to extend such benefits to private school students. Since 1965, the provisions relating to private school student participation in Title I have become increasingly explicit, and there has been a general inclusion of private school students in most federal education programs.[23]

An example of this more explicit directive appeared in the Vocation Education Act of 1968, which required the states to ensure that nonprofit private school students, whose education needs were of the type for which vocational programs were designed, received services on an equitable basis with public school students.

The Education Consolidation and Improvement Act of 1981 (ECIA) was designed as legislation whose purpose was to continue to aid state and local education, but to do so by eliminating unnecessary federal supervision, direction, and control. The services now given are: Chapter I—the same provisions formerly granted under Title I: compensatory education; and Chapter II—the consolidation of 28 of the smaller categorical programs into a block grant.

Another federal program, not included in these chapter arrangements, is delivered through the Handicapped Children Act of 1975. The states must provide satisfactory assurance that, to the extent consistent with the number and location of handicapped children in the state who are enrolled in private elementary and secondary schools, provision will be made for participation of such children in programs assisted by this Act.[24]

There is little accurate information available on the degree of Catholic school participation in these federal programs. Catholic school participation in Chapter I programs, which focus on aiding educationally disadvantaged children, is declining, but, seemingly only in proportion to the general Catholic school enrollment decline. The majority of Catholic schools receive library book loans, but a much smaller percentage participate in the innovate projects available. Participation in federal vocational education programs is very low because so few Catholic schools have vocational education programs. Some research indicates that, although federal rules provide guidelines and criteria for program operation, it was the local interpretation of guidelines that determined the extent of private school involvement in most federal programs.

Other reasons for low private school participation in federal programs are the failure of the state to monitor LEA assurances that private schools are being equitably treated, failure to provide technical assistance to private schools, the competitive nature of a few of the programs, and the unwillingness of private schools to actively pursue their fair share of the funds. In addition, private school officials were found to be generally uninformed about some of the planning and design programs available to them.[25]

Federally-funded programs for education, either in the public or private sector, have always been limited in scope. Public schools have relied on state and local support. Catholic schools have relied on tuition, subsidies, contributed services, cooperative ventures with public schools, fund-raising, and development for their support. In addition, Catholic school participation, in a meaningful way in federal programs, appears to be on the decline. If Catholic schools are to be helped financially to any great extent by the federal government, new initiatives in public funding will need to be found.

Public Funding—New Initiatives

When proposals for public support for private school children are introduced, discussions are value-laden, usually emotional and politically charged. But, there is no compelling reason to believe that the only way for the government to support education is to own and operate schools.[26]

There are some educators today who argue for less government sponsorship of education. Their basic contention is that the state need not operate schools. The state monies could be given to other agencies, private companies as an example, to train students in special skill areas. A computer company or a business firm, with trained personnel and specialized equipment, could do an excellent job in training computer technicians and business managers for the future. These leaders feel that it is unwise to continue to spend money within the public school system when private educational enterprise might be a better investment. Greater expenditure in the public sector, in their opinion, is somewhat like spending money to "fine tune the stagecoaches." This may be considered radical thinking in some circles, but it is introduced to show that the present public school monopoly is not something that has to exist. Examples of business and school partnerships are already in place in some communities. The Houston public school-private sector partnership and the Connecticut mathematics project are examples of this forward thinking.

The Political Process

Financial help of any kind and at whatever level, state or national, will be sprung loose as a result of a *political decision*. Catholic school parents, teachers, and administrators must enter new territory, form educational alliances, join political coalitions, and generally make themselves heard in the political arenas.

Catholic parents and educators should realize at the outset that it is not a foregone conclusion that government aid will be good for them. But, what must be insisted upon, is that others do not make this decision for them. Catholic parents, exercising their choice, should determine what is good or bad for their children and their schools.

Catholic parents and educators must not permit themselves to be ignored. Moynihan states that the "best" people in educational circles think that Catholic schools have no right to seek financial help from government sources. They think it so strongly that they don't even think it is necessary to say so.[45] There are people in key positions who do not think that Catholic schools should exist, so they act as if the schools did not exist. Catholic educators cannot sit idly by and be ignored.

Catholic parents and educators must not permit the threat of unconstitutionality to snuff out the debate. This, again, is a political question, and not a constitutional issue. The constitutional facts are obvious enough. The government today is cooperating with religious groups to further secular purposes in a variety of ways—cooperating, that is, with the single exception of private elementary and secondary schools. Federal funds provide support for Baptist and Jewish hospitals and Catholic colleges. Federal foreign aid funds provide resources for relief work for Protestant agencies in developing countries. Medicare benefits are not denied to the patient who chooses a Lutheran rest home. Catholic education needs spokespersons who will make the Catholic school position the political issue of the moment.

Two important considerations should be kept in mind by Catholics in their quest for government support. One has to do with their relationship to the public sector. The second concerns what might be happening within their own group.

The best position of the Catholic, who is debating the issue of federal funds for private school parents, is to support movements which will strengthen both public and private education. Private school should not attempt to make gains at the expense of the public sector. Voucher reimbursements to parents should be modest enough so as not to upset the stability of the public schools. Tax credits should be large enough to help private school parents, but not so large that a sharp trend to private schools may be anticipated. That is the political process.

Alliances must be formed with public schools where feasible. Public schools should align with private schools, instead of each system viewing the other with suspicion and hostility. Supporters of the public school system might gain, both financially and politically, by looking to the private sector for allies in the effort to adopt a strategy of support for education as a whole.[46]

The thrust for government support for schools within the Catholic community may have ramifications that many fail to anticipate. Catholic leaders are becoming more and more involved with political issues. Most Catholic pronouncements on social matters will be found on the liberal points of the political compass. But, support among Catholics for aid to parents is coming from political conservatives. This latter group may not be in agreement with much of the contemporary Catholic thought on social issues.

Moynihan, speaking on Catholic tradition and social change in 1984, warns that if it should become clear to a significant number of the Catholic community that support for their schools is concentrated in one sector of political opinion, the social commitments of those furthering social concerns will become hostage to the political supporters of Catholic schools.[47]

As Catholics enter the political process at the government level, they cannot ignore the political divisions that exist within their own group. Aid for school children is a need that transcends parties and labels. Bonds of trust, understanding, and cooperation must be established within the Catholic community. If aid to private schools becomes strictly a Republican, or Democrat, or liberal, or conservative position, there is little chance of school children ever receiving aid. The gap between the forces who are moving for general social change and the forces who are moving for specific educational change must not widen. Estrangement among these leaders will lead to failure of both.

The political arena is new territory for most Catholic school educators. However, it is familiar ground to public school educators, who have been involved in the political process for many years. The National Education Association (NEA) is now one of the most powerful lobby groups in the country. This organization, and its state affiliates, exert enormous influence on educational legislation, and on the activities of state departments of education. In many state legislatures, NEA members are very prominent and serve on education committees. In Minnesota, for example, during the debate in 1984 for an increase in the tax deduction allowance, approximately 38 people in public education were voting members of the legislature. In many states also, the principal officers of the departments of education are selected directly from the ranks of these state educational associations.

This is the political process. Catholic schools need to be represented in it. Teachers and administrators at the local level must become involved in their communities. Alliances must be formed which will help to further the cause of private schools. At the diocesan levels, consideration should be given to sending full-time lobbyists to their state capitals.

Educators should consider the suggestion that it may be their duty to become involved in the political process on certain issues. Politics, according to some, is inescapably a moral enterprise. Those who participate in it are—whether they know it or not, and whether they admit it or not—moral actors. The word "moral" here does not mean

that what happens in politics is always morally approvable or in accord with what is right. It means only that the questions engaged are questions that have to do with what is right or wrong, good or evil. Whatever moral dignity politics may possess, depends upon its being a process of contention and compromise among moral actors, not simply a process of accommodation among individuals in pursuit of their interests.[48] Catholic educators are not to be interested in legislating morality, but should be interested in the morality of legislation.

These are some of the ways that Catholic parents and educators can respond to the challenges of political decision-making. Good debate will need to take place as plans surface which design interventions into Catholic schools, a place once very private. The Catholic community must be informed, alert, vocal. No one really knows what the outcome of parent choice with public funding will be. The point is that those involved close at hand, parents and educators, must be involved in the decisions which will determine the future educational opportunities of their children.

Notes

22. *Private Elementary and Secondary Education*, Congressionally Mandated Study of School Finance, Vol. 2 (Washington, DC: U.S. Government Printing Office, 1983-421-054:151), p. 25.
23. Ibid., p. 25.
24. Ibid., p. 27.
25. Ibid., p. 33.
26. Marsha Levine and Denis Doyle, "Private Meets Public: An Examination of Contemporary Education," *Meeting Human Needs*, John A. Myer, Editor (Washington, DC: American Enterprise Institute for Public Policy Research, 1982), p. 314.
45. Daniel P. Moynihan, "Senator Moynihan Speaks Out on Aid to Education," *Catholic League for Religious and Civil Rights Newsletter* (August, 1977, Supplement), p. 3.
46. Denis P. Doyle, "Public Funding and Private Schooling," *Private Schools and the Public Good*, Edward M. Gaffney, Editor (South Bend, Ind.: University of Notre Dame Press, 1981), p. 78.
47. Daniel P. Moynihan, "Catholic Tradition and Social Change," Second Annual Seton-Newman Lecture, May 7, 1984 (Washington, DC: USCC Department of Education), pp. 20-21.
48. Richard J. Neuhaus, *The Naked Public Square* (Grand Rapids, Mich.: William B. Eerdman Publishing, 1984), p. 125.

Government Programs

United States Department of Education, Office of Private Education. 1992.
Handbook on serving private school children with federal education programs, 12–13, 78–80. Washington, D.C.

Brief History of Federal Legislation Affecting Private Schools

Historically, the federal government has had a limited role in education. The Bureau of the Census, in "Public Education Finances: 1989–90," reports that the federal government contributed 5.9 percent of funding for elementary and secondary education. The remainder of education funding came from the states (47.5 percent) and localities (46.6 percent). However, U.S. Education Department assistance to the states and leadership in elementary and secondary educational reform remain important to the education system.

In 1965, the Congress passed the **Elementary and Secondary Education Act (ESEA),** which authorized programs to benefit educationally deprived elementary and secondary students living in areas with high concentration of children from low-income families. It also provided grants for many types of supplementary materials and services, including library materials, audiovisual equipment, and remedial services. In theory, private school students were included in these programs in accordance with the principle that all eligible children, whether they attended public or private schools, should be the beneficiaries of federal education programs, but private schools receive no direct aid from these programs. All program funds were granted to the public authorities who were responsible for serving public and private school children on an equitable basis.

Over the years, the act has undergone significant modifications. Chapter 2, a program of local, state, and federal partnership for school improvement, remains one of the major programs authorized under ESEA. New mathematics and science education programs for elementary and secondary school students and teachers were added under the **Dwight D. Eisenhower Mathematics and Science Education Program,** formerly Title II of the Education for Economic Security Act. In 1986, Congress passed the **Drug-Free Schools and Communities Act,** which subsequently became part of ESEA. The last reauthorization of ESEA was in 1988; the act will be considered for reauthorization again in 1993. Largely because of the programs authorized under ESEA, the largest single type of recipient category of federal education aid is the local education agency which received 40 percent of Department of Education outlays in fiscal year 1992 (see exhibit 4).

Many other laws affect elementary and secondary education in the United States. For example, Public Law 94-142, the **Education of the Handicapped Act (EHA),** requires that all handicapped children be given a free, appropriate public education. This act was reauthorized in 1990 under the title **Individuals with Disabilities Education Act (IDEA).** Under IDEA (and EHA before it) a student can attend private school and receive services from the public school for the disabling condition(s) at the same time. Programs administered under this act are administered by the U.S. Department of Education.

The **Asbestos Hazard Protection and Control Act,** passed in 1980, established a program of inspection and detection of hazardous asbestos materials in all public and private elementary and secondary schools. It also provided for loans to assist with the removal or containment of friable asbestos. In 1986, Congress passed the **Asbestos Hazard Emergency Response Act (AHERA),** which called for every school to formulate an asbestos management plan based on visual inspections and building materials sampling by a certified asbestos contractor. In 1984, the **Asbestos School Hazard Abatement Act (ASHAA)** was passed to provide funding to help public and private schools in complying with AHERA. ASHAA was reauthorized in 1990. These programs are administered by the Environmental Protection Agency.

The **Child Care and Development Block Grant Program** was enacted in 1990. This program is administered by the Department of Health and Human Services. The block grants to states support two separate programs. The first program helps states improve and expand child care. The second part of the block grant funds a state-developed program of child care certificates which are distributed to eligible low-income families to pay for child care, including school-age care, in the setting of their choice.

Appendix A
Federal Programs of Other Agencies That Affect Private Schools

1. **Child Nutrition Programs: U.S. Department of Agriculture**
    National School Lunch Program and National School Breakfast Program (P.L. 79-396 and P.L. 89-642): These programs provide assistance to schools that serve meals that meet the dietary requirements of the statute. Through this program, schools provide free or reduced-price meals to students that qualify under the poverty guidelines of the program. Other children may purchase meals at cost.
    Special Milk Program (P.L. 89-642): The Special Milk Program reimburses participating schools for a portion of their expenditures in providing milk to students of all income ranges. Students may qualify for free or reduced-price milk under this program. Schools not participating in other federally-funded food programs may participate.

Exhibit 4—Department of Education Outlays, by Type of Recipient, Fiscal Year 1992.

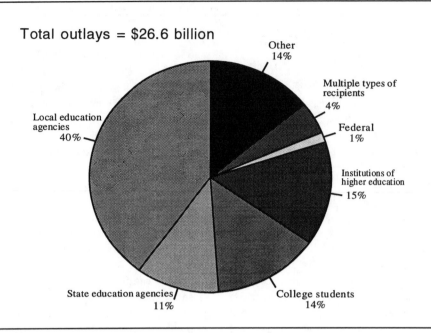

Total outlays = $26.6 billion

Other 14%

Multiple types of recipients 4%

Federal 1%

Institutions of higher education 15%

College students 14%

State education agencies 11%

Local education agencies 40%

For further information on participation, contact your state Child Nutrition Program coordinator.

2. Environmental Hazards: U.S. Environmental Protection Agency

Several programs and statutes under the Environmental Protection Agency (EPA) apply to all schools, K-12.

Asbestos Hazard Emergency Response Act (AHERA): The best known EPA program that applies to schools is the AHERA program. Under AHERA, the EPA requires each elementary and secondary school to perform an inspection for asbestos-containing building material and to prepare an asbestos management plan. The AHERA regulations further require a reinspection of the asbestos-containing building material at least once every three years. For further information, contact your SEA asbestos coordinator or your regional representative. Regional asbestos coordinators are listed at the end of this appendix. EPA has published a manual for reinspection titled A *Guide to Performing Reinspections Under the Asbestos Hazard Emergency Response Act (AHERA)*, publication number EPA 700/B-92/001. Copies are available from EPA, Office of Pollution Prevention and Toxics, Washington, DC 20460; (202) 260-3557.

Asbestos School Hazard Abatement Act (ASHAA): ASHAA provides grants to help schools remove or contain asbestos. The grants are administered through the SEA; the private school allotment is determined by the percentage of private versus public schools in the state. Grants are awarded annually. The regional asbestos coordinator can also provide information about ASHAA.

Lead in Drinking Water: The Lead Contamination Act requires inspection of water coolers and replacement of any water cooler on the list of lead-lined water coolers

prohibited under this act. Also, the statute recommends that the school's water supply be checked for lead level. To receive more information about lead in drinking water, contact the EPA's Drinking Water Hot Line at 1-800-426-4791. For information on water cooler replacement, contact the manufacturer.

Radon: Radon inspection is required in specified geographical areas known to have high concentrations of radon. For information about any requirements that may pertain to your school, contact your state radon office. The brochure *Radon in Schools: Every School Should Take This Simple Test*, publication number EPA 520/1-89-027, contains basic, useful information. If your school tests positively for the presence of radon, consult *Radon Reduction Techniques in Schools: Interim Technical Guidance*, publication number EPA 520/1-89-020. Both publications are available from EPA, Office of Radiation Programs, Office of Research and Development, Washington, DC 20460.

Underground Storage Tanks: Underground storage tanks can pose an environmental hazard if they begin to leak. For further information regarding underground storage tanks, contact EPA's Underground Storage Tank hot line at 1-800-424-9346.

3. Child Care and Development Block Grant of 1990 (CCDBG): U.S. Department of Health and Human Services

The block grant program is administered by each state through a lead agency, the Department of Social Services or a similar agency. Two programs are funded under this program. The first part funds state efforts for expansion and improvement of child care services. States may apply this to preschool or school-age child care.

Religious providers are not eligible for this portion of block-grant funding.

The second part of the block-grant program provides vouchers for low-income parents to purchase preschool or school-age child care. Vouchers can be used at public or private, religious or nonreligious, and center or home-based care. Child care programs that participate must comply with state requirements for registration or licensing. Private providers of preschool or school-age programs should contact the state lead agency. For general information about the CCDBG Act, contact the Child Care Division of the Children's Bureau at the Department of Health and Human Services at (202) 401-9326.

4. U.S. Department of Energy

The *National Energy Conservation Policy Act (1978)* established the Institutional Conservation Program, which provides energy conservation grants to schools and hospitals to improve energy efficiency in buildings and reduce cost. The grant requires a match of funds by the school receiving the grant. Private schools can usually qualify for a lower match requirement because they are not tax supported. For further information and applications, contact your state energy officer.

In addition, the U.S. Department of Energy offers a wide variety of educational programs on the national and regional levels. These programs are offered for preschool through grade 12. The Energy Department also offers graduate programs. For a copy of "U.S. Department of Energy Education Program Catalog," contact the Office of Scientific and Technical Information, P.O. Box 62, Oak Ridge, TN 37831, Attention: Information Services; (615) 576-8401. For more information on specific programs of the U.S. Department of Energy, call the Office of Special Projects at (202) 586-4953.

5. Federal Emergency Management Agency (FEMA)

FEMA provides grants to facilities affected by a major disaster. Private schools are eligible to apply for assistance if they meet the definition of a private, nonprofit organization. FEMA defines a private, nonprofit organization in 44 CFR 206.221 as "any nongovernmental agency or entity that currently has: (1) an effective ruling letter from the U.S. Internal Revenue Service, granting tax exemption under sections 501 (c), (d), or (e) of the Internal Revenue Code of 1954, or (2) satisfactory evidence from the state that the nonrevenue producing organization or entity is a nonprofit one organized or doing business under state law."

6. Other

A variety of discretionary grant competitions are held by other agencies. For information on programs in the fine arts, contact the *National Endowment for the Arts* at (202) 682-5400. The *National Endowment for the Humanities* can be contacted at (202) 786-0438. The contact number for the *National Science Foundation* is (202) 357-5000.

Technology and Chapter 1:[*]
Solutions for Catholic School Participation

Brigham, F. H. 1993. 7, 10, 18, 19. Washington, D.C.: National Catholic Educational Association.

Features of a Good Technology System

◆ **Flexible.** Can be upgraded or added to as time and changing needs require.

◆ **Industry Standards.** Conforms to standard hardware and software specifications to avoid obsolescence.

◆ **Open Architecture.** Allows the addition of third-party materials, as desired.

◆ **Ease of Operation.** Can be operated by existing personnel, not only by highly trained specialists.

◆ **Solid Curriculum.** Helps students learn in a high-interest format.

◆ **Legal Guidelines.** Complies with *Felton* restrictions and the regulations and guidance for the Title 1 program. Technology is one of the few available instructional methods not challenged in court.

Historically, curricular emphasis in Title 1 programs had been placed on remedial and basic skills instruction. The 1988 Amendments to Title 1, however, called for a new focus on critical thinking and higher-order thinking skills within this program. This change in emphasis is becoming a key issue during the current debate on the 1993 reauthorization of the Title 1 program.

Early technology-based curricula provided primarily drill and practice activities for remedial instruction. As adjustments were made in Title 1 instructional theory, similar changes were also being introduced into the technology and courseware. Today, more and more software developers are offering curriculum which places the primary emphasis on developing the thinking skills of students, and secondary emphasis on reinforcing their retention of basic skills information.

Exciting new developments in technology and courseware are incorporating such innovative approaches as multimedia programming. With these programs, students are routinely expected to develop their skills in analytical thinking, inferencing, and even aesthetic evaluation. Many educators believe that this emphasis on metacognition has the potential to make the difference between success or failure for Title 1 students.

Technology Enhances the Classroom Program

Appropriate technology-based curriculum should be selected to correlate directly to the coursework being taught in the regular classroom. Classroom teachers can gain significant insight into the needs and learning patterns of their Title 1-eligible students through involvement with management reports, which effective systems can generate. Educators should look for technology systems which have easy-to-read reports which can be generated by teachers.

Good communication between public school Title 1 personnel and the nonpublic school classroom teacher is essential. Technology can enhance this communication via the telephone or through electronic mail systems. Coordination is critical, in order to provide the best possible educational opportunities for the nonpublic school Title 1 students.

In some cases, through lease arrangements with the public school district, additional student stations may be added to the Title 1 system. If purchased or leased by the nonpublic school, these additional stations allow other students in the school access to the same curriculum, while providing Title 1 students with the extra educational assistance they need. In this way, the program becomes a real link between the Title 1 services and existing classroom work. This is an uncommon approach and must be thoroughly examined by public and nonpublic school legal staff prior to implementation.

Parental involvement is a key component throughout all phases of the Title 1 program, recognizing that home attitudes toward learning have a major impact on student achievement. Technology can provide a sharing opportunity for students and parents to discuss schoolwork.

Programs which allow computers and software to be taken home strengthen this opportunity even further. This type of program eliminates any concern about the supplemental instruction being provided on the nonpublic school premises, and encourages family learning opportunities. These programs may be tied directly to the classroom curriculum, or used as an intensive tutoring project.

Glossary

There are any number of terms with which educators may not be familiar. While not all of these terms were used in this publication, those which educators are most likely to encounter are described here.

Title 1 Terms

Basic Grant—Title 1 allocations given to local school districts based upon a formula derived from the numbers

---

[*]   Editor's note: Chapter 1 of the Elementary and Secondary Education Act (ESEA) is now called Title 1. The text has been updated to reflect this change.

of poor students within the area and the state average per pupil expenditures for public education.

Capital Expenses—Funding available to local public school districts to help offset the additional cost of providing Title 1 services to nonpublic school students after *Aguilar v. Felton.*

Title 1—Title I of the Elementary and Secondary Education Act (ESEA), as amended. Title 1 was last amended in 1988 and [was reauthorized in 1994]. Title 1 provides special supplementary services to educationally disadvantaged children residing in areas with high concentrations of low-income families.

Title 1-Eligible—Public schools which are in an area of high concentration of low-income families are designated as Title 1-eligible schools. Students residing within these school attendance areas who are educationally disadvantaged, based on standards set locally, are Title 1-eligible students.

Concentration Grant—Additional Title 1 funding given to those districts which have the highest concentrations of poor students.

Educationally Disadvantaged—Students who achieve below the minimum standards set by either the district or state and applied in a consistent manner.

***Felton* decision**[*]—U.S. Supreme Court case in 1985 which found the provision of Title 1 services by public school instructional personnel on religious nonpublic school premises unconstitutional.

Technology Terms

CAI—Computer-assisted instruction is a generic term used to describe curriculum material presented via computer.

CD-ROM—Similar in appearance to the CDs used to deliver music, a compact disc read-only-memory is a storage device for data. Information can be accessed quickly and randomly, and a single CD can hold the equivalent of more than 450 floppy discs.

Courseware—Computer software designed for instructional purposes.

Distance Learning—Instructional programs that are transmitted electronically via computer networks, teleconferencing systems, phone lines, television transmission, or satellite systems.

Hardware—Mechanical and electronic equipment associated with computers.

ILS—An *integrated learning system* is an educational computer package combining hardware, courseware, and a management system. Computers are generally linked to form a network. Typically such a system is integrated into existing classroom curriculum and covers many grade levels. The management system produces a variety of reports and can correlate the curriculum to local or state learning objectives.

Interactive—Computer program that allows the user to "communicate" with the computer. The computer reads the user's input and then responds accordingly.

Peripheral—Hardware items, such as modems or printers, which are not required for the basic operation of the computer.

Software—The program which gives the computer hardware its operating instructions. In an educational setting, the software would contain the desired curriculum.

---

[*] Editor's note: In June 1997, another Supreme Court case, the *Agostini* case, reversed the *Felton* decision.

Integrating Technology in Education: The Principal's Role

Gettys, D. J. 1994. *Principal* 73(4):52–53. Alexandria, VA: National Association of Elementary School Principals.

Over the last ten years there have been an increasing number of articles in education journals dealing with the integration of technology and education, most of them directed at teachers. But there has been surprisingly little written about the principal's role in the integration process. Perhaps the lack of attention being paid to the issue of leadership in this area is a clue to why so little progress has been made.

There is no question that technology should be integrated into education. But if this integration is to be taken seriously, what is the role of the principal in the process?

One way to explore this question is to examine a range of principals' viewpoints, ranging from total lack of interest to total participation in the integration process.

1. The Uninvolved Principal

This principal is removed from the integration process for any of several reasons. He or she may believe that technology changes so fast that by the time today's students graduate, what they have experienced in school will serve little purpose.

This principal may also believe, given limited resources, that technology is an area that can be ignored at the elementary level. To those who argue that children need to be exposed to technology before high school, there is a convenient response: "Students learn to drive in high school without prior experience."

Other possible reasons for a principal's lack of interest: impending retirement; preoccupation with attaining other school goals; insecurity about his or her own technological knowledge; and an unwillingness to take risks.

2. The Passive Principal

This principal does not hinder anyone from implementing technology, but does not help teachers seek out ways to use technology as an instructional tool. He or she lacks a vision of how technology can support education, knows little about technology applications, and makes little or no effort to find out.

The principal's lack of encouragement often affects teachers who experience difficulty or failure in attempting to use technology in their classrooms, causing them to abandon their efforts. Worse yet, the next time a teacher wants to try something new, the principal's response is, "Well, you know So-and-So tried that and it didn't work."

3. The Supportive Principal

This principal gives moral and financial support (if resources are available) to staff members and students who express interest in using technology as a learning tool. The principal may not be personally involved in integrating technology, but is enthusiastic about what he or she has seen at conferences or at other schools. There is encouragement of staff participation in meetings, workshops, and seminars on educational technology.

The supportive principal may not know a great deal about the specifics of technology but recognizes the importance of integrating technology and gives it top priority in budget planning. He or she visits regularly with teachers to discuss their needs, and with students to learn about their successes and get their input on future applications.

Supportive principals have good intentions, but because they are not willing to be technologically literate they must rely on their staffs to provide them with the necessary information for making purchasing and application decisions.

4. The Participating Principal

This principal not only encourages teachers and students to view technology as a valuable tool, but incorporates technology into his or her own life and actively participates in the school's technology program. He or she takes the level of support one step further than the supportive principal by being an active user of spreadsheets for budget projections, word processing for communication, and instructional software for presentations.

The participating principal may have brought technology experience into the school or may have "caught the bug" from someone in the building. In either case, the principal uses modeling—one of the most powerful teaching strategies—to help students and staff accept technology for what it is: an everyday set of tools essential to facilitating learning.

Which of these roles do you fill? Let's examine some of the shortcomings of the first three.

To argue that the *uninvolved principal* can be an effective leader in the integration of technology and education is indefensible in this decade. Those who argue that technology changes too rapidly, or that it is not needed in elementary school, should be aware that the thinking and problem-solving processes that can be developed with today's technology transcend any such excuses.

The *passive principal* may reflect administrative preparation programs that focus on school business rather than the visionary aspects of education (Tye 1992). As a result, it is difficult for some principals to envision how technology can help their schools make the leap into the 21st century. But if vision and leadership do not come from the principal, do not expect them to come from the trenches.

As for the *supportive principal*, his or her failure to become personally involved with technology sends the message that, while technology provides useful tools to learn about and use in school, they are not relevant or applicable to the "real world." With the best of intentions, this principal asks teachers and students to become something he or she is not—technologically literate.

How to Be a Participating Principal

If the integration of technology and education is to be successfully pursued, principals must be actively involved and support active involvement by teachers, students, and support staff. Here are some suggestions that may help you become a *participating principal*.

◆ *Identify your present role.* Most principals can easily identify where they fit on the continuum from lack of involvement to total participation. Once you know your current position, you can begin to pinpoint specific attitudes or practices that should be changed or strengthened.

◆ *Be a risk-taker.* Making the transition to active participation involves asking questions, trying new ideas, and making mistakes.

◆ *Find a "tech-buddy."* Network with another principal who is interested in learning more about technology. You can help each other by sharing knowledge and information.

◆ *Find a "tech mentor."* Identify someone in the building who is technologically literate—it could be a teacher or the custodian—and ask for help.

◆ *Ask questions.* In today's technologically saturated world, no one person has all the answers; don't hesitate to ask for information from anyone at any time.

◆ *Attend technology sessions at conferences.* Most education conferences include at least a few sessions on technology applications. You may find some of them overwhelming at first, but eventually you'll begin to understand the terminology and the pieces will start to fall into place.

◆ *Encourage sharing of both successes and failures.* If your staff is going to feel comfortable learning something new, you must convince them that their mistakes are acceptable as part of the learning process.

◆ *Attend beginner classes on word processing and other basic applications.* And strongly encourage your staff to do the same.

◆ *Cultivate support of central office administrators.* As you gather information about technology applications, share it with the central office. Invite district personnel to visit the school to see first-hand the technological accomplishments of students, teachers, and administrators.

◆ *Beware of the "glitz" trap.* It's easy to get caught up in the glamour of technology and feel that you have to buy the latest product. Use some benchmark, such as school goals or district objectives, to measure the value of any piece of technology. If the proposed acquisition does not support a desirable end result, then you probably should not consider purchasing it.

It's important to realize that not all schools integrate technology and education in the same manner. Some schools use technology to empower teachers; others feel more strongly about empowering students; and still others use technology to build new instructional delivery systems.

The important thing is to define what educational needs exist and then determine what technologies can help meet those needs. Who carries out the integration plans may vary depending on the situation, but it is the principal who must provide the visionary leadership.

References

Darling-Hammond, L. "Reframing the School Reform Agenda." *Phi Delta Kappan,* 74 (June 1993).

Maley, D. "How to Keep Up with Technology and Improve Technology Education." *NASSP Tips for Principals* (February 1991).

Snider, R.C. "The Machine in the Classroom." *Phi Delta Kappan,* 74 (December 1992).

Solomon, G. "The Computer as Electronic Doorway: Technology and the Promise of Empowerment." *Phi Delta Kappan,* 74 (December 1992).

Tye, K.A. "Restructuring Our Schools: Beyond the Rhetoric." *Phi Delta Kappan,* 74 (September 1992).

Computers in the School: Working Hard or Hardly Working?

Kabat, M., M. C. Valenteen, and W. Langley. 1991. In *Capital wisdom: Papers from the Principals Academy 1991,* 45–47. Washington, D.C.: National Catholic Educational Association.

In many school environments, principals are dealing with a wide range of computer hardware. Teachers on staff have varied computer experiences and, at times, principals encounter attitudes that are resistant to technology. Some teachers think that computers are a "frill" and just something "more" to teach or use in their classrooms.

Teachers need to understand that computers are central to the technological reality of the 21st century. In order to facilitate an acceptance of this reality, principals need to model the use of technology in their work. Principals must keep their staff from utilizing computers for drill and practice only. Teachers should be guided to the understanding that computers are a tool for teaching and developing higher level thinking skills.

Therefore, administrators should:

◆ develop ongoing staff in-service in the use of computers
◆ demonstrate effective use of computers for the teachers
◆ provide for the integration of computers into the learning process
◆ assume responsibility for the proper evaluation of computer usage in the instructional process

In order to initiate changes in the use of computers, the principal needs to become a role model, facilitator/motivator, and an instructional leader.

Role model

The principal needs to be the primary role model in promoting the use of the computer in the total school program through such activities as producing school bulletins, creating reports, designing birthday banners, and publishing school calendars.

Furthermore, the administrator should personally assess the current level of computer usage in the school, experience the software given to the students, and be an active participant in computer program in-service. Computer literacy is not a requirement just for students and staff.

Facilitator/motivator

In the role of facilitator/motivator, the principal needs to:

◆ provide each teacher with access to a computer
◆ encourage teachers to use release time for computer in-service
◆ compensate teachers who attend computer conferences
◆ solicit volunteers to expedite copying software
◆ allow teachers to take computers home during holiday periods
◆ have teachers share successes and failures at faculty meetings
◆ give awards and compliments for effective computer usage
◆ brainstorm with teachers on how to promote better teaching strategies
◆ develop opportunities for interdisciplinary projects

Instructional leader

As instructional leader in the school, the principal has specific tasks regarding the integration of computer use in the school. The principal needs to clarify the roles and expectations of each staff member. For example, when a computer lab is established in the school under the direction of a coordinator, that role is to be understood by all as one of *coordination*. The coordinator does not assume that which is the direct responsibility of the teacher. The teacher retains the responsibility for teaching the curriculum while using the lab and its technology to facilitate the learning process.

Furthermore, the principal oversees the integration of the computer in the curriculum by requiring teachers to indicate computer use clearly in their lesson planning. Should this lesson planning be vague or inadequate, the principal needs to provide additional training. The principal can also provide assistance and encouragement by requiring teachers to use the computer for such things as record keeping.

The goal is to make sure that the computer becomes an integral tool in the educational process.

Teachers become primary role models for their students by utilizing the computer and demonstrating the proper care of computer equipment and software. Teachers can use computers to reinforce and enrich the educational objectives already taught in their classrooms.

Resources

A number of magazines, journals, and professional organizations provide information and resources to facilitate growth in computer use. Local computer using groups (CUEs) are a great resource for sharing and information. Join a national organization, such as the National Educational Computer Conference (NECC) or the Institute for the Society of Technological Education (ISTE). Subscribe to a couple of magazines from the following list:

> *Microsoft Works in Education*
> *Educational Technology*
> *Electronic Learning*
> *Educational Leadership*
> *Journal of Educational Computing Research*
> *The Computing Teacher*
> *Instructor*
> *Learning*
> *Technology & Learning*
> *Educational Researcher*
> *Teaching & Computers*

Sharing the Light of Faith:
National Catechetical Directory for Catholics in the United States

National Conference of Catholic Bishops. 1979. Nos. 17, 20, 22.
Washington, D.C.: United States Catholic Conference.

Chapter I.*
Some Cultural and Religious Characteristics Affecting Catechesis in the United States

Part B. Science and Technology

17. Science and technology

The rapid progress of science and technology in the United States has put into human hands unprecedented power to reap great benefit for the human race or to sow disaster upon the earth. Men and women have new capacities to attempt to solve some of the persistent problems confronting the people of the entire world; but, they have also new power to deny human dignity and even survival to much of humanity.

Science and technology hold out the promise of improving the world food supply, curing diseases and plagues, and distributing the world's goods more equitably. They can also be used to violate human freedom, curtail human rights, and kill vast numbers of people.

20. Technology

Technological progress has had contradictory effects on life in this country. In becoming highly mobile and migratory, people, especially families, have been drawn further apart; yet, in another sense, the almost universal coverage of modern communications media has brought people into increasingly constant and immediate contact.

22. Communications

The impact of the communications revolution, especially television, is very powerful in the United States. The influx of information is overwhelming. A person living in the United States today is said to be exposed to more information in a week than his or her counterpart of two centuries ago was in a year.

Many find that they are given more information than they can assimilate or evaluate. People need to acquire "literacy" in relation to the new media—that is, they need to grow in their ability to evaluate television and other contemporary media by critical standards which include gospel values.

Yet another threat to the human dignity and privacy is posed by the enormous capacity of computers and data banks to store billions of data indefinitely and retrieve them readily. All manner of records, medical, personal, educational, financial, have now become available to government and even private agencies. Such records can be helpful in many ways and can work to the advantage of many people; yet at the same time the invasion of personal, corporate, and institutional privacy can pose a very real threat to human rights. Solutions lie not only in the physical protection of data banks and in legal sanctions, but also in the moral order of justice.

---

* Editor's note: Chapter notation refers to this excerpt.

The Managing Principal: Using Technology to Share the Power

Schuster, J. 1993. *Electronic Learning* 12(8):26–28, 30.

Technology can make better managers of principals. But it can also help them build a teamwork infrastructure that empowers teachers. Here's the story of one technology-using principal and the remarkable school he helped to create.

It's almost 8 a.m. and Roger Coffee stands off-camera in Webster Elementary School's cramped TV newsroom like a satisfied station manager, arms folded and beaming as 6-year-old Renata Wright faces a camera and reads the weather: "It is chilly this morning." (Never mind that it's Florida.)

Two other girls read the day's school news, fed to them by a small boy flipping cue cards almost as big as he is. Two more girls work the TV cameras of station "WEBS," while a couple of boys twist knobs and flip switches on the complex videotaping, sound-monitoring, and "word-over" editing equipment.

Leaving the newsroom after the eight-minute show, Coffee asks, "Would you ever think this age group would be doing this kind of thing?" Later on he adds, "It's a relief not to be doing the morning announcements anymore and to give them to the students. They have the ability and the power to do them."

That's a telling statement from the principal of the St. Augustine K-5 school, because it reveals something about his management philosophy: Coffee believes in sharing his power, and technology is the means by which he does it.

Empowering teachers is a popular idea these days, and Coffee himself likes to talk about the concept. But if you look at how Coffee has implemented technology in his school, you'll see that, in practice, Webster has gone beyond teacher empowerment. Teamwork isn't just a fashionable phrase; it's the infrastructure of the school.

Webster Elementary, located in St. John's County, is one of five model technology schools set up by the state in 1988 to lead other Florida schools on how to successfully implement technology. To provide that kind of leadership, Coffee says he's tried to create a school environment in which teachers feel "they've been given the opportunity to be a major player," he says, "I would hope that nobody feels like they work for me. I hope they feel like we work together."

The One-Computer Principal

#1 Steal Your Superintendent's Computer

Four years ago, when Jennifer Dolan became principal at Farragut Middle School in Hastings, N.Y., she promptly usurped her superintendent's IBM computer that sat dormant on his desk.

"When I took this job, there was no communication to parents on a regular basis," Dolan says. "One of the first things I was asked to do was improve that communication." Dolan convinced her superintendent that she would use the computer more than he did.

"If I had not had access to a word processor, I would have written to parents differently than I do," Dolan says about her monthly newsletter to parents that she creates using *Q&A*, an integrated works package from Symantec.

"The quality of what I'm sending out has been significantly better because of the technology. And it has given me the opportunity to store [ideas] in a document as I think of them, so it takes less time to do the next month's letter."

Dolan belongs to the school of thought that believes principals must model technology use for their teachers.

"As instructional leaders," Dolan believes, "principals are expected to guide and lead others. You can't supervise somebody properly if you don't know what the range of materials is that the person is working with."

Dolan says that novice technology-using principals should "connect with people who have the skills." For instance, when you're hiring someone to be a library aide, Dolan advises, hire someone who's familiar with technology even if they don't know the library. "You can teach them about the library," she says. "You can't teach them the technology. When we hired a media specialist, knowledge of technology was at the top of my list."

While Dolan's school is still in the early stages of technology integration—they have a couple of IBM labs and non-networked Apple IIs in classrooms—she is an avid technology user at home, where she has a laptop (which she also takes to conferences), a fax/modem, and a scanner. Her entire family uses technology, which Dolan has found to be an important source of support. "The fact that my family has all gotten involved has made learning about technology much easier," she says.

In fact, the biggest issue in getting principals to use technology, Dolan says, is that "it takes a lot of time [to learn]. But principals have to be willing to invest that time to get the paybacks."

—By Isabelle Bruder

Product Information
Q&A, Symantic Corp., Cupertino, Calif., (800) 441-7234

Communication backbone

Building a "team environment" has influenced nearly all of Coffee's management and technology decisions. Case in point: When Webster first received the technology grant, Coffee's number one goal was to improve communication. "We had to have some way of bringing us all together," said Coffee of his 53-person teaching staff that is scattered across three building wings and a dozen "relocatables" (mobile trailers) that sit behind the school. Not surprisingly, teachers had the same idea as Coffee. "When I asked the teachers what was most important to them, they all said communication."

The backbone of Webster's communication system is the schoolwide AppleShare network, which links each teacher to one another and to Coffee. Each teacher has a Macintosh SE (some have LCs) connected to the network; Coffee has a Mac IIcx. The secret weapon on the network is *Microsoft Mail*, an electronic mail package which Coffee credits as being the most important technology in his school.

"With e-mail, teachers don't just share conversation," says Coffee. "They can share lesson plans, entire files of teaching ideas. With a phone, you can't call everyone at once. With e-mail, I can."

Coffee says that communication between him and his staff has improved dramatically since e-mail. "Before, if a teacher wanted to tell me something, she had to catch me in my office, or in the hallway, or write me a note and wait for my reply," he says. "Now, I check my e-mail constantly, and I can reply to teachers sometimes within minutes."

Starving the rumor mill

E-mail also enables Coffee to issue a daily newsletter to update teachers and staff on the day's activities. (Since Webster entertains over 2,000 visitors a year, one of the de facto purposes of the bulletin has been to inform teachers who will be invading their classrooms that day.)

"The bulletin lets teachers know exactly what's going on. When a school has morale problems," Coffee says, "99 percent of the time it's because of a lack of communication. The rumor mill feeds the gossip chain and before you know it, people feel left out of the information loop. The network gives me open communication with teachers."

Technology has given Coffee open communication with parents as well. Coffee sends home a professional-looking weekly newsletter to parents that he creates using *PageMaker*. This spring he's starting a quarterly parent newsletter that relates in-depth what the teaching teams

---

The One-Computer Principal

#2 Get a Simple Data Base

If you think you need fancy equipment and robust networks to effectively start using technology, think again. As Allan Carnes, principal at McDowell Intermediate High School, Millcreek Township, Pa., demonstrates even a data base can make a big difference in managing your school.

Carnes says he would like to have all the computers in the administrative offices networked. He would like to store all student data on his computer so that when a parent calls, he has the information at his fingertips. He would like to have his staff use electronic calendars so he can easily set up meetings.

That's what Carnes would like to do. What he actually does falls more under the category of "back-to-basics." Carnes uses *Microsoft Works* to effectively and efficiently manage some of his more routine, previously time-consuming tasks. Here are a few management tasks Carnes accomplishes in a so-called "low-tech" environment.

◆ *Faculty information.* Carnes uses a data base to track teacher observation schedules—to see when a teacher was last observed, who did it, and when the next observation is scheduled. Tracking inservice is also simpler using a data base, Carnes found. Since there's a mandated number of inservice hours for teachers, Carnes keeps easily updatable records of each teacher's hours.

◆ *Discipline tracking.* Carnes can keep track of student detention, counseling for discipline problems, and more, on a data base. He tracks counselor caseloads, which students are repeat offenders, which teachers refer them to his office. He also easily prints out discipline reports for teachers and parents.

◆ *Student obligation.* If students lose school equipment, they pay a fine. Before student loan information was computerized, the school waited until the end of the year to send out letters telling students and parents about the obligation. Now, by adding a "student obligation" data field in the student data base, the school can easily keep track of who owes money and send out letters on a quarterly basis. Carnes says this eliminates the end-of-the-year rush, and it's proven more effective in getting students to pay up.

◆ *Locker tracking.* Carnes' office uses the computer to keep track of all locker assignments and lock combinations. Any principal knows how often students forget their locker number or combination. The information can be accessed on computer before the student even has a chance to come up with a good excuse.

—*By Judy Schuster*

Product Information
Microsoft Works, Microsoft Corp., Redmond, Wash.; (800) 227-4679

---

are doing at each grade level. "That way, parents with a child in kindergarten have a sense of what their child will be doing in first grade." That kind of prior knowledge helps make for better-informed and more involved parents, Coffee says.

In addition, Webster has a parent-school voice messaging system called the Home-School Communicator, in which parents can call into their kids' teachers' voice mail. They can leave messages for the teacher and pick up messages (such as daily homework assignments). There's also a schoolwide mailbox that provides information on topics such as field trips, assemblies, and the daily lunch menu.

"Before we put in this system, the first calls I would get in the morning were questions about lunch," Coffee says.

Teacher experts

All the hardware and software notwithstanding (Webster has spent about $800,000 over the past four years on technology), here's the most impressive fact about Webster Elementary—it has 100 percent teacher participation in the technology grant. According to an outside evaluator last year, Webster was the only one of the Florida model schools (indeed, it may be the only school in the country) to have achieved that level of teacher involvement.

How did they do that?

"My feeling all along was that technology had to be at the teacher level," says Coffee. "Then it would naturally—and it has—go right down to the student level. I'd been in too many schools where lots of money had been spent on computers that were sitting under dust."

To avoid dust-gathering, Coffee created something he calls the teacher-expert model, a staff development infrastructure that ended up being not only the heart of his technology plan but the soul of his management philosophy.

Here's how the model works: Every teacher is expected to be an expert on some aspect of the technology. It can be as simple as being the laserdisc player expert or as sophisticated as being the copyright law expert. The experts then share their knowledge with fellow teachers, formally in after-school workshops (two times a week) and informally via e-mail.

What Coffee has built through this model is a professional staff of knowledgeable technology users who collectively understand every aspect of the system. It's the essence of a cooperative team. "The only way to run an organization is to use the many talents of the team," says Coffee, who employed team teaching even before the technology grant. "Anything that goes on in our school works toward the common goals of the system. In our school it's the 'we' thing."

The teacher-expert model has generated some interesting side benefits. For one, Coffee saved about $27,000 in training fees the first year alone, because the teacher-experts were training each other. (Also, teachers can take their computers home, a staff development strategy that saves countless dollars in inservice training.)

Two, Webster teachers have become experts outside their school. They are regular presenters at regional and national conferences. And each summer Webster teachers (not administrators) train over 400 of their fellow teachers

---

The One-Computer Principal

#3 Walk Softly & Carry a Big Keyboard

When students at Farragut Middle School get sent to the principal's office for disruptive behavior, they find themselves telling their stories to a computer.

A new form of artificial intelligence? Hardly. Behind the computer screen is principal Jennifer Dolan, quietly typing the students' stories as they speak.

There's a method to her madness. As the children watch their words appear on the screen, Dolan encourages them to think through how those words conform to what actually happened. Not surprisingly, the students refine their statements and suggest changes to the document.

"I'm a visual learner," says Dolan, "so I know seeing your words on a computer screen helps." The process, she believes, takes away some of the anxiety about "going to the principal's office" and gives kids a way to work through their emotions to arrive at a more rational view of the conflict.

Once the conflict has been defined to the satisfaction of both parties, Dolan and the students agree on a behavioral contract. The kids watch again as Dolan types up a set of expectations. If she writes something that either student doesn't agree with, she quickly makes editing changes. ("I'm a very fast typist," Dolan admits. "I'm no stranger to office work.")

Editing the contract with input from the students "shows them that I'm flexible and willing to work with them to resolve the conflict," says Dolan. It also provides a model for the students on how to negotiate and compromise.

When the contract is finished, Dolan prints out a copy then and there, and everybody signs. The immediacy of producing the contract, she believes, is a key factor in getting students to conform to the expectations.

"What most people do [with conflict resolution] is have a routine verbal structure where one child agrees not to do this and one agrees not to do that," says Dolan. "With middle school [students], there's a different sense of commitment involved when you get something on paper and someone signs their name to it. The immediacy of going from talking about something to having a printed copy in you hand; it's unequaled. The issues become so much clearer for people."

—J.S.

---

from across Florida on integrating technology into their classrooms.

St. John superintendent Gary Mathews believes that the teacher-expert model embodies "a new paradigm of leadership. I think they've set a model that we'd like to emulate throughout the state," Mathews says.

Streamlining paperwork

Coffee may be an unusual principal in some aspects, but in one respect he is like every one of his colleagues: He hates the paperwork associated with his job. From his command-post office, Coffee uses technology to streamline a variety of paper-based management tasks, including:

◆ *Forms:* Coffee creates many of the school's forms (field trip requests, letters to parents, and so on) with *Microsoft Works* and puts them on the network. Teachers download the forms, fill them out, and send them back, all via the network. Not only is this method quicker, it has reduced errors.

◆ *Scheduling:* Coffee uses *MacDraw* to set up schedules for classes such as physical education, music, and art. "You don't need a sophisticated scheduling program for that," he says, "just a graphical depiction of the time slots."

◆ *Building schematics:* Again, Coffee uses *MacDraw* to develop schematics for fire drill cards showing exit routes by each classroom. He also uses schematics to keep current the school's facility surveys.

◆ *Student data:* Main student data is housed at the district office (to which Coffee is connected via a Unisys terminal in his office). At Webster, they use *FileMaker Pro* to download student data from the district office and add information they want (for instance, parents' daytime phone numbers).

Coffee strongly believes that he can't expect his teachers to be technology users if he isn't one himself. "It's a proven fact school administrators have to be out in front, not only leading, but pushing and pulling," he says. "If we don't believe in technology ourselves and feel comfortable with it, we can't expect our teachers to use it."

Teachers as curriculum developers

On every Webster teacher's hard drive resides *Microsoft Works*, *PageMaker*, *Print Shop*, *MacDraw*, *MacPaint*, and *HyperCard*, to list a few titles. All the teachers have learned to use the programs to create their own curriculum materials.

"It's no longer canned empowerment, where curriculum is given to teachers and they deliver it," says Coffee. "Now, teachers have the power to shape instruction, using materials that they've created. It's allowed them to meet the needs of a lot of students they wouldn't have been able to." As a result, Webster teachers "truly feel like professionals," says Coffee.

Don't be fooled into thinking, however, that teachers immediately bought into the technology. In fact, many of them fought it.

Scarlet Harriss, who teaches one of the two gifted classes at Webster, says at first each beep of the computer scared her. The many meetings and training sessions were exhausting. "We all griped. Let me tell you, we griped: 'I can't believe he's making us do this. Doesn't he know we've got kids to teach?'" Harriss says. "But let me tell you, it paid off."

Now she says that without her computer she'd probably quit. "I'm not saying that jokingly. I mean, my whole life is on these disks. Just like you can't describe how much you love somebody, you can't describe how much this does for you."

Coffee believes that teachers' willingness to learn depends on a flexible environment in which "they feel they can take a risk. Hopefully, we have created that atmosphere," he says.

As for Coffee's plans for the future (the grant ends next year), he wants to share what he understands about technology with colleagues who have a leg up on him on other aspects of school reform. This year he's begun an exchange with a Kentucky principal who runs a non-graded elementary school, something Coffee is interested in learning about. "First thing, though," he says, "I've got to get him on the Internet."

Coffee says he's "at the age where I should probably think about retiring, but I'm too excited about everything that's going on." He pauses, "Have you ever had the feeling that things are predestined in your life? One little thing happens, then another, and before you know it, you're in the middle of something that feels absolutely right."

Product Information

AppleShare Network, Apple Computer, Inc., Cupertino, Calif.; (408) 996-1010

FileMaker Pro, HyperCard, MacDraw, MacPaint, Claris Corp., Santa Clara, Calif.; (800) 747-7483

Home School Communicator, Assessment Technology, Inc., Tallahassee, Fla.; (904) 893-8258

Microsoft Mail, Microsoft Works, Microsoft Corp., Redmond, Wash.; (800) 227-4679

PageMaker, Aldus Corp., Seattle, Wash.; (206) 628-4511

Print Shop, Broderbund Software, Novato, Calif.; (800) 521-6263

Finance and Development

Finance and Development in Catholic Schools

Joel Konzen, SM

Finance and Catholic school principals

Financial management and development are twin components in a single enterprise for preserving Catholic schools: assuring the viability of a school's essential activities. Financial management entails providing the funding needed to accomplish the necessary elements of the school's operation. Development encompasses planning for the adequacy of school resources. The principal needs to be prepared to take ownership and leadership in both of these tasks. Together financial management and development ensure the existence of the school and the continuation of its religious and academic mission.

Acquiring and managing the school's financial resources may be the least appealing and the most frightening and mysterious of tasks for which Catholic school principals are responsible. People aspiring to lead Catholic schools are often attracted to administration because they view it as a ministry that promotes the faith development of students, parents, and faculty (Ciriello 1993). It is common for Catholic school administrators to feel less than confident in their financial expertise (Ciriello 1991, 1992) and to bemoan their dearth of preparation for overseeing the fundamental business aspects of a school. Becoming the chief administrator of a school, nevertheless, often necessitates designing, managing, and balancing a six- or seven-figure school budget. This can be the occasion for some of the most challenging, immediate, and critical learning an aspiring or new principal is likely to encounter.

Successful handling of financial management and development responsibilities requires the principal to implement a variety of skills in both leadership and management. Bryk, Holland, Lee, and Carriedo (1984) found that effective Catholic schools had, among other qualities, principals who

recognized and dealt effectively with the complex demands of their school situations. These principals were aware of and capable of addressing the diverse conditions in which their schools were expected to thrive.

Leadership behaviors which directly influence a Catholic school's viability and growth include

- establishing a vision,
- maintaining qualitative and quantitative goals,
- cultivating responsible leadership within the school,
- inculcating cooperation and productivity,
- acting decisively, and
- realizing a comprehensive plan for school improvement.

Financial management

Financial management entails two things: first, knowing the school's present and future needs and, second, mapping a strategy for funding all of those needs. It requires the principal to work according to existing policies of the diocese and in conjunction with the school's board, pastor (in parish schools), finance committee, development committee, in-school business personnel (where available), and diocesan administrators.

Burke (1984) states that "budgeting is the key to financial control" (p. 22). Beginning with a clear understanding of the mission and philosophy of the school the budgeting process seeks to establish the cost-per-pupil of operating the school and then to project the income for meeting those costs. The per-pupil costs should accurately reflect all the expenses involved in providing the school program. The principal undertakes the budgeting process in concert with an established finance committee of the parish or the school board. In parish schools, the pastor approves the final budget. In non-parish schools approval is granted by the finance committee of the school's governing group. In both cases, the principal needs to have sufficient input into the budgeting process to represent the perceived and documented needs of all school programs.

Once the budget is determined, the principal ensures that the various budgeted funding goals are met and that spending does not exceed prescribed outlays. If the principal is not successful in these two primary responsibilities, budgeted programs and personnel necessary to the school's mission will be in jeopardy.

The pastor and/or the finance committee are involved in regularly monitoring progress in maintaining an approved budget. They will want to see the budget steered along a predictable and healthy course. The principal who welcomes the assistance of members of the finance committee with expertise in financial planning and management (accountants, bankers, consultants, or corporate managers) will be at an advantage in achieving financial objectives.

A principal's insistence on systematic procedures in accounting and on acknowledging every transaction assures both the school's governing entity and the public that all resources are respected. Frequently when prudence is neglected in this area and money is mishandled, the result is a crisis in confidence, and other funding is either withheld or withdrawn. Loss of trust in the administrator's business management skills often signals impending decline for a school.

Many dioceses through their business offices are prepared to lend assistance to principals. Diocesan officials prefer helping neophyte principals with financial management rather than coming to the rescue of schools in trouble which have not availed themselves of existing resources. If no organized orientation to financial management is offered, a new principal should inquire which diocesan personnel might be called upon for help and advice. Principals should not hesitate to request assistance as needed.

Special expense considerations

Certain items deserve particular attention because of the role they play in determining the size as well as the year-to-year predictability of the annual budget.

Salaries and Benefits

Labor costs make up the greatest part of any school's budget. Some questions to consider in budgeting these costs are

- What is your long-term objective or strategy regarding compensation?
- How does your compensation package compare with other Catholic, non-public, and public schools?
- Is the salary scale in use effective or in need of revision?
- Are there compensation issues requiring attention beyond the standard scales and benefit provisions?
- Are there personnel assignments to be funded for the first time?
- How is all this addressed in this budget?

Additional Personnel

Months before the annual budget is actually approved, discussions should take place (with pastor, board, committees, and councils) about the need for additional personnel and the likelihood of being able to acquire them. Agreement should be reached on the additional personnel before the preliminary budget is drawn up.

Financial Aid

If the school has a plan for allocating tuition reductions or other grants-in-aid, a total amount of aid available and a formula for its distribution will need to be determined. A budget cannot be balanced if this figure is allowed to expand during the course of the school year. The principal will do well to rely on the services of a screening company or committee, which recommends aid amounts according to school-established criteria for all applicants. Further reasonable but firm deadlines and procedures should be in place for the dispensing of funds.

Books and Materials

Costs of replacing and purchasing new instructional materials, especially student texts, should be staggered systematically over a number of years. Ideally the outlay for these materials would be roughly comparable each year. General directions regarding appropriate review criteria and suggested replacement schedules are often provided by staff and diocesan guidelines and/or from accrediting agencies. The principal needs to work closely with the school board and professional staff to develop local guidelines to ensure a consistent process for addressing curriculum changes and their consequent materials changes.

Depreciation

An amount is normally included in the budget under the heading "Depreciation." Its purpose is to fund major repair and eventual replacement of facilities. Ideally, this revenue will be set aside in a separate plant fund or capital improvement fund. Usually, a percentage of the entire budget is designated as the depreciation amount.

Utilities

Local and extenuating circumstances (such as weather and natural disasters) from year to year can make utility costs quite volatile. Increasing use of technology in the administration and instructional aspects of the school also can significantly affect utility costs. Wise anticipation and prudent budgeting are called for in this area.

Sources of funding

Addressing Catholic school governance and finance issues for the National Congress: Catholic Schools for the 21st Century, Hocevar (1991) writes:

> Catholic schools have been resourced and financed in numerous ways by the Catholic community. These sources include: the payment of tuition; the contributions of parishioners for their parish school; the contributed salaries and services of . . . religious and lay [faculty]; diocesan, religious community, and parish services and subsidies; short-range fundraising; long-range development efforts; the contributions of Catholics, concerned citizens, and the business and corporate community to diocesan endowment campaigns; federal and state aid in the form of transportation, special educational

services, textbooks, and other opportunities; and the volunteer services of a host of people whose belief in Catholic education has both inspired and supported the efforts of the schools (pp. 10–11).

The majority of funding for schools continues to be derived from tuition. Ideally, the enrollment and corresponding tuition payments would satisfy the school's operations budget, so that raised funds could be applied to special improvement projects and replacement of equipment and facilities. This is often not possible, however, because of faltering enrollments or a conscious decision to keep tuition at a level affordable to the broadest possible range of students and parents. As a result, most Catholic schools continue to rely on additional funding sources—subsidy, annual fundraising activities, endowment/investment, or a development program —to meet some operational costs.

Tuition

Since every dollar earned through enrollment is a dollar that does not have to be raised, the first order in tuition management is assuring that enrollment exceeds or, at the very least, meets the number projected. In a very real sense, recruitment of new students is a primary element of financial stability and, as such, is one of the principal's most pressing responsibilities.

Thus, it is incumbent upon the principal to see that attention be given to retaining enrolled students. Monetti-Souply (1990) offers the following recruitment and retention strategies:

■ providing welcome and orientation processes,
■ monitoring carefully students' academic progress,
■ offering counseling and advising services,
■ responding to parent concerns in a timely and professional fashion,
■ developing leadership opportunities for students,
■ maintaining varied and appropriate student activities,
■ reviewing regularly the curriculum to be sure it is serving the school's students well, and
■ conducting exit interviews with departing students and their families.

The principal, working with the financial advisory body, determines fair policies for collecting all funds owed to the school and establishes a process for dealing with postponed or waived payments. Sometimes schools contract with a company which acts as the collector of its tuition monies (see end of article). Consistency in tuition collection is more important than the specific method employed. Principals who fail to collect owed funds abet the school's financial problems by sending a message that stipulated payments are not acutely needed—a premise that will prove lethal when the school seeks additional funds.

Subsidy

Sponsoring parishes often allocate some operating monies to their parish schools. Ideally, this support is seen by the parish to be a ministerial service provided its parishioners and others interested in a religiously based education. Often subsidy is the factor allowing the school to remain viable while charging a reasonable tuition. Dioceses, too, sometimes supply selected schools with funds for operations. Schools sponsored by religious communities may receive support through community contributions or the contributed services (less than full salaries) of community members at the school.

In the last twenty years, this form of funding has declined precipitously. Parish subsidy of Catholic schools has decreased an average of roughly 1 percent a year nationwide since 1973—from more than half a school's budget to 34 percent in 1991 (Harris 1992, Kealey 1992). Discretionary funds for all church entities are being stretched to address concerns which were unheard of or of a lower priority a generation ago. Hence, principals who rely too heavily on subsidy for bridging the gap between revenue and costs restrict the school's vision to what such limited and threatened support can finance.

Fundraisers

Catholic schools have long epitomized the "every-penny-counts" operation that misses no opportunity for raising funds through sales, games, or socials. In many schools, the place of bingo or an annual festival which generates significant revenue is regarded as essential. Such activities usually offer the school a social benefit, as well, by uniting parents, students, and others in garnering support.

But fundraisers are not without their drawbacks. They require a constant resupply of dedicated volunteers. In all but the largest events, such as an auction or ball, fundraisers secure roughly the amount of money produced the year before. Thus, while the fundraiser is, depending on the quality of volunteer help, a somewhat stable source of funding, it is often unable to promise meaningful growth in revenue to the school.

Endowment and Foundation Income

Schools which have been able to establish an endowment, or which derive income from a diocesan or other locally established foundation, meet some of their expenses through accrued interest paid according to a set formula. The establishment of this type of funding source, based on invested principal contributed to a trust, is the sign of a mature development effort in a school or locale.

Although amounts from foundation and endowment income sources are small in the early years of their growth, they are extremely stable. An endowment for the individual school, or participation in a diocesan educational foundation, is a recommended goal for every Catholic school. These revenues are protected against the shifts in funding brought about by local economic conditions, enrollment declines, church personnel changes, and fundraising failures. Kealey (1992) reports that 32 percent of Catholic elementary schools had established endowments by 1991.

Development

Of all the Catholic school's funding sources, a development program has the greatest potential for expanding the school's resources. It is a renewable funding source with the capacity to grow annually, even as subsidy sources may be in decline. Because it seeks funding from all those who can afford to contribute to the mission of Catholic schools, it allows the schools to keep tuition levels lower than would be possible relying on traditional income providers.

The Chicago consulting firm of Gonser, Gerber, Tinker, and Stuhr defines *development* as the "total effort on the part of the institution to

- analyze its educational or programmatic philosophy and activities,
- crystallize its objectives,
- project them into the future, and
- take the necessary steps to realize them" (Gonser et al. 1977, p. 4).

A successful development program in a Catholic school is likely to include

- a strategic or long-range plan that is drawn up by the school's board, managed by the principal, and revised at regular intervals;
- an enrollment and marketing strategy managed by the principal and a committee;
- an annual giving campaign involving mail, telephone, and face-to-face (direct) solicitation of the school's potential contributors: graduates, parents, grandparents, businesses, and friends of Catholic education;
- securing of planned gifts through such instruments as wills, trusts, and insurance policies for the sake of establishing and enlarging an endowment or foundation;
- the assistance of development professionals: a paid consultant, a member of the school's staff, or both;
- the empowerment of the school board for the purpose of skilled involvement in moving the direction of the school's plans and advancement programs;
- a comprehensive program of public relations which informs the school's constituents and larger community of the school's essential mission and the steps it is taking to realize that mission.

A primary responsibility of the principal, after having become well-informed about the details and possibilities of development programs, is to educate everyone concerned with the school—including pastor, board, financial advisers, faculty, parents, and students—about the role this mechanism can play in securing the future of the Catholic school. Once others are aware of how development works and what it can provide, the principal can plan aggressively for implementing the various components.

Development and fundraising are distinct entities with different purposes. Fundraising efforts often entail a series of finite events. Schools whose energies are directed primarily to fundraisers such as bingo, raffles, suppers, and candy sales usually rely on volunteer leadership and coordination for handling these events. Principals approve plans, attend events, and sometimes designate the proceeds for various needs.

A development program, on the other hand, is an ongoing, systematic effort that requires a greater commitment from the principal. Some larger Catholic schools may have an administrator whose chief responsibility is to oversee the development program; that official is generally called "president."

The role of the principal in schools without designated personnel concerned primarily with development is

- to see that a program is initiated,
- to secure capable volunteer and/or funded personnel,
- to educate all at the school about the aims and practice of development,
- to (work with a committee) to devise and implement a workable development plan (Konzen 1991).

In schools with ambitious development efforts, it is not unrealistic to project that about 40 percent of a principal's time will be spent in development-related tasks. Most principals will find that the only way they can make such a block of time available is by delegating some leadership responsibilities to others in the school. Thus, in order to advance the goals of comprehensive development, the principal may be forced—and this is not necessarily bad—to ask: Can someone on my staff handle other aspects of administration such as scheduling substitute teachers, managing attendance and health concerns, sharing in the handling of discipline matters, assisting in classroom observations, preparing weekly schedules, or being responsible for liturgy and lunchroom supervision?

Unless a principal is convinced of the need for considerable personal involvement in development projects and is willing to create time for managing the development effort, the program will be doomed to remain an add-on that is not integral to advancing the school's mission properly and profoundly. Principals can be assisted significantly by appointing a paid or volunteer development officer for the school. This person oversees much of the planning and actual operation of development efforts, thus freeing the principal to concentrate on setting goals, recruiting effective volunteers, energizing the board and its committees, and making personal calls on those who can help the school realize its development objectives.

The principal (along with the development officer, where one has been appointed) works in conjunction with a development committee. This committee can be an independent committee of carefully selected volunteers, a standing committee of the school's board, or a combination of these two groups. Together with the principal, the committee establishes annual goals and comes to agreement on methods to attain the goals. It is the principal's responsibility to lead in executing the group's plans and to report regularly on progress (La Riviere 1993).

Various publications exist which may assist principals in learning more about development's purposes and methods. Many of them are listed in the resources. In addition to the annual development conference held in conjunction with NCEA's Easter-week convention, conferences and symposia for Catholic school leaders are conducted by other sponsors throughout the year. Attendance at an NCEA convention may be the best opportunity for principals to become acquainted with the considerable resources available in development.

Technical assistance

A principal must press as persistently as necessary for the technical equipment needed to handle the school's business affairs professionally. Good computer software managed by a knowledgeable professional will aid a principal considerably in financial management and development. Keeping accurate records of incoming and outgoing monies is an absolute necessity for monitoring the budget and forecasting needed revenue. As the development program becomes more sophisticated, computer software can assist in tracking and analyzing giving patterns.

The principal sees, too, that, if financial record-keeping is not otherwise available from existing parish administrative staff or school personnel, an individual with appropriate time and expertise undertakes the bookkeeping required for sound fiscal conduct.

Consulting services are also proving to be valuable resources for Catholic schools, especially as they forge long-range plans and move energetically toward campaigns in annual support, capital improvements, and planned giving. The principal, working with the development committee, does well to become acquainted with and to weigh carefully the advantages and disadvantages of incorporating such services.

Public relations and the principal

Public relations efforts go hand in hand with successful development programs. Catholic schools in many parts of the country are the "best-kept secrets" in the local area. Excellent programs go unacknowledged and unappreciated by the surrounding community because the school has not carefully crafted a systematic program of communication about itself. No educational institution has ever failed because of over-saturating a community with appropriate information concerning the merits of its programs. In some areas of the country professional marketing programs for Catholic schools are producing enrollments increased by 10 percent or more.

Public relations asks

- What do we want people to know?
- Who should hear the message about our school?
- How will we go about getting the message to them?

As the school's chief spokesperson, the principal uses every means available to inform the public about a school's history, mission, and current offerings and events. Unless their children attend the school, most people in parishes have little knowledge of the particular features of a parish school. Others in the community have even less idea of what the typical, local Catholic school does or whom it serves. Simply put, seats will go vacant as long as a school does not inform the public why those seats should be occupied. Every empty seat is lost revenue for the school and a missed opportunity for a youngster.

The principal should see that a marketing committee is established, either as an adjunct to the board or development committee or as a free-standing group. Members of the committee assist the principal in designing and implementing a thorough plan for informing all publics about the school, including parish members, parents of potential students, the business community, and the community at large. The marketing committee also takes responsibility for implementing a retention program at the school, tracking patterns of enrollment and reasons for withdrawal and then seeking to address weaknesses likely to result in removal of enrolled students.

The need for planning and evaluation

Just as Catholic colleges and universities have for decades engaged in strategic planning to ensure the academic quality and financial health of their institutions, so, too, Catholic elementary and secondary schools are beginning to initiate professional and systematic planning for and continual evaluation of their operations.

In her book on school planning Stone (1993) suggests, "Planning activities in independent schools respond to both the *need* and the *desire* to engage in strategic thinking," which "combines both creative and analytic processes, leads to the definition of broad guidelines for future direction (both new and continuing), and to specific actions to implement and assess results" (p. 10). This "strategic thinking" is basic to preparing a school for sound financial management and for development programs. This planning must take place within the context of the school's defined mission. Peter Drucker's famous quip, "If you don't know where you're going, any plan will do" (Bryson 1990, p. 93), is a reminder that unplanned evolution may bring devastating results.

Every Catholic school has a distinctive mission —one that is, ideally, updated regularly and propounded aggressively within the school community. This unique mission shapes even the subtlest notion of where the school needs to be heading and should be the basis for all planning in the school. Bryson (1990) says "developing the [mission] statement begins a habit of focusing a discussion on what is truly important" (p. 97). It is the primary mission, often expressed in simple but compelling terms, which helps school planners to focus on the most important, and hence most urgent, aspects for attention and improvement.

Vaill (1984) says that in "high-performing systems" (p. 85) members have "pictures in their heads which are strikingly congruent" (p. 86). Such organizations usually have a universally understood and agreed-upon mission. Consequently, all who are responsible for growth and direction refer to these common "pictures" for some avenue to the future.

The effective Catholic school principal takes care to assemble a group of cooperators—school board members, volunteer leadership, and school staff—who can find satisfaction in the "pictures" of where the school is headed and can energetically assist in realizing the design proposed in the school's plan. It is essential that the school's board be composed of people who bring real skills in leadership, analysis, and business. The board exists to provide advice and movement *not* ordinarily available from staff or assigned personnel. Although board members' goals should be congruent with those of the school's designated leadership, their backgrounds should not mimic those of people already at work in the school.

Once the plan is formulated, regular revisions are necessary, as is evaluation to chart the success of implementing the plan. At least once a year, a formal evaluation of progress on meeting long-range objectives should be conducted. Generally, this takes place within the context of the school board, with input sought from faculty, parents, and the public. Surveys and marketing studies can be helpful in determining whether changes brought about through planned improvements are achieving the desired effects.

Resources in print

In addition to texts mentioned elsewhere, the following resources can serve to acquaint a principal with many of the aspects entailed in finance and development responsibilities:

■ Catholic School Management's bimonthly newsletter for administrators which often treats topics related to the fiscal concerns of principals.
■ Planning and management guides: local bookstores and college libraries are brimming with texts that outline basic principles and practices for managers and can be adapted to the Catholic

school setting. Especially helpful are publications geared toward nonprofit organizations.

- Research studies and statistical reports published through NCEA, in NCEA's *Momentum* magazine, independently as doctoral dissertations or as scholarly articles (available through electronic search services), or by the Council for the Advancement and Support of Education (CASE). NCEA publishes updated statistics on Catholic elementary and secondary school finances every two years.

- Publications from professional organizations: NCEA's Fastback series on many aspects of development; CASE's monthly *Currents* and topical treatments of public relations, giving campaigns, and other development concerns; the National Center for Nonprofit Boards' newsletter and books; planning and accounting guides from the National Association of Independent Schools; and *Ideas and Perspectives*, a newsletter from Independent School Management.

- *Effective Funding of Catholic Schools* by Thompson and Flynn (1988), which offers research and methodology on increasing the extraordinary funding (beyond tuition and subsidies) for Catholic schools.

- *Building Better Boards* by Lourdes Sheehan, RSM (1990), and other board-related materials from NCEA.

Quality as the touchstone

A reliable starting point for a beginning principal is to be certain that the education offered at the school is worth at least as much as the tuition charged. While a host of recent studies (Bryk 1984, Chubb 1990, Coleman 1987, Yeager 1985) have confirmed that Catholic schools in general offer an environment and academic preparation in many ways preferable or superior to that in other schools with a greater per-pupil cost, it cannot be assumed that every Catholic school automatically delivers such premium performance for its students. The principal, as well as the school board and, as applicable, the pastor, serve as the guardians and constructive critics to ensure that the school is offering a Catholic education of the highest quality to all its students. Such deliberative action goes a long way to guarantee that funds sought in the name of and on behalf of the school support a worthy educational opportunity. Further, careful stewardship demands that all resources be treated fairly, ethically, and imaginatively to enhance the mission of the institution.

Assuring quality experiences in all aspects of the school's operations will easily attract the cooperators and volunteers necessary for success in finance and development efforts. The principal who is pursuing a vision of excellence for all the school's features has no time for lamenting the lack of interest or support from one constituency or another because that principal will be busy creating whatever is lacking and, in the process, creating the means whereby the school will not just survive but will become exemplary.

Reflection Questions

1. What resources will you need to prepare yourself and others to understand and lead in Catholic school financial management and development?

2. In order to construct and maintain the school budget, how will you see the activities of financial management and development as complementary?

3. How can working with finance and development committees enhance the principal's budgeting abilities?

4. How can the variety of funding sources be tapped for availability in the school's operations?

5. Why is a development program unlikely to succeed unless others at the school are sympathetic to its aims and methods?

6. Why is delegation of duties often important to principals embarking on a development program in their schools?

7. Principals need not and should not "go it alone" in the areas of financial management and development. Explain.

8. How is public relations pivotal in maintaining the viability of and engendering growth in Catholic schools?

9. What is the role of student recruitment and retention in advancing a financially healthy operation for Catholic schools?

10. A principal without a comprehensive long-range plan for the school is apt to feel vulnerable and unsteady. Explain.

11. In what sense is *quality* the umbrella under which so many of the school's plans and hopes are assembled?

Resources

Brigham, F. H. 1993. *United States Catholic elementary and secondary schools 1992–93*. Washington, D.C.: National Catholic Educational Association.

Bryk, A. S., P. B. Holland, V. E. Lee, and R. A. Carriedo. 1984. *Effective Catholic schools: An exploration*. Washington, D.C.: National Catholic Educational Association.

Bryson, J. M. 1990. *Strategic planning for public and nonprofit organizations*. San Francisco: Jossey-Bass Publishers.

Burke, R. 1984. *Elementary school finance manual*. Washington, D.C.: National Catholic Educational Association.

Bushman, E. M., and G. J. Sparks, eds. 1990. *The Catholic school administrator: A book of readings*. Portland, Ore: Catholic Leadership Co.

Catholic schools face fiscal facts. 1993. Editorial. *America* 169(18):3.

Chubb, J. E., and T. M. Moe. 1990. *Politics, markets, and America's schools*. Washington, D.C.: The Brookings Institution.

Ciriello, M. J. 1991. *Catholic principals' survey concerning their role and the future of Catholic education in the Archdiocese of Boston*. Boston: Catholic Schools Office.

———. 1992. *Attitudes of Catholic school administrators of the Diocese of Honolulu concerning their role and the future of Catholic education on the Islands*. Honolulu, Hawaii: Catholic School Department.

Ciriello, M. J., and J. J. Convey. 1993. Catholic higher education and diocesan school departments: Collaborating to strengthen leadership. *Current Issues in Catholic Higher Education* 14(1):34–39.

Coleman, J. S., and T. Hoffer. 1987. *Public and private high schools: The impact of communities*. New York: Basic Books.

Donaldson, F. 1991. *Catholic school publications: Unifying the image*. Washington, D.C.: National Catholic Educational Association.

Gary, B. S. 1986. *Seeking foundation grants*. Washington, D.C.: National Catholic Educational Association.

Gonser, Gerber, Tinker, and Stuhr. 1988. On Development. Chicago.

Guerra, M. J. 1993. *Dollars and sense: Catholic high schools and their finances 1992*. Washington, D.C.: National Catholic Educational Association.

Harris, J. C. 1992. Is the American Catholic Church getting out of the elementary school business? *Chicago Studies* 31(1):81–92.

———. 1994. Catholics can too afford schools. *America* 170(8):22–24.

Hocevar, R. 1991. Catholic school governance. In *Catholic school governance and finance*. Washington, D.C.: National Catholic Educational Association.

Kealey, R. 1992. *United States Catholic elementary schools and their finances 1991*. Washington, D.C.: National Catholic Educational Association.

Konzen, J. 1991. The role of the principal in development. Washington, D.C.: National Catholic Educational Association.

La Riviere, A. 1993. *The development council: Cornerstone for success*. Washington, D.C.: National Catholic Educational Association.

McCormick, M. T. 1994. Close, but no cigar. *America* 170(8):24–26.

Monetti-Souply, M. 1990. *A year-round recruitment and retention plan*. Washington, D.C.: National Catholic Educational Association.

Oldenburg, R. L. 1991. *Conducting the phonathon*. Washington, D.C.: National Catholic Educational Association.

Peterson, J. 1990. *How to hire a development officer: From defining needs to ensuring successful performance*. Washington, D.C.: National Catholic Educational Association.

Sheehan, L. 1990. *Building better boards*. Washington, D.C.: National Catholic Educational Association.

———. 1991. Governance. In *Catholic school governance and finance*. Washington, D.C.: National Catholic Educational Association.

Stangl, A. 1990. *The one-person development office*. Washington, D.C.: National Catholic Educational Association.

Stone, S. C. 1987. *Strategic planning for independent schools*. Boston: National Association of Independent Schools.

———. 1993. *Shaping strategy: Independent school planning in the '90s*. Boston: National Association of Independent Schools.

Tedesco, J. 1991. *Catholic schools and volunteers: A planned involvement*. Washington, D.C.: National Catholic Educational Association.

Thompson, L. A., and J. A. Flynn. 1988. *Effective funding of Catholic schools*. Kansas City, Mo.: Sheed and Ward.

Tracy, M. 1990. *Steps in direct solicitation: Preparation, presentation, and follow-up*. Washington, D.C.: National Catholic Educational Association.

Vaill, P. B. 1984. The purposing of high-performing systems. In *Leadership and organizational culture*, ed. T. J. Sergiovanni and J. E. Corbally, 85–104. Urbana: University of Illinois Press.

Yeager, R. J., P. L. Benson, M. J. Guerra, and B. V. Manno. 1985. The Catholic high school: A national portrait. Washington, D.C.: National Catholic Educational Association.

These organizations offer administrative resources, workshops, publications, or consultants:

Catholic Education Marketing Initiative
    629 N. Fairview Avenue
    St. Paul, MN 55104

Catholic Leadership Company
    5470 S.W. Dover Loop
    Portland, OR 97225

Catholic School Management
    24 Cornfield Lane
    Madison, CT 06443

Council for Advancement and
    Support of Education (CASE)
    Suite 400
    11 Dupont Circle
    Washington, DC 20036-1261

Independent School Management
    1315 N. Union Street
    Wilmington, DE 19806-2594

Institute of School and Parish Development
    Suite 703
    2026 St. Charles Avenue
    New Orleans, LA 70130

These organizations, among others, contract with Catholic schools in the management of tuition payments or financial aid screening:

F.A.C.T.S. Tuition Management
    P. O. Box 67037
    Lincoln, NE 68506

SMART Tuition Management Services
    Suite 2300
    95 Wall Street
    New York, NY 10005

Tuition Aid Data Services
    Suite 104
    2305 Ford Parkway
    St. Paul, MN 55116

Area of Responsibility: Finance and Development

Kay Alewine and Maria Ciriello, OP, Ph.D.

Members of the National Congress: Catholic Schools for the 21st Century (*Executive Summary*, Guerra, Haney, and Kealey 1992) stated,

> Effective leadership is critical to the mission of the church and the future of Catholic schools (p. 29).

This statement is relevant to the financial situation of Catholic schools. Catholic school leaders who are convinced of the need for and dedicated to the mission of Catholic schools will be cognizant of their pivotal role in garnering support for them.

Catholic schools, along with all educational institutions, are feeling the pinch of inflation and loss of revenues. In addition, other circumstances endanger the financial stability of Catholic schools. Bryk and Holland (1984) specify four issues that must be addressed to secure the future of Catholic schools:

- declining subsidies from the contributed services of religious personnel;

- increasing physical plant cost due to a long history of deferred maintenance;

- the need for substantial improvement in the very low faculty salaries; and

- the likely need to increase expenditures in response to a nation-wide concern about improving the quality of schools (p. 83).

The financial management of the school affects students and their families. It impacts every employee and all aspects of the school's educational program. Without an adequate financial foundation, even with the best of intentions, the comprehensive educational program will be in precarious circumstances.

The traditional means of supporting the schools have been tuition, subsidy from parishes or religious communities, and fund raising. These means are no longer adequate in themselves. Additional financial resources must be sought beyond the local school, parish, and religious communities. Development programs, long-range planning, marketing, and public relations programs are becoming essential to maintain the financial viability of Catholic schools.

Directional statements and beliefs adopted by the participants of the National Congress: Catholic Schools for the 21st Century (*Executive Summary*, Guerra, Haney, and Kealey 1992) present a financial vision and agenda for those in Catholic school leadership:

Beliefs (p. 25):

- The financial future of Catholic schools demands securing new and available resources.

- Catholic schools are essential to the life and future of the church in the United States and require the support of the entire Catholic community.

- Catholic schools should be available and financially accessible to Catholic families and to others who support the mission.

Directional Statements (p. 26):

- We will challenge the entire Catholic community and others to make a radical commitment to Catholic schools and generous investment in them.

- We will immediately initiate long-range strategic planning processes for Catholic schools at the local, diocesan, and national levels.

- We will implement in every school just compensation plans for all Catholic school personnel.

■ We will implement and evaluate comprehensive development programs at the local, diocesan, and national levels.

The principal as manager of finances and development planning in a Catholic school is called to the following expectations:

D1. To demonstrate skill in managing a school's *financial resources* and developing and monitoring an annual *budget*

D2. To understand the basic strategies of *long-range* and *strategic planning* and apply them to a school

D3. To provide for *development* in the broadest sense, including an effective *public relations* program and a school *marketing* program in parishes and the broader community.

D4. To seek *resources* and support *beyond the school* and parish(es)

The following pages address each expectation regarding finance and development separately. In an introduction, a rationale is presented to clarify the importance of the expectation as a basic competency for the Catholic school administrator. Learning activities, including readings and interactions with experienced professionals, are prescribed. To foster optimum growth and insight, the learner is encouraged to seek a mentor and to make every effort to interact with personnel actively involved in the day-to-day functioning of Catholic educational institutions. A written record (journal) of all related readings and activities is integrated to enhance personal development and to provide a systematic chronicle of professional experiences. Finally, outcome activities are listed to give the learner opportunities to demonstrate mastery of the specific competency.

Role: Principal as Manager

Area: Finance and Development

Competency: D1
Financial Resources and Budget

In 1931, Hughes and Ubben noted that schools were big businesses. Imagine what they might say about our schools today! Burke (1985) makes a strong case for establishing and maintaining an effective bookkeeping and budgeting system in every Catholic school: budgeting is basic to maintaining financial control and accountability. Administrators, pastors, parishes, board members, parents, and donors have a vested interest in our schools. As the Church, we must be able to demonstrate that we are making responsible decisions as good stewards in the ministry of education. Effective budgets are based on the philosophy, mission statement, and priorities established by school administration and boards in long-range planning.

Ordinarily the principal will be responsible for developing initial budget projections based on the previous year's income and expenses. Subsequently the principal will confer with groups whose input is needed to make the final decisions. The specific groups consulted will depend on the sponsorship of the school. For parish schools, it will be the pastor and parish finance committee and, where instituted, the school board. Private schools usually work with a board. Diocese-sponsored schools also have specific guidelines and policies for school budgeting.

Sr. Mary Benet McKinney, in *Sharing Wisdom* (1987), speaks to the need for collaboration: each person has a "piece of the wisdom." It is in working together that more can be learned and accomplished. The budgeting process provides an excellent occasion to share collective wisdom in exercising good stewardship.

To support and give evidence of professional growth in planning and managing a school's financial resources and developing and monitoring an annual budget, the learner will engage in the listed activities under the direction of the diocese (Model I) or through a self-directed program and/or with the guidance of a mentor (Model II).

The primary means of keeping a consistent record of activities is to keep an ongoing JOURNAL which would contain

1) a *Dated Log* section recording when activities were undertaken and completed,

2) a *Reading/Response* section in which notes from suggested readings and the response reactions are systematically organized, and

3) an *Experience(Activity)/Reflection* section in which one records ideas and insights gained through interacting with people or seeking out additional information in the course of completing the activities.

Learning Activities: D1
Financial Resources and Budget

1. Read the following and respond with reactions in a journal.* Ideally, you should discuss these readings and your reactions with a mentor. These integral readings are reprinted for your convenience on pages 274–90.

Burke, R. 1984. The annual budget. In *Elementary school finance manual*, 22–27, 28, 31, 43, 45, 49, 54–59. Washington, D.C.: National Catholic Educational Association.

McLaughlin, T. 1985. *Catholic school finance and Church-State relations*. Washington, D.C.: National Catholic Educational Association, 19.

Sheehan, L. 1990. The role of the board in finances. In *Building better boards: A handbook for board members in Catholic education*. Washington, D.C.: National Catholic Educational Association, 26–31.

Also, read the following sections from the *Catechism*.

Libreria Editrice Vaticana. 1994. *Catechism of the Catholic Church*. Washington, D.C.: United States Catholic Conference.

Nos. 2426–34: Economic activity is related to social justice. Economic life should be aimed at the service of persons and the human community. Everyone has the right to draw from work a reasonable means of support.

* In your journal, note your insights concerning the budgeting process and its components. How

do (or should) budgets reflect the school's philosophy, mission statement, and five-year plan? What principles have you developed to prioritize expenses? What criteria are appropriately applied when a preliminary budget must be pared down? How should budgets be adjusted when emergencies preclude planned purchases? What ideas have you formulated regarding the relationship of total dollars spent and cost per pupil? What changes have occurred in financial management of Catholic schools in the last 10 to 20 years? What future trends do you see in planning and managing financial resources for Catholic schools? What further questions do you have?

2. Visit one or two Catholic schools to learn about the budgeting process.
    a. Who has the ultimate responsibility for preparing and monitoring the school budget?
    b. What is the role of the school board in this process?
    c. What specific steps involve the principal in the process?
    d. Besides the annual budget, is there any provision for long-range financial planning, such as a three- or five-year plan?
    e. What provisions has the school made for unexpected emergencies?
    f. What are the most significant concerns or problems of the principal regarding the school's budgeting process?
    g. Does the principal feel he or she had good financial management skills as a new principal? If so, how were the skills acquired? If not, what did the principal do to learn them?
    h. What sources of assistance are available to the principal in attending to the financial details of the school?
    i. Do negative attitudes affect the development and approval of the budget? How does the principal circumvent or improve the situation?
    j. What advice would the principal give to a new principal regarding the budgeting process?

    Whether personal or institutional, discussing financial details is always a delicate matter. For good reasons, some principals might be reluctant to share specific financial documents and details. You may need to ask the diocesan office to aid you in finding examples and resources to learn about this important aspect of school management.

3. Through your contact with the principal(s), try to obtain a copy of
    ■ the school's annual budget process,
    ■ the school's current budget,
    ■ a sample of the monthly spreadsheet or financial summary report, and
    ■ the school's philosophy and mission statement.

    After you have read the materials, respond to the following questions:
    a. How does the budget reflect the school's philosophy, mission statement, and (if applicable) five-year plan?
    b. What examples of sound business management, good stewardship, and accountability have you noticed?
    c. What questions do you have in interpreting the spreadsheet? How are specific amounts determined for the expense budget? for the income budget?
    d. How are tuition rates developed and approved?
    e. What resources generate income inside the local school and parish and outside the local school and community?
    f. For parish schools: Is there a parish subsidy? What percentage of the school budget is subsidized? What percentage of the parish budget goes to support the school? What do these figures say about the parish-school relationship, and what extenuating circumstances, if any, are there?
    g. What have you discovered about the major line-item costs of the budget?

    As a result of this reflection and activity, how do you assess your skills for understanding the budgeting process and utilizing the spreadsheet? In which areas do you need further development? How will you acquire these skills?

4. If the diocese has a principal's handbook, examine the sections that deal with the financial management of the school's resources. (You

might even be able to secure some time with a diocesan consultant, who could further explain the procedures.) To what extent have the steps in planning and monitoring an annual budget been standardized for the diocesan schools (timelines for the process, guidelines as to who participates in developing the budget, etc.)? What and how much flexibility is allowed to individual schools? What training or preparation is offered to assist principals in becoming more adept in financial management? Can you determine how much responsibility individual principals have for day-to-day management (writing checks or purchase orders, making independent decisions on purchases, etc.)? Does this vary from school to school? If so, in what ways? How would you summarize the responsibility of the principal in planning and managing financial resources?

As a result of study, reflection, and interaction with knowledgeable individuals, the learner will be able to complete the following activities. The quality of response to these activities should give some indication of the level of expertise the learner is able to bring to the situation.

Outcome Activities: D1
Financial Resources and Budget

1. List and discuss qualities of sound business management within the context of Christian stewardship and the level of accountability expected of those who serve in the ministry of Catholic school administration.

2. *Scenario*

   Note: This case depicts an elementary parish school situation. However the questions regarding budgeting problems are similar for any level of Catholic education. In the case of a private school, the board would make decisions similar to those of the bishop and pastor.

   You are the principal of an elementary school with 250 students in grades pre-school through eight. You have submitted the budget to the pastor for the final reading. At that meeting, you and the pastor discussed developments that have occurred since your submission of the preliminary budget. Some revisions must be made before final approval is sought from the finance committee.

   The bishop mandated that health insurance be provided at school expense to all full-time diocesan school employees who request it. (This is employee coverage only—dependent coverage must be provided by the employee.) You have just been informed that health insurance rates for the next school year will increase by 18 percent per employee, and that will cost an additional $3,500. Staffing is stable for the following year at this time. You estimate that ten staff members who chose the plan last year will remain on it, and no additional staff members will request the plan.

   Utility rates have skyrocketed. You estimate this will require an additional $5,000.

   The parish offertory collections are down because of the continuing recession. You anticipated this and have already projected a possible lower enrollment and made the appropriate adjustment in the amount of anticipated tuition. The pastor informs you that current collections indicate that the parish subsidy will be $12,000 less than he had committed to you previously, (*or*, in the case of a private school, the interest on the endowment is down, and the anticipated income to the school will be $12,000 less than formerly projected).

Further Points for Consideration

You have reviewed the entire budget and determined that any cuts must come from the areas listed below. After you determine how much must be cut, decide where you will make cuts. List the cuts you would make, and give a brief rationale for each decision.

Staff

You have determined that grade-level teaching staff cannot be cut. You need every homeroom teacher to meet class size requirements. Additional staff salaries are as follows:

- Computer teacher, full-time (10)* ND** $12,500
- Librarian, full-time (3) ND $9,500
- PE coach, full-time, (2) $14,500
- Pre-school teacher (3-year-old class), part-time, (10) degree in progress $7,000
- Pre-school teacher (4-year-old class), part-time, (2), B.A., M.A. $8,900.
- Band instructor, part-time, grades 5–8 (3) ND $3,000
- Choral music instructor, part-time, (3) ND $5,000
- Art instructor, part-time, $5,000
- Secretary, full-time, (7) $9,000
- Secretary, part-time, (2) $4,500
- Clerical/instructional aide, full-time, ND $7,000
- Maintenance man, full-time (2) $10,000
- Maintenance man, part-time (15) $5,000
- One-third of parish accountant salary, (manages tuition, issues checks, etc.) $4,500

* Number in parentheses indicates years of service at your school.

** ND = non-degreed, but meets diocesan requirements for job and field experience or special skills experience; does not affect accreditation.

Books and Materials

To follow diocesan guidelines, textbook series in each subject area should be updated once every five years. You are one year ahead of schedule. The language arts series and a new math series have been purchased this year. Next year, a new science series should be added, with social studies and religion planned for the year after. The estimates for the two favored science series for all grades are
- $6,000 for texts only, and
- $10,000 for a laser disc instruction program, equipment, and accompanying text.

Both series have advantages and disadvantages, but during curriculum and text review meetings, both you and the staff strongly favored the laser disc program. To allow for the laser disc program, you have trimmed all possible fat from other books and materials purchases. New accreditation standards stress the use of technology, as well as hands-on

instruction. You had planned $2,000 for a much-needed science lab materials update.

Since the library holdings are generally inadequate at all levels, particularly in the pre-school and primary grades, you planned to update those areas. New accreditation requirements for libraries will be mandated in two years; your accreditation visit is in three years, but you are having an interim visit this fall. Because of other program and staffing needs, library needs have been minimally funded for many years. Stacks have been cleared, and outdated texts were removed. A small grant has helped somewhat, but the approximate cost of meeting new library requirements is $8,500.

Plant Operation

The building is 50 years old and has no long-range plan for updating equipment. Each year for the past five years, approximately $15,000 to $18,500 has been needed to repair or replace equipment, such as air conditioners and a heating unit. A new roof had to be installed on one of the outer buildings last year. The maintenance man said that two air-conditioning units may need to be replaced this coming year ($5,000 each). One individual room heater ($3,000) may last the winter. Those items (a total of $13,000) were entered into the preliminary budget. Because of rising costs and need for more supplies, an additional $3,000 was added to the preliminary budget.

Note: All possible expected income has been included in the income portion of the budget. The changes are not optional; they must be made to have a balanced budget.

How would you revise the budget? What cuts will be necessary to balance the budget? What additional sources of revenue would be required to keep the original projections? How would you acquire those funds?

a) Discuss how you would prioritize what must remain in this year's budget, and what might be delayed. Provide a rationale for each decision made.

b) Discuss possible additional sources of revenue that would allow more flexibility in the budget.

Role: Principal as Managerial Leader

Area: Finance and Development

Competency: D2
Long-Range and Strategic Planning

In the absence of clearly defined goals, we are forced to concentrate on activity and ultimately become enslaved in it.

—*Chuck Coonradt*

Goals describe where we want to go. Plans provide the way to get there. In organizational theory, planning is considered the most reliable means of realizing goals (Castetter 1992). Patterson, Purkey, and Parker (1986) concisely capture the essence of strategic planning:

> The goal of strategic planning is to produce a stream of wise decisions designed to achieve the mission of the organization. Emphasis shifts from product to process. Just as the planning process builds in flexibility for adaptation to changing conditions in and out of the organization, it also accepts the possibility that the final product may not resemble what was initially intended (p. 61).

More than 25 years ago the U.S. Catholic bishops (1973), in their influential educational statement *To Teach as Jesus Did*, supported the value of long-range planning for the future of the schools:

> While it is difficult to define and plan the Church's educational mission in this period of rapid institutional change, the effort must continue. Educational needs must be clearly identified; goals and objectives must be established which are simultaneously realistic and creative; programs consistent with these needs and objectives must be designed carefully, conducted efficiently, and evaluated honestly (no. 138).

Those involved in the National Congress endorsed long-range strategic planning to address the future of Catholic schools. This prophetic stance frees the leadership of Catholic schools to embrace creative new ways to make schools available and financially accessible to all who support the mission. With effective long-range planning, schools will avoid the pitfalls that result from crisis-based management and last-minute decisions. Long-range planning anticipates and prioritizes needs while allowing time to acquire the financial resources to meet those needs.

Ideally, the Catholic school principal will not be totally responsible for the creation and implementation of such plans. Depending on the sponsorship of the school, various groups and personnel will be available and should be invited to join the process. However, the principal frequently serves as the inspirational catalyst and a professional resource who lends guidance so that an effective plan is developed, implemented, and updated in a timely fashion.

To support and give evidence of professional growth in understanding the strategies of long-range planning and applying them to a school, the learner will engage in the listed activities under the direction of the diocese (Model I) or through a self-directed program and/or with the guidance of a mentor (Model II).

The primary means of keeping a consistent record of activities is to keep an ongoing JOURNAL which would contain

1) a *Dated Log* section recording when activities were undertaken and completed,
2) a *Reading/Response* section in which notes from suggested readings and the response reactions are systematically organized, and
3) an *Experience(Activity)/Reflection* section in which one records ideas and insights gained through interacting with people or seeking out additional information in the course of completing the activities.

Learning Activities: D2
Long-Range and Strategic Planning

1. Read the following and respond with reactions in a journal.* Ideally, you should discuss these readings and your reactions with a mentor. These integral readings are reprinted for your convenience on pages 291–95.

Burke, R. 1984. Long-range planning. In *Elementary school finance manual*, 84–89. Washington, D.C.: National Catholic Educational Association.

Sheehan, L. 1990. Planning. In *Building better boards: A handbook for board members in Catholic education*, 7–9. Washington, D.C.: National Catholic Educational Association.

* In your journal, note insights concerning (a) the roles of the pastor, principal, and school board in developing and monitoring a long-range plan; (b) the questions that must be addressed in developing the plan; and (c) strategies for developing a timeline and procedures for implementing a long-range plan. How does the long-range plan reflect the school's philosophy and mission statement? What knowledge and skills are needed by the administrator to develop "job descriptions," or strategies, for board members and others who will gather data and help formulate the plan? What is the relationship of the long-range plan to the other major financial management areas: the annual budget, tuition, fund raising, and development?

2. Visit one or two Catholic schools to learn about the long-range planning process.

   a. What are the major societal and economic changes that have necessitated long-range strategic planning in the past 10 to 20 years?

   b. What are the most difficult aspects of designing a long-range plan?

   c. How does the principal gather the data for the financial history of the school?

   d. How are future needs determined in light of the school's financial history?

   e. What skills did the principal have when long-range planning became necessary? What new skills, if any, had to be acquired, and how was this accomplished?

   f. What advice would the principal give to a new principal regarding long-range and strategic planning?

3. Through your contact with a principal, obtain copies of the forms used to gather and report data for the initial long-range plan. Ask the principal to discuss the rationale for the areas of information used to develop a long-range plan. See if the principal will share data projection sheets with you. (How are the school's philosophy and mission statement reflected in projections?) If this is not possible, ask the principal to explain how he or she feels the mission statement and school philosophy are reflected in the plans. In your discussions with the principal, what examples of sound business management and good Christian stewardship have you noted? What skills might you need to acquire to develop an effective long-range plan?

4. Visit with a representative from the diocesan office of schools. What kinds of training are available to local school administrators, boards of education, and pastors through the diocesan office? How is this training provided, and who bears the costs? Are there inservice training programs or mentors assigned to new principals to help them learn the dynamics of strategic planning? Are there any regional or diocese-wide support groups or other cooperative efforts to distribute information regarding this crucial aspect of administration? How can data from diocesan annual reports and statistical reports published by the National Catholic Educational Association assist principals in writing a long-range plan?

As a result of study, reflection, and interaction with knowledgeable individuals, the learner will be able to complete the following activity. The quality of response to this activity should give some indication of the level of expertise the learner is able to bring to the situation.

Outcome Activity: D2
Long-Range and Strategic Planning

Scenario

You have just been hired as the new principal of a school that was founded 45 years ago. The school, which once thrived, has declined in enrollment from 400 students to 125 students. The pastor who hired you, the school board, the parent organization, and the staff are all eager to keep the school viable. They want it to thrive again.

Although much historical, financial, and other school data is accessible in the school and the diocesan office, past administrators did not incorporate long-range or strategic planning into the school's program. Few people connected with the school seem to have any idea what long-range planning is, much less how to help develop and implement it.

a. What would be your major goals for the first year in beginning long-range planning? Give a rationale for selecting each goal, and discuss how each goal would relate to the staff, the school board, and the pastor or parish.

b. What strategies would you use during the first year of your principalship to realize these goals and develop a long-range plan for the school? Prioritize your strategies, and give a rationale for each.

c. Provide a timeline for implementation of goals and strategies in the first year of your long-range planning. Be specific about what needs to be accomplished and by whom.

Role: Principal as Managerial Leader

Area: Finance and Development

Competency: D3
Development, Public Relations, Marketing

Thompson and Flynn (1988) assert that the term "development" was first used in educational circles in 1923 by Thomas A. Gonser at Northwestern University, who "used it to describe a function in the university meaning 'the development of the whole institution.'" Gonser later joined with Gerber, Tinker, Stuhr of Chicago to create a development consulting firm that is the pioneer in Catholic school development. A summary of their philosophy of development is as follows:

> The overall concept of development holds that the highest destiny of an institution can be realized only by a total effort on the part of the institution to analyze its educational or programmatic philosophy and activities, to crystallize its objectives, project them into the future, and take the necessary steps to realize them (Gonser et al. 1977, p. 4).

Catholic school leaders must cultivate a development program that encompasses two types of planning: for stability and for advancement (Konzen 1991). Stability requires generating funds for operating expenses, including scholarship funds. Advancement includes planning for improvement and expansion of the educational program and the physical plant (Konzen 1991). The backbone of a comprehensive development program is a systematic public relations and marketing effort.

Bagin (1994) specifies that "educational public relations is management's systematic, continuous, two-way, honest communication" between the school and its publics (p. 14). The purpose of public relations is "to improve and maintain student achievement and to build public support" (Holliday 1988, p. 12). Parents in particular, and Catholics in general, are publics of concern to the Catholic school principal. Marketing, or specifically promoting the value of the school to the community, is one facet of the public relations program. Getting the message out about the school is an important way to instill pride and loyalty in the community. Drawing on the community's knowledge, pride, and loyalty toward the school, the principal has a sound basis on which to appeal for support of the school. The current economic circumstances of the average Catholic school necessitate deliberate efforts by the principal to ensure the school's prospects.

To support and give evidence of professional growth in understanding development in the broadest sense, including an effective public relations program and a school marketing program, the learner will engage in the listed activities under the direction of the diocese (Model I) or through a self-directed program and/or with the guidance of a mentor (Model II).

The primary means of keeping a consistent record of activities is to keep an ongoing JOURNAL which would contain

1) a *Dated Log* section recording when activities were undertaken and completed,

2) a *Reading/Response* section in which notes from suggested readings and the response reactions are systematically organized, and

3) an *Experience(Activity)/Reflection* section in which one records ideas and insights gained through interacting with people or seeking out additional information in the course of completing the activities.

Learning Activities: D3
Development, Public Relations, Marketing

1. Read the following and respond with reactions in a journal.* Ideally, you should discuss these readings and your reaction with a mentor. These integral readings are reprinted for your convenience on pages 296–304.

Balfe, M., M. Lanning, A. Meese, and A. M. Walsh. 1991. Enrollment: Securing our future. In *Capital wisdom: Papers from the Principals Academy*, 11–20. Washington, D.C.: National Catholic Educational Association.

Sheehan, L. 1990. Public relations. In *Building better boards: A handbook for board members in Catholic education*, 40–44. Washington, D.C.: National Catholic Educational Association.

Yeager, R. J. 1985. Steps toward development. In *Elementary school finance manual*, 120–23. Washington, D.C.: National Catholic Educational Association.

* In your journal, note your insights about the importance of implementing development programs at both elementary and secondary levels of Catholic education, the responsibility of the principal as leader in establishing this process, and the importance of developing a team approach for the process during the initial stage of implementation.

2. Visit one or two Catholic schools with functioning development programs. Request copies of the support materials developed for the program (school brochures, case statement, advertisements, newspaper articles, etc.).

Ask the principal to describe the public relations and marketing efforts of the school and explain how they relate to the development efforts of the school. In addition, ask the principal to show you any literature that relates to these programs. In particular, learn the answers to these questions:

a. What is the role of the principal in the establishment and implementation of the programs? Did this person establish these programs? What does this person do to ensure their effectiveness?

b. At what stage of evolution is the public relations and marketing program? When was it established? What impact has it had on the development program of the school?

c. What local factors indicated the need for a development program? When was the decision made to have a development program? What strategies were utilized to initiate the process, and by whom?

d. How much responsibility does the principal have in these areas? How does managing these responsibilities impact the other duties he or she has as principal?

e. To what extent and how is the principal active in the broader community on behalf of the school?

f. What skills are most important to be effective in public relations, marketing, and development efforts?

g. How did the principal become skilled in these areas?

h. How does the diocesan school office, the chancery, or a diocese-wide marketing and development group (if it exists) assist principals in beginning these programs?

i. Are there any diocesan programs providing financial assistance to struggling families and schools or inner-city schools?

j. Does the principal have additional personnel to attend to public relations, marketing, and development responsibilities? How are team members selected and roles defined?

3. If there is a separate school staff member for public relations, request a meeting with that person. If not, focus on these aspects of public relations with the principal:

a. What local factors are considered in shaping public relation campaigns?

b. What strategies are used with the local media to keep the school, its programs, staff accomplishments, and other areas of interest before the public?

c. How do the development program and the public relations program work together to seek other sources of funding for the school?

d. What strategies are used to reach the broader public—beyond the parish and school community? How have publics been identified, researched, and approached, and who has been reached through these efforts?

e. What are the major accomplishments of the school marketing program? What strategies have been successful? What has not worked as well?

4. If there is a separate development director, request an interview. If not, pursue these questions with the principal:

   a. How is the development program organized? Is there a separate board?

   b. What are the accomplishments of the development program or board during the past year or two? since being established?

   c. Is there an established alumni association, and how has it contributed to the development program? What are some of the major steps and possible problems in establishing an active alumni organization? What concerns are peculiar to the elementary school? the secondary school?

   d. To what extent have businesses, foundations, or major gift prospects been approached on behalf of the school?

   e. Has an endowment program been established?

   f. Which of these efforts are functioning at present: annual fund drive, estate planning, insurance gifts, catalog of gift opportunities, capital campaign drives?

   g. How are the major areas of development —quality education, sound business management, long-range planning, and public relations—reflected in the actions and accomplishments of the development program or board?

   h. How and when is the annual report developed? By whom and to whom is it distributed?

5. If there is an established development board, development director, or development office in the school, ask permission to attend a meeting or visit the director. Study the agenda and minutes, if possible. Note the roles played by board members and how they interact.

   a. How are the school philosophy and mission reflected in the board's activities?

   b. What committees are functioning? How and by whom are their duties defined?

   c. What leadership qualities are most evident during the meeting?

   What conclusions did you come to regarding the principal's role in initiating and sustaining public relations, marketing, and development programs on behalf of the school?

As a result of study, reflection, and interaction with knowledgeable individuals, the learner will be able to complete the following activity. The quality of response to this activity should give some indication of the level of expertise the learner is able to bring to the situation.

Outcome Activity: D3
Development, Public Relations, Marketing

Even though knowledge of development and public relations programs, along with their importance to Catholic schools, has been discussed for a number of years, there is still a strong possibility a principal will enter a school where little or no public relations and development effort is in place.

Scenario

You have recently been hired as principal of a Catholic school. The school is struggling, having declined in enrollment from 500 students to 158 students.

There have been frequent changes in educational leadership. You are the first lay principal and the third principal in the past four years. The present pastor has been at the parish less than a year. He succeeds the founding pastor, who was at the parish for 25 years. The former pastor had been ailing for some time but died suddenly of a heart attack last year. Consequently, the school and parish are suffering tremendously from a lack of stable educational leadership and inertia.

The former pastor was good-hearted and supportive of the school. The parish has been subsidizing 75 percent of the school budget. The parish has minimally supported its CCD program, which serves 80 percent of the parish children without a DRE. The parish has not been able to afford adult education programs, ministry to the elderly or sick, or other programs ministering to the needs of the parish.

The new pastor is supportive of Catholic education but concerned about the needs of all his parishioners. He realizes that the parish can no longer support the school to the extent that it did in the past. Those presently involved in the school are fanatically loyal to it. The rest of the parish is apathetic. Some are resentful because it drains so much of the parish resources. A persistent and growing group favors closing the school because of declining enrollment. The parish is becoming polarized. Rumblings have even resulted in front-page exposure in the local newspaper of rumors that the school is in imminent danger of closing.

The new priest is strongly committed to collaborative leadership and is willing to work with you on behalf of the school in an attempt to change parish attitudes. But he is also adamant that other ways to finance the school must be found. He has already told you that the next year the subsidy to the school will be reduced by 20 percent. He intends to reduce the subsidy each year until the parish is contributing no more than 25 percent of the school budget. His plan is to reach that goal in five years.

There are some wealthy and influential parishioners whose children, now grown, attended the school. Some have grandchildren in the school. They would like to see it continue. The staff, although in disarray from frequent changes in leaders and leadership styles, have voiced their loyalty and commitment to the school and you as the new principal.

The parent organization has dwindled in numbers, but its commitment to the school is fierce. It is willing to do whatever is necessary to keep the school.

The previous pastor ignored the directive of the diocese to establish a parish council and a school board. The new pastor is willing to establish a school board. He knows little about school administration and virtually nothing about public relations and development programs in schools.

You believe that a systematic development program for the school is the only chance for it to become financially viable. Since school problems have become parish-wide and community-wide knowledge, you have decided that you must assume leadership in public relations to reach both publics. You understand that a sound public relations program will bolster the chances of success in the development efforts. You will have to bear the major responsibility of development and public relations efforts until you get to know your people, educate them, and form a team to assist you.

a. Prepare a list of goals for the first year of public relations and development training, with accompanying rationale.

b. List strategies for achieving each goal, using a timeline format to indicate projected completion dates.

c. Decide what committees will be necessary to accomplish these goals, and include committee job assignments for the coming year.

d. List what you personally must do during this first year to lead these public relations and development efforts and begin turning the negatives about the school into positives.

e. Using the school calendar of events, design a public relations program that will utilize all forms of media in your community to reach parish and civic groups.

 i) How would you keep your school *positively* represented to the community throughout the school year?

 ii) How will you inform the parish about the school and reach out to the parish community?

Role: Principal as Managerial Leader

Area: Finance and Development

Competency: D4
Resources beyond the School

As we look at the history of Catholic schools in America, we realize that the concept of going beyond the local school and parish in search of resources and support is relatively new. Traditionally, the schools were supported by the parishes or parents whose children attended them. However, economic factors continue to impact our schools at alarming rates. Few schools can operate today on tuition alone, or tuition plus a parish subsidy. As tuition skyrockets, volunteer programs are decimated by the loss of parents who must work outside the home to provide Catholic education to their children.

Going beyond the school and parish to seek resources and support is no longer an option for the majority of our schools. It is a mandate—a matter of survival.

A major focus of development programs is seeking outside resources to provide major gifts to our schools. Whether the gifts are financial or in the form of support services, the assistance they provide eases the financial burden on parents and parish.

Total development programs include efforts to reach alumni, establish endowments, build school-business partnerships, seek grants from foundations and industry, and create committees that solicit major gifts through estate planning, insurance giving, annual fund drives, and capital campaigns. Identifying, researching, and approaching prospective donors—whether they are individuals, foundations, or businesses—is both a science and an art. Establishing "blue ribbon committees" of affluent and influential individuals committed to Catholic education will bring in dollars that will ensure the financial viability of a school for years to come. These efforts must "emphasize the school's mission," according to Yeager (1985). Donors will want to know why the school exists and be convinced of its excellence before they give money or services.

To support and give evidence of professional growth in understanding the principles of seeking resources and support beyond the school and parish(es), the learner will engage in the listed activities under the direction of the diocese (Model I) or through a self-directed program and/or with the guidance of a mentor (Model II).

The primary means of keeping a consistent record of activities is to keep an ongoing JOURNAL which would contain

1) a *Dated Log* section recording when activities were undertaken and completed,

2) a *Reading/Response* section in which notes from suggested readings and the response reactions are systematically organized, and

3) an *Experience(Activity)/Reflection* section in which one records ideas and insights gained through interacting with people or seeking out additional information in the course of completing the activities.

Learning Activities: D4
Resources beyond the School

1. Read the following and respond with reactions in a journal.* Ideally, you should discuss these readings and your reactions with a mentor. These integral readings are reprinted for your convenience on pages 305–08.

McLaughlin, T. 1985. *Catholic school finance and Church-State relations.* Washington, D.C.: National Catholic Educational Association, 28, 53–54.

Yeager, R. J. 1985. Steps toward development. In *Elementary school finance manual*, 123–26. Washington, D.C.: National Catholic Educational Association.

* In your journal, note insights concerning (a) the process of identifying, researching, and approaching prospective major donors; (b) how and what strategies and materials are developed to assure the potential donor that the school is a wise investment; (c) the differences between fund-raising programs and seeking major gifts, materials, and services; and (d) suggested methods of subsequent communication with the donors contacted.

2. Obtain the annual reports of one or more schools. Pay particular attention to the format and design of each report (use of pictures, styles of printing, graphic art, quality of paper, color composition, etc.). How does the report reflect the school's mission? Are additional investment opportunities listed? If so, how are they presented? (Note the language or terminology of the written report.) How are communications from the administration and school or development board officers presented? In what ways are donors recognized? Study the detailed report of the year's gifts and investments. Are investors local, regional, or national in nature? Is there diversity among the types of donors—businesses, foundations, individuals? What percentage of the gifts come from the various sources listed—grants, annual fund drives, capital giving campaigns, insurance giving, estate planning, foundations, individuals? List any other sources in addition to these, along with the percentages of their gifts.

3. Research local school-business partnerships that are active in your community. Discuss the following: What goods and services are available to schools from businesses? What financial resources or grants are also available? What strategies are used in identifying and establishing school-business partnerships? Support your assertions by making references to authorities in the field.

4. In your parish or community, identify potential donors, whether individuals, business and industry, or foundations. How can you identify donors? What information is necessary to create a profile of each donor? Give a rationale for each strategy chosen, and for using each kind of information.

5. Visit the diocesan school office. What help, if any, is provided by the chancery, the diocesan board of education, or the diocesan school office to help schools reach resources and support beyond the local school? What, if any, efforts at the diocesan level are under way to require parishes without schools to financially assist parishes with schools?

As a result of study, reflection, and interaction with knowledgeable individuals, the learner will be able to complete the following activities. The quality of response to these activities should give some indication of the level of expertise the learner is able to bring to the situation.

Outcome Activities: D4
Resources beyond the School

1. Develop a general plan for soliciting support from outside sources:
   a. List at least ten potential contacts in your area, including alumni, businesses, industries, and foundations, that might be potential supporters of a Catholic school.
   b. Specify the types of support these sources could supply.
   c. Plan a generic strategy that might be used as the initial approach to each source. Include a protocol for the initial phone or personal contact and a draft of the initial written contact.
   d. Specify the steps to take once initial contact is made.
   e. List follow-up steps to be taken once the donor has committed.

2. Major gifts result from studied, persistent effort in identifying and cultivating potential donors.

Scenario

You have been principal at a high school for three years. The development efforts you began when you arrived have progressed slowly. An endowment goal of $1 million has been established for the school. Through a multi-faceted program, about $135,000 has been raised.

Though new to the community, you have made many efforts to become active and learn who might be a potential donor. You have discovered that several alumni in the area are very affluent and are involved in community endeavors. You have noted their names as substantial donors to the local symphony, the art museum, and the Little League baseball teams. You have met several of these people informally at social events. Some have commented that they are hearing good things about the school.

The alumni association at the school has not been very active. You realize that this resource has great potential.

a. Discuss the steps you would take to put some life into the alumni association.

b. Provide a rationale for each step. Why do you think that particular step is important? List steps in sequence, from beginning to end.

c. Outline the steps you would take to cultivate people who have an interest in or connection to the school and might be particularly able to support it (parents, alumni, friends, etc.).

i) How would you determine the amount of money you would ask for?

ii) How would you present the case of need?

iii) How would you make the contact?

iv) If your approach is not successful, what steps would you take next regarding the same donor?

Finance and Development Bibliography

Role: Principal as Managerial Leader

Area of Responsibility:
Finance and Development

Introduction

Bryk, A. S., P. B. Holland, V. E. Lee, and R. A. Carriedo. 1984. *Effective Catholic schools: An exploration*. Washington, D.C.: National Catholic Educational Association.

Guerra, M., R. Haney, and R. Kealey, eds. 1992. *National congress: Catholic schools for the 21st century: Executive summary*. Washington, D.C.: National Catholic Educational Association.

D1. Demonstrates skills in planning and managing the school's financial resources toward developing and monitoring an annual budget

Burke, R. 1984. The annual budget. In *Elementary school finance manual*. Washington, D.C.: National Catholic Educational Association, 21–27.

Hughes, L. W., and G. C. Ubben. 1978. *The elementary principal's handbook*. Boston, Mass.: Allyn and Bacon.

Libreria Editrice Vaticana. 1994. *Catechism of the Catholic Church*. Washington, D.C.: United States Catholic Conference, nos. 2426–34.

McKinney, M. B. 1987. *Sharing wisdom: A process for group decision making*. Valencia, Calif.: Tabor Publishing.

McLaughlin, T. 1985. *Catholic school finance and Church-State relations*. Washington, D.C.: National Catholic Educational Association, 19.

Sheehan, L. 1990. *Building better boards: A handbook for board members in Catholic education*. Washington, D.C.: National Catholic Educational Association.

Speigle, C., and J. A. Haudan. 1985. Maximizing dollars through money management. *Momentum* 16(3):56–58.

Walter, J. K., and G. D. Marconnit. 1989. *The principal and fiscal management*. Elementary Principal Series #6. Bloomington, Ind.: Phi Delta Kappa Educational Foundation.

D2. Understands the basic strategies of long-range/strategic planning and applies them in developing plans for the school

Burke, R. 1984. Long-range planning. In *Elementary school finance manual*, 84–89. Washington, D.C.: National Catholic Educational Association.

Castetter, W. B. 1992. *The personnel function in educational administration*. 5th ed. New York: Macmillan.

Convey, J. J., and M. J. Ciriello. 1996. *Strategic planning for Catholic schools: A diocesan model for consultation*. Washington, D.C.: United States Catholic Conference.

National Conference of Catholic Bishops. 1973. *To Teach as Jesus did*. Washington, D.C.: United States Catholic Conference.

Neck, J. A. 1985. Entry points in development for Catholic elementary schools. *Momentum* 16(3): 20–21.

Patterson, J., S. Purkey, and J. Parker. 1986. *Productive schools systems for a non-rational world*. Alexandria, Va.: Association for Supervision and Curriculum Development.

Sheehan, L. 1990. *Building better boards: A handbook for board members in Catholic education*. Washington, D.C.: National Catholic Educational Association, 7–14.

Stone, S. C. 1987. *Strategic planning for independent schools*. Boston: National Association of Independent Schools, 8–42, 57–61.

Yeager, R. J. 1986. In justice, the times demand development. In *Personnel issues and the Catholic school administrator*, 153–56. Washington, D.C.: National Catholic Educational Association.

D3. Provides for development in the broadest sense, including effective public relations programs [parish(es), Church, and broader community] and a school marketing program

Abella, M. 1989. The exciting world of public relations. *Momentum* 20(1):38–39.

Bagin, D., D. R. Gallagher, and L. W. Kindred. 1994. *The school and community relations*. 5th ed. Boston: Allyn and Bacon.

Balfe, M., M. Lanning, A. Meese, and A. M. Walsh. 1991. Enrollment: Securing our future. In *Capital wisdom: Papers from the Principals Academy*, 11–21. Washington, D.C.: National Catholic Educational Association.

Clark, D., and E. Kujawa. 1985. Are you ready? The preconditions of development. *Momentum* 16(3):14–15.

Gonser, Gerber, Tinker, Stuhr. 1977. *On development*. Chicago.

Holliday, A. E. 1988. In search of an answer: What is school public relations? *Journal of Educational Public Relations* 11(2):12.

Jarc, J. A. 1985. *Development and public relations for the Catholic school*. Washington, D.C.: National Catholic Educational Association, 1–60.

Konzen, J. M. 1991. *The role of the principal in development*. Washington, D.C.: National Catholic Educational Association.

LaRiviere, A. 1993. *The development council: Cornerstone for success*. Washington, D.C.: National Catholic Educational Association.

Leahy, M. A. 1989. A new determination. *Momentum* 20(3):48–51.

Pawlas, G., and K. Meyers. 1989. *The principal and communication*. Elementary Principal Series #3. Bloomington, Ind.: Phi Delta Kappa Educational Foundation.

Peterson, J. 1990. *How to hire a development officer: From defining needs to ensuring successful performance*. Washington, D.C.: National Catholic Educational Association.

Reck, C. 1988. *The small Catholic elementary school: Advantages and opportunities*. Washington, D.C.: National Catholic Educational Association, 99–108.

Sheehan, L. 1990. *Building better boards: A handbook for board members in Catholic education*. Washington, D.C.: National Catholic Educational Association, 40–44.

Thompson, L. A., and J. A. Flynn. 1988. *Effective funding of Catholic schools*. Kansas City, Mo.: Sheed and Ward.

Webster, W. E. 1989. *The new principal learning about your school and community*. Elementary Principal Series #2. Bloomington, Ind.: Phi Delta Kappa Educational Foundation.

Yeager, R. J. 1984. Steps toward development. In *Elementary school finance manual*. Washington, D.C.: National Catholic Educational Association, 120–23.

D4. Seeks resources and support beyond the school [and parish(es)]

Donaldson, F. 1991. *Catholic school publications: Unifying the image*. Washington, D.C.: National Catholic Educational Association.

Hofbauer, G. 1984. Fundraising. In *Elementary school finance manual*. Washington, D.C.: National Catholic Educational Association, 103–17.

McLaughlin, T. 1985. *Catholic school finance and Church-State relations*. Washington, D.C.: National Catholic Educational Association, 28, 53–54.

Stuhr, R. L. 1985. What makes a successful development program? *Momentum* 16(3):10–12.

Yeager, R. J. 1985. Steps toward development. In *Elementary school finance manual*, 123–26. Washington, D.C.: National Catholic Educational Association.

Integral Readings for Finance and Development

The Annual Budget

Burke, R. 1984. In *Elementary school finance manual*, 22–27, 28, 31, 43, 45, 49, 54–59.
Washington, D.C.: National Catholic Educational Association.

Introduction

Budgeting is the key to financial control. In other areas, the process might be called "model building." Both terms connote the same objective; that is, the simulation of operating results, given certain assumptions and conditions. Proper budgeting requires care, thought and adequate information. It involves a number of areas indirectly related to finances including philosophy, mission statement, organizational structure, communications and reporting. The budget process positions the school board and administration to tailor spending priorities and to support the school's philosophy and mission statement.

The budgeting process should begin with a clear understanding, on the part of both the school board members and the administration, of the philosophy and mission statement of the school. Priorities, usually established in a five-year planning process (see chapter on long-range planning), should be articulated by the school board in advance of the annual budgeting process. Based on those priorities, the school administrator should establish the initial expenditure budget. Expenditure budgets should be considered not only in terms of total dollars to be spent, but also in terms of the cost-per-pupil in relation to schools of similar size and structure, both on a diocesan and on a national level.

With expenditure budget established, an income should be planned by the administration, with the participation of the pastor. Careful attention must be paid to the financing mix as well as the relationships among parish support, tuition, fees and assessments, fund raising and development. The preliminary budget should be reviewed and eventually approved by the school board. It cannot be stressed too strongly at the outset, that the annual operating budget should be reflective of, and based on, the school's philosophy, mission statement and five-year plan.

In order to prepare an effective annual operating budget, school board members and administrators must rely on an effective bookkeeping system. Such a system usually requires the separation of school and church accounts. It records cash receipts and cash disbursements on a daily basis. An effective bookkeeping system also provides receipt and disbursement summaries on a monthly basis.

Reasons for Effective Bookkeeping and Budgeting

Writing in the August 1982 issue of *Management Accounting*, two certified public accountants seriously questioned church accounting practices. In an article entitled, "Closing the GAAP in Church Accounting," Terry L. Arndt, CPA, Ph.D., and Richard W. Jones, CPA, Ph.D., said in part, "It's time for houses of worship to cast aside their haphazard budgetary techniques in favor of proper financial management procedures." They went on to challenge not only budgetary techniques, but bookkeeping, accounting and financial reporting procedures as well. Catholic school administrators would do well to follow their recommendations.

An effective bookkeeping and budgeting system is needed in every parish elementary school for the following reasons:

◆ To ensure orderly financial management, displaying income and expenses in such a way as to focus attention on program priorities;

◆ To provide financial information to administrators, school board members and diocesan departments in a consistent, easy-to-understand and easy-to-use format; and

◆ To provide assurance to the school's many publics that the school administration is responsible and is exercising good stewardship.

Preparing the Annual Budget

Annual operating budgets should be prepared by the school administration, with participation of the pastor and school board. The final budget should be approved by the board in time to sign teacher contracts and set tuition rates for the upcoming year. It is generally recommended that the budget development process be completed by April 30 for a budget to become effective July 1.

Shown below are some general guidelines which should be observed during the budget preparation process.

◆ Budget figures should be realistic and not "padded." A contingency account should be established to meet unanticipated expenses.

◆ Make realistic allowances for inflation.

◆ The budget format should follow the standard "Chart of Accounts" (see Appendix A).

◆ Projected expenses should have supporting documentation to justify the planned expenditure.

◆ Projected income items should have a supporting plan to ensure that the income can, in fact, be realized.

◆ The budget should reflect the priorities of the board and administration. New programs or expanded programs should not be forced into a preestablished budget.

◆ Budget carefully for all expenditure items. Budgeted figures should be based on actual expectations using the most recent expenditure data. Avoid basing line item budgets on the prior year's budgets.

The following points outline the budget development process for a parish elementary school. It is important that these steps be followed sequentially in an effort to provide for an orderly preparation and to ensure as broad a participation as possible.

Month	Person Responsible—Task
July	*Principal with monthly monitoring by school board*—Begin implementation of current year's budget.
August	No budgeting activity.
September (and each succeeding month)	*Principal and School Board*—Board reviews monthly and year-to-date actual performance against budget.
October	*School Board's long-range plan committee*—Five-year plan is updated by long-range plan committee of the school board. New assumptions are presented to the budget development committee no later than December.
	Principal/School Board; School Board budget or finance committee—Principal convenes budget planning committee for review of basic assumptions set forth in the long-range plan.
December	*Principal/School Board finance committee*—Begin actual preparation of annual budget based on revised long-range plan.

Principal presents school board finance committee members with budget preparation forms and "Charts of Accounts." Responsibility for various sections of the budget are assigned.

Assumptions are developed by administration in the areas of enrollment and staffing, to be presented to committee in January.

January	*Principal*—Finalize enrollment and staffing assumptions, including salary schedules and fringe benefits.
	Principal—Back-up forms should be used detailing faculty by name, grade taught, salary base, and additional information.
	Principal—Distribute budget request information to faculty for use in preparing textbook, supply, and departmental requests.
February	*Principal and School Board finance committee*— Develop line-by-line expenditure budget using faculty and departmental requests, as well as assumptions built into long-range plan.
	List all salary costs, including fixed charges and fringe benefits. This will be the largest single expenditure in the operating budget. It should be refined and finalized at this point.
	Building repairs and improvements should be detailed for the operating budget from the five-year plan. The finance committee should review the priorities established for repairs and maintenance.
March	*Principal and School Board finance committee*—Develop line-by-line income assumptions including tuitions, fund-raising, parish subsidy and development income.

It is essential that each of the income accounts mentioned above have a back-up form prepared showing how the income will be achieved. The back-up forms should show all formulas, calculations and projects used in deriving the income total.

Assumptions for tuition and/or fee increases should be clearly stated since they will need to be presented to the full school board for approval along with the completed budget.

With the income assumptions completed, the school board's finance committee will meet with the administration to review the preliminary budget. It is essential that efforts be made at this point to balance the budget, with income equaling or exceeding expenditures.

If expenditures exceed income, the administration should make recommendations for expenditure cuts, and/or adjustments for investment opportunities (see long-range plan chapter) and/or increased income.

Month	Person Responsible—Task
April	*Principal and School Board finance committee*—Present tentative budget to the school board for approval.
	Back-up information on specific income should also be provided to the board, particularly in the areas of tuition and fund-raising.
May	*Principal*—Calendarize budget for control purposes and develop a monthly cash flow (see Appendix C).
June	*Principal*—Publish budget in annual report.

The Chart of Accounts and Budget Preparation

With regard to the line items presented in the budget, the cardinal rule is consistency. That is, financial reports should, as much as possible, be prepared in similar, if not identical, formats from one year to the next. Line items of revenue and expense should be identified by clearly understandable, descriptive titles. This series of line items is called the "Chart of Accounts." It is generally recommended that revenue items be segmented into categories of tuition, fees and assessments, subsidies, parent and student fund-raising activities, formal development programs and contributed services. Some provision should also be made for miscellaneous income. Expenditure categories should be subtotaled in order to provide the reader with an overview of at least the following: administrative costs, instructional costs, library costs, operational costs (plant and facilities), convent costs, fixed costs and capital expenditures.

A sample Chart of Accounts is included as Appendix A. A sample financial report is included as Appendix B.

Budget Reporting

With an effective budget developed, it is important that the budget be reported to the various publics with which the school deals. One of the best vehicles for such reporting is the annual report.

The annual report, as the name suggests, should be published every year, following the close of the school year. Effective annual reports are usually published in booklet form, and contain not only financial information. The annual report should include the school's goals and objectives which were established for the preceding year, along with a detail of activities which took place in an effort to meet those objectives. Goals and objectives for the upcoming year should also be outlined in the annual report. The report should detail what new resources will be required to meet those goals and objectives.

Financially, the annual report should present the budget prepared at the beginning of the preceding year, along with the actual income and expenses shown in comparison to that budget. The budget for the upcoming year should be presented and shown in juxtaposition to the prior year's budget.

In developing its own list of publics, a school would want to make annual reports available to at least the following:

- ◆ Pastor and parish priest
- ◆ Pastors and priests of neighboring parishes served by the school
- ◆ Members of the parish council
- ◆ Parishioners
- ◆ Parents
- ◆ Diocesan educational officials
- ◆ Individual and business donors
- ◆ Agencies and foundations making grants to the school

Budget Format

Catholic elementary school financial reports, which are intended for publication and use by various publics, should be designed to reflect as much professionalism as possible. Specifically, the Catholic school financial reports at year-end should be prepared with five columns. A sample columnar format is shown below.

(1)	(2)	(3)	(4)	(5)
1984-85 Actual	1984-85 Plan	Fav/(Unfav) to Plan	1985-86 Plan	$ Amount of Increase/(Decrease) from 1984-85 Actual
		(Col. 1 minus Col. 2)		

As shown, the first column is designed to show actual income and expenses, while the second column shows income and expenses as they were budgeted prior to the beginning of the school year. The third column reflects the variances between the line items in the planned budget and the actual budget. The fourth column is designed to provide the reader with budget information for the upcoming year, while the fifth column is designed to show changes between actual revenues and expenses, and those budgeted for the following year.

Calendarized Budget and Cash Flow

Cash management may be defined as the ability to track and control changes in cash position due to generation of income or expenses. Since effective cash management is essential in the Catholic elementary school, the annual operating budget should be used as a control document. Not only should the control document prove useful to the school's principal on a regular basis, but the air of control that it represents should prove extremely useful in the school's development efforts. Potential funding sources will be impressed by solid financial control and adequate reporting to publics served.

Preparation of a calendarized budget is the most effective way of achieving a monthly control document. Development of a calendarized budget for both income and expense will allow school administrators to develop a monthly cash flow using the techniques described below. The purpose of a cash flow projection is to ensure that the projected income for each month will cover expenditures for that month.

The following is a detail of specific tasks to be handled by pastors, principals and bookkeepers as a calendarized budget and cash flow system is implemented.

Pastor

◆ Participate in the budget development process with the principal and appropriate committee.
◆ Secure the services of an accountant to prepare the calendarized (nonlinear) budget and cash flow system to cover the fiscal year.
◆ Review the calendarized budget in detail and approve the cash flow.
◆ Review the self-audit statements, on a monthly basis, with the principal and bookkeeper.

Principal

◆ Participate in the budget development process with the pastor and appropriate committee.
◆ Provide input to the accountant with regard to the preparation of the calendarized budget.
◆ Review the calendarized budget in detail.
◆ Approve all invoices prior to payment.
◆ Make spending adjustments as necessary.
◆ Review and analyze the monthly self-audit statements.

Bookkeeper

◆ Provide input to the accountant with regard to the preparation of the calendarized budget.

◆ Review the calendarized budget in detail.
◆ Maintain the checking account, cash receipts journal, and cash disbursements journal accurately.
◆ At the end of the month, close the books of original entry and reconcile the checking account with the bank statement.
◆ Reconcile the checking account with the cash receipts and cash disbursements journals.
◆ Complete the monthly self-analysis statement, transferring the actual income and expenses from the cash receipts and cash disbursements journals to the monthly self-analysis statement.
◆ With the monthly information transferred and balanced, complete the year-to-date section of monthly self-analysis statement.
◆ Copy the monthly self-analysis statement for the pastor, principal and accountant.
◆ Retain a copy of the monthly self-analysis statement with the appropriate notations to assist in the refinement of the calendarized budget for the next year.

Additional information concerning the calendarized budget and cash flow system for schools can be obtained in the December 1978 issue of *Momentum*, the NCEA journal.

Shown in Appendix C are sample calendarized expense, income and cash flow sheets. Appendix D consists of a monthly budget analysis of both income and expenses.

The following charts are excerpted from the original Appendices A-D in the *Elementary School Finance Manual*. The learner is encouraged to contact the Diocesan Financial Office to obtain the appropriate school financial forms to use in studying this material.

Appendix A
(Partial) Chart of Accounts—
Description of Operating Accounts

Receipts

This section contains the definitions of school accounts listed as *Receipts* in the *Chart of Accounts*. These definitions are to be used to determine the proper allocation of cash received during the current year.

0100 Series—Tuition

The accounts in this series are to be used to record Tuition Payments made by students to the school.

0110—IN-PARISH TUITION—Record here any current year tuition received from students in the parish or in parishes affiliated with the school.

0120—OUT-OF-PARISH TUITION—Record here any current year tuition received from students who are from parishes not affiliated with the school or who are not affiliated with any parish. Also record here any tuition received from students who are non-Catholic.

0135—KINDERGARTEN TUITION—Use this account to record receipts of Kindergarten tuition.

0136—PRE-SCHOOL TUITION—Use this account to record receipts of Pre-School tuition.

0140—PRIOR YEARS' TUITION—This account is to be used to record monies received from those who pay tuition from previous years.

0150—OTHER TUITION—Record here any tuition payments from students whose classification does not fit the above listed accounts.

0160—CONTINGENCY FOR UNCOLLECTIBLE TUITION—This account is a planning account only and should not be used for anything except budgetary purposes during the budget-making process. It will always be a negative figure.

0200 Series—Subsidies/Assessments/Special Funds

Subsidies and assessments are monies given to the school for either its operation as an educational institution or, in specific cases, as a sum allocated as scholarships for financial assistance to the students.

0210—PARISH SUBSIDY—(applicable to parish schools) Record here any monies received from the parish as part of full payment of its subsidy to the parish school. Any payments of past-due subsidies are to be recorded here as well.

0220—PARISH ASSESSMENTS—(applicable to regional schools) Record here any monies received from the parish as part of full payment of its subsidy to the parish school. Any payments of past-due assessments are to be recorded here as well. Also, include any assessments which are earmarked as scholarship aid.

0230—SPECIAL REGIONAL FUNDING—(R.C.E.F.) This account is to be used by schools to record receipts of any area Catholic education fund.

0240—SPECIAL FUNDS FROM THE DIOCESE—Record here any special receipts from the Diocese for emergency situations and special purposes. This is a restricted account.

0250—OTHER—Record here any other assessments or subsidies not provided for in other accounts of this series.

0700 Series—Exchange Funds

0710—EXCHANGE ACCOUNT—This account is to be used to record all receipts of income which are held for a specific purpose and which will be matched by an *identical* expense. The *identical* expense account is Account #2410. An example is money collected for a group purchase of books from a book club.

0800 Series—Scholarships from Endowment

0810—SCHOLARSHIPS FROM ENDOWMENT FUND—This account is to be used only to record transfers of funds from the Endowment Fund—for the purpose of scholarships.

Expenses

This section contains the definitions of school accounts listed as *Expenses* in the *Chart of Accounts*. These definitions are to be used to determine the proper allocation of cash expenditures disbursed during the school year.

1101 Series—Instruction

Instruction, as a general term for this series of accounts, consists of those activities which deal with or aid in the teaching of students or improve the quality of teaching. The activities of the teacher, principal, guidance personnel, and librarian are included here.

1101—RELIGIOUS PROFESSIONAL PERSONNEL—Charge to this account any salaries paid to religious personnel engaged in teaching, guidance, library, administration, etc.

1103—LAY PROFESSIONAL PERSONNEL—Charge to this account any salaries paid to lay personnel engaged in teaching, guidance, library, administration, etc.

1105—SALARIES—SUBSTITUTE TEACHERS—Record in this account any salaries paid to teachers who are substituting for other teachers who are absent from duties.

1107—SALARIES—TEACHER AIDES—Charge to this account any salaries paid to aides or other para-professionals.

1125—INSTRUCTIONAL MATERIALS—Record in this account all expenditures for consumable and non-consumable instructional materials. Items which should be recorded here are expenditures for all departmental supplies which are actually or constructively consumed in the teacher-learning process, including freight and cartage on them. Items which should be included are books, periodicals, documents, pamphlets, photographs, reproductions, pictorial or graphic works, musical scores, maps, charts, globes, sound recordings, processed slides, transparencies, films, filmstrips, kinescopes, videotapes and educational computer software. Also included are printed and published instructional materials as well as portable instructional equipment, suitable for and to be used by children and teachers in elementary schools. The term also includes the following: tests, chalk, paper, test tubes, ink, pencils, paints, paint brushes, crayons, chemicals, food for the instructional program, and other instructional supplies. *Note:* The term *does not* include furniture, non-portable equipment or items normally affixed to the realty or forming a part of the building structure.

School Financial Report Form—Elementary Schools

SCHOOL _____ ADDRESS _____ DATE _____

	(1) 1984-85 Actual	(2) 1984-85 Plan	(3) VARIANCE Fav/Unfav (to Plan)	(4) 1985-86 Plan	(5) $ Amount of Increase/ (Decrease) from 84-85 Actual
SCHOOL INCOME			*(Col. 1 minus Col. 2)*		*(Col. 4 minus Col. 1)*
0100 Series—Tuition *(Note individual rates on pg. 52)*					
0100—In Parish Tuition					
0102—Out of Parish Tuition (Tuition From Students in Other Parishes)					
0135—Kindergarten Tuition					
0136—Pre-School Tuition					
0140—Prior Years' Tuition					
0150—Other Tuition					
0160—Contingency for Uncollectible Tuition					
1. TOTAL All Items Minus Acct. #0160					
0200 Series— Subsidies/Assessments/ Special Funds					
0210—Parish Subsidy (applicable to parish schools)					
0220—Parish Assessments (applicable to regional schools)					
0230—Special Regional Funding					
0240—Special Funds From Diocese					
0250—Other					
2. TOTAL					
0300 Series—Third Source Income					
0310—Receipts From Home/School Association					
0315—Bingo					
0320—Donations, Gifts, Bequests					

SCHOOL INCOME	(1) 1984-85 Actual	(2) 1984-85 Plan	(3) VARIANCE Fav/Unfav (to Plan)	(4) 1985-86 Plan	(5) $ Amount of Increase/ (Decrease) from 84-85 Actual
			(Col. 1 minus Col. 2)		*(Col. 4 minus Col. 1)*
0500 Series—Transfer From Capital Improvement Fund					
6. 0545—Transfer From Capital Improvement Fund					
0600 Series—Transfer From Savings					
7. 0610—Transfer From Savings					
0700 Series—Exchange Funds					
8. 0710—Exchange Account					
0800 Series—Scholarships From Endowment Fund					
9. 0810—Scholarships From Endowment					
10. TOTAL School Income— Lines 1 through 4					
11. Pupil Transportation—Line 5					
12. TOTAL Income— Add Lines 10 and 11					
13. GRAND TOTAL: All Income— Add Lines 6, 7, 8, 9 & 12					

EXPENSES

01100 Series—Instruction

1101—Salaries—Relig. Prof. Personnel					
1103—Salaries—Lay Prof. Personnel					
1105—Salaries—Substitute Teachers					
1107—Salaries—Teachers' Aides					
1122—Textbooks					
1125—Instructional Materials					
1129—Guidance and Testing					

	(1)	(2)	(3)	(4)	(5)
SCHOOL INCOME	1984-85 Actual	1984-85 Plan	VARIANCE Fav/Unfav (to Plan)	1985-86 Plan	$ Amount of Increase/ (Decrease) from 84-85 Actual
			(Col. 1 minus Col. 2)		*(Col. 4 minus Col. 1)*
2300 Series—Supplies & Textbook for Resale					
2301—Supplies & Textbooks	____	____	____	____	____
2305—Other Expenses	____	____	____	____	____
24. TOTAL	____	____	____	____	____
25. 2410—Exchange Account	____	____	____	____	____
2500 Series—Transfer to Savings Account					
26. 2510—Transfer to Savings	____	____	____	____	____
2600 Series—Transfer to Capital Improvement Fund					
27. 2610—Transfer to Capital Improvement Fund	____	____	____	____	____
2700 Series—Transfer to Endowment Fund					
28. 2710—Transfer to Endowment Fund	____	____	____	____	____
29. TOTAL School Expenses: Add Lines 14 through 24	____	____	____	____	____
30. Pupil Transportation: Add TOTAL from page 51	____	____	____	____	____
31. Faculty Residence Expenses: Add TOTAL from page 51	____	____	____	____	____
32. TOTAL Expenses: Add Lines 29, 30 & 31	____	____	____	____	____
33. GRAND TOTAL: All Expenses— Add Lines 25, 26, 28 & 32	____	____	____	____	____

Appendix C

Expenses
Sample Calendar
1984–85

	Total Budget	July	Aug.	Sept.	Oct.	Apr.	May	June
INSTRUCTIONAL SALARIES								
a. Lay teachers & lay principal	$98,738	8,714	8,714	8,131	8,131	8,131	8,131	8,131
b. Religious teachers & prin.	10,496	833	833	833	833	833	833	833
c. Substitutes.	1,300	—	—	100	100	50	50	—
d. Social Security	7,790	691	691	639	639	636	636	632
e. Lay Employment Benefit Program .	7,300	608	608	609	608	608	608	609
f. Unemployment Compensation	—	—	—	—	—	—	—	—
TOTAL a, b, c, d, e, f	125,624	10,846	10,846	10,312	10,311	10,258	10,258	10,205
INSTRUCTION OTHER								
a. Textbooks & Workbooks—Secular . .	7,000	—	—	5,500	1,000	—	—	—
b. Textbooks & Workbooks—Religious	2,500	—	—	1,500	1,000	—	—	—
c. Library Books & Supplies	1,500	—	—	1,000	—	—	—	—
d. Teaching Supplies & AV.	3,800	—	—	1,500	1,500	—	—	—
e. Office Supplies & Expenses.	1,700	—	400	400	300	200	—	—
TOTAL a, b, c, d, e	16,500	—	400	9,900	3,800	200	—	—
OPERATIONS SALARIES								
a. Custodian	7,764	897	897	597	597	597	597	597
b. Office Staff	8,480	707	707	706	707	707	707	706
TOTAL a, b	16,244	1,604	1,604	1,303	1,304	1,304	1,304	1,303
OPERATIONS OTHER								
a. Fuel.	15,000	—	—	—	—	2,000	—	—
b. Other Utilities.	7,000	400	400	600	600	600	600	600
c. Custodial Supplies	1,700	200	300	—	400	300	—	—
d. Custodial Services	3,000	190	190	910	190	190	190	190
TOTAL a, b, c, d	26,700	790	890	1,510	1,190	3,090	790	790
MAINTENANCE								
a. Building Repairs	1,500	—	300	300	300	300	—	—
b. Scheduled Maintenance	3,000	—	—	—	—	—	—	—
c. Repair/Repl. of Furn., Equip.	1,000	—	300	500	200	—	—	—
TOTAL a, b, c	5,500	—	600	800	500	300	—	—
FIXED CHARGES								
a. Property Insurance.	3,000	—	—	—	—	—	—	—
b. Pupil Insurance	200	—	—	—	200	—	—	—
c. Teacher Inservice	900	—	—	500	—	—	—	—
d. Other Fixed Costs	1,300	—	500	—	200	300	—	—
TOTAL a, b, c, d	5,400	—	500	500	400	300	—	—
STUDENT SERVICES								
a. Cafeteria—Milk.	4,000	—	—	400	400	400	400	400
b. Extracurricular Activities	800	—	—	200	—	200	—	200
c. Other—Miscellaneous	1,200	—	—	—	—	—	—	1,000
TOTAL a, b, c	6,000	—	—	600	400	600	400	1,600
TOTAL SCHOOL EXPENSES	$201,968	13,240	14,840	24,925	17,905	16,052	12,752	13,898
CONVENT—Auto.	334	—	—	33	33	33	33	37
—Reimbursement to Parish	6,666	555	555	555	555	555	555	561
TOTAL CONVENT EXPENSES	7,000	555	555	588	588	588	588	598
TOTAL EXPENSES SCHOOL & CONVENT	$208,968	13,795	15,395	25,513	18,493	16,640	13,340	14,496

Income

Sample Calendar
1984–85

	Total Budget	July	Aug.	Sept.	Oct.	Apr.	May	June
TUITION								
a. Parishioners	$54,585	4,000	8,000	6,500	2,000	2,000	5,000	5,085
b. Non-Parishioners	7,060	500	2,000	500	500	1,000	—	60
c. Non-Catholics	36,505	1,000	8,000	5,000	1,000	3,000	500	3,005
(Estimated Delinquency)	(4,900)	(200)	(1,000)	(200)	—	(200)	(100)	(800)
TOTAL a, b, c	93,250	5,300	17,000	11,800	3,500	5,800	5,400	7,350
ASSESSMENT FROM PARISHES OF NON-PARISHIONERS ..	4,000	—	—	—	1,000	—	—	—
FEES	300	—	—	—	100	—	—	100
GIFTS, ENDOWMENTS......	9,726	—	—	—	9,726	—	—	—
SUBSIDY FROM PARISH.....	72,924	5,500	—	10,000	10,000	7,500	7,500	10,034
OTHER INCOME								
a. Cafeteria—Milk	4,000	—	—	400	400	400	400	400
b. Collection Drives—School	—	—	—	—	—	—	—	—
c. Parent/Student Fund Raising	22,500	—	—	—	6,000	3,000	—	500
d. Other Sources	2,500	—	—	250	250	250	250	250
TOTAL a, b, c, d	29,000	—	—	650	6,650	3,650	650	1,150
CATHOLIC SCHOOLS COLLECTION GRANT.......	—	—	—	—	—	—	—	—
TOTAL SCHOOL INCOME....	$209,200	10,800	17,000	22,450	30,976	16,950	13,550	18,634

Cash Flow

Sample Calendar
1984–85

	Total Budget	July	Aug.	Sept.	Oct.	Apr.	May	June
Beginning Balance	$4,960	4,960	—	—	—	—	—	—
TOTAL INCOME	209,200	10,800	17,000	22,450	30,976	16,950	13,550	18,634
TOTAL EXPENSES	208,968	13,795	15,395	25,513	18,493	16,640	13,340	14,496
VARIANCE FAV/(UNFAV).....	5,192	1,965	1,605	(3,063)	12,483	310	210	4,138
CUMULATIVE CASH FLOW...	NA	1,965	3,570	457	12,890	944	1,104	5,192

Appendix D

Income
Monthly Budget Analysis

Item	Month—September 19xx			Year-to-Date		
	Plan	Actual	Variance	Plan	Actual	Variance
TUITION						
a. Kindergarten	$ —			$ —		
b. Parishioners	6,500	4,782.50	(1,717.50)	18,500	13.565.50	(4,934.50)
c. Non-Parishioners	500	2,174.00	1,674.00	3,000	4,434.00	1,434.00
d. Non-Catholics	5,000	5,507.63	507.63	14,000	12,736.13	(1,263.87)
(Estimated Delinquency)	(200)	—	200.00	(1,400)	—	1,400.00
TOTAL a, b, c, d	11,800	12,464.13	664.13	34,100	30,735.63	(3,364.37)
ASSESSMENT FROM PARISHES OF NON-PARISHIONERS	—	—	—	—	200.00	200.00
FEES	—	—	—	—	—	—
GIFTS, ENDOWMENTS	—	9,726.60	9,726.60	—	9,726.60	9,726.60
SUBSIDY FROM PARISH	10,000	273.40	(9,726.60)	15,500	5,773.40	(9,726.60)
ALL OTHER INCOME						
a. Cafeteria	400	—	(400.00)	400	—	(400.00)
b. Collection drives for school	—	—	—	—	—	—
c. Parent/student fund raising	—	—	—	—	—	—
d. Other sources	250	78.11	(171.89)	250	137.31	(112.69)
TOTAL a, b, c, d	650	78.11	(571.89)	650	137.31	(512.69)
CATHOLIC SCHOOLS COLLECTION GRANT	—	—	—	—	—	—
Beginning Balance	—	—	—	4,960	3,707.95	(1,252.05)
TOTAL SCHOOL BALANCE	$23,100	22,542.24	(479.65)	$55,860	50,418.20	1,286.94
Total Expenses	25,563	23,886.73	1,676.27	54,753	49,169.78	5,583.22
Variance Gain/(Loss)	$ (2,463)	(1,344.49)	(1,196.62)	$1,107	(1,248.42)	(4,251.28)

+-------------------------------------+
| **TOTAL UNPAID BILLS** |
| **$1,272.00** |
+-------------------------------------+

Checkbook Balance as of Sept. 1	$3,707.95
Gain/(Loss)	1,344.49
Checkbook Balance as of Oct. 1	$2,363.46

Expenses
Monthly Budget Analysis

Item	Month—September 19xx			Year-to-Date		
	Plan	Actual	Variance	Plan	Actual	Variance
INSTRUCTIONAL SALARIES						
a. Lay teachers & prin.	$8,131	7,836.83	294.17	$25,559	22,630.75	2,928.25
b. Rel. teachers & prin.	883	883.00	—	2,549	2,549.68	(.68)
c. Substitutes	100	—	100.00	100	—	100.00
d. Social Security	639	618.54	20.46	2,021	1,841.46	179.54
e. Lay Employee Benefits	609	710.61	(101.61)	1,825	1,508.12	316.88
f. Unemployment Comp.	—	—	—	—	—	—
TOTAL a, b, c, d, e, f	10,362	10,048.98	313.02	32,054	28,530.01	3,523.99
INSTRUCTION OTHER						
a. Textbooks—Secular	5,500	4,965.15	534.85	5,500	5,289.14	210.86
b. Textbooks—Religious	1,500	—	1,500.00	1,500	—	1,500.00
c. Library books	1,000	82.25	917.75	1,000	117.47	882.53
d. Teaching & AV supplies	1,500	663.77	836.23	1,500	800.65	699.35
e. Office supplies & exp.	400	300.55	99.45	800	595.15	204.85
TOTAL a, b, c, d, e	9,900	6,011.72	3,888.28	10,300	6,802.41	3,497.59
OPERATIONS SALARIES						
a. Custodian	597	1,116.40	(519.40)	2,391	2,242.40	148.60
b. Office Staff	706	678.33	27.67	2,120	2,011.69	108.31
TOTAL a, b	1,303	1,794.73	(419.73)	4,511	4,254.09	256.91
OPERATIONS, OTHER						
a. Fuel	—	—	—	—	—	—
b. Elect, wtr, gas, phone	600	540.34	59.66	1,400	1,242.95	157.05
c. Custodial supplies	—	811.92	(811.92)	500	1,101.57	(601.57)
d. Custodial services	910	79.00	(831.00)	1,290	315.69	974.31
TOTAL a, b, c, d	1,510	1,431.26	(1,583.26)	3,190	2,660.21	529.79
MAINTENANCE						
a. Building repairs	300	27.20	272.80	600	326.22	273.78
b. Scheduled Maint.	—	—	—	—	—	—
c. Repair/repl. furn-equip.	500	323.75	176.25	800	412.91	387.09
TOTAL a, b, c	800	350.95	449.05	1,400	739.13	660.87
FIXED CHARGES						
a. Property Insurance	—	2,951.00	(2,951.00)	—	2,951.00	(2,951.00)
b. Pupil Insurance	—	—	—	—	—	—
c. Teacher Inservice	500	540.00	(40.00)	500	540.00	(40.00)
d. Other	—	95.00	(95.00)	500	95.00	405.00
TOTAL a, b, c, d	500	3,586.00	(3,086.00)	1,000	3,586.00	(2,586.00)
STUDENT SERVICES						
a. Cafeteria—Milk	400	—	400.00	400	—	400.00
b. Extracurricular activ.	200	—	200.00	200	—	200.00
c. Other	—	93.09	(93.09)	—	93.09	(93.09)
TOTAL a, b, c	600	93.09	506.91	600	93.09	506.91
SUBTOTAL SCHOOL EXPENSES	24,975	23,316.73	(3,431.73)	53,055	46,664.94	6,390.06
CONVENT—Auto	33	15.00	18.00	33	15.00	18.00
—Reimb. to Parish	555	555.00	—	1,665	555.00	1,110.00
TOTAL CONVENT EXPENSES	588	570.00	18.00	1,698	570.00	1,128.00
TOTAL EXPENSES SCHOOL & CONVENT	$25,563	23,886.73	(3,413.73)	$54,753	47,234.94	7,518.06

Catholic School Finance and Church-State Relations

McLaughlin, T. 1985. 19. Washington, D.C.: National Catholic Educational Association.

Summary

1. Public schools are financed generally by combinations of state aid, local tax support, federal programs, and business support.

2. In Catholic schools, tuition covers only a percentage of the total student cost, so other funding is needed. Independent schools usually peg the tuition at the total educational cost.

3. One pricing formula which permits the parents to be involved in tuition price-setting is called "negotiated tuition," or "fair share tuition." An agreement on the amount to be paid is reached between the parents and the school representative.

4. A "prepaid tuition plan" is being used in some areas of the country today. The money is invested, and the interest is used in lieu of increasing tuition. Parents who cannot afford to pay the entire tuition in advance are granted bank loans at a favorable interest rate.

5. Some schools charge no tuition. The parish supports the school from church funds. Parents may realize some tax advantage because of their contributions to the parish through this procedure.

6. There appears to be stronger emphasis being placed on the need to have the total Catholic community support the Catholic school system today.

The Role of the Board in Finances

Sheehan, L. 1990. In *Building better boards: A handbook for board members in Catholic education*, 26–31. Washington, D.C.: National Catholic Educational Association.

Catholic schools are funded from a combination of tuition, subsidies (parish, diocesan, religious congregation, and contributed services), fund-raising, and development. Public schools on the other hand, are funded from state, local, and federal taxes.

The current funding trend in the public schools is toward more state aid rather than local aid in order to equalize educational opportunities for all public school students in the state.

On the other hand, Catholic school funding remains dependent on tuition, with assistance from subsidy and increasing development efforts. However, several state conferences of Catholic bishops in pastoral letters have restated that the financing of Catholic schools is the responsibility of the total Catholic community—not just users and staff.

School boards should always include provisions for some financial aid in budgets so that Catholic schools remain available to students regardless of their family's socioeconomic status.

The manner in which the board is constituted will certainly determine who has authority to make final decisions. Whether the board is constituted as consultative or one with limited jurisdiction, it is involved in two major areas of financial management: the annual budget and tuition.

Budget

The annual budget is the key to financial control and is based on the philosophy, mission statement and long-range plan of the school.

The expenditure budget is prepared by the finance committee of the board and the principal, and considers the total amount of money to be spent and the cost per pupil in relation to schools of similar size and situation, both on a diocesan and national level. The *Elementary School Finance Manual* and the *Self-Study Guide for Catholic High Schools*, both published by NCEA, are resources for this information.

The income budget is prepared by the finance committee of the board and the principal, in conjunction with the pastor and the finance council of the parish or parishes involved. At the diocesan school, or private Catholic school, appropriate diocesan and religious congregation personnel should be involved. The income budget considers the financial mixes and relationship among subsidies, tuition, fees and assessment, fund-raising, and development.

The amount of subsidy which the school receives is determined by the parish, diocese, or religious congregation. The finance committee of the parish school board should meet with the finance council of the parish and the pastor to determine the amount the total parish will invest in the school. The school subsidy is part of the parish budget and is approved with the total parish budget according to diocesan and parish policies and practices. The approval of the school budget is the responsibility of the school board according to its procedures and guidelines. Other schools' subsidy is determined by diocesan and religious congregation policies.

Budget Preparation Guidelines

1. Budget figures should be realistic and not "padded." A contingency account should be established to meet unanticipated expenses.
2. The budget makes realistic allowances for inflation.
3. The budget format should follow the standard "Chart of Accounts" (NCEA *Elementary School Finance Manual*, 1984, or other approved charts of accounts).
4. Projected expenses should have supporting documentation to justify the planned expenditure.
5. Projected income items should have a supporting plan to ensure that the income can, in fact, be realized. Do not budget uncertain income.
6. The budget should reflect the priorities of the board and administration. New programs or expanded programs should not be forced into a preestablished budget.
7. The budget includes all expenditure items. Budgeted figures should be based on actual expectations using the most recent expenditure data. Avoid basing line item budgets on the prior year's budget.
8. The budget should include money for financial aid to families who cannot afford the tuition.

Budget Calendar

A regular, scheduled approach to budget preparation through the use of a calendar can provide the necessary structuring to the budget process for a school. In NCEA's *Elementary School Finance Manual*, the following calendar is suggested:

Month	Responsible Party and Tasks
July	*Principal with monthly monitoring by school board*—Begin implementation of current year's budget.
August	No budgeting activity.
September *(and each succeeding month)*	*Principal and school board*—Review monthly and year-to-date actual performance against budget.
October	*School board's long-range plan committee*—Update five-year plan. Present new assumptions to the budget development committee no later than December. Principal/school board; school board budget or finance committee—Convene budget planning committee for review of basic assumptions set forth in the long-range plan.
December	*Principal/school board finance committee*—Begin actual preparation of annual budget based on revised long-range plan. *Principal*—Present school board finance committee members with budget preparation forms and "Chart of Accounts." Assign responsibilities for various sections of the budget.

Develop assumptions in the areas of enrollment and staffing presentation to the committee in January.

January	*Principal*—Finalize enrollment and staffing assumptions, including salary schedules and fringe benefits. Use back-up forms detailing faculty by name, grade taught, salary base, and additional information. Distribute budget request information to faculty for use in preparing textbook, supply, and departmental requests.
February	*Principal and school board finance committee*—Develop line-by-line expenditure budget using faculty and departmental requests, as well as assumptions built into long-range plan. List all salary costs, including fixed charges and fringe benefits. This will be the largest single expenditure in the operating budget. It should be refined and finalized at this point. Detail building repairs and improvements for the operating budget from the five-year plan. The **finance committee** should review the priorities established by the board for repairs and maintenance.
March	*Principal and school board finance committee*—Develop line-by-line income assumptions including tuitions, fundraising, subsidies, and development income.
April	*Principal and school board finance committee*—Present tentative budget to the school board for approval. Provide back-up information on specific income to the board, particularly in the areas of tuition and fund-raising.
May	*Principal*—Calendarize budget for control purposes and develop a monthly cash flow. (See Appendix C of Elementary School Finance Manual included with Burke's Budgeting article, in this text.)
June	*Principal*—Publish budget in annual report.

Budget Approval

Ordinarily, a board with limited jurisdiction has authority to approve the annual budget. A consultative board will need the enactment of the pastor or comparable diocesan or religious congregation person before the budget can be implemented by the principal.

The process for approval should be determined in the operating procedures of the board. It is appropriate that the pastor and parish finance and pastoral councils be involved in determining the amount of parish subsidy to the school. This is also an appropriate role for the diocesan education office or religious congregation in the case of many diocesan and private Catholic schools. The school board should be responsible for factoring the subsidy into the total balanced budget and submitting that for the approval of the pastor, diocesan office, or religious congregation.

Budget Reporting

Usually, the budget is presented in the annual report, which includes—in addition to the approved budget—the school's goals and objectives which were established for the preceding year and the activities which took place in meeting those objectives. It also should include plans for the following year and resources needed to accomplish them. A final item is the financial statement, which compares actual income and expenses with the projected budget.

The annual report is made available to those persons and groups who are involved in the school: for example, the pastor or pastors who subsidize the school, members of the parish pastoral council(s), diocesan office, bishop and religious congregations for diocesan and private schools, parents, parishioners, and donors. It is also important to note there should be a monthly financial report to the board so that the budget can be monitored responsibly.

Tuition

The questions which need to be addressed regarding Catholic school tuition are: What share of the actual cost per pupil is to be borne by parents who choose Catholic schools for their children, and who makes this determination?

Traditional Approach

The most traditional approach to tuition used by over 90 percent of Catholic elementary schools defines tuition in the following way: The tuition charge is the cost per pupil, less the subsidy, less operating revenue per pupil (fund-raising, interest earned, etc.). That figure equals the per-pupil user cost or the traditional tuition charged. The advantage of this system is its simplicity. The two major disadvantages are that this approach usually ignores capital costs and provides the same subsidy to each student whether the subsidy is needed or wanted.

Alternative Methods

There are several alternative methods of determining tuition and financing schools that are being used in some dioceses. All of these seem to fall into the category of negotiated or fair share tuition charges. In these methods, the actual per-pupil cost is presented to parents who are asked to consider seriously how much of this amount they can pay as tuition. Persons selected to meet with parents should be known in the community for their commitment to the school and their ability to maintain confidences. These approaches are based on the following assumptions:

1. Communication is necessary. When people totally understand the financial facts, they are more likely to respond.
2. People have a need to give. When they have an ever so slight amount of discretionary funds, they will support the self-perceived needs and good causes.

3. The preservation of Catholic education for all. Catholic schools should not be available only to those who can afford increasing costs.

Strategies

If a group is considering an alternative means of determining tuition, such as negotiated or fair share, there are certain strategies which should be considered for implementation.

This is also true if a parish is considering instituting a program of sacrificial giving and operating a tuition-free school.

The first point to remember is the good will of people and their need to give. Parents should be informed and involved in this new approach from the beginning. The second important strategy is the essential component of leadership, that is, the principal and pastor(s) **must** be behind this effort. The third strategy involves the importance of presenting the actual per-pupil cost and marketing the effort and determining the time relationship between marketing and the actual implementation. The fourth strategy includes the selection and training of a limited number of negotiators who ought to be known for prudence and discretion. And the last strategy is the significance of communicating the changed approach with parents.

Tuition Collection

Another consideration of the board is determining when tuition should be collected. The traditional practice requires that tuition and fees be paid by the end of the academic year. This is called a post-paid plan. More schools are moving toward some type of prepaid tuition plan or variations to this approach. For example, some schools use the entirely prepaid and discounted approach while others use the prepaid and discounted approach with commercial or credit union borrowing available. Some schools are allowing parents to prepay tuition by using a major credit card, while others are assisting parents through arrangements with a local bank to assume low-interest loans to repay tuition. Additional information concerning some alternative plans can be found in the appendix.

Daily Financial Management

Although the board is not engaged in the daily financial management of the school, it is essential that this phase of the school's operation is organized and functioning adequately; therefore the board may want to develop adequate policies which will ensure such an efficient operation.

Principles:
1. The system should be clear, concise, and repetitive.
2. The procedures should be governed by the policies of the diocese, religious congregation, or parish. This would include bonding of all persons who handle money. All school savings and checking accounts

should require more than one person's signature for issuing checks and withdrawing money; and the actual daily financial "set-up" should be designed to allow for the preparation of the following types of information:

a. cost per pupil;
b. revenues and expenses incurred for a given time-period; and
c. comparison of actual revenues and expenses with budgeted amounts.

3. It is preferable that the school have a separate financial account. However, if school funds are mingled with parish, diocesan, or religious congregation funds, then the school should have a means of generating regular financial reports for its own operation.

4. The roles and responsibilities of those involved in financial management should be clearly stated (school bookkeeper, parish bookkeeper, pastor, principal, board, and parish finance council).

Long-range Planning

Burke, R. 1984. In *Elementary school finance manual*, 84–89.
Washington, D.C.: National Catholic Educational Association.

Introduction

Long-range planning is not simply a necessary component of good development and effective budgeting. Planning is critically important to the ability of Catholic schools to survive and to flourish through the 1980s, 1990s, and beyond. It is an exercise of prudence, leadership, and vision. Planning both articulates the goals of Catholic education for the school and organizes all available resources into a plan to attain those goals. Long-range planning as an act of true Christian stewardship strives to preserve and to pass on to future generations the treasure of vital Catholic educational institutions.

As budgets are considered a financial expression of the institution's priorities, so too, long-range plans are meant to express the priorities and projections of the school in the areas of enrollment, curriculum, staffing, facilities, finance, and development.

It is essential that all considerations in each of the above planning areas are based on and tied to the school's philosophy. *To Teach As Jesus Did* (1972 Pastoral Message of the American Bishops), *The Catholic School* (1977 Statement of the Vatican Congregation for Catholic Education) and diocesan policies and guidelines form the basis for each school's revised philosophy.

As our society continues to experience rapid and frequent changes, long-range planning for elementary school is increasingly of paramount importance. Long-range planning helps Catholic elementary school administrators avoid crises situations and last-minute decision making. The five-year plan process outlined in this chapter is designed for maximum participation. It is structured to allow problems and opportunities to be anticipated in advance.

Use of the long-range plan process described in this chapter assumes that the school has a good bookkeeping system and can obtain statistical and financial information on a timely basis. However, it assumes that the bookkeeping system is used not simply to record historical data, but to allow administrators and board members to monitor and manage the school's operations.

Roles and Responsibilities

The long-range plan process described in this chapter is designed to be implemented with the involvement of the pastor, principal, and school board. Specific roles are outlined for each.

The Pastor's Role

From a financial management point of view, the pastor's role with regard to the parish school is clearly defined in Canon Law. He is canonically responsible for the fiscal operation of the parish, including the parish school. In short, he is ultimately responsible, at the parish level, for the overall management functions. While his responsibility is huge, the pastor is encouraged, under the principle of subsidiarity (that principle which holds that no decision should be made at a higher management level when it can effectively be made at a lower hierarchical level) to delegate duties and responsibilities. It is, in fact, this delegation which brings to light the role of other individuals and groups.

Given this premise, the pastor's primary responsibility is to commission the preparation of a formal, long-range plan. This is usually done in writing to the school board and principal, followed by a personal presentation by the pastor to the principal and board members. With the planning process underway, the pastor offers his candid input to the board with regard to parish finances, parishioner attendance trends, and parish goals and directions. It is, of course, most helpful if the pastor outlines any "non-negotiables" at the onset of the planning process.

The Principal's Role

It is the role of the principal, as the school's administrator, to initiate the planning process and to guide it to completion. While the pastor and school board are involved in the planning process throughout, the principal's primary role is that of catalyst. The suggested chronology for the planning process outlined in this chapter details the main steps in the process and the activities involved for the principal and board members.

The School Board's Role

The primary role of the school board is to receive input from the school's faculty and administration, to discuss and test options, and to develop assumptions that will be included in the long-range plan. The school board should at all times work to place assumptions within a policy framework, and not become involved in the administrative tasks of operating the school.

Plan Format

The long-range plan (five-year plan) is designed not only to provide a direction for the school, but also a historical perspective for that direction. As a result, the narrative section of the long-range plan should be completed in such a way that each major topic area discusses the historical perspective, the current situation, and the assumptions which have been adopted for the future. In short, the narrative should attempt to answer these questions:

◆ Where have we been?
◆ What factors have influenced our historical development?
◆ Where are we today and why?
◆ Where are we going and why?
◆ How are we going to get there?

Each of these questions should be related to the philosophy of Catholic education generally and to the individual school particularly. In addition, the narrative should support the projections made in each section of the plan (enrollment, curriculum, staffing, facilities, finance, and development).

Again, it should be emphasized that care should be taken during each phase of the plan's creation, to involve various individuals who have particular interest in, and responsibility for, that section of the plan.

Developing the Long-Range Plan

The following suggested chronology and back-up forms may be used by individual school boards and principals for developing a comprehensive long-range plan.

Month	Person Responsible—Task
July	*Principal*—Set aside time for dreaming and goal setting. What problems and opportunities exist for the school? What should it be doing better? What ought it to emphasize now to be more faithful to its philosophy?
August	*Principal/Board Chairperson*—Issue recommitment invitation to board members. Make committee assignments. Note: During initial year, provide board members with *To Teach As Jesus Did, The Catholic School, Teach Them,* and the school's philosophy.

Arrange and conduct Board Preservice Program—include discussion of:
❖ Philosophy
❖ Roles and Responsibilities
❖ Distinction between policy-making and administration

Pastor/Principal—Pastor and principal issue letter to board commissioning long-range plan.

| September | *Principal/Board Chairperson/School Board*—Convene board or long-range plan development committee. Review basic assumptions, constraints, and timetable. Administrator shares dreams, problems, and possibilities for school with board. Board reviews school position in light of documents listed above, diocesan goals, and school philosophy. |
| October | *Principal with School Board*—Board reviews enrollment history and enrollment mix. It begins creation of narrative, citing reasons for enrollment changes (Appendices A and B). |

Enrollment and/or Data Committee

❖ Collect and study prior five-year enrollments by grade (Appendix A) and by religious category (Catholic parishioners, Catholic non-parishioners, non-Catholics) (Appendix B).
❖ Collect and study baptismal records for parish(es) for last five years.
❖ Compare baptismal records to "Parishioner enrollment" for appropriate years.
❖ Secure pertinent data from local public school officials concerning population trends in public school enrollment projections.
❖ Secure population trend information from Census Bureau, Chamber of Commerce, and telephone company.
❖ Build a five-year enrollment projection based on all of the above. The projection should list enrollments first by grade and then by religious mix. Be sure to consider current demographics, trends, and health and fire codes as well as class size (Appendix C).
❖ Outline plans for market research as required.

| November | *Principal with Board*—Board prepares enrollment projections for five years by grade level with accompanying narrative (Appendix C). A marketing plan for school "image" and enrollment should accompany enrollment projections in order to ensure ability to achieve projections. (See *Catholic School Management Letter*, Volume I, 3 and *Momentum*, May, 1979, pages 42–45.) |
| December | *Principal/Faculty*—Curriculum section of five-year plan to be completed by principal and faculty and presented for review by board. |

❖ Review and revise the school philosophy in light of *To Teach As Jesus Did, The Catholic School,* and other documents cited including diocesan guidelines.
❖ Review current curriculum in light of diocesan guidelines and build a five-year plan for curriculum, updating as necessary.

- Include assumptions concerning textbooks (purchasing and replacement), library books, workbooks, equipment, teaching aids, audiovisual equipment, laboratory supplies, etc.
- Build a catalog of investment opportunities based on the dreams of the principal and staff (See *Catholic School Management Letter*, Volume IV, 3).
- Evaluate program offerings including specialized areas; e.g., physical education, music, art, etc.

January *Principal*—Principal, by reviewing current personnel records on all teachers prepares a historical perspective and overview of current staffing situations, including qualifications, experience, salary, benefits, etc. This perspective is reviewed by the board (Appendix D).

Principal reviews staffing assumptions for next five years and prepares a summary for board (Appendix E).

Principal/Pastor/Board—Based on enrollment and staffing assumptions, the principal and board prepare a five-year projection for staffing by grade and/or department. Assumptions should be made in the areas of salaries and fringe benefits.

February *Principal/Pastor Board Facilities Committee*—Initial plan for plant and facilities should be completed by a subcommittee of the board working with the principal.

- Make a complete survey of all physical facilities available, including school buildings, residences, and grounds. Based on current fire and health codes, list all necessary and desirable repairs and capital improvements.
- Develop a five-year plan to complete improvements. Include cost estimates. Survey should be specific as to the number of classrooms and specialized areas to be utilized.
- Build a catalog of investment opportunities based on capital improvements and repairs to buildings, grounds, furniture, and equipment (See *Catholic School Management Letter*, Volume, IV, 3).

March *Principal/Pastor Board Finance Committee*—Review school costs of the last three years using annual reports.

- Ensure that all line items are exclusively those of the school and are not attributable to other parish or religious education programs.

- Develop an expenditure budget based on enrollment, curriculum, staffing, and plant and facility considerations. (Financial growth assumptions should be clearly stated in footnotes or in the assumptions section of the plan.) Include provision for some level of student assistance (Appendix F).

April *Principal/Pastor Board Finance Committee*—Develop a five-year income plan with realistic assumptions in the areas of tuition, subsidies, traditional fund-raising, and investment opportunities (Appendix G).

Create a five-year development plan (Appendix H).

May *Board*—Review the completed five-year plan including projections and accompanying narrative in the areas of philosophy, enrollment, curriculum, staffing, plant and facilities, and finances and development.

- Approval of five-year plan by board.

June *Principal/Board*—Preparation of summary "Case Statement" and Development Plan, based on five-year plan, to be used in promoting the school to various publics. (Note: may take more than one month.) (See *Catholic School Management Letter*, Volume V, 2.)

- Identify Case Statement. Summarize history, philosophy, vision, and objectives of school, in a manner that invites credibility and investment. This statement should stress the unique and desirable characteristics of the total educational program, especially through elements related to its identity as a Catholic school.

Identify for past five years:
- Alumni relations
- Public relations
- Special gifts
- Publics being served
- Endowments
- Foundation grants
- Business/Industry participation
- Estate planning (bequests)
- Insurance gifts
- Fund-raising projects
- Identify priorities for next five years.
- Project realistic involvement and dollar increase to support Finance Committee projections.
- Establish appropriate committees to respond to five-year priority selections.

Note: It is assumed that in fulfillment of the planning role assigned to him/her above, the principal will involve the faculty, through frequent consultation and other appropriate ways.

Using the Long-range Plan

With the five-year plan completed, it becomes a basic guideline document for the principal, pastor, and board. The plan should be reviewed, refined, and updated on an annual basis, so that it continually looks four years into the future.

It should be pointed out that the full five-year plan is not designed for "public consumption." For that purpose, a "Case Statement" based on the five-year plan should be prepared which summarizes the assumptions made in each of the areas including enrollment, curriculum, staffing, plant finance, and development. The philosophy and mission statement of the school should also be clearly stated.

It is, of course, understood that every effort should be made during the planning process to ensure that the curriculum and all aspects of the plan are reflective of the philosophy, and that the values of Catholic education are well integrated with the curriculum.

From the school board's point of view, the long-range plan becomes the guiding document from which annual budgets are developed. These budgets should, on an annual basis, be based on and reflective of, the school's long-range plan.

Finally, five-year planning should be seen, not as an end in itself, but as a prerequisite to, and part of, good development, and as an important help to the school in attaining its goals.

Annual Update of Long-range Plan

It is essential that the five-year plan be annually updated in each succeeding year. In order to simplify the annual update, all of the data used to prepare the plan must be carefully documented and available for future use.

In order to ensure that the projections are updated annually, it is recommended that the school board formally adopt a policy requiring that the update take place. During the updating process, every effort should be made not only to develop an additional year's projection, but also to revise and to refine the assumptions used throughout the plan.

Planning

Sheehan, L. 1990. In *Building better boards: A handbook for board members in Catholic education*, 7–9. Washington, D.C.: National Catholic Educational Association.

Catholic schools are involved in planning activities in a variety of ways. For example, each year the faculty plans inservice opportunities and curriculum development. The school itself usually participates in a type of planning in conjunction with its regular evaluation and accreditation process. The board, usually through its long-range planning committee, assesses where the school is currently and where it hopes to be in the next three to five years. The rationale for board planning is best expressed in the adage, "If you don't know where you're going, any plan will do" (Drucker). Long-range or strategic planning is an absolute necessity for Catholic schools, especially in terms of development and effective budgeting. The chair of the long-range planning committee is a member of the board, but committee members need not be.

Some Pitfalls of Planning

◆ If preparations are not made carefully, planning can cause groups to focus on problems without ever coming up with solutions. Some problems seem so insurmountable that people give up. Planning has to be done in such a way that the group has small successes along the way.

◆ Planning may heighten interpersonal tensions within a group or organization. When these tensions surface, they may obstruct the planning process. Some means has to be built in that will diffuse interpersonal problems.

◆ Planning can allow people to concentrate on paper solutions or on ideas instead of action. Sometimes organizations get so caught up in the planning process that they never get to the implementation stage. It is very easy to push paper around; it is not as easy to motivate and lead people.

◆ Planning that involves goal setting and the writing of objectives (for example, management by objective) can tend to lower standards after it has been used more than one year. People recognize very quickly that they will be judged only on the objectives they write. Therefore, they tend to write objectives that will not make as many demands on them as the ones they wrote in the previous year. Management by objectives usually works very well the first year, but tends to help people slide into mediocrity thereafter.

◆ Planning can lead to inflated budgets. People tend to budget according to all the contingencies they thought of during the planning process, which in turn tends to raise the amount of money they request for any given project. Group planning includes good budgeting, which will help keep the budget realistic.

One Practical Planning Approach

Successful planning includes the steps listed below in the order they are given. The amount of time that any group spends on each of the steps is a part of the planning process. The board is responsible for its own planning and

---

should work closely with the principal in planning for the school.

A. Develop ideal goals

The best way to start out any planning process is to develop the ideal picture of what things should look like at the end of the plan. Starting off with the best situation or scenario stops people from killing good ideas before they ever get off the ground. It is also good to remember that it is much easier to tone down an exciting idea than it is to enhance one that is not exciting or interesting.

In planning, the group can write as many ideal goals as necessary but should cover all aspects of the situation. An example of an ideal goal for a school would be that there will be full enrollment for the coming year, or that there will be no deficit for the coming year.

B. Identify and describe the influences and constraints

Once the ideal picture has been established, the group can come back to earth and deal with constraints. These could be technical, financial, legal, moral, political, social, or demographic limitations. The key during this stage is to concentrate on what is and not what should be.

For example, to have no deficit for next year, the school would have to raise $100,000 through either tuition or third-source funding.

C. Set attainable goals

Attainable goals are the result of adjusting the ideal goals in light of the influences and constraints.

Once the new goals have been written, it is important to see whether or not they have maintained their exciting nature.

An example for an attainable goal might be to have no school deficit three years in the future.

D. Develop alternatives for reaching goals

There is never just one way to do anything. Creativity and imagination are the key factors here. Even the most outlandish ideas must not be dismissed too quickly. The key to success is brainstorming and a ban on all comments like "That's not practical," "We've never done it that way before," "We don't have the time." Just the fact that there is a backup plan increases confidence and the chances that the preferred plan will be successful.

For example, if the group locks in on only tuition as a solution, the goal may not be attained; they should look at all aspects of raising funds and cutting expenses.

E. Do a cost-effective analysis

After the alternatives have been identified and established, it is important for the group to decide on the most effective alternative. The choice is between a) what are the costs, and b) what are the benefits. Cost does not just mean money; it can refer to money, time, space, morale, public relations.

For example, it may be possible to raise tuition to eliminate the deficit, but the school may lose 30 students.

It is always necessary to have a detailed written time schedule for each plan. Without it, there is no accountability.

F. Establish fallback positions for failed plans

No group is infallible. It is always possible that the best plans will not succeed. The future is not predictable, no matter how good the plan. Thus, it is important to plan for contingencies, that is, to have fallback positions in the event that the future does not turn out the way it is projected. For example, suppose the pastor who is very supportive of the school is transferred and the new pastor is not as supportive; what happens then?

G. Implement and evaluate the plan

Use the timetable previously established to begin implementation of the plan. The group itself should monitor the plan closely to see that there is constant evaluation. Usually the principal and the board chairperson have the responsibility for seeing that evaluation takes place. On a yearly basis, there should be a more in-depth and formal evaluation of the long-range plan.

Roles and Responsibilities in Planning

As the canonical administrator of the parish which includes the parish school, the pastor's primary responsibility in planning is to commission the preparation of a formal long-range plan. This commission is usually done in writing to the school board and principal, and when the process is under way, the pastor provides information to the board regarding parish finances, attendance trends, and parish goals and directions. At the beginning, it is helpful if the pastor communicates any "non-negotiables" that the board should keep in mind.

Enrollment: Securing Our Future

Balfe, M., M. Lanning, A. Meese, and A. M. Walsh. 1991. In *Capital wisdom: Papers from the Principals Academy 1991*, 11–20. Washington, D.C.: National Catholic Educational Association.

Did you ever think that news of Catholic schools would make the front page of the *Wall Street Journal*? Or that Peter Jennings would feature Catholic schools on a segment of "American Agenda"? Well, it was and he did!

These things happen because Catholic schools are realizing the importance and benefit of sharing our story. This is marketing.

We believe that Catholic schools are a gift to our nation and our world and that this message needs to be proclaimed. Awareness of the contributions of Catholic schools will help increase and maintain enrollment. It is imperative that individual schools, regions, and diocesan systems plan and implement marketing strategies in order to secure their future.

We offer here an effective plan for the formation of an enrollment committee and give practical strategies to help your committee fulfill its goals. The committee will address both the areas of recruitment (attracting new students) and retention (keeping present students until graduation). Four tasks are necessary for the establishment and implementation of this committee.

Assessment

Determine the needs of your specific school through the use of a survey instrument (see Appendix A). Before you can effectively market any product, it is necessary to know the product and the prospective clientele. Perceptions are not always realities, but it is important to be aware of both. By conducting a survey, you will be able to understand clearly what the needs of your clientele are, as well as their perceptions about your school. Any effective survey needs to be custom-made for the local community.

Planning

Developing an enrollment program for your school will involve a variety of people. If you have a development person on staff, he/she can assume leadership of the program. If not, the principal can be the initiator.

The principal chooses a chairperson for the enrollment committee. This person needs to be carefully selected. A person with a strong commitment to the school and its future, as well as one possessing the necessary skills and a willingness to work hard, is the ideal chairperson.

The chairperson and principal review the results of the survey. From the information gleaned, they set goals and objectives and begin to put together the enrollment committee.

This commitment should consist of four to 12 members, depending on needs. Choose committee members based on skills and areas of expertise. Consider people who have "connections."

A marketing skills background is helpful in this selection but not essential.

The purpose of the enrollment committee is to work with the principal to increase the enrollment of the school or to maintain its current enrollment through the development of a plan of action. Refer to Appendix B for a sample plan of action and to Appendix C for the elements of a successful recruitment/retention plan.

Implementation of the plan

The entire committee chooses specific activities and develops a timeline. A myriad of recruitment and retention activities have been shared in recent educational publications. Some examples are: Open House, Spirit Day, Catholic Schools Week activities, direct mailings to various groups, student newspapers, and intramural sports. We have included a list of suggested activities in Appendix C. Tap the creative energy of your committee members to develop your own list.

The chairperson asks for or assigns a coordinator from the committee members for each individual activity. Each coordinator recruits volunteers to carry out the work of his/her activity. This provides yet another opportunity to draw people into the life of the school and thus helps to secure its future. The coordinators are responsible for completing the Project Profile (Appendix D) and communicating progress to the principal and chairperson. The Profile provides an ongoing record of the project and serves as an evaluative tool.

Some additional tips that you might find helpful are:

◆ Attempt to be faithful to your timeline.
◆ All committee members are ambassadors; be positive ambassadors.
◆ Estimate costs for every activity.
◆ Make frequent progress reports.
◆ Inform committee of any comments from the community regarding the school.
◆ Have courage and confidence!

Evaluation

At different points during the plan of action and at the end of the year, both informal and formal evaluation should be made by the committee at large. The following questions might be helpful in the process of evaluation.

- Are the goals and objectives being met?
- Has there been any change in enrollment?
- What comments have been made by the school/parish community with regard to the efforts of the enrollment committee?
- Are available resources being used to their full potential?

Our hope is that the formation of an enrollment committee will enable you to spread the Good News of your school and secure your future. Who knows—your school may be the next feature on Peter Jennings' "American Agenda!"

Appendix A: Sample Survey

These are sample questions which would be used on a parent survey. It is essential for each school to develop its own questionnaire.

Directions: Check all appropriate items.

1. How did you first hear about St. Philomena School?
   ___ a. Through a friend who has had children in the school
   ___ b. From a relative who has had children in the school
   ___ c. From my children or their friends
   ___ d. Referral from a nursery school or previous school
   ___ e. Through the telephone directory
   ___ f. Through the media, e.g., newspaper ads or photos
   ___ g. Through my parish
   ___ h. Other (please specify)_____

2. Why did you consider St. Philomena School for your child?
   ___ a. Interested in a Catholic education
   ___ b. Wanted a more diversified program
   ___ c. Wanted a value-centered curriculum
   ___ d. Desired a greater academic challenge
   ___ e. Qualified, caring faculty
   ___ f. Wanted more personal attention for my child
   ___ g. Tuition cost
   ___ h. Other_____

3. How many children do you have?
   ___ a. One
   ___ b. Two
   ___ c. Three
   ___ d. Four
   ___ e. Five or more

4. How many children ages 5–13 do you have?
   ___ a. One
   ___ b. Two
   ___ c. Three
   ___ d. Four
   ___ e. Five or more

5. If you have children ages 5–13 who are not enrolled at St. Philomena School, please indicate where they currently attend school.
   ___ a. Public school
   ___ b. Private school
   ___ c. Catholic school

6. If your children (5–13) are not enrolled at St. Philomena School, please indicate why.

7. Now that your child is attending St. Philomena School, to what degree have your initial expectations been fulfilled?
   ___ a. Very satisfied
   ___ b. Satisfied
   ___ c. Dissatisfied

8. Please grade the school in the following areas, by circling appropriate letter.
   A = Excellent B = Very Good C = Good
   D = Fair E = Needs Improvement

a. Academic program	A B C D E
b. Athletic program	A B C D E
c. Art/music programs	A B C D E
d. Atmosphere/tone of school	A B C D E
e. Class size	A B C D E
f. Child's value development	A B C D E
g. Diversity of student body	A B C D E
h. Extracurricular activities	A B C D E
i. Helpfulness of report cards	A B C D E
j. Improvement over previous school	A B C D E
k. Parent/teacher communication	A B C D E
l. Parent involvement in school	A B C D E
m. Peer relationships among students	A B C D E
n. Preparation for secondary school	A B C D E
o. Quality of faculty	A B C D E
p. Religious instruction	A B C D E
q. School's facilities	A B C D E

9. Generally speaking, how do you rate the school's performance in developing your child?
   Academically
   ___ a. Excellent
   ___ b. Good
   ___ c. Fair
   ___ d. Poor
   ___ e. Not sure
   Spiritually
   ___ a. Excellent
   ___ b. Good
   ___ c. Fair
   ___ d. Poor
   ___ e. Not sure

10. Do you feel that there is a good working relationship between:

The students and the principal?
___ a. Yes
___ b. No
___ c. Not Sure

The students and the faculty?
___ a. Yes
___ b. No
___ c. Not Sure

11. What is your single best source of information about the school?
___ a. Personal contact with teachers
___ b. My children or other students
___ c. Other parents
___ d. Principal's letters
___ e. Parents Club

12. Do you feel that you receive enough information about the school on a regular basis?
___ a. Yes
___ b. No
If no, how do you think communication between the school and parents could be improved?

13. What are the main strengths of St. Philomena School?

14. What areas of school life need improvement?

15. Additional comments.

Appendix B: Plan of Action

Activity	Coordinator
July	
Planning meeting of enrollment committee	Enrollment committee
August	
Parent meeting/new students	Principal/pastor
Orientation of new students	Student council/faculty/pastor
September	
Room mothers meeting	Volunteer 1
PTA meeting/open house	PTA president/volunteer
October	
School display of students' creative writing	Volunteer 2
November	
Article about school in parish newsletter	Volunteer 3/principal
December	
January	
Catholic Schools Week activities in parish and school	Volunteers 4 and 5/staff
February	
Distribute brochure to parents, parishioners, community leaders	Volunteer 6
March	
Mail survey to school parents	Volunteer 7
Direct mail campaign to parents of parish's 4- and 5-year old children	Volunteer 8
April	
Open House for prospective students/parents	Volunteer 9
May	
Grandparents' Day	Volunteer 10/staff
June	
Evaluation of year's activities	Enrollment committee

Appendix C: Elements for a Successful Recruitment/Retention Program

I. Involvement of many people
   A. Students (past and present)
   B. Parents (past and present)
   C. Faculty
   D. Administrators
   E. Development director (local and/or diocesan)
   F. School secretary/support staff
   G. Community people/professionals/business/clergy

II. Get your message out through
   A. Media
   B. Newspapers: local, diocesan, school/parish
   C. TV: cable, local
   D. Public service announcements (PSA)
   E. Word of mouth
   F. Parish bulletin
   G. Billboards
   H. Special school/parish publications
   I. Brochures/other printed material

III. Create a salable product
   A. Programs
      1. Quality academics based in Christian values
      2. Varied extracurricular activities
      3. Extended care programs, if needed
      4. Effective athletic and fine arts programs
      5. Learning centers utilizing modern technology
      6. Special needs
      7. Service
   B. Climate
      1. Warm and caring
      2. Welcoming and enthusiastic secretary/faculty/students
      3. Spirit of cooperation between parish, school, and community
      4. Willingness by principal/faculty/staff to become involved in community affairs
   C. Physical facility
      1. Warm reception area (entrance hall)
      2. Well-maintained building, grounds
      3. Attractive, meaningful displays
      4. Sufficient space to meet educational needs

Suggested activities for recruitment and retention
- Home visits to parents with students entering kindergarten
- Camps (athletic or academic) for students grades 5–8
- Quarterly school publication to all parishioners
- Preschool story hours
- Invite parents of each homeroom to family-style lunch
- Second-graders send First Communion notes to CCD second-graders
- Breakfast for all First Communion students sponsored by the school or by the enrollment committee
- Develop A.V. presentation for civic groups/cable television
- Sponsor Grandparents' Day
- Open House including information, tour, and social gathering
- Parish bulletin announcements/local media/newspaper coverage
- Visits (and printed materials) to day care centers and nursery schools
- Kindergarten visit day for prospective students and their parents
- Tours of school readily available for interested parents
- Personally invite parishioners from parishes without school to home/school meetings and/or school activities
- Write letters/cards to parish shut-ins/nursing home residents
- Student participation in community educational fairs and contests
- Send "happy baptismal" cards to all babies and their families
- Provide car-pooling plans for parents
- Congratulatory notes to students who make the news
- Distribute printed materials to real estate offices, doctors, dentists, etc.

Appendix D: Project Profile

Project: _____

Beginning date:_____   Ending date:_____

Captain: _____

Target: _____

Goal: _____

Coordinate with other activities: _____

_____

Budget: _____

Names and phone numbers of volunteers: _____

_____

Needs from school office:_____

_____

Ideas/suggestions: _____

_____

Evaluation: _____

_____

Public Relations

Sheehan, L. 1990. In *Building better boards: A handbook for board members in Catholic education*, 40–44. Washington, D.C.: National Catholic Educational Association.

The role of the board in public relations is primarily to provide direction; that is, the board should be involved in determining what should be done, not the specifics of how public relations should be accomplished. Public relations is both an art and a science. As an art, it enables people to understand the school, and to stimulate their support of it in its mission. It is the science of selecting the appropriate media, materials, and events to connect effectively with audiences with which the school wishes to establish goodwill. One can characterize public relations as the sum of all that a school or person does or does not do which affects how it is perceived and supported by various groups or publics in a community.

Handling Crisis Moments

The school board has a responsibility to be sure that appropriate plans and procedures are in place to handle the public relations aspects of the various crisis moments which develop in school communities. How such events are reported can result in positive or negative publicity for the school. Some examples of crisis moments for which the board ought to have policies and procedures in place are:

1. Emergencies involving suspected cases of child abuse, serious injury, or student death
2. Announcements of program cutbacks, school closings, mergings
3. Response to parent concerns about curriculum, discipline

Careful planning, reflection, formulation of positions, and determining who will speak with confidence and clarity are the keys to handling such crisis situations.

Everyday Public Relation Opportunities—How Do You Use Them?

Every school community has a personality, which it reveals by how it handles everyday occurrences with its publics. Recognizing that administration is the responsibility of the principal, a public relations committee could reflect with the principal on the following questions in light of present practices and the impact they have on parents, students, parishioners, neighbors, and inquirers.

◆ How are telephones answered?
◆ How are visitors welcomed to the building? Do signs point the way to the school office?
◆ How are halls decorated? Do they communicate something about the Catholic education happening there? What is their message?
◆ How do office staff respond to visitors? When are parents welcome in the building? How are they involved in the school's life?

◆ How are students recognized for achievements?
◆ What kinds of orientation programs exist for new students, for new staff?
◆ How many opportunities do you offer for neighbors, parishioners, and other members of the community to participate in the school's life?
◆ How are concerns of parents handled by teachers and administrators?
◆ How are concerns of neighbors voiced about students' behavior handled?
◆ In what ways does the school secretary see him/herself as an important part of the school's public relations effort?
◆ In what ways are students, parents, and faculty encouraged to be goodwill ambassadors for the school?
◆ How would you rate parent-teacher conferences in terms of creating goodwill?
◆ How are schedule changes communicated to parents and faculty?
◆ How do you gather the advice of experts in your community to improve instruction and other school activities?
◆ What kind of image do your school handbooks and publications convey?
◆ How do you provide for feedback in your building? from parents? from graduates?

Marketing

Marketing is an important function in the overall development of the school. By some, marketing is equated with sales, and so student recruiting and public relations are assumed to be marketing. In reality, these are strategies of the marketing program, and marketing is a strategy of the development program.

Marketing begins with the notion that people have needs which they must meet. The school is meeting a need people have to educate their children. If, however, the school is to succeed, it must analyze whose needs it serves, what service these people are looking for, and how the school can meet that particular need.

Thus marketing starts from an exchange relationship, where something of value is traded between at least two parties. Marketing, then, is the managing of these exchange relationships. The program begins outside the school with external needs. Only if the school is in tune with external needs will its marketing programs succeed.

Beginning a Marketing Effort

The following are the first four steps to begin a marketing program.

1. **Establish a Marketing Committee.** Whether this committee is a formal or an ad hoc board committee, it is important that it have high-level support and involvement, that it has broad representation, that it be chaired by someone influential in the school who has had some marketing knowledge, and that someone be responsible for carrying out the decisions of the committee as approved by the board. At least the chair of the marketing committee should be a board member.

2. **Develop a Good Data Base.** Conduct a marketing audit of the school. Remember to be as objective, systematic, and comprehensive as possible, but also remember to be realistic. Everything cannot be identified in a single audit. In fact, some schools will simply not have answers to many of the questions asked. Don't worry about it now, but do remember that these unanswered questions are areas in which the school needs to do additional work.

The following marketing audit for Catholic schools will be helpful.

The Marketing Environment
1. What effect will the short-term economic situation have on the school, and its ability to achieve its mission and objectives?
2. What effect will trends in the size, age, distribution, birthrate, and religious preference in the local area have on the school?
3. What are the public's attitudes toward the school and its present (curriculum)?
4. What changes are occurring in the market size and demographic distribution of the school's student market?
5. How do current and prospective students and their parents rate the school and its competitors with respect to each element of the school's offerings? What are the needs, wants, and benefits desired from the school? How do these market segments (potential clients) reach a decision on which school a student will attend?
6. Who are the school's competitors in attracting these students? What are the school's perceived strengths and weaknesses? What are the competition's perceived strengths and weaknesses?

Marketing Strategy
1. Are the mission and objectives of the school clearly stated, and do they logically lead to the marketing objectives for the school?
2. Are the marketing objectives for students/parents/donors and other markets clearly stated in order to guide marketing, planning, implementation, and control?
3. Are the marketing objectives appropriate, given what is known about the market, competition, and the school's resources?
4. What are the school's marketing strategies?

5. Are the school's resources adequate to carry out these strategies and achieve the desired objectives?
6. Are these resources optimally allocated to different market segments and the different elements of the marketing mix?

Marketing Activities
1. How does the marketing process work at the school? Are there ways to increase its effectiveness and/or efficiency?
2. What is the marketing approach like, and what marketing activities of the school are occurring at each stage of the process?
3. How are the marketing efforts organized and staffed at the school? Why? Is there a high-level marketing individual with adequate authority and responsibility over all marketing activities that affect parent/student satisfaction?
4. Is there a marketing research, or marketing information, system at the school? Is the system providing accurate and timely information on the market, and present and prospective parents/students/donors? Is the system measuring the effectiveness and efficiency of the school's marketing efforts?
5. Is there an annual planning process adequate to direct the school's marketing efforts? Is it tied to a control system to measure if annual objectives are being met?
6. Have specific objectives and strategies been established for each of the school's marketing efforts, and is the effectiveness of each being measured?
7. Are the school's various marketing efforts, and especially the promotion effort, being integrated into a unified effort to project a clear, attractive, and realistic image of the school? Are any of these efforts in conflict with any of the others?

3. **Identify Opportunities and Problems.** As a result of the marketing audit, the marketing committee will be able to identify a number of opportunities and problems facing the school, develop a prioritized list of these opportunities and problems related to marketing, and identify those that need to be addressed immediately.

4. **Develop Prioritized Marketing Objectives.** Develop a list of prioritized marketing objectives that address the opportunities and problems identified. Make these specific and measurable. For example, if declining enrollment is a problem, a marketing objective might be to identify specific cause(s) of the decline within 90 days through a survey of student families. These objectives should focus the efforts of the marketing committee, and should be in accord with the overall planning efforts of the board. How many objectives can be dealt with in a given year will depend on the magnitude of the objectives, and the time and funding available.

Steps Toward Development

Yeager, R. J. 1985. In *Elementary school finance manual*, 120–23.
Washington, D.C.: National Catholic Educational Association.

Introduction

Many Catholic elementary schools are already moving in the direction of development; many others are just planning to begin and often suffer from confusion about the proper directions to take. It is interesting to note that many private schools have had flourishing development programs for years. Some of them enroll students in pre-kindergarten through only Grade 2 or 3. This fact points toward the possibility of good development practices at any level of education.

Concept of Development

As administrators begin to "jump into development" they must carefully understand that development is not simply one more form of fund-raising. As Richard Burke points out "development is not synonymous with fund raising, but rather a long-term process which grows out of institutional planning."[1] Robert Stuhr also notes that "Development is more than fundraising strengthened by marketing tools."[2]

For success, good development requires:

◆ understanding
◆ commitment
◆ involvement
◆ long-range planning
◆ a well thought out and thoroughly enunciated case statement
◆ creation of a funded endowment for both current and special projects

At the risk of being overly philosophical, it must be pointed out immediately that development as conceived for American Catholic elementary schools is defined as the overall concept which holds that the highest destiny of an institution can be realized only by a total effort on the part of the entire institution to *analyze* its philosophy of mission and activities, to crystallize its objectives, project them into the future, take the necessary steps to realize them, and continually follow through to see that the objectives are realized.

Development Process Elements

This concept of development is implemented in elementary schools through a process which:

◆ evidences quality Catholic education;
◆ evidences good business management practices;
◆ practices effective marketing techniques; and
◆ attracts the support both of people and money.

It should be evident already that development cannot be done only by those who have responsibility and concern for Catholic elementary schools.

Development is a *team effort*. The team must include administrators (pastor and principal), teachers, students, board of education members, parents, grandparents, and others interested in the promotion of education at the local level. There is no way in which a principal or pastor can "do development" by themselves. They may serve as the spark which initially ignites the fire, but ultimately all those names here will have roles to play. Just as in an orchestra, not all can be directors or all play first violin; so too the differentiation of roles in the total development program is necessary.

Beginnings

As elementary school administrators become convinced of the importance of a development program for their school, they often feel there is a period of time during which they are moving "toward a full development program" but are not yet ready to hire a development director full- or part-time. During this period it is especially important that the administrator, pastor, board of education, and other interested parties act in ways which will ultimately be helpful to the fledgling development program when it is launched. All those involved in this phase will begin to grow in knowledge of and especially interest in a full development program.

The following are suggestions of some possible activities which might be pursued in this phase. No priority is intended in this list—neither is it suggested that a particular school necessarily engage in all of them.

Suggestion 1: Begin to inservice pastor, board of education members, and school staff with materials that give information about the true nature of development as described in this chapter. Any techniques which can be used to cause small and large group discussion about the "possible" application of the concept of development to this school will be most helpful.

Suggestion 2: Continue all current fund-raising activity but especially review to make sure that it is being done with a goal in mind and that all ethical concerns are being met. Questions should be asked about the use of students for "sales" and the impact this has on the whole educational philosophy of the institution.

Suggestion 3: Review all materials sent to various publics from the school, especially those sent to parents. Are they presented in a form which clearly and actually states the message that is intended? Are regular news releases on school matters sent to the parish bulletins and local and diocesan newspapers? What about the same to local radio and television stations? Personal contacts with publishers and newspersons will enhance one's basic position. News needs to be sent on a regular basis, not only in a crisis situation. Keep your school before all parties that could possibly find interest.

Suggestion 4: How are address records of current students' payments kept? What about alumni, especially recent ones? A special list of grandparents of current students should be readily available which lists all grandchildren by name. Another list worth developing is that of graduates who have succeeded especially well or become well known locally, regionally, or nationally. In time you will want to contact them to tell the story of their "roots." In the meantime there is time to do thorough research on them.

Suggestion 5: Find out about any operational development programs in your immediate area. If there are some on either elementary or high school level make contact with the development officer. Spend some time with this person finding out the first steps used in the program as well as current strategies and techniques.

Suggestion 6: Prepare an up-to-date history of your school from the very beginning. It is important to show the real community needs that *this* school has met over the years of its existence. Who are some of the outstanding people who were educated in *this* institution? At what points in time and under what particular circumstances did this school make an impact on the community? Sources for this information may include parish yearbooks and information on file in the diocesan education office or chancery. Do not forget to look in back copies of local newspapers available through the public library. The total result of this historical narrative when completed should form the basis for a case statement.

Program Personnel

Suggestion 7: Somewhat akin to suggestion 6, one could begin to gather anecdotal information from graduates which shows a meaningful relationship to the school. Some of this information might be used in the history. It might also be used as a way of discovering and cultivating future donors.

Suggestion 8: Anything done to increase the professional manner in which communication is carried on between school and home will be helpful. Written information sent home with students need not be elaborately done, but should be well written and attractively designed and presented. Notices of school activities which invite parental presence should state very clearly what the parents are being asked to do including time, date, length of meeting, and location.

Suggestion 9: Grandparents are a great asset to an elementary school and often have the time and resources to be involved in a program. Some elementary schools regularly have a program for grandparents just prior to Thanksgiving. This is a splendid opportunity to teach about one's "roots" with a spirit of gratitude for all that older generations have done for a child. The invitations can well be written by the students themselves. The program will include all students and might showcase classroom activities as well as a more general assembly type program. A half day ending with the grandparent having lunch with the grandchild is very effective. Grandparents certainly have many opportunities to spread the good word about the school.

Suggestion 10: Volunteers in some elementary schools have prepared excellent slide and cassette programs showing campus, classrooms, and activities of the school. The programs are useful for recruiting new students, but also for spreading the news of "what goes on" at the local Catholic elementary school. Some groups have been invited to present such a program to local service clubs, e.g., Rotary, Kiwanis, and Knights of Columbus.

Suggestion 11: Buy a school camera. Begin to take pictures showing students and staff involved in all types of school experiences. Make a point to get each student in some kind of picture during the first month of school each fall. Be sure to keep negatives for further use and label them well, so that you can easily recognize all people and what they are doing. It is equally important to get the pastor and/or associate pastors in some of these activity pictures.

School Mission

When the development program is begun there must be a person whose time and energies will be devoted in large part if not exclusively to development. Development will not succeed if it is just one more activity undertaken by an already overcommitted principal and/or pastor. The development director's position will take various institutional formats. But regardless of the differences, the position must not be tacked on to someone already overburdened.

Development must emphasize the school's mission. For an individual school this means that the local development program must make a convincing argument why *this individual* Catholic elementary school exists in this city right now. Donors and those who can grow in interest for an individual school are mission oriented. They want to know

- why this school exists
- why its program is important to the church and civic communities it purports to serve
- what its production or results are—translated into what is going on with students while they are enrolled and where they enroll for high school

- whom this school serves, not just in terms of numbers and from whence they come, but what particular special interest groups of the civic community are served by this school.

Notes

1. Richard J. Burke, *Catholic School Management Letter*, Richard J. Burke & Associates, Hartford, CT, May 1982, Vol. IV, 1, p. 1.
2. Robert L. Stuhr, *Bulletin on Public Relations & Development for Independent Schools*, Gonser Gerber Tinker Stuhr, Chicago, IL, June 1982, p. 1.

Catholic School Finance and Church-State Relations

McLaughlin, T. 1985. 28, 53–54. Washington, D.C.: National Catholic Educational Association.

Summary

1. Subsidies—funds which are transferred to the school operation from parish, diocese, or religious order sources—are the greatest financial resources for Catholic elementary schools generally.

2. There is increasing pressure on parish councils to provide funding for many parish activities other than schools. The impact of a possible subsidy reduction on school financing will vary from school to school. Much will depend upon how strong a case can be made by the school administration for continued strong support.

3. The dollar value to the school for the donated services of religious community members and diocesan clergy is called "contributed services."

4. "New money" must be found as the older sources of school finance become overworked. Creative fundraising, development, grants, and foundation sources must be explored.

5. Cooperative programs with other private schools is a possibility. In general, schools established by different religious denominations are not in competition with one another for students.

6. Catholic schools, because of their local management and sense of community, are in a favorable position to initiate cooperative programs with the business and, also possibly, the industrial community.

7. Good financial management is a must if the schools are to be effective. This financial management must include a review of teacher salaries. Schools cannot remain healthy if teachers remain underpaid.

Summary

1. Examples of local level Catholic and public school cooperation are the "shared-time" and "dual-enrollment" programs. They work best when there is a financial benefit to the public school (state aid formula adjustment) and to the Catholic school (less payroll).

2. One form of *state* aid to parents of private school children is the "tax deduction," an *indirect* reduction, which reduces the sum on which the parents' total state tax liability is computed.

3. A "tax credit," a *direct* reduction in the amount of tax the parents would pay on their *federal* income tax, has been proposed, but is not yet available.

4. There is increased debate today on the best way to finance public education and on whether private schools should be part of new initiatives in school finance. Some innovators are asking for less government involvement in education and more involvement with business partnerships.

5. The general thrust of the "new thinking" in educational finance is that consumers (parents) be given more choice in education and that more control reside at the local level.

6. The popular debate on actual proposals to assist private school children with federal funding surfaces four general justifications for such assistance: service equity, financial equity, choice and diversity in education, and competition and improvement to the quality of education.

7. Critics of aid to private education argue that the decision to incur the added cost of private education and to forgo the benefits of available public education is a decision of the individual that does not warrant compensation through tax credits or the expenditure of public funds.

8. The reply of the Catholic parent is that the state demands that their children attend school. The state offers an educational program devoid of some of the values parents may wish for their children.

9. The important point to remember is that in such proposed legislation as *tax credits*, the parent receives the benefit directly. No money leaves any program targeted for the public schools, and no money goes to the private schools.

10. *Vouchers* provide assistance directly to parents for tuition costs, are provided at the time parents select and "pay" for the child's education. The GI Bill of Rights, whereby a veteran is given a government subsidy to be spent for an education in the high school or college of his/ her choice, is an example of a successful voucher plan.

11. It must be realized that financial help of any kind and at any level, state or national, will be sprung loose as a result of a *political decision*.

12. The best position for the Catholic in debating the issue of federal funds for private school parents is to support movements which will strengthen both public and private education. Private schools should not attempt to make gains at the expense of the public sector. If support for Catholic schools is concentrated in only one sector of political opinion, failure will be the result. Aid for school children is a need that transcends parties and labels.

Steps Toward Development

Yeager, R. J. 1985. In *Elementary school finance manual*, 123–26.
Washington, D.C.: National Catholic Educational Association.

Planning—Short and Long Range

Every school should have at least a five-year plan showing income and expenditure for that five-year period. Projected enrollment is also part of this same planning process.

Members of the local school board play a very important part in the development program. Some members will no doubt wear the dual hat of board member as well as be a parent of current students. These people will bring an important dimension to the development effort. It is very necessary that board members be given continued "in-service" on various areas of information related to development, so that they may make a significant contribution to its success. From the very outset board members should know the necessity of five-year planning, be a part of its implementation, and serve on groups forming a case statement. Informed involvement is the surest way of creating interest.

Continual work with annual and long-range goals, together with a written plan for their implementation, is a logical activity in which to include board members. This is an ongoing activity if done properly. Goal yielding is sometimes difficult for Catholic elementary schools, who may in the past have had more of a siege mentality. Much of our national past history shows that we built out of "reaction to" rather than as a logical step which was attempting to achieve a long-range goal. In goal planning primary emphasis must be on students served by the school and on the donors who support the program.

Development Director as Marketing Manager

The development director serves as a marketing manager in a local elementary school. We have passed from the time in which the Pastor could ascend the pulpit on the third Sunday of August and remind all parents that under pain of refusing them the sacraments they were "commanded" to send their children to the local parish school beginning the day after Labor Day. We are now in a buyers' market, and in some places in a market in which there is a reaction to the earlier scenario.

The development director as marketing manager sets the general marketing plan (within the annual school plan), directs its implementation, and controls its operation. The focus must be on the institution's service and program, on those who benefit by it, and on activities to reach their special interests.

This involves, along with other activities, the basics of development procedure:

1. *Obtaining the Facts*—about your programs, their contribution to your publics—your "customers" or donors.

2. *Re-articulating Your Mission and "Product."*

3. *Listing Your Objectives.*

4. *Selecting Your Target Markets*—Schools identify their "publics"—groups of people with common views or expectations. Markets are simply those publics to which the school wishes to appeal to obtain support. Too little time has traditionally been spent in analyzing these markets or segmenting them into various submarkets. Alumni are a good example. Often there is important variance among alumni groups according to age, location, or occupation as to their interest in the school or what appeals to them. "Segmenting markets" or separating groups such as alumni, parents, the local community, major donors into subgroups with varied interests will help the administrator be more efficient and productive. Analyzing their market potential will help establish priorities in time and budget.

5. *Planning Your Approach*—Reaching each segment of your market by the means most likely to appeal. For instance: Do the alumni of the 1960s or 70s react as favorably to class agent appeals and class comparisons as do the alumni of the 1930s and 40s? Do alumni who received financial support while in school have a special interest in giving financial aid today? Each market requires a special understanding and approach.

6. *Constructing a Written Development (or Marketing) Plan*—A written plan helps to obtain consensus. The very effort of planning brings institutional groups together.

7. *Involving All Parts of Your Institution*—The development concept emphasizes that building a greater institution

is everyone's job. The marketing concept holds that all parts of the organization must work together to produce the right product, at the right price, to make it available at the right place, and support it with the right promotion.

Donor Cultivation

In this, the marketing approach and concept strengthen the development concept. And both are more than fund-raising.

One of the opportunities which an ongoing development provides for a Catholic elementary school is that of cultivating gifts and gift givers on a regular basis. Although the management of the ongoing effort to identify, cultivate, and solicit prospects should ultimately be a top priority of the development director, in reality, the preliminary groundwork will be laid by principal and/or pastor.

For the school moving in the direction of development, it is important for all connected to the program to identify a program of donor cultivation. Every community has persons whose interest and resources can be cultivated for the benefit of the school. Obtaining gifts is not a one-time casual effort. The process must be continuous and includes researching, planning, strategizing, scheduling, cultivating, and asking for the gift. Even the basic research step is not easy, as wealth is not easy to guess.

Obtaining gifts above all requires teamwork as noted earlier. The pastor must be willing to allot time to make calls on top prospects. The principal (or director of development) will coordinate all parties concerned. The members of the Board of Education should lend assistance in advising and supporting the pastor and principal. They may also be involved in making calls on actual donors. Other persons may volunteer who are willing to use their influence with prospects.

Ultimately it is the development officer who must organize the process, monitor and inspire the effort to search out, cultivate, and see that major prospects are asked to support major projects and programs by making gifts.

Process of Obtaining Gifts

The process of obtaining gifts requires a planned strategy.[1] Gifts don't just happen—someone makes them happen as a result of a well-thought-out plan.

The sequential steps in this process are these:

◆ *Effective research* by the development staff among the school's key interested publics to identify individuals, foundations, or corporations capable of making a commitment to the school's programs.

◆ *Evaluation* of the prospect's interests, resources, and potential. How much could the prospect give? What form might the gift take? Cash, appreciated property, stocks and bonds, life insurance. What interests does the prospect have?

◆ *Cultivation* of the prospect to bring him/her into a close relationship with the school and its programs. Volunteers are especially useful at this step.

◆ *Involvement* of the prospect in the life of the school through participation on a committee, as a guest speaker on some occasion such as graduation, parents/students banquets, as a member of Board of Education.

◆ *Ask for the gift*! Some gifts are never received simply because the "ask" never occurs. When the time is right, the most influential person (Pastor, Principal, Volunteer) must make a presentation and ask for a special gift.

◆ *Extend proper acknowledgment to the donor* for the gift. Be prompt, be thorough, be appropriate, and then

◆ *Provide recognition to the donor.* Make sure you know that the recognition is to the donor's liking. Not all donors want a public fanfare over a gift, yet nearly everyone desires some degree of recognition.

Each step prepares the way for the next step if it is successful. If a step is not successful different ways of reaching the next step must be found. Continuous activity is important. When the top step is reached, it is usually time to repeat the process.

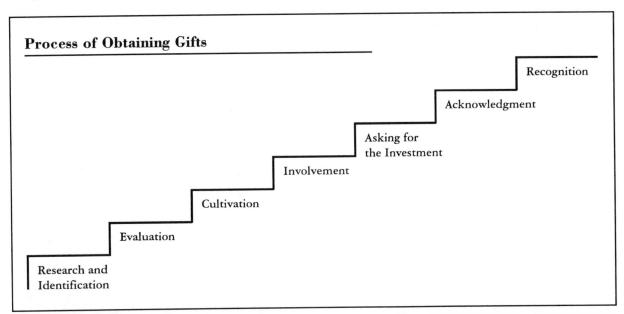

Process of Obtaining Gifts

Recognition

Acknowledgment

Asking for the Investment

Involvement

Cultivation

Evaluation

Research and Identification

A Word on Volunteers

While continuous and aggressive staff (Pastor, Principal, and Development Director) work is needed to obtain major gifts, the role of the volunteers is an equally potent force. Every elementary school has board members, alumni, parents, and other friends who can advise concerning approaches to prospective gift-givers and, even more, support the efforts to contact and "sell" the prospect.

Such volunteers are available, but they must be given the staff help to use their talents most effectively in a way which will conserve their time and efforts. Volunteers are very busy persons in their own lives. Their time is a precious and expensive commodity. It must be treated as such when used in a development program.

The initiative to suggest "moves" and next steps must come from the staff members. There are many ways volunteers can use their "clout" in moving up the steps to success with a donor, but staff members must suggest them, recommend them, and make it possible for the volunteer to assist.

Summary

The NCEA will offer a full seminar on development-related topics in conjunction with its annual convention for the next several years beginning in April 1984. Also in preparation are further print materials on the various parts that make up development. All of this information can form the basis for successful development programs in local institutions. The NCEA will continue to act as a national clearinghouse on the topic of development for Catholic elementary and secondary schools. Member schools are always welcome to seek further information on this emerging trend by contacting the author of this chapter.

Note

1.   This process and explanation is presented with the permission of its source—Gosner Gerber Tinker Stuhr, Chicago, IL.

Bibliography and Appendices

General Bibliography

Abella, M. 1989. The exciting world of public relations. *Momentum* 20(1):38–39.

Albert, L., W. Roy, and A. LePage. 1989. *Cooperative discipline*. Circle Pines, Minn.: American Guidance Service.

Bagin, D., D. R. Gallagher, and L. W. Kindred. 1994. *The school and community relations*. 5th ed. Boston: Allyn and Bacon.

Bailey, R., U. Butler, and M. Kearney. 1991. Development of the Catholic school board. In *Capital wisdom: Papers from the Principals Academy 1991*. Washington, D.C.: National Catholic Educational Association.

Balfe, M., M. Lanning, A. Meese, and A. M. Walsh. 1991. Enrollment: Securing our future. In *Capital wisdom: Papers from the Principals Academy*. Washington, D.C.: National Catholic Educational Association.

Barth, R. S. 1991. *Improving school from within*. San Francisco: Jossey-Bass.

Belenky, M. F., B. M. Clinchy, N. R. Goldberger, and J. M. Tarule. 1986. *Women's ways of knowing*. New York: Basic Books, Inc., Publishers.

Bennis, W. A. and B. Nanus. 1985. *Leaders: The strategies for taking charge*. New York: Harper and Row.

Benson, P. L., and M. J. Guerra. 1985. *Sharing the faith: The beliefs and values of Catholic high school teachers*. Washington, D.C.: National Catholic Educational Association.

Brigham, F. H. 1993a. *Technology and Chapter 1: Solutions for Catholic school participation*. Washington, D.C.: National Catholic Educational Association.

———. 1993b. *United States Catholic elementary and secondary schools 1992–93*. Washington, D.C.: National Catholic Educational Association.

Brookfield, S. 1986. *Understanding and facilitating adult learning*. San Francisco: Jossey-Bass.

Bryk, A. S., and M. E. Driscoll. 1988. *The high school as community: Contextual influences and consequences for students and teachers*. Madison, Wis.: Wisconsin Center for Educational Research.

Bryk, A. S., P. B. Holland, V. E. Lee, and R. A. Carriedo. 1984. *Effective Catholic schools: An exploration*. Washington, D.C.: National Catholic Educational Association.

Bryk, A. S., V. E. Lee, and P. B Holland. 1993. *Catholic schools and the common good*. Cambridge, Mass.: Harvard University Press.

Bryson, J. M. 1990. *Strategic planning for public and nonprofit organizations*. San Francisco: Jossey-Bass.

Burke, R. 1984a. The annual budget. In *Elementary school finance manual*. Washington, D.C.: National Catholic Educational Association.

Burke, R. 1984b. Long-range planning. In *Elementary school finance manual*. Washington, D.C.: National Catholic Educational Association.

Bushman, E. M., and G. J. Sparks, eds. 1990. *The Catholic school administrator—A book of readings*. Portland, Ore.: Catholic Leadership Co.

Canter, L., and M. Canter. 1976. *Assertive discipline*. Santa Monica, Calif.: Canter and Associates.

Canon Law Society of America. 1983. *Code of Canon Law: Latin-English edition*. Washington, D.C.: Canon Law Society of America.

Cappel, C. 1989. A reflection on the spirituality of the principal. In *Reflections on the role of the Catholic school principal*, ed. R. J. Kealey. Washington, D.C.: National Catholic Educational Association.

Castetter, W. B. 1986. *The personnel function in educational administration*. 4th ed. New York: MacMillan.

———. 1992. *The personnel function in educational administration*. 5th ed. New York: MacMillan.

Catholic schools face fiscal facts, editorial. 1993. *America* 169(18):3.

Chubb, J. E., and T. M. Moe. 1990. *Politics, markets, and America's schools*. Washington, D.C.: The Brookings Institution.

Ciriello, M. J. 1988. *Teachers in Catholic school: A study of commitment*. Ph.D. diss., The Catholic University of America, 1987. Abstract in *Dissertations Abstracts International* 48:8514A.

———. 1991. *Catholic principals' survey concerning their role and the future of Catholic education in the Archdiocese of Boston*. Boston: Catholic Schools Office. [Workshop and report to the Archdiocese of Boston Strategic Planning Study for Schools. Washington, D.C.: The Catholic University of America.]

———. 1992. *Attitudes of Catholic school administrators of the Diocese of Honolulu concerning their role and the future of Catholic education on the Islands*. Honolulu, Hawaii: Catholic School Department. [Workshop and report to the Diocese of Honolulu Strategic Planning Study for Schools. Washington, D.C.: The Catholic University of America.]

Ciriello, M. J., and J. J. Convey. 1993. Catholic higher education and diocesan school departments collaborating to strengthen leadership. *Current Issues in Catholic Higher Education* 14(1):34–39.

Clark, D., and E. Kujawa. 1985. Are you ready? The preconditions of development. *Momentum* 16(3):14–15.

Clifton, D., and P. Nelson. 1992. *Soar with your strengths*. New York: Delacourte Press.

Code of ethics for the Catholic school teacher. 1982. Washington, D.C.: National Catholic Educational Association.

Coleman, J. S., and T. Hoffer. 1987. *Public and private high schools: The impact of communities*. New York: Basic Books.

Congregation for Catholic Education. 1977. *The Catholic school*. Washington, D.C.: United States Catholic Conference.

———. 1982. *Lay Catholics in schools: Witnesses to faith.* Boston: Daughters of St. Paul.

Convey, J. J. 1992. *Catholic schools make a difference.* Washington, D.C.: National Catholic Educational Association.

Convey, J. J., and M. J. Ciriello. 1996. *Strategic planning for Catholic schools: A diocesan model for consultation.* Washington, D.C.: United States Catholic Conference.

Corr, M. A. 1986. Justice in teacher termination. In *Personnel issues and the Catholic school administrator.* Washington, D.C.: National Catholic Educational Association.

Covey, S. R. 1989. *The seven habits of highly successful people: Restoring the character ethic.* New York: Simon and Schuster.

———. 1991. *Principle-centered leadership.* New York: Summit Books.

Cunningham, W. G., and D. W. Gresso. 1994. *Cultural leadership: The culture of excellence in education.* Needham, Mass.: Allyn and Bacon.

Daresh, J. C. 1992. *Supervision, a proactive process.* New York: Longman.

Dombart, P. 1992. A job to suit up for. *Educational Leadership* 49(5):83.

Donaldson, F. 1991. *Catholic school publications: Unifying the image.* Washington, D.C.: National Catholic Educational Association.

Doyle, R., N. Kinate, A. Langan, and M. Swanson. 1991. Evaluation of the school's Catholicity. In *Capital wisdom: Papers from the Principals Academy 1991.* Washington, D.C.: National Catholic Educational Association.

Drahmann, T. 1985. *Governance and administration in the Catholic school.* Washington, D.C.: National Catholic Educational Association.

Drahmann, T., and A. Stenger. 1989. *The Catholic school principal: An outline for action.* Rev. ed. Washington, D.C.: National Catholic Educational Association.

Droel, W. 1989. *The spirituality of work: Teachers.* Chicago: National Center for the Laity.

Fielding, G., and H. D. Schalock. 1985. *Promoting the professional development of teachers and administrators.* School Management Digest Series. Eugene, Ore.: ERIC Clearinghouse on Educational Management, College of Education, University of Oregon.

Fuller, F. F. 1969. Concerns of teachers: A developmental conceptualization. *American Educational Research Journal* 6:207–26.

Gall, M. D., G. D. Fielding, H. D. Schalock, W. W. Charters Jr., and J. M. Wilczynski. 1984. *Involving the principal in teachers' staff development: Effects on the quality of mathematics instruction in elementary schools.* Eugene, Ore.: University of Oregon Center for Educational Policy and Management.

Gary, B. S. 1986. *Seeking foundation grants.* Washington, D.C.: National Catholic Educational Association.

Gettys, D. J. 1994. Integrating technology in education: The principal's role. *Principal* 73(4):52–53.

Gilbert, J. 1983. *Pastor as shepherd of the school community.* Washington, D.C.: National Catholic Educational Association.

Gilligan, C. 1982. *In a different voice: Psychological theory and women's development.* Cambridge, Mass.: Harvard University Press.

Glatthorn, A.A., and C. R. Shields. 1983. *Differentiated supervision for Catholic schools.* Washington, D.C.: National Catholic Educational Association.

Glickman, C. D. 1990. *Supervision of instruction.* Boston: Allyn and Bacon.

Gonser, Gerber, Tinker, Stuhr. 1977. *On development.* Chicago.

Goodman, D. 1992. Strategies for staying up-to-date. *Inc: The Office Technology Advisor* 14(12): 8–11, 14–15.

Governal, M. A. 1986. Effective principaling in the Catholic school. In *The Catholic school administrator—A book of readings,* ed. E. M. Bushman and G. J. Sparks, 161–64. Portland, Ore.: Catholic Leadership Company.

Guerra, M. J. 1993. *Dollars and sense: Catholic high schools and their finances 1992.* Washington, D.C.: National Catholic Educational Association.

Guerra, M., R. Haney, and R. Kealey, eds. 1992. *National congress: Catholic schools for the 21st century: Executive summary.* Washington, D.C.: National Catholic Educational Association.

Harris, J. C. 1992. Is the American Catholic Church getting out of the elementary school business? *Chicago Studies* 31(1):81–92.

———. 1994. Catholics can too afford schools. *America* 170(8):22–24.

Hendricks, W. 1989. *How to manage conflict.* Leadership Success Series. Shawnee Mission, Kans.: National Press.

Hennessey, C., C. A. Solomon, K. Mitchell, S. Plasek, D. A. Clifford, and T. Bogar. 1997. *Administrator's handbook of regulations.* Houston, Tex.: Catholic School Office, Diocese of Galveston-Houston.

Hersey, P., and K. H. Blanchard. 1984. *The management of organizational behavior.* 4th ed. Englewood Cliffs, N.J.: Prentice Hall.

Hind, J. F. 1989. *The heart and soul of effective management: A Christian approach to managing and motivating people.* Wheaton, Ill.: Scripture Publications Press, Inc.

Hocevar, R. 1991. Catholic school governance. In *Catholic school governance and finance.* Washington, D.C.: National Catholic Educational Association.

Hofbauer, G. 1984. Fundraising. In *Elementary school finance manual.* Washington, D.C.: National Catholic Educational Association, 103–17.

Holliday, A. E. 1988. In search of an answer: What is school public relations? *Journal of Educational Public Relations* 11(2):12.

Hughes, L. W., and C. G. Ubben. 1978. *The elementary principal's handbook.* Boston, Mass.: Allyn and Bacon.

Hunter, J. O. 1992. Technological literacy: Defining a new concept for general education. *Educational Technology* March:28–29.

James, R., J. Perkowski, and M. Sesko. 1991. In the beginning: Orientation of the new teacher. In *Capital wisdom: Papers from the Principals Academy 1991*. Washington, D.C.: National Catholic Educational Association.

Jarc, J. A. 1985. *Development and public relations for the Catholic school*. Washington, D.C.: National Catholic Educational Association.

John, R., and M. J. Wagner. 1991. Looking for saints: Hiring Catholic school teachers. In *Capital wisdom: Papers from the Principals Academy 1991*. Washington, D.C.: National Catholic Educational Association.

Kabat, M., M. C. Valenteen, and W. Langley. 1991. Computers in the school: Working hard or hardly working? In *Capital wisdom: Papers from the Principals Academy 1991*. Washington, D.C.: National Catholic Educational Association.

Kambeitz, T. 1991. Teaching and stewardship. *The Living Light* 27(4):334–38.

Kealey, R. J. 1992. *United States Catholic elementary schools and the finances 1991*. Washington, D.C.: National Catholic Educational Association.

Kealey, R. J., and K. C. Collins. 1993. *Stewardship and the Catholic school tuition program*. Washington, D.C.: National Catholic Educational Association.

Kehoe, W. V. 1986. Influence of personality traits: Staffing, interpersonal relations and teaching/learning styles. In *The Catholic school administrator—A book of readings*, ed. E. M. Bushman and G. J. Sparks. Portland, Ore.: Catholic Leadership Company.

Knowles, M. S. 1970. *The modern practice of adult education*. New York: Association Press.

———. 1984. *Andragogy in action*. San Francisco: Jossey-Bass.

Knox, A. B. 1990. *Helping adults learn*. San Francisco: Jossey-Bass.

Konzen, J. M. 1991. *The role of the principal in development*. Washington, D.C.: National Catholic Educational Association.

LaRiviere, A. 1993. *The development council: Cornerstone for success*. Washington, D.C.: National Catholic Educational Association.

Larson, C. E., and F. M. LaFasto. 1991. *Teamwork*. Newbury Park, Calif.: Sage Publication.

Leahy, M. A. 1989. A new determination. *Momentum* 20(3): 48–51.

Leak, L., B. McKay, P. Splain, P. Walker, and C. Held. 1990. *Professional development resource book for school principals*. College Park, Md.: University of Maryland Printing Service.

Lewis, A. 1991. Turning theories into research and practice. In *Learning styles: Putting research and common sense into practice*. Alexandria, Va.: American Association of School Administrators.

Lunenburg, F. C., and A. C. Ornstein. 1991. *Educational administration: Concepts and practices*. Belmont, Calif.: Wadsworth.

MacNaughton, R. H., and F. A. Johns. 1991. Developing a successful schoolwide discipline program. *NASSP Bulletin* 75(536):52–56.

Maeroff, G. I. 1993. Team building. *Phi Delta Kappan* 74 (7):512–19.

McBride, A., Rev. 1981. *The Christian formation of Catholic educators, A CACE monograph*. Washington, D.C.: National Catholic Educational Association.

McCormick, M. T. 1994. Close, but no cigar. *America* 170(8):24–26.

McKinney, M. B. 1987. *Sharing wisdom: A process for group decision making*. Valencia, Calif.: Tabor Publishing.

McLaughlin, T. 1985. *Catholic school finance and Church-State relations*. Washington, D.C.: National Catholic Educational Association.

Michelon, L. C. 1972. *The myths and realities of management*. Cleveland, Ohio: Republic Education Institute.

Monetti-Souply, M. 1990. *A year-round recruitment and retention plan*. Washington, D.C.: National Catholic Educational Association.

Monahan, F. J. 1991. Non-public schools and public policy. In *Political action, public policy and Catholic schools*. Washington, D.C.: National Catholic Educational Association.

Morvay, M., and C. von Buelow. 1990. *Show me the way: A teacher support program for beginning teachers*. Louisville, Ohio.

National Conference of Catholic Bishops. 1973. *To teach as Jesus did*. Washington, D.C.: United States Catholic Conference.

———. 1979. *Sharing the light of faith: National catechetical directory for Catholics of the United States*. Washington, D.C.: United States Catholic Conference.

———. 1990. *In support of Catholic elementary and secondary schools*. Washington, D.C.: United States Catholic Conference.

Neck, J. A. 1985. Entry points in development for Catholic elementary schools. *Momentum* 16(3):20–21.

O'Brien, J. S., ed. 1987. *A primer on educational governance in the Catholic Church*. CACE/NABE Governance Task Force. Washington, D.C.: National Catholic Educational Association.

Oldenburg, R. L. 1991. *Conducting the phonathon*. Washington, D.C.: National Catholic Educational Association.

Patterson, J., S. Purkey, and J. Parker. 1986. *Productive schools systems for a non-rational world*. Alexandria, Va.: Association for Supervision and Curriculum Development.

Pawlas, G., and K. Meyers. 1989. *The principal and communication*. Elementary Principal Series #3. Bloomington, Ind: Phi Delta Kappa Educational Foundation.

Peterson, J. 1990. *How to hire a development officer: From defining needs to ensuring successful performance*. Washington, D.C.: National Catholic Educational Association.

Poplin, M. S. 1992. The leader's role: Looking to the growth of teachers. *Educational Leadership* 49(5):10–11.

Purkey, S. C., and M. S. Smith. 1985. School reform: The district policy implications of the effective schools literature. *Elementary School Journal* 85:353–89.

Reck, C. 1988. *The small Catholic elementary school: Advantages and opportunities*. Washington, D.C.: National Catholic Educational Association.

Reid, D. G., ed. 1990. *Dictionary of Christianity in America*. Downers Grove, Ill.: Intervarsity Press.

Ristau, K. 1989. The role of the principal in the ongoing education of teachers. In *Reflections on the role of the Catholic school principal*, ed. R. J. Kealey. Washington, D.C.: National Catholic Educational Association.

Saphier, J., and R. Gower. 1997. *The Skillful Teacher: Building Your Teaching Skills*. 5th ed. Carlisle, Massachusetts: Research for Better Teaching, Inc.

Schein, E. 1992. *Organizational culture and leadership*. 2nd ed. San Francisco: Jossey-Bass.

Schuster, J. 1993. The managing principal: Using technology to share the power. *Electronic Learning* 12(8):26–30.

Secretan, L. H. K. 1993. *Managerial moxie*. Rocklin, Calif.: Prima Publishing.

Sergiovanni, T. J. 1987. *The principalship: A reflective practice perspective*. Boston: Allyn and Bacon.

———. 1990. *Value-added leadership*. New York: Harcourt Brace Jovanovich.

———. 1992. *Moral leadership*. San Francisco: Jossey-Bass.

———. 1994. *Building community in schools*. San Francisco: Jossey-Bass.

Shaughnessy, M. A. 1989. *School handbooks: Some legal considerations*. Washington, D.C.: National Catholic Educational Association.

———. 1990. *Catholic schools and the law*. Mahwah, N.J.: Paulist Press.

———. 1991. *A primer on school law: A guide for board members in Catholic schools*. Washington, D.C.: National Catholic Educational Association.

Shea, M. 1986. Personnel selection. In *Personnel issues and the Catholic school administrator*. Washington, D.C.: National Catholic Educational Association.

Sheehan, L. 1986. Policies and practices of governance and accountability. In *Personnel issues and the Catholic school administrator*, 1–11. Washington, D.C.: National Catholic Educational Association.

———. 1990a. *Building better boards: A handbook for board members in Catholic education*. Washington, D.C.: National Catholic Educational Association.

———. 1990b. Hiring the right person. *Momentum* 21(2): 31–33.

———. 1991. Governance. In *Catholic school governance and finance*. Washington, D.C.: National Catholic Educational Association.

Silver, H. F., and J. R. Hanson. 1980. *Teacher self-assessment*. Moorestown, N.J.: Hanson Silver and Associates, Inc.

Smith, W. F., and R. L. Andrews. 1989. *Instructional leadership: How principals make a difference*. Alexandria, Va.: Association for Supervision and Curriculum Development.

Sparks, G. J. 1986. The Catholic school administrator. In *The Catholic school administrator—A book of readings*, ed.

E. M. Bushman and G. J. Sparks. Portland, Ore.: Catholic Leadership Company.

Speigle, C., and J. A. Haudan. 1985. Maximizing dollars through money management. *Momentum* 16(3):56–58.

SRI Gallup. 1991. *Themes of the Catholic school teacher*. The Catholic School Principal Perceiver. Lincoln, Neb.: Human Resources for Ministry Institute.

SRI Gallup. 1990. *Themes of the Catholic school principal*. The Catholic School Principal Perceiver. Lincoln, Neb.: Human Resources for Ministry Institute.

Stangl, A. 1990. *The one-person development office*. Washington, D.C.: National Catholic Educational Association.

Stone, S. C. 1987. *Strategic planning for independent schools*. Boston: National Association of Independent Schools.

———. 1993. *Shaping strategy: Independent school planning in the '90s*. Boston: National Association of Independent Schools.

Stuhr, R. L. 1985. What makes a successful development program? *Momentum* 16(3):10–12.

Tarr, H. C. 1990a. *Teacher values and commitment orientations*. A Report to the Archdiocese of Boston Strategic Planning Study for Schools, October 29, 1990. Washington, D.C.: The Catholic University of America.

———. 1990b. *Teacher satisfaction, attitudes and attributions*. A Report for the Archdiocese of Boston Strategic Planning Study for Schools, December 21, 1990. Washington, D.C.: The Catholic University of America.

Tarr, H. C., M. J. Ciriello, and J. J. Convey. 1993. Commitment and satisfaction among parochial school teachers: Findings from Catholic education. *Journal of Research on Christian Education* 2(1):41–63.

Tedesco, J. 1991. *Catholic schools and volunteers: A planned involvement*. Washington, D.C.: National Catholic Educational Association.

Thomas, J. A., and B. Davis. 1989. The principal as part of the pastoral team. In *Reflections on the role of the Catholic school principal*, ed. R. J. Kealey. Washington, D.C.: National Catholic Educational Association.

Thomas, J. A., and J. Haudan. 1984. Tuition. In *Elementary school finance manual*. Washington, D.C.: National Catholic Educational Association.

Thompson, L. A., and J. A. Flynn. 1988. *Effective funding of Catholic schools*. Kansas City, Mo.: Sheed and Ward.

Tracy, M. 1990. *Steps in direct solicitation: Preparation, presentation, and follow-up*. Washington, D.C.: National Catholic Educational Association.

Truitt, M. R. 1991. *The supervisor's handbook*. Shawnee Mission, Kans.: National Press.

United States Catholic Conference. 1991. *Political responsibility: Revitalizing American democracy*. Washington, D.C.: United States Catholic Conference.

United States Department of Education. 1992. *Handbook on serving private school children with Federal education programs*. Washington, D.C.: United States Department of Education, Office of Private Education.

Vaill, P. B. 1984. The purposing of high-performing systems. In *Leadership and organizational culture*, ed. T. J.

Sergiovanni and J. E. Corbally, 85–104. Urbana, Ill.: University of Illinois Press.

Walker, J. E. 1990. The skills of exemplary principals. *NASSP Bulletin* 74:48–55.

Walter, J. K., and G. D. Marconnit. 1989. *The principal and fiscal management.* Elementary Principal Series #6. Bloomington, Ind.: Phi Delta Kappa Educational Foundation.

Watts, G. D., and S. Castle. 1992. Electronic networking and the construction of professional knowledge. *Phi Delta Kappan* 73(9):684–89.

Webster, W. E. 1989. *The new principal learning about your school and community.* Elementary Principal Series #2. Bloomington, Ind.: Phi Delta Kappa Educational Foundation.

Williams, L. P., ed. 1994. *State laws affecting private schools.* Washington, D.C.: United States Department of Education, Office of Private Education.

Yeager, R. J. 1985. Steps toward development. In *Elementary school finance manual.* Washington, D.C.: National Catholic Educational Association.

———. 1986. In justice, the times demand development. In *Personnel issues and the Catholic school administrator,* 143–61. Washington, D.C.: National Catholic Educational Association.

Yeager, R. J., P. L. Benson, M. J. Guerra, and B. V. Manno. 1985. *The Catholic high school: A national portrait.* Washington, D.C.: National Catholic Educational Association.

Young, M. 1986. New wine in new wineskins: Challenge to administrators. In *Personnel issues and Catholic school organization,* 66–70. Washington, D.C.: National Catholic Educational Association.

Yukl, G. 1994. *Leadership in organizations.* Englewood Cliffs, N.J.: Prentice Hall.

Organizations which offer administrative resources, workshops, publications, or consultants:

Catholic Education Marketing Initiative
629 N. Fairview Avenue
St. Paul, MN 55104

Catholic Leadership Company
5470 SW Dover Loop
Portland, OR 97225

Catholic School Management
24 Cornfield Lane
Madison, CT 06443

Council for Advancement and Support
of Education (CASE)
Suite 400
11 Dupont Circle
Washington, DC 20036-1261

Independent School Management
1315 N. Union Street
Wilmington, DE 19806-2594

Institute of School and Parish Development
2026 St. Charles Avenue
Suite 703
New Orleans, LA 70130

These organizations, among others, contract with Catholic schools in the management of tuition payments or financial aid screening:

F.A.C.T.S.
Tuition Management
P. O. Box 67037
Lincoln, NE 68506

SMART
Tuition Management Services
95 Wall Street
Suite 2300
New York, NY 10005

Tuition Aid Data Services
2305 Ford Parkway
#104
St. Paul, MN 55116

Appendix A.
Integral Readings

This appendix is a compilation of all integral readings cited.
They are listed by competency topic within each area of responsibility.

I. Personnel Issues

P1. Staff Recruitment Selection/Orientation

James, R., J. Perkowski, and M. Sesko. 1991. In the beginning: Orientation of the new teacher. In *Capital wisdom: Papers from the Principals Academy 1991*, 22–25. Washington, D.C.: National Catholic Educational Association.

John, R., and M. J. Wagner. 1991. Looking for saints: Hiring Catholic school teachers. In *Capital wisdom: Papers from the Principals Academy 1991*, 55–59. Washington, D.C.: National Catholic Educational Association.

Shea, M. 1986. Personnel selection. In *Personnel issues and the Catholic school administrator*, ed. J. S. O'Brien and M. McBrien, 25–27. Washington, D.C.: National Catholic School Educational Association.

P2. Principals of Adult Development and Motivation

Fielding, G., and H. D. Schalock. 1985. *Promoting the professional development of teachers and administrators*. School Management Digest Series. Eugene, Ore.: ERIC Clearinghouse on Educational Management, College of Education, University of Oregon, 7–9, 13–15.

Knox, A. B. 1990. Understanding adult learners. In *Helping adults learn*, 15–31. San Francisco: Jossey-Bass.

Lewis, A. 1991. Turning theories into research and practice. In *Learning styles: Putting research and common sense into practice*, 19–32. Arlington, Va.: American Association of School Administrators.

National Conference of Catholic Bishops. 1979. *Sharing the light of faith: National catechetical directory for Catholics of the United States*. Washington, D.C.: United States Catholic Conference, nos. 182–89.

Ristau, K. 1989. The role of the principal in the ongoing education of teachers. In *Reflections on the role of the Catholic school principal*, ed. R. J. Kealey, 60–65. Washington, D.C.: National Catholic Educational Association.

Silver, H. F., and J. R. Hanson. 1980. Understanding myself as a learner. In *Teacher self-assessment*, 63–81 [Chapter V]. Moorestown, N.J.: Hanson Silver and Associates, Inc.

———. 1980. Understanding myself as a teacher. In *Teacher self-assessment*, 95–110 [Chapter VI]. Moorestown, N.J.: Hanson Silver and Associates, Inc.

P3. Delegation and Communication

Cappel, C. 1989. A reflection on the spirituality of the principal. In *Reflections on the role of the Catholic school principal*, ed. R. J. Kealey, 26–27. Washington, D.C.: National Catholic Educational Association.

Fielding, G., and H. D. Schalock. 1985. *Promoting the professional development of teachers and administrators*. School Management Digest Series. Eugene, Ore.: ERIC Clearinghouse on Educational Management, College of Education, University of Oregon, 66–67.

Libreria Editrice Vaticana. 1994. *Catechism of the Catholic Church*. Washington, D.C.: United States Catholic Conference, nos. 1897–1917.

Smith, W. F., and R. L. Andrews. 1989. *Instructional leadership: How principals make a difference*. Alexandria, Va.: Association for Supervision and Curriculum Development, 46–48.

Sparks, G. J. 1986. The Catholic school administrator. In *The Catholic school administrator—A book of readings*, ed. E. M. Bushman and G. J. Sparks, 283–91. Portland, Ore.: Catholic Leadership Company.

Truitt, M. R. 1991. Time management. In *The supervisor's handbook*, 55–57, 61–63. Shawnee Mission, Kans.: National Press.

P4. Group Process

Libreria Editrice Vaticana. 1994. *Catechism of the Catholic Church*. Washington, D.C.: United States Catholic Conference, nos. 1724, 1738, 1886–88.

Sheehan, L. 1990. Decision making. In *Building better boards: A handbook for board members in Catholic education*, 70–74. Washington, D.C.: National Catholic Educational Association.

Thomas, J. A., and B. Davis. 1989. The principal as part of the pastoral team. In *Reflections on the role of the Catholic school principal*, ed. R. J. Kealey, 45–54. Washington, D.C.: National Catholic Educational Association.

Truitt, M. R. 1991. *The supervisor's handbook*. Shawnee Mission, Kans.: National Press, 16–20.

P5. Managing Conflicts

Drahmann, T. 1985. Kill the Umpire. In *Governance and administration in the Catholic school*, 27–30. Washington, D.C.: National Catholic Educational Association.

Hendricks, W. 1989. *How to manage conflict*. Leadership Success Series. Shawnee Mission, Kans.: National Press, 1–3, 6–14, 15–22.

Libreria Editrice Vaticana. 1994. *Catechism of the Catholic Church*. Washington, D.C.: United States Catholic Conference, nos. 1822–29, 2302–06.

Shaughnessy, M. A. 1989. *School handbooks: Some legal considerations*. Washington, D.C.: National Catholic Educational Association, 76.

P6. Evaluating Staff

Glatthorn, A. A., and C. R. Shields. 1983. Credo for supervision in Catholic schools. In *Differentiated supervision for Catholic schools*, 2, 8–12. Washington, D.C.: National Catholic Educational Association.

Hind, J. F. 1989. Treat others with tough love and a tender touch. In *The heart and soul of effective management: A Christian approach to managing and motivating people*, 113–17. Wheaton, Ill.: Scripture Press Publications, Inc.

Shaughnessy, M. A. 1989. *School handbooks: Some legal considerations*. Washington, D.C.: National Catholic Educational Association, 19–20, 28–30.

Truitt, M. R. 1991. Preparation • Presentation • Follow-up: Keys to constructive criticism. In *The supervisor's handbook*, 46–49. Shawnee Mission, Kans.: National Press.

❖❖❖❖❖❖❖❖❖❖❖❖❖❖

II. Institution Issues

I1. Orderly School Environment and Discipline

Doyle, R., N. Kinate, A. Langan, and M. Swanson. 1991. Evaluation of the school's Catholicity. In *Capital wisdom: Papers from the Principals Academy 1991*, 1–6. Washington, D.C.: National Catholic Educational Association.

Drahmann, T., and A. Stenger. 1989. *The Catholic school principal: An outline for action*. Rev. ed. Washington, D.C.: National Catholic Educational Association, 25–26.

Governal, M. A. 1986. Effective principaling in a Catholic school. In *The Catholic school administrator—A book of readings*, ed. E. M. Bushman and G. J. Sparks, 161–64. Portland, Ore.: Catholic Leadership Company.

Libreria Editrice Vaticana. 1994. *Catechism of the Catholic Church*. Washington, D.C.: United States Catholic Conference, no. 2030.

Saphier, J., and R. Gower. 1997. Classroom climate: Community and mutual support, risk taking and confidence, influence. In *The Skillful Teacher: Building Your Teaching Skills*, 357–394. 5th ed. Carlisle, Mass.: Research for Better Teaching, Inc.

Shaughnessy, M. A. 1989. *School handbooks: Some legal considerations*. Washington, D.C.: National Catholic Educational Association, 24–27, 62–68.

I2. Governance Structures/ Catholic School Boards

Bailey, R., U. Butler, and M. Kearney. 1991. Development of the Catholic school board. In *Capital wisdom: Papers from the Principals Academy 1991*, 39–44. Washington, D.C.: National Catholic Educational Association.

National Conference of Catholic Bishops. 1979. *Sharing the light of faith: National catechetical directory for Catholics of the United States*. Washington, D.C.: United States Catholic Conference, Chapter 10.

Shaughnessy, M. A. 1991. *A primer on school law: A guide for board members in Catholic schools*. Washington, D.C.: National Catholic Educational Association, 29–34.

Sheehan, L. 1990. What is a Catholic school board? In *Building better boards: A handbook for board members in Catholic education*, 1–5. Washington, D.C.: National Catholic Educational Association.

Sparks, G. J. 1986. Preparing a presentation for the board of education. In *The Catholic school administrator—A book of readings*, ed. E. M. Bushman and G. J. Sparks, 293–95. Portland, Ore.: Catholic School Leadership Company.

I3. Relationship with Diocesan Office

Drahmann, T. 1985. *Governance and administration in the Catholic school*. Washington, D.C.: National Catholic Educational Association, 15–16.

Hennessey, C., C. A. Solomon, K. Mitchell, S. Plasek, D. A. Clifford, and T. Bogar. 1992, 1988. *Administrator's handbook of regulations*. Houston, Tex.: Catholic School Office, Diocese of Galveston-Houston, 7–10.

Sheehan, L. 1986. Policies and practices of governance and accountability. In *Personnel issues and the Catholic school administrator*, ed. J. S. O'Brien and M. McBrien, 1–11. Washington, D.C.: National Catholic Educational Association.

I4. Relationship with Religious Congregation(s)

Drahmann, T. 1985. *Governance and administration in the Catholic school*. Washington, D.C.: National Catholic Educational Association, 16–18.

Drahmann, T., and A. Stenger. 1989. *The Catholic school principal: An outline for action*. Rev. ed. Washington, D.C.: National Catholic Educational Association, 17.

I5. Civil and Canon Law

CACE/NABE Governance Task Force. 1987. *A primer on educational governance in the Catholic Church*, ed. J. S. O'Brien. Washington, D.C.: National Catholic Educational Association, 7–16.

Libreria Editrice Vaticana. 1994. *Catechism of the Catholic Church*. Washington, D.C.: United States Catholic Conference, nos. 707–710, 2104–06.

Shaughnessy, M. A. 1991. *A primer on school law: A guide for board members in Catholic schools*. Washington, D.C.: National Catholic Educational Association, 5–13, 16–22.

———. 1989. *School handbooks: Some legal considerations*. Washington, D.C.: National Catholic Educational Association, 1–3, 11–15.

I6. State Requirements and Government-Funded Programs

Hennessey, C., C. A. Solomon, K. Mitchell, S. Plasek, D. A. Clifford, and T. Bogar. 1997. *Administrator's handbook of regulations*. Houston, Tex.: Catholic School Office, Diocese of Galveston-Houston. [Federal Programs Section 1–4, Special Education Section 1–4.]

McLaughlin, T. 1985. *Catholic school finance and Church-State relations*. Washington, D.C.: National Catholic Educational Association, 34–37, 44–52.

United States Department of Education, Office of Private Education. 1992. Government programs. In *Handbook on serving private school children with federal education programs*, 12–13, 78–80. Washington, D.C.

I7. Technologies

Brigham, F. H. 1993. *Technology and Chapter 1: Solutions for Catholic school participation*. Washington, D.C.: National Catholic Educational Association, 7, 10, 18–19.

Gettys, D. J. 1994. Integrating technology in education: The principal's role. *Principal* 73(4): 52–53.

Kabat, M., M. C. Valenteen, and W. Langley. 1991. Computers in the school: Working hard or hardly working? In *Capital wisdom: Papers from the Principals Academy 1991*, 45–47. Washington, D.C.: National Catholic Educational Association.

National Conference of Catholic Bishops. 1979. *Sharing the light of faith: National catechetical directory for Catholics of the United States*. Washington, D.C.: United States Catholic Conference, nos. 17, 20, 22.

Schuster, J. 1993. The managing principal: Using technology to share the power. *Electronic Learning* 12(8): 26–28, 30.

❖ ❖ ❖ ❖ ❖ ❖ ❖ ❖ ❖ ❖ ❖ ❖ ❖ ❖

III. Finance and Development

D1. Financial Resources

Burke, R. 1984. The annual budget. In *Elementary school finance manual*, 22–27, 28, 31, 43, 45, 49, 54–59. Washington, D.C.: National Catholic Educational Association.

Libreria Editrice Vaticana. 1994. *Catechism of the Catholic Church*. Washington, D.C.: United States Catholic Conference, nos. 2426–34.

McLaughlin, T. 1985. *Catholic school finance and Church-State relations*. Washington, D.C.: National Catholic Educational Association, 19.

Sheehan, L. 1990. The role of the board in finances. In *Building better boards: A handbook for board members in Catholic education*. Washington, D.C.: National Catholic Educational Association, 26–31.

D2. Long-Range/Strategic Planning

Burke, R. 1984. Long-range planning. In *Elementary school finance manual*, 84–89. Washington, D.C.: National Catholic Educational Association.

Sheehan, L. 1990. Planning. In *Building better boards: A handbook for board members in Catholic education*, 7–9. Washington, D.C.: National Catholic Educational Association.

D3. Development, Public Relations, and Marketing

Balfe, M., M. Lanning, A. Meese, and A. M. Walsh. 1991. Enrollment: Securing our future. In *Capital wisdom: Papers from the Principals Academy 1991*, 11–20. Washington, D.C.: National Catholic Educational Association.

Sheehan, L. 1990. Public relations. In *Building better boards: A handbook for board members in Catholic education*, 40–44. Washington, D.C.: National Catholic Educational Association.

Yeager, R. J. 1985. Steps toward development. In *Elementary school finance manual*, 120–23. Washington, D.C.: National Catholic Educational Association.

D4. Resources Beyond the School

McLaughlin, T. 1985. *Catholic school finance and Church-state relations*. Washington, D.C.: National Catholic Educational Association, 28, 53–54.

Yeager, R. J. 1985. Steps toward development. In *Elementary school finance manual*, 123–26. Washington, D.C.: National Catholic Educational Association.

Appendix B.
Learning Activities

This appendix is a compilation of all learning activities listed.
They are listed by competency topic within each area of responsibility.

I. Personnel Issues

P1. Staff Recruitment Selection/Orientation

1. Readings with log entries
2. School visit to talk to principal: Strategies to attract teachers
3. Teacher interviews
4. Diocesan office contact: for forms: job application, interviewing protocols, contract, policies to critique

P2. Principles of Adult Development and Motivation

1. Readings with log entries
2. School visit: Perceptions of principals about importance of principles of adult learning

P3. Delegation and Communication

1. Readings with log entries
2. Reflection on personal experience with application to delegation processes
3. School visit to talk to principal: Management practices/administrative organization
4. Obtain samples of school communications to critique
5. Diocesan office contact: Diocesan principal handbook to analyze

P4. Group Process

1. Readings with log entries
2. School visit or talk to principals: Group processes utilized with various groups
3. Interview group chairs/officers of organizations about responsibilities and decision making
4. School observation: Attending meetings to analyze interactions and processes

P5. Managing Conflicts

1. Readings with log entries
2. Interview: School and or parish leadership regarding problem solving and conflict management processes
3. Interview: Employees or volunteers about sources of conflict and preferred resolution processes in their activities
4. List components of effective crisis management plan

P6. Evaluating Staff

1. Readings with log entries
2. Reflection on personal experience on being evaluated
3. School visit or talk to principals regarding evaluation processes
4. Classroom observation with a principal
5. Diocesan office contact: Diocesan forms/policies regarding teacher evaluation

❖ ❖ ❖ ❖ ❖ ❖ ❖ ❖ ❖ ❖ ❖ ❖ ❖ ❖

II. Institution Issues

I1. Orderly School Environment and Discipline

1. Readings with log entries
2. School visit to experience and understand elements of the environment
3. Obtain copies of school handbooks: Focus on safety, security, discipline
4. Interview: Employees, consumers of Catholic Education about safety, security measures

I2. Governance Structures/ Catholic School Boards

1. Readings with log entries
2. Diocesan office contact: Guidelines, policies about Boards/Commissions
3. Attend parish Catholic school board meeting/Interview member

I3. Relationship with Diocesan Office

1. Readings with log entries
2. Diocesan office visit to learn "inner workings," structure, support afforded
3. Interview: Acting principals about their perspectives of diocesan services

I4. Relationship with Religious Congregation(s)

1. Readings with log entries
2. School visit where there are vowed Religious on the staff
3. School visit where vowed Religious are no longer present
4. Diocesan contact: About the historical/[future] role/ contribution of religious congregations
5. [Visit with leadership of Religious Congregation]

I5. Civil and Canon law

1. Readings with log entries
2. School visit: Ascertain general level of awareness/ knowledge
3. Obtain local school policies/material re: Teacher assessment
4. Obtain student and faculty handbooks: Critique

I6. State Requirements and Government-Funded Programs

1. Readings with log entries
2. School visit: Participation on government programs
3. Diocesan office contact: Interview with appropriate personnel

I7. Technologies

1. Readings with log entries
2. School visit: Use of technology
3. Research/evaluate packages suited to school technology needs

III. Finance and Development

D1. Financial Resources

1. Readings with log entries
2. School visit: Budgeting processes
3. Obtain school documents related to financial planning and accountability; critique
4. Diocesan office contact: Principal's Handbook or other pertinent financial materials/guidelines

D2. Long-Range/Strategic Planning

1. Readings with log entries
2. School visit: Evidence of long-range planning
3. School visit: Interview principal/obtain school documents relating to planning
4. Diocesan office contact: What support is there to do planning?

D3. Development, Public Relations, and Marketing

1. Readings with log entries
2. School visit: Interview principal about role in development program/obtain written materials
3. School visit: Interview public relations personnel about processes and strategies
4. School visit: As applicable interview those directly involved in development
5. School visit: As applicable interview those directly involved in development; interview various members of boards responsible for development and public relations

D4. Resources Beyond the School

1. Readings with log entries
2. Obtain copies of annual reports/case statements; critique
3. Research instances of present school/business partnerships in local area
4. Develop list of potential resources that could be cultivated
5. Diocesan office contact: Ascertain resources and policies available

Appendix C.
Outcome Activities

This appendix is a compilation of all outcome activities listed.
They are listed by competency topic within each area of responsibility.

I. Personnel Issues

P1. Staff Recruitment Selection/Orientation

1. Situation: Member of committee to review/revise policies
2. Design a formal staff/faculty orientation program

P2. Principles of Adult Development and Motivation

1. Situation: Describe strategies used to get to know situation
2. Proposal to diocese on a process to orienting new administrators

P3. Delegation and Communication

1. Generate list of qualities for sound organizational management
2. Scenario: Meeting with previous principal who outlines "problem" and tasks needing attention; calls on application of various management skills

P4. Group Process

1. Generate list of group roles and responsibility of the leader

2. Reflection on qualities and costs involved in striving for consensus
3. Elementary scenario: Friend wants advice about uniform problem
4. Secondary scenario: New principal addressing instructional strategies problem

P5. Managing Conflicts

1. Prepare intervention plan for each scenario
   a. Difference in styles between new and veteran teachers
   b. Difficult teacher with colleagues
   c. Distraught teacher with student problem
   d. Dissatisfied parent

P6. Evaluating Staff

1. Critique of diocesan procedures for evaluation
2. Comment on merits of supervision models application of models to specific teachers
   a. Experienced, non-Catholic new to the school
   b. Sister teaching 25 years
   c. Older beginning teacher, not Catholic
   d. Four high school teachers
   e. Young beginning teacher, a vowed religious
   f. Three experienced mature teachers

❖ ❖ ❖ ❖ ❖ ❖ ❖ ❖ ❖ ❖ ❖ ❖ ❖ ❖ ❖

II. Institution Issues

I1. Orderly School Environment and Discipline

1. Develop a check list of security measures to be used for evaluation
2. Develop a list of standards to evaluate a school discipline code
3. Design a hearing process for due process cases
4. Elementary scenario: Dealing with complaints and expectations
5. Secondary scenario: Dealing with student alleged misbehavior in the community

I2. Governance Structures/ Catholic School Boards

1. Develop a plan for an information night for those wanting to get more involved in the school
2. Situation: Develop a proposal for the institution of a separate school board

I3. Relationship with Diocesan Office

1. Compare/contrast management responsibilities of public and Catholic school administrators
2. Develop an organization chart of diocesan school office
3. Assessment of services available versus the needs of the individual

I4. Relationship with Religious Congregation(s)

1. Scenario: Recognition of religious on the staff
2. Scenario: Strategies to keep the school linked to the heritage
3. Scenario: Lay person assuming leadership in a school sponsored by a religious community

I5. Civil and Canon law

1. Scenario: New principal needs to educate Board on legal issues
2. Scenario: Lack of appropriate documentation with legal consequences

I6. State Requirements and Government-Funded Programs

1. Listing of government programs available to the school in the particular area
2. Reflection on the basic rights of students/families to access to government programs with strategies available when rights are denied or ignored
3. Devise a staff development session on legal and governmental issues

I7. Technologies

1. Develop a philosophy and rationale for incorporating technology in the school with ramifications to leadership
2. Scenario: New on site at a place that is technologically backward

❖ ❖ ❖ ❖ ❖ ❖ ❖ ❖ ❖ ❖ ❖ ❖ ❖ ❖

III. Finance and Development

D1. Financial Resources

1. List qualities of sound business management
2. Scenario: Situation presented problem: Devise the budget

D2. Long-Range/Strategic Planning

Scenario: New principal of a troubled school: Devise a "turn-around" plan

D3. Development, Public Relations, and Marketing

Scenario: New principal in a declining school in need of a public relations plan

D4. Resources Beyond the School

1. Generate a plan to draw on outside support
2. Scenario: A school in need of alumni organization

About the Authors

Kay Alewine, mother of four children and grandmother of six, has maintained a multifaceted career throughout her professional life. Before assuming the principal position at Our Lady of Fatima in Texas City, she taught special education classes for fourteen years and was a lay missionary and teacher in northern China. She has frequently presented sessions at NCEA conventions. She also serves as an educational clinician and motivational speaker for both public and Catholic schools and various civic organizations. She earned her M.S. in education at East Texas State University.

Sr. Maria Ciriello, OP, Ph.D., is presently the dean of the School of Education of the University of Portland in Oregon. Sister Maria spent eight years teaching and fourteen years in elementary and secondary school administration before pursuing her doctorate at The Catholic University of America. In 1987 she joined the faculty at Catholic University. As an associate professor, she taught in the areas of teacher education and education administration. She also collaborated nationally on strategic planning and evaluation studies of diocesan school systems. She earned her master's degree in education administration at the University of Dayton.

(Ann) Nancy Gilroy is an assistant superintendent at the Division of Catholic Schools in the Archdiocese of Baltimore. Prior to her position with the archdiocese, she was a principal and teacher in Staten Island, New York. She received her master's degree from the City University in New York and is presently pursuing doctoral studies at Morgan State University.

Fr. Joel Konzen, SM, assistant to the Marist Provincial, was formerly the president/principal at St. Michael's Academy in Austin, Texas. He has been involved in Catholic school administration since 1980 as admissions director, headmaster, and president of Marist School, Atlanta, Georgia. He is the author of the NCEA paperback *The Role of the Principal in Development* and has presented workshops and training sessions on development practice and Catholic school boards. His M.A. in educational administration is from The Catholic University of America.

Lawrence E. Leak, Ph.D., is an associate professor in the teacher education and administration department at Morgan State University. Prior to joining the faculty at Morgan, he was a member of the graduate faculty at the University of Maryland at College Park where he also received his doctorate in 1988.

Sr. Lourdes Sheehan, RSM, currently the executive director of CACE (Chief Administrators of Catholic Education of the National Catholic Educational Association), has served as a Catholic school teacher, principal, diocesan superintendent of schools, and secretary for education of the United States Catholic Conference. Immediately before assuming her current position, Sr. Lourdes was the director of the Alliance for Catholic Education, a teacher service initiative at the University of Notre Dame. She is the author of the NCEA publication *Building Better Boards.* She earned her master's degree in colonial history from the University of Pennsylvania and her doctorate in educational administration from Virginia Tech.